# Lecture Notes in Computer Science 4625

*Commenced Publication in 1973*
Founding and Former Series Editors:
Gerhard Goos, Juris Hartmanis, and Jan van Leeuwen

T0217260

Rainer Stiefelhagen   Rachel Bowers
Jonathan Fiscus (Eds.)

# Multimodal Technologies for Perception of Humans

International Evaluation Workshops
CLEAR 2007 and RT 2007
Baltimore, MD, USA, May 8-11, 2007
Revised Selected Papers

 Springer

Volume Editors

Rainer Stiefelhagen
Universität Karlsruhe (TH)
Institut für Theoretische Informatik
Am Fasanengarten 5, 76131 Karlsruhe, Germany
E-mail: stiefel@ira.uka.de

Rachel Bowers
Jonathan Fiscus
National Institute of Standards and Technology (NIST)
100 Bureau Drive, Stop 8940, Gaithersburg, MD 20899, USA
E-mail: {rachel.bowers,jfiscus}@nist.gov

Library of Congress Control Number: 2008930167

CR Subject Classification (1998): I.4, I.5, I.2.10, I.3.5, I.2.6, F.2.2

LNCS Sublibrary: SL 6 – Image Processing, Computer Vision, Pattern Recognition, and Graphics

ISSN 0302-9743

ISBN 978-3-540-68584-5 Springer Berlin Heidelberg New York

Springer is a part of Springer Science+Business Media

springer.com

© Springer-Verlag Berlin Heidelberg 2008

Typesetting: Camera-ready by author, data conversion by Scientific Publishing Services, Chennai, India
Printed on acid-free paper       SPIN: 12275588       06/3180       5 4 3 2 1 0

# Preface

The second annual Classification of Events Activities and Relationships (CLEAR) and the 2007 Rich Transcription (RT) evaluations took place during the winter and early spring of 2007. This was a co-location of complementary evaluation efforts; CLEAR for the evaluation of human activities, events, and relationships in multiple multimodal data domains (e.g., meetings, surveillance, etc.); RT for the evaluation of speech transcription-related technologies from meeting room audio collections. Through these collaborative speech-and video-based evaluation tasks, we hope to provide resources that help the speech and vision research communities establish a base for fostering more multimedia research efforts in the future.

CLEAR targets the evaluation of systems for the perception of people, their identities, activities, interactions, and relationships in human-to-human interaction and related scenarios in various multimodal data domains (meetings, surveillance, etc.). RT targets the evaluation of meeting domain speech technologies including: speech-to-text transcription, "who-spoke-when" speaker diarization, and speaker attributed speech-to-text. As part of the evaluation, two workshops were held, during May 8–9, 2007 for CLEAR, and May 10–11, 2007 for RT, in Baltimore, Maryland, where the participating systems were presented and the evaluation results were discussed in detail. Both CLEAR and RT were open to any institution interested in participating and drew over 50 participants for their individual workshops.

The book is broken down into two sections: CLEAR and RT. Each gives an overview of the data, evaluation protocol, the individual evaluation tasks, and the participants' results. This is followed by the papers that describe details of the algorithms that were scored.

Though you may be drawn to the proceedings from a specific workshop we encourage you to explore all the work presented in this publication. There are complementary aspects between the research evaluated in CLEAR and RT, which we hope will stimulate new ideas for multimedia-based research, as well as new multimedia evaluation.

Finally, we would like to thank the reviewers of the CLEAR and RT papers, the CLEAR Task Leaders, the sponsoring projects and funding agencies, those responsible for the evaluation workshop management and organization, contributors to the development of the CLEAR/RT proceedings, and most importantly, the participants of the CLEAR/RT evaluations and workshops.

January 2008

Rainer Stiefelhagen
Jonathan Fiscus
Rachel Bowers

# Organization

## CLEAR Workshop Chairs

Rainer Stiefelhagen      Universität Karlsruhe (TH), Germany
Rachel Bowers      National Institute of Standards and Technology
(NIST), USA

## RT Workshop Chair

Jonathan Fiscus      National Institute of Standards and Technology
(NIST), USA

## Workshop Organization

Travis Rose      NIST, USA
Jerome Ajot      NIST, USA
Teresa Vicente      NIST, USA

## CLEAR Evaluation Task Organizers

Keni Bernardin      Universität Karlsruhe (TH), Germany
Rachel Bowers      NIST, USA
Hazim Ekenel      Universität Karlsruhe (TH), Germany
Djamel Mostefa      ELDA, Paris, France
Aristodemos Pnevmatikakis      Athens Information Technology, Greece
Ramon Morros      Universitat Politecnica de Catalunya, Spain
Jean-Marc Odobez      IDIAP Research Institute, Switzerland
Travis Rose      NIST, USA
Andrey Temko      Universitat Politecnica de Catalunya, Spain
Michael Voit      Universität Karlsruhe (TH), Germany

## Sponsoring Projects and Institutions

### Projects

- CHIL, Computers in the Human Interaction Loop, http://chil.server.de
- VACE, Video Analysis Content Extraction,
  https://control.nist.gov/dto/twiki/bin/view/Main/WebHome
- AMI, Augmented Multiparty Interaction, http.//www.amiproject.org

**Institutions**

- European Commission, through the Multimodal Interfaces objective of the Information Society Technologies (IST) priority of the Sixth Framework Programme
- US National Institute of Standards and Technology (NIST), http://www.nist.gov/speech

# Table of Contents

# Person and Vehicle Tracking on Surveillance Data

# Vehicle and Person Tracking Aerial Videos

# Person Identification

## Head Pose Estimation

## Acoustic Event Detection

## RT 2007

## Speech-to-Text

## Speaker Diarization

# CLEAR 2007

# The CLEAR 2007 Evaluation

Rainer Stiefelhagen[1], Keni Bernardin[1], Rachel Bowers[2], R. Travis Rose[3],
Martial Michel[3,4], and John Garofolo[3]

[1] Interactive Systems Lab, Universität Karlsruhe, 76131 Karlsruhe, Germany
{stiefel, keni}@ira.uka.de
[2] Naval Research Laboratory, 4555 Overlook Ave. S.W., Washington, DC 20375
[3] NIST, 100 Bureau Dr - MS 8940, Gaithersburg, MD 20899, USA
[4] Systems Plus, Inc., 1370 Piccard Drive - Suite 270, Rockville, MD 20850, USA

**Abstract.** This paper is a summary of the 2007 CLEAR Evaluation
on the Classification of Events, Activities, and Relationships which took
place in early 2007 and culminated with a two-day workshop held in
May 2007. CLEAR is an international effort to evaluate systems for the
perception of people, their activities, and interactions. In its second year,
CLEAR has developed a following from the computer vision and speech
communities, spawning a more multimodal perspective of research evaluation. This paper describes the evaluation tasks, including metrics and
databases used, and discusses the results achieved. The CLEAR 2007
tasks comprise person, face, and vehicle tracking, head pose estimation,
as well as acoustic scene analysis. These include subtasks performed in
the visual, acoustic and audio-visual domains for meeting room and surveillance data.

## 1 Introduction

CLassification of Events, Activities and Relationships (CLEAR) is an international
effort to evaluate systems that are designed for perceiving people's identities, activities, interactions and relationships in human-human interaction scenarios, and
related scenarios. The first CLEAR evaluation workshop was held in spring 2006
(see [23] for a complete description of CLEAR'06). It hosted a variety of tasks, evaluated on challenging, realistic scenarios, and brought together a number of research
institutions from around the world. Prompted by the success of the first evaluation,
another round was conducted from January through April 2007, culminating with
a 2-day workshop in Baltimore, MD, where system details and results were presented and discussed. The CLEAR 2007 workshop was collocated with the 2007
Rich Transcription (RT) workshop to provide an opportunity for members of both
the vision and speech research communities to participate in discussions related to
multimedia based evaluations.

### 1.1 Motivation

Many researchers, research labs and in particular a number of major research
projects worldwide – including the European projects CHIL, Computers in the

R. Stiefelhagen et al. (Eds.): CLEAR 2007 and RT 2007, LNCS 4625, pp. 3–34, 2008.
© Springer-Verlag Berlin Heidelberg 2008

Human Interaction Loop [1], and AMI, "Augmented Multi-party Interaction" [2], as well as the US programs VACE, "Video Analysis and Content Extraction" [3], and CALO, "Cognitive Assistant that Learns and Organizes" [4] – are working on technologies to analyze people, their activities, and their interaction. However, common benchmarks for such technologies are usually not available. Most researchers and research projects use their own data sets, annotations, task definitions, metrics and evaluation procedures. As a consequence, comparing the advantages of research algorithms and systems is virtually impossible. Furthermore, this leads to a costly multiplication of data production and evaluation efforts for the research community as a whole.

CLEAR was created to address this problem. Its goal is to provide a common international evaluation framework for such technologies, and to serve as a forum for the discussion and definition of related common benchmarks, including the definition of tasks, annotations, metrics and evaluation procedures. The expected outcomes for the research community from such a common evaluation forum are:

- the definition of widely adopted metrics and tasks
- greater availability of resources achieved by sharing the data collection and annotation burdens
- the provision of challenging multimodal data sets for the development of robust perceptual technologies
- comparability of systems and approaches
- faster progress in developing improved and robust technologies

## 1.2   Background

CLEAR is a collaborative effort between the US Government funded Video Analysis and Content Extraction (VACE), and the European Commission funded, Computers in the Human Interactive Loop (CHIL) programs, but 2007 has expanded this collaboration to include an evaluation task from the Augmented Multiparty Interaction (AMI) program. As in 2006, this new round of evaluations targeted technologies for tracking, identification, and analysis of human-centered activities, on challenging multimodal databases from various meeting and surveillance domains. As before, the evaluations were open and interested sites not part of the initiating projects were invited to participate.

## 1.3   Scope and Evaluation Tasks in 2007

The CLEAR 2007 evaluation was organized in conjunction with the Rich Transcription (RT) 2007 evaluation [5], their deadlines were harmonized and this year the workshops were collocated. While the evaluations conducted in RT focus on content-related technologies, such as speech and text recognition, CLEAR is more about context-related multimodal technologies such as person tracking, person identification, head pose estimation, analyzing focus of attention, interaction, activities and events.

The evaluation tasks in CLEAR 2007 can be broken down into four categories:

- tracking (faces/persons/vehicles, 2D/3D, acoustic/visual/audio-visual)
- person identification (acoustic, visual, audio-visual)
- head pose estimation (single view data, multi-view data)
- acoustic scene analysis

These tasks and their various subtasks are described in Section 4. As in the 2006 evaluations, part of the tasks were organized by CHIL and others by VACE, depending on the partner that originally defined them, and on the datasets used. The tasks were run independently in parallel, although care was taken to harmonize task definitions, annotations and metrics wherever possible. In contrast to 2006, the face detection and tracking task was run using the same annotations and metrics for both the CHIL and VACE related subtasks. In addition, the multiple object tracking metrics (see section 3), which were first agreed on in 2006, were further harmonized, and used without exception in all 2007 tracking tracking tasks and subtasks.

## 1.4   Contributors

As in the previous year, many people and institutions worldwide contributed to the success of CLEAR 2007. Again, the organizers were the Interactive Systems Labs of the Universität Karlsruhe, Germany (UKA) and the US National Institute of Standards and Technology (NIST). The participants and contributors included: the Research and Education Society in Information Technologies at Athens Information Technology, Athens, Greece, (AIT), the Interactive Systems Labs at Carnegie Mellon University, Pittsburgh, PA, USA, (CMU) the Evaluations and Language resources Distribution Agency, Paris, France (ELDA), the IBM T.J. Watson Research Center, RTE 134, Yorktown Heights, USA (IBM), the Centro per la ricerca scientifica e tecnologica at the Fundacione Bruno Kessler, Trento, Italy (FBK-IRST), the Universitat Politécnica de Catalunya, Barcelona, Spain (UPC), the Laboratoire d'Informatique pour la mécanique et les sciences de l'ingénieur at the Centre national de la recherche scientifique, Paris, France (LIMSI), Pittsburgh Pattern Recognition, Inc., Pittsburgh, PA, USA (PittPatt), the department of Electronic Engineering of the Queen Mary University of London, UK (QMUL), the Computer Science and Technology Department of Tsinghua University, Beijing, China (Tsinghua), the Department of Computer Science of the University of Maryland, MD, USA (UMD), the University of Central Florida, USA (UCF), the Institute of Signal Processing of the Technical University of Tampere, Finland (TUT), the Breckman Institute for Advanced Science and Tech. at the University of Illinois Urbana Champaign, USA (UIUC), the IDIAP Research Institute, Martigny, Switzerland (IDIAP), the MIT Lincoln Laboratory, Lexington, MA, USA (MIT), the Institute for Robotics and Intelligent Systems of the University of Southern California, USA (USC), the Institute for Infocomm Research, Singapore (IIR).

UKA, FBK-IRST, AIT, IBM and UPC provided several recordings of "interactive" seminars, which were used for the 3D person tracking tasks, for face detection, for the person identification tasks and for acoustic event detection. UKA and IDIAP provided several annotated recordings for the head pose estimation task. UPC and FBK-IRST provided different databases with annotated acoustic events used for acoustic event recognition.

Visual and acoustic annotations of the CHIL Interactive Seminar data were mainly done by ELDA, in collaboration with UKA, CMU, AIT, IBM, FBK-IRST and UPC. Packaging and distribution of data coming from CHIL was handled by UKA. The data coming from VACE was derived from a single source for the surveillance data - the Imagery Library for Intelligent Detection Systems (i-LIDS) [6]. The meeting room data was a collection derived from data collected at CMU, the University of Edinburgh (EDI), NIST, the Netherlands Organisation for Applied Scientific Research (TNO), and Virginia Tech (VT). The evaluation scoring software for VACE tasks was contributed by the University of South Florida (USF).

The discussion and definition of the individual tasks and evaluation procedures were moderated by so-called "task-leaders". These were Keni Bernardin (UKA, 3D person tracking), Ramon Morros (UPC, CHIL-related 2D Face tracking), Rachel Bowers, Martial Michel and Travis Rose (NIST, VACE-related 2D face tracking, 2D person tracking, 2D vehicle tracking), Hazim Ekenel (UKA, visual person identification), Djamel Mostefa (ELDA, acoustic identification), Aristodemos Pnevmatikakis (AIT, audio-visual identification), Michael Voit and Jean-Marc Odobez (UKA and IDIAP, head pose estimation), Andrey Temko (UPC, acoustic event recognition). The tasks leaders were responsible for scoring the evaluation submissions. For CHIL tasks, they were also centrally scored by ELDA.

Note that original plans called for the inclusion of a person detection and tracking task in the unmanned aerial vehicle (UAV) domain using data contributed by the Defense Advanced Research Projects Agency (DARPA) Video Verification of Identity (VIVID) [7] program. Unfortunately, the annotation of this data proved to be too difficult to perform with the sufficient level of consistency required for the purposes of this evaluation. Therefore, the UAV Person Detection and Tracking task was eliminated from the evaluation.

The remainder of this paper is organized as follows: Section 2 first gives a brief overview of the used data sets and annotations, followed by an introduction to the evaluation metrics in Section 3. Section 4 then presents the various evaluation tasks with an overview of the achieved results and discusses some of the outcomes and potential implications for further evaluations. Finally, Section 5 summarizes the experiences gained from the CLEAR'07 evaluation.

Further details on the tasks definitions and data sets can be found in the evaluation plans available on the CLEAR webpage [8].

## 2    Evaluation Corpora

### 2.1    CHIL Interactive Seminars

The CHIL-sponsored evaluation tasks of 3D person detection, person identification, face detection and tracking, and acoustic event recognition were carried out using the CHIL Interactive Seminar database. This database features recordings of small seminars with 3 to 8 participants, recorded at 5 different CHIL sites with greatly varying room characteristics. The "lecture-type" Seminar database still used in CLEAR'06 [23], figuring recordings of a lecturer in front of an audience, and focused toward single person analysis were dropped completely in favor of the multiple person scenario. A minimum common sensor setup in the recording rooms guaranteed a certain level of standardization to ease algorithm development and testing. The visual sensor setup includes 4 fixed cameras with overlapping views installed in the room corners and one fisheye ceiling camera. The audio setup includes at least three 4-channel T-shaped microphone arrays and at least one MarkIII 64-channel linear microphone array on the room walls, as well as several close-talking and table top microphones. All data is synchronized, with highest priority on the audio channels which can be used for acoustic source localization and beamforming. A detailed description of the recording rooms, sensors, scenarios and procedures is given in [19]. A total of 25 seminars were recorded in 2006, which were separated into 100 minutes of development and 200 minutes of evaluation data (see Table 1).

**Table 1.** CHIL Interactive Seminar data used in CLEAR'07

| Site | Development | Evaluation |
|------|-------------|------------|
| AIT | 1 Seminar (20m segment) | 4 Seminars (2x 5m segments each) |
| IBM | 1 Seminar (20m segment) | 4 Seminars (2x 5m segments each) |
| IRST | 1 Seminar (20m segment) | 4 Seminars (2x 5m segments each) |
| UKA | 1 Seminar (20m segment) | 4 Seminars (2x 5m segments each) |
| UPC | 1 Seminar (20m segment) | 4 Seminars (2x 5m segments each) |

For the person identification task, the same development and evaluation seminars were used, but the training and test segments were chosen from different time points to better suit the requirements of the task, as explained in Section 4.5. All video recordings are provided as sequences of single JPEG images at 640x480, 768x576, 800x600 or 1024x768 pixels resolution and at 15, 25 or 30fps, depending on the recording site and camera. The audio recordings are provided as single channels sampled at 44.1kHz, 24 bits per sample, in the WAV or SPHERE formats, depending on the recording sensor. In addition, information about the calibration of every camera, the location of every sensor, the recording room dimensions, and a few empty room images for background modeling are supplied for each seminar. The development and evaluation segments are annotated, providing 3D and 2D head centroid locations, face bounding boxes, facial features such as the eyes and nose bridge, and audio transcriptions of speech and other acoustic events. Fig. 1 shows example scenes from the 2007 Interactive Seminar database.

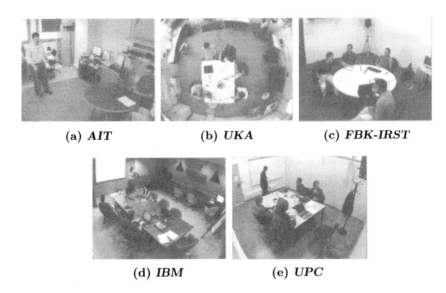

(a) *AIT*          (b) *UKA*          (c) *FBK-IRST*

(d) *IBM*          (e) *UPC*

**Fig. 1.** Scenes from the 2007 CHIL Interactive Seminar database

## 2.2   VACE Related Datasets

The evaluation data were assembled using two databases, multi-site meetings and surveillance data (Table 2). The surveillance data originate from the 2006 Imagery Library for Intelligent Detection Systems (i-LIDS) [6], distributed by the United Kingdom's Home Office via collaboration with NIST. All videos are in MPEG-2 format using either 12 or 15 I-frame rate encoding. The annotations are provided in ViPER (the Video Performance Evaluation Resource tool) format [16,18]. The Multi-Site Meetings are composed of datasets from different sites, samples of which are shown in Fig. 2:

1. CMU (10 Clips)
2. EDI (10 Clips)
3. NIST (10 Clips)
4. TNO (5 Clips)
5. VT (10 Clips)

Sample annotations for the moving vehicle and the person tracking in surveillance tasks are shown in Figs. 3 and 4.

**Table 2.** Evaluation data

| Data | Raw data | Training | Evaluation |
|------|----------|----------|------------|
| Multi-Site Meetings | 160GB | 50 Clips (Face) | 45 Clips (Face) |
| i-LIDS Surveillance | 38GB | 50 Clips (Person) | 50 Clips (Person) |
| i-LIDS Surveillance | 38GB | 50 Clips (Moving Vehicle) | 50 Clips (Moving Vehicle) |

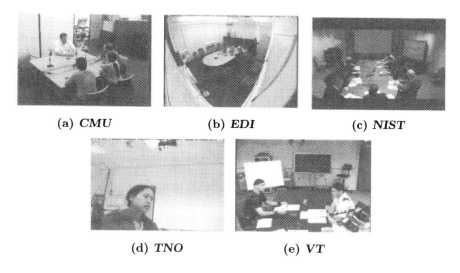

(a) *CMU*          (b) *EDI*          (c) *NIST*

(d) *TNO*          (e) *VT*

**Fig. 2.** Scenes from Multi–Site Meetings

### 2.3   Other Datasets

In addition to the above described databases, some tasks were carried out using other datasets more suited to their requirements. The Head Pose Estimation task was performed on two databases: One recorded at UKA, using 4 corner cameras with overlapping views of the room, and one extracted from the AMI Meeting database, featuring single views of a meeting table. These databases and their annotations are explained further in Section 4.6. For the Acoustic Event Recognition task, although development and evaluation was mostly based on the CHIL Interactive Seminar database, 2 databases of isolated acoustic events, recorded at UPC and ITC, which were also used in the CLEAR 2006 evaluation, were included in the development set. More details are given in Section 4.7.

## 3   About Tracking Metrics

The reason tracking metrics are specifically presented here is because these same metrics were used in many of the CLEAR tasks, including 3D visual, acoustic and audio-visual person tracking, face tracking, and 2D person and vehicle tracking. As opposed to other tasks, such as face identification, for which well known and widely accepted metrics exist, there is yet no common standard in the tracking community for the evaluation of multiple object trackers. Most measures are designed with the characteristic of a specific domain in mind (e.g. merges and splits in 2D visual tracking, coming from the tradition of 2D foreground blob analysis), and are not suited for application to other domains (such as e.g. acoustic tracking, 3D tracking, etc). For the first CLEAR evaluation in 2006, an effort was undertaken to harmonize the metrics used in the different tracking

**Fig. 3.** Sample annotation for vehicle. MOBILE objects are marked by black boxes. STATIONARY objects are marked by white boxes. The shaded region indicates where mobile vs. stationary is ambiguous.

tasks under consideration in the CHIL and VACE communities. The resulting metrics, the Multiple Object Tracking Precision ($MOTP$) and the Multiple Object Tracking Accuracy ($MOTA$), should for the first time offer a general framework for the evaluation of multibody trackers in all domains and for all modalities. The $MOT$ metrics are only briefly sketched in the following. For a detailed explanation, the reader is referred to [11,14,22]. The metrics used in the person identification, head pose estimation and acoustic event recognition tasks are described together with the respective task descriptions in Section 4.

### 3.1   The MOT Tracking Metrics

The Multiple Object Tracking ($MOT$) metrics build upon a well defined procedure to calculate the basic types of errors made by multiple object trackers over a tracking sequence: Imprecisions in the estimated object locations, failures to estimate the right number of objects, and failures to keep a consistent labeling of these objects in time. Given that for every time frame $t$ a multiple object tracker outputs a set of hypotheses $\{h_1 \ldots h_m\}$ for a set of visible objects $\{o_1 \ldots o_n\}$, let $c_t$ be the number of object-hypothesis correspondences made for frame $t$ and $d_t^i$ be the distance between object $o_i$ and its corresponding hypothesis. Let further $g_t$ be the number of objects and $fp_t$, $m_t$ and $mme_t$ be the number of false positives, misses, and track ID mismatch errors made for frame $t$. Then the $MOTP$ is defined as:

$$MOTP = \frac{\sum_{i,t} d_t^i}{\sum_t c_t} \tag{1}$$

and the $MOTA$ as:

**Fig. 4.** Sample annotation for a person in surveillance

$$MOTA = 1 - \frac{\sum_t (m_t + fp_t + mme_t)}{\sum_t g_t} \qquad (2)$$

For the distance $d_t^i$ between an object and a tracker hypothesis, various measures can be used without changing the general framework. For the CLEAR 3D person tracking tasks, e.g., the Euclidian distance on the ground plane between annotated and tracked object centroids was used, whereas for the 2D face, person and vehicle tracking tasks, the spatial overlap between annotated and tracked bounding boxes, $G_t^i$ and $D_t^i$, was used.

$$d_t^i = \frac{|G_t^i \cap D_t^i|}{|G_t^i \cup D_t^i|} \qquad (3)$$

## 4    CLEAR 2007 - Evaluation Tasks and Results

The CLEAR tasks can be broken down into four main categories: tracking tasks, identification tasks, head pose estimation and acoustic event recognition. Table 3 shows the different CLEAR 2007 tasks.

### 4.1    3D Person Tracking

The objective of the 3D person tracking task is to estimate the trajectories on the ground plane of the participants in CHIL Interactive Seminar recordings (see Fig. 5). As in the previous evaluation, it is broken down into 3 subtasks: Visual, acoustic and multimodal tracking. For all subtasks, the $MOTP$ and $MOTA$ metrics described in Section 3 are applied, evaluating both localization precision and tracking accuracy. The database for evaluation consisted of 200

**Table 3.** CLEAR'07 tasks

| Task name | Organizer | Section | Database |
|---|---|---|---|
| Tracking | | | |
| 3D Person Tracking (A,V,AV) | CHIL | 4.1 | Interactive Seminars |
| 2D Face Det. & Tracking (V) | CHIL/VACE | 4.2 | Int. Sem./Multi-Site Meetings |
| 2D Person Tracking (V) | VACE | 4.3 | Surveillance Data |
| 2D Vehicle Tracking (V) | VACE | 4.4 | Surveillance Data |
| Person Identification (A,V,AV) | CHIL | 4.5 | Interactive Seminars |
| Head Pose Estimation (V) | CHIL/AMI | 4.6 | Seminars[1], AMI Meetings |
| Acoustic Event Recognition | CHIL | 4.7 | Int. Sem., Isolated Events |

minutes of recordings from 5 different CHIL sites and included the streams from 4 corner cameras and a panoramic ceiling camera, from at least 12 audio channels coming from 3 T-shaped microphone arrays, and from at least 64 more audio channels captured by a MarkIII microphone array. The scenes figured 3 to 8 seminar participants engaged in natural interaction, and were cut out as 5 minute segments from various points inside the seminars, such that they did often not include the starting phase, where persons enter the room. Trackers therefore had to be capable of acquiring person tracks at any point in the sequence, of adapting their person models, and had to automatically cope with the variability of all CHIL rooms without room specific tuning.

Some notable changes to the CLEAR'06 tracking task should be mentioned here:

- First of all, the single person tracking scenarios (lecture scenarios) were dropped completely. Only scenarios involving the tracking of multiple persons were considered.
- The acoustic subtask was extended and required trackers to automatically detect segments of speech in addition to performing localization. This means that segments of silence or noise were now included in the evaluation data. Segments containing cross-talk, though, were still considered as "don't care" segments.
- The multimodal subtask was redefined and the conditions *A* and *B* from CLEAR'06 were dropped. The goal in this evaluation was to audio-visually track the last known speaker. This implies that the tracking target has to be determined acoustically, tracked audio-visually, segments of silence have to be bridged using only the visual modality, and the target has to be switched automatically when a new speaker becomes active. The defined task cannot be solved well using monomodal trackers. This change in the task definition was made to achieve a better balance of the modalities and to better show the advantages of multimodal fusion.

---

[1] For this task, a number of interactive seminars were recorded and annotated in 2006. These seminars, however, were not part of the dataset used for the tracking and identification tasks.

**Fig. 5.** Example screenshot of a 3D person tracking system running on Interactive Seminar data (Image taken from [15])

Fig. 6 shows the results for the visual subtask. A total of 7 systems from 4 sites participated. Various approaches, such as particle filters, Kalman filters, and heuristic-based trackers were represented and a variety of features, gained from the multiple views, were used. These include foreground segmentation support maps, person colors, body or face detections, edge contours, etc. The best performing system in terms of accuracy (78.36%) was a particle filter based tracker using as sole feature a 3D voxelized foreground support map, computed from the various views. The most performant system in terms of precision (91 mm) was based on the intelligent tracking and combination of detected faces in the 2D views. According to the runtime information provided in the system descriptions, almost all these systems performed at close to realtime.

Fig. 7 shows the results for the acoustic subtask. A total of 8 systems from 5 sites participated. The approaches were based on the computation of the Generalized Cross-Correlation (GCC-PHAT) between microphone pairs or of a Global Coherence Field (GCF or SRP-PHAT) using the information from all arrays. While some systems still tackled speech segmentation and localization separately, others did use a combined approach. The best performing system overall was a Joint Probabilistic Data Association Filter (JPDAF) - based tracker, which performed speech segmentation by thresholding localization uncertainties. It reached a precision of 140mm and an accuracy of 54.63%. Most systems proved to be capable of realtime or close to realtime operation.

Fig. 8 shows the results for the multimodal subtask. A total of 6 systems from 4 sites participated. These systems are a combination of the visual and acoustic trackers presented earlier. Almost all systems perform modality fusion

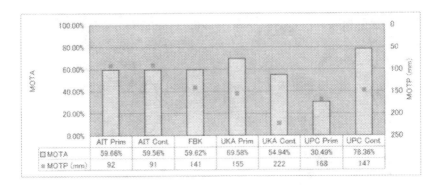

**Fig. 6.** 3D Person Tracking – Visual subtask. The light bars represent the $MOTA$ in percent and the dark dots represent the $MOTP$ in mm.

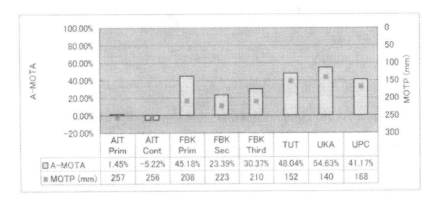

**Fig. 7.** 3D Person Tracking – Acoustic subtask

by post-processing the outputs of the monomodal trackers and combining at the decision level. The only exception is the lead system in terms of accuracy (58.49%), which fused the audio and visual information at the feature level to initiate, update, and terminate person tracks.

In general, the biggest challenge facing visual tracking systems in the CLEAR scenarios is still the reliable detection of persons in various poses, with partial occlusions, from a variety of viewing angles, in natural uncontrolled environments. Compared to systems presented in 2006, the approaches were much more advanced this year, fusing far more features and more types of detectors to achieve higher robustness. The best $MOTA$ score improved from 62.79% to 78.36%, despite the much higher variability caused by the inclusion of more recording sites (for comparison, the best system from 2006, $UKA$ $Cont$ [12,13], achieved only 54.94% $MOTA$ on the 2007 data). Similarly, the challenge on the acoustic side relies on the proper detection and segmentation of speech in the presence of irregular, non-uniform noise sources, reverberation and crosstalk. While the

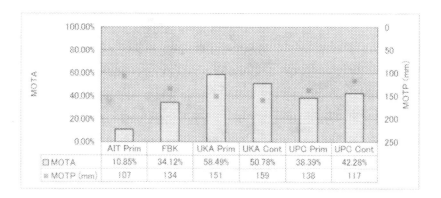

**Fig. 8.** 3D Person Tracking – Multimodal subtask

best acoustic performance seems to have dropped from 64% in 2006 to 54.63% in 2007, one must remember that the task this year involved also the automatic segmentation of speech, while last year systems were only evaluated on manually annotated segments of clean speech. On the whole, scores for all systems were much higher, showing that basic difficulties previously encountered could be overcome to some extent. Undoubtedly, though, a great deal of work must still be done to further increase the robustness of acoustic systems. On a last note: The best multimodal $MOTA$ score for 2007, 58.49%, can not be directly compared to the best 2006 multimodal scores (37.58% for condition $A$, 62.20% for condition $B$), as the task definitions, and therefore the goals and difficulties for trackers differ. Also, the 2007 multimodal scores cannot be directly compared to the 2007 monomodal visual or acoustic scores for the same reasons. At the very least, one can observe that an early fusion of audio-visual features seems to bear some advantages, as shown by this year's best performing system. Only the scoring of monomodal acoustic trackers on periods of silence, just as in the multimodal task, could clearly show the advantages gained by the addition of visual features[2]. The problem of objectively measuring the advantages of multimodal fusion, especially in natural, application-near scenarios such as in CLEAR, still poses some difficult questions that must be investigated.

Appendix $A$ graphically shows a more detailed analysis of the results for the CLEAR 2007 3D person tracking task, for the audio, visual and multimodal subtasks.

### 4.2 2D Face Detection and Tracking

The purpose of this task is to measure the accuracy of face tracking for meeting and lecture room videos. The objective is to automatically detect and keep track

---

[2] While the scoring of such trackers on silence-only periods is useful for diagnostic purposes in determining the contribution from audio tracking to the multimodal task, it is not representative of a real-world task.

**Fig. 9.** Example screenshot for the face tracking task on Interactive Seminar data (Image taken from [20])

of all visible faces in a video sequence, estimating both their position and their extension (see Fig. 9).

The task was evaluated on two databases, the CHIL Interactive Seminars and the VACE Multi-Site Meetings. While for the Multi-Site Meeting database, detection and tracking could only be performed separately in the multiple camera views, the Interactive Seminar database offered exact calibration information between views, allowing to use 3D geometric reasoning about scene locations of faces to increase accuracies (this was not exploited by any of the participating systems, though). In both cases, the overall performance is computed as the average of 2D tracking performances across all views. Face sizes in the CLEAR databases are extremely small (down to 10x10 pixels), faces are rarely oriented directly toward a camera, lighting conditions are difficult and faces are often occluded, making standard skin color segmentation or template matching techniques unusable. Thus, the difficulty of the dataset drives the development of innovative techniques for this research field.

In contrast to CLEAR'06, the task was better harmonized, with respect to the CHIL and VACE datasets, notably concerning the annotation of face extensions, the definition of visible faces, and the metrics used. Faces are considered visible if of the three annotated features, the left eye, the right eye and the nose bridge, at least two are visible. They are regarded as "don't care" objects, which are ignored in scoring, if only one feature is visible. As for all tracking tasks in CLEAR'07, the *MOT* metrics were adopted, using the overlap between annotated and tracked face bounding boxes as distance measure.

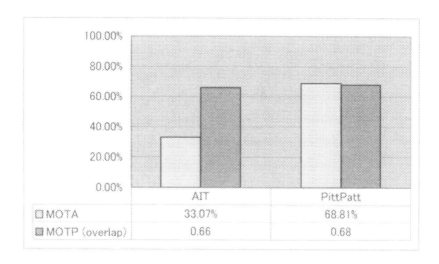

**Fig. 10.** 2D Face Tracking – CHIL Interactive Seminar database

**2D Face Tracking on the CHIL Interactive Seminar Database** The results for face tracking on the Interactive Seminar database are shown in Fig. 10. As in 2006, two sites participated on this dataset. The best system used a 3-stage algorithm consisting of a frame-based face detection step, a motion-based tracking step, and a subsequent track filtering step. It reached a precision of 68% overlap and an accuracy of 68.81%. These results are slightly better than those in 2006 (best $MOTP$: 0.64, best $MOTA$: 68.32%), although in 2006 tracking errors resulting from track ID switches were not counted, and in 2007 the conditions were more challenging due to an increase in the amount of seminar participants involved.

**2D Face Tracking on the Multi-Site Meeting Database.** The results on the Multi-Site Meeting database appear in Fig. 11. 5 systems from 3 different sites participated in the evaluation. The leading system here also used a 3-stage approach consisting of face detection using a hierarchical multi-view face detector, particle filter-based tracking, and filtering of the resulting tracks. It reached scores of 70% $MOTP$ and 85.14% $MOTA$.

For both datasets, the main difficulties still stemmed from very small or hardly identifiable faces, extreme views of faces, and blurred or highly compressed video. Another important factor is that the quality of annotations is also affected by these same problems. A fair portion of false positives can (for example) be attributed to cases where faces are tracked in extreme poses in which none of the facial features were clearly visible, and were therefore annotated as invisible. The converse also holds for ambiguous cases which were judged visible based on facial feature annotations, but only contain fractions of a face, resulting in a miss by the tracker. In both cases, better guidelines for the annotation of "don't care" faces, and some form of rating for the difficulty of the underlying video

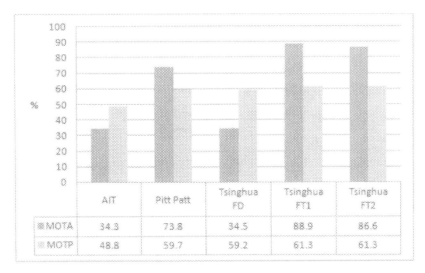

| | AiT | Pitt Patt | Tsinghua FD | Tsinghua FT1 | Tsinghua FT2 |
|---|---|---|---|---|---|
| MOTA | 34.3 | 73.8 | 34.5 | 88.9 | 86.6 |
| MOTP | 48.8 | 59.7 | 59.2 | 61.3 | 61.3 |

**Fig. 11.** Face tracking in meeting room

sequence may reveal a much higher performance of presented tracking systems than the actual numbers suggest.

For all VACE-sponsored tasks, a unified evaluation methodology was applied, as task definitions, annotations and metrics were very similar. This methodology should be briefly mentioned here: Each participating site electronically submitted system output for scoring using the USF_DATE software[3]. Submissions were evaluated using a batch process that involved two main stages: a data validation step, followed by application of the metrics.

To run the scoring software, it was verified that the submissions were compliant with the Viper Document Type Definition [16,18] and would successfully be parsed. This required normalization of all submissions to complete validation of their data. In the following cases, sites were notified and asked to resubmit corrected files:

- Wrong object types: this occurred when submissions contained custom keywords for objects.
- No object in submission: either the submission file contained no object at all, or no object relevant to the task being scored was present in the file.
- Using a 2006 index file: cases where submitted files matched CLEAR 2006 index files.
- Incomplete submission: when a submitted system output was not complete, such as a malformed XML file.
- Not a Viper file: some submissions were not in Viper format.

---

[3] USF_DATE is USF (University of South Florida) DATE (Detection and Tracking Evaluation).

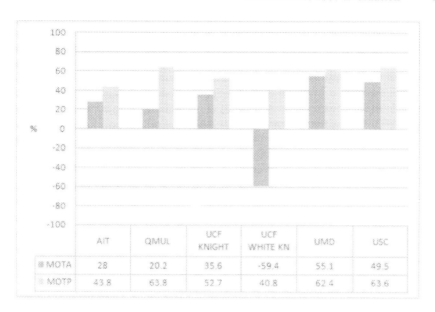

**Fig. 12.** Person tracking in surveillance video

Each submission was evaluated against the ground truth using the metrics described in Section 3. In cases where the submission could not be scored due to limitations in USF_DATE, the clip was marked as being problematic. Finally, the set of all clips that were successfully scored for all submissions was used to obtain the MOTA and MOTP scores, i.e. the same clips were used in these calculations for all submissions, and scores were calculated only with respect to the objects retained in the test set.

### 4.3    2D Person Tracking

The purpose of this task it is to track persons in a surveillance video clip. The annotation of a person in the Surveillance domain comprises the full extent of the person (completely enclosing the entire body including the arms and legs). Specific annotation details about how a person is marked appear in the guidelines document [21]. The person tracking in surveillance video results appear in Fig. 12.

### 4.4    2D Vehicle Tracking

The goal of the moving vehicle task is to track moving vehicles in a given video clip. For the annotation, only vehicles that have moved at any time during the clip are marked. Vehicles are annotated at the first frame where they move. For specific details see [21].

For this evaluation task, the vehicle has to be moving and must be clearly visible (i.e., should not be occluded by other objects). In the i-LIDS dataset

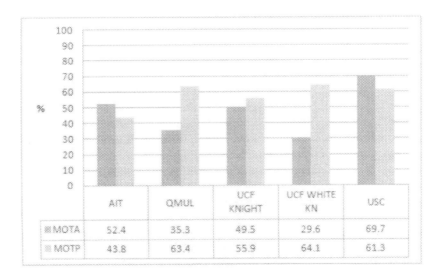

| | AIT | QMUL | UCF KNIGHT | UCF WHITE KN | USC |
|---|---|---|---|---|---|
| MOTA | 52.4 | 35.3 | 49.5 | 29.6 | 69.7 |
| MOTP | 43.8 | 63.4 | 55.9 | 64.1 | 61.3 |

**Fig. 13.** Vehicle tracking in surveillance video

there are regions where vehicles are not clearly visible due to tree branches or where the sizes of vehicles are very small. These regions are marked accordingly (as "don't care" regions). The vehicle tracking in surveillance video results are summarized in Fig. 13.

### 4.5  Person Identification

The person identification task in the CLEAR evaluation was designed to measure the performance of visual and acoustic identification systems operating under far-field[4] conditions in realistic meeting and seminar scenarios (see Fig. 14).
  The task was that of closed set identification and was evaluated on the CHIL Interactive Seminar database. Only corner camera views and the MarkIII microphone array channels were available. For each participant to be identified, training, validation and testing data was provided. The training data consisted of 15 and 30 second audio-visual data segments extracted from the original sequences. Testing was then made on segments of varying length, from 1 to 20 seconds, to measure the improvements to be achieved by temporal fusion. A major improvement over the CLEAR'06 evaluations is that the evaluation segments were much more carefully chosen to offer a better balance between the audio and visual modalities. Care was taken that, for each segment, at least a certain amount of frontal non-occluded views of the head were available in addition to clean speech, eliminating the artificial bias toward the audio modality

---

[4] The "far-field" condition implies that only fixed microphones placed on the room table or walls are to be used, as opposed to close talking or lapel microphones, which are worn directly by the users. This causes for a significantly lower signal to noise ratio, making the task much more challenging.

**Fig. 14.** Example screenshot of a face identification system running on Interactive Seminar data (Image taken from [17])

observed in 2006. Visual annotations were also of higher frequency and accuracy, with face bounding box, left eye and right eye labels provided every 200ms. The evaluation set comprised 28 individuals in total (up from 26 in 2006). Figs. 15, 16 and 17 show the results for the visual, acoustic and multimodal subtasks respectively.

For the visual subtask, 7 systems from 3 sites were represented. As manual labels for face bounding boxes and eyes of the concerned participant for a segment were provided, systems did not need to perform tracking, but just to align and crop faces for recognition. Two systems did use some form of preprocessing, though, e.g. interpolating between 200ms label gaps to obtain more facial views. Many types of feature extraction algorithms were used, including Principle Component Analysis (PCA), Linear Discriminant Analysis (LDA), block-based Discrete Cosine Transform (DCT), and variants or combinations thereof. Classification was mostly done using nearest neighbor classifiers. The best results in all train and test conditions were reached by a local appearance based approach using only labeled faces, DCT features, and nearest neighbor classification. It achieved 84.6% accuracy for the hardest condition in terms of data availability (15s train, 1s test) and 96.4% for the easiest condition (30s train, 20s test). This is a major improvement over 2006, where the best results obtained in the 30s train, 20s test condition were 83.7%.

While some of the improvement stems from algorithm design, some part of it must no doubt also be attributed to better labeling and segmentation of the visual data, as described above. Because of the differences in the preprocessing and classification techniques, it is difficult to directly compare the strengths of the feature extraction algorithms. Looking at the results from both CLEAR

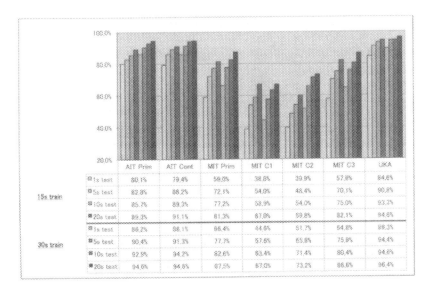

**Fig. 15.** Recognition rates for Person Identification – Visual subtask. Results are shown for 15 and 30 second training, and for 1, 5, 10 and 20 second test segment lengths. Shown are the Correct Recognition Rates in percent.

2006 and 2007, however, one may find that using local models of appearance does offer some advantages over other techniques. A more thorough experimental investigation is necessary, though, before general conclusions could be made.

A total of 11 systems from 6 sites participated in the acoustic subtask. The approaches were based on Gaussian Mixture Models (GMMs), adapted Universal Background Models (UBMs) or Support Vector Machines (SVMs), and used Mel-Frequency Cepstral Coefficient (MFCC) or Perceptually-weighted Linear Predictive (PLP) features, their derivatives, or combinations thereof. Systems also differed in the amount of microphone channels used and the way they were fused in pre- or post-processing. The best overall results in the 15s training condition were achieved by a system using PLP coefficients from one single channel and a UBM model. It reached 98.2% for the 20s test condition. The best overall results in the 30s training condition came from a system using UBM-GMM classifiers separately on 7 channels, and fusing at the decision level. It reached 100% accuracy for the 20s test condition. On the whole, it seems that PLP features, used stand-alone or in combination with others, outperform other features, and that adapted UBM models outperform speaker specific GMMs. It was also observed that, contrary to expectations, pre-processing multiple channels through beamforming to produce a cleaner signal degrades performance. The more promising path seems to be the combination of classifier outputs at the post-decision level. In comparison with 2006, clear improvements could be noticed only in the 15s training condition.

Four sites participated in the multimodal subtask. All systems used post-decision fusion of the monomodal recognizer outputs, with different strategies

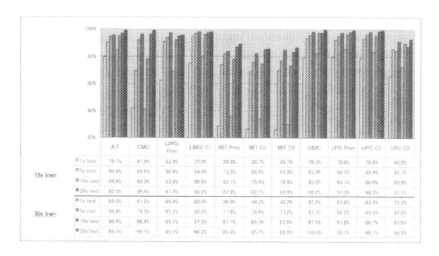

**Fig. 16.** Recognition rates for Person Identification – Acoustic subtask. Shown are the Correct Recognition Rates in percent.

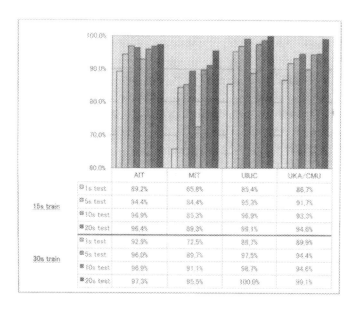

**Fig. 17.** Recognition rates for Person Identification – Multimodal subtask. Shown are the Correct Recognition Rates in percent.

for the weighting of audio and visual inputs. The best performing system in the multimodal case was also based on the best overall acoustic system. It used an appearance based technique for face identification, which was not evaluated separately in the visual subtask. For 20s test segments, it reached 99.1% and

100% accuracies for the 15s and 30s train conditions, respectively. Overall, the perfomance of acoustic systems was quite high, such that the advantages of multimodal fusion could only be observed in the 1s test condition, where the best results improved from 79.7% and 85.6% (15s, 30s train) to 89.2% and 92.9%. When the availability of both modalities is guaranteed, the strength of multimodal approaches clearly lies in the smaller amount of observations required, more than in the accuracies to be reached.

Appendix *B* summarizes the best results for the person identification task in CLEAR 2007, and shows the progress achieved since CLEAR 2006, for the audio, visual and multimodal subtasks, and for all evaluation conditions.

## 4.6  Head Pose Estimation

The objective in the head pose estimation task is to continuously estimate the pan, tilt, and roll orientations of a person's head using using visual information from one or more cameras.

**Fig. 18.** Example screenshot for the head pose estimation task on the AMI Meeting Corpus (Image taken from [10])

The task was subdivided into two subtasks, determined by the datasets used: The first subtask was built on the AMI Meeting Corpus [10], and offered single views of meeting participants interacting around a table (see Fig. 18). It contained 16 one minute segments, extracted individually for 16 different subjects, of which 10 were to be used for training, and 6 for evaluation. The task required automatically tracking the head of one of the participants, in addition to estimating its orientation. The second subtask involved a data corpus captured in the CHIL-UKA smart room and offered 4 synchronized and calibrated views, which could be combined to derive head orientations in the room coordinate frame. In contrast to the AMI database, head sizes were relatively small and manual annotations for the head bounding box were provided, such that no tracking was necessary. A total of 15 subjects was considered, 10 for training and 5 for evaluation, with a 3 minute segment provided per person. For both subtasks, the ground truth head orientations were captured with high precision using "Flock of Birds" magnetic sensors. This constitutes a great improvement over the previous evaluation, where only manual annotations into 45° pan classes were available. The metrics used were the mean absolute pan, tilt and roll errors, as well as the mean angular error between annotated and estimated head orientation vectors. Figs. 19 and 20 show the mean absolute pan/tilt/roll errors for the AMI and the CHIL corpus, respectively.

For the first subtask, 3 systems from 2 sites participated. The best systems achieved errors rates of less than 10° in all dimensions. The overall best performing system used a specially designed particle filter approach to jointly track the head location and pose. It reached 8.8° pan, 9.4° tilt and 9.8° roll error.

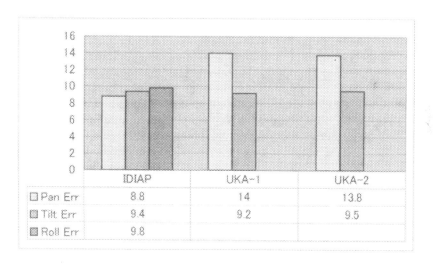

|  | IDIAP | UKA-1 | UKA-2 |
|---|---|---|---|
| ☐ Pan Err | 8.8 | 14 | 13.8 |
| ☐ Tilt Err | 9.4 | 9.2 | 9.5 |
| ☐ Roll Err | 9.8 | | |

**Fig. 19.** Head Pose Estimation – AMI Meeting database

A total of 5 sites participated in the second subtask. The best error rates were remarkably low, even compared to the previous subtask, although face sizes in this database were notably smaller. This is due in part to the availability of several camera views for fusion, but undoubtedly also to the availability of head bounding box annotations, which allow for optimal head alignment. Only two systems attempted location and pose tracking jointly, while the best performing systems relied on the manual annotations. The best overall system relied

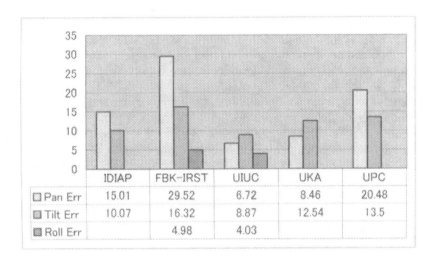

**Fig. 20.** Head Pose Estimation – CHIL database

on a special person-independent manifold representation of the feature space, constructed by synchronizing and embedding person-specific sub-manifolds, and estimated head poses using a k-nearest neighbor classifier. It reached error levels as low as 6.72° pan, 8.87° tilt and 4.03° roll.

### 4.7  Acoustic Event Recognition

As in 2006, the 2007 CLEAR evaluations featured an acoustic event recognition task, in which non-speech noises occurring in a seminar scenario were to be identified. A definite change compared to 2006, is that classification of pre-segmented events was not considered anymore. Instead, evaluation was performed on the CHIL Interactive Seminar database, on the same segments as used in the 3D Person Tracking, Person Identification, and 2D Face Tracking tasks. This is a major extension to the previous evaluation, where only one full-valued seminar was considered, aside from isolated event databases. In addition to *classification*, systems had to automatically *detect* acoustic events, possibly overlapped with speech or other acoustic events. 12 event classes were considered, including "door knock", "steps", "chair moving", "paper work", "phone ring", "applause", "laugh", etc. The recognition of the "speech" and "unknown" classes was not evaluated. For development, one seminar was taken per recording site, as well as the 2 isolated event databases from 2006. The test data was chosen from the remaining seminars and comprised 20 five minute segments from 4 sites, for a total of 6000 seconds, of which 36% were classified as acoustic events of interest, 11% as silence, and 53% as speech or "unknown" events. The Interactive seminars offered a challenging testbed, as 64% of acoustic events in the evaluation data were overlapped with speech and 3% were overlapped with other acoustic events. Two new metrics were defined for this evaluation, the $AED - ACC$,

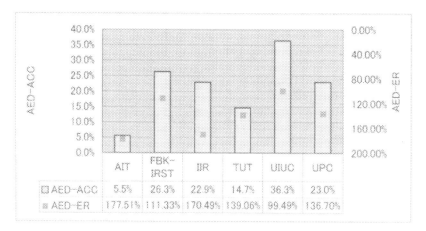

**Fig. 21.** Acoustic Event Recognition – site-independent systems. The light bars represent the $AED - ACC$ and the dark dots represent the $AED - ER$.

measuring event detection accuracy, and the $AED - ER$, measuring how precisely the temporal boundaries of acoustic events are found. They are defined as follows:

$$AED - ACC = \frac{(1 + \beta^2) * P * R}{\beta^2 * P + R},$$

where

$$P = Precision = \frac{number\ of\ correct\ system\ output\ AEs}{number\ of\ all\ system\ output\ AEs}$$

$$R = Recall = \frac{number\ of\ correctly\ detected\ reference\ AEs}{number\ of\ all\ reference\ AEs}$$

and $\beta$ is a weighting factor that balances precision and recall. In this evaluation, the factor $\beta$ was set to 1.

$$(AED - ER) = \frac{\sum_{all\ seg} dur(seg) * (max(N_{REF}, N_{SYS} - N_{correct}(seg)))}{\sum_{all\ seg} dur(seg) * N_{REF}(seg)}$$

where, for each segment $seg$ (defined by the boundaries of both reference and hypothesized AEs): $dur(seg)$ is the duration of $seg$, $N_{REF}(seg)$ is the number of reference AEs in $seg$, $N_{SYS}(seg)$ is the number of system output AEs in $seg$ and $N_{correct}(seg)$ is the number of reference AEs in $seg$ which correspond to system output AEs in $seg$. Notice that an overlapping region may contribute to several errors. The results of the Acoustic Event Recognition task are shown in Fig. 21.

Six sites participated in the evaluation. From the presented systems, 5 are Hidden Markov Model (HMM) or Gaussian Mixture Model (GMM) based, and one is based on Support Vector Machines (SVMs). Half of the systems use multiple microphones, and the other half (including the best performing system) use only a single microphone. As can be seen, the overall scores are quite low, showing that there is still much room for improvement in spontaneous meeting room AED. The best system reached just 36.3% accuracy and almost 100% $AED - ER$ error. An analysis revealed that, on average, more than 71% of errors occur in overlapped segments as, e.g, low-energy acoustic classes, such as "chair moving", "paper work" or "steps", proved difficult to detect in the presence of speech. In occurence, the "step" class accounted for 40% of all acoustic events in the test data. Leaving out segments of overlap, the error rate of most systems would be around 30–40%. No doubt, more research is necessary to overcome the problems caused by overlap. One direction that was not explored could be to build AED systems as a set of isolated recognizers. Other improvements could be expected from the more efficient use of multiple microphones to better isolate events, or from audio-visual analysis.

## 5 Summary

This paper summarized the CLEAR 2007 evaluation, which started early in 2007 and was concluded with a two day workshop in May 2007. It described the evaluation tasks performed in CLEAR'07, including descriptions of metrics and used databases, and also gave an overview of the individual results achieved by the evaluation participants. Further details on the individual systems can be found in the respective system description papers in the proceedings of the evaluation workshop.

The goal of the CLEAR evaluation is to provide an international framework to evaluate multimodal technologies related to the perception of humans, their activities and interactions. CLEAR has been established through the collaboration and coordination efforts of the European Union (EU) Integrated Project CHIL - Computers in the Human Interactive Loop - and the United States (US) Video Analysis and Content Extraction (VACE) programs. After a successful first round in 2006, the evaluations were launched again with new challenging tasks and datasets, better harmonized metrics, and with the inclusion of a new head pose estimation task, sponsored by the European Augmented Multiparty Interaction (AMI) project. The CLEAR 2007 workshop took place in May, after more than half a year of preparations, where large amounts of data were collected and annotated, task definitions were redefined, metrics were discussed and harmonized, evaluation tools were developed, and evaluation packages were distributed to participants all over the world. In CLEAR'07, seventeen international research laboratories participated in 13 evaluation subtasks.

An important contribution of the CLEAR evaluations on the whole, is the fact that they provide an international forum for the discussion and harmonization of related evaluation tasks, including the definition of procedures, metrics and guidelines for the collection and annotation of necessary multimodal datasets.

Another important contribution of CLEAR and the supporting programs is also the fact that significant multimedia datasets and evaluation benchmarks have been produced over the course of several years, which are now available to the research community. Evaluation packages for the various tasks, including datasets, annotations, scoring tools, evaluation protocols and metrics, are available through the Evaluations and Language Distribution Agency (ELDA)[9] and NIST.

While we consider CLEAR'06 and '07 as a great success, we think that the evaluation tasks performed - mainly tracking, identification, head pose estimation and acoustic scene analysis - do yet only scratch the surface of automatic perception and understanding of humans and their activities. As systems addressing such "lower-level" perceptual tasks are becoming more mature, we expect that further tasks, addressing human activity analysis on higher levels, will become part of future CLEAR evaluations.

## Acknowledgments

The work presented here was partly funded by the European Union (EU) under the integrated project CHIL, Computers in the Human Interaction Loop (Grant number IST-506909) and partial funding was also provided by the US Government VACE program.

VACE would additionally like to thank the following groups for the use of tools and resources developed under CLEAR 2006:

- The University of Maryland, for their VIPER video annotation tool
- Video Mining, for their video data annotation efforts
- The University of South Florida, for their evaluation scoring tool

The authors also thank Padmanabhan Soundararajan of the University of South Florida for his participation in developing the CLEAR metrics and his kind assistance in the use of the evaluation scoring tool.

*Disclaimer: Certain commercial equipment, instruments, software, or materials are identified in this paper in order to specify the experimental procedure adequately. Such identification is not intended to imply recommendation or endorsement by the National Institute of Standards, nor is it intended to imply that the equipment, instruments, software or materials are necessarily the best available for the purpose they were presented.*

## References

1. CHIL - Computers In the Human Interaction Loop, http://chil.server.de
2. AMI - Augmented Multiparty Interaction, http://www.amiproject.org
3. VACE - Video Analysis and Content Extraction,
   https://control.nist.gov/dto/twiki/bin/view/Main/WebHome

4. CALO - Cognitive Agent that Learns and Organizes,
   `http://caloproject.sri.com/`
5. NIST Rich Transcription Meeting Recognition Evaluations,
   `http://www.nist.gov/speech/tests/rt/rt2006/spring/`
6. The i-LIDS dataset,
   http://scienceandresearch.homeoffice.gov.uk/hosdb/cctv-imaging-technology/
   video-based-detection-systems/i-lids/
7. DARPA VIVID, http://www.vividevaluation.ri.cmu.edu/datasets/PETS2005/
   PkTest02/index.html
8. CLEAR evaluation webpage, `http://www.clear-evaluation.org`
9. ELRA/ELDA's Catalogue of Language Resources, `http://catalog.elda.org/`
10. Ba, S.O., Odobez, J.M.: Evaluation of head pose tracking algorithm in indoor
    environments. In: International Conference on Multimedia & Expo, ICME 2005,
    Amsterdam, Netherlands (2005)
11. Bernardin, K., Elbs, A., Stiefelhagen, R.: Multiple object tracking performance
    metrics and evaluation in a smart room environment. In: 6th IEEE Int. Workshop
    on Visual Surveillance, VS 2006 (May 2006)
12. Bernardin, K., Gehrig, T., Stiefelhagen, R.: Multi- and single view multiperson
    tracking for smart room environments. In: Stiefelhagen, R., Garofolo, J.S. (eds.)
    CLEAR 2006. LNCS, vol. 4122, Springer, Heidelberg (2007)
13. Bernardin, K., Gehrig, T., Stiefelhagen, R.: Multi-level particle filter fusion of fea-
    tures and cues for audio-visual person tracking. In: Multimodal Technologies for
    Perception of Humans, Joint Proceedings of the CLEAR 2007 and RT 2007 Eval-
    uation Workshops, Baltimore, MD, USA. LNCS, vol. 4625, Springer, Heidelberg
    (2007)
14. Bernardin, K., Stiefelhagen, R.: Evaluating multiple object tracking performance:
    The CLEAR MOT Metrics. EURASIP Journal on Image and Video Processing,
    Special Issue on Video Tracking in Complex Scenes for Surveillance Applications
    (submitted)
15. Canton-Ferrer, C., Salvador, J., Casas, J.R., Pardas, M.: Multi-person tracking
    strategies based on voxel analysis. In: Multimodal Technologies for Perception of
    Humans, Joint Proceedings of the CLEAR 2007 and RT 2007 Evaluation Work-
    shops, Baltimore, MD, USA. LNCS, vol. 4625, Springer, Heidelberg (2007)
16. Doermann, D., Mihalcik, D.: Tools and techniques for video performances evalua-
    tion. In: International Conference on Pattern Recognition, pp. 167–170 (2000)
17. Ekenel, H.K., Jin, Q., Fischer, M., Stiefelhagen, R.: ISL Person Identification Sys-
    tems in the CLEAR 2007 Evaluations. In: Multimodal Technologies for Perception
    of Humans, Joint Proceedings of the CLEAR 2007 and RT 2007 Evaluation Work-
    shops, Baltimore, MD, USA. LNCS, vol. 4625, Springer, Heidelberg (2007)
18. Mariano, V.Y., Min, J., Park, J.-H., Kasturi, R., Mihalcik, D., Doermann, D.,
    Drayer, T.: Performance evaluation of object detection algorithms. In: International
    Conference on Pattern Recognition, pp. 965–969 (2002)
19. Mostefa, D., Moreau, N., Choukri, K., Potamianos, G., Chu, S.M., Tyagi, A.,
    Casas, J.R., Turmo, J., Christoforetti, L., Tobia, F., Pnevmatikakis, A., Mylonakis,
    V., Talantzis, F., Burger, S., Stiefelhagen, R., Bernardin, K., Rochet, C.: The
    chil audiovisual corpus for lecture and meeting analysis inside smart rooms. In:
    Language Resources and Evaluation, vol. 41, Springer, Heidelberg (2007)
20. Nechyba, M.C., Brandy, L., Schneiderman, H.: Pittpatt face detection and tracking
    for the clear 2007 evaluation. In: Multimodal Technologies for Perception of Hu-
    mans, Joint Proceedings of the CLEAR 2007 and RT 2007 Evaluation Workshops,
    Baltimore, MD, USA. LNCS, vol. 4625, Springer, Heidelberg (2007)

21. Raju, H., Prasad, S.: Annotation guidelines for video analysis and content extraction (VACE-II). In: CLEAR Evaluation Workshop (2006)
22. Stiefelhagen, R., Bernardin, K., Bowers, R., Garofolo, J., Mostefa, D., Soundararajan, P.: The CLEAR 2006 Evaluation. In: Stiefelhagen, R., Garofolo, J.S. (eds.) CLEAR 2006. LNCS, vol. 4122, Springer, Heidelberg (2007)
23. Stiefelhagen, R., Garofolo, J.S. (eds.): CLEAR 2006. LNCS, vol. 4122. Springer, Heidelberg (2007)

# Appendix A: Result Graphs for 3D Person Tracking

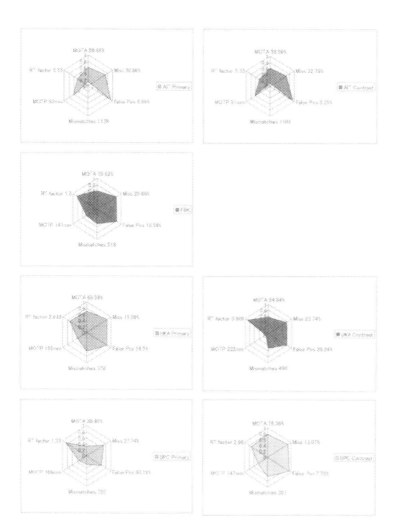

**Fig. 22.** 3D Person Tracking – Visual subtask: Radar Charts

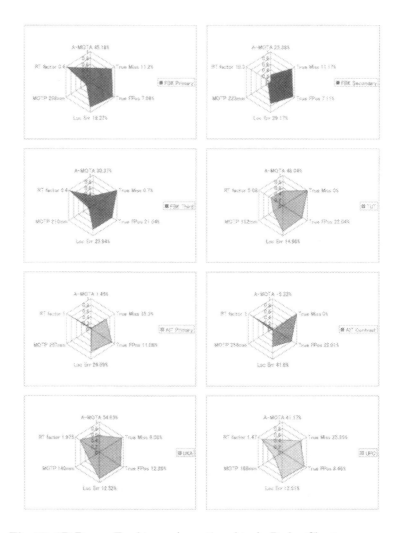

**Fig. 23.** 3D Person Tracking – Acoustic subtask: Radar Charts

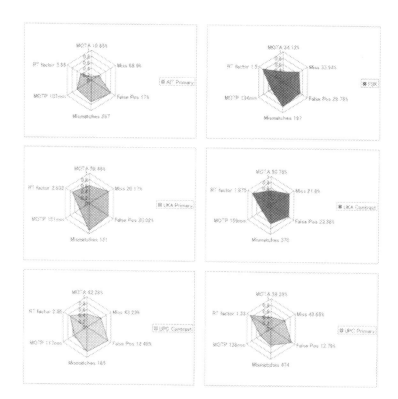

**Fig. 24.** 3D Person Tracking – Multimodal subtask: Radar Charts

# Appendix B: Progress Charts for Person Identification

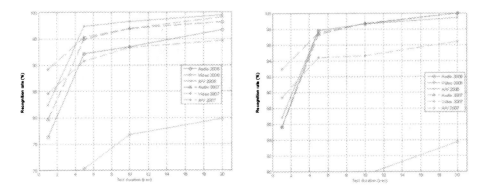

**Fig. 25.** Person Identification – Visual subtask: Progress Chart

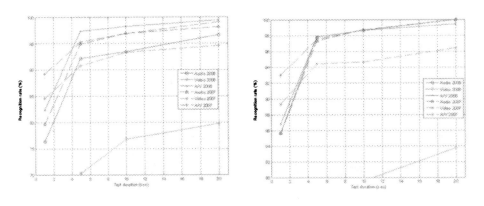

**Fig. 26.** Person Identification – Acoustic subtask: Progress Chart

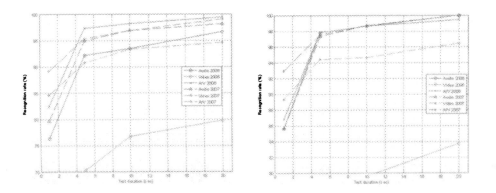

**Fig. 27.** Person Identification – Multimodal subtask: Progress Chart

# The AIT 3D Audio / Visual Person Tracker for CLEAR 2007

Nikos Katsarakis, Fotios Talantzis,
Aristodemos Pnevmatikakis, and Lazaros Polymenakos

Athens Information Technology, Autonomic and Grid Computing,
P.O. Box 64, Markopoulou Ave., 19002 Peania, Greece
{nkat, fota, apne, lcp}@ait.edu.gr
http://www.ait.edu.gr/research/RG1/overview.asp

**Abstract.** This paper presents the Athens Information Technology system for 3D person tracking and the obtained results in the CLEAR 2007 evaluations. The system utilizes audiovisual information from multiple acoustic and video sensors. The proposed system comprises a video and an audio subsystem whose results are suitably combined to track the last active speaker. The video subsystem combines in 3D a number of 2D face localization systems, aiming at tracking all people present in a room. The audio subsystem uses an information theoretic metric upon an ensemble of microphones to estimate the active speaker.

## 1 Introduction

Three dimensional person tracking from multiple synchronized audiovisual sensors has many applications, like surveillance, security, smart spaces [1], pervasive computing, and human-machine interfaces [2] to name a few. In such trackers, body motion is the most widely used video cue, while speech is the audio cue. As speech is not always present for all people present in the monitored space, a stand-alone audio tracker cannot provide continuous tracks. A video tracker on the other hand can loose track of the people due to clutter from other people and the background. In this case the audio cue can help resolve the tracks.

In this paper an audiovisual approach towards 3D tracking is employed. The stand-alone video tracker aims at tracking all people present in the monitored space from the synchronized recordings of multiple calibrated cameras [3] to produce 3D tracks from multiple 2D face trackers [4]. The audio tracker aims at finding the active speaker. It employs an information theoretic approach [5] for direction-of-arrival estimation, as this can be combined using multiple clusters of microphones [6]. The multimodal tracker combines the two into a system that tracks the last active speaker, even after he or she has stopped talking.

This paper is organized as follows: In sections 2 to 4 the audio, video and multimodal combination modules of the tracker are detailed. The results on CLEAR 2007 evaluations are presented and discussed in section 5. Finally, in section 6 the conclusions are drawn, followed by some indications for further work.

R. Stiefelhagen et al. (Eds.): CLEAR 2007 and RT 2007, LNCS 4625, pp. 35–46, 2008.
© Springer-Verlag Berlin Heidelberg 2008

## 2 Audio 3D Tracker

An audio-based localization system is typically employed in a reverberant environment and it considers $M$ microphones arranged in $P$ pairs. The sound source that the system attempts to locate and track is assumed to be in the far field of the microphones. Therefore, we can approximate the spherical wavefront emanating from the source as a plane wavefront of sound waves arriving at the microphone pairs in a parallel manner. The discrete signal recorded at the $m$-th microphone ( $m = 1, 2$ ) of the $p$-th pair at time $k$ is:

$$x_{mp}(k) = h_{mp}(k) * s(k) + n_{mp}(k), \quad p = 1, 2, \ldots, P \tag{1}$$

where $s(k)$ is the source signal, $h_{mp}(k)$ is the room impulse response between the source and $m$-th microphone, $n_{mp}(k)$ is additive noise, and $*$ denotes convolution. The length of $h_{mp}(k)$, and thus the number of reflections, is a function of the reverberation time $T_{60}$ (defined as the time in seconds for the reverberation level to decay to 60 dB below the initial level) of the room and expresses the main problem when attempting to track an acoustic source. This is because when the system is used in reverberant environments, the source location can be estimated in a spurious location created by the reflections.

Most of the localization systems are required to operate in real time. Therefore we assume that data at each sensor $m$ are collected over $t$ frames of data $\mathbf{x}_{mp}^{[t]} = \left[ x_{mp}(tL), x_{mp}(tL+1), \ldots, x_{mp}(tL+L-1) \right]$ of $L$ samples. So, we can have a representation of the microphone data until time frame $t$ by forming the array:

$$\mathbf{x}_{1:t} = \begin{bmatrix} \mathbf{x}_{11}^{[1]} & \mathbf{x}_{11}^{[2]} & \cdots & \mathbf{x}_{11}^{[t]} \\ \mathbf{x}_{21}^{[1]} & \mathbf{x}_{21}^{[2]} & \cdots & \mathbf{x}_{21}^{[t]} \\ \vdots & \vdots & & \vdots \\ \mathbf{x}_{1p}^{[1]} & \mathbf{x}_{1p}^{[2]} & \cdots & \mathbf{x}_{1p}^{[t]} \\ \mathbf{x}_{2p}^{[1]} & \mathbf{x}_{2p}^{[2]} & \cdots & \mathbf{x}_{2p}^{[t]} \end{bmatrix} \tag{2}$$

Since the microphones of each pair reside in different spatial locations, their corresponding recordings will be delayed with respect to each other by a relative time delay $\tau_p$. The first aim of localization systems is to retrieve this Time Delay Estimate (TDE) between the two microphones of each pair $p$. This typically performed by looking for the delay that maximizes some criterion amongst some set of candidate delays. Using all estimated $\tau_p$ the localizer can then provide an estimate of the source location. Traditional systems typically do this by converting $\tau_p$ to a line along which the estimated source position is. The problem of localization then reduces to finding the location which minimizes the distance to each intersection points of the bearing lines [7]. In the context of the present work we use an alternative approach. We still collect all $\tau_p$ but these serve as a feed to a Particle Filter (PF) that has an embedded

Voice Activity Detection (VAD) functionality. PFs allow us to integrate the properties of human motion while the VAD module helps us to deal with the silence periods existing in the utterances of the active speaker.

The following paragraphs describe separately the sub-systems of the audio tracker. First the general PF framework for localization is presented. Then we briefly describe the TDE estimation method and finally we review the VAD system.

## 2.1  State-Space Estimation Using Particle Filters

Assuming a first order model for the source dynamics, the source state at any frame $t$ is given as:

$$\mathbf{a}_t = \left[ X_t, Y_t, Z_t, \dot{X}_t, \dot{Y}_t, \dot{Z}_t \right]^T \tag{3}$$

where $s_{\mathbf{a}_t} = \left[ X_t, Y_t, Z_t \right]$ is the source location and $\left[ \dot{X}_t, \dot{Y}_t, \dot{Z}_t \right]$ the corresponding source velocity. If we could calculate the conditional density $q\left(\mathbf{a}_t | \mathbf{x}_{1:t}\right)$, we could then find the source location by choosing the state that is more likely given the sensor data until frame $t$. We can perform this by using [8]:

$$q\left(\mathbf{a}_t | \mathbf{x}_{1:t}\right) \propto q\left(\mathbf{x}_t | \mathbf{a}_t\right) q\left(\mathbf{a}_t | \mathbf{x}_{1:t-1}\right) \tag{4}$$

where we have set $\mathbf{x}_t \equiv \mathbf{x}_{t:t}$. Also, $q\left(\mathbf{x}_t | \mathbf{a}_t\right)$ is the likelihood and $q\left(\mathbf{a}_t | \mathbf{x}_{1:t-1}\right)$ is known as the prediction density and it is given as [8]:

$$q\left(\mathbf{a}_t | \mathbf{x}_{1:t-1}\right) = \int q\left(\mathbf{a}_t | \mathbf{a}_{t-1}\right) q\left(\mathbf{a}_{t-1} | \mathbf{x}_{1:t-1}\right) d\mathbf{a}_{t-1} \tag{5}$$

where $q\left(\mathbf{a}_t | \mathbf{a}_{t-1}\right)$ is the state transition density, and $q\left(\mathbf{a}_{t-1} | \mathbf{x}_{1:t-1}\right)$ is the prior filtering density. The solution to (4) and (5) can be found using a Monte-Carlo simulation of a set of particles with associated discrete probability masses that estimate the source state. For this we require a model of how the source propagates from $\mathbf{a}_{t-1}$ to $\mathbf{a}_t$. To keep consistent with the literature we will use the Langevin model [9]. We also need a function to measure the likelihood of the microphone data, which is [9]:

$$q\left(\mathbf{x}_t | \mathbf{a}_t\right) = \prod_{p=1}^{P} q_p\left(\mathbf{x}_t | \mathbf{a}_t\right) \tag{6}$$

where

$$q_p\left(\mathbf{x}_t | \mathbf{a}_t\right) = \max\left( R_p^{[t]}\left(\tau_p^{[\mathbf{a}_t]}\right), p_0 \right)^2 \tag{7}$$

and $p_0$ is some prior probability that none of the potential source locations is the true one. $R_p^{[t]}$ is a TDE function evaluated only at a set of candidate delays given as:

$$\tau_p^{[\mathbf{a}_t]} = \left( \left\| s_{\mathbf{a}_t} - \mathbf{m}_{1p} \right\| - \left\| s_{\mathbf{a}_t} - \mathbf{m}_{2p} \right\| \right) / c \tag{8}$$

where $\mathbf{m}_{mp}$ denotes the location of the $m$-th microphone at the $p$-th pair and $c$ is the speed of sound.

There are occasions where reverberation or noise sources can trap the particles in a spurious location. For this we use an external PF $\mathbf{e}_t$ that has the same architecture as the main one $\mathbf{a}_t$ but it is initialized at every frame $t$. If these new particles estimate a source location that is $d_e$ away from the main PF for a significant amount of time $T_e$ then we reset the locations of the particles of the main PF to those of the external.

## 2.2   Time Delay Estimation

A variety of methods like GCC [10] exist for TDE. For any pair $p$ the GCC-PHAT variant $R_t(\tau)$ is defined as the cross correlation of $\mathbf{x}_{1p}^{[t]}$ and $\mathbf{x}_{2p}^{[t]}$, filtered by a weighting function g for a range of delays $\tau$. Let $X_{1p}^{[t]}(\omega)$, $X_{2p}^{[t]}(\omega)$ and $G(\omega)$ denote the $L$-point discrete Fourier transforms of the microphone signals and the g function for the $p$-th pair at frame $t$. Since the TDE analysis is independent of the data frame, we drop $t$ to express frames simply as $X_{mp}^{[t]}(\omega)$ for any $t$. In the context of our model, and for any set of frames, we may then write $X_{1p}(\omega) = X_{2p}(\omega)e^{-j\omega\tau_p}$. Thus, the problem is essentially to estimate the correct value of $\tau_p$ for which the two recordings are synchronized. We can express $R_t(\tau)$ as:

$$R_t(\tau) = \frac{1}{2\pi}\sum_{\omega} G(\omega) X_{1p}(\omega) X_{2p}^*(\omega) e^{j\omega\tau} \qquad (9)$$

with

$$G(\omega) = 1/\left|X_{1p}(\omega) X_{2p}^*(\omega)\right| \qquad (10)$$

Ideally, $R_t(\tau)$ exhibits a global maximum at the lag value which corresponds to the correct $\tau$. Thus, an estimation of $\tau_p$ can be obtained by $\tau_p = \arg\max_\tau R(\tau)$.

## 2.3   Voice Activity Detection

The VAD employed for the purposes of our system is presented in [11]. It is a conceptually simple system that operates fast enough to be used in conjunction with real-time implementations like our speaker localization system. More particularly the used VAD extends the use of statistical models in speech detection by employing a decision-directed parameter estimation method for the likelihood ratio test that defines the presence of speech. This is combined with an effective hang-over scheme which considers the previous observations by a first-order Markov process modeling of speech occurrences. This serves as an improvement to typical VAD algorithms which normally operate on heuristics.

We then fuse the VAD decision with the tracking system in the same manner authors did in [12]. This is done by noting that the probability $1 - p_0$ corresponds to the likelihood of the acoustic source being active i.e. the result returned by the VAD. Thus, we can choose $p_0$ to vary in time in accordance to the result of the VAD as $p_0^{[t]} = 1 - a^{[t]}$ with $a^{[t]} \in [0,1]$ the return value of the VAD with 1 denoting presence and 0 absence of speech in time frame $t$.

The summary of the proposed algorithm can be itemized as follows:

1) Start with a set of particles $a_0^{[i]}, i = 1...N$ with uniform weights $w_0^{[i]}, i = 1...N$. For every new frame of data perform steps 2-7.

2) Resample the particles from state $a_{t-1}^{[i]}$ using some resampling method [13] (we used the *residual resampling* algorithm) and form the resampled set of particles $\tilde{a}_{t-1}^{[i]}, i = 1...N$.

3) Using the Langevin model, propagate $\tilde{a}_{t-1}^{[i]}$ to predict the current set of particles $a_t^{[i]}$.

4) Take a set of frames of $L$ samples from each microphone and convert them into the frequency domain to get $X_{mp}(\omega), m = 1, 2, p = 1...P$.

5) For every pair of microphones calculate the MI only at the time delays corresponding to $a_t^{[i]}$, using the delays found by (8).

6) Weight the particles using the likelihood function i.e. $w_t^{[i]} = p(x_t | a_t^{[i]}), i = 1...N$ and normalize the weights so that they add up to unity.

7) The source location for the current frame is then given as the weighted average of the particles: $s_t = \sum_{i=1}^{N} w_t^{[i]} s_a$. If the external PF $e_t^{[i]}$ source estimate remains at a distance greater than $d_e$ for more than $T_e$ sec then set $a_t^{[i]} = e_t^{[i]}, i = 1...N$.

## 3   Video 3D Tracker

The video 3D tracker employs multiple instances of the AIT 2D face tracker [4], each operating on the synchronized video streams of multiple calibrated cameras [3]. Possible associations of the different views of a face are constructed by projecting a grid of 3D points onto the different image planes and collecting face evidence. A stochastic tracker then selects the best association. Additionally, a panoramic camera view is also processed by the AIT body tracker [14] used in the CLEAR 2006 evaluations. The 3D locations of the people estimated by associating the faces are projected onto the panoramic camera plane and are validated by the tracked bodies in that camera view.

### 3.1   Face Tracker

The 2D face localization system is detailed in [4]. Face localization is constrained in the body areas provided by the AIT body tracker [14]. Three face detectors for frontal and left/right profile faces provide candidate face regions in the body areas. They are of the cascades of simple features type, trained with AdaBoost. The face candidates are validated using the probability scores from a Gaussian Mixture Model trained from texture and color properties of faces. The surviving candidates are checked for possible merging, as both the profile detectors and the frontal one can detect different portions of the same face if the view is half-profile. The resulting face candidates are associated with faces existing in the previous frame and also with tracks that currently have no supporting evidence and are pending to either get an association, or be eliminated. Any faces of the previous frame that do not get associated with candidate faces at the current frame have a CAM-Shift tracker initiated to attempt to track similarly colored regions in the current frame. If CAM-Shift also fails to track, then these past faces have their track in pending status for $F_p$ frames. Finally, all active face tracks are checked for duplicates, i.e. high spatial similarity. In the following subsections, the various modules of the system are detailed.

### 3.2 Mapping of Faces in 2D into Heads in 3D

Our approach for 3D tracking utilizes the 2D face localization system presented in the previous section, applied on multiple calibrated [3] and synchronized cameras. To solve the problem of associating the views of the face of the same person from the different cameras, a 3D space to 2D image planes approach is utilized. The space is spanned by a 3D grid. Each point of the grid is projected onto the different image planes. Faces whose centers are close to the projected points are associated to the particular 3D point. 3D points that have more than one face associated to them are used to form possible associations of views of the face of the same person from the different cameras. If in each camera view $c$ there are $n_c$ faces then the $k$-th association (of the total $K$ ones) that span the 3D space is of the form $a^{(k)} = \left\{ i_1^{(k)}, \ldots, i_C^{(k)} \right\}$, where $C$ is the number of available cameras and $i_c^{(k)} \in \{0, 1, \ldots n_c\}$. A value $i_c^{(k)} = 0$ corresponds to no face from the $c$-th camera in the $k$-th association, while any other value corresponds to the membership of a face from those in the $c$-th camera in the $k$-th association. Obviously $\forall c \in \{1, \ldots, C\}$, $i_c^{(k_1)} > 0$ and $k_1 \neq k_2$, it is $i_c^{(k_1)} \neq i_c^{(k_2)}$, i.e. the same face in a camera view cannot be a member of different valid associations This condition renders some of the associations mutually exclusive. After eliminating duplicate associations, the remaining ones are grouped into possible sets of mutually exclusive associations and sorted according to a weight that depends on the distance of each association from the face center and on the number of other associations that contradict it.

All the $M$ mutually exclusive sets of possible associations $a^{(k)}$ are validated using a Kalman filter in the 3D space. For each new frame, all possible solutions are compared to the state established on the previous frame, penalizing solutions which fail to detect previously existing targets, or in which there are detections of new targets in the scene. While this strategy reduces the misses and false positives, it does not prevent new targets from appearing, as in the case of new people entering the room, all solution pairs will include that new target and thus will be equally penalized.

## 4   Audiovisual 3D Tracker

The audiovisual tracker uses the synchronized outputs of both Audio 3D and Video 3D person trackers to generate the audiovisual output. It constantly keeps track of all provided video tracker positions for the current frame. However, no output is provided, unless the voice activity detector of the audio tracker indicates that only one person is talking at the time period under consideration. On the other hand, whenever the audio tracker indicates that there is a person talking, the system tries to find the closest match between the provided speaker position and any of the recently updated video states. If there is such an association, the person is tracked by the video tracker, keeping consistent track id over time, otherwise the system outputs the position given by the audio localizer. A flowchart of the system is shown in Figure 1.

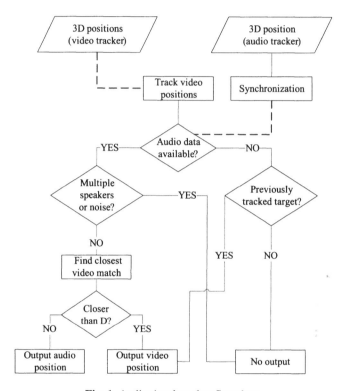

**Fig. 1.** Audiovisual tracker flowchart

## 5   CLEAR 2007 Evaluation Results

The video, audio and audiovisual trackers presented in sections 2, 3 and 4 are evaluated using the CLEAR 2007 multimodal recordings. Typical results are shown in Figure 2.

The quantitative evaluation of the proposed system follows the CLEAR2007 evaluation protocol [15]. According to it, the tracking system outputs (hypotheses) are mapped to annotated ground truths based on centroid distance and using the Hungarian algorithm [16]. The metrics for face tracking are five [15]. The Multiple Object Tracking Precision (MOTP) is the position error for all correctly tracked persons over

**Fig. 2.** Operation of the individual 2D face trackers on the four corner cameras and association of the 2D evidence into 3D tracks. The detected faces are marked by bounding boxes. The IDs of the tracks are of the form AIT_XXX shown at the projection of the tracked head centroids on the floor. The tracks are also projected to a panoramic camera (not used by the system) for better visualization.

**Table 1.** Video-based person tracking performance of the system on all 38 seminars, averaged per site

| Site | MOTP (mm) | MOTA (%) | Misses (%) | False positives (%) | Mismatches (%) |
|------|-----------|----------|------------|---------------------|----------------|
| AIT | 81.22 | 60.15 | 33.67 | 3.57 | 2.61 |
| IBM | 93.56 | 60.39 | 29.39 | 8.47 | 1.75 |
| ITC | 97.73 | 59.66 | 30.45 | 6.83 | 3.06 |
| UKA | 94.85 | 50.75 | 40.72 | 5.86 | 2.67 |
| UPC | 88.70 | 65.13 | 23.77 | 8.47 | 2.63 |
| **Overall** | **91.51** | **59.66** | **30.86** | **6.99** | **2.50** |

all frames. It is a measure of how well the system performs when it actually finds the face. There are three kinds of errors for the tracker, false positives, misses and track identity mismatches. They are reported independently and also jointly in an accuracy metric, the Multiple Object Tracking Accuracy (MOTA). The MOTA is the residual of the sum of these three error rates from unity. For the audio system, there is no

**Table 2.** Video-based person tracking performance of the system on all 38 seminars, averaged per site, including panoramic camera

| Site | MOTP (mm) | MOTA (%) | Misses (%) | False positives (%) | Mismatches (%) |
|------|-----------|----------|------------|---------------------|----------------|
| AIT | 80.11 | 58.65 | 36.29 | 2.50 | 2.56 |
| IBM | 92.44 | 61.19 | 30.50 | 6.56 | 1.75 |
| ITC | 97.73 | 59.66 | 30.45 | 6.83 | 3.06 |
| UKA | 96.00 | 46.79 | 48.46 | 2.39 | 2.36 |
| UPC | 88.74 | 67.69 | 23.28 | 6.46 | 2.57 |
| **Overall** | **91.22** | **59.56** | **32.78** | **5.25** | **2.42** |

**Table 3.** Audio-based person tracking performance of the system on all 40 seminars, averaged per site

| Site | MOTP (mm) | A-MOTA (%) | Misses (%) | False positives (%) |
|------|-----------|------------|------------|---------------------|
| AIT | 229.00 | 25.85 | 51.45 | 22.70 |
| IBM | 266.76 | 10.16 | 66.10 | 23.74 |
| ITC | 269.99 | -12.46 | 56.97 | 55.49 |
| UKA | 316.70 | -27.65 | 66.05 | 61.60 |
| UPC | 214.19 | 11.60 | 64.32 | 24.08 |
| **Overall** | **256.89** | **1.46** | **61.39** | **37.15** |

**Table 4.** Audiovisual person tracking performance of the system on all 38 seminars, averaged per site

| Site | MOTP (mm) | MOTA (%) | Misses (%) | FPs (%) | Mismatches (%) |
|------|-----------|----------|------------|---------|----------------|
| AIT | 93.32 | 29.02 | 60.57 | 6.67 | 3.74 |
| IBM | 144.62 | 5.34 | 83.49 | 8.83 | 2.34 |
| ITC | 122.21 | 2.29 | 64.19 | 28.80 | 4.72 |
| UKA | 83.62 | -4.48 | 67.27 | 35.00 | 2.20 |
| UPC | 98.37 | 21.68 | 66.13 | 9.25 | 2.94 |
| **Overall** | **107.12** | **10.85** | **68.90** | **17.00** | **3.24** |

penalty for identity switches, hence the MOTA only have two components: The misses and the false positives. The quantitative performance of the video, audio and audiovisual systems is summarized in Tables 1-4.

It is instructive to compare the MOTA obtained by the 2D face localization system, to that of the 3D person tracking system. This way we understand the benefit of combining the 2D information into 3D. This is done in Figure 5 for all seminars. Obviously, for seminars where the 2D MOTA has been low, there is a lot to gain. Only rarely the 3D MOTA is lower than the 2D, since misses, false positives and identity switches can be constrained by combining all four cameras. It is also important to understand which component of the 2D face tracking MOTA is more correlated with the 3D person tracking MOTA, affecting it the most: the misses or the false positives.

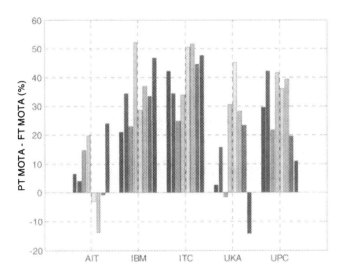

**Fig. 3.** Improvement of the 3D visual person tracking MOTA over the 2D face tracking MOTA. There is significant gain from combining the 2D face locations into the 3D locations.

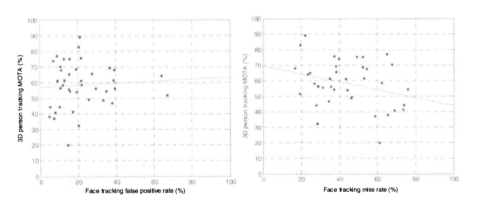

**Fig. 4.** Correlation of the 3D person tracking MOTA to the 2D face tracking false positives and misses. As the slope of the linear regression shows, the most important factor affecting the 3D MOTA is the 2D face misses.

The scatter plots of Figure 6 address this question. It is evident from the scatter and the slope of the linear regression that the 3D MOTA is not strongly correlated to the 2D false positives. On the other hand there is a strong correlation of the 3D MOTA to the 2D misses.

## 6   Conclusions

In this paper we have presented and evaluated a 3D audiovisual tracking system that employs multiple audio and video sensors. The video subsystem exhibits good performance, consistent among the different test sites. On the other hand, the audio tracker does not perform as expected, especially on 2 out of the 5 test sites. Preliminary analysis of the results shows that a main cause of errors is the voice activity detection module. The audiovisual module improves the performance of the audio tracker, showing that further development of the latter will bring promising results.

## Acknowledgements

This work is sponsored by the European Union under the integrated project CHIL, contract number 506909. The authors wish to thank the people involved in data collection, annotation and overall organization of the CLEAR 2007 evaluations for providing such a rich test-bed for the presented algorithms.

## References

[1] Waibel, A., Steusloff, H., Stiefelhagen, R., et al.: CHIL: Computers in the Human Interaction Loop. In: 5th International Workshop on Image Analysis for Multimedia Interactive Services (WIAMIS), Lisbon, Portugal (April 2004)

[2] Pnevmatikakis, A., Talantzis, F., Soldatos, J., Polymenakos, L.: Robust Multimodal Audio-Visual Processing for Advanced Context Awareness in Smart Spaces. In: Artificial Intelligence Applications and Innovations, Peania, Greece (June 2006)

[3] Zhang, Z.: A Flexible New Technique for Camera Calibration, Technical Report MSR-TR-98-71, Microsoft Research (August 2002)

[4] Stergiou, A., Karame, G., Pnevmatikakis, A., Polymenakos, L.: The AIT 2D face detection and tracking system for CLEAR2007. In: CLEAR 2007. LNCS, vol. 4625. Springer, Heidelberg (2008)

[5] Talantzis, F., Constantinides, A.G., Polymenakos, L.: Estimation of Direction of Arrival Using Information Theory. IEEE Signal Processing 12(8), 561–564 (2005)

[6] Talantzis, F., Constantinides, A.G., Polymenakos, L.: Real-Time Audio Source Localization Using Information Theory. In: Joint Workshop on Multimodal Interaction and Related Machine Learning Algorithms (MLMI 2006) (May 2006)

[7] Brandstein, M.S., Adcock, J.E., Silverman, H.: A Closed-Form Location Estimator for Use with Room Environment Microphone Arrays. IEEE Trans. on Acoust. Speech and Sig. Proc. 5, 45–50 (1997)

[8] Gordon, N.J., Salmond, D.J., Smith, A.F.M.: Novel approach to nonlinear/nongaussian bayesian state estimation. IEE Proceedings-F (Radar and Signal Processing) 140(2), 107–113 (1993)

[9] Vermaak, J., Blake, A.: Nonlinear filtering for speaker tracking in noisy and reverberant environments. In: Proc. IEEE Int. Conf. on Acoustics, Speech and Signal Processing, Salt Lake City, USA, May 2001, vol. 5, pp. 3021–3024 (2001)

[10] Knapp, C.H., Carter, G.C.: The generalized correlation method for estimation of time delay. IEEE Trans. Acoust., Speech, Signal Process. ASSP-24(4), 320–327 (1976)

[11] Sohn, J., Kim, N.S., Sung, W.: A statistical model-based voice activity detection. IEEE Signal Processing Letters 6, 1–3 (1999)

[12] Lehmann, E.A., Johansson, A.M.: Particle Filter with Integrated Voice Activity Detection for Acoustic Source Tracking. EURASIP Journal on Advances in Signal Processing 2007 Article ID 50870 (2007)

[13] Bolic, M., Djuric, P.M., Hong, S.: New Resampling Algorithms for Particle Filters. In: Proceedings of the IEEE International Conference on Acoustics, Speech, and Signal Processing, Hong Kong, vol. 2, pp. 589–592 (2003)

[14] Pnevmatikakis, A., Polymenakos, L.: 2D Person Tracking Using Kalman Filtering and Adaptive Background Learning in a Feedback Loop. In: Stiefelhagen, R., Garofolo, J.S. (eds.) CLEAR 2006. LNCS, vol. 4122, Springer, Heidelberg (2007)

[15] Mostefa, D., et al.: CLEAR Evaluation Plan, document CHIL-CLEAR-V1.1-2006-02-21 (February 2006)

[16] Blackman, S.: Multiple-Target Tracking with Radar Applications, ch. 14. Artech House, Dedham (1986)

# A Person Tracking System for CHIL Meetings

Alessio Brutti*

FBK-irst,
Via Sommarive 18,
38050 Povo di Trento,
Italy
brutti@itc.it

**Abstract.** This paper presents the audio based tracking system designed at FBK-irst laboratories for the CLEAR 2007 evaluation campaign. The tracker relies on the Global Coherence Field theory that has proved to efficiently deal with the foreseen scenarios. Particular emphasis is given to the post-processing of localization hypotheses which guarantees smooth speaker trajectories and is crucial for the overall performance of the system. The system is also equipped with a speech activity detector based on Hidden Markov Models. The performance delivered by the proposed tracker presents a considerable gain with respect to the previous evaluation. An attempt to devise a multimodal tracker based on merging outputs of a video and an audio trackers is also described.

## 1 Introduction

The goal of an audio based person tracker is to estimate the position of an active speaker from a set of acoustic measurements. This paper presents the algorithm designed at FBK-irst laboratories to participate to the CLEAR 2007 evaluation campaign on multi-person audio tracking. The proposed tracker is a direct evolution of the system adopted in the previous evaluation [12] and hence its core consists in the computation, and maximization, of sound maps representing the acoustic activity in a given environment. In particular the system was modified in order to fit the new meeting scenario and the new metrics [1]. Given a traditional Global Coherence Field (GCF) [20] framework that efficiently handle multi-channel audio inputs, the novelties of this work are represented by a Speech Activity Detection (SAD) module based on Hidden Markov Models (HMM), which is in charge with triggering the tracker, and a final post-processing module, whose goal is to deliver smooth and regular speaker trajectories and remove outliers. Figure 1 shows the overall system block diagram and highlights the role of the SAD module and of the post-processing.

This paper is organized as follows: section 2 introduces the peculiarities of the mutli-person acoustic tracking task in CLEAR 2007; section 3 describes the modules that constitute the proposed tracking system; section 4 includes evaluation results and conclusions and section 5 briefly describes a multimodal tracker that combines the outcomes of an audio and a visual trackers.

---

\* This work was partially supported by the EU under the CHIL and DICIT projects.

R. Stiefelhagen et al. (Eds.): CLEAR 2007 and RT 2007, LNCS 4625, pp. 47–56, 2008.

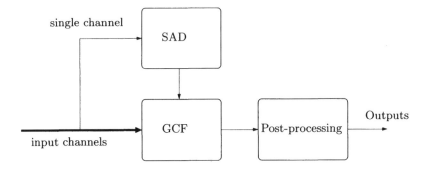

**Fig. 1.** Block diagram of the proposed tracking system. The SAD module activates the sound map computation and the post-processing filter elaborates the GCF peaks.

## 2   CLEAR 2007

The CLEAR 2007 evaluation is focused on meetings that are held in smart rooms equipped with a Distributed Microphone Network (DMN) as envisioned in the CHIL project [2]. In particular, the adopted DMN implementation consists in a set of T-shaped microphone arrays and the 64 channel NIST Mark-III linear array. The 40 audio chunks taken in consideration for the evaluation are excerpts of real meetings recorded in the 5 smart rooms (CHIL rooms) arranged by the CHIL partners. Recordings involve 4 or 5 participants with considerably different levels of interaction. In some cases silence and noise sources are predominant while in other cases speech is present most of the time. As in the previous evaluation, a reference file, including speaker coordinates and speech/silence information, was available for each meeting with $1\,s$ time resolution. A deep description of the CHIL data collections can be found in [10]. Being recordings of real meeting, the database presents some peculiarities that differentiate this tracking task from more traditional formulations. As a matter of fact, in the given scenario a tracking system has to deal with the effects of spontaneous speech, with coherent noise sources introduced by electronic devices and with interferences generated by the attendees to the meetings.

The performance is measured in terms of localization precision (MOTP) and localization accuracy (A-MOTA), the latter accounting for gross errors, misses and false positives. It is worth underling that the evaluation tools take into account also frames labeled as silence and penalize tracking systems that deliver hypotheses during those frames. In this perspective, the SAD module was introduced. Refer to the evaluation plan [1] for further details about the metrics.

## 3   Person Tracking Based on Global Coherence Field

Almost all the localization algorithms presented in the literature rely on an analysis of the time difference of arrivals (TDOAs) at two or more microphones which, in far field conditions, is directly related to the direction of arrivals

(DOAs) of the acoustic waves. The most common approach exploits the phase of the cross-spectrum of the received signals through the well-known Generalized Cross Correlation PHAse Transform (GCC-PHAT) [16,18]. Let us assume that a sensor pair $i$, consisting of the microphones $m_{i1}$ and $m_{i2}$, is available and let us denote as $x_{i1}(n)$ and $x_{i2}(n)$ the digitalized sequences captured by the sensors, where $n = 0, \ldots, L-1$ and $L$ is the analysis window length. The GCC-PHAT at microphone pair $i$ and time instant $t$ is computed as follows:

$$C_i(t,l) = FFT^{-1} \left\{ \frac{FFT(x_{i1}(n)) \cdot FFT^*(x_{i2}(n))}{|FFT(x_{i1}(n))| \cdot |FFT(x_{i2}(n))|} \right\} \tag{1}$$

where $l$ is the time lag. GCC-PHAT delivers a measure of similarity, or coherence measure, between signals realigned according to the time delay $l$. In ideal conditions, GCC-PHAT presents a prominent peak in correspondence to the actual TDOA [25]. Although several alternative solutions to the TDOA estimation problem have been investigated over the years [5,8,14,23], GCC-PHAT remains the technique of choice among the sound source localization community. The reasons of its success are mainly its rather simple and direct implementation and the proved robustness to highly adverse and noisy environments. Anyway it must be taken into account that as soon as the level of reverberation increases and reflections get stronger, the performance of GCC-PHAT decreases [6].

When a DMN is available as in the addressed scenario, the contributions of each microphone pair are combined to derive a single estimation of the source position. The combination can be performed at the TDOAs level using one among several approaches: a maximum likelihood or least square framework, triangulation, spherical interpolation [24], spherical intersection [22], linear interpolation [3] and so on. Conversely, "direct approaches" derive the source position estimation performing a search, in a beamformer-like [4] fashion, over a grid $\Sigma$ of potential source positions $\mathbf{p}$ and maximizing an objective function based either on coherence or energy. Within this class, a very efficient approach is the GCF that was introduced in [21] and that exploits the coherence measure contribution of each microphone pair. In the given multi-microphone scenario, where sensors are distributed all around the room, GCF has proved to efficiently handle and manage the information provided by the sensor network yielding satisfactory performance in the single speaker case [12,19]. Let us consider a set of $M$ microphone pairs and the corresponding set of theoretical time delays $\tau_i(\mathbf{p})$ $(i = 0, \ldots, M-1)$ measured at microphone pair $i$ if the source is in $\mathbf{p}$. GCF is a function defined over the grid $\Sigma$ and computed as follows:

$$GCF(t, \mathbf{p}) = \frac{1}{M} \sum_{i=0}^{M-1} C_i(t, \tau_i(\mathbf{p})) \tag{2}$$

GCF represents the plausibility that an active sound source is present in $\mathbf{p}$ and its maximum corresponds to the source position estimation $\hat{\mathbf{p}}$:

$$\hat{\mathbf{p}} = \arg\max_{\mathbf{p} \in \Sigma} GCF(t, \mathbf{p}) \tag{3}$$

It is worth mentioning that this approach does not make any assumption about far or near field conditions and can hence be directly applied to any position in the space of the potential solutions. The SRP-PHAT [7] and the theory of realizable delay vectors [13] are based on very similar concepts but commonly applied to compact microphone clusters rather than DMNs.

## 3.1  GCF Computation

As already mentioned, the core of the presented tracking system is the computation of GCF sound maps whose peaks identify the estimated source positions. In order to find out a trade-off between accuracy and tracking capabilities the analysis window for both GCC-PHAT and GCF computation was set to $2^{14}$ samples with an overlap factor 4. Given a $44.1\,kHz$ sampling rate, this is equivalent to a $0.09\,s$ time step, corresponding to about 10 sound map computations per second. Since GCC-PHAT delivers a coherence measure only at integer time delays, an oversampling of factor 2 was introduced in order to increase the overall accuracy. The GCF function was computed frame by frame independently, on a plane parallel to the floor at $130\,cm$ height. The spatial resolution of $\Sigma$ was set to $2\,cm$ on both coordinates. The GCF map was computed exploiting each horizontal microphone pair available in the T-shaped arrays. Restricting to seminars recorded in UPC and ITC-irst rooms, 8 channels of the NIST Mark-III linear array, corresponding to 4 further microphone pairs, were also exploited.

## 3.2  Speech Activity Detection

The SAD module is derived from an Acoustic Event Detector (AED) based on HMM whose features are the traditional 38 coefficients adopted in speech recognition applications. The proposed AED, that is fully described in [26] and was adopted to participate to the corresponding CLEAR 2007 task, is able to detect, i.e. to recognize time boundaries, and classifies 13 different acoustic events including speech. The module extracts the features from a fixed single channel that is selected on the basis of experiments conducted on the development set. It is worth underling that this implementation is site-dependent since a set of event models is trained for each CHIL room. According to localization experiments conducted on the development data set, the AED was forced to recognize presence of speech when there are not enough clues to derive a safe classification. The role of this module is crucial for the system performance since it allows the tracker to skip silence frames reducing also the impact of outliers.

## 3.3  The Smoothing Filter

Due to the particular characteristics of the given scenario in terms of spontaneous speech, interfering noise sources and acoustics of the environments, GCC-PHAT and GCF peaks may result less prominent or less reliable than in ideal conditions. For this reason, a post-processing on the sound map peaks was introduced, which implements an adaptive smoothing filter [9] in an effort to remove outliers and increase the robustness of the system. The smoothing process was specifically designed to handle multiple slowly moving sources that, as observed in the training set, characterize the addressed scenario. With this purpose, the smoothing filter is very static but ready to move to a new area of the room as soon as there are cues that a new source is currently active. First of all, the system considers the spatial distance $d(n, n-1)$ between the current GCF peak $\mathbf{u}(n)$ and the last confirmed localization hypothesis $\tilde{\mathbf{u}}(n-1)$. If $d(n, n-1)$ is higher than the threshold $T_d$, the current GCF peak is skipped. Otherwise, the new localization estimate $\tilde{\mathbf{u}}(n)$ is computed as follows:

$$\begin{cases} \tilde{\mathbf{u}}(n) = \alpha\mathbf{u}(n) + (1-\alpha)\tilde{\mathbf{u}}(n-1) & \text{if } d(n, n-1) < T_d \\ \text{skip frame} & \text{otherwise} \end{cases} \quad (4)$$

The parameter $\alpha \in [0.12, 1]$ is adapted according to the following equation:

$$\alpha = \begin{cases} \alpha/1.5 & \text{if } d'(n, n-1) < T_\alpha \\ 1.05\alpha & \text{otherwise} \end{cases} \quad (5)$$

where $d'(n, n-1)$ is the euclidean distance between $\tilde{\mathbf{u}}(n)$ and $\tilde{\mathbf{u}}(n-1)$, while the threshold $T_\alpha$ is commonly set to $0.4T_d$. Notice that the filter does not take into account the actual temporal distance between $\tilde{\mathbf{u}}(n-1)$ and $\mathbf{u}(n)$ in case several GCF peaks are skipped or long pauses occur. In order to enable the tracker to switch to different areas when a new speaker takes turn, the whole process is reset and moved when a given number $(N_w)$ of GCF peaks gather in the same area with a range equal to $T_d$.

Since each CHIL room presents peculiar acoustic characteristics and different DMN implementations, the tracker loads different parameter configurations depending on the room it is dealing with. Parameters are tuned on the basis of experiments conducted on the development set. Typical values are $T_d = 30-50\,cm$ and $N_w = 7-10$.

As an alternative to the proposed solution, audio source tracking is commonly tackled using either Kalman Filtering [15] or Particle Filtering [11].

## 4    Results and Conclusions

The tracking performance was evaluated on 40 segments, each one 5 minutes long, extracted from a set of meetings recorded in 5 CHIL rooms. The evaluation data set covers different phases of meetings. i.e. beginning, single speaker presentations, discussions, pauses and so on, resulting in a wide variety of acoustic activities.

Table 1 reports on the results obtained in the CLEAR 2007 evaluation campaign by the proposed tracking system on both the test and development data sets.

As a first comment, it is worth noting that an even simple smoothing process as the one adopted in this work, whose computational requirements are considerably low and fit eventual real-time constraints, is able to guarantee satisfactory

**Table 1.** Evaluation results for the proposed system. The tracker is evaluated on both the test and development data sets.

| SET | MOTP | A-MOTA | Miss Rate | False Pos | Err>50cm |
|-----|------|--------|-----------|-----------|----------|
| TEST | 20.8cm | 45.18% | 29.47% | 25.35% | 18.27% |
| DEV | 20.5 | 48.65% | 20.71% | 30.64% | 19.23% |

performance. It is anyway worth mentioning that, even if performance is encouraging for further works in this direction, there seems to be room for more improvements. Moreover, an analysis on single segments highlights that performance varies hugely depending on the conditions the system is facing. Picture 2 reports on the performance in terms of A-MOTA and MOTP for each of the 40 evaluated segments. Notice the variability of the results in particular referring to A-MOTA. Going more into details, in contrast with the development set where speech was almost always present, it can be observed that those meetings where silences or non-speech sounds are predominant are characterized by very bad performance that affects the overall scores. From this point of view, further investigations aimed at increasing the reliability and robustness of the tracker must be conducted.

On the other hand table 2 confirms that performance is not really influenced by the particular set-up and by the different acoustic features of the CHIL rooms.

**Table 2.** Tracking performance averaged per site

| Site | MOTP | A-MOTA | Miss Rate | False Pos |
|------|------|--------|-----------|-----------|
| AIT | 23.06 | 39.85% | 25.88% | 35.56% |
| IBM | 21.51 | 50.81% | 25.98% | 23.21% |
| ITC | 22.22 | 33.63% | 37.85% | 28.53% |
| UKA | 22.40 | 30.15% | 40.26% | 19.56% |
| UPC | 17.03 | 43.80% | 26.09% | 30.11% |

In order to have a direct understanding of the improvements obtained from the previous evaluation, table 3 compares the 2007 performance with the results obtained by the ITC-irst system in CLEAR 2006. In this case the evaluation criteria are the same as 2006 and silences are neglected. Notice the considerable gain in terms of A-MOTA and the consistent reduction of "Miss Rate". On the other hand the precision, represented by the metrics MOTP, shows only a little and not significant improvement. Since the GCF computation is more or less the same and there is no significant gain in terms of precision, it is reasonable to assume that the improvement is mainly to ascribe to the new adaptive post-processing.

Moreover the AED seems to provide satisfactory performance even if it is responsible of at least a 7% drop in terms of A-MOTA. However this is only a

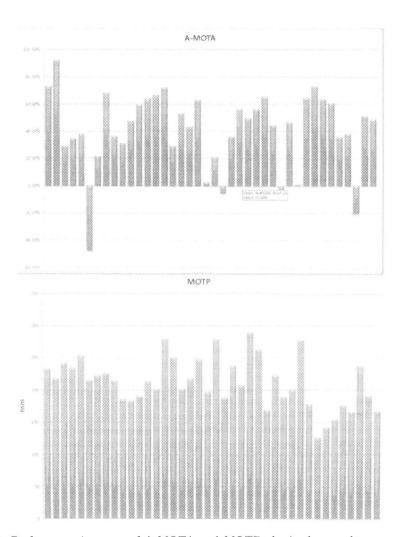

**Fig. 2.** Performance in terms of A-MOTA and MOTP obtained on each segment of the test set

**Table 3.** Comparison between the performance obtained in 2006 and 2007 CLEAR evaluations in the multi-person tracking task. Silences are neglected as foreseen in the 2006 metrics.

| System | MOTP | A-MOTA | Miss Rate | False Pos |
|--------|------|--------|-----------|-----------|
| 2006 | 21.8cm | 15.6% | 65% | 19% |
| 2007 | 20.8cm | 52.26% | 29.47% | 18.27% |

rough estimation as the whole localization system is influenced by the behaviour of the SAD module.

### 4.1 Computational Load

As for the computational load of the tracker, the overall real time factor is 0.4, as measured on a Pentium 2.4 GHz machine. In particular, GCC-PHAT computation of one single microphone pair is responsible for 0.3, while the remaining localization process, including both GCF search and post-processing, contributes with 0.1. Notice that GCC-PHAT computations can be parallelized in order to save computational load. In case this was not possible, a measure of the computational load due to the GCC-PHAT computation would not be feasible since it depends on the number of exploited pairs. Finally, the algorithm is single-pass and fully automatic.

## 5   Multimodal Person Tracking

The FBK-irst multimodal person tracker combines independently computed outputs of a visual [17] and an acoustic tracking systems, which is described in detail in the previous sections. Acoustic events trigger the dumping of the most likely visual track segment that may have generated it. Once speech activity is detected and located by the audio based system, the multimodal tracker selects the spatially closest visual track as multimodal output. Once the speech activity has terminated, the system keeps the last selected visual track until a new acoustic activity is detected. The multimodal system exploits the same data as the acoustic and visual trackers. Computational overhead for the above described fusion strategy is negligible with respect to the single modality computational loads.

### 5.1 Results and Conclusions

Table 4 reports on the results obtained by the multimodal system. Since the task considerably differs from the 2006 one, a deeper analysis of the results is not feasible. It is anyway clear that this kind of approach suffers the weaknesses of both systems. A real multimodal system, that treats the audio contribution as an extra source of likelihood, as presented in [12] would be more suitable to the given scenario.

**Table 4.** Performance obtained by the multimodal tracker

| MOTP | MOTA | Miss | False Pos | Mismatches |
|------|------|------|-----------|------------|
| 13.4mm | 34.12% | 33.94% | 29.78% | 197(2.15%) |

# References

1. http://www.clear-evaluation.org/
2. http://server.chil.de/
3. Brandstein, M., Adcock, J., Silverman, H.: A closed-form location estimator for use with room environment microphone arrays. IEEE Transactions on Speech and Audio Processing 5(1), 45–50 (1997)
4. Brandstein, M., Ward, D. (eds.): Microphone Arrays. Springer, Heidelberg (2001)
5. Capon, J.: High-resolution frequency-wavenumber spectrum analysis. Proceeding of IEEE 57(8), 1408–1418 (1969)
6. Champagne, B., Bedard, S., Stephenne, A.: Performance of time-delay estimation in the presence of room reverberation. IEEE Transactions on Speech and Audio Processing 4(2), 148–152 (1996)
7. DiBiase, J.: A High-Accuracy, Low-Latency Technique for Talker Localization in Reverberant Environments Using Microphone Arrays. PhD thesis, Brown University (May 2000)
8. Doclo, S., Moonen, M.: Robust time-delay estimation in highly adverse acoustic environments. In: Proceeding of IEEE WASPAA, New Platz, NY, USA, October 21-24, 2001, pp. 59–62 (2001)
9. Abad, A., et al.: Audio person tracking in a smart-room environment. In: Proceedings of Interspeech, Pittsburgh, PA, USA, September 17-21, 2006, pp. 2590–2593 (2006)
10. Mostefa, D., et al.: The chil audiovisual corpus for lecture and meeting analysis inside smart rooms. Journal for Language Resources and Evaluation (2007)
11. Antonacci, F., et al.: Tracking multiple acoustic sources using particle filtering. In: Proceedings of the European Signal Processing Conference, Florence, Italy, September 4-8 (2006)
12. Brunelli, R., et al.: A generative approach to audio-visual person tracking. In: Stiefelhagen, R., Garofolo, J.S. (eds.) CLEAR 2006. LNCS, vol. 4122, pp. 55–68. Springer, Heidelberg (2007)
13. Griebel, S., Brandstein, M.: Microphone array source localization using realizable delay vectors. In: IEEE WASPAA, New Platz, NY, USA, October 21-24, 2001, pp. 71–74 (2001)
14. Huang, Y., Benesty, J., Elko, G.: Adaptive eigenvalue decomposition algorithm for real time acoustic source localization system. In: Proceedings of IEEE ICASSP, Phoenix, AZ, USA, March 15-19, 1999, vol. 2, pp. 937–940 (1999)
15. Klee, U., Gehrig, T., McDonough, J.: Kalman filters for time delay of arrival-based source localization. In: Proceedings of Interspeech, Lisbon, Portugal, September 4-8, 2005, pp. 2289–2292 (2005)
16. Knapp, C., Carter, G.: The generalized correlation method for estimation of time delay. IEEE Transactions on Acoustic, Speech and Signal Processing 24(4), 320–327 (1976)
17. Lanz, O., Brunelli, R.: An appearance-based particle filter for visual tracking in smart rooms. In: Second International Evaluation Workshop on Classification of Events, Activities and Relationships, CLEAR 2006. LNCS, Springer, Heidelberg (2007)
18. Omologo, M., Svaizer, P.: Use of Crosspower-Spectrum Phase in acoustic event location. IEEE Transactions on Speech and Audio Processing 5(3), 288–292 (1997)
19. Omologo, M., Svaizer, P., Brutti, A., Cristoforetti, L.: Speaker localization in CHIL lectures: Evaluation criteria and results. In: Renals, S., Bengio, S. (eds.) MLMI 2005. LNCS, vol. 3869, pp. 476–487. Springer, Heidelberg (2006)

20. Omologo, M., Svaizer, P., DeMori, R.: Spoken Dialogue with Computers, ch. 2. In: Acoustic Transduction, Academic Press, London (1998)
21. Omologo, M., Svaizer, P.: Use of the crosspower-spectrum phase in acoustic event localization. Technical Report 9303-13, ITC-irst Centro per la Ricerca Scientifica e Tecnologica (1993)
22. Schau, H., Robinson, A.: Passive source localization employing intersecting spherical surfaces from time-of-arrival differences. IEEE Transaction on Acoustics, Speech and Signal Processing 35(12), 1661–1669 (1987)
23. Schmidt, R.: A Signal Subspace Approach to Multiple Emitter Location and Spectral Estimation. PhD thesis, Stanford University (1981)
24. Smith, J., Abel, J.: Closed-form least-square source location estimation from range-difference measurements. IEEE Transaction on Acoustics, Speech and Signal Processing 35(12), 1661–1669 (1987)
25. Svaizer, P., Matassoni, M., Omologo, M.: Acoustic source location in a three-dimensional space using crosspower spectrum phase. In: Proceedings of IEEE ICASSP, Munich, Germany, April 21-24, 1997, vol. 1, pp. 231–234 (1997)
26. Zieger, C.: An HMM based system for acoustic event detection. In: Second International Evaluation Workshop on Classification of Events, Activities and Relationships, CLEAR 2007. LNCS, vol. 4625. Springer, Heidelberg (2008)

# An Appearance-Based Particle Filter for Visual Tracking in Smart Rooms

Oswald Lanz, Paul Chippendale, and Roberto Brunelli

Bruno Kessler Foundation - irst
Via Sommarive 18, 38050 Povo di Trento, Italy
{lanz,chippendale,brunelli}@itc.it

**Abstract.** This paper presents a visual particle filter for tracking a variable number of humans interacting in indoor environments, using multiple cameras. It is built upon a 3-dimensional, descriptive appearance model which features (i) a 3D shape model assembled from simple body part elements and (ii) a fast while still reliable rendering procedure developed on a key view basis of previously acquired body part color histograms. A likelihood function is derived which, embedded in an occlusion-robust multibody tracker, allows for robust and ID persistent 3D tracking in cluttered environments. We describe both model rendering and target detection procedures in detail, and report a quantitative evaluation of the approach on the 'CLEAR'07 3D Person Tracking' corpus.

## 1 Introduction

People tracking from video is one of the key enabling technologies for recent applications in the field of Domotics, Ambient Intelligence, Surveillance, Traffic Analysis, Control and Automation and Human-Computer Interaction. While the demand for perceptual components able to provide detailed reports on human activity within the environment arises directly from the task that such applications aim to perform, they could in theory work on many different modalities such as audio, video, infra-red, active source triangulation, etc. The huge amount of information carried by images about the scene and the fact that no special devices need to be worn have made video-based solutions an appealing framework.

While the visual intelligence of animals can handle by far more complicated tasks, designing an algorithm that works in general circumstances still remains surprisingly difficult. After more than two decades of research [16] we still lack robust solutions that can handle many of the scientific challenges present in natural scenes such as occlusions, illumination changes and high-dimensional motion. Traditional approaches [9,5,6,8] can work well under certain assumptions or when system parameters are tuned to the characteristics of the scene under analysis. Recently, generative approaches [11,18] have gained increased attention by the community because they allow us to overcome some of the limitations of traditional approaches by explicitly modeling the observation process implemented in a camera. The basic idea is to generate a set of likely hypotheses

R. Stiefelhagen et al. (Eds.): CLEAR 2007 and RT 2007, LNCS 4625, pp. 57–69, 2008.

and to compare the actual observation with a synthetic view of them *rendered* using explicit models of the different components of the scene such as the targets as well as the background. While powerful in principle because important features such as articulation constraints [7] or occlusions [14] may be included, their success rests on reliable yet efficient design of these models which in practice is often difficult. However, the potentials of such approaches have been demonstrated e.g. in a recent international evaluation campaign, CLEAR'06 [1], where the best performing 3D single person tracker has been a color-based particle filter [3]. This paper [1] builds upon that work, extending the appearance model proposed there to a 3D model able to capture viewpoint-specific variations and proposing a new, fully automatic acquisition procedure.

## 1.1 Overview

The scenarios addressed in the CLEAR evaluation exhibit a number of peculiarities which turn the visual tracking problem into a scientific challenge. Among the most important ones we can cite:

- Variable number of targets. Actors are free to enter the monitored room and leave it during the recordings: determining and updating the number of targets to be tracked is part of the task.
- Dynamic background. Moving objects, door opening/closing, dynamic projections (displays, slide projectors, graphical interfaces, etc.) continuously change the appearance of scene constituents which are not of direct interest to the analysis. Such changes may be 'kept unknown' to the system, leading to a background scene which appears to be dynamic.
- Static targets. Comprehensive analysis requires that all tracked participants be continuously monitored, even if they are not actively contributing to the current interaction. Such passive targets are difficult to handle by traditional approaches based on background suppression.
- Occlusions. As interactions arise among several targets who can move freely in a limited space, visual features of interest may disappear in the images according to the current constellation of the targets and the viewing direction considered. This causes loss of information in the data: analysis must consider all targets jointly to interpret data consistently.
- Changing lighting conditions. Room illumination may change significantly across the scene, and also over time, due to slide projections and non-uniform illumination.

All these issues are of major concern when using classical approaches based on the typical processing chain: background suppression - morphological noise filtering - blob classification. Robust solutions usually require the engineering of complex cascades of low-level filters whose behavior is difficult to understand and which require the tuning of many parameters to the particular scene conditions.

[1] Research partly funded by the European Union under project IP 506909: CHIL - Computers in the Human Interaction Loop.

We address these problems by adopting a principled Bayesian approach which remains simple and whose performance is largely unaffected by most of the issues mentioned above. The core of the tracker is a likelihood function built upon a generative model of its visual appearance. Its purpose is to assign scores to hypothetical target poses by analysing a set of calibrated input images. Tracking is then formulated as a stochastic filtering problem, and solved by propagating the best-scored hypotheses according to a simple model of target dynamics. For the purpose of this paper, a hypothesis is specified in terms of the target's 2D position on the floor, its horizontal body orientation, and a binary label for specifying a sitting or standing pose.

The paper is organized as follows. The next section presents a multi-view appearance model for tracking applications; a model acquisition procedure is presented in Sec. 4. Sec. 5 reports experiments aimed to validate the model and its acquisition procedure, and to demonstrate its suitability for tracking, while Sec. 6 presents the conclusions and discusses possible improvements.

## 2   Modeling Visual Appearance

Modeling human appearance in unconstrained situations is challenging and a research topic by itself [12,17]. There is a trade-off between the level of detail one is interested in, the robustness to be achieved against non-modeled effects, and the computational load that can be afforded by the application. For the purpose of location tracking it is sufficient to resort to low-dimensional descriptions, which then marry well with the real-time demand common in many applications. To be usable with local search methods such as mean-shift [5] or particle filtering [2], the likelihood function built on top of it should render comparable hypotheses to comparable scores, thus be a smooth function of target position. At the same time, however, it should be able to absorb background clutter while remaining sufficiently discriminative to distinguish between different targets so as to maintain target identity.

Our approach addresses all these issues and is characterized by the use of two components:

- a coarse, volumetric, description of the shape of an upright standing person;
- body part- and viewpoint-based representation of target color, in form of head, torso and legs histograms.

The shape model is responsible for consistently mapping a hypothetic position into a triple of image patches where target head, torso and legs are expected to appear under that hypothesis. Using histograms to describe the appearance within these patches guarantees invariance to small spatial offsets and non-modeled articulated motion, and robustness to slight illumination changes. Part-based definition of the model highlights appearance independence that usually exists between the different body parts due to skin color and clothing. This allows the system to discriminate between background clutter and the actual target, and between targets wearing different clothes or of different size.

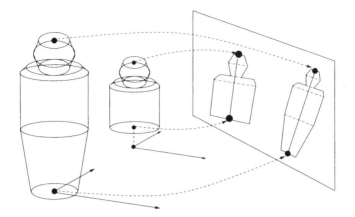

**Fig. 1.** 3D shape model of a standing and sitting person, and the approximate, but efficient, rendering implementation which maintains imaging artefacts such as perspective distortion and scaling

## 2.1   Shape

A coarse, part-based 3D model identifying the scene volume covered by a person standing upright is adopted for shape, similar to the generalized-cylinder model proposed in [11]. This model is shown in Fig. 1 and is assembled from a set of horizontally elongated cone truncs. It can be calibrated to a specific target by adapting two parameters: target height and width. To obtain the image projection of this 3D model when placed in a specific 3D position $x$ of the scene we proceed as follow. Firstly, we compute a pair of 3D points which represent the center of feet and top of head of the model. In case of $x$ describing the 2D position with respect to the floor plane and $h$ being the height of the target, these two points are simply given by $x$ enhanced by a third coordinate which has value 0 and $h$, respectively. These two points are then projected onto the camera reference frame by means of a calibrated camera model. The segment joining these two image points defines the axis around which the contour is drawn with piece-wise linear offset. This offset is further multiplied by a constant scale factor $s(o) \in [0.7 : 1.0]$ that accounts for profile width changing with the relative orientation $o$ of the target to the camera. Precisely, $s(o) = 0.7 + 0.3|\cos o|$. For a sitting pose we set the height of the 3D hip centre to the typical height of a chair and ignore the leg trunks. This rendering procedure is fast and sufficiently accurate on near-horizontal views such as the ones captured by cameras placed at the corners of a room.

## 2.2   Color

The projected silhouette is further decomposed into three body parts: head, torso and legs. Within these parts, the appearance of the target is described by one color histogram per part. In our implementation we quantize the RGB

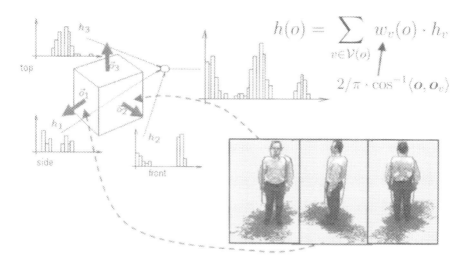

**Fig. 2.** Histogram synthesis. The cube faces represent pre-acquired top, front and side view of the object as seen from a new viewpoint. A weight is assigned to each view according to its amount of visible area (which is proportional to the cosine angular offset to the new views). New object appearance is then generated as a weighted interpolation of these histograms.

color space uniformly in $8 \times 8 \times 8$ bins (thus we have histograms of size 512). We follow a view-based rendering approach to synthesize the appearance of a given hypothesis, based on the idea of embedding the high-dimensional manifold of target appearance in a small, linear histogram subspace. The basic idea is to record a set of key views of the target, to extract the corresponding descriptions (i.e. color histograms) for each body part, and to generate the descriptions for a new view by interpolation from these key views. How to acquire such key views for a target will be discussed later. The histogram rendering procedure for a specific pose works for each body part as depicted in Fig. 2. When generating the appearance for a new hypothesis, the object orientation $o$ with respect to the camera is taken into account. The set of neighboring model views $\mathcal{V}(o)$ is identified and contributes to the new histogram $h(o)$ according to

$$h(o) = \sum_{v \in \mathcal{V}(o)} w_v(o) \cdot h_v. \tag{1}$$

Interpolation weights $w_v(o)$ sum up to 1 over the set $\mathcal{V}(o)$ and account linearly for the angular offset from the current viewing direction

$$w_v(o) \propto 2/\pi \cdot \cos^{-1} \langle o, o_v \rangle. \tag{2}$$

Here $\langle o, o_v \rangle$ denotes the scalar product between the 3D versors pointing in the direction of pose orientation $o$ and key view orientation $o_v$. This method supports histogram rendering from any viewing orientation, including top-down views. In setups where only lateral views are available (typically cameras placed in the corners of a room) it is sufficient to acquire key view histograms for side views only (like those seen in Fig. 2), and interpolation for a new view can be achieved on the two closest ones. We have used this faster rendering strategy in the implementation of the tracker.

## 3   Tracking Multiple Targets with Known Appearance

An occlusion robust particle filter [14] is implemented to jointly track the locations of a number of targets. The basic idea behind particle filtering is to propagate a sample-based representation of the posterior probability density over all possible target locations. Such posterior is obtained recursively by propagating the previous estimate to current time and updating it by integrating the evidence contained in the current image.

### 3.1   Likelihood

The likelihood function used in the update step is built upon the presented appearance model and computes as follows. To score a given pose hypothesis $\mathbf{x}$ on a new input image, we design a likelihood function based upon the proposed shape and color model. To do so, hypothetic body parts are identified within the image by means of the shape model rendered for $\mathbf{x}$. Candidate color histograms are then extracted from these areas. To assign a score to $\mathbf{x}$, these histograms are compared with the interpolated histograms of the model rendered for that pose, using a similarity measure derived from Bhattacharyya-coefficient based distance. If $a^h, a^t, a^l$ are the area of body part projections and $h_z^h, h_z^t, h_z^l$ and $h_m^h, h_m^t, h_m^l$ denote normalised extracted and modelled histograms respectively, the assigned likelihood is

$$\exp\left\{ - (a^h d^2(h_z^h, h_m^h) + a^t d^2(h_z^t, h_m^t) + a^t d^2(l_z^t, l_m^t)) / 2\sigma^2(a^h + a^t + a^l)\right\} \quad (3)$$

with histogram distance $d$ given by (index i scans all color bins)

$$d^2(h, k) = 1 - \sum_i \sqrt{h_i k_i}. \quad (4)$$

Parameter $\sigma$ can be used to control the selectivity of this function and is set empirically to 0.12.

### 3.2   Dynamics

For the purpose of prediction, the pose vector $\mathbf{x}$ is enhanced with the 2D velocity of the target on the floor plane. A pose hypothesis, or particle, is thus embodied by an 5-dimensional vector, plus one binary dimension for sitting/standing. The particle set representing the probabilistic estimate at time $t$ is projected to time $t + 1$ by a first order autoregressive process: each particle's location is linearly propagated along its velocity according to the time elapsed, and zero-mean Gaussian noise is added to all components to account for nonlinear behavior. After prediction, particle likelihoods are computed on the different views available and particle weights are assigned as the product of their likelihoods over the different views. Weighted re-sampling is applied in a straightforward manner.

# 4   Target Detection, Model Acquisition, and Target Release

The performance of an appearance-based tracker depends strongly on the quality of the model it searches for in the video. In constrained scenarios, such as the monitoring of meetings or lectures in a dedicated room, it may be possible to acquire accurate models for each participant a priori in an enrollment phase, through the target visiting a *hot spot* area. Stable and robust tracking can then be achieved in spite of occlusions and cluttered environments [19].

## 4.1   Target Detection

To cope with unconstrained scenarios recorded in the CLEAR07 corpus, we built upon the detection procedure proposed in [3] to account for sitting and standing pose, occlusions, and limited visual coverage of each camera. Furthermore, the procedure has been integrated with the tracking. Again, a Bayesian approach is adopted. The tracking domain is collapsed into a regular 2D grid, with each grid corner representing the possible location of a new target. At each position, a number of hypotheses are created for different target heights and widths, body orientations, and pose. Given a set of input images capturing the current room configuration, a likelihood is assigned to each such hypothesis, calculated as the product of responses computed independently on each single view. Only those views providing responses above a threshold are hereby considered. Relevant features in each view derive from:

- coverage of foreground blobs extracted using an adaptive background model,
- match of projected model contour and observed edges, and
- horizontal color symmetry of the upper body.

If the largest likelihood response on the detection grid is above a given threshold, a new target is detected. Note that occluded views are implicitly filtered out because the matching with unobserved contours invalidate them for the detection. Body part histograms are then extracted from all unoccluded views by rendering the shape model for that configuration, and stored as the key views of the target's appearance model (annotated with the relative viewing angles derived from body orientation), together with the target's physical width and height. Appearance model, shape parameters and current position are transmitted to the tracker which allocates a new track to it.

**Fig. 3.** Updated background models at the end of sequence ITC_20060922B_B. In spite of moved objects (chairs and laptop) and persistent foreground blobs (static targets) the models still describe the background scene at an acceptable accuracy.

To speed-up the acquisition process, a multi-resolution approach is implemented. At the coarse level, a subset of configurations (undersampled grid, one height/width level only) are tested on all available views (including the ceiling camera), considering only foreground blob coverage. The neighborhood of hypotheses with significant likelihood are analyzed at the finer level, and tested at full resolution by considering all three visual features. To avoid re-acquisition of already tracked targets, the neighborhood of their currently estimated location is removed from the set of detection hypotheses before each iteration.

### 4.2   Detection Likelihood

It remains to show how the three components of single-view responses are computed. A background model in Y-Cb-Cr color space is maintained for each camera [4]. It is bootstrapped from a set of empty room images, and updated at pixel-level by temporal filtering: $B_t[i,j] = \alpha B_{t-1}[i,j] + (1-\alpha)I_t[i,j]$. Parameter $\alpha$ may vary with the framerate, but is kept constant for the evaluation. An image mask is computed at each iteration to update the model on stable background image regions only. It accounts for persistent motion (accumulated frame-by-frame difference + morphological filtering) and image regions supported by the current tracks (identified by rendering the shape model for the current estimates), which are then neglected in the background update (see Fig.3). The coverage likelihood term for a given hypothesis is computed as the percentage of projected silhouette area currently covered by foreground blobs (simple Y-Cb-Cr thresholding). The contour likelihood is computed as follows. Canny edge detection is performed on the input image to extract candidate edges. Such edges are validated through connected component analysis and morphological noise cleaning. To each detection hypothesis a score is assigned according to the amount of overlap between measured and expected edges. To compute this term, the shape model is rendered and its contour matched with the validated edge map. The log-value of the resulting score is composed of two terms. The first one is computed as the sum over model contour pixels $u$ of their Euclidean distance to the nearest validated edge, normalized w.r.t. the length of the contour under

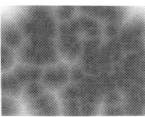

**Fig. 4.** Validated motion edges, their distance transform, and the projected 3D shape exhibiting the highest contour likelihood. Note that detection is unaffected by the presence of other people in the room.

consideration. The second term penalizes edges whose orientation does not match with the contour normal $N(u)$. To limit the influence of missing edges, the contribution of contour pixels that exceed 30% of projected body width are set to a maximum value. Fast scoring can be achieved by limiting edge analysis to image regions-of-interest (ROI) which can be determined by pre-rendering of the detection hypotheses. Within such ROIs, Euclidean distances are pre-compiled into lookup tables obtained by means of the Distance Transform (DT) of edge images (see Fig. 4). If $\Delta(\mathbf{x})$ denotes projected body width, $\mathcal{C}(\mathbf{x})$ describes its contour, $D(u)$ is the DT of the validated edge map and $G(u)$ is the gradient versor of the closest edge in $u$, the likelihood assigned is

$$\exp\left(-\frac{1}{\text{length}\{\mathcal{C}(\mathbf{x})\}}\int_{\mathcal{C}(\mathbf{x})}\min\{1,\frac{D(u)}{0.3\Delta(\mathbf{x})}\}-0.5\langle N(u),G(u)\rangle\,du\right). \quad (5)$$

Similar shape likelihoods have been proposed for tracking, e.g in [10]. In [10] edges are searched for only along a small predefined set of contour normals. While this formulation is computationally cheaper when the number of hypotheses to be tested is limited, the overhead introduced through the computation of DT in our approach becomes negligible for a large search task such as high-resolution target detection. In addition, our measure is more accurate as it considers continuous contours. The third likelihood term, color symmetry of the upper body, is computed as the $L_1$ distance between left and right part RGB histograms extracted from the current image.

### 4.3 Target Release

To decide whether to propagate an existing track or not, views of the ceiling camera are analyzed. Foreground blobs are extracted by considering significant differences to the background model (Y-Cb-Cr thresholding + morphological filtering). If the neighborhood of a track remains unsupported for a number of subsequent iterations (1 second) the track is terminated.

**Table 1.** Tracking scores on the CLEAR07 corpus VPT task: overall, best case is IBM_20060815_B, worse case is AIT_20061020D_B

|            | MOTP   | MISSRATE | FALSEPOS | MISSMATCH    | MOTA    |
|------------|--------|----------|----------|--------------|---------|
| overall    | 141 mm | 20.7 %   | 18.6 %   | 518 (1.1 %)  | 59.6 %  |
| best case  | 107 mm | 3.2 %    | 6.2 %    | 12 (0.1 %)   | 90.5 %  |
| worse case | 212 mm | 31.2 %   | 76.6 %   | 12 (0.1 %)   | -7.9 %  |
| avg. AIT   | 209 mm | 20.1 %   | 26.6 %   | 128 (1.9 %)  | 51.4 %  |
| avg. IBM   | 126 mm | 11.9 %   | 10.8 %   | 92 (0.8 %)   | 76.4 %  |
| avg. ITC   | 123 mm | 23.4 %   | 15.3 %   | 55 (0.6 %)   | 60.7 %  |
| avg. UKA   | 124 mm | 25.4 %   | 19.8 %   | 203 (1.8 %)  | 53.0 %  |
| avg. UPC   | 145 mm | 24.5 %   | 22.7 %   | 133 (1.2 %)  | 51.7 %  |

## 5   Evaluation Results

The complete system implements a one-pass algorithm with no pre- and post-processing. For the tracking of an acquired target only the four corner cameras are used. The top-down view of the scene is used solely to trigger target detection and model acquisition, and to terminate unsupported tracks. The system output is computed as the expectation over the current, weighted particle set. No manual intervention is needed, no parameters have been changed to process sequences from different sites.

The sequences have been processed at a real time factor of 1.5 on a Intel Xeon 2.3 Ghz DualCore biprocessor, using up to 80% of the processing capacity. Most of the time, with 4-5 tracked targets, it works at about 60-70% of CPU load, including reading and uncompressing images. The tracker works at a variable frame rate, according to the uncertainty present in the data. It implements a mechanism to adapt the number of particles needed to consistently represent the probabilistic estimates [15]. It is therefore not possible to express the efficiency in cputime/frame. The slowest part is detection, which requires the system to run slower than real time. Again, the detection processing time cannot be specified by a constant cputime/frame factor, as it depends linearly on the size of foreground blobs detected in the ceiling camera which are not covered by any of the active tracks. Thus, detection time varies with complex factors such as the effectivness of background model adaptation and the tracking performance of already acquired targets. It ranges from a few milliseconds (when all targets are tracked) to up to several seconds (when background model adaptation failed and no tracks are active). Typically, a new target is detected in less than half a second. The tracking is easily accommodated in real time.

Table 1 reports the performance of the proposed approach on the 'CLEAR'07 3D Person Tracking' corpus (see [13] for a presentation of the error metrics). We throw the following conclusions.

**Fig. 5.** Visual coverage in AIT sequences: the ceiling camera provides rich information; corner cameras have narrow FoVs with limited overlap

- **Significant challenges are posed to detection algorithms**. The corpus contains sequences with very different dynamics, ranging from empty room segments to sequences starting with all people sat down (IBM_20060810_B), to situations in which five people enter the scene almost simultaneously (UKA_20061207_A). Target detection in such situations is challenging due to untracked occlusions and limited visual coverage. The acquisition of poor appearance models then directly impacts on the overall tracking performance.
- **Occlusions are not a major concern for the tracking**. The frequency of visual occlusions in the corpus is low. Most of the time people are sat down, thus corner cameras, as well as the ceiling camera, observe no or only small occlusions. There is no significant gain in pursuing occlusion reasoning at the cost of more intense computations, as implemented in our system [14].
- **Sensing geometry varies significantly with the different sites**. For AIT setup (see Fig. 5) the ceiling camera delivers highly informative and undistorted views of the scene; corner cameras have very narrow vield-of-views, where targets are visible only partially, many times even only in one camera. This makes the target model acquisition very difficult. On the other hand, IBM room has good coverage from the corner cameras, but the ceiling view exhibits significant distortion at the peripheral regions. Also, the cameras' color responses are very different.

In summary, the performance of the presented system is bounded by the limited detection efficiency. The system builds upon a robust multi target tracker, recently extended to handle online detection and model acquisition. As a consequence of this, there is space for significant improvements, especially in target model adaptation and non-instantaneous acquisition. Fully integrated use of the ceiling camera is also expected to provide measurable improvements, and may require a more flexible management of target models.

## 6   Conclusion and Future Work

A multi-view appearance model for tracking humans has been described, which is derived according to imaging principles using a 3-dimensional part-based shape model of a standing person. Within each part the color appearance is generated by weighted histogram interpolation to account for relative orientation, considering the set of closest key views. To acquire such key views, a target is detected within a hot spot region by exhaustive search driven by a model-based contour likelihood. The resulting appearance model is discriminative and fast, supporting real-time tracking of several people while maintaining their identity. Future work will address online model acquisition and adaptation, a challenging problem in the multi-target context due to occlusion and target similarity.

# References

1. CLEAR 2006 evaluation campaign [Online], http://www.clear-evaluation.org/
2. Arulampalam, S., Maskell, A., Gordon, N., Clapp, T.: A tutorial on particle filters for on–line non–linear/non–gaussian bayesian tracking. IEEE Trans. Signal Processing 50(2) (2002)
3. Brunelli, R., Brutti, A., Chippendale, P., Lanz, O., Omologo, M., Svaizer, P., Tobia, F.: A generative approach to audio-visual person tracking. In: Stiefelhagen, R., Garofolo, J.S. (eds.) CLEAR 2006. LNCS, vol. 4122, Springer, Heidelberg (2007)
4. Chippendale, P.: Towards automatic body language annotation. In: Intl. Conf. Automatic Face and Gesture Recognition (2006)
5. Comaniciu, D., Ramesh, V., Meer, P.: Real-time tracking of non-rigid objects using mean-shift. In: Intl. Conf. Computer Vision and Pattern Recognition (2000)
6. Cucchiara, R., Grana, C., Tardini, G., Vezzani, R.: Probabilistic people tracking for occlusion handling. In: Int. Conf. Pattern Recognition (2004)
7. Deutscher, J., Blake, A., Reid, I.: Articulated body motion capture by annealed particle filtering. In: Int. Conf. Computer Vision and Pattern Recognition (2000)
8. Dockstader, S., Tekalp, A.M.: Multiple camera tracking of interacting and occluded human motion. Proc. of the IEEE 89(10) (2001)
9. Haritaoglu, I., Harwood, D., Davis, L.S.: W4: Real-time surveillance of people and their activities. IEEE Trans. Pattern Analysis and Machine Intelligence 22(8) (2000)
10. Isard, M., Blake, A.: Condensation – conditional density propagation for visual tracking. Int. Journal of Computer Vision 29 (1998)
11. Isard, M., MacCormick, J.: BraMBLe: A bayesian multiple-blob tracker. In: Int. Conf. Computer Vision (2003)
12. Jepson, A.D., Fleet, D.J., El-Maraghi, T.: Robust online appearance models for visual tracking. IEEE Trans. on Pattern Analysis and Machine Intelligence 25(10) (2003)
13. Elbs, A., Bernardin, K., Stiefelhagen, R.: Multiple object tracking performance metrics and evaluation in a smart room environment. In: IEEE International Workshop on Visual Surveillance (2006)
14. Lanz, O.: Approximate bayesian multibody tracking. IEEE Trans. Pattern Analysis and Machine Intelligence 28(9) (2006)
15. Lanz, O.: An information theoretic rule for sample size adaptation in particle filtering. In: Intl Conf. Image Analysis and Processing (ICIAP 2007) (2007)
16. Moeslund, T.B., Granum, E.: A survey of computer vision-based human motion capture. Computer Vision and Image Understanding 81(3) (2001)

17. Sidenbladh, H., Black, M.J.: Learning the statistics of people in images and video. Int. Journal of Computer Vision 54(1) (2003)
18. Zhao, T., Nevatia, R.: Tracking multiple humans in complex situations. IEEE Trans. on Pattern Analysis and Machine Intelligence 26(9) (2004)
19. SmarTrack (patent pending) showcased at the IST 2006 event [Online]: http://tev.itc.it/TeV/Technologies/SmarTrack_atIST06.html

# Multi-level Particle Filter Fusion of Features and Cues for Audio-Visual Person Tracking

Keni Bernardin, Tobias Gehrig, and Rainer Stiefelhagen

Interactive Systems Lab
Institut für Theoretische Informatik
Universität Karlsruhe, 76131 Karlsruhe, Germany
{keni, tgehrig, stiefel}@ira.uka.de

**Abstract.** In this paper, two multimodal systems for the tracking of multiple users in smart environments are presented. The first is a multi-view particle filter tracker using foreground, color and special upper body detection and person region features. The other is a wide angle overhead view person tracker relying on foreground segmentation and model-based blob tracking. Both systems are completed by a joint probabilistic data association filter-based source localizer using the input from several microphone arrays. While the first system fuses audio and visual cues at the feature level, the second one incorporates them at the decision level using state-based heuristics.

The systems are designed to estimate the 3D scene locations of room occupants and are evaluated based on their precision in estimating person locations, their accuracy in recognizing person configurations and their ability to consistently keep track identities over time.

The trackers are extensively tested and compared, for each separate modality and for the combined modalities, on the CLEAR 2007 Evaluation Database.

## 1 Introduction and Related Work

In recent years, there has been a growing interest in intelligent systems for indoor scene analysis. Various research projects, such as the European CHIL or AMI projects [20,21] or the VACE project in the U.S. [22], aim at developing smart room environments, at facilitating human-machine and human-human interaction, or at analyzing meeting or conference situations. To this effect, multimodal approaches that utilize a variety of far-field sensors, video cameras and microphones to obtain rich scene information gain more and more popularity. An essential building block for complex scene analysis is the detection and tracking of persons.

One of the major problems faced by indoor tracking systems is the lack of reliable features that allow to keep track of persons in natural, unconstrained scenarios. The most popular visual features in use are color features and foreground segmentation or movement features [2,1,3,6,7,14], each with their advantages and drawbacks. Doing e.g. blob tracking on background subtraction maps is error-prone, as it requires a clean background and assumes only persons are moving. In real environments, the foreground blobs are often fragmented or merged with others, they depict only parts of occluded persons or are produced by shadows or displaced objects. When using color information, the problem is

R. Stiefelhagen et al. (Eds.): CLEAR 2007 and RT 2007, LNCS 4625, pp. 70–81, 2008.

to find appropriate color models for tracking. Generic color models are usually sensitive and environment-specific [4]. If no generic model is used, color models for tracked person need to be initialized automatically at some point [3,7,13,14]. In many cases, this still requires the cooperation of the users and/or a clean and relatively static background.

On the acoustic side, although actual techniques already allow for a high accuracy in localization, they can still only be used effectively for the tracking of one person, while this person is speaking. This naturally leads to the development of more and more multimodal techniques.

Here, we present two multimodal systems for the tracking of multiple persons in a smart room scenario. A joint probabilistic data association filter uses the audio streams from a set of microphone arrays to detect speech and determine active speaker positions. For the video modality, we compare the performance of 2 approaches: A particle filter approach using several cameras and a variety of features, and a simple blob tracker relying on foreground segmentation features gained from a wide angle top view. While the former system fuses the acoustic and visual modalities at the feature level, the latter does this at the decision level using a state-based selection and combination scheme on the single modality tracker outputs. All systems are evaluated on the CLEAR'07 3D Person Tracking Database.

The next sections introduce the multimodal particle filter tracker, the single-view visual tracker, the JPDAF-based acoustic tracker, as well as the fusion approach for the single view visual and the acoustic tracking systems. Section 6 shows the evaluation results on the CLEAR'07 database and section 7 gives a brief summary and conclusion.

## 2  Multimodal Particle Filter-Based 3D Person Tracking

The multimodal 3D tracking component is a particle filter using features and cues from the four room corners cameras and the wide angle ceiling camera, as well as source localization hypotheses obtained using the room's microphone arrays. The tracker automatically detects and tracks multiple persons without requiring any special initialization phase or area, room background images, or a-priori knowledge about person colors or attributes, for standing, sitting or walking users alike.

### 2.1  Tracking Features

The features used are adaptive foreground segmentation maps and upper body region colors gained from all 5 camera images, resampled to 320x240 resolution, as well as upper body detection cues from the room corner cameras, person region hints from the top camera, and source localization estimates gained from the T-shaped microphone arrays.

– The foreground segmentation is made using a simple adaptive background model, which is computed on grayscale images as the running average of the last 1000 frames. The background is subtracted from the current frame and a fixed threshold is applied to reveal foreground regions.

- The color features are computed in a modified HSV space and modeled using a specially designed histogram structure, which eliminates the usual drawbacks of HSV histograms when it comes to modeling low saturation or brightness colors.

The color space is a modified version of the HSV cone. First, colors for which the brightness and saturation exceed 20% are set to maximum brightness . This reduces the effect of local illumination changes or shadows. The HSV values are subsequently discretized as follows: Let *hue*, *sat* and *val* be the obtained HSV values, then the corresponding histogram bin values, $h$, $s$ and $v$, are computed as:

$$v = val \tag{1}$$

$$s = sat * val \tag{2}$$

$$h = hue * sat * val \tag{3}$$

The effect is that the number of bins in the hue and saturation dimensions decreases towards the bottom of the cone. There is, e.g., only one histogram bin to model colors with zero brightness. This is in contrast to classical discretization techniques, where e.g. grayscale or nearly grayscale values, for which the hue component is either undefined or ill-conditioned, are spread over a large number of possible bins. At the large end of the cone, a maximum of 16 bins for hue, 10 bins for saturation, and 10 for brightness are used. Figure 1 shows a graphical representation of the resulting discretized HSV space.

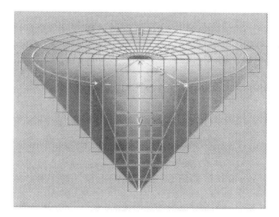

**Fig. 1.** The discretization of the HSV cone into histogram bins. Colors with zero saturation or brightness have a unique mapping although their hue value, e.g., is undefined.

The color features for tracking are gained from the detected upper body regions of subjects, as well as their immediatly surrounding background. One upper body and one background histogram are kept per camera and track. Upper body histograms for corner cameras are adapted with each upper body detection from pixels inside the detection region. The upper body histograms for the top camera are obtained using colors sampled from a 60cm diameter region centered around the tracked person position. They are continuously adapted with each frame, but only after valid color histogram models for the corner cameras could be created. This is because the track is only considered reliable enough for continous color model adaptation after it has been confirmed at least once by a direct upper body detection in a corner camera. The background histograms for all views, in turn, are continuously adapted in every frame, with the adaptation learnrate set such as to achieve a temporal smoothing window of approximately 3 seconds.

All upper body histograms are continuously filtered using their respective background histograms. Let $H$ be an upper body and $H_{neg}$ a background histogram. Then the filtered histogram $H_{filt}$ is obtained as:

$$H_{filt} = minmax(H) * (1 - minmax(H_{neg})),\qquad(4)$$

with all operations performed bin-wise. For the $minmax$ operator, the min value is set to 0 and the max value is set to the maximum bin value of the respective histogram.

The effect of histogram filtering is to decrease the bin values for upper body colors which are equally present in the background. The motivation is that since several views are available to track a target, only the views where the upper body is clearly distinguishable from the immmediately surrounding background should be used for tracking. The use of filtered histograms was found to dramatically increase tracking accuracies.

– The upper body detections in the fixed corner camera images are obtained by exhaustive scanning with Haar-feature classifier cascades, such as in [8,9]. Using camera calibration information, the 3D scene coordinates of the detected upper body as well as the localization uncertainty, expressed as covariance matrix, are computed from the detection window position and size. This information is later used to associate detections to person tracks, update color models, and to score particles.

– Person regions are found in the top camera images through the analysis of foreground blobs, as described in [12]. It is a simple model-based tracking algorithm that dynamically maps groups of foreground blobs to possible person tracks and hypothesizes a person detection if enough foreground is found within a 60cm diameter region for a given time interval. The motivation for detecting person regions in this way is that top view images present very little overlap between persons, making a simple spatial assignment of blobs to tracks plausible.

– The acoustic features fed to the particle filter are the 3D source localization estimates from the JPDAF tracker described in section 4. Currently, only the active source with the smallest localization uncertainty at a given time is considered. As the source is assumed to be located at the mouth region of a speaking subject, its 3D coordinates are used to associate it to tracks, score particles, and to deduce appropriate upper body regions in each view for updating color models. Acoustic features can therefore lead to the initialization of person tracks with increasingly accurate color models even in the absence of visual upper body detections.

## 2.2   Intialization and Termination Criteria

For automatic detection of persons and initialization of tracks, a fixed number of "scout" particle filter trackers are maintained. These are randomly initialized in the room and their particles are scored using the foreground, color, and detection features described above. A person track is initialized when the following conditions are met:

- The average weight of a scout's particle cloud exceeds a fixed activation threshold $T$. This threshold is set such that initialization is not possible based on the foreground feature alone, but requires the contribution of at least an upper body detection, person region hint or source localization estimate.
- The spread of the particle cloud, calculated as the variance in particle positions, is below a threshold $T_2$.
- The tracked object's color is balanced throughout all camera images. For this, color histograms are computed in each view by sampling the pixel values at the scout's particles' projected 2D coordinates, and histogram similarity is measured using the bhattacharyya distance.
- The target object is sufficiently dissimilar to its surrounding background in every view. Again, the bhattacharyya distance is used to measure similarity between the target object histograms and the corresponding background histograms. For the latter, colors are sampled in each view from a circle of 60cm diameter, centered around the scout track's position and projected to the image planes. This last condition helps to avoid initializing faulty tracks on plane surfaces, triggered e.g. by false alarm detections or shadows, or when the target's upper body color is not distinct enough from the surrounding background to allow stable tracking.

Tracks are deleted when their average weight, considering only color, audio-visual detection and person region contributions, falls below a certain threshold, or the spread of their particle cloud exceeds a fixed limit.

## 2.3   Particle Filtering

The tracking scheme used here maintains a separate particle filter tracker for each person. In contrast to conventional implementations, in this framework a particle represents the hypothesized $(x, y, z)$ scene coordinates of one single point on the target object, not necessarily its center. Consequently, the foreground and color feature scores of a particle in each camera image are not computed using a projected kernel or person window, but rather by using only one pixel value: The particle's 3D position, shifted by -20cm in the z-axis, is projected to the image. The corresponding pixel coordinates and color value are then used, together with the foreground segmentation map and the track's color histogram, to derive the foreground and color scores respectively. The particle's 3D position, on the other hand, is used together with available upper body detection, person region hint or acoustic source positions and uncertainties to derive a detection score. A weighted combination of these scores using predefined fixed weights then yields the final particle score. In this way, the computational effort for an individual particle's score is kept at a minimum, notably requiring no time consuming histogram comparisons or backprojections.

After scoring, normalization and resampling, the mean of the particles' positions is taken as the track center. Propagation is then done by adding gaussian noise to the resampled positions in the following way: The particles are first split into 2 sets. The first set comprises the highest scoring particles, the "winners" of the resampling step, and contains at most half of the particle mass. The rest of the particles comprises the second set. The speed of propagation is then adjusted differently for each set, such that the high scoring particles stay relatively stable and keep good track of still targets, while the low scoring ones are heavily spread out to scan the surrounding area and keep track of moving targets. A total of only 75 particles is used per track.

Since the system maintains a separate particle filter for every track, some mechanism is required to avoid initializations on already supported tracks or accumulations of filters on the same track. This is accomplished as follows: A "repellent" region of 60cm diameter is defined around the center of each track. The weight of all other tracks' particles which fall into the repellent region are then set to 0 if their current weight does not exceed the repellent track's average weight. Additionally, absolute priority is given to valid tracks over scout tracks. In this way, particles from distinct tracks which share the same space are penalized and tracks with higher confidence repel less confident ones.

The system implementation is distributed over a network of 5 machines to achieve real-time computation speed. It was extensively tested and achieved high accuracy rates, as shown in section 6. Figure 2 shows a graphical output of the particle filter tracking system.

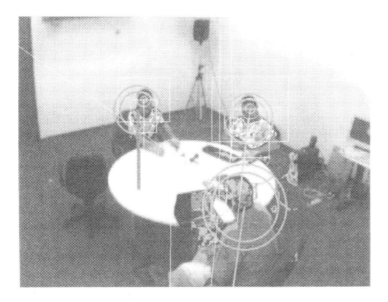

**Fig. 2.** A graphical output of the particle filter based tracking system. The white rectangles show upper body detection hits and the areas used for sampling foreground and background colors. The histogram backprojection values are shown for each track, superimposed on the image as grayscale values, with brighter colors indicating higher probabilities of belonging to the person track.

## 3   Single-View Model-Based Person Tracking on Panoramic Images

In contrast to the above presented system, the panoramic camera tracker relies solely on the wide angle images captured from the top of the room. The advantage of such images is that they reduce the chance of occlusion by objects or overlap between persons. The drawback is that detailed analysis of the tracked persons is difficult as person-specific features are hard to observe. This system has already been tested in the CLEAR 2006 evaluation, and is described in detail in [12]. No modifications to the system or its parameters, and no tuning on the 2007 data was done, to provide an accurate baseline for comparisons. The following gives only a brief system overview.

The tracking algorithm is essentially composed of a simple but fast foreground blob segmentation followed by a more complex EM algorithm for association of blobs to person models.

At first, foreground patches are extracted from the images by using a dynamic background model. The background model is created on a few initial images of the room and is constantly adapted with each new image using an fixed adaptation factor $\alpha$. Background subtraction, thresholding and morphological filtering provide the foreground blobs for tracking.

The subsequent EM algorithm tries to find an optimal assignment of the detected blobs to a set of active person models. Person models are composed of an image position $(x, y)$, velocity $(vx, vy)$, radius $r$ and a track ID, and are instantiated or deleted based on the foreground blob support observed over a certain time window.

The approach results in a simple but fast tracking algorithm that is able to maintain several person tracks, even in the event of moderate overlap. By assuming an average height of 1m for a person's body center, and using calibration information for the top camera, the positions in the world coordinate frame of all tracked persons are calculated and output.

The system makes no assumptions about the environment, e.g. no special creation or deletion zones, about the consistency of a person's appearance or about the recording room. It runs at a realtime factor of 0.91, at 15fps, on a Pentium 3GHz machine.

## 4   JPDAF-Based Acoustic Source Localization

The acoustic source localization system is based on a joint probabilistic data association filter (JPDAF) [15,19]. This is an extension to the IEKF used in previous approaches [18], that makes it possible to track multiple targets at once and updates each of the internally maintained IEKFs probabilistically. It also introduces a "clutter model" that models random events, such as door slams, footfalls, etc., that are not associated with any speaker, but can cause spurious peaks in the GCC of a microphone pair, and thus lead to poor tracking performance. Observations assigned with high probability to the clutter model do not affect the estimated positions of the active targets.

First of all the timedelays and corresponding correlation values are calculated for all possible microphone pairs within each of the T-arrays and 14 pairs of the available MarkIIIs by calculating the GCC-Phat [16,17] of the frequencies below 8000 Hz. The timedelays are estimated 25 times per second resulting in a hamming window size of 0.08 ms with a shift size of 0.04ms. For the GCC, a FFT size of 4096 points is used. The maximum search in the resulting correlation function is restricted to be in the valid range of values as conditioned on the room size and the microphone positions.

Then, for each of the seminars and each of the used microphone pairs, a correlation threshold is estimated separately by calculating the histogram of all correlation values of that pair and seminar and using the value that is at 85% of it, i.e. the smallest value that is greater than 85% of the correlation values.

The JPDAF is then fed with one measurement vector for each time instant and microphone array that is made up of the TDOAs of those microphone pairs of that array with a correlation higher than the previously estimated one. As observation noise we used 0.02ms. The measurement vector is only used for position estimation if it has at least 2 elements.

The first step in the JPDAF algorithm is the evaluation of the conditional probabilities of the *joint association events*

$$\boldsymbol{\theta}(t) = \bigcap_{i=1}^{m_t} \theta_{ik_i}, \quad t = 0, \ldots, T \tag{5}$$

where the atomic events are defined as

$$\theta_{ik} = \{\text{observation } i \text{ originated from target } k\} \tag{6}$$

Here, $k_i$ denotes the index of the target to which the i-th observation is associated in the event currently under consideration. In our case we chose the maximum number of targets to be $T \leq 3$ and the maximum number of measurements per step to be $m_t \leq 1$. From all the theoretically possible events only *feasible events* are further processed. A feasible event is defined as an event wherein

1. An observation has exactly one source, which can be the clutter model;
2. No more than one observation can originate from any target.

An observation is possibly originating from a target when it falls inside the target's validation region given by the innovation covariance matrix and a gating threshold of 4.0.

Applying Bayes' rule, the conditional probability of $\boldsymbol{\theta}(t)$ can be expressed as

$$P\{\boldsymbol{\theta}(t)|\mathcal{Y}_t\} = \frac{P\{\mathbf{Y}(t)|\boldsymbol{\theta}(t), \mathcal{Y}_{t-1}\}P(\boldsymbol{\theta}(t)}{P\{\mathbf{Y}(t)|\mathcal{Y}_{t-1}\}} \tag{7}$$

where the marginal probability $P\{\mathbf{Y}(t)|\mathcal{Y}_{t-1}\}$ is computed by summing the joint probability in the numerator of (7) over all possible $\boldsymbol{\theta}(t)$. The conditional probability of $\mathbf{Y}(t)$ required in (7) can be calculated from

$$P\{\mathbf{Y}(t)|\boldsymbol{\theta}(t), \mathcal{Y}_{t-1}\} = \prod_{i=1}^{m_t} p(\mathbf{y}_i(t)|\theta_{ik_i}(t), \mathcal{Y}_{t-1}) \tag{8}$$

The individual probabilities on the right side of (8) can be easily evaluated given the fundamental assumption of the JPDAF, namely,

$$\mathbf{y}_i(t) \sim \mathcal{N}(\hat{\mathbf{y}}_{k_i}(t|\mathcal{Y}_{t-1}), \mathbf{R}_{k_i}(t)) \tag{9}$$

where $\hat{\mathbf{y}}_{k_i}$ and $\mathbf{R}_{k_i}(t)$ are, respectively, the predicted observation and innovation covariance matrix for target $k_i$. The prior probability $P\{\boldsymbol{\theta}(t)\}$ in (7) can be readily evaluated through combinatorial arguments [15, §9.3] using a detection probability of 85%. Once the posterior probabilities of the joint events $\{\boldsymbol{\theta}(t)\}$ have been evaluated for all targets together, the state update for each target can be made separately according to the update rule of the PDAF [15, §6.4].

As the JPDAF can track multiple targets, it was necessary to formulate rules for deciding when a new track should be created, when two targets should be merged and when a target should be deleted. The JPDAF is initially started with no target at all. A new target is created every time a measurement can not be assigned to any previously existing target. A new target is always initialized with a start position in the middle of the room and a height of 163.9cm and a diagonal state error covariance matrix with a standard deviation that is essentially the size of the room for x and y and 1m for z. This initialization is allowed to take only 0.1s otherwise the target is immediately deleted. The initialization is said to be finished when the target is detected as active. This is when the volume of the error ellipsoid given by the state error covariance matrix is smaller than a given threshold. If a target didn't receive any new estimates for 5s, it is labeled as inactive and deleted. If two targets are less than 25cm apart from each other for at least 0.5s the target with the larger error volume is deleted.

To allow speaker movement, the process noise covariance matrix is dynamically set to a multiple of the squared time since the last update. For stability reasons, the process noise as well as the error state covariance matrix are upper bounded.

Since the filter used for each of the targets is built on top of the IEKF, there are at most 5 local iterations for each update.

The selection of the active speaker out of the maintained targets is done by choosing the target with the smallest error volume that has a height between 1m and 1.8m. Additionally, an estimate is only output when it is a valid estimate inside the physical borders of the room.

The JPDAF algorithm used here is a fully automatic two-pass batch algorithm, since the correlation thresholds are first estimated on the whole data and then the position is estimated using the precalculated time delays. If those correlation thresholds would be used from previous experiments, it would be a fully automatic one-pass online algorithm. The algorithm runs at realtime factor 1.98 on a Pentium 4, 2.66GHz machine.

## 5   State-Based Decision-Level Fusion

For the panoramic camera system, the fusion of the audio and video modalities is done at the decision level. Track estimates coming from the top camera visual tracker and the JPDAF-based acoustic tracker are combined using a finite state machine, which considers their relative strengths and weaknesses. Although the visual tracker is able to keep several simultaneous tracks, in scenarios requiring automatic initialization it can fail to detect persons completely for lack of observable features, poor discernability from the background, or overlap with other persons. The acoustic tracker, on the other hand, can precisely determine a speaker's position only in the presence of speech, and does not produce accurate estimates for several simulaneous speakers or during silence intervals.

Based on this, the fusion of the acoustic and visual tracks is made using a finite state machine weighing the availability and reliability of the single modalities:

- State 1: An acoustic estimate is available, for which no overlapping visual estimate exists. Here, estimates are considered overlapping if their distance is below 500mm. In this case, it is assumed the visual tracker has missed the speaking person and the acoustic hypothesis is output. The last received acoustic estimate is stored and continuously output until an overlapping visual estimate is found.
- State 2: An acoustic estimate is available, and a corresponding visual estimate exists. In this case, the average of the acoustic and visual estimates is output.
- State 3: After an overlapping visual estimate had been found, an acoustic estimate is no longer available. In this case, it is assumed the visual tracker has recovered the previously undetected speaker and the position of the last overlapping visual track is continuously output.

# 6  Evaluation on the CLEAR'07 3D Person Tracking Database

The above presented systems for visual, acoustic and multimodal tracking were evaluated on the CLEAR'07 3D Person Tacking Database. This database comprises recordings from 5 different CHIL smartrooms, involving 3 to 7 persons in a small meeting scenario, with a total length of 200 minutes.

Table 1 shows the results for the Single- and Multi-view visual systems (Particle Filter, Top Tracker), for the acoustic tracker (JPDAF), as well as for the corresponding mutimodal systems (Particle Filter Fusion, Decision Level Fusion). For details on the Multiple Object Tracking Precision (MOTP) and Multiple Object Tracking Accuracy (MOTA) metrics, the reader is referred to [11].

**Table 1.** Evaluation results for the 3D person tracking systems

| System | $MOTP$ | $miss$ | $falsePos$ | $mism.$ | $(A-)MOTA$ |
|---|---|---|---|---|---|
| Particle Filter | 155mm | 15.09% | 14.50% | 378 | 69.58% |
| Top Tracker | 222mm | 23.74% | 20.24% | 490 | 54.94% |
| JPDAF | 140mm | 20.60% | 24.78% | - | 54.63% |
| Particle Filter Fusion | 151mm | 20.17% | 20.02% | 121 | 58.49% |
| Decision Level Fusion | 159mm | 21.80% | 23.38% | 370 | 50.78% |

As can be seen in Table 1, the particle filter tracker clearly outperforms the baseline top view system, while still remaining competitive in terms of computational speed.

Factors that still affect tracking accuracies can be summed up in 2 categories:

- Detection errors: In some cases, participants showed no significant motion during the length of the sequence, rarely spoke, were only hardly distinguishable from the background using color information, or could not be detected by the upper body detectors, due to low resolution, difficult viewing angles or body poses. This accounts for the rather high percentage of misses.

The adaptation of the used detectors on CLEAR recording conditions or the inclusion of more varied features for detection should help alleviate this problem.
- False tracks: The scarce availability of detection hits for some targets lead to a system design that aggressively initializes person tracks whenever a detection becomes available and keeps tracks alive for extended periods of time even in the absence of such. This unfortunately can lead to a fair amount of false tracks which can not be distinguished from valid tracks and effectively eliminated based on color or foreground features alone. Again, the design of more reliable person detectors should help reduce the number of false tracks.

The MOTP numbers range from 222mm for the top camera visual system to 140mm for the acoustic tracker. The acoustic tracker reached an accuracy of 55%, with the main source of errors being localization uncertainty. On the visual and the multimodal side, the particle filter based feature level fusion approach (70%, 58%) clearly outperformed the baseline approach (55%, 51%). In the particle filter approach, the fusion of both modalities could improve tracking accuracy, compared to acoustic only tracking results, even though in the multimodal subtask the speaker additionally had to be tracked through periods of silence.

## 7  Summary

In this work, two systems for the multimodal tracking of multiple users were presented. A joint probabilistic data association filter for source localization is used in conjunction with two distinct systems for visual tracking: The first is a particle filter using foreground, color, upper body detection and person region cues from multiple camera images. The other is a blob tracker using only a wide angle overhead view, and performing model based tracking on foreground segmentation features. Two fusion scheme were presented, one at feature level, inherent in the particle filter approach, and one at decision level, using a 3-state finite-state machine to combine the output of the audio and visual trackers. The systems were extensively tested on the CLEAR 2007 3D Person Tracking Database. High tracking accuracies of up to 70% and position errors below 15cm could be reached.

## Acknowledgments

The work presented here was partly funded by the *European Union* (EU) under the integrated project CHIL, *Computers in the Human Interaction Loop* (Grant number IST-506909).

## References

1. Khalaf, R.Y., Intille, S.S.: Improving Multiple People Tracking using Temporal Consistency. MIT Dept. of Architecture House_n Project Technical Report (2001)
2. Niu, W., Jiao, L., Han, D., Wang, Y.-F.: Real-Time Multi-Person Tracking in Video Surveillance. In: Pacific Rim Multimedia Conference, Singapore (2003)

3. Mittal, A., Davis, L.S.: M2Tracker: A Multi-View Approach to Segmenting and Tracking People in a Cluttered Scene Using Region-Based Stereo. In: Heyden, A., Sparr, G., Nielsen, M., Johansen, P. (eds.) ECCV 2002. LNCS, vol. 2350, pp. 18–33. Springer, Heidelberg (2002)
4. Checka, N., Wilson, K., Rangarajan, V., Darrell, T.: A Probabilistic Framework for Multi-modal Multi-Person Tracking. In: Workshop on Multi-Object Tracking (CVPR) (2003)
5. Comaniciu, D., Meer, P.: Mean Shift: A Robust Approach Toward Feature Space Analysis. IEEE PAMI 24(5) (May 2002)
6. Haritaoglu, I., Harwood, D., Davis, L.S.: W4: Who? When? Where? What? A Real Time System for Detecting and Tracking People. In: Third Face and Gesture Recognition Conference, pp. 222–227 (1998)
7. Raja, Y., McKenna, S.J., Gong, S.: Tracking and Segmenting People in Varying Lighting Conditions using Colour. In: 3rd. Int. Conference on Face & Gesture Recognition, p. 228 (1998)
8. Viola, P., Jones, M.: Rapid Object Detection using a Boosted Cascade of Simple Features. In: IEEE CVPR (2001)
9. Lienhart, R., Maydt, J.: An Extended Set of Haar-like Features for Rapid Object Detection. In: IEEE ICIP 2002, September 2002, vol. 1, pp. 900–903 (2002)
10. Gehrig, T., McDonough, J.: Tracking of Multiple Speakers with Probabilistic Data Association Filters. In: CLEAR Workshop, Southampton, UK (April 2006)
11. Bernardin, K., Elbs, A., Stiefelhagen, R.: Multiple Object Tracking Performance Metrics and Evaluation in a Smart Room Environment. In: Sixth IEEE International Workshop on Visual Surveillance, in conjunction with ECCV 2006, Graz, Austria, May 13th (2006)
12. Bernardin, K., Gehrig, T., Stiefelhagen, R.: Multi- and Single View Multiperson Tracking for Smart Room Environments. In: CLEAR Evaluation Workshop 2006, Southampton, UK, April 2006. LNCS, vol. 4122, pp. 81–92 (2006)
13. Tao, H., Sawhney, H., Kumar, R.: A Sampling Algorithm for Tracking Multiple Objects. In: International Workshop on Vision Algorithms: Theory and Practice, pp. 53–68 (1999)
14. Wren, C., Azarbayejani, A., Darrell, T., Pentland, A.: Pfinder: Real-Time Tracking of the Human Body. IEEE Transactions on Pattern Analysis and Machine Intelligence 19(7), 780–785 (1997)
15. Bar-Shalom, Y.: Tracking and data association. Academic Press Professional, Inc., San Diego (1987)
16. Knapp, C.H., Carter, G.C.: The Generalized Correlation Method for Estimation of Time Delay. IEEE Trans. Acoust. Speech Signal Proc. 24(4), 320–327 (1976)
17. Omologo, M., Svaizer, P.: Acoustic Event Localization Using a Crosspower-spectrum Phase Based Technique. In: Proc. ICASSP, vol. 2, pp. 273–276 (1994)
18. Klee, U., Gehrig, T., McDonough, J.: Kalman Filters for Time Delay of Arrival-Based Source Localization. EURASIP Journal on Applied Signal Processing (2006)
19. Gehrig, T., McDonough, J.: Tracking Multiple Simultaneous Speakers with Probabilistic Data Association Filters. LNCS, vol. 4122, pp. 137–150 (2006)
20. CHIL - Computers In the Human Interaction Loop, http://chil.server.de
21. AMI - Augmented Multiparty Interaction, http://www.amiproject.org
22. VACE - Video Analysis and Content Extraction, http://www.ic-arda.org
23. OpenCV - Open Computer Vision Library, http://sourceforge.net/projects/opencvlibrary

# Multispeaker Localization and Tracking in Intelligent Environments*

C. Segura, A. Abad, J. Hernando, and C. Nadeu

Technical University of Catalonia, Barcelona, Spain
{csegura,alberto,javier,climent}@gps.tsc.upc.edu

**Abstract.** Automatic speaker localization is an important task in several applications such as acoustic scene analysis, hands-free videoconferencing or speech enhancement. Tracking speakers in multiparty conversations constitutes a fundamental task for automatic meeting analysis. In this work, we present the acoustic Person Tracking system developed at the UPC for the CLEAR'07 evaluation campaign. The designed system is able to track the estimated position of multiple speakers in a smart-room environment. Preliminary speaker locations are provided by the SRP-PHAT algorithm, which is known to perform robustly in most scenarios. Data association techniques based on trajectory prediction and spatizal clustering are used to match the raw positional estimates with potential speakers. These positional measurements are then finally spatially smoothed by means of Kalman filtering. Besides the technology description, experimental results obtained on the CLEAR'07 CHIL database are also reported.

## 1 Introduction

The automatic analysis of meetings in multisensor rooms is an emerging research field. In this domain, localizing and tracking people and their speaking activity play fundamental roles in several applications, like scene analysis, hands-free videoconferencing or speech enhancement techniques.

Many approaches to the task of acoustic source localization in smart environments have been proposed in the literature. The main differences between them lie in the way they gather spatial clues from the acoustic signals, and how this information is processed to obtain a reliable 3D position in the room space. Spatial features, like the Time Difference of Arrival (TDOA) [8] between a pair of microphones or the Direction of Arrival (DOA) to a microphone array, can be obtained on the basis of cross-correlation techniques [1], High Resolution Spectral Estimation techniques [3] or by source-to-microphone impulse response estimation [2].

Conventional acoustic localization systems include a tracking algorithm that smoothes the raw positional measurements to increase precision. Furthermore,

---

* This work has been partially sponsored by the EC-funded project CHIL (IST-2002-506909) and by the Spanish Government-funded project ACESCA (TIN2005-08852).

the localization of multiple speakers simultaneously becomes severely complicated due to speech overlap of participants, since the localization techniques based on the cross-correlation like TDOA estimation assume one impinging wavefront. The task becomes specially difficult in the case of multiple moving speakers. Prior research on speaker tracking usually deals with a single speaker [10], however recently, multispeaker tracking [11] using Kalman [4] and particle [13] filtering techniques has gained interest in the context of smart meeting rooms.

The UPC acoustic localization system proposed in this work is based on the SRP-PHAT [5] localization method. The SRP-PHAT, algorithm although being very robust in reverberant environments, is not very well suited for the case of multiple concurrent speakers. The PHAT weighting introduces a masking effect of dominant acoustic sources over other sources of sound. This is desirable for increasing the robustness of the localization system by masking multipath acoustic propagation and reverberation, but it also hinders the localization of multiple acoustic sources. However, in the case of using a short analysis window (∼23ms), we have observed that the positional estimates produced by the SRP-PHAT jump from one speaker to another at a very high rate due to the nonstationarity of the voice.

In our work we use a multiperson tracker based on the Kalman filter, which models a simple Newtonian motion of the source. The tracker carries out the tasks of detecting potential acoustic sources using spatial clustering and also assigning the raw location estimates to their corresponding speaker tracks using data association techniques. Then the measures assigned to each individual track are spatially smoothed by means of the corresponding Kalman filter [12], acording with the measure error variance estimation method defined in the next section.

## 2    Acoustic Source Localization

The SRP-PHAT algorithm [5] tackles the task of acoustic localization in a robust and efficient way. In general, the basic operation of localization techniques based on SRP is to search the room space for a maximum in the power of the received sound source signal using a delay-and-sum or a filter-and-sum beamformer. In the simplest case, the output of the delay-and-sum beamformer is the sum of the signals of each microphone with the adequate steering delays for the position that is explored. Concretely, the SRP-PHAT algorithms consists in exploring the 3D space, searching for the maximum of the contribution of the PHAT-weighted cross-correlations between all the microphone pairs. The SRP-PHAT algorithm performs very robustly due the the PHAT weighting, keeping the simplicity of the steered beamformer approach.

Consider a smart-room provided with a set of $N$ microphones from we choose $M$ microphone pairs. Let $\mathbf{x}$ denote a $\mathbf{R}^3$ position in space. Then the time delay of arrival $TDOA_{i,j}$ of an hypothetic acoustic source located at **x** between two microphones $i, j$ with position $\mathbf{m}_i$ and $\mathbf{m}_j$ is:

$$TDOA_{i,j} = \frac{\| \mathbf{x} - \mathbf{m}_i \| - \| \mathbf{x} - \mathbf{m}_j \|}{s}, \tag{1}$$

where $s$ is the speed of sound.

The 3D room space is then quantized into a set of positions with typical separation of 5-10cm. The theoretical TDOA $\tau_{\mathbf{x},i,j}$ from each exploration position to each microphone pair are precalculated and stored.

PHAT-weighted cross-correlations [1] of each microphone pair are estimated for each analysis frame. It can be expressed in terms of the inverse Fourier transform of the estimated cross-power spectral density ($G_{m_1 m_2}(f)$) as follows,

$$R_{m_i m_j}(\tau) = \int_{-\infty}^{\infty} \frac{G_{m_i m_j}(f)}{|G_{m_i m_j}(f)|} e^{j 2\pi f \tau} df, \tag{2}$$

The estimated acoustic source location is the position of the quantized space that maximizes the contribution of the cross-correlation of all microphone pairs:

$$\hat{\mathbf{x}} = \underset{\mathbf{x}}{\operatorname{argmax}} \sum_{i,j \,\in\, \mathbb{S}} R_{m_i m_j}(\tau_{\mathbf{x},i,j}), \tag{3}$$

where $\mathbb{S}$ is the set of microphone pairs. The sum of the contributions of each microphone pair cross-correlation is assumed to be well-correlated with the likelihood of the estimation given. Hence, this value is compared to a fixed threshold (depending on the number of microphone pairs used) to reject/accept the estimation. The threshold has been experimentally fixed to 0.5 for each 6 microphone pairs. It is important to note that in the case of concurrent speakers or acoustic events, this technique will only provide an estimation for the dominant acoustic source at each iteration.

## 3   Multiple Speaker Tracking

One of the major problems faced by acoustic tracking systems is the lack of a continuous stream of features provided by the localization module. Moreover, in the case of spontaneous speech, we have to deal with acoustic events that are sporadic and others that are concurrent.

The proposed method makes use of spatial segmentation to detect tracks and associate incoming raw estimates to them. Each tracked acoustic source has an associated acceptance region and a Kalman filter. When a raw estimate falls within a region of a track, it is asigned to that track and then used by the Kalman filter. If no measurement falls within this acceptance region, then the predicted position is used as the measurement for the Kalman filter.

We have no constraint on the number of acoustic sources that the algorithm is able to track. The method dynamically estimates the number of sources based on a birth/death system. The track detection uses a spatial segmentation algorithm to group locations that are close to each other in space and time. When a minimum number of locations $N_b$ are found in a space region over a defined time window $T_b$, the tracking system decides it is a new track. Similarly, if a track does not have any measurements that fall within its acceptance region for a given amount of time $T_d$, then the track is dropped. The ratio between $T_b$ and $N_b$ used in the track detection module is a design parameter. It must be high enough to filter out noises and outliers, but also not too high in order to be able to detect sporadic acoustic events. In our experiments $N_b$ is set to 4, $T_b$ is $460ms$ and $T_d$ is also $460ms$.

## 3.1   Kalman Filter

The Kalman filter [12] has been widely used in tracking applications.

The motion of a specified talker is modelled by a simple Newtonian model defined by the state difference equation:

$$\mathbf{s}_{k+1} = \phi_k \mathbf{s}_k + \mathbf{\Gamma}_k \mathbf{w}_k, \tag{4}$$

where $\mathbf{s}_k$ is the system state, $\phi_k$ is the transition matrix that propagates the state, $\mathbf{w}_k$ is the process noise vector and $\mathbf{\Gamma}_k$ is the gain matrix.

In this work we have chosen the state, as a 6-component vector consisting in the 2-dimensional source position, velocity and acceleration:

$$\mathbf{s}_k = [x_k \ y_k \ \dot{x}_k \ \dot{y}_k \ \ddot{x}_k \ \ddot{y}_k]^T. \tag{5}$$

The process noise vector, $\mathbf{w}_k = [w_{x,k} \ w_{y,k}]^T$, whose components are uncorrelated, zero-mean Gaussian variables with equal variance $\sigma_w$, is used to model variations in the acceleration of the source motion. The transition matrix $\phi$ and the gain matrix $\mathbf{\Gamma}$ are defined by:

$$\phi = \begin{pmatrix} \mathbf{I}_2 & \Delta t \mathbf{I}_2 & \frac{\Delta t^2}{2} \mathbf{I}_2 \\ \mathbf{0}_2 & \mathbf{I}_2 & \Delta t \mathbf{I}_2 \\ \mathbf{0}_2 & \mathbf{0}_2 & \mathbf{I}_2 \end{pmatrix}, \tag{6}$$

$$\mathbf{\Gamma} = \left( \frac{\Delta t^3}{6} \mathbf{I}_2 \Big| \frac{\Delta t^2}{2} \mathbf{I}_2 \Big| \Delta t \mathbf{I}_2 \right)^T, \tag{7}$$

where $\Delta t$ is the time period between positional measures provided by the localization system, $\mathbf{I}_2$ is the identity matrix and $\mathbf{0}_2$ is a zero matrix.

In the other hand, the source positional observation at the $k^{th}$ iteration, $\mathbf{z}_k$ is modelled in the conventional as the true 2D source position corrupted by the measurement noise $\mathbf{v}_k$.

$$\mathbf{z}_k = \mathbf{H} \mathbf{s}_k + \mathbf{v}_k. \tag{8}$$

In this work, the measurement matrix is given by:

$$\mathbf{H} = [\mathbf{I}_2 | \mathbf{0}_2 | \mathbf{0}_2]. \tag{9}$$

The covariance matrix of the measurement noise $\mathbf{R}_k = E\left[\mathbf{v}_k \mathbf{v}_k^T\right]$ is calculated as a function of the estimated source location, sensor position and environmental conditions as proposed in [14], where the error covariance of the localization estimation is computed as a function of the variances of the TDOAs estimation and a pure geometrical weight matrix:

$$\mathbf{R}_k = \left(\mathbf{M}^T \cdot \mathbf{V} \cdot \mathbf{M}\right)^{-1}, \tag{10}$$

$$\mathbf{V} = \begin{pmatrix} \frac{1}{\sigma_{\tau_1}^2} & & & \\ & \frac{1}{\sigma_{\tau_2}^2} & & \\ & & \ddots & \\ & & & \frac{1}{\sigma_{\tau_N}^2} \end{pmatrix}, \tag{11}$$

where the weight matrix $\mathbf{M}$ [14] models the sensitivity of the microphone array at the estimated position of the speaker and $\mathbf{V}$ is the diagonal matrix consisting of the inverse of the TDOA variances $\sigma_{\tau_i}^2$ at the microphone pair $i$. The figure 1 shows a simulation of the error variance for the rooms at UKA and UPC.

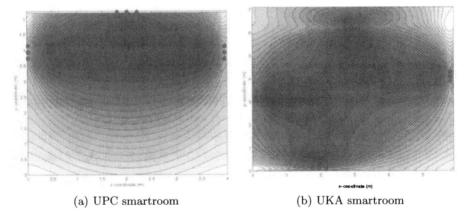

(a) UPC smartroom        (b) UKA smartroom

**Fig. 1.** Simulation of the localization error variance at heigh= $1.7m$ for UPC and UKA CHIL-Rooms. The brightness in the figure is related to the predicted error at a given position. Brighter zones are more prone to localization errors.

The SRP-PHAT algorithm does not provide an estimation of the variance of the time differences of arrival, because the TDOAs $\hat{\tau}_{\hat{\mathbf{x}},i,j}$ are estimated indirectly calculating the distance differences from the detected location of the acoustic source to each microphone. The only measure available is the value of the cross-correlation $\rho = R_{m_i m_j}(\hat{\tau}_{\hat{\mathbf{x}},i,j})$ at each microphone pair. In principle, lower values of the cross-correlation function should correspond with high variance TDOA estimation. Preliminary experimental results have led us to propose an exponential function to model the relationship between $\rho$ and $\sigma_\tau^2$ :

$$\sigma_\tau^2 = e^{-\frac{\rho}{\delta}} \cdot \beta. \tag{12}$$

The parameter $\delta$ must be set according with the microphone array configuration, since microphones that are closer exhibit a higher cross-correlation. In our work we have chosen $\delta = 0.05$ and $\beta = 5 \cdot 10^{-4}$.

## 3.2 Data Association

In situations dealing with multiple, possibly moving, concurrent speakers, the purpose of the data association method is to assign raw location measures to a specific acoustic source and also to filter out outliers that appear due to noise and reverberation. This is done through the use of acceptance regions [15]. The acceptance region is a segment of the space around the position predicted by the corresponding track. The region size is set dynamically according to the measure noise variance and state estimation uncertainty:

$$\left(\mathbf{z} - \mathbf{z}_k^-\right)^T \cdot \mathbf{S}_k^- 1 \cdot \left(\mathbf{z} - \mathbf{z}_k^-\right) \leq \gamma. \tag{13}$$

The variable $\mathbf{z}$ defines the acceptance region in space, $\gamma$ is a fixed bound value , $\mathbf{z}_k^-$ is the source position predicted by the Kalman filter and $\mathbf{S}_k$ is the covariance matrix of the positional observations, that can be formulated recursively as follows:

$$\mathbf{S}_k = \mathbf{H} \cdot \mathbf{P}_k^- \cdot \mathbf{H}^T + \mathbf{R}_k, \tag{14}$$

where $\mathbf{P}_k^-$ is a matrix provided by the Kalman filter, that predicts the error covariance of the estimated state. A high value of the measure noise covariance matrix $\mathbf{R}_k$ or a high uncertainty in the estimation of the state, for instance due motion of the source, yields to a bigger acceptance region.

# 4 Evaluation

Audio Person Tracking evaluation is run on an extract of the data collected by the CHIL consortium for the CLEAR 07 evaluation. The data consists of meetings recorded at each partner site involving presentations and discussions. A complete description of the data and the evaluation can be found in [7].

## 4.1 Summary of the Experimental Set-Up

**Data Description.** Room set-ups of the contributing sites present two basic common groups of devices: the *audio* and the *video* sensors.

Audio sensors set-up is composed by 1 (or more) NIST Mark III 64-channel microphone array, 3 (or more) T-shaped 4-channel microphone cluster and various table-top and close-talk microphones.

**Evaluation Metrics.** Two metrics are considered for evaluation and comparison purposes:

*Multiple Object Tracking Precision (MOTP) [mm]* This is the precision of the tracker when it comes to determining the exact position of a tracked person in the room. It is the total Euclidian distance error for matched *ground truth-hypothesis* pairs over all frames, averaged by the total number of matches made. It shows the ability of the tracker to find correct positions, and is independent of its errors in keeping tracks over time, estimating the numbers of persons, etc.

*Multiple Object Tracking Accuracy (A-MOTA) [%]* This is the accuracy of the tracker when it comes to keeping correct correspondences over time, estimating the number of people, recovering tracks, etc. It is one minus the sum of all errors made by the tracker, false positives, misses, over all frames, divided by the total number of ground truth points. This metric is like the *video* MOTA in which all mismatch errors are ignored and it is used to measure tracker performance only for the active speaker at each point in time for better comparison with the acoustic person tracking results (where identity mismatches are not evaluated).

## 4.2   Audio Person Tracking Results

We have decided to use all the *T-clusters* available in the different seminars and only to use the *MarkIII* data for the sites (ITC, UKA and UPC). In general, only microphone pairs of eather the same *T-cluster* or within the *MarkIII* array are considered by the algorithm. In the experiments where the *MarkIII* is used, 16 microphone channels are selected for GCC-PHAT computation The pairs selected out of the *MarkIII* are 42 in total, spanning an inter-microphone separation of 16cm, 24cm, and 32cm. The number of microphones pairs used in *MarkIII* is greater than those used of the *T-Clusters*, thus a corrective weight is given to the *MarkIII* contribution to the SRP-PHAT algorithm in order to have approximately the same importance as one *T-Cluster*

In Table 1 individual results for each data set and average results for the Acoustic Person Tracking tasks are shown. Notice that the average results are not directly the mean of the individual results, since the scores are recomputed jointly.

**Table 1.** Results for acoustic person tracking

| Site | MOTP | Misses | False Positives | A-MOTA |
|------|------|--------|-----------------|--------|
| AIT data | 201mm | 48.15% | 8.17% | 43.68% |
| IBM data | 206mm | 35.01% | 18.09% | 46.91% |
| ITC data | 157mm | 38.31% | 38.97% | 22.72% |
| UKA data | 175mm | 41.55% | 22.56% | 35.89% |
| UPC data | 117mm | 30.35% | 13.69% | 55.96% |
| Total Average | 168mm | 37.86% | 20.97% | 41.17% |

# 5   Conclusions

In this paper we have presented the audio Person Tracking system developed by UPC for the CLEAR evaluation campaign. A method for estimating the localization error covariance matrix of the SRP-PHAT algorithm has been presented, that can be used in conjuction with a Kalman tracking filter to add robustness to scenario and environment variables. Results show that the use of the *MarkIII* data yields a better precision but more false positives, which may be attributable to non-speech acoustic sources. Improvement of the Kalman filtering and association rules and the introduction of a SAD algorithm, are expected to enhance the tracking system.

# References

[1] Omologo, M., Svaizer, P.: Use of the crosspower-spectrum phase in acoustic event location. IEEE Trans. on Speech and Audio Processing (1997)
[2] Chen, J., Huang, Y.A., Benesty, J.: An adaptive blind SIMO identification approach to joint multichannel time delay estimation. In: Proc. IEEE Int. Conf. Acoustics, Speech, Signal Processing (ICASSP), Montreal (May 2004)
[3] Potamitis, I., Tremoulis, G., Fakotakis, N.: Multi-speaker doa tracking using interactive multiple models and probabilistic data association. In: Proceedings of Eurospeech 2003, Geneva (September 2003)
[4] Sturim, D.E., Brandstein, M.S., Silverman, H.F.: Tracking multiple talkers using microphone-array measurements. In: Proc. IEEE Int. Conf. Acoustics, Speech, Signal Processing (ICASSP), Munich (April 1997)
[5] DiBiase, J., Silverman, H., Brandstein, M.: Microphone Arrays, ch. 8. In: Robust Localization in Reverberant Rooms, Springer, Heidelberg (2001)
[6] CHIL Computers In the Human Interaction Loop. Integrated Project of the 6th European Framework Programme (506909) (2004-2007),
   http://chil.server.de/
[7] The Spring 2007 CLEAR Evaluation and Workshop,
   http://www.clear-evaluation.org/
[8] Brandstein, M.S.: A Framework for Speech Source Localization Using Sensor Arrays. Ph.D. Thesis, Brown University (1995)
[9] Bernardin, K., Gehring, T., Stiefelhagen, R.: Multi- and Single View Multiperson Tracking for Smart Room Environments. In: Stiefelhagen, R., Garofolo, J.S. (eds.) CLEAR 2006. LNCS, vol. 4122, Springer, Heidelberg (2007)
[10] Vermaak, J., Blake, A.: Nonlinear filtering for speaker tracking in noisy and reverberant environments. In: Proc. IEEE Int. Conf. Acoustics, Speech, Signal Processing (ICASSP) (2001)
[11] Claudio, E., Parisi, R.: Multi-source localization strategies. In: Brandstein, M.S., Ward, D.B. (eds.) Microphone Arrays: Signal Processing Techniques and Applications, ch. 9, pp. 181–201. Springer, Heidelberg (2001)
[12] Welch, G., Bishop, G.: An introduction to the Kalman filter. TR 95-041, Dept. of Computer Sc., Uni. of NC at Chapel Hill (2004)

[13] Checka, N., Wilson, K., Siracusa, M., Darrell, T.: Multiple person and speaker activity tracking with a particle filter. In: Proc. IEEE Int. Conf. on Acoustics, Speech and Signal Processing (ICASSP), Montreal (May 2004)

[14] Brandstein, M.S., Adcock, J.E., Silverman, H.F.: Microphone array localization error estimation with application to optimal sensor placement. J. Acoust. Soc. Am. 99(6), 3807–3816 (1996)

[15] Bar-Shalom, Y., Fortman, T.E.: Tracking and Data association. Academic Press, London (1988)

# Multi-person Tracking Strategies Based on Voxel Analysis

C. Canton-Ferrer, J. Salvador, J.R. Casas, and M.Pardàs

Technical University of Catalonia, Barcelona, Spain
{ccanton,jordi,josep,montse}@gps.tsc.upc.edu

**Abstract.** This paper presents two approaches to the problem of simultaneous tracking of several people in low resolution sequences from multiple calibrated cameras. Spatial redundancy is exploited to generate a discrete 3D binary representation of the foreground objects in the scene. Color information obtained from a zenithal camera view is added to this 3D information. The first tracking approach implements heuristic association rules between blobs labelled according to spatiotemporal connectivity criteria. Association rules are based on a cost function which considers their placement and color histogram. In the second approach, a particle filtering scheme adapted to the incoming 3D discrete data is proposed. A volume likelihood function and a discrete 3D re-sampling procedure are introduced to evaluate and drive particles. Multiple targets are tracked by means of multiple particle filters and interaction among them is modeled through a 3D blocking scheme. Evaluation over the CLEAR 2007 database yields quantitative results assessing the performance of the proposed algorithm for indoor scenarios.

## 1 Introduction

The current paper addresses the problem of detecting and tracking a group of people in an indoor scenario using a multiple camera setup. Robust, multi-person tracking systems are employed in a wide range of applications, including SmartRoom environments, surveillance for security, health monitoring, as well as providing location and context features for human-computer interaction.

A number of methods for camera based multi-person 3D tracking have been proposed in the literature [5]. A common goal in these systems is robustness under occlusions created by the multiple objects cluttering the scene when estimating the position of a target. Single camera approaches [2] have been widely employed but are more vulnerable to occlusions, rotation and scale changes of the target. In order to avoid these drawbacks, multi-camera tracking techniques [9] exploit spatial redundancy among different views and provide 3D information as well. Integration of features extracted from multiple cameras has been proposed in terms of image correspondences [3], multi-view histograms [11] or voxel reconstructions [6].

R. Stiefelhagen et al. (Eds.): CLEAR 2007 and RT 2007, LNCS 4625, pp. 91–103, 2008.
© Springer-Verlag Berlin Heidelberg 2008

We propose two methods for 3D tracking of multiple people in a multi-camera environment. Both methods share the initial steps, where redundancy among cameras is exploited to obtain a binary 3D voxel representation of the foreground objects in the scene as the input of the tracking system. The first approach processes the information as follows: a time-consistent label is assigned to each blob corresponding to a person in the room and the 3D position of the person is updated at every frame. All the processing in this step is performed using heuristic criteria such as closest blob, most similar color, etc.

The second approach uses filtering techniques to add temporal consistency to tracks. Kalman filtering approaches have been extensively used to track a single object under Gaussian uncertainty models and linear dynamics [9]. However, these methods do not perform accurately when facing noisy scenes or rapidly maneuvering targets. Particle filtering has been applied to cope with these situations since it can deal with multi-modal *pdf*s and is able to recover from lost tracks [1]. In the second tracking system proposed, a particle filter is implemented to track a target estimating its 3D centroid. No motion model has been assumed to keep a reduced state space. Particle weights are evaluated through a volume likelihood function measuring whether a particle falls inside or outside a volume. A 3D discrete re-sampling technique is introduced to propagate particles and to capture object shifts. Multiple targets are tracked assigning a particle filter to every one. In order to achieve the most independent set of trackers, we consider a 3D blocking method to model interactions. It must be noted that this second tracking system with particle filtering has been already introduced in [4].

Finally, the effectiveness of both proposed algorithms is assessed by means of objective metrics defined in the framework of the CLEAR07 [7] multi-target tracking database.

## 2  System Overview

This section aims to briefly describe the main blocks composing our multi-person tracking system. The input data are images captured by five calibrated cameras and their respective calibration data. Four of those cameras are placed at the corners of a meeting room and the fifth is installed as a zenithal camera. The system is depicted in Fig. 1.

The first block in our system is an adaptive foreground segmentation block based on the Stauffer-Grimson method [13] applied on each of the input images. It consists of two different working phases: the initialization step, when the segmentation algorithm does not know yet the contents of the background and the adaptive loop, when some model of the background has already been acquired but it still needs to be updated to cope with phenomena such as slow ambient light variations.

After this first block, a Shape from Silhouette algorithm applied on the obtained foreground masks delivers a 3D reconstruction of the foreground volumes

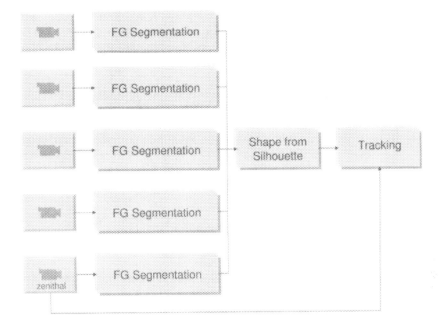

**Fig. 1.** UPC tracking system

in the scene by testing voxel occupancy on each of the available foreground masks corresponding to each camera view. In order to obtain useful foreground volumes, voxel visibility is considered in each one of the camera views for foreground/background classification of voxels out of the common visibility volume for all five camera views.

The third and final block consists in the tracking of 3D connected components, or blobs. This block gets 3D binary foreground volumes from the previous Shape from Silhouette stage (also the color image from the zenithal camera, in the case where color features are considered). Two systems are proposed for the tracking of the 3D blobs:

- *Heuristics Based Tracking:* In the first approach, a time-consistent label is assigned to each blob corresponding to a person in the room. The 3D position of the person is updated at every frame and a cost function based on heuristic criteria such as closest 3D blob, with most similar color, etc. is used to solve the temporal correspondence problem.
- *Tracking with Particle Filters:* The second approach employs a particle filtering strategy using only the information coming from the reconstruction (thus not taking into account color information). A particle filter is assigned to each person and connectivity criteria are employed to drive the particles. Finally, an exclusion criterion is employed to separate particles among different filters.

The next subsections describe the common steps (Foreground Segmentation and Shape from Silhouette) for both tracking methods presented. The two tracking approaches themselves are described in the subsequent sections 3 and 4.

## 2.1 Foreground Segmentation

As mentioned above, foreground segmentation follows Stauffer-Grimson [13] in two phases. During initialization, the method needs to be fed with images containing only background elements (without people). The initial algorithm estimates both the mean YUV values of every pixel of the background and their variances, assuming a single modal Gaussian behavior for each pixel.

The adaptive loop can also be divided in two phases: firstly it decides whether to classify a pixel in an image as background or foreground by using the available Gaussian model. The decision of belonging to the foreground will only be taken when the difference in chrominance with respect to the mean in the Gaussian model is higher than a threshold computed from the variance of the latter and the pixel's luminance is below a certain threshold, because of the unreliability of the chrominance vector for high luminance values. The second phase consists in updating the Gaussian model for each pixel classified as background with the new data from the current frame. Thus, foreground segmentation is able to adapt to slight variations in the light condition of the captured sequence by continuously learning the background.

## 2.2 Shape from Silhouette

Before the actual tracking step, a 3D model of the scene foreground is generated as the result of a Shape from Silhouette (SfS) algorithm [8] delivering voxelized foreground blobs from a set of foreground segmentation masks in the calibrated camera views. The algorithm applies a consistency check on the projection of the elementary spatial analysis unit (a voxel in this case) over the five cameras to decide whether the voxel belongs to the foreground of the scene. In this case, the consistency check analyzes whether the projected voxel overlaps the foreground masks in the camera views.

For simplicity, the consistency check of the algorithm only uses the projection of voxels' geometrical centers on the five camera views. To speed up the execution time, a look-up table (LUT) containing the pixel coordinates of the projection of every voxel center on every camera image is generated using the calibration data prior to the actual analysis. Another LUT, containing the camera visibility for every voxel in a completely empty space is computed for the visibility-aware consistency check.

Finally, a non-linear function is applied to decide whether a voxel is occupied by a foreground element. As not all the voxels are seen by all the cameras, the threshold in the consistency check is adapted to the number of cameras that see each voxel. A voxel is considered as part of the foreground if:

1. The voxel is seen by all five cameras and the consistency check on the five camera views is positive

2. The voxel is seen by only four cameras and the consistency check on the four camera views is positive
3. The voxel is seen by only three cameras and the consistency check on the three camera views is positive

Otherwise, the voxel is considered as part of the background. This technique delivers 3D models for the foreground of the scene with enough accuracy, even in areas with low camera visibility, thanks to the visibility LUT. Effects such as occlusion by background elements, i. e. tables or chairs, are not correctly dealt with in this approach but, as mentioned above, the results obtained are accurate enough for our target application.

# 3   Heuristics Based Tracking

The heuristic tracker receives binary voxelized masks of 3D blobs from the Shape from Silhouette step as well as the camera images from the zenithal camera. As a first step, an analysis of connected components on the input volume is performed, in order to get an identification label for each blob. Spurious (unconnected) foreground voxels are also removed in this first step.

## 3.1   Blob Classification

For each 3D connected component, its volume, the position of its centroid and its height are computed to obtain a first classification for the foreground blobs of the scene. This classification takes into account the following rules:

1. If the blob has a volume smaller than a given threshold, it is considered as an object, otherwise it is marked as a person
2. If the blob is marked as a person and it is taller than a certain height (140 cm), the blob is marked as a standing person, otherwise it is marked as a sitting person

## 3.2   Color Model for Blobs

In addition to the geometric features mentioned above, a color model of the blob is obtained from the information contained in the zenithal camera view. Keeping in mind that our system is designed to be fast enough to deliver results for real-time applications, we decided to create a color model using only the color of a layer of voxels for each blob. In addition, we also wanted those layers to be as much populated as possible. This condition led us to the decision of choosing a layer of voxels at a height of 100 cm for sitting persons and 150 cm for standing persons, heights at which the sections of the body in those poses present the largest areas. Thus, in the case of blobs classified as a standing person, the color model is obtained from the projection over the zenithal camera of the centers of the voxels at a height of 150 cm. Similarly the color samples of a sitting person are obtained from the voxels at a height of 100 cm.

The color model obtained through the mentioned sampling is an RGB histogram with a parametric number of bins. In our tests, a number of 16 bins per channel delivered the best results.

### 3.3  Heuristic Tracking

The tracking algorithm for the heuristic tracker is based on the application of heuristic rules. Once the relevant features (blob classification, color model) have been extracted, a cost function is computed from the available data from tracked blobs in the previous time instant and (candidate) blobs in the current time instant.

Firstly, a marginal cost is computed as the 2D euclidean distance between each pair composed by a tracked and candidate blob. If the distance is shorter than a certain speed times the time difference between frames, assuming that such speed is the maximum speed of a person in a meeting room, this first marginal cost is set to zero. Otherwise, if the distance is longer than the maximum distance but smaller than twice such maximum distance, a cost is set from the formula [distance / mindistance - 1]. If the distance is larger than twice the maximum distance, the cost is set to 1. Thus, the marginal cost for the euclidean distance is set as a value comprised in the range [0, 1]. This extension to the maximum possible speed of a person (up to twice the expected value) is aimed to balance the effects of merging blobs, usually implying a high speed of blobs' centroids.

A second marginal cost is computed as the 1-complementary of the Bhatacharyya distance computed from the histograms of each tracked-candidate pair, resulting in a value also comprised in the range [0, 1], although in general the dynamic range of this type of distance is much smaller than the whole range.

With these two marginal costs for distance and color and the remaining information from the blob classification (volume of the blobs), a cost table is generated. The aim is to compute the potential association among any two candidate blobs from two sequential frames. If a tracked blob has only one candidate blob with a distance cost smaller than 1, then the marginal cost for the euclidean distance is used for all the pairs formed with this tracked blob. If there are several candidates with a distance cost smaller than 1 for a given tracked blob, then for those tracked-candidate pairs the color marginal cost is used instead of the distance cost. Furthermore, if the candidate is classified as an object instead of as a person, a penalty is applied by multiplying by 2 the color cost.

When the cost table is filled in, the candidate blob with less cost is assigned to each track. If a candidate is assigned to more than one tracked blob, then a special group ID is added to the label of each of the tracked blobs to allow a correct separation later. Otherwise, if a candidate is only assigned to one tracked blob, the color model for that track is updated by averaging its previous histogram with the candidate's position. If a candidate is not assigned to any tracked blob and the blob classification reported it as being a person, a new track is added to the list with the features extracted in the current time instant. Finally, if a track does not have any matching candidate (cost smaller than 1), it is removed from the list of tracked blobs.

## 4    Particle Filtering Applied to 3D Tracking

Particle Filtering is an approximation technique for estimation problems where the variables involved do not hold Gaussian uncertainty models and linear dynamics. Person tracking can be tackled by means of Particle Filters (PFs) to estimate the 3D position of a person $x_t = (x, y, z)_t$ at time $t$, taking as observation a set of binary voxels representing the 3D scene up to time $t$ denoted as $z_{1:t}$. Multi-person tracking might be dealt with by assigning a PF to each target and defining an interaction model to ensure track coherence.

For a given target $x_t$, a PF approximates the posterior density $p(x_t|z_{1:t})$ with a sum of $N_s$ Dirac functions:

$$p(x_t|z_{1:t}) \approx \sum_{j=1}^{N_s} w_t^j \delta(x_t - x_t^j), \qquad (1)$$

where $w_t^j$ and $x_t^j$ are the weights and positions associated to the particles. For this type of tracking problem, a Sampling Importance Re-sampling (SIR) Particle Filtering is applied to drive particles across time [1]. Assuming importance density to be equal to prior density, weight update is recursively computed as:

$$w_t^j \propto w_{t-1}^j \, p(z_t|x_t^j). \qquad (2)$$

SIR Particle Filtering avoids the particle degeneracy problem by re-sampling at every time step. In this case, weights are set to $w_{t-1}^j = 1/N_s, \forall j$, therefore

$$w_t^j \propto p(z_t|x_t^j). \qquad (3)$$

Hence, the weights are proportional to the likelihood function that will be computed over the incoming volume $z_t$ as defined in Sec.4.1. The re-sampling step derives the particles depending on the weights of the previous step. Then all the new particles receive a starting weight equal to $1/N_s$, which will be updated by the next volume likelihood function.

Finally, the best state at time $t$ of target $m$, $X_t^m$, is derived based on the discrete approximation of Eq.1. The most common solution is the Monte Carlo approximation of the expectation as

$$X_t^m = \mathbb{E}\left[x_t|z_{1:t}\right] \approx \frac{1}{N_s} \sum_{j=1}^{N_s} w_t^j x_t^i. \qquad (4)$$

A major limitation of Particle Filtering, and specially SIR ones, is the capability of the particle set of representing the *pdf* when the sampling density of the state space is low. Scenarios with a high number of degrees of freedom require a large number of particles to yield an efficient estimation, with the consequent increase in terms of computational cost.

Up to the authors' knowledge, the novelty of the proposed scheme is to employ the minimum unit of the scene, the voxel, to redefine state space sampling. Our volume being a discrete representation, particles are constrained to occupy a single voxel and to move with displacements on a 3D discrete orthogonal grid.

### 4.1  Likelihood Evaluation

Function $p(\mathbf{z}_t|\mathbf{x}_t)$ can be defined as the likelihood of a particle belonging to the volume corresponding to a person. For a given particle $j$ occupying a voxel, its likelihood may be formulated as

$$p(\mathbf{z}_t|\mathbf{x}_t^j) = \frac{1}{|\mathcal{C}(\mathbf{x}_t^j,q)|} \sum_{\mathbf{p}\in\mathcal{C}(\mathbf{x}_t^j,q)} d(\mathbf{x}_t^j,\mathbf{p}), \qquad (5)$$

where $\mathcal{C}(\cdot)$ stands for the neighborhood over a connectivity domain $q$ on the 3D orthogonal grid and $|\mathcal{C}(\cdot)|$ represents its cardinality. Typically, connectivity in 3D discrete grids can be 6, 14 and 26 and in our research $q = 26$ provided accurate results. Function $d(\cdot)$ measures the distance between a foreground voxel $\mathbf{p}$ in the neighborhood and the particle.

Ideally, particles placed inside the volume of the target achieve maximum likelihood while those being on the surface of the volume attain a non-zero value. Volumes belonging to people would be completely solid but, in practice, there are holes introduced as the effect of segmentation inaccuracies during the SfS reconstruction.

### 4.2  3D Discrete Re-sampling

The re-sampling step has been defined according to the condition that every particle is assigned to a foreground voxel. In other words, re-sampling has usually been defined as a process where some noise is added to the position of the re-sampled particles according to their weights [1]. The higher the weight, the more replicas will be created. In our current tracking scenario, re-sampling adds some *discrete* noise to particles only allowing motion within the 3D discrete positions of adjacent foreground voxels as depicted in Fig.2a. Then, non populated foreground voxels are assigned to re-sampled particles. In some cases, there are not enough adjacent foreground voxels to be assigned, then a connectivity search finds closer non-empty voxels to be assigned as shown in Fig.2b.

(a)                                   (b)

**Fig. 2.** Discrete re-sampling example (in 2D)

No motion model has been assumed in the state space in order to keep a reduced dimensionality of our estimation problem. However, object translations are captured within the re-sampling step by means of this particle set expansion leading to satisfactory results.

### 4.3   Multi-person PF Tracking

Challenges in 3D multi-person tracking from volumetric scene reconstruction are basically twofold. The first is finding an interaction model in order to avoid mismatches and target merging. The second is filtering out spurious objects that appear in the volumetric scene reconstruction and discarding non-relevant objects such as chairs or furniture. In our Particle Filtering approach, the first problem is managed by the blocking strategy described below, whereas the second problem is tackled at the initialization step, where objects which are not likely to be a person are not allowed to initialize a new PF.

Several approaches have been proposed for multi-target tracking using PFs [2, 11] but the joint Particle Filtering presented in [10] explicitly models the domain knowledge that two targets cannot occupy the same space, and targets actively avoid collisions. However, its computational load increases dramatically with the number of targets to track since every particle estimates the location of all targets in the scene simultaneously. The proposed solution is to use a split PF per person, which requires less computational load at the cost of not being able to solve some complex cross-overs. However, this situation is alleviated by the fact that cross-overs are restricted to the horizontal plane in our scenario (see Fig.3a).

Let us assume that there are $M$ independent PF trackers, being $M$ the number of humans in the room. Nevertheless, they are not fully independent since each PF can consider voxels from other tracked targets in both the likelihood evaluation or the 3D re-sampling step resulting in target merging or identity mismatches. In order to achieve the most independent set of trackers, we consider a blocking method to model interactions by extending the blocking proposals in 2D tracking related works [10,12] to our 3D case. Blocking methods penalize particles that overlap zones with other targets. Hence, blocking information can be also considered when computing the particle weights as:

$$ w_t^j = \frac{1}{N_s} \, p(z_t|x_t^j) \prod_{\substack{k=1 \\ k \neq m}}^{M} \beta \left( X_{t-1}^m, X_{t-1}^M \right), \tag{6} $$

where $M$ is the total number of trackers, $m$ the index of the evaluated tracker and $X$ is the estimated state. Term $\beta(\cdot)$ is the blocking function defining exclusion zones that penalize particles falling into them. For our particular case, considering that people in the room are always sitting or standing up (the scenario is a meeting room, so we assume that they never lay down), a way to define an exclusion region modeling the human body is by using an ellipsoid with fixed $x$ and $y$ axes. The $z$ axis is a function of the estimated centroid height. An example of this exclusion technique is depicted in Fig.3. Particles spreading in the ellipsoid (exclusion zone) of the neighboring track are penalized by the blocking function. Tracked objects that come very close can be successfully tracked even if their volumes are partially overlapped.

Initialization of a new PF is decided as follows. First, a connected component analysis is performed on the incoming voxels of the reconstructed scene in order

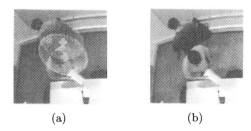

(a)                              (b)

**Fig. 3.** Particles from the tracker $A$ (yellow ellipsoid) falling into the exclusion zone of tracker $B$ (green ellipsoid) will be penalized by a multiplicative factor $\alpha \in [0, 1]$

to compute parameters for each connected component (or blob) such as volume (number of voxels), centroid position and the highest (top) and lowest (bottom) extent in the $z$ axis. Voxel regions falling into the exclusion zone (ellipsoid) of the already existing tracks are discarded. The remaining blobs are then checked by a classifier which allows discarding objects whose parameters of volume, top and bottom are not likely to correspond to those of a person. The classifier is trained on previously annotated samples from the development data. A new filter is initialized for each blob accepted by the classifier, as it fulfils the minimum criteria

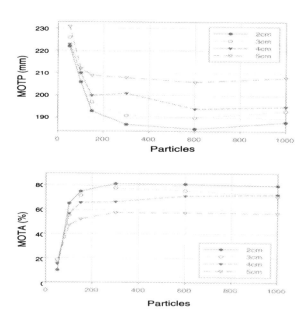

**Fig. 4.** PF tracking system performance. *MOTP* and *MOTA* scores for various voxel sizes and numbers of particles. Low MOTP and high MOTA scores are preferred indicating low metric error when estimating multiple target 3D positions and high tracking performance.

(a) Experiments with $\nu = 5$cm and $\nu = 2$cm. 300 particles employed.

(b) Experiments with 100 and 300 particles. Voxel size set to $\nu = 2$cm.

**Fig. 5.** PF tracking system zenital view of two comparative experiments. In (a), two tracking runs showing that large voxel reconstructions miss some objects. In (b), two tracking runs in a scene involving sudden motion showing how a reduced number of particles per filter lose track of one target.

to be a person (minimum volume, appropriate height,...). For the deletion, if the efficiency of a filter (measured as the number of particles with a weight different than zero) is below a given threshold, the filter is deleted.

### 4.4 Parameter Tunning

Two parameters drive the performance of the algorithm: the voxel size $\nu$ and the number of particles $N_P$. Experiments carried out explore the influence of these two variables on the $MOTP$ and $MOTA$ scores as depicted in Fig.4. This plot shows how scenes reconstructed with a large voxel size do not capture well all spatial details and may miss some objects, thus decreasing the performance of the tracking system. Furthermore, the larger the number of particles, the more accurate the performance of the algorithm; however, no substantial improvement is achieved for more than 600 particles due to the restriction imposed that every particle occupies the size of one voxel. Visual results of these effects are depicted in Fig.5.

These experiments, carried out over the development dataset, allowed setting the two main parameters of the algorithm for the test phase as follows: $\nu = 3$ and $N_P = 300$.

## 5  Results and Conclusions

Results for the two proposed systems are shown in Table 1. The PF tracker provides better performance over the heuristic tracker in terms of misses, false positives and mismatches. This effect is achieved since the PF keeps information about the multimodal structure of the pdf of the tracked object, rendering it more robust to poor observations. Please notice that the PF tracker works only from the voxelized 3D masks, without any color information, as is the case of the heuristic tracker. Obviously, the introduction of color features for the PF tracker is the next target in our future work.

**Table 1.** Quantitative results with voxel size of 3 cm. Legend: misses ($\overline{m}$), false positives ($\overline{fp}$) and mismatches ($\overline{mme}$).

| System | MOTP | $\overline{m}$ | $\overline{fp}$ | $\overline{mme}$ | MOTA |
|---|---|---|---|---|---|
| Heuristic Tracker | 168 | 27.74% | 40.19% | 1.58% | 30.49% |
| PF Tracker | 147 | 13.0% | 7.78% | 0.79% | 78.36% |

## References

1. Arulampalam, M.S., Maskell, S., Gordon, N., Clapp, T.: A tutorial on particle filters for online nonlinear/non-Gaussian Bayesian tracking. IEEE Trans. on Signal Processing 50(2), 174–188 (2002)
2. Bernardin, K., Gehrig, T., Stiefelhagen, R.: Multi and Single View Multiperson Tracking for SmartRoom Environments. In: Stiefelhagen, R., Garofolo, J.S. (eds.) CLEAR 2006. LNCS, vol. 4122, Springer, Heidelberg (2007)
3. Canton-Ferrer, C., Casas, J.R., Pardàs, M.: Towards a Bayesian Approach to Robust Finding Correspondences in Multiple View Geometry Environments. In: Sunderam, V.S., van Albada, G.D., Sloot, P.M.A., Dongarra, J. (eds.) ICCS 2005. LNCS, vol. 3515, pp. 281–289. Springer, Heidelberg (2005)
4. López, A., Canton-Ferrer, C., Casas, J.R.: Multi-Person 3D Tracking with Particle Filters on Voxels. In: IEEE Int. Conf. on Acoustics, Speech and Signal Processing (ICASSP) (2007)
5. Checka, N., Wilson, K.W., Siracusa, M.R., Darrell, T.: Multiple person and speaker activity tracking with a particle filter. In: Proc. IEEE Int. Conf. on Acoustics, Speech and Signal Processing (ICASSP), vol. 5, pp. 881–884 (2004)
6. Cheung, G.K.M., Kanade, T., Bouguet, J.Y., Holler, M.: A real time system for robust 3D voxel reconstruction of human motions. In: IEEE Conf. on Computer Vision and Pattern Recognition (CVPR), vol. 2, pp. 714–720 (2000)
7. CLEAR Evaluation Workshop (2006 and 2007), http://www.clear-evaluation.org
8. Dyer, C.R.: Volumetric scene reconstruction from multiple views. In: Davis, L.S. (ed.) Foundations of Image Understanding, pp. 469–489. Kluwer, Dordrecht (2001)
9. Focken, D., Stiefelhagen, R.: Towards vision-based 3D people tracking in a smart room. In: IEEE Int. Conf. on Multimodal Interfaces (ICMI), pp. 400–405 (2002)
10. Khan, Z., Balch, T., Dellaert, F.: Efficient particle filter-based tracking of multiple interacting Targets using an MRF-based motion model. In: Proc. Int. Conf. on Intelligent Robots and Systems, vol. 1, pp. 254–259 (2003)

11. Lanz, O.: Approximate Bayesian Multibody Tracking. IEEE Trans. on Pattern Analysis and Machine Intelligence 28(9), 1436–1449 (2006)
12. MacCormick, J., Blake, A.: A Probabilistic Exclusion Principle for Tracking Multiple Objects. Int. Journal of Computer Vision 39(1), 57–71 (2000)
13. Stauffer, C., Grimson, W.E.L.: Learning patterns of activity using real-time tracking. IEEE trans. on Pattern Analysis and Machine Intelligence 22(8) (August 2000)

# TUT Acoustic Source Tracking System 2007

Teemu Korhonen and Pasi Pertilä

Tampere University of Technology,
Institute of Signal Processing, Audio Research Group
P.O.Box 553, 33101, Tampere, Finland
{teemu.korhonen, pasi.pertila}@tut.fi

**Abstract.** This paper is a documentation of the acoustic person tracking system developed by TUT. The system performance was evaluated in the CLEAR 2007 evaluation. The proposed system is designed to track a speaker position in a meeting room domain using only audio data. Audio data provided for the evaluation consists of recordings from multiple microphone arrays. The meeting rooms are equipped with three to seven arrays.

Speaker localization is performed by mapping pairwise cross-correlations of microphone signals into a three dimensional likelihood field. The resulting likelihood is used as source evidence for a particle filtering algorithm. A point estimate for the speaker position for each time frame is derived from the resulting sequential process. Results indicate an 85 % success rate of localization with 15 cm average precision.

## 1 Introduction

The CLEAR 2007 evaluation campaign was composed of multiple different tracking and identification tasks. This work proposes a system tackling the 3D person tracking subtask using the provided audio data. The audio recordings contain data sets from different meeting room environments. Each setting comprises of multiple microphone arrays with known coordinates. Performance of the system is evaluated by outside party of TUT using metrics measuring both accuracy and precision.

The TUT source tracking system is based on Bayesian framework where measurement update is done using likelihoods inferred by pairwise cross-correlations of microphone signals. Source tracking algorithm is based on particle filtering where distributions are presented as set of weighted points.

The following section deals with evaluation tasks and metrics associated with them. Section 3 describes the TUT acoustic person tracking system with details of its implementation. The results are given in Section 4 with related discussion in Section 5. The work is concluded in Section 6.

## 2 Evaluation

### 2.1 Tasks

One of the CLEAR 2007 evaluation tasks is the 3D person tracking, which has been further divided into subtasks using audio or video data, or a combination

R. Stiefelhagen et al. (Eds.): CLEAR 2007 and RT 2007, LNCS 4625, pp. 104–112, 2008.
© Springer-Verlag Berlin Heidelberg 2008

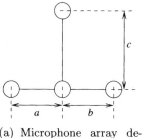

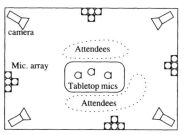

(a) Microphone array design

(b) Example room layout

**Fig. 1.** Geometry related to data gathering is illustrated. The geometry of a four microphone T-array is presented in panel 1(a). Dimensions $a$ and $b$ are 20 cm and $c$ is 30 cm for every site except IBM, where the corresponding dimensions are 26 cm and 40 cm. Panel 1(b) illustrates a basic recording room layout for a meeting, equipped with different sensors. Microphone arrays, used by the TUT system, are mounted to the walls.

of both. The TUT system participates in "Acoustic Person Tracking" task where the goal is detection and tracking of a speaker using available far-field microphones [1].

## 2.2 Data

A short description about the data used in system development and a performance evaluation is given here. For further details refer to the evaluation plan [1] or description of the CHIL audiovisual corpus [2].

**Table 1.** Information about the data used in the evaluation is presented. The smart rooms used in the evaluation are: Society in Information Technologies at Athens Information Technology, Athens, Greece (AIT); the IBM T.J. Watson Research Center, Yorktown Heights, USA (IBM); the Centro per la ricerca scientica e tecnologica at the Instituto Trentino di Cultura, Trento, Italy (ITC-irst); the Interactive Systems Labs of the Universitat Karlsruhe, Germany (UKA); and the Universitat Politecnica de Catalunya, Barcelona, Spain (UPC). [2]

| Site | T-arrays | Data length [minutes] | | Room size [m] | | | Recording type |
| | | Dev set | Eval set | $x$ | $y$ | $z$ | |
|---|---|---|---|---|---|---|---|
| UKA | 4 | 44 | 8 * 5 | 5.9 | 7.1 | 3.0 | Meeting |
| ITC | 7 | 31 | 8 * 5 | 4.7 | 5.9 | 4.5 | Meeting |
| IBM | 4 | 37 | 8 * 5 | 7.2 | 5.9 | 2.7 | Meeting |
| UPC | 3 | 23 | 8 * 5 | 4.0 | 5.2 | 4.0 | Meeting |
| AIT | 3 | 31 | 8 * 5 | 5.0 | 3.7 | 2.6 | Meeting |

The CHIL corpus is a collection of video and audio recordings from different meeting room settings collected during years 2003–2006. Accompanying the corpus is a manually generated annotation for any notable activities. the 3D person tracking task uses a set of recordings from five different sites listed in Table 1.

The basic setting for each site consists of microphone arrays of different geometries and sizes. The smaller arrays have four microphones in a two dimensional upside-down T-shaped form (Fig. 1). These arrays have been mounted on the walls and Table 1 documents their number per site. Larger array housing 64-microphones in a linear setup is not used by the TUT system.

The audio data has been divided into development and testing sets. The development set accompanied by complete annotation is 2.8 hours in length. The testing set contains eight recordings per site. Each recording is five minutes in length (with total of 3.3 hours of data). The nature of the recordings is interactive seminar, where the active speaker can switch between attendees.

The audio data was sampled at 44.1 kHz with 24 bit resolution. The reference data for active speaker 3D location was given with time resolution of 1.0 s.

## 2.3  Metrics

The CLEAR 2007 Evaluation uses a set of metrics for analyzation of the system performance. Proposed metrics measure performance in terms of precision and accuracy. Further details and discussion can be read from [1].

Acoustic person tracking accuracy is evaluated with the metrics similar to video person tracking task. However, identity mismatches are removed from the calculations since audio tracking is not expected to distinguish between different speakers. Following notations are used for different metrics and related types of error:

- MOTP [mm]: Multiple Object Tracking Precision
- MISS [%]: number of misses out of ground truth points
- FALSEPOS [%]: number of false positives out of ground truth points
- A-MOTA [%]: (Audio-) Multiple Object Tracking Accuracy

The MOTP metric is defined as an average Euclidean distance for correctly tracked positions. Errors are divided into misses and false positives and classified using a threshold set to 500 mm. The ground truth points without a tracker hypothesis within the threshold are classified as misses. False positives are, on the other hand, hypothesis points without ground truth support. The combination of both of the errors is reflected in the A-MOTA metric.

## 3  System Description

The proposed acoustic source tracking system is based on Bayesian framework utilizing particle filtering. Audio signals from microphones are processed pairwise within each array using a derivative cross-correlation method. Combination of the resulting likelihoods follows in a room-encompassing spatial likelihood field which the particle filtering algorithm processes as a source evidence. A point estimate can be extracted from the filtering process for each frame of interest.

## 3.1 Sound Source Likelihood Estimation

It is assumed that when an active speaker is present the received signals between spatially separate microphones inside an array differ mainly in the reception time. The microphone data is processed in frames of length $L$. The signal from microphone $i$ belonging to array $a \in [1, N]$ is denoted $x_i^a(t) = [x_i^a(t - L + 1), \ldots, x_i^a(t)]^{\mathrm{T}}$. The similarity of two signals from spatially separated microphones $i, j$ from array $a$ is estimated using the generalized cross-correlation (GCC) with the PHAT weighting algorithm [3]

$$r_{i,j}^a(\tau) = \mathcal{F}^{-1}\left\{ \frac{X_i^a(\omega_u)X_j^{a*}(\omega_u)}{|X_i^a(\omega_u)X_j^{a*}(\omega_u)|} \right\}, \omega_u = 0, \ldots, L - 1, \tag{1}$$

where $\mathcal{F}^{-1}\{\cdot\}$ denotes inverse discrete Fourier transform (IDFT) and $X_i^a(\omega_u)$ is the DFT of microphone signal $x_i^a(t)$, $\omega_u$ is the $u$th frequency sample, $\{\cdot\}^*$, $\{\cdot\}^{\mathrm{T}}$ denote complex conjugate transpose and transpose respectively, and $t, \tau$ are discrete time indices. The window length was set to 44100 samples and an overlap of 22050 samples was used. The system therefore produces location estimates at the rate of 0.5 second. The resulting GCC values are normalized between zero and one.

From any hypothetical point $\mathbf{h}$ a discrete time difference of arrival (TDOA) value $\Delta\tau_{\mathbf{h},i,j}^a$ can be calculated between a microphone pair $i, j$ in array $a$

$$\Delta\tau_{\mathbf{h},i,j}^a = Q\left[ \frac{f_s \cdot (\| \mathbf{h} - \mathbf{m}_i^a \| - \| \mathbf{h} - \mathbf{m}_j^a \|)}{c} \right], \tag{2}$$

where $c$ is the speed of sound, $f_s$ is the sampling rate, $\mathbf{m}_i^a$ denotes the microphone $i$ position and $Q[\cdot]$ is a quantization operator. Here $c$ was set to 343 m/s.

The similarity function (Eq. 1) is indexed with the TDOA value (Eq. 2) to get a likelihood of source location $\mathbf{h}$ from a single pairwise similarity measure

$$L(\mathbf{h}(t)|\mathbf{x}_i^a(t), \mathbf{x}_j^a(t)) = r_{i,j}^a(\Delta\tau_{\mathbf{h},i,j}^a). \tag{3}$$

The likelihoods from all pairwise similarities for point $\mathbf{h}$ are combined via multiplication. The multiplication of normalized likelihoods can be interpreted as a logical "and" operation. Only points in which all pairwise similarities are significant the source likelihood can be significant. This differs from the approach of summing up non-negative likelihood values [4][5] which can be interpreted as a logical "or" operation. This approach has not been used previously elsewhere according to the knowledge of the authors. The pairwise similarity estimation (Eq. 1) is performed for every microphone pair within each microphone array. Each array consists of four microphones. A total of six microphone pairs are used per array. The pairwise similarity values for point $\mathbf{h}$ are first multiplied together between all pairs inside each microphone array. Then the resulting array likelihoods are combined. The likelihood of a sound source existing in point $\mathbf{h}(t)$ at discrete time $t$ can now be written as

$$L\left(\mathbf{h}(t)|\mathbf{X}^1(t),...,\mathbf{X}^N(t)\right) = \prod_{a=1}^{N} \prod_{\substack{i=1, \\ j=i+1}}^{i=3,j=4} r_{i,j}^a \left(\Delta\tau_{\mathbf{h},i,j}^a\right), \tag{4}$$

where $r_{i,j}^a$ denotes pairwise similarity of microphone signals $i,j$ from array $a = 1,\ldots,$N and the data from array $a$ is written as

$$\mathbf{X}^a(t) = \left[\mathbf{x}_1^a(t),\ldots,\mathbf{x}_4^a(t)\right].$$

## 3.2   Source Tracking

The source tracking was performed using sequential Monte Carlo method known as particle filtering. Specifically, the Sampling Importance Resampling (SIR) algorithm is used [6] where transition prior is used as importance function.

Particle filtering approximates a probability density function (pdf) with a set of $M$ weighted random samples $\mathcal{X}_t = \{\mathbf{s}_t^{(n)}, w_t^{(n)}\}_{n=1}^{M}$ for each time instant $t$. The samples known as particles are propagated over time and resampled according to their fit on the evidence from measurements. A point approximation from the particle set can be evaluated with many different methods. Here, a median of particle positions $\mathbf{s}_t$ is used due to its robustness. Median is calculated separately for each of the three dimensions.

The initial set of particles $\mathcal{X}_0$ is sampled from an uniform distribution constrained within room coordinates and at the height of 1.2 to 1.8 m. The number of particles is constant for any frame and set to $M = 50\,000$. During each iteration particles are sampled from importance function modeled as multi-Gaussian prior (with deviations of 50 mm and 200 mm). Particle weights indicating fitness of each particle are calculated from the spatial likelihood field given by (4) and the particles are resampled according to the weights gained. A defensive strategy is implemented resampling 5% of the particles uniformly into the room boundaries. This resampling is also applied to particles falling out of the room limits.

## 3.3   System Output

The system outputs a speaker location hypothesis every 0.5 second interval. The results from TUT source tracking system were evaluated against annotation from 3D labels for acoustic person tracking subtask.

## 4   Results

Evaluation scores were calculated using metrics specified in 2.3 and results are presented in Table 2 with specifics in Table 4.

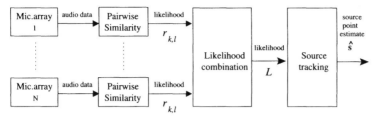

**Fig. 2.** A block diagram showing flow of information within presented system. Microphone signals are processed pairwise to produce source likelihoods. The combination of those likelihoods is then used as measurement evidence for source tracking system.

### 4.1 Computation time

The system was implemented and run in Matlab using only internal libraries. The computer used was a 3.20 GHz Intel Pentium 4 with 2 GB of RAM. Running environment was Linux based. The total processing time is given in Table 3.

A realtime factor (RT) of 5.08 was achieved with given setup using the eval data set. If all processed data is modeled as a single concatenated mono channel (equaling 206296 s), the RT factor would be 0.30.

## 5   Discussion

The task evaluated was 3D tracking of multiple persons using acoustic recordings from a set of microphones. Applied system performed well regardless the lack of speech activity detection (SAD). This naturally reflects directly as a degradation of the false positives metric when every frame is tagged as source. Large number of false positives also affect the A-MOTA metric directly.

Detailed evaluation results with recording specific metrics are given in Table 4. The false positives metric is maximized due to the lack of a SAD and therefore has been omitted from the table.

**Table 2.** TUT system's evaluation scores for the both data sets. The tasks are defined in Section 2.1 and the metrics are defined in Section 2.3. The scores for the CLEAR 2006 evaluation are presented for comparison: acoustic multiple person tracking (MPT-A) and single person tracking (SPT-A).

| MOT Scores | CLEAR 2007 | | CLEAR 2006 | |
|---|---|---|---|---|
| | eval | dev | MTP-A | SPT-A |
| MOTP [mm] | **152** | 165 | 334 | 245 |
| MISS [%] | **14.96** | 7.91 | 83.32 | 27.93 |
| FALSEPOS [%] | **37.00** | 24.23 | 83.22 | 27.86 |
| A-MOTA [%] | **48.04** | 67.85 | -66.53 | 44.21 |

**Table 3.** The total processing times of the TUT system. The IO overhead is the time spent by the system while loading audio data and is accounted for in the RT factor estimation.

| | |
|---|---|
| + GCC-PHAT | 25992 s |
| − IO overhead | 5492 s |
| + Particle filter | 40365 s |
| = | 60865 s |

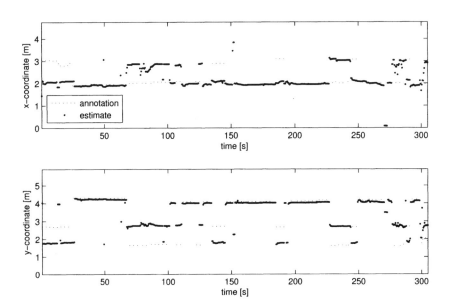

**Fig. 3.** Resulting track estimate (*points*) and accompanying annotation (*dotted line*) from the sixth ITC site recording. A conversation between three participants is visualized in x- and y-axis. There is a clear disagreement between estimate and annotation concerning two of the speakers (*two lowermost estimate trajectories of the y-coordinate*) which is evident in the complementary nature of switching activities.

Comparison between system output and the annotation reveals a recurring bias in the z-axis where the estimates appear roughly 5 – 10 cm below the annotation. The bias is site-independent. The speaker reference position is the head centroid [1] while the system focuses on the sound source origin: the mouth of the speaker.

Sixth recording from the AIT site ("AIT_20061020D_B") results in a very high miss percent score and low precision with the described system. The annotation, however, contains only a fraction of ground truth points compared to other recordings and this could compromise the result.

An anomaly in the sixth ITC recording ("ITC_20060927_B") is presented in Fig. 3. Both the estimated position and the reference position result from a

**Table 4.** The CLEAR 2007 evaluation results for the proposed system presenting accuracy and precision separated between sites and recordings. Anomalous results with values over twice the evaluation score have been boldfaced for clarity.

| Site | Metric | Recording | | | | | | | |
|------|--------|------|------|------|------|------|------|------|------|
| | | 1 | 2 | 3 | 4 | 5 | 6 | 7 | 8 |
| AIT | MISS [%] | 12.7 | 8.8 | 13.1 | 16.3 | 13.3 | **60.5** | 24.4 | 15.8 |
| | MOTP [mm] | 178 | 166 | 207 | 156 | 164 | 263 | 243 | 213 |
| IBM | MISS [%] | 19.2 | 22.1 | 11.5 | 7.5 | 16.1 | 4.6 | 3.2 | 4.5 |
| | MOTP [mm] | 198 | 184 | 171 | 154 | 227 | 112 | 213 | 202 |
| ITC | MISS [%] | 6.2 | 6.7 | 4.1 | **40.6** | 13.3 | **47.0** | 16.6 | 9.9 |
| | MOTP [mm] | 105 | 138 | 113 | 106 | 123 | 94 | 135 | 134 |
| UKA | MISS [%] | 7.8 | 9.1 | 7.1 | 8.8 | **48.4** | 7.8 | **30.2** | 15.6 |
| | MOTP [mm] | 128 | 107 | 88 | 123 | 97 | 101 | 145 | 123 |
| UPC | MISS [%] | 8.3 | 8.2 | 10.2 | 8.5 | 15.6 | **44.3** | 23.7 | 14.8 |
| | MOTP [mm] | 142 | 128 | 128 | 147 | 169 | 282 | 160 | 143 |

conversation between multiple participants, but disagree on the identity of the active speaker. This disparity is evident in the complementary nature of two speakers switching between interpretations.

Rest of the irregularities follow from various disturbances or from increased dynamics of the active sources. The presented system is unable to distinguish speech from other sound sources and assumes relaxed system dynamics.

# 6   Summary

A system for acoustic person tracking was presented complying the task presented in CLEAR 2007 evaluation. The acoustic tracking system uses data provided by microphone arrays with known coordinates. Measurements are processed pairwise within each microphone array with cross-correlation producing a similarity value for each time delay. The similarity values are processed as spatial likelihoods and combined over all microphone pairs. Resulting likelihood is used in particle filtering algorithm as speaker location evidence. A point estimate for speaker location is derived from the sequential process. The system is precise to 15 cm for roughly 85 % of the time.

### Acknowledgments

The authors wish to thank Mikko Parviainen, Tuomo Pirinen, Sakari Tervo and Ari Visa for their efforts in the development of the presented acoustic person tracking system.

# References

1. Bernardin, K.: Clear 2007 evaluation plan v.1.0 (2007), http://isl.ira.uka.de/clear07/downloads/?download=CLEAR07-3DPT-2007-03-09.pdf
2. Mostefa, D., Moreau, N., Choukri, K., Potamianos, G., Chu, S.M., Tyagi, A., Casas, J.R., Turmo, J., Christoforetti, L., Tobia, F., Pnevmatikakis, A., Mylonakis, V., Talantzis, F., Burger, S., Stiefelhagen, R., Bernardin, K., Rochet, C.: The CHIL audiovisual corpus for lecture and meeting analysis inside smart rooms (accepted for publication, Kluwer Academic publishers). Journal of Language Resources and Evaluation (2007)
3. Knapp, C., Carter, G.: The generalized correlation method for estimation of time delay. IEEE Trans. on Acoustics, Speech, and Signal Processing 4, 320–327 (1976)
4. Aarabi, P.: The Fusion of Distributed Microphone Arrays for Sound Localization. EURASIP Journal on Applied Signal Processing 4, 338–347 (2003)
5. DiBiase, J., Silverman, H., Brandstein, M.: Microphone Arrays, ch. 8. Springer, Heidelberg (2001)
6. Gordon, N., Salmond, D., Smith, A.: Novel approach to nonlinear/non-Gaussian Bayesian state estimation. Radar and Signal Processing, IEE Proceedings F 140, 107–113 (1993)

# The AIT 2D Face Detection and Tracking System for CLEAR 2007

Andreas Stergiou, Ghassan Karame,
Aristodemos Pnevmatikakis, and Lazaros Polymenakos

Athens Information Technology, Autonomic and Grid Computing,
P.O. Box 64, Markopoulou Ave., 19002 Peania, Greece
{aste, gkar, apne, lcp}@ait.edu.gr
http://www.ait.edu.gr/research/RG1/overview.asp

**Abstract.** This paper describes the AIT system for 2D face tracking and the results obtained in the CLEAR 2007 evaluations. The system is based on the
complementary operation of a set of face detectors and a deterministic tracker
based on color. To minimize false positives, the system is applied on the body
regions provided by a stochastic body tracker, and utilizes a detection validation
scheme based on color and texture modeling of the faces.

## 1  Introduction

Tracking and recognizing people is very important for applications such as surveillance, security and human-machine interfaces. In the visual modality, faces are the
most commonly used cue for recognition. Finding the faces also helps resolve human
bodies that are merged into one by the tracker. Hence face localization is of paramount importance in many applications.

Face localization can be done on a single camera frame by means of a detector, or
across multiple frames using a tracker. Any of the two tasks can become very difficult
in far-field unconstrained recording conditions. Low resolution faces suffering from
pose, illumination and expression variations, as well as occlusions can only be detected sporadically. The misses need to be accounted for by a tracker, whose model
needs frequent update to cope with the ever-changing face. Also, such face detectors
suffer from false alarms that need to be constrained as much as possible.

Face detection can be very accurate [1,2], given large resolution, almost frontal
pose and long processing time allowance. Unfortunately, none of these apply to the
intended application, where resolution is low, pose can be arbitrary and processing
has to be real-time. Cascades of simple classifiers [3] can detect small faces in arbitrary background and are fast. An ensemble of such cascades can be trained, each
with different poses, together serving as a multi-view face detector.

Two approaches can be used in face tracking: stochastic and deterministic. Stochastic trackers are based on recursive Bayesian filtering, either in its exact form for
Gaussian states and linear dynamics, the Kalman filter [4], or in its numerical approximation for non-linear dynamics, the particle filter [5]. Deterministic tracking on
the other hand minimizes a cost function related to template matching between the

R. Stiefelhagen et al. (Eds.): CLEAR 2007 and RT 2007, LNCS 4625, pp. 113–125, 2008.
© Springer-Verlag Berlin Heidelberg 2008

object and a candidate region. In Mean-Shift [6] face tracking, or its continuously adaptive variant (CAM-Shift) [7] the template is a color histogram, that is very suitable for non-rigid objects. In both cases, the open question is the means and frequency of model update [8].

In [9], a system that utilizes a detector to find faces and a tracker to cope with misses operates in the whole image, increasing processing time and potentially false positives. In [10] foreground segmentation is also utilized. That system has been successfully tested in the Classification of Events, Activities and Relationships (CLEAR2006) evaluation [11,12].

In this paper, we enhance such systems in a number of ways. Three face detectors find frontal and left/right profile faces. Also, false alarms are minimized by applying the detectors on the body areas provided by a body tracker, by validating detections using a Gaussian Mixture Model (GMM) of face parameters and by merging frontal with profile detections.

The rest of the paper is organized as follows: In section 2, the face detection and tracking system is described, comprising the body tracker, the face detectors, the detection validation and merging scheme and the deterministic face tracker. In Section 3, the performance of the proposed system in the CLEAR 2007 evaluations [12] is analyzed. Finally, in Section 4 the conclusions are drawn.

## 2 Face Detection and Tracking System

The 2D face localization is constrained in the body areas provided by a body tracker. Three face detectors for frontal and left/right profile faces provide candidate face regions in the body areas. The face candidates are validated using the probability scores from a GMM. The surviving candidates are checked for possible merging, as both the profile detectors and the frontal one can detect different portions of the same face if the view is half-profile. The resulting face candidates are associated with faces existing in the previous frame and also with tracks that currently have no supporting evidence and are pending to either get an association, or be eliminated. Any faces of the previous frame that do not get associated with candidate faces at the current frame have a CAM-Shift tracker [7] initiated to attempt to track similarly colored regions in the current frame. If CAM-Shift also fails to track, then these past faces have their track in pending status for $F_p$ frames. Finally, all active face tracks are checked for duplicates, i.e. high spatial similarity. The block diagram of the 2D face detection and tracking system is shown in Figure 1. In the following subsections, the various modules of the system are detailed.

### 2.1 Body Tracking Module

The goal of the body tracker is to provide the frame regions occupied by human bodies. Any subsequent face detection and tracking is performed within these body regions. The tracker is based on a dynamic foreground segmentation algorithm [13,14] that utilizes adaptive background modeling with learning rates spatiotemporally controlled by the states of a Kalman filter [4]. It comprises three modules in a feedback configuration: adaptive background modeling based on Stauffer's algorithm [15]

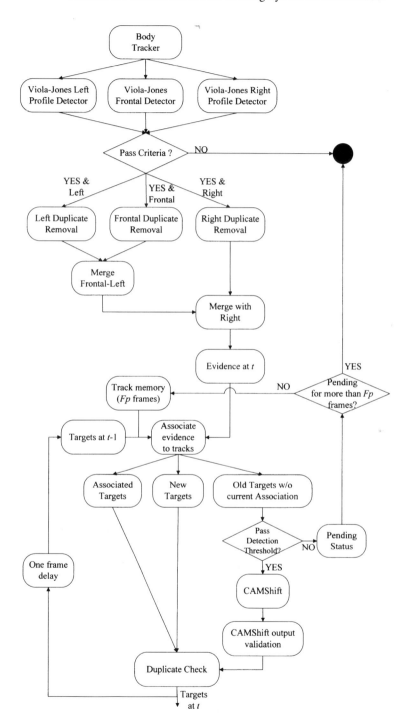

**Fig. 1.** Block diagram of the complete face localization system

provides the pixels that are considered foreground to the evidence formation module. The later combines the pixels into body evidence blobs, used for the measurement update state of the Kalman filter module. The states of the Kalman filter are used to obtain an indication of the mobility of each target, as a combination of translation motion and its size change. Also the position and size of the targets are contained in the states of the Kalman filter. This information is fed back to the adaptive background modeling module to adapt the learning rate in the vicinity of the targets: frame regions that at a specific time have a slow-moving target have smaller learning rates.

The proposed spatiotemporal adaptation of the learning rate of the adaptive background modeling module solves the problem of Stauffer's algorithm when foreground objects stop moving. Without it, targets that have stopped moving are learnt into the background. With the proposed feedback configuration this process is halted long enough for the intended application, i.e. tracking people in a meeting. For the details of the body tracking algorithm and its application both for in-doors and out-doors tracking, see [13,14].

### 2.2  Face Detection and Validation Module

The goal of the face detection and validation module is to find possible faces in a given face without the use of any temporal information, and to validate them in order to reduce the false detections. Many face detectors can be found in the literature [1-3]. They are split into those that attempt to find face features, and from them find the faces themselves, and those that search directly for faces. The former are usually slower, and require adequate resolution for accurate feature detection. As the faces are small compared to the frame size, the natural choice for a detector is the boosted cascade of simple features [3]. Its implementation in OpenCV [16] is chosen, as this is publicly available. We train a left profile and a frontal detector. Right-profiles are detected by flipping the frame and using the left-profile detector. For each detector we use 6,000 positive samples (images with marked faces), 20,000 negative samples (images with no human or animal face present), an aspect ratio of 3/4, minimum feature size 0, 99.9% hit rate and 50% false alarm per cascade stage, horizontal and 45-degrees tilted features, non-symmetric faces and gentle AdaBoost learning [16]. The detector thus trained is applied on the grayscale portions of the frames that are designated as human bodies by the body tracker. Only the upper part of the bodies that has height equal to the body width is examined by the detector to speed up the process.

Unfortunately the face detector suffers from false detections. These are constrained by the fact that the detector is applied on a limited portion of the frames, but nevertheless the detections need to be validated to further reduce false alarms. The face validation module is based on a multivariate Gaussian Mixture Model comprising representative statistics of skin color and brightness of the detected region. The models of Jones and Rehg [17] are used to build the likelihood ratio of human skin versus non-skin. Although detected faces are for the most part expected to contain areas with high skin color likelihood, we need also to account for regions surrounding the eyes and eyebrows that do not exhibit skin-like colors. Furthermore, human faces exhibit a lot of brightness variation due to self-shadowing, and can thus not be uniformly too bright or too dark. Such conditions are implicitly enforced by the GMM, so that false positives on furniture, walls and, to some extent, hand regions can be removed. The likelihood threshold for face validation used by the detectors is determined during the training stage of the GMM so as to correctly validate 99% of the training faces, and is usually somewhat different for frontal and profile faces.

Frequently, the various face detectors yield multiple detections of the same face target, thus resulting in duplicate tracked objects. Such a behavior could be especially detrimental when the face in question is somewhat rotated, either in- or out-of-plane. We remedy this by combining such duplicate detections. That is, matching frontal and left profile detections are first merged into single face targets. The resulting objects are subsequently combined with matching right profile detections. Such a strategy aims at improving the target extension accuracy by preventing direct combination of left and right profile detections. Detections are marked as matching for merging when they meet two conditions: they have to be located within a distance twice the maximum width of the detections in question and the resulting merged detection should have both width and height smaller than a threshold of 80 pixels.

## 2.3  Face Tracking Module

After possible merging, the detected faces are assigned to the tracked targets. This association is done using an optimal greedy algorithm, the Hungarian (or Munkres) algorithm [18], which minimizes the overall Mahalanobis distance between the detections and the targets. Once the detections are assigned to some targets, the targets' records are updated accordingly. On the other hand, in case a detection can not be assigned to any target, a new target is initialized. Finally, if a target is not associated to any detection at a certain frame, for instance due to occlusion, rotation or tilt, then the target's record is examined. If it has more detections associated with it than a threshold, then deterministic tracking based on histogram matching and using the CAM-Shift algorithm [7] is initiated. Otherwise, the target in question enters pending status. The threshold is a decreasing linear function of the age of the target; older targets need smaller detection rates to be kept active.

The CAM-Shift tracker uses a trained color histogram in RGB color space as a representation of the face to be tracked. The training of the color histogram is carried out in the area of the last detection. The histogram is not updated throughout tracking; only the detections that are validated by the GMM are trusted for the task. The pixels that are used for the histogram are the top 75 percentile that match skin color according to the Jones and Rehg skin color model. Utilizing the trained histogram and a probability threshold of 0.05, a binary map of the pixels in a search region around the face location in the previous frame is built. Higher probability thresholds lead more constraint tracked regions. Morphological closing removes any small regions on the binary map. Then the centroid and width of the updated face location is calculated using moments [7]. The height is computed using the aspect ratio of the detected face that initiated the tracker. The CAM-Shift tracked regions are also validated using the same GMM as the regions returned by the detectors; only the threshold is relaxed to account for the looser face framing evident in most CAM-Shift tracked regions.

When the CAM-Shift tracker does not yield any face region, then the track enters pending status. This mechanism accounts for temporary occlusions of the face under tracking; e.g. when the person in question is not facing the camera for some frames. In this case, the target's history is kept in memory for $Fp$ frames, after which, it is erased. If, on the other hand, a detection occurs in the vicinity of the pending track before it is erased, then the track becomes active again. Hence the pending mechanism allows for track continuity while it prevents false alarm faces from being reported.

Finally, all active face tracks are checked for duplicates, in order to prevent duplicate tracking of the same face. The check for target duplicates utilizes both target location and area.

### 2.4  System Variations for the VACE Multisite Meeting Recordings

The localization of faces can in principle be constrained in the body areas provided by a body tracker. Although this approach is followed in [13], it is not used for the VACE multisite meeting recordings section of the CLEAR 2007 evaluations as there is not enough motion in most of these videos for the AIT body tracker [14,15] to initiate the tracks.

The detection validation scheme needs to change. As no part of the VACE multisite meeting recordings, although termed 'training' has the faces annotated to extract the models from, Gaussian Mixture Modeling of color and texture properties of the faces is not possible. Instead, the face validation module is based on a skin likelihood map that enumerates the similarity of the colors in the detected face regions to human skin. The models of Jones and Rehg [17] are used to build the likelihood ratio of any color RGB triplet belonging to human skin versus non-skin. The skin likelihood map corresponding to the whole frame is thresholded, leading to skin-colored patches. To validate a detected face region, then within its bounding box there needs to be a significant percentage of pixels that are active in the thresholded skin likelihood map.

Instead of the deterministic CAM-Shift tracker, a Kalman tracker is used in the VACE multisite meeting recordings. The main reason for changing the tracker is because we have not been very satisfied with the framing of the faces by the CAM-Shift tracker. Also, the histogram of a face is trained using a memory of all past detections associated with the particular track, not only the latest detection. The Kalman tracker uses a constant velocity model and evidence collected from the frame by thresholding a likelihood map that enumerates the similarity of the RGB color triplets of the pixels to the colors found in the face being tracked. To do so, a color histogram in RGB color space is trained as a representation of the face to be tracked. The training of the color histogram is carried out using the pixels of the regions detected by the face detectors. The histogram is not updated throughout tracking; only the detections that are validated are trusted for the task. The histogram update uses memory, placing more confidence to the most recent detections.

## 3  CLEAR 2007 Evaluation Results

The proposed two-dimensional face localization system is tested on the CLEAR 2007 evaluations. Typical results on the multi-camera indoor video sequences coming from the CHIL are shown in Figure 2.

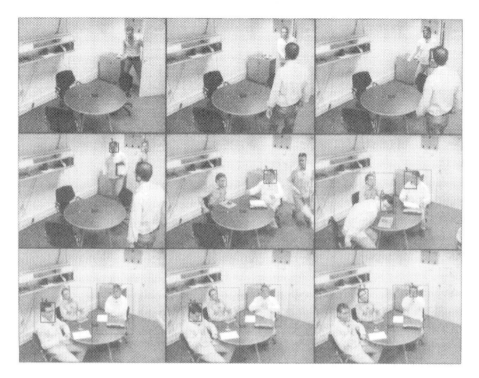

**Fig. 2.** Typical performance of the face localization system. Detections of the three cascades of simple classifiers are marked in red, while faces being tracked by the CAM-Shift tracker are marked in blue. Notice that the latter are occluded or tilted faces.

The quantitative evaluation of the proposed system follows the CLEAR2007 evaluation protocol [11]. According to it, the tracking system outputs (hypotheses) are mapped to annotated ground truths based on centroid distance and using the Hungarian algorithm [18]. The metrics for face tracking are five [11]. The Multiple Object Tracking Precision (MOTP) is the position error for all correctly tracked persons over all frames. It is a measure of how well the system performs when it actually finds the face. There are three kinds of errors for the tracker, false positives, misses and track identity mismatches. They are reported independently and also jointly in an accuracy metric, the Multiple Object Tracking Accuracy (MOTA). The MOTA is the residual of the sum of these three error rates from unity.

The quantitative performance of the system for the multi-camera indoor video sequences coming from the CHIL is summarized in Table 1. It is evident from Table 1 that the easiest CHIL recording site is AIT. This is due to the small size of the room that allows easier detection. Two sites suffer particularly from misses: ITC and UPC. The reasons are different. No faces from ITC have been used in training the detectors, since in the 2006 recordings only the presenter was tracked. Most faces in the ITC recordings are severely tilted, so it is difficult to initiate and maintain face tracks. The

**Table 1.** Face detection performance of the system on all 40 seminars and 4 camera views, averaged per site

| Site | MOTP | Misses (%) | False positives (%) | Mismatches (%) | MOTA (%) |
|------|------|-----------|------------------|--------------|---------|
| AIT | 0.665 | 34.0 | 13.1 | 1.64 | 51.3 |
| IBM | 0.672 | 36.7 | 35.2 | 2.06 | 26.1 |
| ITC | 0.723 | 65.5 | 13.2 | 1.62 | 19.7 |
| UKA | 0.610 | 33.5 | 31.2 | 3.45 | 31.9 |
| UPC | 0.656 | 50.0 | 12.1 | 2.32 | 35.6 |
| **Overall** | **0.656** | **42.5** | **22.1** | **2.29** | **33.1** |

main reason for misses in the UPC recordings is the color of the faces: shadows and darker skin colors cause some faces to fail the detection validation. The severe interlacing of the moving people is a secondary cause.

Two CHIL sites suffer from many false positives: IBM and UKA. For the IBM recordings, the poor performance of the GMM validation scheme is due to the skin-like table-top. On the other hand, for most of the UKA recordings that scheme was turned off entirely. This is due to the 'blue' dominant color in those recordings that renders the general human skin color model unusable. The hit rate versus the false positive rate for each of the 40 seminars is shown in Figure 3. The points are grouped per each of the five recording sites. The false positive rate is constrained mostly below 20% for three sites: AIT, UPC and ITC. While for AIT the hit rate is mostly high, for UPC it varies a lot per seminar and for ITC it is mostly too low. On the other hand the hit rate of IBM and UKA does not vary a lot per seminar, being high for UKA and moderate for IBM. This is due to the very small face sizes in the IBM recordings. On the other hand, for these sites the false positive rate varies a lot per seminar.

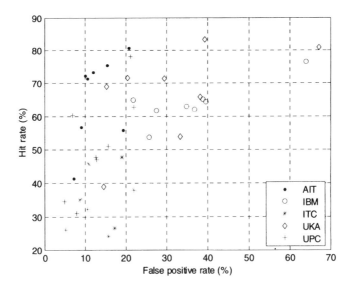

**Fig. 3.** Hit versus false alarm rate for each of the recording five sites and eight seminars per site

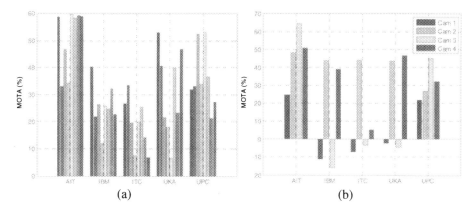

**Fig. 4.** Break-down of MOTA performance in each recording site per seminar (a) and camera (b)

**Fig. 5.** Typical performance of the face localization system. Note the huge scale differences between the different videos. Also note the false positives introduced by the portions of the background that have skin-like color (like the light brown tabletops). Finally note the problems introduced by ceiling cameras.

It is instructive to explore the variation of the MOTA of the system across the five different CHIL sites and four different recording segments per site. This is done in Figure 4.a. The variation of performance per camera in each site is also important. This is shown in Figure 4.b. Obviously, cameras 1 and 3 are problematic in the IBM,

**Table 2.** Face detection performance of the system on all 40 seminars and 4 camera views, averaged per site

| Site | Camera | MOTA | MOTP | MODA | MODP |
|------|--------|------|------|------|------|
| CMU | 1 | 0.754117 | 0.389168 | 0.760345 | 0.39108 |
| | 2 | 0.610005 | 0.471459 | 0.613843 | 0.481971 |
| | 3 | 0.10886 | 0.470489 | 0.113903 | 0.481669 |
| | 4 | 0.066071 | 0.272116 | 0.094017 | 0.267079 |
| | 1 | 0.854083 | 0.356301 | 0.862888 | 0.362882 |
| | 2 | 0.164589 | 0.574879 | 0.170599 | 0.594912 |
| | 3 | -0.33799 | 0.493185 | -0.33201 | 0.510621 |
| | 4 | 0.685068 | 0.547175 | 0.687984 | 0.556083 |
| | 4 | 0.378129 | 0.55109 | 0.380567 | 0.56138 |
| EDI | 1 | 0.825202 | 0.391323 | 0.891429 | 0.391323 |
| | 2 | 0.917533 | 0.356488 | 0.956667 | 0.356488 |
| | 3 | 0.96356 | 0.539589 | 0.985795 | 0.539589 |
| | 4 | 0.826019 | 0.469796 | 0.839599 | 0.469796 |
| | 6 | -0.46557 | 0.518283 | -0.46358 | 0.520069 |
| | 1 | 0.915931 | 0.555009 | 0.944251 | 0.555009 |
| | 2 | 0.857769 | 0.442454 | 0.912913 | 0.442454 |
| | 3 | 1 | 0.533721 | 1 | 0.533721 |
| | 5 | -1.09589 | 0.444647 | -1.09246 | 0.438951 |
| | 6 | -3.89232 | 0.367822 | -3.88942 | 0.360969 |
| IDI | 1 | 0.880132 | 0.374985 | 0.88716 | 0.374985 |
| | 2 | 1 | 0.608063 | 1 | 0.608063 |
| | 4 | 0.8125 | 0.598335 | 0.8125 | 0.598335 |
| | 6 | 0.341924 | 0.605769 | 0.341924 | 0.605839 |
| | 7 | -0.18336 | 0.605199 | -0.18287 | 0.616589 |
| NIST | 1 | -51.9672 | 0.547779 | -51.9672 | 0.576739 |
| | 2 | -0.41419 | 0.480783 | -0.41419 | 0.481809 |
| | 6 | 0.529101 | 0.478348 | 0.542627 | 0.49683 |
| | 7 | 0.463855 | 0.486226 | 0.463855 | 0.486226 |
| | 2 | 0.57988 | 0.562361 | 0.589633 | 0.565895 |
| | 3 | 0.37452 | 0.575775 | 0.375184 | 0.56464 |
| | 6 | 0.93782 | 0.649301 | 0.93782 | 0.647581 |
| | 7 | 0.998567 | 0.548702 | 1 | 0.548702 |
| TNO | 1 | 1 | Not defined | 1 | Not defined |
| | 5 | -1.62702 | 0.367315 | -1.62559 | 0.361337 |
| | 5 | -0.12322 | 0.297492 | -0.12322 | 0.295899 |
| | 6 | 0.352629 | 0.459642 | 0.353383 | 0.443571 |
| VT | 2 | 0.273996 | 0.423164 | 0.279825 | 0.427221 |
| | 3 | 0.242871 | 0.553586 | 0.243547 | 0.554587 |
| | 4 | -0.24323 | 0.256464 | -0.22691 | 0.256464 |
| | 5 | 0.613096 | 0.436159 | 0.621802 | 0.430904 |
| | 6 | 0.003308 | 0.354638 | 0.021053 | 0.36074 |
| | 1 | 0.058727 | 0.339733 | 0.062937 | 0.33558 |
| | 2 | -0.34652 | 0.336181 | -0.33235 | 0.348369 |
| | 3 | 0.636678 | 0.446199 | 0.636678 | 0.451405 |
| | 5 | 0.355096 | 0.43923 | 0.364042 | 0.444365 |
| | 7 | 0.404306 | 0.430923 | 0.411417 | 0.433509 |
| Median values | | 0.39122 | 0.47049 | 0.39599 | 0.48167 |

ITC and UKA recordings. This does not affect performance greatly, since these are the camera views with the smallest number of ground truth faces.

Typical results on the VACE multisite meeting recordings are shown in Figure 5. The quantitative performance is summarized in Table 2, and the MOTA per site are presented in Figure 6. It is evident from that and Table 1 that the EDI and IDI are the easiest sites, CMU, NIST and VT are about as hard as all the sites pooled together, and TNO is the most difficult. The reason for EDI and IDI being the easier sites is because those recordings have many near-field cameras. On the other hand, the difficult TNO recordings have skin-like colors in the background, rendering the rejection of false positives useless. This ranking is based on the median values, but due to the variation of the results across the different cameras and the limited number of recordings analyzed per site, there is large uncertainty about the estimation of the median values, rendering the ordering of the difficulty statistically risky.

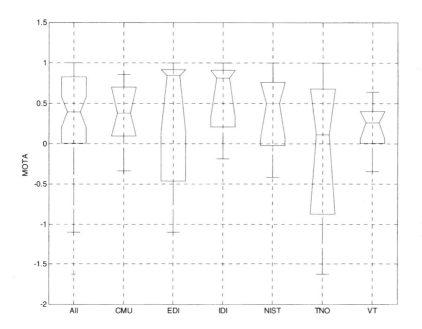

**Fig. 6.** Boxplot of the MOTA of all the sites pooled together, and site-specific. EDI has the highest median MOTA, but also the largest variation and uncertainty in the estimation of the median.

## 4  Conclusions

In the proposed face localization system, a CAM-Shift tracker complements three detectors based on cascades of simple features. The CLEAR evaluations have shown that the system should be improved by reducing misses and false positives. Both can be achieved employing better detectors, based on FloatBoost [19] or Schneiderman's detector [20,21]. Also, better modeling of faces versus non-face patches can help eliminate false positives. Finally, the performance of the overall system using the

CAM-Shift and the Kalman trackers should be assessed on the same dataset for comparison. This comparison should be extended to the use of a particle filter tracker.

## Acknowledgements

This work is sponsored by the European Union under the integrated project CHIL, contract number 506909. The authors wish to thank the people involved in data collection, annotation and overall organization of the CLEAR 2007 evaluations for providing such a rich test-bed for the presented algorithm.

## References

[1]  Li, S.-Z., Lu, J.: Face Detection, Alignment and Recognition. In: Medioni, G., Kang, S. (eds.) Emerging Topics in Computer Vision (2004)
[2]  Hsu, R.-L., Abdel-Mottaleb, M., Jain, A.K.: Face Detection in Color Images. IEEE Transactions on Pattern Analysis and Machine Intelligence 24, 696–706 (2002)
[3]  Viola, P., Jones, M.: Rapid Object Detection using a Boosted Cascade of Simple Features. In: IEEE Conf. on Computer Vision and Pattern Recognition, p. 511 (December 2001)
[4]  Kalman, R.E.: A New Approach to Linear Filtering and Prediction Problems. Transactions of the ASME – Journal of Basic Engineering 82 (Series D), 35–45 (1960)
[5]  Arulampalam, S., Maskell, S., Gordon, N., Clapp, T.: A Tutorial on Particle Filters for On-line Non-linear Non-Gaussian Bayesian Tracking. IEEE Transactions on Signal Processing 20, 174–188 (2002)
[6]  Jaffré, G., Crouzil, A.: Non-rigid object localization from color model using mean shift. In: International Conference on Image Processing (ICIP 2003) (September 2003)
[7]  Bradski, G.: Computer Vision Face Tracking for Use in a Perceptual User Interface. Intel Technology Journal 2 (1998)
[8]  Zhou, S., Chellappa, R., Moghaddam, B.: Visual tracking and recognition using appearance-adaptive models in particle filters. IEEE Transactions on Image Processing 13, 1491–1506 (2004)
[9]  Yang, T., Li, S.-Z., Pan, Q., Li, J., Zhao, C.: Reliable and Fast Tracking of Faces under Varying Pose. In: 7th International Conference on Automatic Face and Gesture Recognition (FGR 2006), April 2006, pp. 421–426 (2006)
[10] Bernardin, K., Gehrig, T., Stiefelhagen, R.: Multi- and Single View Multiperson tracking for Smart Room Environments. In: Stiefelhagen, R., Garofolo, J.S. (eds.) CLEAR 2006. LNCS, vol. 4122, pp. 81–92. Springer, Heidelberg (2007)
[11] Stiefelhagen, R., Bernardin, K., Bowers, R., Garofolo, J., Mostefa, D., Soundararajan, P.: The CLEAR 2006 Evaluation. In: Stiefelhagen, R., Garofolo, J.S. (eds.) CLEAR 2006. LNCS, vol. 4122, pp. 1–44. Springer, Heidelberg (2007)
[12] http://www.clear-evaluation.org
[13] Pnevmatikakis, A., Polymenakos, L.: Kalman Tracking with Target Feedback on Adaptive Background Learning. In: Renals, S., Bengio, S., Fiscus, J.G. (eds.) MLMI 2006. LNCS, vol. 4299, Springer, Heidelberg (2006)
[14] Pnevmatikakis, A., Polymenakos, L.: Robust Estimation of Background for Fixed Cameras. In: International Conference on Computing (CIC 2006) (2006)
[15] Stauffer, C., Grimson, W.E.L.: Learning patterns of activity using real-time tracking. IEEE Transactions on Pattern Analysis and Machine Intelligence 22, 747–757 (2000)
[16] Bradski, G., Kaehler, A., Pisarevsky, V.: Learning-Based Computer Vision with Intel's Open Source Computer Vision Library. Intel Technology Journal 9 (2005)

[17] Jones, M., Rehg, J.: Statistical color models with application to skin detection. In: Proceedings of IEEE Conference on Computer Vision and Pattern Recognition, pp. 274–280 (1999)
[18] Blackman, S.: Multiple-Target Tracking with Radar Applications, ch. 14. Artech House, Dedham (1986)
[19] Li, S.-Z., Zhang, Z.Q.: FloatBoost Learning and Statistical Face Detection. IEEE Transactions on Pattern Analysis and Machine Intelligence 26, 1112–1123 (2004)
[20] Schneiderman, H.: Feature-Centric Evaluation for Efficient Cascaded Object Detection. In: Proceedings of IEEE Conference on Computer Vision and Pattern Recognition (June 2004)
[21] Nechyba, M., Schneiderman, H.: PittPatt Face Detection and Tracking for the CLEAR 2006 Evaluation. In: Stiefelhagen, R., Garofolo, J.S. (eds.) CLEAR 2006. LNCS, vol. 4122, pp. 161–170. Springer, Heidelberg (2007)

# PittPatt Face Detection and Tracking for the CLEAR 2007 Evaluation

Michael C. Nechyba, Louis Brandy, and Henry Schneiderman

Pittsburgh Pattern Recognition
40 24th Street, Suite 240, Pittsburgh, PA 15222, USA
michael@pittpatt.com,
http://www.pittpatt.com

**Abstract.** This paper describes Pittsburgh Pattern Recognition's participation in the face detection and tracking tasks for the CLEAR 2007 evaluation. Since CLEAR 2006, we have made substantial progress in optimizing our algorithms for speed, achieving better than real-time processing performance for a speed-up of more than 500× over the past two years. At the same time, we have maintained the high level of accuracy of our algorithm. In this paper, we first give a system overview, briefly explaining the three main stages of processing: (1) frame-based face detection; (2) motion-based tracking; and (3) track filtering. Second, we report our results, both in terms of accuracy and speed, over the CHIL and VACE test data sets. Finally, we offer some analysis on both speed and accuracy performance.

## 1 System Description

Similar to our work for the CLEAR 2006 evaluation [1], our processing for CLEAR 2007 proceeds in three stages: (1) frame-based face detection; (2) motion-based tracking; and (3) track filtering. However, over the past couple of years, we have introduced a large number of changes and additions targeted at accelerating speed performance while maintaining system accuracy.

### 1.1 Frame-Based Face Detection

**Face finding:** At the heart of our system lies PittPatt's robust face finder, available for single-image testing through our web demo at http://demo.pittpatt.com.[1] Conceptually, this current version of the detection algorithm builds on the approach described in [2][3]; however, we have implemented large-scale improvements, both at the algorithm and code level, to dramatically boost speed

---

[1] For the evaluation, two parameter settings differ from the default settings on the web demo. First, we configured the face finder to search for faces with an inter-ocular distance as small as four pixels, approximately 50% smaller than for the web demo. Second, we set our normalized log-likelihood ($ll$) threshold to be -0.75 (instead of 0.0). While this lower setting generates more false alarms, it also permits more correct detections. Later processing across frames (described in Secs. 1.2 and 1.3) is able to eliminate most of the introduced false alarms, while preserving more correctly detected faces.

R. Stiefelhagen et al. (Eds.): CLEAR 2007 and RT 2007, LNCS 4625, pp. 126–137, 2008.
© Springer-Verlag Berlin Heidelberg 2008

performance. First, the detector has been radically re-designed to speed up performance algorithmically through:

1. Sharing of common computation across multiple poses;
2. Reduced stage-1 complexity within the detector;[2]
3. Replaced vector quantization with sparse coding;
4. Reduced probability model size to minimize memory bottlenecks; and,
5. Improved termination of the classifier search in late stages of the detector.

Second, we re-engineered substantial portions of the code to minimize computational bottlenecks. This effort has paid off most significantly for expensive inner-loop computations (e.g. the wavelet transform) which have been largely re-written directly in assembly. When practical, these new code segments parallelize vector computations through Intel's SSE instruction set extensions, and minimize cache misses through improved memory access patterns.

Third, we have implemented two distinct parallelization schemes that allow the detector to exploit the resources of multi-core and/or multi-CPU platforms. For real-time systems, where response time is critical, parallelization occurs at the video-frame level, such that processing for each frame is distributed across all available processors and video frames are processed in order. The main disadvantage of this approach, however, is that this type of parallelization introduces communication overhead between processors, and does not trivially scale to large core/CPU counts. Therefore, we implemented a second buffered parallelization scheme for stored media that allocates one video frame per processor. While this can result in short-term, out-of-order processing of video frames, and, consequently, requires buffering of the input video, this approach vastly reduces communication overhead and, as such, is highly scalable to a large number of processors. The speed results reported in this paper correspond to this second, buffered implementation.

For each detected face, we retain the following: (1) face-center location $(x, y)$; (2) face size $s$; (3) one of five possible pose categories – namely, frontal, right/left profile, and $\pm 30°$ tilted; and (4) classifier confidence $c$, $c \geq 0.25$.[3]

**Selective Visual Attention:** For previous evaluations, the face finder processed every video frame at all positions and scales, independent of previous-frame detection results or the level of change between consecutive video frames. This approach is quite wasteful in terms of computation, since video contains an enormous amount of visually redundant information across time. As such, for the CLEAR 2007 evaluation, we implemented *selective visual attention*, an algorithm that focuses computational effort for the detector on the most necessary (i.e. changed) parts of each frame. In broad terms, the algorithm proceeds as follows. First, we periodically process a full frame independent of the properties of the input data. These *key frames* provide a reference point for subsequent frames and

---

[2] Earlier stages in the detector typically consume more CPU cycles since they have to process all and/or larger portions of the image position-scale space.
[3] Classifier confidence $c$ is related to the detection log-likelihood $ll$ by $c = ll + 1$.

prevent detection errors from propagating beyond limited time spans. For this evaluation, we set the key-frame rate to 15. Then, for all *intermediate frames*, we determine those regions that have changed sufficiently since the last key frame so as to require examination by the face finder. We apply the face finder only to these regions of change, and then merge the resulting partial face-finder output with the full-frame results from the last processed key frame.

Fig. 1 illustrates our selective attention algorithm for two sample video frames. While this example results in only one region of change [Fig. 1(a)-(e)], the selective attention algorithm frequently generates multiple, spatially disjoint regions, which our system trivially accommodates. In the merging of partial results with key-frame results [Fig. 1(f)-(h)], we arbitrate the combined output to eliminate possible duplicate detections for the same face.

### 1.2   Motion-Based Tracking

In motion-based tracking, we exploit the spatio-temporal continuity of video to combine single-frame observations into face tracks, each of which is ultimately associated with a unique subject ID. For this evaluation, the tracking algorithm is substantially different from the algorithm applied in prior evaluations. First, the new algorithm is *causal*; previously we tracked both forward and backward in time [1]. Second, we now utilize a globally optimal matching algorithm [4] [5] for associating observations across frames, similar to that used for matching ground truth data to system output by CLEAR evaluators. Third, we have re-engineered the code for faster performance, primarily through the implementation of efficient,

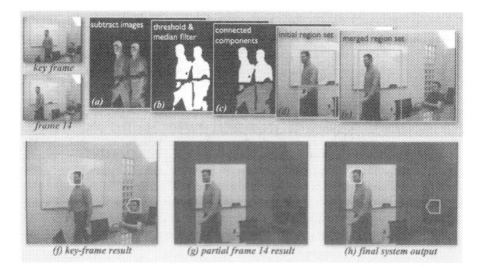

**Fig. 1.** Selective visual attention algorithm: (a)-(e) determine regions of change; (f)-(h) detect faces for selected regions and merge results with key-frame detection results

dynamic data structures. Below, we describe the revised tracking algorithm in greater detail.

**Motion Model:** Let $(z_t, c_t)$, $z_t = [x_t, y_t, s_t]^T$, denote the face location and size, and the classifier confidence in frame $t$ for a given person. Now, assume that we have a collection of these observations for that person for $t \in [0 \ldots T]$, and, furthermore, assume that the person's motion is governed by a second-order motion model:

$$\hat{z}_t = a_0 + a_1 t + a_2 t^2 \tag{1}$$

the parameters of which – $a_0$, $a_1$ and $a_2$ – must be updated with each new frame. To do this update for frame $t$, we minimize $J$:

$$J(a_0, a_1, a_2) = \sum_{k=0}^{t} c_k \lambda^{t-k} ||z_k - \hat{z}_k||^2, \ t \in [0 \ldots T]. \tag{2}$$

Note that each term in the above sum is weighed by two factors: (1) the classifier confidence, thus giving more weight to higher-confidence detections, and (2) an *exponential decay* $\lambda$, $0 < \lambda < 1$, giving more weight to more recent observations (we set $\lambda = 0.75$). The minimization of eqs. (2) can be solved recursively through the *square root information filter (SRIF)* algorithm [6]. This algorithm is mathematically equivalent to weighted recursive least squares, but requires no matrix inversion. We define *track confidence* $m_t$ as:

$$m_t = 1/\sqrt{|\hat{\Sigma}|} \tag{3}$$

where $\hat{\Sigma}$ denotes the estimated covariance in $z_t$, thereby incorporating both *classifier* confidence and *motion-model* confidence into $m_t$.

**Data Association:** The above discussion assumes that the data association problem – the correct matching of IDs across frames – is solved; this is, however, not the case when multiple faces are present. Let us assume that we have a set of partial face tracks $Z_{t-1} = \{z_{t-1}^i\}$, $i \in \{1 \ldots M\}$, through frame $(t-1)$, and a set of unassociated detector observations $Z_t = \{z_t^j\}$, $j \in \{1 \ldots N\}$, for frame $t$. To associate the existing tracks with the new observations for frame $t$, we first predict $\hat{Z}_t = \{\hat{z}_t^i\}$, $i \in \{1 \ldots M\}$, using the current motion-model parameters $(a_0^i, a_1^i, a_2^i)$ and eq. (1). Next, we map all observations $\hat{z}_t^i$ and $z_t^j$ to bounding boxes $\hat{B}_t^i$ and $B_t^j$, respectively.[4] For these bounding boxes, we then compute the following confidence-weighted association measure $J_{i,j}$ for prediction $\hat{z}_t^i$ and detector observation $z_t^j$:

$$J_{i,j} = \begin{cases} \sqrt{c_{t-1}^i c_t^j} \times r_{i,j} & \text{if } r_{i,j} \geq \rho_{thresh} \\ 0 & \text{if } r_{i,j} < \rho_{thresh} \end{cases} \tag{4}$$

---

[4] A bounding box $B$ is fully defined from observation $z$ and the canonical dimensions of a given detector – $32 \times 24$ for frontal faces, $40 \times 32$ for profile faces.

where

$$r_{i,j} = \frac{\hat{B}_t^i \cap B_t^j}{\hat{B}_t^i \cup B_t^j} = \text{area overlap ratio.} \tag{5}$$

The threshold $\rho_{thresh}$ disallows associations for weak spatial overlaps. Given $\boldsymbol{J} = \{J_{i,j}\}$, $i \in \{1 \ldots M\}$, $j \in \{1 \ldots N\}$, we apply the Hungarian algorithm [4] [5] to compute the globally optimal association between predictions $\hat{\boldsymbol{Z}}_t$ and new observations $\boldsymbol{Z}_t$. If no appropriate match is found for $\hat{z}_t^i$, we set $c_t^i = 0$.

**Track Initiation and Termination:** New tracks are initiated for any observation $z_t^j$ that is not associated with an existing face track through $\boldsymbol{J}$. A track only becomes valid, however, once the classifier confidence $c_t$ and the track confidence $m_t$ exceed acceptance thresholds $c_{accept}$ and $m_{accept}$, respectively. A valid track is terminated if (1) no new detector observation has been associated with that track for at least three frames or (2) $c_t$ and $m_t$ fall below rejection thresholds $c_{reject}$ and $m_{reject}$, respectively. In our system configuration:

$$c_{reject} < c_{accept} \quad \text{and} \quad m_{reject} < m_{accept}. \tag{6}$$

## 1.3   Track Filtering

After motion-based tracking, we finalize our results with a few additional processing steps. While motion-based tracking can successfully track through very short-term (i.e. a few frames) occlusions or missed detections, the track confidence $m_t$ deteriorates quickly for longer time gaps, due to the exponential decay $\lambda$. As a result, incorrect ID splits occur. Therefore, we merge the subject ID of tracks if they meet certain spatial consistency criteria and do not overlap temporally. We apply three principal spatial consistency tests: (1) mean distance between two tracks; (2) covariance-weighted mean distance between two tracks; and (3) distance between the start and end locations of two tracks.

Second, we delete low-confidence tracks. Through extensive experiments on development data, we observe that false alarm tracks that survive motion-based tracking are typically characterized by low classifier confidence $c_t$ throughout. Therefore, we eliminate all tracks for which the maximum classifier confidence $c_t$ is less than 2.3 *and* does not rise above 2.0 for at least 10% of the track's existence. This two-tiered criteria was found to be the most discriminating between false alarm tracks and true face tracks.

Third, we delete tracks that exhibit very little movement throughout the lifetime of the track as long as they do not meet a more stringent confidence test. As with the confidence-based tests above, we observed through experiments that near-stationary tracks are much more likely to be persistent false alarm tracks than true positive tracks. Finally, we adjust the face bounding boxes output by our system through a constant mapping to better conform to the annotation guidelines for CHIL and VACE-supported tasks, respectively, as specified in Fig. 2. This final step is the only difference in processing between the CHIL and VACE tasks.

| | | VACE | CHIL |
|---|---|---|---|
| Size scaling | Frontal | 0.70 | 0.90 |
| | Profile | 0.70 | 0.70 |
| | Tilted | 0.70 | 0.80 |
| Aspect-ratio scaling | Non-tilted | 0.70 | 1.10 |
| | Tilted | 0.70 | 1.00 |
| Horizontal offset | Right profile | 0.50 | 0.20 |
| | Left profile | -0.50 | -0.20 |
| Vertical offset | All poses | 0.25 | 0.05 |

**Fig. 2.** Bounding-box adjustments for the VACE and CHIL tasks. The horizontal and vertical offsets are relative to the absolute width and height of the bounding box, respectively.

## 2  System Performance

### 2.1  Accuracy

Here, we report accuracy performance over the VACE and CHIL test data sets for face detection and tracking. Fig. 3 summarizes our results by data set. *VACE-1* results exclude clips #04, #28, #31 and #37 (per the scoring protocol at NIST),

| | Data Size | | | Detection | | | Tracking | |
|---|---|---|---|---|---|---|---|---|
| | $N_F$ | $N_O$ | $N_T$ | DP | FAP | AOR | TDP | MMP |
| VACE-1 | 13341 | 23907 | 146 | 74.48% | 5.08% | 0.607 | 69.86% | 0.06% |
| VACE-2 | 12867 | 22196 | 122 | 79.64% | 5.19% | 0.608 | 79.51% | 0.07% |
| CHIL | 49220 | 77042 | 610 | 80.17% | 10.27% | 0.691 | 88.20% | 0.68% |
| AIT | 9832 | 12413 | 114 | 89.96% | 11.17% | 0.694 | 84.21% | 0.73% |
| IBM | 9744 | 19140 | 142 | 63.80% | 5.18% | 0.706 | 82.39% | 0.33% |
| ITC | 9900 | 9393 | 88 | 78.90% | 12.03% | 0.657 | 84.09% | 0.49% |
| UKA | 9788 | 16110 | 125 | 84.76% | 18.47% | 0.702 | 92.80% | 0.61% |
| UPC | 9956 | 19986 | 141 | 86.66% | 7.13% | 0.685 | 95.74% | 1.13% |

**Fig. 3.** Accuracy performance: $N_F$ = # of evaluation frames; $N_O$ = # of ground-truth objects; $N_T$ = # of ground-truth tracks; $DP$ = detection pct. = $100 \times N_D/N_O$, where $N_D$ = # of detected objects; $FAP$ = false alarm pct. = $100 \times N_{FA}/N_O$, where $N_{FA}$ = # of false alarms; $AOR$ = avg. area overlap ratio; $TDP$ = track detection pct. = $100 \times N_{TD}/N_T$, where $N_{TD}$ = # of tracks at least partially detected; $MMP$ = mismatch pct. = $100 \times (N_S + N_M)/N_O$, where $N_S$ = # of incorrect ID splits and $N_M$ = # of incorrect ID merges.

while *VACE-2* results exclude three additional clips from a fish-eye overhead camera (#15, #18 and #19), which contain faces in very atypical poses – poses which our system is not trained to detect. In fact, similar points-of-view are specifically omitted from the CHIL face detection and tracking task (i.e. cam5). The results in Fig. 3 were generated using PittPatt's internal evaluation software and subsequently verified with version 5.1.6 of the USF evaluation software.[5] For the CHIL data, we enforced the agreed-upon criterion that at least two of the three annotated landmarks (i.e two eyes, nose bridge) be visible in order to be considered a valid ground-truth object. For both the CHIL and VACE data, a ground-truth object and system object must have an overlap ratio of at least 0.2 to be considered a valid correspondence.

### 2.2   Speed

In Fig. 4 we report speed performance over the VACE and CHIL test data sets.[6] All evaluation runs were performed on a standard PC with a Dual 3GHz Intel Xeon 5160 processor, 4GB of RAM, and a Seagate Barracuda 500GB SATA II (3.0GB/s) hard drive, running the Ubuntu 6.06 operating system (Linux). In Fig. 4, note that real-time factors (RTF) greater than 1.0 correspond to better-than-real-time performance. Over the entire CLEAR 2007 test data (VACE and CHIL combined), our system processed 15.1 hours of video in approximately 9.4 hours for an average RTF of 1.6.

## 3   Speed Performance Analysis

### 3.1   Speed Improvements

In Fig. 5, we illustrate the algorithmic speed improvement for our system since the VACE 2005 and CLEAR 2006 evaluations. The average RTF of 1.6 for the CLEAR 2007 evaluation represents a **200×** speed-up since CLEAR 2006, and a **500×** speed-up since VACE 2005. For example, it would have taken our system approximately 4700 hours of CPU time in 2005 to process 15 hours of video. Spread over 10 CPUs, that corresponds to approximately 20 days; by contrast, for this evaluation, it took less than 10 hours on a single multi-core PC.

Since 2005, about 1.5× of the overall improvement in speed performance is due to better hardware performance and compilers. The remaining speed-up is

---

[5] Very minor discrepancies exist between our results and those produced by the VACE/CHIL evaluators. We compared against ground truth using real-valued vertices for face bounding boxes, while the ViPER and CHIL system-output format conventions force conversion to integer-valued vertices. This difference is the most likely cause for these discrepancies.

[6] The RTF's reported herein differ from those submitted with our evaluation results in March because of an error in computing the SSD's for some of the test data. Moreover, for the VACE data, the numbers reported herein correspond to video-frame I/O in JPEG format, while the numbers submitted in March correspond to video-frame I/O in PGM format.

| | Source Video Statistics | | | Processing Time | |
|---|---|---|---|---|---|
| | Resolution | FPS (Hz) | SSD (min) | TPT (min) | RTF |
| VACE-1 | 720×480 | 29.97 | 89.34 | 65.41 | 1.37 |
| VACE-2 | 720×480 | 29.97 | 86.55 | 63.02 | 1.37 |
| CHIL | | | 818.18 | 503.74 | 1.62 |
| AIT | 640×480 | 30 | 163.34 | 105.89 | 1.54 |
| IBM | 640×480 | 15 | 161.92 | 99.80 | 1.62 |
| ITC | 800×600 | 15 | 164.82 | 77.98 | 2.11 |
| UKA | 640×480 | 15 | 162.67 | 58.19 | 2.80 |
| UPC | 768×576 | 25 | 165.42 | 161.88 | 1.02 |

**Fig. 4.** Speed performance: $FPS$ = frames per second; $SSD$ = source signal duration; $TPT$ = total processing time (including all initialization and I/O); $RTF$ = real-time factor = $SSD/TPT$ (values greater than 1.0 correspond to better-than-real-time processing).

attributable to the algorithm/code improvements discussed in Section 1.1 and breaks down as follows:

1. Face-finder optimizations (algorithmic/code-level optimizations): $\approx 10\times$
2. Parallelization of code for multi-core platform (4 cores): $\approx 4\times$
3. Selective visual attention: $\approx 6\times$

We examine the impact of selective visual attention in greater detail in the following section.

### 3.2 Selective Visual Attention

Here, we demonstrate the effect of selective visual attention on both the speed and accuracy of the overall system. Fig. 6 illustrates the speed-up gained through selective attention, while Fig. 7 illustrates the accuracy difference between full-frame processing and processing with selective attention. With regard to speed, we note that the average speed-up factor (6.16) is less than the theoretical maximum (1/11.39% $\approx$ 8.78) due to the computational cost of the selective attention algorithm itself and the overhead associated with processing image regions in the face finder. We have also tested the algorithm on more dynamic video, with moving cameras and frequent scene breaks, and have observed smaller, but still substantial savings, both in terms of the percentage of pixels processed ($\approx 25\%$) as well as the net speed-up factor ($\approx 3$). Therefore, the applicability of the selective attention algorithm extends well beyond static/fixed camera scenarios.

In terms of accuracy, the overall difference in performance is very small and may not be statistically significant in light of the ground-truth annotation limitations discussed in Section 4.1.

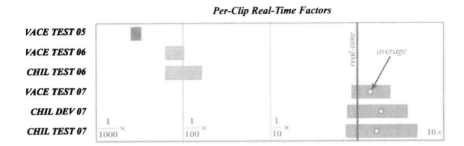

**Fig. 5.** Algorithm speed improvement from 2005 to present. Each bar indicates the range of real-time factors (RTF's) for the indicated data sets on a per-clip basis.

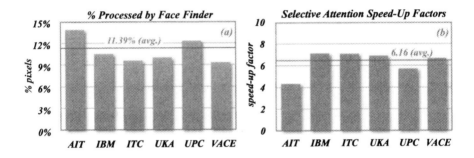

**Fig. 6.** (a) percent of pixels processed by face-finder after selective attention; (b) net speed-up of overall algorithm due to selective attention.

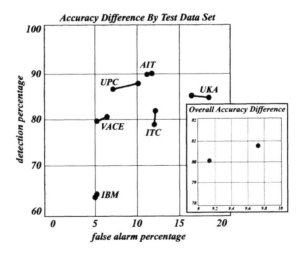

**Fig. 7.** Accuracy comparison between full-frame processing and processing with se-lective attention. Red points correspond to full-frame processing, while green points correspond to selective-visual attention processing.

# 4    Accuracy Performance Analysis

## 4.1    Ground-Truth Limitations

In analyzing how the accuracy of our re-designed algorithm has changed from previous evaluations, it is important to first understand the limitations of the ground-truth annotations against which our algorithms are evaluated. Any errors or inconsistencies in the ground truth introduce uncertainty in the accuracy results. Performance comparisons between different algorithms across common source data must therefore be judged in the presence of this uncertainty.

Given the large amount of data that has been annotated for the CLEAR 2007 evaluation (approximately 100,000 video frames), we recognize that human-generated ground truth will contain errors, as in "to err is human." As such, this discussion is not meant to criticize the evaluation organizers, but rather to highlight the challenges in interpreting the results of such a large-scale evaluation.

Our analysis of the ground-truth annotations is based on extracting and visually inspecting every scored miss and false alarm for our system output (e.g. 15,278 misses, 7,909 false alarms over the CHIL test data). This process has led us to conclude that a non-negligible number of faces are either improperly annotated, or not annotated at all. The vast majority of these suspect annotations correspond to faces that are visually ambiguous to varying degrees. Typically, one or more of the following factors contribute to this visual ambiguity: (1) poor image quality due to compression artifacts; (2) motion blur or video interlacing; (3) substantial occlusion; (4) small face size; and (5) extreme poses, such as profiles turned substantially more than $\pm 90°$ from the camera, and downward-looking faces. Suspect annotations fall into two broad categories: (1) faces (visually ambiguous or not) that are not annotated at all; and (2) visually ambiguous faces marked as "visible" (e.g., for CHIL annotations, two or more valid landmarks exist in the ground truth). Fig. 8 gives a few examples of both.

For our system output over the CHIL test data, we conservatively identified 3,805 scored false alarms, where a face is clearly contained within the system-output bounding box.[7] This corresponds to roughly 48% of all reported false alarms. Interestingly, if we factor these false alarms out of our results, the aggregate false alarm percentage over the CHIL data would drop to 5.33%, which is much closer to the VACE results (5.19%), where fewer of this type of error are evident. For VACE, visually ambiguous faces are marked as such and are treated as Don't Care Objects (DCOs); the CHIL protocol does not, however, contemplate the marking of DCOs. The absence of DCOs in the CHIL annotations most likely accounts for many of the suspect annotations.

Given our ground-truth analysis, it is highly probable that the "true" false alarm percentage is lower, and the "true" detection percentage is higher than what is reported. Moreover, *small* accuracy variations across algorithms may well be within the noise of the annotation errors and, therefore, do not offer sufficient evidence of the relative ranking of algorithms in terms of accuracy.

---

[7] We did not aggregate similar statistics for misses, since these tend to be more subjective.

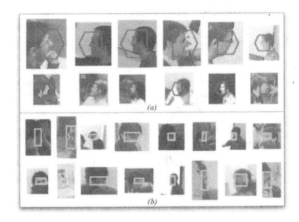

**Fig. 8.** Suspect ground-truth annotations: (a) faces that are not annotated but detected by our system (red boxes), resulting in erroneous false alarms; (b) visually ambiguous faces scored as misses (cyan boxes are ground truth).

## 4.2   CLEAR 2006 vs. CLEAR 2007

Here, we examine accuracy differences between our current algorithm and those run for the CLEAR 2006 evaluation. To get an apples-to-apples comparison, we ran our current algorithm on the CHIL 2006 test data, for which we have results

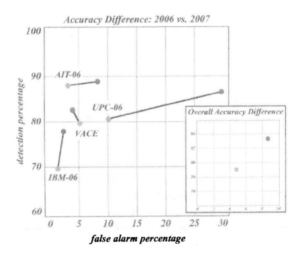

**Fig. 9.** Accuracy comparison between CLEAR 2006 and CLEAR 2007 algorithms. Red points correspond to 2006 results, while green points correspond to newly generated 2007 results.

from CLEAR 2006 [1].[8] Fig. 9 reports detection results for the VACE and three CHIL 2006 data sets.

Overall, these results suggest that our current algorithm operates at a lower false alarm percentage and a correspondingly lower detection percentage than our 2006 algorithms, although the total error rate (i.e. misses + false alarms) differs by less than 1%. The largest accuracy difference occurs for the UPC-06 data set, where our current algorithm dramatically reduces the false alarm percentage from 29.7% to 10.1%, and the IBM-06 data set, where the detection rate drops from 77.9% to 69.6%. This drop in detection accuracy is most likely related to more aggressive stage-1 elimination thresholds in the face finder, which allow fewer low-confidence stage-1 detections through to later, and more accurate processing stages. The more aggressive settings were selected to speed up later-stage processing in the face finder. Since the faces occurring within the IBM-06 videos are, on average, very small, and consequently lower confidence, those data are most susceptible to the new settings. Given our ground-truth analysis, however, further investigation is required to more completely characterize accuracy differences across diverse video sources.

## Acknowledgment

This research was funded (in part) by the U.S. Government VACE program.

## References

1. Nechyba, M.C., Schneiderman, H.: PittPatt face detection and tracking for the CLEAR 2006 evaluation. In: Stiefelhagen, R., Garofolo, J.S. (eds.) CLEAR 2006. LNCS, vol. 4122, pp. 161–170. Springer, Heidelberg (2007)
2. Schneiderman, H.: Feature-centric evaluation for efficient cascaded object detection. CVPR 2, 29–36 (2004)
3. Schneiderman, H.: Learning a restricted Bayesian network for object detection. CVPR 2, 639–646 (2004)
4. Munkres, J.R.: Algorithms for the assignment and transportation problems. J. SIAM 5, 32–38 (1957)
5. Fredman, M.L., Tarjan, R.E.: Fibonacci heaps and their uses in improved network optimization algorithms. J. ACM 34(3), 596–615 (1987)
6. Bierman, G.: Factorization Methods for Discrete Sequential Estimation. Academic Press, New York (1977)

---

[8] The VACE test data is identical for CLEAR 2006 and CLEAR 2007.

# Tsinghua Face Detection and Tracking for CLEAR 2007 Evaluation

Yuan Li, Chang Huang, and Haizhou Ai

Department of Computer Science and Technology
Tsinghua University, Beijing 100084, China
ahz@mail.tsinghua.edu.cn

**Abstract.** This paper presents the algorithm and evaluation results of a face detection and tracking system. A tree-structured multi-view face detector trained by Vector Boosting is used as the basic detection module. Once a new face are detected, a track is initialized and maintained by detection confidence and Lucas-Kanade features, which are fused by particle filter. Additionally, a post process is adopted to eliminate low confidence tracks and connect track fragments which are likely to belong to the same target. Evaluation results are given on video data of CLEAR 2007 test set.

## 1 Task Overview

The objective of face detection and tracking task of CLEAR 2007 Evaluation is to output the bounding box (including in-plane rotation angle) of each face in the scene, and in addition, for tracking the identity of each face should be maintained, too. Test data are videos captured in six meeting rooms (CMU, EDI, IDI, NIST, TNO, VT), in different time and by cameras at different positions (Fig. 1). 50 sequences are specified to be the testing set, each of the length of about 3000 to 5000 frames. The evaluation is done by the official software usf_date (version 5.1.6), and the metrics are MODA, MODP, MOTA and MOTP [1].

In the following section, we describe our detection and tracking algorithm; Section 3 gives the evaluation results and analysis; And Section 4 concludes the paper.

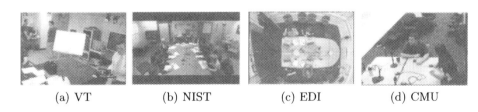

(a) VT  (b) NIST  (c) EDI  (d) CMU

**Fig. 1.** Video data samples

R. Stiefelhagen et al. (Eds.): CLEAR 2007 and RT 2007, LNCS 4625, pp. 138–147, 2008.

## 2   Algorithm

A tree-structured multi-view face detector trained by Vector Boosting [2] is adopted as the basic detection module. Since our first concern is accuracy, detection is performed every frame so that newly emerging (either entering or recovering from tracking loss) faces can be found as quickly as possible.

Face detection result is fed into a tracking module which integrates face detection confidence and Lucas-Kanade feature tracker [3] by particle filter. We choose to use Lucas-Kanade feature to complement the face detection cue because it is local, and therefor less vulnerable to partial occlusion or difficult poses of face, while face detection might fail in such cases. Particle filter performs the Bayesian temporal inference and ensures tracking efficiency by its sampling manner.

After all tracks are generated, a post process is added to eliminate false tracks by thresholding on the average face detection confidence of each track. And tracks which may belong to the same target are connected by analyzing their spatial and temporal distance.

### 2.1   Detection

The tree-structured detector covers a detection range of $\pm 90°$ out-of-plane rotation (yaw) and $\pm 45°$ in-of-plane rotation (tilt). The detector accomplishes two tasks at one time: to distinguish faces and non-faces and to distinguish different poses. A width-first-search tree structure is used to balance these two aspects as well as to enhance the detector in both accuracy and speed (Fig. 2). Each node of the tree is a strong classifier boosted from numerous weak classifiers using Sparse features, and it decides whether an input image patch should be rejected or passed to one or more of its son nodes. In one detection run, an image patch starts from the root node and travels along tree paths by width-first search, and is accepted as face if and only if it passes one or more leaf-node.

To train branch nodes which are responsible for not only rejecting non-faces but also identifying poses, the Vector Boosting algorithm is extended from the Real AdaBoost. In Vector Boosting the output of classifiers are vectors rather

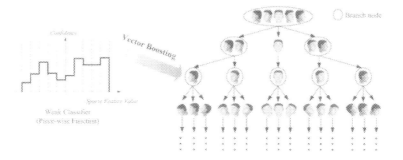

**Fig. 2.** Weak classifier and the tree structure face detector

than scalars, with each dimension of the output vector accounting for one tree branch (one pose subspace).

When an image is detected for faces, all patches within a certain range of size are scanned and those which passed are collected. Passed patches are clustered according to size and position, each cluster results in a detected face. In order to reduce false alarm, for the face detection task we only output faces whose corresponding cluster contains at least two passed image patch. Detection result is also input to the tracking algorithm for initialization of tracks.

## 2.2   Tracking

The basic framework for tracking is particle filter [4]. Denote the state of each face and the observation at time $t$ by $\mathbf{x}_t$ and $\mathbf{z}_t$. We define $\mathbf{x}_t = \langle x_t, y_t, s_t \rangle$, where $\langle x_t, y_t \rangle$ is the centroid of the face square region, and $s_t$ is the side length of the square. Observation model outputs $p(\mathbf{z}_t|\mathbf{x}_t)$ for each input candidate $\mathbf{x}_t$. Particle filters works in the famous two-step recursion:

$$\text{Prediction}: p(\mathbf{x}_t|\mathbf{Z}_{t-1}) = \int p(\mathbf{x}_t|\mathbf{x}_{t-1})p(\mathbf{x}_{t-1}|\mathbf{Z}_{t-1})d\mathbf{x}_{t-1} \tag{1}$$

$$\text{Update}: p(\mathbf{x}_t|\mathbf{Z}_t) \propto p(\mathbf{z}_t|\mathbf{x}_t)p(\mathbf{x}_t|\mathbf{Z}_{t-1}) \tag{2}$$

And the target distribution $p(\mathbf{x}_t|\mathbf{Z}_t)$ is simulated by a set of weighted particles $\{\mathbf{x}_{f,t}^{(i)}, w_{f,t}^{(i)}\}_{i=1}^{N}$. From here on we suppress the subscript $t$ when there is no ambiguity.

Two observation models are adopted, one is based on detection confidence: $p(\mathbf{z}^{face}|\mathbf{x})$, the other is based on Lucas-Kanade (LK) feature tracker: $p(\mathbf{z}^{lk}|\mathbf{x})$. Overall observation likelihood is formulated as

$$p(\mathbf{z}|\mathbf{x}) = p(\mathbf{z}^{face}|\mathbf{x})p(\mathbf{z}^{lk}|\mathbf{x}). \tag{3}$$

**Face Likelihood.** Conventionally, detector only outputs a binary value: pass or reject. Here we model the tree-structured detector output into real-valued likelihood. For an input $\mathbf{x}$, we can obtain the number of layers $h$ that $\mathbf{x}$ passes and the confidence $c$ given by the last strong classifier it passed. The observation likelihood is given by

$$p(\mathbf{z}^{face}|\mathbf{x}) \propto 1/\left(1 + \phi_h \exp(-c)\right), \tag{4}$$

where $\phi_h$ is the a priori ratio of negative samples to positive samples for the strong classifier in the $h$-th layer (obtained during training process). It decreases as $h$ increases to reflect the fact that the more layers $\mathbf{x}$ passes, the more likely it is the true target. For detailed derivation of (4) please refer to [5].

**Lucas-Kanade Feature Likelihood.** For each tracked face, a set of LK features are selected within the facial region. Denote the LK feature set as $\mathbf{P}$, and each feature by $\mathbf{p} = \langle px, py, rx, ry \rangle$, where $\langle px, py \rangle$ is its position in the image, and $\langle rx, ry \rangle$ is the relative position to the face it belongs to. When the features are initialized or updated (when face confidence is high), $\langle rx, ry \rangle$ is calculated and recorded as reference.

While updating particle weight at time $t$, we obtain $p(\mathbf{z}^{lk}|\mathbf{x})$ by measuring the consistency between each face particle $\mathbf{x} = \langle x, y, s \rangle$ and the tracked LK features $\mathbf{P} = \{\mathbf{p}_i\}_{i=1}^{M}$. It is done by calculating the relative position of each $\mathbf{p}_i$ to $\mathbf{x}$ and compare it with the reference relative position:

$$\Delta rx = \frac{(px_i - (x + s/2))}{s} - rx_i, \tag{5}$$

$$\Delta ry = \frac{(py_i - (y + s/2))}{s} - ry_i, \tag{6}$$

$$\Delta rd = \sqrt{\Delta rx^2 + \Delta ry^2}. \tag{7}$$

The LK likelihood is defined intuitively as the proportion of "consistent" features:

$$p(\mathbf{z}^{lk}|\mathbf{x}) \propto \frac{\sum_{i=1}^{M} \delta(\Delta rd < \tau)}{M}, \tag{8}$$

where $\delta(expression) = 1$ when $expression$ is true, else $\delta(x) = 0$. $\tau$ is empirically set to 0.1.

Table 1 gives the complete tracking algorithm.

## 2.3  Post Process

In the tracking phase, we set the thresholds $\Gamma_{face}$ and $\Gamma_{lk}$ to relative low values, to ensure that most face tracks are preserved. After all tracks are obtained, the following steps are done to generate final tracking result:

1. For each face track, calculate the frame-average face likelihood. Eliminate tracks with likelihood lower than threshold $\Gamma_{low}$.
2. Connect face tracks which are close in both temporal and spatial domain to reduce identity switch. For each track $A$, search in the rest tracks for a track $B$ to connect with $A$. If the end point of $A$ is at frame $t_A$ with face $\mathbf{x}_A = (x_A, y_A, s_A)$, and the starting point of $B$ is at frame $t_B$ with face $\mathbf{x}_B = (x_B, y_B, s_B)$, $B$ should satisfy that

$$\sqrt{(x_A - x_B)^2 + (y_A - y_B)^2} < \min(s_A, s_B) \cdot \eta_d, \tag{9}$$

$$\frac{s_A}{s_B} < \eta_s, \frac{s_B}{s_A} < \eta_s, \tag{10}$$

and $(t_B - t_A)$ is minimized (the interval between two tracks should not be too long). If such $B$ exist then connect $B$ at the end of $A$. Empirically we choose $\eta_d = 1.0$ and $\eta_s = 1.2$.

3. For each face track, calculate again the frame-average face likelihood, and eliminate tracks with likelihood lower than $\Gamma_{high}$.

Note that if we do not eliminate low likelihood tracks before connecting, some false alarm tracks might be connected with true tracks and cannot be eliminated later (or they may cause some true tracks to be eliminated). Therefore we choose to do the filtering twice with two different thresholds.

**Table 1.** The tracking algorithm

---

Assume that from the $(t-1)$-th frame, the set of faces which are being tracked is denoted as $F$, and for each $f \in F$, a weighted particle set is maintained: $\{\mathbf{x}_{f,t-1}^{(i)}, w_{f,t-1}^{(i)}\}_{i=1}^{N}$, also a set of LK features $\mathbf{P}_{f,t-1}$. The output of full-frame face detector result at the $t$-th frame is a set of faces $G$, which is also input to the tracking system.
Proceed as follows in the $t$-th frame:

– **Track each $f \in F$ by particle filter**
  - Track LK features $\mathbf{P}_{f,t-1}$ to get $\mathbf{P}_{f,t}$.
  - Do the Resample and Prediction steps of PF to obtain new particle set $\{\mathbf{x}_{f,t}^{(i)}, 1\}_{i=1}^{N}$.
  - For each particle $\mathbf{x}_{f,t}^{(i)}$, calculate its face likelihood $w_{f,face}^{(i)}$ and Lucas-Kanade tracker likelihood $w_{f,lk}^{(i)}$.
  - Calculate $W_{f,face} = \sum_{i=1}^{N} w_{f,face}^{(i)}$, and $W_{f,lk} = \sum_{i=1}^{N} w_{f,lk}^{(i)}$.
  - If $W_{f,face} > \Gamma_{face}$ and $W_{f,lk} > \Gamma_{lk}$, let $w_{f,t}^{(i)} = w_{f,face}^{(i)} \cdot w_{f,lk}^{(i)}$, face $f$ is tracked, and is "visible";
  - Elseif $W_{f,face} > \Gamma_{face}$, let $w_{f,t}^{(i)} = w_{f,face}^{(i)}$, face $f$ is tracked, and is "visible";
  - Elseif $W_{f,lk} > \Gamma_{lk}$, let $w_{f,t}^{(i)} = w_{f,lk}^{(i)}$, face $f$ is tracked, but is "invisible";
  - Else face $f$ is lost.
  - If face $f$ is tracked, calculate estimation $\hat{\mathbf{x}}_t = \frac{\sum_{i=1}^{N} w_{f,t}^{(i)} \cdot \mathbf{x}_{f,t}^{(i)}}{\sum_{i=1}^{N} w_{f,t}^{(i)}}$.
– **Check faces**
  - **Check for disappearance**: if some tracked face $f \in F$ has been "invisible" for $Q$ frames, mark it as lost and discard it.
  - **Check for appearance**: if some detected face $g \in G$ is not tracked currently, initialize a new face by $g$, let $F = F \cup g$.
  - **Update LK features**: if some tracked face $f \in F$ has high face confidence, update its LK features' relative position to the face.
– **Output tracking result** for each $f \in F$.

---

# 3  Evaluation Results

## 3.1  Overview

There are originally 50 test clips, among them clip #4, #28, #31, #37 are excluded by the organizers. Therefore all results are for the rest 46 clips.

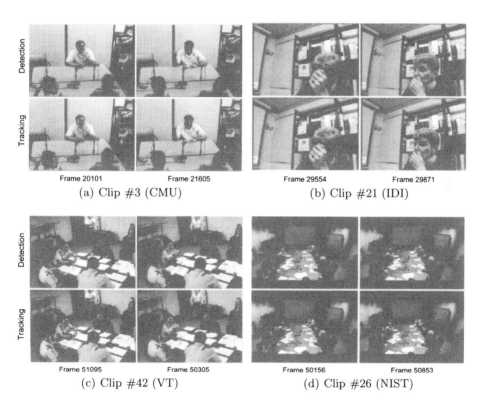

(a) Clip #3 (CMU)          (b) Clip #21 (IDI)

(c) Clip #42 (VT)          (d) Clip #26 (NIST)

**Fig. 3.** A few snapshots of detection and tracking results

The evaluation is done by the usf_date software (version 5.1.6). The metrics listed here are MODA (Multiple Object Detection Accuracy), MODP (Multiple Object Detection Precision), MOTA (Multiple Object Tracking Accuracy) and MOTP (Multiple Object Tracking Precision)[1], DP (detected objects / groundtruth objects), FAP (false alarms / groundtruth objects)[2].

The result is shown in Table 2. Both tracking and detection results are included, together with results classified by meeting sites. It can be seen that MODA and MODP of tracking is higher than frame-based detection. Also the

---

[1] These four metrics are obtained by **usf_date GT_file SO_file Face -clear**.

[2] These two metrics are obtained by **usf_date GT_file SO_file Face -sfdat 0.2 -stdat 0.2 -binthres** according to [1].

DP (detection percentage) is about 6% higher than that of detection, and the FAP (false alarm percentage) is reduced by about 12% compared with detection.

Fig. 3 gives some sample results of detection and tracking. It can be seen that in some occasion, tracking is able to reduce false alarm and fill detection gaps due to occlusion or difficult poses. But still identities switches can be observed when track is lost and renewed.

**Table 2.** Evaluation scores (overall average and averages for each dataset)

|            | MODA   | MODP   | MOTA   | MOTP   | DP      | FAP     |
|------------|--------|--------|--------|--------|---------|---------|
| **Tracking** | **0.8521** | **0.5843** | **0.8514** | **0.5774** | **87.41%** | **4.21%** |
| CMU        | 0.9345 | 0.6440 | 0.9336 | 0.6323 | 96.35%  | 3.62%   |
| EDI        | 0.7749 | 0.5829 | 0.7746 | 0.5603 | 77.70%  | 0.38%   |
| IDI        | 0.9334 | 0.6185 | 0.9324 | 0.6176 | 97.88%  | 5.73%   |
| NIST       | 0.8796 | 0.6541 | 0.8790 | 0.6520 | 94.40%  | 5.86%   |
| TNO        | 0.8978 | 0.5388 | 0.8973 | 0.5461 | 91.40%  | 5.05%   |
| VT         | 0.7741 | 0.4771 | 0.7735 | 0.4777 | 76.65%  | 6.18%   |
| **Detection** | **0.7014** | **0.5611** | -      | -      | **81.49%** | **16.20%** |
| CMU        | 0.5998 | 0.6268 | -      | -      | 89.26%  | 24.96%  |
| EDI        | 0.7129 | 0.5720 | -      | -      | 74.42%  | 15.35%  |
| IDI        | 0.8340 | 0.5429 | -      | -      | 91.85%  | 12.03%  |
| NIST       | 0.8026 | 0.6416 | -      | -      | 89.61%  | 9.71%   |
| TNO        | 0.7611 | 0.5162 | -      | -      | 81.33%  | 11.05%  |
| VT         | 0.6101 | 0.4539 | -      | -      | 69.97%  | 18.51%  |

### 3.2   Scenario Analysis

**Results on Data Classified by Face Condition.** From Table 2 we can see that the difficulty of test clips from various sites are different, mainly due to the variation in face condition and background complexity. We further classify the test clips by face condition into three groups: large face, medium-sized face and tiny or omni-directional face[3]. And the tracking scores of each group is shown in Fig. 4(a), and Fig. 4(b) shows a few data samples from each group. It is clear that for the "large face" group, the system performs best (with MOTA at 0.9760 and DP at 99.41%). But the scores for "tiny/omni-directional" group are very low.

**Typical Failure Cases.** There are four test clips whose MOTA is lower than 0.6, they are #15 (0.5397), #19 (0.2269), #20 (0) and #46 (0.1058). The snapshots of groundtruth and tracking result of our system is shown in Fig. 5. The low scores for these cases are mainly due to miss detection when face is up-side-down

---

[3] #11-#14, #16-#18, #21-#23, #30, #35 and #36 contain single large face (width at 50-150 pixels); #1-#3, #5-#10, #24-#27, #29, #32-#34 and #38-#50 contain multiple medium-sized faces (width at 20-50 pixels); #15 and #20 contain small omni-directional faces (up-side-down), faces in #19 is very tiny (width about 10 pixels).

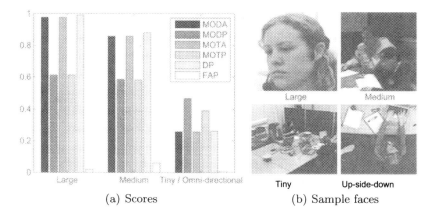

(a) Scores    (b) Sample faces

**Fig. 4.** Evaluation scores of tracking for test videos grouped by face condition. 13 clips are grouped as "large face", with face width at 50-150 pixels; 30 clips as "medium-sized face", face width 20-50 pixels; 3 clips contain tiny or omni-directional faces, with face width at about 10 pixels.

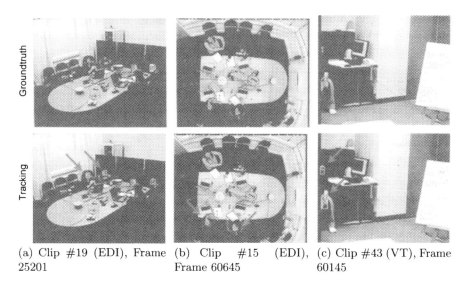

(a) Clip #19 (EDI), Frame 25201    (b) Clip #15 (EDI), Frame 60645    (c) Clip #43 (VT), Frame 60145

**Fig. 5.** Partial and enlarged snapshots of groundtruth and tracking failure. Red arrows points to miss tracked faces.

(clip #15 and #20), partially out of image region (clip #46), small and blurry (clip #19) or difficult pose (clip #15, #19 and #20).

Difficult or blurry faces (as in clip #19) can be detected and tracked if we reduce the face confidence threshold. However, this will largely increase the false alarms in other test videos.

**Possible Improvements.** For videos which contain non-upright faces, we can adopt omni-directional face detector which is obtained by rotating the original face detector. We have applied such detector on clip #15 and #20. MOTA of #15 is improved from 0.5397 to 0.8930 and MOTA of #20 from 0 to 0.1442. But it should also be noted that using omni-directional detector will induce extra time complexity and false alarms, too. See Fig. 6 For a few tracking result using omni-directional face detection.

Additionally, to detect and track faces that are partially out of image boundary (and hence not included in the search region of detector), it is a possible solution to add a black margin to the image, so that they will be equivalent to partially occluded faces, which may be handled by the detector and tracker when occlusion is not severe. Currently we have not implemented this.

Clip #15, Frame 40618        Clip #20, Frame 32175        Clip #20, Frame 33107

**Fig. 6.** Tracking result by using omni-directional detector Yellow arrows points to tracked faces

### 3.3    Processing Speed

The system is developed in C++. The processing speed is tested on a PC with Pentium 4 CPU 2.80GHz, 2.00GB memory (although the application uses 50M-100M memory). The processing time is reported in Table 3. The whole system runs at about 1.45fps.

Since accuracy is of first concern here, we choose to perform full detection in each frame, therefore the time for detection takes up a large part (70.4%) of the total system running time. In fact, the tracking module is originally designed for real-time online tracking. In its original setting, detection is performed only partially in each frame to discover new target, and its tracking speed can achieve more than 20fps for QVGA-sized video.

**Table 3.** Processing Time of each module (Total frames processed: 175949)

| Module | Total Time (s) | Time per Frame (s) | Percentage |
|---|---|---|---|
| Detection | 85503.943 | 0.486 | 70.4% |
| Tracking | 35857.874 | 0.204 | 29.6% |
| Post Process | 68.953 | 0.0004 | 0.0% |
| Total | 121430.770 | 0.690 | - |

## 4   Conclusion

We implemented a face detection and tracking system and reported its performance following CLEAR 2007 evaluation routines. For face detection task, the average MODA is 0.7014, detection percentage is 81.49%, and false alarm percentage is 16.20%. For face tracking task, the average MOTA is 0.8514, detection percentage is 87.41%, and false alarm percentage is 4.21%.

From the evaluation, it is observed that the proposed detector and tracker is vulnerable to difficult poses including non-upright faces, as well as blurry, small or partially occluded ones, especially those on image boundary. We have discussed a few possible improvements. Besides, it may be interesting to reduce id switch by enhancing the post process to connect track fragments by matching appearance (as in retrieval or recognition algorithms).

## Acknowledgements

This work is supported in part by National Science Foundation of China under grant No.60332010, No.60673107, National Basic Research Program of China under Grant No.2006CB303100, and it is also supported by a grant from Omron Corporation.

## References

1. Kasturi, R., Goldgof, D., Manohar, V., Boonstra, M., Korzhova, V.: Performance evaluation protocol for face, person and vehicle detection and tracking in video analysis and content extraction (vace-ii) clear - classification of events, activities and relationships (2006)
2. Huang, C., Ai, H., Li, Y., Lao, S.: High performance rotation invariant multiview face detection. IEEE Transactions on Pattern Analysis and Machine Intelligence 29(4), 671–686 (2007)
3. Tomasi, C., Kanade, T.: Detection and tracking of point features. Technical Report CMU-CS-91-132, Carnegie Mellon University (1991)
4. Isard, M., Blake, A.: Condensation – conditional density propagation for visual tracking. International Journal on Computer Vision 28(1), 5–28 (1998)
5. Li, Y., Ai, H., Huang, C., Lao, S.: Robust head tracking based on a multi-state particle filter. In: IEEE International Conference on Automatic Face and Gesture Recognition (2006)

# The AIT Outdoor Tracker for Vehicles and Pedestrians in CLEAR2007

Andreas Stergiou, Aristodemos Pnevmatikakis, and Lazaros Polymenakos

Athens Information Technology, Autonomic and Grid Computing,
P.O. Box 64, Markopoulou Ave., 19002 Peania, Greece
{aste, apne, lcp}@ait.edu.gr
http://www.ait.edu.gr/research/RG1/overview.asp

**Abstract.** This paper presents the tracking system from Athens Information Technology that participated to the pedestrian and vehicle surveillance task of the CLEAR 2007 evaluations and the obtained results. The system is based on the CLEAR 2006 one, with some important modifications that are detailed. Since the test data in CLEAR 2006 and 2007 are the same, it is easy to quantify the obtained performance gain from the older system to the proposed one.

## 1 Introduction

Target tracking in video streams has many applications, like surveillance, security, smart spaces [1], pervasive computing, and human-machine interfaces [2] to name a few. In these applications the objects to be tracked are either humans, or vehicles. To track objects we first need to detect them. The detected objects are used to initialize the tracks and provide measurements to the tracking algorithm, usually of the recursive Bayesian filtering [3] type. This is a very hard problem, one that remains unsolved in the general case [3]. If a shape or a color model of the objects were known a-priori, then detection can be done using active contours [4] or variations of the mean-shift algorithm [5]. Unfortunately such approaches can only be applied in limited application domains; the shape and color richness of all possible people and vehicles prohibit their use in unconstrained applications like surveillance or smart rooms.

The solution to the detection problem is a common property of such targets: sooner or later they move, which produces evidence that distinguishes them from the background and identifies them as foreground objects. The segmentation of foreground objects can be accomplished by processing the difference of the current frame from a background image. This background image can be static [6] or can be computed adaptively [7]. The drawback of the static background image is that background does change. In outdoor scenes natural light changes and the wind causes movement of trees and other objects. In indoor scenes, artificial light flickers and pieces of furniture may be moved around. All such effects can be learned by an adaptive background algorithm like Stauffer's [8] and of its modifications [9,10]. Such an algorithm detects targets as segments different from the learned background, but depends on the targets' movement to keep a fix on them. If they stop, the learning process fades them into the background.

R. Stiefelhagen et al. (Eds.): CLEAR 2007 and RT 2007, LNCS 4625, pp. 148–159, 2008.

Once a target is initialized, a tracking system should be able to keep a fix on it even when it remains immobile for some time. In this paper, we propose a novel tracking system that addresses this need by utilizing a feedback mechanism from the tracking module to the adaptive background module which in turn provides the evidence for each target to the tracking module. We control the adaptive background parameters on a pixel level for every frame (spatiotemporal adaptation), based on a prediction of the position of the target. Under the assumption of Gaussian target states and linear dynamic models, this prediction can be provided by a Kalman filter [11].

The proposed tracker system comprises of the feedback configuration of three modules, namely the adaptive background, the image processing for evidence generation and the Kalman filtering. A fourth module operates on the tracks in a temporal window of 1 second, by checking their consistency.

This paper is organized as follows: In section 2 the four modules of the system are detailed. The results on the VACE person and vehicle surveillance tasks of the CLEAR 2006 evaluations are presented and discussed in section 3. Finally, in section 4 the conclusions are drawn, followed by some indications for future enhancements.

## 2   Tracking System

The block diagram of the tracking system is shown in Figure 1. It comprises four modules: adaptive background, image processing for evidence generation, Kalman filtering and track consistency. Evidence for the targets is generated once difference from the estimated background is detected. The estimation of the background is dynamic; background is learnt in a different manner for different portions of the frame, depending on whether they belong to existing targets, the target size and its speed.

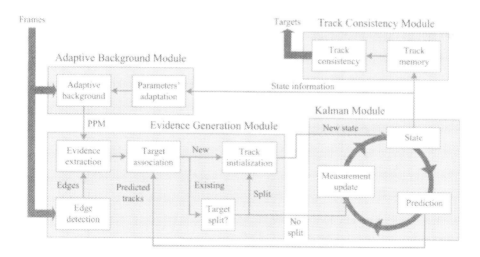

**Fig. 1.** Block diagram of the complete feedback tracker architecture. Frames are input to the adaptive background and evidence generation modules, and targets are output from the track consistency module.

The dynamic estimation in the CLEAR 2007 system is applied on a blurred version of the original frame, to reduce the effect of flicker. The evidence is used to initialize and update tracks. Tracks that are persistent for 10 out of the 15 past frames are promoted to targets, and are reported by the system. Given that the frame rate of all the VACE person and vehicle surveillance videos is 30 frames per second, the introduced lag is a small penalty to pay for the added robustness to false alarms. Initialized tracks have their new position predicted by the state update step of the Kalman filter. The predictions are used to associate evidence with tracks and perform the measurement update step of the Kalman filter. Tracks are also eliminated is they have no evidence supporting them for 15 frames. The states of the Kalman filter, i.e. the position, velocity and size of the targets, are fed back to the adaptive background module to spatio-temporally adapt the learning rate. They are also fed forward to the track consistency module to obtain the reported tracks of the system and the decision whether they correspond to vehicles or pedestrians. In the following subsections, we present the four modules in detail.

## 2.1 Adaptive Background Module

The targets of the proposed system (vehicles and pedestrians) are mostly moving. The changes in subsequent video frames due to movement are used to identify and segment the foreground (pixels of the moving targets) from the background (pixels without movement). If a background image were available, this segmentation is simply the difference of the current frame from the background image. The foreground pixels thus obtained are readily grouped into target regions. A static image of the empty scene viewed by the (fixed) camera can be used for background [6]. Unfortunately this is not practical for outdoors applications, or even for long term indoors applications, hence adaptive background approaches are adopted [7-10] primarily for two reasons: First, such an empty scene image might not be available due to system setup. Second and most important, background (outdoors and indoors) also changes: Natural light conditions change slowly as time goes by; the wind causes swaying movements of flexible background object (e.g. foliage); fluorescent light flickers at the power supply frequency; objects on tabletops and small pieces of furniture are rearranged and projection areas display different content. All these changes need to be learnt into an adaptive background model.

Stauffer's adaptive background algorithm [8] is capable of learning such changes with different speeds of change by learning into the background any pixel, whose color in the current frame resembles the colors that this pixel often had in the history of the recording. So no changes, periodic changes or changes that occurred in the distant past lead to pixels that are considered background. To do so, a number of weighted Gaussians model the appearance of different colors in each pixel. The weights indicate the amount of time the modeled color is active in that particular pixel. The mean is a three dimensional vector indicating the estimated color for that model and that pixel, while the covariance matrix indicates the extend around the mean that a color of that pixel is to be considered similar to the one modeled. Colors in any given pixel similar to that modeled by any of the Gaussians of that pixel lead to an update of that Gaussian, an increase of its weight and a decrease of all the weights of the other Gaussians of that pixel. Colors not matching any of the Gaussians of that pixel lead to the introduction of a new Gaussian with minimum weight. Hence the possible updates of the weight of the $i$-th Gaussian of the pixel located at $(x, y)$ at time $t$ are

$$w_i(x,y,t) = \begin{cases} a & \text{new Gaussian} \\ (1-a)w_i(x,y,t-1) & \text{non-matching Gaussians} \\ (1-a)w_i(x,y,t-1)+a & \text{matching Gaussians} \end{cases} \tag{1}$$

where $a$ is the learning rate.

Some variations of the Stauffer algorithm found in the literature deal with the way covariance is represented (single value, diagonal of full matrix) and the way the mean and covariance of the Gaussians are updated [9]. Some further variations of the algorithm address the way the foreground information is represented. The original algorithm and most of the modifications lead to a binary decision for each pixel: foreground or background [8,9]. In [10], the Pixel Persistence Map (PPM) is used instead. This is a map of the same dimension as the frames with a value at each location $(x, y)$ equal to the weight of the Gaussian matching the current color of the pixel at $(x, y)$. Small PPM values indicate foreground objects, while large indicate background. The foreground/background threshold is left unspecified though.

The drawback of all the existing variations of Stauffer's algorithm is that stationary foreground objects tend to fade in the background with rate $a$. Small background learning rates fade foreground objects slowly, but are also slow in adapting to the background changes. Large rates favor background adaptation but tend to fade a target into the background when it stops. This fading progressively destroys the region of the tracked object, deforms its perceived shape and finally leads to loosing track of the object altogether. When the target resumes moving, foreground pixels will be marked only at the locations not previously occupied by the stationary target. When a target remains stationary long enough, or has fairly uniform coloration, the new evidence will be far apart from the last evidence of the track, either in time, or in space or in both. Then the track is lost; the track is terminated and another is initiated when movement resumes.

We address the problem of the fading of stationary foreground objects using a feedback tracking architecture. The edges of the frame that coincide with values of the PPM below a threshold serve as target evidence to the Kalman filter. The states of the Kalman filter provide ellipses that describe every target. The learning rate is modified in regions around these targets, based on their speed and size. Thus, instead of a constant value, a spatiotemporal adaptation of the learning rate is used:

$$a(x,y,t) = \begin{cases} 0.04 & \text{if } (x, y) \text{ not a target pixel at time } t \\ a(\hat{v},C) & \text{if } (x, y) \text{ a target pixel at time } t \end{cases} \tag{2}$$

where $C$ is the covariance matrix of the target (hence $\det(C)$ relates to its size) and $\hat{v}$ is the mobility of the target, which is related to the change of the position of its centroid and the change of its size. The latter indicates an approaching or receding target and is quantified using the determinant of the covariance matrix of the target. Thus the mobility is defined as follows:

$$\hat{v} = T_f \sqrt{\|v\|_2} + \sqrt{\frac{\max\left(C_t, C_{t-T_f}\right)}{\min\left(C_t, C_{t-T_f}\right)}} \tag{3}$$

where $v$ is the velocity vector and $T_f$ is the inverse of the frame rate. Then, the learning rate $a(\hat{v}, C)$ of a pixel belonging to a target is:

$$a(\hat{v}, C) = \begin{cases} 0.04 & \text{if } \det(C) \leq 8 \cdot 10^5 \text{ and } \hat{v} \geq 2 \\ \dfrac{0.04}{4} & \text{if } \det(C) > 8 \cdot 10^5 \text{ and } \hat{v} \geq 2 \\ 0.0044 \cdot \tan\left(\dfrac{\hat{v} \cdot \pi}{4.3}\right) & \text{if } \det(C) \leq 8 \cdot 10^5 \text{ and } \hat{v} < 2 \\ \dfrac{0.0044}{4} \cdot \tan\left(\dfrac{\hat{v} \cdot \pi}{4.3}\right) & \text{if } \det(C) > 8 \cdot 10^5 \text{ and } \hat{v} < 2 \end{cases} \tag{4}$$

This choice for $a(\hat{v}, C)$ progressively delays fading of the targets as they become slower. It also delays fading of large targets by setting the learning rate to $1/4$ of its value if the target is too large. This is useful for large vehicles, where their speed can be large, but their uniform colors can lead to fading into the background.

The second major proposed modification of Stauffer's algorithm addresses extreme flickering situations often encountered in night vision cameras. In such scenes the PPM needs to be binarized by a high threshold in order not to consider flickering pixels as foreground. The high threshold on the other hand tends to discard actual foreground pixels as well. The proposed solution is to adapt the threshold $T$ in a spatiotemporal fashion similar to the learning rate in (2). i.e.

$$T(x, y, t) = \begin{cases} 0.25 & \begin{array}{l} \text{if } (x, y) \text{ not a target pixel at time } t \\ \text{or a target with } \det(C) < 500 \end{array} \\ 0.5 & \text{elsewhere} \end{cases} \tag{5}$$

This way flickering pixels are avoided far from the targets, while the targets themselves are not affected. To avoid a delayed detection of new very small targets, the threshold of pixels belonging to such targets with $\det(C) < 500$ is not affected.

These proposed feedback mechanisms on the learning rate and PPM binarization threshold lead to robust foreground regions regardless of the flickering in the images or the lack of target mobility, while they do not affect the adaptation of the background around the targets. When such flickering and mobility conditions occur, the resulting PPM is more suitable for target region forming that the original version of [10]. The forming of target regions is the goal of the evidence generation module, detailed next.

## 2.2 Evidence Generation Module

The evidence generation module finds foreground segments, assigns their pixels to known targets or initializes new ones and checks targets for possible splitting. The information for new targets or targets to be updated is passed to the Kalman module.

The binary mask obtained by adaptively thresholding the PPM is passed through a shadow detector based on [12]. It is then merged with the binary mask obtained by the edge detector using the AND operator. The resulting mask contains the foreground edges. Edges are used to add robustness to the system: The PPM can have filled segments if the object has entered the camera view after initialization and moves sufficiently. On the other hand an object can manifest itself by parts of its outline if it has been present in the scene at initialization. The use of edges provides the contours of objects in both cases, so they no longer need to be treated by different image processing modules. The foreground edge map is dilated to form regions. The dilation is such that edges that lie up to 10 pixels apart are merged into a single segment. Should these regions contain holes, they are filled, providing solid regions. This modification of the CLEAR 2007 system compared to the CLEAR 2006 one is important, as it results to robust estimation of the Kalman filter states.

The association of the evidence to targets is the major modification of the CLEAR 2007 system. While the CLEAR 2006 association was done on a per segment basis, it is performed on a per pixel basis in the CLEAR 2007 system. The advantage of this per pixel approach is robustness to:

- target splits, when the evidence of a target is split into more than one segment due to similarity to the background color, and
- collision handling, when targets touch and their evidences produce one big segment that can be shared between multiple targets.

The states of the targets contain their mean and the covariance matrix, hence the Mahalanobis distance of any evidence pixel from a target can be found. The association of the evidence to the targets utilizes this Mahalanobis distance as follows:

- Allocate to every existing target all evidence pixels that have Mahalanobis distance smaller than 1. By doing so pixels can be allocated to more than one target, while others can be left unallocated.
- For every unallocated evidence pixel, find the closest target. If the distance is less than 2, associate it to the target. Each of these pixels is hence either allocated to a single target, or it still remains unallocated.
- If a distinct region of evidence pixels has none of its member pixels allocated to a target, then this region is used to initialize a new target.

After the association of evidence pixels to targets, the regions of the targets are checked for possible split. A split is allowed if the target is big enough (in terms of number of pixels) and its modeling with a two-dimensional Gaussian density is not good enough. The fitness of the two-dimensional Gaussian model is enumerated by the total probability of the associated pixels. If this falls below 0.5, the target is split in two using k-means.

## 2.3  Kalman Filtering Module

The Kalman filtering module maintains the states of the targets. It creates new targets should it receive a request from the evidence generation module and performs measurement update based on the foreground segments associated to the targets. The states of the targets are fed back to the adaptive background module to adapt the learning rate and the threshold for the PPM binarization. States are also eliminated if they have no foreground segments associated to them for 15 frames.

Every target is approximated by an elliptical disc that is obtained by the mean $\mathbf{m}$ and the covariance matrix $\mathbf{C}$ of the target, i.e. it is described by a single Gaussian.

$$\mathbf{m} = \left[ m_x, m_y \right]^T$$
$$\mathbf{C} = \begin{bmatrix} C_{11} & C_{12} \\ C_{12} & C_{22} \end{bmatrix} \tag{6}$$

If the eigenvectors and the eigenvalues of $\mathbf{C}$ are $\mathbf{v}_i$ and $\lambda_i$ respectively, with $i = 1,2$, then the axes of the ellipse are the $\mathbf{v}_i$ and the radii are $2\sqrt{\lambda_i}$ .

The target states are seven-dimensional; they comprise of the mean of the Gaussian describing the target (horizontal and vertical components), the velocity of the mean (horizontal and vertical components) and the three independent terms of the covariance matrix. Hence the state vector is:

$$\mathbf{s} = \left[ m_x, m_y, v_x, v_y, C_{11}, C_{22}, C_{12} \right]^T \tag{7}$$

The prediction step uses a loose linear dynamic model of constant velocity [17] for the update of the mean position and velocity. As for the update of the three covariance terms, their exact model is non-linear, hence cannot be used with the Kalman tracker; instead of using linearization and an extended Kalman tracker, the covariance terms are modeled as constant. The variations of the velocity and the covariance terms are permitted by the state update variance term. This loose dynamic model permits arbitrary movement of the targets. It is very different to the more elaborate models used for tracking aircraft. Aircraft can perform a limited set of maneuvers that can be learned and be expected by the tracking system. Further, flying aircraft can be modeled as rigid bodies thus strict and multiple dynamic models are appropriate and have been used extensively in Interacting Multiple Model Kalman trackers [18,19]. Unlike aircraft, street vehicles and especially humans have more degrees of freedom for their movement which includes apart from speed and direction changes obstacles arbitrarily, rendering the learning of a strict dynamic model impractical. A strict dynamic model in this case can mislead a tracker to a particular track even in the presence of contradicting evidence [3].

## 2.4  Track Consistency Module

The track consistency module has two roles: Firstly, it manages the tracks for possible elimination and merging. Secondly, it classifies the targets into pedestrians and vehicles. The input to the track management is the states of the Kalman filtering module. The processed tracks are the input to the target type classification.

Track management begins with elimination of tracks when they are:

- very short (in duration),
- not spanning any distance (immobile objects are mostly false positives), and
- mainly existing inside other targets (such targets are usually vehicle fragments inside a larger vehicle bounding box).

Then, adjacent tracks are merged, to avoid identity switches. To do so, the starting and ending points of tracks are considered in time-space. If the temporal proximity is less than 0.6 sec (18 frames) and the spatial proximity is less than 30 pixels, then the tracks are merged.

The decision about the type of target is based on the velocity, size and the distance covered by the target. A vehicle confidence is built using the product of these metrics. If the product is large enough, then the target is considered a vehicle. This approach fails when vehicle tracks are fragmented by some occlusion. Then a track that is too short (in space) can lead to wrong classification.

## 3   CLEAR 2007 Evaluation Results

The outdoor videos that the CLEAR 2007 system is tested on are the same as those of CLEAR 2006. Figure 2 contains typical frames from these recordings, with the detected targets and their tracks superimposed. The recordings are 50 in total depicting two different sites at different whether conditions. The main difference between the two sites is the motion of the vehicles; in site 2 they park/un-park performing slow and jerky

**Fig. 2.** Typical frames from the outdoor recordings with the tracked targets superimposed. Dashed bounding boxes and lines correspond to vehicles and their tracks.

maneuvers. In site 1 there are some videos with adverse whether conditions: wind is moving the background a lot, and possibly the camera a bit, while very bright sunlight casts long shadows. For this reason the results are grouped in these three categories.

The quantitative evaluation of the system is based on the metrics described in [20]. The primary metrics for face tracking are two: The Multiple Object Tracking Precision (MOTP) is the position error for all correctly tracked targets over all frames. It is a measure of how well the system performs when it actually finds the target. There are three kinds of errors for the tracker, false positives, misses and track identity mismatches. They are reported jointly in an accuracy metric, the Multiple Object Tracking Accuracy (MOTA). The MOTA is the residual of the sum of these three error rates from unity. The mean MOTA of the CLEAR 2007 system is compared to that of the CLEAR 2006 in Table 1. Table 2 summarizes the MOTP.

Evidently the MOTA has improved overall and per site, conditions and target type. The only exception is the adverse conditions in site 1, where the MOTA is a bit decreased for pedestrians only. The most impressive performance gains can be found in site 2 for pedestrians and site 1 (adverse conditions) and site 2 for vehicles. The CLEAR 2007 system for vehicle tracing performs similarly across sites and conditions. The same system for pedestrians is still short on performance for site 2. Excluding site 2 for pedestrians, the system tracks equally well pedestrians and vehicles.

**Table 1.** Mean MOTA of the CLEAR 2007 tracking system, compared to that of 2006 for the different sites and conditions

| Recordings | Pedestrians | | Vehicles | |
|---|---|---|---|---|
| | 2006 | 2007 | 2006 | 2007 |
| All | 0.00277 | 0.255 | 0.312 | 0.511 |
| Site 1, normal | 0.526 | 0.574 | 0.517 | 0.556 |
| Site 2 | -0.906 | -0.261 | 0 | 0.456 |
| Site 1, adverse | 0.489 | 0.462 | 0.242 | 0.477 |

Regarding tracking precision, the MOTP of the CLEAR 2007 system for pedestrians has dropped compared to the 2006 one. This is mainly due to the inclusion of more targets, which due to their location are harder to track. Regarding vehicles, precision has increased, indicating a better framing of vehicles by the new system. The MOTA is consistent across sites and target types, with the only exception of the adverse conditions in site 1. The long shadows caused by the bright sunlight in these recordings result to looser framing of the pedestrians.

**Table 2.** Mean MOTP of the CLEAR 2007 tracking system, compared to that of 2006 for the different sites and conditions

| Recordings | Pedestrians | | Vehicles | |
|---|---|---|---|---|
| | 2006 | 2007 | 2006 | 2007 |
| All | 0.525 | 0.434 | 0.385 | 0.434 |
| Site 1, normal | 0.556 | 0.429 | 0.561 | 0.447 |
| Site 2 | 0.461 | 0.456 | 0 | 0.412 |
| Site 1, adverse | 0.577 | 0.395 | 0.491 | 0.432 |

The spread of the MOTA scores is analyzed by the boxplot of the MOTA per target type depicted in Figure 3. Evidently the spread is reduced in the CLEAR 2007 system compared to the 2006 one.

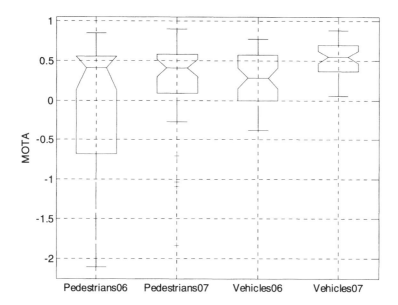

**Fig. 3.** Boxplot comparison of the MOTA per target type in the CLEAR 2006 and 2007 evaluations. The improvement of the median value of the MOTA for pedestrians is not statistically significant, even though the newer system has negative MOTA only for the outliers. The improvement of the median value of the MOTA for vehicles is statistically significant.

## 4   Conclusions

The AIT system for pedestrian and vehicle tracking for CLEAR 2007 evaluations has superior performance to that for the CLEAR 2006. The most important modifications are the way the evidence is associated to the tracked targets, and the track consistency module that manages the tracks and classifies targets into pedestrians and vehicles.

A number of issues remain open. Firstly, the degraded performance on pedestrians for the site 2 recordings needs to be analyzed. To do so, the MOTA score needs to be broken down to its components: the miss, false positive and identity switch rates. Secondly, color information can be incorporated in the evidence generation. Finally, a tracker based on particle filters and the CONDENSATION [21] algorithm can be incorporated in the feedback loop of the filter.

## Acknowledgements

This work is sponsored by the European Union under the integrated project CHIL, contract number 506909. The authors wish to thank the people involved in data collection, annotation and overall organization of the CLEAR 2007 evaluations for providing such a rich test-bed for the presented algorithm.

# References

[1] Waibel, A., Steusloff, H., Stiefelhagen, R., et al.: CHIL: Computers in the Human Interaction Loop. In: 5th International Workshop on Image Analysis for Multimedia Interactive Services (WIAMIS), Lisbon, Portugal (April 2004)

[2] Pnevmatikakis, A., Talantzis, F., Soldatos, J., Polymenakos, L.: Robust Multimodal Audio-Visual Processing for Advanced Context Awareness in Smart Spaces. In: Maglogiannis, I., Karpouzis, K., Bramer, M. (eds.) Artificial Intelligence Applications and Innovations (AIAI 2006), pp. 290–301. Springer, Heidelberg (2006)

[3] Forsyth, D., Ponce, J.: Computer Vision - A Modern Approach, pp. 489–541. Prentice Hall, Englewood Cliffs (2002)

[4] MacCormick, J.: Probabilistic modelling and stochastic algorithms for visual localisation and tracking, PhD Thesis, University of Oxford, section 4.6 (2000)

[5] Jaffré, G., Crouzil, A.: Non-rigid object localization from color model using mean shift. In: International Conference on Image Processing (ICIP 2003), Barcelona, Spain (September 2003)

[6] Ekenel, H., Pnevmatikakis, A.: Video-Based Face Recognition Evaluation in the CHIL Project – Run 1. In: Face and Gesture Recognition, Southampton, UK, pp. 85–90 (March 2006)

[7] McIvor, A.: Background Subtraction Techniques, Image and Vision Computing, New Zealand (2000)

[8] Stauffer, C., Grimson, W.E.L.: Learning patterns of activity using real-time tracking. IEEE Trans. on Pattern Anal. and Machine Intel. 22(8), 747–757 (2000)

[9] KaewTraKulPong, P., Bowden, R.: An Improved Adaptive Background Mixture Model for Real-time Tracking with Shadow Detection. In: Proc. 2nd European Workshop on Advanced Video Based Surveillance Systems (AVBS 2001), (September 2001)

[10] Landabaso, J.L., Pardas, M.: Foreground regions extraction and characterization towards real-time object tracking. In: Renals, S., Bengio, S. (eds.) MLMI 2005. LNCS, vol. 3869, Springer, Heidelberg (2006)

[11] Kalman, R.E.: A New Approach to Linear Filtering and Prediction Problems. Transactions of the ASME – Journal of Basic Engineering 82 (Series D), 35–45 (1960)

[12] Xu, L.-Q., Landabaso, J.L., Pardas, M.: Shadow Removal with Blob-Based Morphological Reconstruction for Error Correction. In: IEEE International Conference on Acoustics, Speech, and Signal Processing (March 2005)

[13] Blackman, S.: Multiple-Target Tracking with Radar Applications, ch. 14. Artech House, Dedham (1986)

[14] Zhang, Z.: A Flexible New Technique for Camera Calibration, Microsoft Research, Technical Report MSR-TR-98-71 (August 2002)

[15] Jones, M., Rehg, J.: Statistical color models with application to skin detection. Computer Vision and Pattern Recognition, 274–280 (1999)

[16] Viola, P., Jones, M.: Rapid Object Detection using a Boosted Cascade of Simple Features. In: IEEE Conf. on Computer Vision and Pattern Recognition (2001)

[17] Herman, S.-M.: A particle filtering approach to joint passive radar tracking and target classification, PhD thesis, University of Illinois at Urbana-Champaign, 51–54 (2002)

[18] Bloom, H.A.P., Bar-Shalom, Y.: The interactive multiple model algorithm for systems with Markovian switching coefficients. IEEE Trans. Automatic Control 33, 780–783 (1988)

[19] Watson, G.A., Blair, W.D.: IMM algorithm for tracking targets that maneuver through coordinated turns. In: Proc. of SPIE Signal and Data Processing of Small Targets, vol. 1698, pp. 236–247 (1992)

[20] Kasturi, R., et al.: Performance evaluation protocol for face, person and vehicle detection & tracking in video analysis and content extraction (VACE-II), University of South Florida (January 2006)

[21] Isard, M., Blake, A.: CONDENSATION - conditional density propagation for visual tracking. Int. J. Computer Vision 29, 5–28 (1998)

# Objective Evaluation of Pedestrian and Vehicle Tracking on the CLEAR Surveillance Dataset

Murtaza Taj, Emilio Maggio, and Andrea Cavallaro

Queen Mary, University of London
Mile End Road, London E1 4NS (United Kingdom)
{murtaza.taj,emilio.maggio,andrea.cavallaro}@elec.qmul.ac.uk
http://www.elec.qmul.ac.uk/staffinfo/andrea/

**Abstract.** Video object detection and tracking in surveillance scenarios is a difficult task due to several challenges caused by environmental variations, scene dynamics and noise introduced by the CCTV camera itself. In this paper, we analyse the performance of an object detector and tracker based on background subtraction followed by a graph matching procedure for data association. The analysis is performed based on the CLEAR dataset. In particular, we discuss a set of solutions to improve the robustness of the detector in case of various types of natural light changes, sensor noise, missed detection and merged objects. The proposed solutions and various parameter settings are analysed and compared based on 1 hour 21 minutes of CCTV surveillance footage and its associated ground truth and the CLEAR evaluation metrics.

## 1 Introduction

People and vehicle tracking in surveillance scenarios is an important requirement for many applications like traffic analysis, behaviour monitoring and event detection. The tracking task is usually performed in two steps: first objects of interest (targets) are detected in each frame of the sequence, next the detections are linked from frame to frame in order to obtain the track of each targets.

In real-world surveillance scenarios the biggest challenges are due to sensor noise, inter-target occlusions and natural environmental changes in the scene. The environmental changes are usually caused by global illumination variations due to the night-and-day cycle, passage of clouds, cast and self shadows, vehicle headlights and street lamps. Also, movement of vegetation due to wind, rain and snow fall can have a major impact on the reliability of an object detector.

### 1.1 Object Detection

Object detectors can be divided into two main classes, namely *background model* based and *object model* based. In the first class the detection is performed by learning a model of the background and then by classifying as objects of interest connected image regions (blobs) that do not fit the model [1,2,3]. This solution is mainly used to detect moving objects in the scene. In the second class the

R. Stiefelhagen et al. (Eds.): CLEAR 2007 and RT 2007, LNCS 4625, pp. 160–173, 2008.
© Springer-Verlag Berlin Heidelberg 2008

detector learns a model of the objects of interest and then the model is used by a classifier that is generally applied to each frame of the sequence [4]. Although this approach is also appropriate in applications with non-static cameras, it can only detect object classes belonging to the training dataset.

A popular *background model* based adaptive method uses Gaussian Mixture Models (GMM) [5,6,7]. The distribution of a colour of each pixel is approximated by a Gaussian mixture where the parameters are updated to cope with slow changes in natural light conditions. However, when an object becomes static it is gradually assimilated into the background model. The update speed for the parametric model is usually a trade-off between a fast update required to cope with sudden illumination changes and a slow update necessary to allow the detection of slow or stopping objects. A possible solution is to modify the learning rate in the region around a moving object depending on its speed [5]. Also, edge information can help detecting objects when they become static [6]. Once the edge structure of the background is learned, a pixel is classified as foreground by comparing its gradient vector with the gradient distribution of the background model.

A major problem with background-based detection algorithms is the difficulty to deal with object interactions, such as object proximity and occlusions. In such a case, two objects that are close are likely to generate a merged foreground region that produces one detection only, instead of multiple detections. However, when an occlusion is partial, projection histograms can be used to split the merged objects [5]. Also, motion prediction based on trajectory data can help to estimate the likelihood of an occlusion thus allowing a single blob to represent two objects [8].

Unlike background model based methods, *object model* based techniques [4,9] learn local representative features of the object appearance and perform detection by searching for similar features in each frame. Edgelets [10] or Haar wavelets [11] are used in Adaboost algorithms as weak object classifiers that combined in a cascade form a strong classifier [12]. Approaches based on learned classifiers are also used after background subtraction to categorize the detections (i.e. to differentiate pedestrians from vehicles) [13]. Similarly, Support Vector Machines using simple object features, such as object size and object width-height ratio, can be used [8].

## 1.2   Object Tracking

Once object detection is performed, data association is needed to link different instances of the same object over time. Generating trajectories requires an estimate of the number of targets and of their position in the scene. As modelling of all the possible object interactions is (in theory) necessary, the tracking problem has a complexity that is exponential with the number of targets in the scene. Joint probabilistic data association filter (JPDA) [14] is a widely used data association technique. An alternative is to model the problem with a graph [15]

(a)                                        (b)

**Fig. 1.** CLEAR dataset scenarios for the pedestrian and vehicle tracking task. (a) Scenario 1: Broadway Church (BC). (b) Scenario 2: Queensway (QW).

where the nodes are associated to the detections and the edges represent the likelihood that two detections in consecutive frames are generated by the same object. Smoothing or target state estimation can be performed by initializing a Kalman Filter for each target [5] and by assuming Gaussianity of the posterior density at every time step. This limiting assumption can be alleviated by using Particle Filters [7]. An alternative to probabilistic methods is Mean Shift (MS), a non-parametric kernel-based method used for target localization [8]. Smoothing and clutter filtering can also be performed prior to data association using a Probability Hypothesis Density (PHD) filter [16], a Bayesian recursive method with linear complexity (with the number of targets). The PHD filter approximates the multi-target statistics by propagating only the first order moments of the posterior probability.

### 1.3  Detection and Tracking Algorithm Under Evaluation

The detection and tracking algorithm we evaluate in this paper [2] performs object detection using a statistical background model [3] and data association using graph matching [15]. Because performance varies depending on different environmental conditions, the testing and evaluation of a detection and tracking algorithm requires a large amount of (annotated) data from real word scenarios. The CLEAR dataset provides a large testbed making it easier to evaluate how different features impact on the final detection and tracking results.

In this paper we analyse the results of a total of 13 runs on the complete CLEAR dataset consisting of 50 sequences with ground truth annotation, for a total of 121.354 frames per run (i.e., approximately 1 hour 21 minutes of recorded video). To reduce the computational time we processed the sequences at a half the original resolution (i.e., 360x240 pixels). The dataset consists of outdoor surveillance sequences of urban areas (Fig. 1) and the annotation provides the bounding boxes of pedestrians and vehicles in the scene. The complexity of the

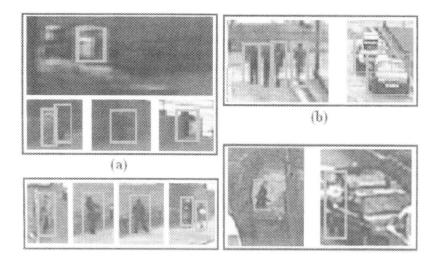

**Fig. 2.** Examples of challenging situations for the pedestrian and vehicle detection and tracking task in the CLEAR dataset (the ground-truth detection are shown in green). (a) Objects in low visibility regions. (b) Objects in close proximity. (c) Objects with low contrast compared to the background. (d) Occluded objects.

CLEAR dataset is related to the challenges discussed earlier in this section. A set of samples illustrating these difficult situations is shown in Fig. 2: objects with low visibility located in the shade generated by a building (Fig. 2 (a)); merged detections (Fig. 2 (b)) due to either the physical closeness or to the camera perspective view; objects with little contrast compared to the background (Fig. 2 (c)); partial and total occlusions (Fig. 2 (d)).

The detection and tracking performance is measured by means of a set of scores (i.e., Multi-Object Detection Precision (MODP), Detection Accuracy (MODA), Tracking Precision (MOTP) and Tracking Accuracy (MOTA)) defined by the CLEAR evaluation protocol [17]. These scores give a weighted summary of the detection and tracking performance in terms of False Positives (FP), False Negatives (FN) and object identity switches.

## 1.4 Organization of the Paper

This paper is organized as follows. Section 2 discusses the improvements in the detection algorithm under natural environmental changes (using background model update and edge analysis), illumination flickering (using spatio-temporal filtering), sensor noise (using noise modelling), miss-detections and clutter (using the PHD filter), and merged objects (using projection histograms). Finally, in Section 3 we discuss the results and we draw the conclusions.

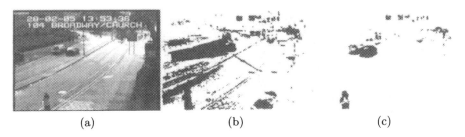

(a)                                  (b)                                  (c)

**Fig. 3.** Comparison of background subtraction results with and without update of the background model. (a) Original scene, (b) sample result without background update and (c) sample result with background update.

## 2   Performance Evaluation

### 2.1   Natural Environmental Changes

As described in Section 1, rapidly changing illumination conditions and inappropriate background modelling can lead to a situation where most of the pixels are classified as foreground pixels (Fig. 3). For background modelling, we use a linear update strategy with a fixed update factor. At time $t$ the background model $I_{t-1}^{(bk)}$ is updated as $I_t^{(bk)} = \alpha I_t + (1 - \alpha) I_{t-1}^{(bk)}$, where $I_{t-1}$ is the previous frame and $\alpha$ is the update factor. The choice of $\alpha$ depends on a trade-off between update capabilities and resilience to merging stopped or slow foreground objects in the background model. Figure 4 shows the performance comparison varying $\alpha$ in the range $[0.00005, 0.005]$. Increasing $\alpha$ from $\alpha = 0.00005$ to $\alpha = 0.0005$ precision and accuracy improve (Fig. 4); FPs are reduced without a significative

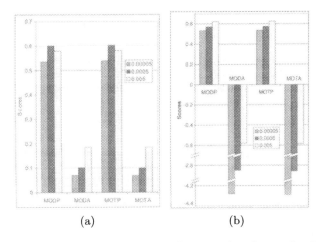

(a)                                  (b)

**Fig. 4.** Comparison of tracking results with different update factors for the background model. (a) Pedestrian tracking. (b) Vehicle tracking.

$\alpha = 0.00005$          $\alpha = 0.0005$          $\alpha = 0.005$

**Fig. 5.** Sample tracking results with different update factors for the background model. A reduction of False Positives is observed by increasing $\alpha$ (from left to right). When $\alpha = 0.005$ no False Positives are returned at the cost of one False Negative.

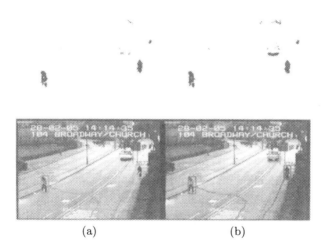

(a)                          (b)

**Fig. 6.** Sample tracking results with and without change detection enhanced by edge analysis (EA). (a) Without edge analysis, (b) with edge analysis.

increase of FNs. However, when increasing $\alpha$ to 0.005, the accuracy improves but the precision decreases for pedestrian tracking. Figure 5 shows how the model update manages to reduce FPs; however, the car that stopped on the road becomes part of the background model thus producing a FN. A value of $\alpha = 0.005$ is therefore a good compromise between accuracy and precision.

To avoid erroneously including slow moving objects into the background, we use Edge Analysis (EA). EA enhances the difference image obtained after background subtraction using an edge detector. In our implementation we compute

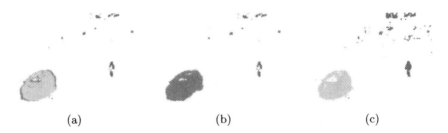

(a)                              (b)                              (c)

**Fig. 7.** Comparison of background subtraction results obtained with and without edge analysis. (a) Without edge analysis the results contain a large number of spurious blobs. (b) With edge analysis the spurious blobs are partially removed, however this generates holes in the pedestrian and an enlarged mask for the vehicle. (c) Superimposed result showing the extra pixels (halo) around the vehicle.

the edges by taking the difference between consecutive frames. Figure 6 shows an example of a correct detection of a vehicle despite it had stopped. The price to pay for these correct detections is an artificial enlargement of the blobs produced by fast moving objects (Fig. 7).

## 2.2  Flickering Illumination

To reduce the effect on the object detector of short-term illumination variations we use a spatio-temporal filtering (STF) on the result of the frame difference. An $n$-frame window is used to smooth the output using past and future information. Figure 8 shows the comparative results using pixel-wise temporal filtering. The improvements in terms of accuracy and precision are of 58% and 4%, respectively, for vehicle detection and of 2% and 7%, respectively, for pedestrian tracking.

## 2.3  Sensor Noise

The video acquisition process introduces noise components due to the CCTV cameras themselves. To reduce the effect of the sensor noise, the simplest solution is to threshold the frame difference, either using luminance information only or using the three colour channels. The problem with using a fixed threshold is the inability of the algorithm to adapt to different illumination conditions and therefore is not appropriate for long sequences or across different sequences, as manual tuning is necessary. An alternative is to model the noise assuming that its distribution is Gaussian [3,18] or Laplacian [19].

In this work we performed object detection assuming additive white Gaussian noise on each frame and using a spatial observation window [3]. To account for camera perspective and to preserve small blobs associated to objects in regions far from the camera (top of the frame), unlike our previous work [2], we learn or adapt $\sigma$ according to the spatial location [1]. We divide the image into three horizontal regions and apply three different multipliers to $\sigma$, namely 0.75, 1 and

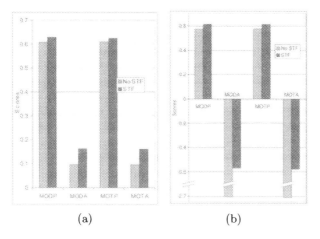

(a)                                    (b)

**Fig. 8.** Comparison of tracking results with and without spatio-temporal filtering (STF). (a) Pedestrian tracking, (b) vehicle tracking. The scores show a significant improvement especially in terms of accuracy.

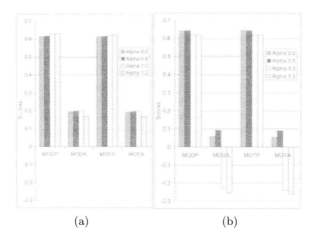

(a)                                    (b)

**Fig. 9.** Comparison of tracking results by changing the model parameter of the sensor noise. (a) Pedestrian tracking. (b) Vehicle tracking.

1.25. The amplitude of the noise ($\sigma = 0.8$) was estimated experimentally. Figure 9 shows the impact of $\sigma$ on vehicle and pedestrian tracking. The value $\sigma = 1.0$ produces better results for pedestrians but also an important performance decrease in terms of accuracy for vehicle tracking. Figure 10 shows sample detection results: the highest value of $\sigma$ does not allow the detection of the pedestrians, whereas with $\sigma = 0.8$ the classification of most of the pixels belonging to the object is correct.

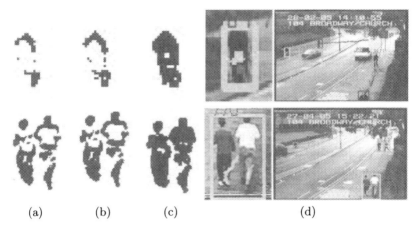

    (a)        (b)        (c)              (d)

**Fig. 10.** Comparison of background masks of pedestrians by changing the model of the sensor noise. (a) $\sigma = 1.2$, (b) $\sigma = 1.0$, (c) $\sigma = 0.8$. (d) Sample tracking results.

### 2.4   Filtering Clutter and Miss-Detections

To mange the intrinsic exponential complexity of the multi-target tracking problem we recently proposed to use the PHD filter, a tracking algorithm that achieves linear complexity by propagating only the first order statistics of the multi-target posterior. This spatio-temporal filter is able to model birth and death of targets, background clutter (i.e., FP), miss detections (i.e., FN) and the spatial noise on the detections. Figure 11 shows the comparative results of introducing the PHD spatio-temporal filtering stage at the detection level. In vehicle tracking, the PHD filter allows for a 6% improvement in accuracy and

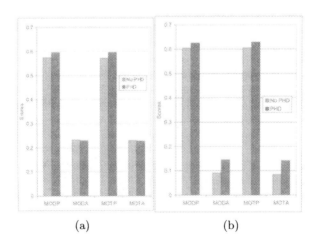

           (a)                    (b)

**Fig. 11.** Comparison of tracking results with and without PHD Filter. (a) Pedestrian tracking: enabling the PHD filter the tracker achieves higher precision scores. (b) Vehicle tracking: the tracker achieves both higher precision and accuracy scores.

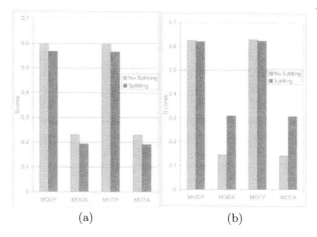

(a)                                (b)

**Fig. 12.** Comparison of tracking results obtained by splitting the blobs associated to more than one target using projection histograms. (a) Pedestrian tracking: small decrease in the scores. (b) Vehicle tracking: large accuracy improvement.

2% improvement in precision. In pedestrian tracking, there is 2% increase in precision whereas there is no significant change in accuracy.

## 2.5   Merged Objects

Multiple objects in proximity to each other may be grouped into one blob only by background subtraction based detection algorithms. In order to maintain a separate identity for these objects, a possible solution is to analyse the histograms

**Fig. 13.** Sample tracking results obtained with and without blob spitting using projection histograms. Top row: without blob splitting. Bottom row: with blob splitting.

**Fig. 14.** Sample tracking results on Broadway Church (BC) and Queensway(QW) scenarios

of the pixels of a blob projected on one of the two Cartesian coordinates [20]. This solution assumes that the modes of the histogram correspond to the different pedestrians that can be split by separating the modes.

Figure 12 shows the tracking performance comparison with and without the use of the projection histograms based blob splitting. The impact of this procedure on the scores is biased by the vehicle-pedestrian classification. As the classification depends on the width-height ratio of the bounding boxes, the splitting allows to assign the correct label to group of pedestrians and therefore the accuracy of vehicle tracking increases by 16%. However, previous errors assigned to the vehicle tracking scores are now transferred to pedestrian tracking. An example of tracks obtained with and without splitting is shown in Figure 13. The merged blobs associated to the two pedestrians on the right are constantly split by analysing the projection histograms.

To conclude, Fig. 14 shows sample detection and tracking results generated by the proposed framework on the BC and QW scenarios under different illumination conditions.

## 2.6   Failure Modes

Figure 15 shows three failure modalities of the proposed tracker. In Fig. 15 (a and b) two objects are merged and the use of the projection histograms based

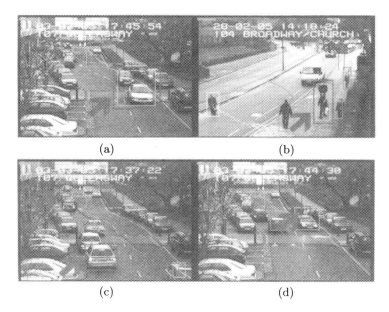

(a)                                    (b)

(c)                                    (d)

**Fig. 15.** Sample failure modalities on the CLEAR Broadway Church (BC) and Queensway (QW) scenarios (red boxes indicate the areas of the frame where the failure occurred). Top row: merged objects. Bottom left: missed detections caused by small objects. Bottom-right: object incorporated into the background model.

splitting does not help as the objects are not merged along the horizontal axis. A possible solution could be the use of a body part detector to estimate the number of targets in a blob. Figure 15 (c) shows missed detections caused by (i) static, (ii) small and (iii) similar-to-the-background objects. Figure 15(d) shows a failure due to an occlusion. To overcome this problem, information from multiple cameras could help disambiguating the occlusion.

## 3   Conclusions

In this paper we analysed major challenges of video tracking in real-world surveillance scenarios. Starting from this analysis and a well-tested tracking platform, we evaluated the inclusion of a set of new features into the framework. The main added features are a background model update strategy, a spatio-temporal filtering, edge analysis, a PHD filtering step and splitting blobs containing nearby objects by means of projection histograms. The evaluation was performed on the CLEAR dataset and showed that the new features improve the accuracy and precision of the tracker by 76% and 50%, respectively. Further work includes the improvement of the vehicle-pedestrian classification step by means of a dedicated object classifier.

## Acknowledgements

The authors acknowledge the support of the UK Engineering and Physical Sciences Research Council (EPSRC), under grant EP/D033772/1.

## References

1. Stauffer, C., Grimson, W.: Learning patterns of activity using real-time tracking. IEEE Trans. Pattern Anal. Machine Intell. 22, 747–757 (2000)
2. Taj, M., Maggio, E., Cavallaro, A.: Multi-feature graph-based object tracking. In: Stiefelhagen, R., Garofolo, J.S. (eds.) CLEAR 2006. LNCS, vol. 4122, pp. 190–199. Springer, Heidelberg (2007)
3. Cavallaro, A., Ebrahimi, T.: Interaction between high-level and low-level image analysis for semantic video object extraction. EURASIP Journal on Applied Signal Processing 6, 786–797 (2004)
4. Wu, B., X., Kuman, V., Nevatia, R.: Evaluation of USC Human Tracking System for Surveillance Videos. In: Stiefelhagen, R., Garofolo, J.S. (eds.) CLEAR 2006. LNCS, vol. 4122, pp. 183–189. Springer, Heidelberg (2007)
5. Pnevmatikakis, A., Polymenakos, L., Mylonakis, V.: The ait outdoors tracking system for pedestrians and vehicles. In: Stiefelhagen, R., Garofolo, J.S. (eds.) CLEAR 2006. LNCS, vol. 4122, pp. 171–182. Springer, Heidelberg (2007)
6. Zhai, Y., Berkowitz, P., Miller, A., Shafique, K., Vartak, A., White, B., Shah, M.: Multiple vehicle tracking in surveillance video. In: Stiefelhagen, R., Garofolo, J.S. (eds.) CLEAR 2006. LNCS, vol. 4122, pp. 200–208. Springer, Heidelberg (2007)
7. Abd-Almageed, W., Davis, L.: Robust appearance modeling for pedestrian and vehicle tracking. In: Stiefelhagen, R., Garofolo, J.S. (eds.) CLEAR 2006. LNCS, vol. 4122, pp. 209–215. Springer, Heidelberg (2007)
8. Song, X., Nevatia, R.: Robust vehicle blob tracking with split/merge handling. In: Stiefelhagen, R., Garofolo, J.S. (eds.) CLEAR 2006. LNCS, vol. 4122, pp. 216–222. Springer, Heidelberg (2007)
9. Viola, P., Jones, M.: Rapid object detection using a boosted cascade of simple features. In: Proc. of IEEE Conf. on Computer Vision and Pattern Recognition, Kauai, Hawaii, pp. 511–518 (2001)
10. Wu, B., Nevatia, R.: Detection of multiple, partially occluded humans in a single image by bayesian combination of edgelet part detectors. In: Proc. of IEEE Int. Conf. on Computer Vision, pp. 90–97. IEEE Computer Society Press, Washington (2005)
11. Viola, P., Jones, M., Snow, D.: Detecting pedestrians using patterns of motion and appearance. In: Proc. of Int. Conf. on Computer Vision Systems, vol. 2, pp. 734–741 (2003)
12. Friedman, J., Hastie, T., Tibshirani, R.: Additive logistic regression: a statistical view of boosting. Technical report, Department of Statistics, Stanford University (1998)
13. Munder, S., Gavrila, D.: An experimental study on pedestrian classification. IEEE Transactions on Pattern Analysis and Machine Intelligence 28(11), 1863–1868 (2006)
14. Herman, S.: A Particle Filtering Approach to Joint Passive Radar Tracking and Target Classification. PhD thesis, University of Illinois at Urbana Champaign (2005)

15. Shafique, K., Shah, M.: A noniterative greedy algorithm for multiframe point correspondence. IEEE Trans. Pattern Anal. Machine Intell. 27, 51–65 (2005)
16. Maggio, E., Piccardo, E., Regazzoni, C., Cavallaro, A.: Particle phd filter for multi-target visual tracking. In: Proc. of IEEE Int. Conf. on Acoustics, Speech, and Signal Processing, Honolulu, USA (2007)
17. Kasturi, R.: Performance evaluation protocol for face, person and vehicle detection & tracking in video analysis and content extraction (VACE-II). Computer Science & Engineering University of South Florida, Tampa (2006)
18. Li, W., Unbehauen, J.L.R.: Wavelet based nonlinear image enhancement for gaussian and uniform noise. In: Proc. of IEEE Int. Conf. on Image Processing, Chicago, Illinois, USA, vol. 1, pp. 550–554 (1998)
19. Aiazzi, B., Baronti, S., Alparone, L.: Multiresolution adaptive filtering of signal-dependent noise based on a generalized laplacian pyramid. In: Proc. of IEEE Int. Conf. on Image Processing, Washington, DC, USA, vol. 1, pp. 381–384 (1997)
20. Hu, W., Hu, M., Zhou, X., Lou, J.: Principal axis-based correspondence between multiple cameras for people tracking. IEEE Trans. Pattern Anal. Machine Intell. 28(4), 663 (2006)

# Person and Vehicle Tracking in Surveillance Video

Andrew Miller, Arslan Basharat, Brandyn White,
Jingen Liu, and Mubarak Shah

Computer Vision Lab at University of Central Florida

## 1 Introduction

This evaluation for person and vehicle tracking in surveillance presented some new challenges. The dataset was large and very high-quality, but with difficult scene properties involving illumination changes, unusual lighting conditions, and complicated occlusion of objects.

Since this is a well-researched scenario [1], our submission was based primarily on our existing projects for automated object detection and tracking in surveillance. We also added several new features that are practical improvements for handling the difficulties of this dataset.

## 2 Previous Approach

Our previous efforts in automated surveillance led to the development of the KNIGHT system[2], which uses a three-stage process. First, the frame is segmented into foreground regions by maintaining an adaptive model of the background appearance[3], [4]. Second, the correspondence between foreground regions in adjacent frames are found using motion and appearance cues[5]. Third, the objects are classified as either vehicles or people by analyzing a Recurrent Motion Image (RMI) that indicates the periodic motion of a person walking.

## 3 Illumination Change Detection

In this dataset, abrupt illumination changes frequently occur when clouds move and obscure the sunlight. This causes a large portion of the frame to be mislabeled as foreground. If the illumination change is sufficiently rapid, then the incorrect foreground regions will remain a problem even for a while after the scene reaches a new steady state.

There is a direct tradeoff between the sensitivity to changing appearance because of moving foreground objects and the robustness to change because of a varying background. This balance is controlled by the learning rate parameter. Trying to increase this parameter to account for illumination changes will tend to cause slow-moving or low-contrast objects to disappear into the background.

R. Stiefelhagen et al. (Eds.): CLEAR 2007 and RT 2007, LNCS 4625, pp. 174–178, 2008.

Our proposed approach to this problem is to detect the occurrence of a global illumination change and temporarily increase the learning rate so that the system recovers quickly once the scene reaches a new steady state. This has the advantage that the system will not suffer in the case of constant illumination, yet a brief change won't cause long-lasting problems.

The challenge in detecting a global illumination change is that they often occur over an inconvenient time interval of about one second, which is too sudden for the background model to update but too gradual to detect using the foreground segmentation image alone. We exploit the observation that such an illumination change will cause a smooth intensity change over a period of 15 to 20 frames and that the change is approximately linear and monotonic. Thus for each pixel, we perform a linear regression of intensity over a temporal window of 20 frames. Pixels with a high correlation coefficient signify an illumination change, while a low correlation coefficient indicates change due to random fluctuation with no monotonic trend. This coefficient is summed over the entire image and then thresholded to trigger a temporary increase in the learning rate. An example of frames and correlation coefficients before and during an illumination change are shown in Figure 1.

(a)          (b)

(c)          (d)

**Fig. 1.** Original frames (left column) and correlation-coefficient maps (right column), before (top) and during (bottom) an illumination change. The illumination change from cloud movement causes an increase in the correlation coefficient of a large number of pixels.

## 4  Particle Swarm Optimization

Nearly all vision algorithms have several adjustable parameters that affect (some-times significantly) performance. Although there are often guidelines or rules-of-thumb for setting typical values, these parameters are normally tuned manually - by trial and error - which is tedious and leads to possibly suboptimal results.

Our proposed solution to this problem is to use an automated machine-learning process [6] to choose the best parameter values for a training sequence. The first step is to prepare ground-truth segmentation images images for approx-imately 5 key frames in a training sequence. Then the background subtraction algorithm is automatically run dozens of times with different combinations of parameters, and scored for how well its output matches the ground truth.

Although theoretically any optimization technique could be used to choose new parameter values (such as gradient descent or simulated annealing), we choose Particle Swarm Optimization because it performs consistently well with few iterations and lots of highly nonlinear parameters.

The Particle Swarm Optimization method involves treating each parameter as a spatial dimension. A specific configuration of parameter values is a position vector in this space. A set of about 10 and 50 particles is initialized, each with a position, velocity, and acceleration vector. In each iteration, the background subtraction is run on the training sequence with each of the particles indicating a parameter configuration. Then the particles are updated with swarm motion equations that combines 'cognitive' and 'social' forces to move each particle towards its own best location and towards the globally best location, with added random entropy:

$$v_t = wv_{t-1} + c_1 r_1 (p_i - x_{t-1}) + c_2 r_2 (p_g - x_{t-1}),$$

$$x_t = x_{t-1} + v_t,$$

where $w$ is an 'inertial' weight, $p_i$ is the particle's previous best location, $p_g$ is the globally best location of the entire population, $r_1$ and $r_2$ are randomly generated noise, and $c_1$ is the cognitive weight, $c_2$ is the social weight.

## 5  Person and Vehicle Classification

The RMI classifier used in KNIGHT depends heavily on precise foreground seg-mentation and object localization. In order to be more robust with respect to partial occlusion and clutter, we chose to use a classification method based on appearance models instead.

Edge histograms are known as an effective cue for object recognition. In our project, we compute the local edge orientation histogram for each chip using the following steps:

1. Convolution with Sobel filters. Sobel filters are applied to each chip in eight directions as shown in Figure 2. The filter that produces strongest response is chosen as the gradient direction of the pixel.

2. Edge pixels detection. The pixels whose magnitude of gradient is larger $\tau$ (in our experiment, it is $0.30 * Gmax$, where $Gmax$ is the maximum magnitude of the edge pixels) are considered as edge pixels.
3. Edge Histogram computation. The edge histogram has eight bins counting the number of edge pixels in eight directions corresponding to the Sobel filters.

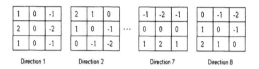

| 1 | 0 | -1 |
|---|---|----|
| 2 | 0 | -2 |
| 1 | 0 | -1 |

Direction 1

| 2 | 1 | 0 |
|---|---|----|
| 1 | 0 | -1 |
| 0 | -1 | -2 |

Direction 2

···

| -1 | -2 | -1 |
|----|----|----|
| 0 | 0 | 0 |
| 1 | 2 | 1 |

Direction 7

| 0 | -1 | -2 |
|---|----|----|
| 1 | 0 | -1 |
| 2 | 1 | 0 |

Direction 8

**Fig. 2.** Oriented Sobel filters

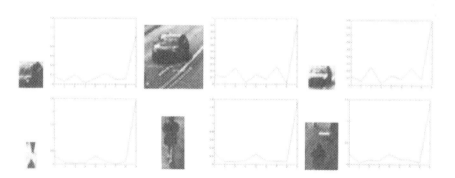

**Fig. 3.** The examples of features of cars or person. The first row shows there different car chips with similar feature distributions. The second row shows three examples of person chips with their feature plots.

Other than the Edge Histogram, another feature we apply is the aspect ratio, which is the height-to-width ratio of the detected chip. Our observation is that vehicles have a generally wide aspect ratio while people have a narrow and tall aspect ratio.

Finally, each detected chip is represented by a nine-dimensional feature vector, which contains eight dimensions of edge histogram and one dimension of aspect ratio. Figure 3 shows some example of chips with their corresponding features. The edge histogram for cars are strong in several directions, while people have mostly only horizontal edges.

Once feature vectors are constructed, we use a linear Support Vector Machine (SVM) to classify each chip. A training set of chips from people and from cars is initially used to find the ideal hyperplane in this nine-dimensional feature space that separates the car vectors from the person vectors.

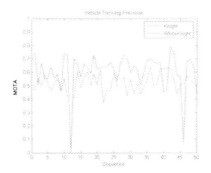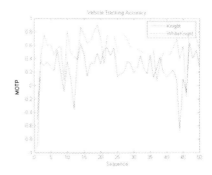

**Fig. 4.** Vehicle tracking results for Knight (using SVM classification) and WhiteKnight (automatic parameter tuning and illumination change detection). Since neither system is better in both accuracy (left) and precision (right), it will take more experiments to evaluate these changes.

## 6    Conclusion

We have presented several extensions to our previous system for object detection and tracking. Ultimately we did not have enough time to fully evaluate our new work, so we submitted two separate system results: one with the SVM classification (Knight), and the other with automated parameter tuning and illumination change compensation (WhiteKnight). As shown in Figure 4, WhiteKnight received a higher precision score, but Knight received a higher accuracy score. It will take further analysis and possibly the generation of a ROC curve to arrive at a meaningful assessment of these.

## References

1. Yilmaz, A., Javed, O., Shah, M.: Object tracking: A survey. ACM Comput. Surv. (2006)
2. Javed, O., Shah, M.: Tracking and object classification for automated surveillance. In: Heyden, A., Sparr, G., Nielsen, M., Johansen, P. (eds.) ECCV 2002. LNCS, vol. 2353, pp. 343–357. Springer, Heidelberg (2002)
3. Javed, O., Shafique, K., Shah, M.: A hierarchical approach to robust background subtraction using color and gradient information. In: IEEE Workshop on Motion and Video Computing, Orlando (2002)
4. Sheikh, Y., Shah, M.: Bayesian modeling of dynamic scenes for object detection. PAMI (2005)
5. Shafique, K., Shah, M.: A noniterative greedy algorithm for multiframe point correspondence. IEEE Trans. Pattern Anal. Mach. Intell. (2005)
6. White, B., Shah, M.: Automatically tuning background subtraction parameters using particle swarm optimization. In: IEEE International Conference on Multimedia and Expo., Beijing, China (2007)

# UMD_VDT, an Integration of Detection and Tracking Methods for Multiple Human Tracking

Son Tran, Zhe Lin, David Harwood, and Larry Davis

UMIACS
University of Maryland
College Park, MD 20740, USA

**Abstract.** We integrate human detection and regional affine invariant feature tracking into a robust human tracking system. First, foreground blobs are detected using background subtraction. The background model is built with a local predictive model to cope with large illumination changes. Detected foreground blobs are then used by a box tracker to establish stable tracks of moving objects. Human detection hypotheses are detected using a combination of both shape and region information through a hierarchical part-template matching method. Human detection results are then used to refine tracks for moving people. Track refinement, extension and merging are carried out with a robust tracker that is based on regional affine invariant features. We show experimental results for the separate components as well as the entire system.

## 1 Overview of UMD_VDT

Most human activity analysis and understanding approaches in visual surveillance take human tracks as their input. Establishing accurate human tracks is therefore very important in many visual surveillance systems. Even though it has been long studied, accurate human tracking is still a challenge due to a number of reasons such as shape and pose variation, occlusion and object grouping. We describe a multiple object tracking system that is an integration of human detection and general object tracking approaches. Our system detects people automatically using a probabilistic human detector and tracks them as they move through the scene. It is able to resolve partial occlusion and merging, especially when people walk in groups.

Figure 1 shows the diagrammatic overview of our system. It consists of three main components: background subtraction, human detection and human tracking. Their details will be discussed in the next sections (Section 2, 3, and 4). In this section, we describe the overall procedure that is built on top of these components.

### 1.1 Algorithm Integration

*Foreground Detection*
First, background subtraction (section 2) is applied to detect foreground blobs. To improve the detection rate, we combine background subtraction with a

R. Stiefelhagen et al. (Eds.): CLEAR 2007 and RT 2007, LNCS 4625, pp. 179–190, 2008.

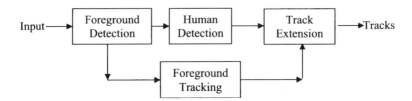

**Fig. 1.** Main components of our human tracking system

short-term frame difference. The background subtraction module is designed to cope with global illumination changes. However, in visual surveillance, lighting changes sometime happen at the local scale such as when a truck casts a large scattered shadow on streets and pavements. In such cases, subtraction from the long-term, trained background model will likely produce many false alarms while frame differencing does not.

The resulting detected foreground boxes are connected to form preliminary tracks, $PT$. Unstable tracks are then eliminated.

*Box Filtering*
The set of these preliminary tracks, $PT$, corresponds to different moving objects in the scene (humans, human groups, cars, car group, etc.). A cascade of filters is applied to eliminate irrelevant moving objects retaining only tracks that correspond to human or human groups. A filter on *location* classifies object position into road and non-road regions. It is trained for each view, for example, based on cars' position. A filter on *object shape* classifies objects into humans, human groups or cars. Its decision is based on human width and height ratio. This filter gives high detection rates for single-person boxes even when shadow is significant. A filter on *track properties* makes the distinction between the tracks of cars and human groups. Their tracks often differ in a number of aspects. For example, cars often move along the road with high velocity, while humans rarely walk in groups along the road. Stacking these filters in a decision tree-like order, we have a composite filter that outputs a set of tracks, $FT$, that correspond to only single humans or human groups. Further elimination of false alarms can be done in combination with human detection described below.

*Human Detection*
In the tracks, $FT$, each individual human in a human group has not yet been segmented and localized accurately. Localization inaccuracy may also exist in a track of single person when there is a strong shadow associated with it. To resolve these problems, a human detection technique (section 3) is applied.

It is difficult to apply the frame-by-frame object detection directly to tracking since the detection task is often time consuming and can only be performed at very low frame rates (e.g. on every fifth or tenth frame of the original sequences). Furthermore, the image quality in surveillance videos is typically low, making it difficult to achieve high detection and low false alarm rates at the same time for every frame.

Here we used the frame-by-frame detection result, $D$, to refine the set $FT = \{FT_i\}$ obtained in the previous section. Let $D_i = \{D_i^1, \ldots, D_i^n\} \in D$ denotes the set of relevant detected humans for $FT_i$. Each $D_i^j$ may be empty or is set of detected boxes that significantly intersect $FT_i$ at time $j$. Algorithm 1 describes the integration of detection results into tracking.

---

**Algorithm 1.** Track Refinement using Human Detection

---

Input: set of tracks $FT$ and human detection result $D$
Output: set of refined tracks $RT$

$RT = \emptyset$
For every track $FT_i \in FT$

1. Compute $D_i \in D$, the set of relevant detected human boxes for $FT_i$.
2. $RT_i = \emptyset$
3. *Forward Tracking*
   From frame $t$ to $t + 1$,
   - For every track $tr \in RT_i$, extend $tr$ to frame $t + 1$, using the tracker in section 4. Stop at the end of $FT_i$.
   - Merge any detected box in $D_i^{t+1}$ that intersects $tr$ significantly.
   - For each un-mergeable box, start a new track $tr$ and add it to $RT_i$.
4. *Backward Tracking*
   - For each track $tr \in RT_i$, using the tracker in section 4, track backward, starting from the first frame in $tr$. Stop at the beginning of $T_i$.
5. Add $RT_i$ to $RT$.

Merge similar tracks in $RT$.

---

In surveillance, it is very common that people with similar appearance walk close to each other. In such cases, accurate object state prediction to limit the tracker's searching range plays an important role in reducing track or identity switch. Therefore, in the forward and backward tracking steps in Algorithm 1, a prediction step is added to the tracker described in section 4. The prediction is based on the movement of the bounding box in $T_i$ and the relative location of the tracked human w.r.t. this bounding box. Since the prediction is only possible within the duration of $T_i$, at this stage, we stop the tracker at the temporal boundary of $T_i$.

In the last step of Algorithm 1, two tracks can be merged if they are not temporally far away from each other and spatially overlap each other. The merging process stops when there are no two tracks that can be merged.

*Track Extension*
Each refined track $RT_i \in RT$ is extended within the temporal limit of the original track $FT_i \in FT$. Usually each $RT_i$ is quite stable and long. Therefore, the velocity of the tracked object can be estimated reliably. Using this estimation as

the prediction on object dynamics, we extend $RT_i$ using the tracker in Section 4. Similar tracks are then merged to form the set of final tracks.

## 1.2   Results

Figure 2 shows sample results of our tracking system on some sequence from the VACE-CLEAR 2007 tracking evaluation dataset. Foreground detection, human detection, and final localization are shown overlaid. As we can see, foreground detection results (green boxes) give rough locations of moving objects in the scene. The human detection results (blue boxes) give better estimation but with occasional misses (Figure 2, left, top). Based on the human detection, the tracker is able to track each individual more accurately even when they walk in groups (Figure 2, left, bottom). Figure 3 shows results from another sequence. Figure 3.b shows some false alarms when the shape of a detected foreground bolob is similar to a human. For this sequence, there is no detection result in the neighborhood

**Fig. 2.** Results on sequence *PVTRA102a01* (VACE-CLEAR07). Foreground detection, human detection, and final localization are show respectively in green, blue and red. On the left are some blowups and on the right is a full view.

a)frame ♯1498                   b)frame ♯1748                   c)frame ♯4999

**Fig. 3.** Results on sequence *PVTRA201c05* (VACE-CLEAR07). Foreground detection, human detection(if present), and final localization are show respectively in green, blue and red.

of frame ♯4999 (fifty frames before and after), but the system was still able to track the object accurately (Figure 3.b).

# 2  Background Subtraction

## 2.1  Introduction

Common approaches to background modeling construct a probability distribution for a pixel's color values or for some local image features. A single or multi-modal distribution such as a Gaussian or mixture of Gaussians ([1]) may be used depending on levels of noise and complexity of the background. Approaches proposed in the literature have difficulties in handling fast response to illumination change. Adaptation using Kalman filter approach ([2]) or caches ([3]) inevitably leads to lag in accommodating to illumination change during which the system is effectively "blind".

Here, we employ the VQ approach ([3]) to background modeling, and motivate the use of a locally linear model to predict and update pixel color codebook values. Our approach is able to deal with large illumination changes using only a small number of codewords per pixel.

## 2.2  Background Modeling Using the Codebook Representation

There are two main observations that motivate our approach. First, in natural outdoor scenes, different surfaces have different irradiant responses when the illumination is changed. To accurately adapt the background model to such changes, a single global set of adaptive parameters, such as suggested by [4], is insufficient. Instead, for each pixel we use a separate set of parameter values that are updated independently as lighting changes. Second, as lighting changes, the color values of individual pixels do not lie on a color line passing through the origin of color space, as assumed by [3] and others. Since camera sensors have limited range [0-255], the response is necessarily saturated at the limits so that locally, changes in color as a function of illumination change will not point

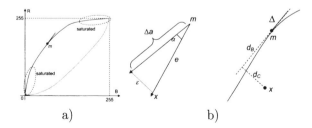

**Fig. 4.** a) Illustration on R-B plane of the response of the camera sensor to changes in lighting intensity. b) Prediction errors and distances in brightness $d_C$ and $d_B$ in color. $\Delta$ is the local tangent and $m$ is the mean at a pixel. $a$ is the global gain. $x$ denotes the observation.

toward the color space origin. This is illustrated in Figure 4. At low light levels all pixels fade to black. At sufficiently high light levels they all tend to white. Between those two extremes they follow a curved trajectory between black and white depending on the reflectance properties of the corresponding surface point. We point out that reaching saturation is quite common, especially for scenes that are under direct and strong sunlight. Models for background adaptation under illumination change have to take a typical camera's non-linear responses into account.

**Background Model Construction.** We construct a locally linear model to update codeword colors as illumination changes. So, at each pixel, we use a tangent vector to that pixel's color trajectory to represent the rate and direction of its color variation. As the lighting changes, both are adjusted to better model the local behavior of a pixel's color.

The overview of our background model adaptation is as follows.

- For each pixel, a codeword model is learned during a training period. Each codeword contains a principle color values and a tangent vector.
- When scene illumination changes, the change is measured through a gain in a global index value. For each codeword, this gain, in combination with the mean and tangent of the codeword, produces a prediction of the codeword color under the changing lighting condition. A new codeword is created if no prediction is close to the observation.

With some additional updating based on secondary technical considerations, these predictions constitute our updated background model.

**Foreground Detection.** Scene illumination will, of course, also change after training the codebook is completed. Therefore, we keep updating the background model in parallel with foreground detection. The algorithm is the same as above with the exception that when the observation for a pixel is far off from its prediction, instead of creating a new code word, we mark that pixel as belonging to the foreground.

## 2.3   Results

We shown here an experiment on an outdoor sequence where the lighting changed extensively during both the training and detection periods. The first 150 frames are used for training. No foreground objects are present during that period. Figure 5 shows the results on three frames from the testing sequence. As we can see, with the same distance threshold, both of the approaches in [3] and [2] produce more false alarms than ours. Note that reducing $r_D$ to exclude false alarms also leads to a reduction in detection rate (i.e. producing more holes in the foreground regions). For example, in [3]'s result for frame ♯400, the foreground (true positive) starts to disappear while the background (false alarms) has not been completely eliminated yet. Note that increasing the adaptation rate also does not necessarily lead to improvements in detection.

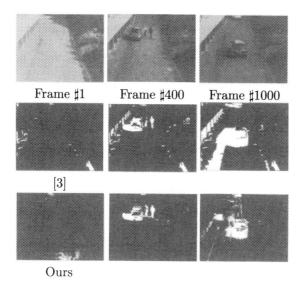

Frame ♯1        Frame ♯400        Frame ♯1000

[3]

Ours

**Fig. 5.** The first row shows three frames of the testing sequence. The remaining rows respectively show the result of [3] and our methods on those three frames.

## 3   Human Detection

### 3.1   Introduction

Local part-based approaches [5][6] detect human parts first and assemble the detected parts for final classification. Global template-based approaches, e.g. [7], use a more direct global shape matching method for human detection. Blob-based approaches [8][9] use an MCMC-based optimization to segment foreground blobs into humans.

### 3.2   Human Detection

**Bayesian MAP Framework.** We formulate the human detection problem as a Bayesian MAP optimization: $\mathbf{c}^* = \arg\max_{\mathbf{c}} P(\mathbf{c}|I)$, where $I$ denotes the original image, $\mathbf{c} = \{\mathbf{h}_1, \mathbf{h}_2, ...\mathbf{h}_n\}$ denotes a human configuration (a set of human hypotheses). $\{\mathbf{h}_i = (\mathbf{x}_i, \theta_i)\}$ denotes an individual hypothesis which consists of foot position $\mathbf{x}_i$ and corresponding model parameters $\theta_i$. Using Bayes Rule, the equation can be decomposed into a joint likelihood and a prior as follows: $P(\mathbf{c}|I) = \frac{P(I|\mathbf{c})P(\mathbf{c})}{P(I)} \propto P(I|\mathbf{c})P(\mathbf{c})$. We assume a uniform prior, hence the MAP problem reduces to maximizing the joint likelihood.

The joint likelihood $P(I|\mathbf{c})$ is modelled as: $P(I|\mathbf{c}) = P_{ol}(\mathbf{c})P_{cl}(\mathbf{c})$, where $P_{ol}(\mathbf{c})$ and $P_{cl}(\mathbf{c})$ denote object-level likelihood and configuration-level likelihood, respectively. Object-level likelihood is further expressed as a product of likelihoods of each hypothesis: $P_{ol}(\mathbf{c}) = \prod_{i=1}^{n} P_{ol}(\mathbf{h}_i) = \prod_{i=1}^{n} P_{ol}(I|\mathbf{x}, \theta_i)$. Also, configuration-level likelihood is calculated as the global coverage density of the

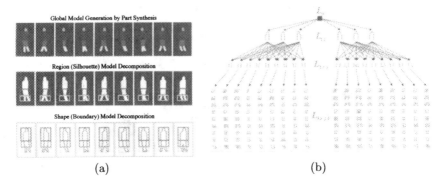

(a)                                        (b)

**Fig. 6.** An illustration of the part-template tree and its construction process. (a) Generation of global shape models by part synthesis, decomposition of global silhouette and boundary models into region and shape part-templates, (b) Part-template tree characterized by both shape and region information.

---

**Algorithm 2.** Hierarchical Part-Template Matching

---

For each pixel $\mathbf{x}$ in the image, we adaptively search over scales distributed around the expected human size $(w_0, h_0)$ estimated by foot-to-head plane homography and an average aspect ratio $\Delta$.

**1)** We match the set of head-torso shape templates with edges and estimate the maximum likelihood solution $\theta_{ht}^*$.

**2)** Based on the part-template estimate $\theta_{ht}^*$, we match the upper leg template models and the lower leg template models with edges to find the maximum likelihood solution for leg layers $\theta_{ul}^*$ and $\theta_{ll}^*$.

**3)** Finally, we estimate global human shapes by combining the maximum likelihood estimates of the local part-templates, and return the synthesized model parameters $\theta^* = \{\theta_{ht}^*, \theta_{ul}^*, \theta_{ll}^*\}$.

---

binary foreground regions: $P_{cl}(\mathbf{c}) = \frac{\Gamma(\mathbf{c})}{\Gamma_{fg}} = \frac{\bigcup_{i=1}^{n} \Gamma(\mathbf{h}_i)}{\Gamma_{fg}}$, where, $\Gamma_{fg}$ denotes the foreground coverage, and $\Gamma(\mathbf{h}_i)$ denotes the coverage by the hypothesis $\mathbf{h}_i$.

**Hierarchical Part-Template Matching.** We first generate a flexible set of global shape models by part synthesis (Figure 6(a)). Next, silhouettes and boundaries are extracted from the set of generated global shape models and decomposed into three parts (head-torso, upper legs and lower legs). The part parameters are denoted as $\theta_{ht}$, $\theta_{ul}$ and $\theta_{ll}$, where each parameter represents the index of the corresponding part in the part-template tree. Then, the tree-structured part-template hierarchy is constructed by placing the decomposed part regions and boundary fragments into a tree as illustrated in Figure 6(b).

For a part-template $j \in ht, ul, ll$, we denote the overall part-template likelihood as $P_{ol}(I|\mathbf{x}, \theta_j)$, the chamfer matching score as the shape likelihood $P_{ol}^s(I|\mathbf{x}, \theta_j)$, and the part foreground coverage density as the region likelihood $P_{ol}^r(I|\mathbf{x}, \theta_j)$. Given the binary foreground image $I_f$ and Canny edge map $I_e$, the likelihoods are calculated as follows:

$$P_{ol}(I|\mathbf{x},\theta_j) = P_{ol}(I_e, I_f|\mathbf{x},\theta_j) = P_{ol}^s(I_e|\mathbf{x},\theta_j)P_{ol}^r(I_f|\mathbf{x},\theta_j), \tag{1}$$

$$P_{ol}^s(I|\mathbf{x},\theta_j) = P_{ol}^s(I_e|\mathbf{x},\theta) = D_{chamfer}(\mathbf{x}, T_{\theta_j}), \tag{2}$$

$$P_{ol}^r(I_f|\mathbf{x},\theta_j) = \gamma(\mathbf{x},\theta_j), \tag{3}$$

where $T_{\theta_j}$ represents the part-template defined by parameter $\theta_j$ and $D_{chamfer}(\mathbf{x}, T_{\theta_j})$ represents the average chamfer distance. The foreground coverage density $\gamma(\mathbf{x},\theta_j)$ is defined as the proportion of the foreground pixels covered by the part-template $T_{\theta_j}$ at candidate foot pixel $\mathbf{x}$. Then, we find the maximum likelihood estimate $\theta_j^*(\mathbf{x})$ as follows: $\theta_j^*(\mathbf{x}) = \arg\max_{\theta_j \in \Theta_j} P_{ol}(I|\mathbf{x},\theta_j)$, where $\Theta_j$ denotes the parameter space of the part $j$, and $P_{ol}(I|\mathbf{x},\theta_j)$ denotes the *part-template likelihood* for candidate foot pixel $\mathbf{x}$ and part-template $T_{\theta_j}$.

Finally, the global object-level likelihood $P_{ol}(I|\mathbf{x})$ for candidate foot pixel $\mathbf{x}$ is estimated as: $P_{ol}(I|\mathbf{x}) = \sum_j w_j P_{ol}(I|\mathbf{x},\theta_j^*(\mathbf{x}))$, where $w_j$ is an importance weight for the part-template $j$. We smooth the resulting likelihood map by a 2D Gausssian filter adaptively and extract local maxima from it. We define the set of local maxima with likelihood larger than some threshold as the set of initial human hypotheses: $C = \{\mathbf{h}_1, ...\mathbf{h}_N\}$.

**Optimization:** A fast and efficient greedy algorithm is employed for optimization. The algorithm works in a progressive way as follows: starting with an empty configuration $\mathbf{c_0} = \phi$, we iteratively add a new, locally best hypothesis from the residual set of possible hypotheses until the termination condition is satisfied. The iteration is terminated when the joint likelihood stop increasing or no more hypothesis can be added. The greedy solution $\mathbf{c}^*$ is used as the final estimate for the human configuration.

### 3.3   Implementation and Results

Given the calibration information and the binary foreground image from background subtraction, we first estimate binary foot candidate regions $R_{foot}$ for efficiently localizing all the human feet. Human vertical axis $\vec{\mathbf{v}}_\mathbf{x}$ is estimated for a foot candidate pixel $\mathbf{x}$ by the calibration information. Then, foot candidate regions $R_{foot}$ are obtained as: $R_{foot} = \{\mathbf{x}|\gamma_\mathbf{x} \geq \xi\}$, where $\gamma_\mathbf{x}$ denotes the proportion of foreground pixels in an adaptive rectangular window $W(\mathbf{x},(w_0,h_0))$ determined by candidate foot pixel $\mathbf{x}$. The window coverage is efficiently calculated using integral images. Figure 7 shows an example of our human detection process.

# 4   Object Tracking

### 4.1   Introduction and Related Work

Developing robust tracking algorithms is challenging due to factors such as noisy input, illumination variation, cluttered backgrounds, occlusion, and object appearance change due to 3D motion and articulation.

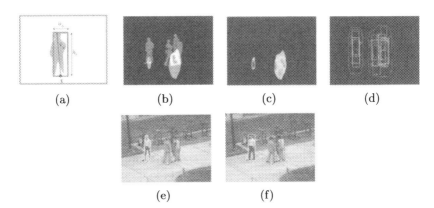

(a) (b) (c) (d)

(e) (f)

**Fig. 7.** An example of the detection process with background subtraction. (a) Adaptive rectangular window, (b) Foot candidate regions $R_{foot}$ (lighter regions), (c) Object-level likelihood map by the hierarchical part-template matching, (d) The set $C$ of human hypotheses overlaid on the Canny edge map, (e) Final human detection result, (f) Final human segmentation result.

There is a vast literature on tracking, and we restrict ourselves to some recent approaches related to our research. To address appearance changes, adaptive modeling of object appearance is typically employed. In [10], object appearance is modeled with a mixture of a fixed number of color-spatial Gaussians. Each mixture is considered as a particle in a particle filter system. This representation is quite similar to the object model in [11], where a variable number of Gaussian kernels is used. The set of kernels is updated between frames using Bayesian sequential filtering. The Gaussian approximation makes these approaches applicable to gradual appearance changes. However, similar to [12], they have difficulties with rapid changes or when changes include both occlusion and dis-occlusion, such as when an object rotates (even slowly).

We use in this work a regional-feature based tracking algorithm designed to cope with large changes in object appearance. The tracking algorithm estimates a time-varying occupancy map of the tracked object which is updated based on local motion models of both the object and the background. The regional features we employ are the MSER features ([13]) that have been used previously for object recognition and wide-baseline stereo matching (see [14]). They are more stable from frame to frame than local features such as corners or lines, making it easier to match them for motion modelling.

## 4.2 Approach Summary

Our approach is motivated by the simple assumption that any image element (feature, pixel ... ) that is close to the object and moves consistently with the object is, with high probability, part of the object. Our approach to updating the model of a tracked object is, then, based on motion of image elements as opposed to appearance matching.

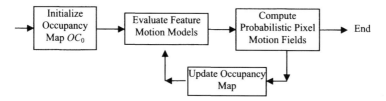

**Fig. 8.** Main components of our tracking algorithm

The summary of our approach is as follows. We represent the object with a probabilistic occupancy map and reduce the problem of tracking the object from time $t$ to $t+1$ to that of constructing the object occupancy map at $t+1$ given the occupancy map at time $t$. We start by computing probabilistic motion models for detected features at time $t$ conditioned on that they belong to the foreground or the background. Feature motion distributions are computed based on the occupancy map at time $t$ and feature similarities across frames. From these feature motions, a probabilistic motion model for each pixel is constructed. The construction starts from the center of the regional features and expands out to cover the entire image. Finally, pixel motion fields are used to construct the object occupancy at $t+1$. Figure 8 shows the flowchart of our tracking algorithm.

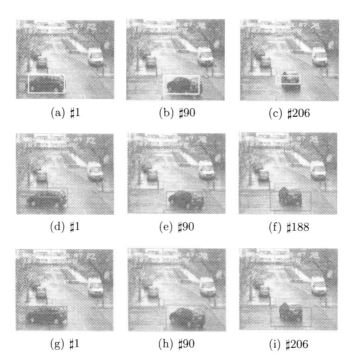

**Fig. 9.** Tracking result on the car sequence. Results of [11] (top), [15] (middle) and our tracker (bottom)

### 4.3  Experimental Results

Figure 9 shows the tracking results on a surveillance video from published domains[1] (rough bounding boxes are shown for better visualization). The challenges in this sequence include cluttered background, partial occlusion, large object shape and size changes as the car turns and moves away.

# References

1. Stauffer, C., Grimson, W.: Adaptive background mixture models for real-time tracking, pp. 245–252. IEEE Computer Society, Washington, DC, USA (1999)
2. Kilger, M.: A shadow handler in a video-based real-time traffic monitoring system. In: Proc. IEEE Workshop Applications of Computer Vision, pp. 11–18. IEEE Computer Society, Los Alamitos (1992)
3. Kim, K., Chalidabhongse, T., Harwood, D., Davis, L.S.: Background modeling and subtraction by codebook construction, pp. 3061–3064. IEEE Computer Society, Washington (2004)
4. Koller, D., Weber, J., Malik, J.: Robust multiple car tracking with occlusion reasoning, pp. 189–196. Springer, London (1994)
5. Wu, B., Nevatia, R.: Detection of multiple, partially occluded humans in a single image by bayesian combination of edgelet part detectors. In: ICCV (2005)
6. Mikolajczyk, K., Schmid, C., Zisserman, A.: Human detection based on a probabilistic assembly of robust part detector. In: Pajdla, T., Matas, J(G.) (eds.) ECCV 2004. LNCS, vol. 3021, pp. 69–82. Springer, Heidelberg (2004)
7. Gavrila, D.M., Philomin, V.: Real-time object detection for smart vehicles. In: ICCV (1999)
8. Zhao, T., Nevatia, R.: Mcmc-based approach for human segmentation. In: CVPR (2004)
9. Smith, K., Perez, D.G., Odobez, J.M.: Using particles to track varying numbers of interacting people. In: CVPR (2005)
10. Wang, H., Suter, D., Schindler, K.: Effective appearance model and similarity measure for particle filtering and visual tracking. In: Leonardis, A., Bischof, H., Pinz, A. (eds.) ECCV 2006. LNCS, vol. 3953, pp. 606–618. Springer, Heidelberg (2006)
11. Han, B., Davis, L.: On-line density-based appearance modeling for object tracking. In: Proc. IEEE ICCV 2005, pp. 1492–1499. IEEE Computer Society, Los Alamitos (2005)
12. Jepson, A., Fleet, D., El-Maraghi, T.: Robust online appearance models for visual tracking. IEEE Trans. PAMI 25(10) (2003)
13. Matas, J., Chum, O., Martin, U., Pajdla, T.: Robust wide baseline stereo from maximally stable extremal regions. In: Proc. BMVC 2002 London, pp. 384–393 (2002)
14. Mikolajczyk, K., Tuytelaars, T., Schmid, C., Zisserman, A., Matas, J., Schaffalitzky, F., Kadir, T., Gool, L.V.: A comparison of affine region detectors. Int'l J. Computer Vision 65(1-2), 43–72 (2005)
15. Collins, R., Liu, Y., Leordeanu, M.: On-line selection of discriminative tracking features. IEEE Trans. PAMI 27(10), 1631–1643 (2005)

---

[1] The ETI-SEO and VACE-CLEAR07 tracking evaluation projects.

# CLEAR'07 Evaluation of USC Human Tracking System for Surveillance Videos

B. Wu, V.K. Singh, C.-H. Kuo, L. Zhang, S.C. Lee, and R. Nevatia

University of Southern California
Institute for Robotics and Intelligent Systems
Los Angeles, CA 90089-0273
{bowu, viveksin, chenghak, zhang11, sungchul, nevatia}@usc.edu

**Abstract.** This paper presents the evaluation results of a system for tracking humans in surveillance videos. Moving blobs are detected based on adaptive background modeling. A shape based multi-view human detection system is used to find humans in moving regions. The detected responses are associated to infer the human trajectories. The shaped based human detection and tracking is further enhanced by a blob tracker to boost the performance on persons at a long distance from the camera. Multi-threading techniques are used to speedup the process. Results are given on the video test set of the CLEAR-VACE surveillance human tracking evaluation task.

## 1 Task and Data Set

The task in this evaluation exercise is to track the 2D locations and regions of multiple humans in surveillance videos. The videos are captured with a single static camera mounted a few meters above the ground looking down towards a street. The test set for the evaluation contains 50 sequences of 150 seconds each, captured from two different sites at various times. The frame size is $720 \times 480$; the sampling rate is 30 frame per second (FPS). Fig.1 shows one frame of each site.

(a) site 1　　　　　　　　(b) site 2

**Fig. 1.** Sample frames

This is a repeat of the evaluation conducted for CLEAR 2006. We follow the same approach as before and described in [2], though there are some differences

R. Stiefelhagen et al. (Eds.): CLEAR 2007 and RT 2007, LNCS 4625, pp. 191–196, 2008.

in the classifier design. For completeness, we give a summary of the method in this paper. One major difference from the earlier system is in improving the computational speed by use of parallel processing. This is described in more detail later in section 3.

## 2   Methodology

We first detect person hypotheses frame by frame, then we track them in videos with a data association method. Shape based tracking is combined with a blob tracker to improve the performance.

We learn a full-body detector for walking/standing humans by the method proposed in [1]. A tree structured multi-view pedestrian detector is learned by boosting edgelet feature based weak classifiers; the earlier version, describe in [2], used a sequential cascade for each view. We do not use the part based representation in [1] for partial occlusion reasoning explicitly, as the local feature based full-body detector can work with partial occlusion to some extent and inter-human occlusions are not strong in this data set.

We constrain the search of humans around motion blobs. Motion is detected by comparing pixel colors to an adaptively learned background model. This reduces the search space of the human detector and prevents false alarms on static scene objects; however, it also prevents detection of static persons in the scene.

Humans are tracked by forming associations between the frame detection responses. This tracking algorithm is a simplified version of that in [1], as only the full-body detector is applied. The affinity between a hypothesis and a responses is calculated based on cues from distance, size, and color. A greedy algorithm is used to associate the hypotheses and the detection responses.

The shape based detector does not work well on persons less than 24 pixel wide, as is the case when the humans are far from the camera. We augment the shape based method with motion based blob tracking. The moving objects with relatively small size are classified as pedestrians; the others to be vehicles.

We use an integration method to combine the shape based tracking and the motion based tracking. For each human track segment $h_s$ from shape based tracking, we search for the motion blob track segments $h_m$ which have large overlap with $h_s$. We then merge the motion blob track segments $h_m$ with the human track segment $h_s$. This combination increases the accuracy of the trajectories. Fig.2 shows an example of the combination.

## 3   Improving the Computational Speed

For the task of online surveillance, a real-time system is desired. We use parallel programming to improve the speed of our system. Two main modules of the system are converted to multi-threading: the background subtraction module and the shape based pedestrian detection module.

| Shape based tracking | Motion based tracking | Combination |

**Fig. 2.** Combination of shape based and motion based tracking

## 3.1 Multi-thread Background Subtraction

A *thread* is a unit of execution in an operating system. A process (or application program) consists of one or more threads and the scheduler in the operating system controls thread task distribution. In our system, the user can control the number of threads and the system divides input stream image into small piece of images based on the number of threads as illustrated in Fig.3.

Then, the system distributes each image region to the threads to perform the adaptive background subtraction operation for smaller size images. Lastly, the system collects and combines the results of background subtraction after all threads finish their tasks. The procedural description of the multi-threaded adaptive background subtraction algorithm is shown below.

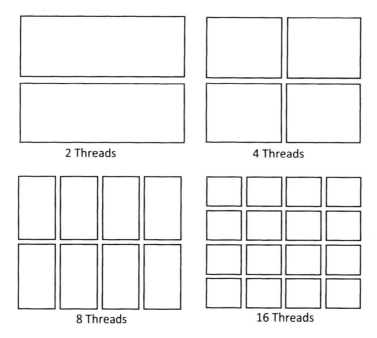

**Fig. 3.** Image division based on the number of threads

Capture a video frame and do the followings:

1. Divide the frame image into multiple images with configuration of Fig. 3 according to the number of threads (user's input)
2. Distribute the segmented image to each thread and dispatch threads to perform the adaptive background subtraction task.
3. Wait until all threads have finished their tasks.
4. Combine all pieces of background subtracted images into one image.

### 3.2   Multi-thread Pedestrian Detection

For pedestrian detection, we implement multi-threading within a sliding window. Suppose we use $k$ threads for pedestrian detection, then the size of sliding window is $k$ frames. The detector is applied to each of the $k$ frames by one thread. As soon as one frame is finished, the sliding window moves forward by a step of one frame. The new frame is sent to the thread that just finished its previous task. This implementation provides load balance among different processors. Table.1 shows the speed of the detection module using various number of threads on a dual core dual processor Intel Xeon machine featured with Hyper-Threading Technology, 3.73GHz CPU and 4.00GB of RAM.

**Table 1.** Speed of pedestrian detection with various number of threads

| Number of threads | 1 | 2 | 4 | 8 |
|---|---|---|---|---|
| Speed (ms per frame) | 1470 | 799 | 546 | 381 |

Our preliminary experiments indicate that we can achieve a speedup factor of about 4 by using eight threads on the dual core dual processor machine. The speed of the current system on the CLEAR-VACE test set is about 1.6 FPS.

## 4   Experiments

We ran our system on the 50 test sequences. The formal evaluation process defines four main metrics for the human tracking task [3]:

1. Multiple Object Detection Precision (MODP) reflects the 2D location precision of detection level;
2. Multiple Object Detection Accuracy (MODA) is the detection accuracy calculated from the number of false alarms and missed detections;
3. Multiple Object Tracking Precision (MOTP) reflects the 2D location precision of the tracking level; and
4. Multiple Object Tracking Accuracy (MOTA) is the tracking accuracy calculated from the number of false alarms, missed detections, and identity switches.

**Table 2.** Evaluation scores. (The scores of previous year's results are computed with the new version of evaluation software. When computing the scores for one sequence of the 50, the new evaluation software crashes, hence the numbers listed are the average of the remaining 49 sequences.)

|          | MODP   | MODA   | MOTP   | MOTA   |
|----------|--------|--------|--------|--------|
| CLEAR'06 | 0.5742 | 0.4768 | 0.5812 | 0.4585 |
| CLEAR'07 | 0.6194 | 0.5148 | 0.6230 | 0.4988 |

(a) Sequence 04 from site 1

(b) Sequence 36 from site 2

**Fig. 4.** Examples of tracking results

Table 2 lists the scores of our current system together with those of the previous evaluation. It can be seen that the current results are slightly better than those we achieved in the CLEAR'06 evaluation [2]. The improvement on accuracy is mainly due to the new detector structure which has similar detection rate but fewer false alarms compared to the previous version. Fig.4 shows some examples of final tracking results.

## 5    Conclusion and Discussion

We applied a fully automatic multiple human tracking method to surveillance videos. The system has achieved reasonable performance on the test sequences.

Our current system still does not run at real time, although some speedup has been obtained by multi-threading with CPU. We plan to investigate the use of Graphics Processing Unit (GPU) for further improvement.

**Acknowledgements.** This research was funded, in part, by the U.S. Government VACE program.

## References

1. Wu, B., Nevatia, R.: Detection and Tracking of Multiple, Partially Occluded Humans by Bayesian Combination of Edgelet based Part Detectors. International Journal of Computer Vision (2007)
2. Wu, B., Song, X., Singh, V.K., Nevatia, R.: Evaluation of USC Human Tracking System for Surveillance Videos. In: CLEAR Evaluation Campaign and Workshop, in conjunction with FG 2006 (2006)
3. Kasturi, R., Goldgof, D., Soundararajan, P., Manohar, V., Boonstra, M., Korzhova, V.: Performance Evaluation Protocal for Face, Person and Vehicle Detection & Tracking in Video Analysis and Centent Extraction (VACE-II) CLEAR - Classification of Events, Activities and Relationships,
http://www.nist.gov/speech/tests/clear/2006/CLEAR06R106EvalDiscDoc/
DataandInformation/ClearEval_Protocol_v5.pdf

# Speed Performance Improvement of Vehicle Blob Tracking System

Sung Chun Lee and Ram Nevatia

University of Southern California, Los Angeles, CA 90089, USA
sungchun@usc.edu, nevatia@usc.edu

**Abstract.** A speed performance improved vehicle tracking system on a given set of evaluation videos of a street surveillance system is presented. We implement multi-threading technique to meet the requirement of real-time performance which demanded in the practical surveillance systems. Through multi-threading technique, we can accomplish near real-time performance. An analysis of results is also presented.

## 1 Introduction

Detection and tracking of vehicles is important for traffic analysis and video surveillance. Our objective is to develop techniques for automatic vehicle tracking to enable the image analysts to cope with exploiting the exponentially growing volume of video imagery available to them.

There are several factors that make this task highly challenging: camera and scene instabilities. Firstly, sometimes, cameras shake, creating false foreground detections and automatic gain control abruptly changes the intensity of the video image causing multiple false detections. Secondly, there exist ambient illumination changes such as due to passing clouds and occluding objects such as trees and traffic signs as illustrated in Fig. 1.

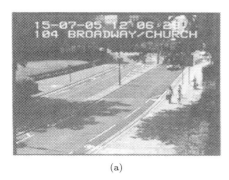 

(a)                                            (b)

**Fig. 1.** Illustration of camera and scene instabilities: (a) A white car (top right) occluded behind a tree and a traffic sign, (b) Intensity of scene dramatically changes due to automatic camera gain change as clouds pass

R. Stiefelhagen et al. (Eds.): CLEAR 2007 and RT 2007, LNCS 4625, pp. 197–202, 2008.

In our previous work [5], we have tried to address these issues and described a robust detection and tracking vehicle system. One of limitations of the work is slow computational performance. Practical surveillance applications demand real time processing performance as an important factor. We applied a multithreading programming approach to improve the computational performance which is the focus of this paper.

## 2   Vehicle Tracking and Detection

Before explaining the speed enhancement, we briefly describe the detection and tracking algorithm from the previous work.

The task is to evaluate the performance of our vehicle detection and tracking algorithm on a set of surveillance videos provided by the VACE project [2]. Objective includes accurate detection, localization and tracking while maintaining the identities vehicles as they travel across different frames.

The videos are of street scenes captured by cameras mounted at light pole heights looking down towards the ground. There is one road running from top to bottom of the image and another one from left to right near the top of the image. Provided videos are from two different cameras at several different times.

We assume vehicles move on a ground plane; we use vehicle motion and vanishing points from scene features to compute an approximate camera model [4]. This process is performed once, in training phase. To distinguish vehicles from walking humans and other motion, we set a minimum size for an object to be considered as a vehicle; this size is set in 3D, its size in image is computed by using the camera parameters.

### 2.1   Background Subtraction

A common way to detect moving objects has been to learn a pixel-wise model of the background and to flag significant variations from it as a moving object occludes the pixel. This approach works well when the camera is stationary. We have used this method to detect and track vehicle blobs in surveillance videos.

We use an adaptive background subtraction method [4]. We first detect temporal color changes in the input video stream and classify as corresponding to moving objects. Then, we filter out isolated points and cluster the detected pixels to form foreground objects. The background model is updated at each frame. In an ideal case, every extracted foreground object would correspond to one vehicle object. However, there might be other cases: merged vehicles, split vehicle, or other moving objects (e.g. human).

### 2.2   Vehicle Tracking and Detection

Our tracking method processes the frames sequentially. We analyze the extracted foreground blobs from background subtraction process as described in Section 2.1. At each new frame, we do following:

1. Apply tracking object's dynamic model to predict its new position
2. Generate an association matrix based on the overlap between the predicted object rectangle and the detected blob rectangle
3. In the association matrix, there are following cases:
   (a) If the track-blob match is one-to-one, we simply update the position of the track.
   (b) If a blob has no match with current tracking objects and its size is comparable to a regular vehicle, a new tracking object is created.
   (c) If there is no blob match for more than a certain number of frames, the track of this object ends.
   (d) If an object matches with multiple blobs, we combine the split blobs into one to match with the object being tracked.
   (e) If multiple objects merge into one blob, we segment the blob based on the appearance model of each involved object. Specifically, we apply a meanshift color tracking method [1] to locate the vehicle in the merged blob.

Some example results are given below in Fig. 2.

**Fig. 2.** Results of vehicle tracking and detection (Yellow box: DCO (Dont Care Object), Green box: Detected ground truth, White box: Detected system output, Blue box: Missed ground truth, Black box: Detected but overlapped with DCO, Magenta box: Occluded ground truth (DCO), Cyan box: Stationary ground truth (DCO))

## 3    Computation Time Improvement

One of the limitations in our approaches was that computation performance was up to 10 times slower than real-time. Our analysis indicated that the adaptive background subtraction task is the most time consuming process in our system. One alternative is the use of a Graphic Processing Unit (GPU); GPUs are very powerful and relatively inexpensive. However, GPU programming can be difficult. Instead, we have chosen to explore the use of multi-processors available in a modern workstation (dual-core dual processors are now common, quad-core machines should become available shortly).

### 3.1    Multithreading Background Subtraction

A *thread* is a unit of execution in an operating system. A process (or application program) consists of one or more threads and the scheduler in the operating system controls thread task distribution. In our system, the user can control the number of threads and the system divides input stream image into small piece of images based on the number of threads as illustrated in Fig. 3.

Then, the system distributes each image region to the threads to perform the adaptive background subtraction operation for smaller size images. Lastly, the system collects and combines the results of background subtraction after all threads finish their tasks. The procedural description of the multi-threaded adaptive background subtraction algorithm is shown below:

Capture a video frame and do the followings:

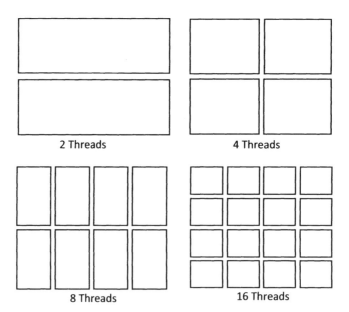

**Fig. 3.** Image division based on the number of threads

1. Divide the frame image into multiple images with configuration of Fig. 3 according to the number of threads (user's input)
2. Distribute the segmented image to each thread and dispatch threads to perform the adaptive background subtraction task.
3. Wait until all threads have finished their tasks.
4. Combine all pieces of background subtracted images into one image.

Our preliminary experiments indicate that we can achieve a speed up of between 2.5 and 4 by using various number of threads. The main limitation seems to be in limited Cache memory that is shared between two processors in dual core chip.

## 4   Experiments and Results

In 2006, we tested our systems on the videos provided by the VACE project. The size of each frame is 720 × 480. The experiments were finished on a regular PC with Intel Pentium 2.6GHZ CPU. The average processing time was 2.85 (frame per second). By using a multithreading background subtraction, We are able to achieve average of 11.9 (frame per second) as shown in Table 1.

**Table 1.** Computation Time using multithreading skill with Intel Xeon CPU with two dual core 64 bit 3.73GHZ CPUs

| Num of Threads | Background Subtraction Speed with Multithreading (second / frame) | Tracking Speed (second / frame) | Final Speed (second / frame) | Final Speed (frame / second) |
|---|---|---|---|---|
| 1 | 0.200 | 0.020 | **0.220** | **4.55** |
| 2 | 0.110 | 0.020 | **0.130** | **7.69** |
| 4 | 0.085 | 0.020 | **0.105** | **9.52** |
| 8 | 0.064 | 0.020 | **0.084** | **11.90** |

We quantitively evaluated our system according to the requirements of the test process. The metrics shown evaluate both the detection and tracking performances. We summarize the metric definitions below; more details may be found in [2].

1. MODP (Multiple Object Detection Precision) measures the position precision of single frame detections;
2. MODA (Multiple Object Detection Accuracy) combines the influence of miss detections and false alarms;
3. MOTP (Multiple Object Tracking Precision) measures the position precision at tracking level;
4. MOTA (Multiple Object Tracking Accuracy) is MODA at tracking level with consideration of ID switches.

Table 2 lists the scores on 50 test video sequences. One observation from the table is that: the difference of MODP and MOTP, or MODA and MOTA is very

**Table 2.** Evaluation scores on 50 test video sequences

| Average MODP | Average MODA | Average MOTP | Average MOTA |
|:---:|:---:|:---:|:---:|
| 0.602 | 0.679 | 0.616 | 0.640 |

small for all the test video sequences. It is mainly because the penalty on object ID change is relatively small. Actually, there is a difference in the number of ID changes in the outputs of different subsets. However, the current defined MOTA and MOTP are not able to reflect this tracking error very well.

## 5 Conclusions

We have presented evaluation results of the detection and tracking accuracy and precision and the speed performance improvement of our vehicle detection and tracking system on a provided set of surveillance videos. The data contains many highly challenging features. The performance of our system is promising though many shortcomings exist and shows near real-time operation.

**Acknowledgements.** This research was funded by VACE program of the U.S. government.

## References

1. Comaniciu, D., Ramesh, V., Meer, P.: Real-time tracking of non-rigid objects using mean shift. In: IEEE Conference on Computer Vision and Pattern Recognition, vol. 1, pp. 511–518 (2001)
2. Kasturi, R., Goldgof, D., Soundararajan, P., Manohar, V., Boonstra, M., Korzhova, V.: Performance Evaluation Protocal for Face, Person and Vehicle Detection Tracking in Video Analysis and Centent Extraction (VACE-II) CLEAR - Classification of Events, Activities and Relationships,
   http://www.nist.gov/speech/tests/clear/2006/CLEAR06-R106-EvalDiscDoc/DataandInformation/ClearEval_Protocol_v5.pdf
3. Liyuan Li, Weimin Huang, Irene Y.H. Gu, and Qi Tian. Foreground Object Detection from Videos Containing Complex Background. ACM Multimedia (2003)
4. Lv, F., Zhao, T., Nevatia, R.: Self-Calibration of a Camera from Video of a Walking Human. In: Proceedings of IEEE International Conference on Pattern Recognition (ICPR) (2002)
5. Song, X., Nevatia, R.: Robust Vehicle Blob Tracking with Split/Merge Handling. In: Stiefelhagen, R., Garofolo, J.S. (eds.) CLEAR 2006. LNCS, vol. 4122, pp. 216–222. Springer, Heidelberg (2007)

# Vehicle and Person Tracking in Aerial Videos

Jiangjian Xiao, Changjiang Yang, Feng Han, and Hui Cheng

Sarnoff Corporation
{jxiao, cyang, fhan, hcheng}@sarnoff.com

**Abstract.** This paper presents two tracking approaches from Sarnoff Corporation to detect moving vehicles and person in the videos taken from aerial platform or plane. In the first approach, we combine layer segmentation approach with background stabilization and post track refinement to reliably detect small moving objects at the relatively low processing speed. Our second approach employ a fast tracking algorithm that has been optimized for real-time application. To classify vehicle and person from the detected objects, a HOG (Hierarchy Of Gradient) based vehicle v.s. person classifier is designed and integrated with the tracking post-processing. Finally, we report the results of our algorithms on a large scale data set collected from VIVID program and the scores evaluated by NIST CLEAR program.

## 1 Introduction

Object tracking is a classic research topic in computer vision and has been investigated by computer vision researchers for a long time[1,2,3,4,5]. With the availability of the low cost video cameras, a huge amount video data is recorded every day to be analyzed. Therefore, a reliable and automated video content analysis process is very important. In such process, object tracking is the fundamental block for the high level content analysis and exploitation. Especially, in the intelligence community, aerial video has been one of the fastest growing data sources and it has been extensively used in intelligence, surveillance, reconnaissance, tactical and security applications[5]. Based on the analysis of the routinely captured video from aerial platform, a series of intelligent content services for intelligence community are provided to greatly improve the analyst's capabilities in motion imagery exploitation and to enhance security against terrorist attack at US installations at home and abroad.

Traditionally, the object tracking includes two parts: moving object detection and tracking the detected object over the frames. The first part is to detect the interesting moving object based on the motion information such as optical flow or background substraction. The second part is to maintain a consistent identity on the object based on the appearance, shape, or kinematic information when the object is either moving or becomes stationary over the frames. In our CLEAR evaluation task, an additional sub-task is required to classify the moving objects into two categories: vehicle and person. Therefore, an appearance based object classifier is needed to be designed for this task.

In this paper, we present two tracking approaches and conduct performance evaluation between these two approaches on a large aerial video data set. Our first approach is layer-based tracker, where the background and foreground moving objects are represented by different layers respectively. During the detection and tracking process, each

R. Stiefelhagen et al. (Eds.): CLEAR 2007 and RT 2007, LNCS 4625, pp. 203–214, 2008.

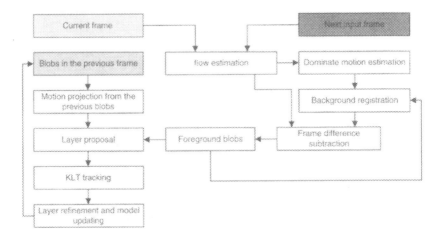

**Fig. 1.** The flow chart of layer-based tracking algorithm. At each time instance, the inputs include two frames and the previous blob set in the previous frame, and the output is the updated blob set with ID information.

layer has maintained an independent appearance and motion model. After performing the tracking process on the video, we also apply a post-tracking refinement process to link the track fragments into a long consistent track ID to further reduce false alarm and increase detection rate. In our second tracking algorithm, SNIFF, we optimize the tracking code and speed up the algorithm for real time applications. This algorithm is based on robust change detection and optical flow based linkage[3]. This algorithm has been successfully deployed on a series of real products in Sarnoff Corporation.

The remainder of this paper is organized as follows. Section 2 discusses the layer based tracking approach and post-tracking refinement. Section 3 presents the fast tracking algorithm broadly used in Sarnoff products. In section 4, a HOG based vehicle v.s. person classifier is discussed. The experimental results and evaluation scores for both vehicle and persion tracking are reported at Section 5.

## 2    Layer-Based Tracker and Post Linking

In our layer-based tracking algorithm, we combine background stabilization and layer representation to detect and track the moving objects. Compared with the ground stationary or PTZ cameras, tracking in aerial video is more challenging due to the significant camera motion and parallax affect[6,7]. In order to reduce the camera motion effect, a frame-to-frame video registration or stabilization process is necessary. In this step, the frames are registered through the background regions excluding the foreground moving objects. However, the video registration may often fail when the camera has a fast motion or strong illumination change. In such case, the detection and tracking process should be temporarily suspended and a motion prediction will fully take control until the reliable registration becomes available.

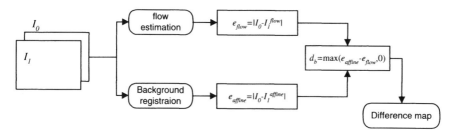

**Fig. 2.** The process of difference subtraction between two image residues, where $I_1^{flow}$ and $I_1^{affine}$ are the warping images of frame $I_1$ respectively. The resulted difference map will be used for the foreground blob detection.

## 2.1   Layer Proposal Generation

Figure 1 shows the flowchart of our layer-based tracking algorithm. In the approach, we first estimate dense optical flow between the new coming video frame and the current reference frame. Then, based on the dominant motion extracted from the optical flow, a global registration is preformed to align the background region. During the alignment, the outlier regions are detected and segmented out from the images by the following subtraction process[8]. Therefore, the registration becomes more robust and the small motion of the moving object can be possibly detected.

Instead of using simple subtraction between the aligned frame, we propose a difference substraction method to reduce motion noise and compensate the illustration change such as automatic gain control. In our approach, two warping images, $I_1^{flow}$ and $I_1^{affine}$, are first computed from affine warping and flow warping as shown in Figure 2. Next, the corresponding residual images, $e_{flow}$ and $e_{affine}$, are obtained by subtraction between $I_0$ with these two warping images. Since the optical flow approach attempts to minimize image residue $e_{flow}$ between two input frames, the image residue for independent moving object will be also reduced by the minimization process and generally is smaller than those in $e_{affine}$. For those occlusion regions, the image residue, $e_{flow}$, is similar to $e_{affine}$, since in both cases there are no exact correspondences to minimize the image residues. Hence, if we subtract the two image residues, $e_{affine}$ and $e_{flow}$, a second order residual difference, $d_b$, are generated such that

$$d_b = \max(e_{affine} - e_{flow}, 0). \qquad (1)$$

In this new residual difference map, the independent moving object will have strong response, and image residues at the occlusion regions will be canceled. This approach can also effectively cancel the illumination inconsistency due to camera motion since both residual images has same response for illumination variations. After applying our difference substraction approach, the image residues due to occlusion regions are filtered out and only the independent moving object has strong response.

After the difference subtraction, the foreground blob can be detected by either simple threshold or graph cut segmentation. In our approach, we apply the more sophisticated graph cut method to segment the foreground object from the background[8]. After that,

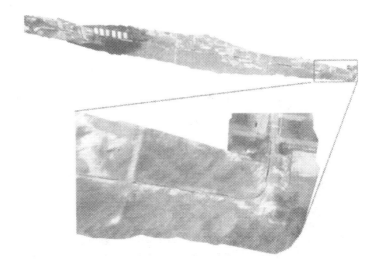

**Fig. 3.** Mosaic of one video sequence. The detected tracks are also overlapped on the mosaic. The bottom is the zoom view of partial mosaic.

a merging process will merge the small blob fragments into a reasonable size based on the motion similarity and in-between distance. Therefore, an initial blob set, $S_1$, is obtained. Then, from the previous frame, we project the previous blob set, $S_0$, by using its corresponding motion parameters into this frame to create a warped blob set, $\tilde{S}_0$. Once two blob sets are obtained, a maximal likelihood association process is applied to associate the blobs and reassign the pixels into the blob set. For remaining un-associated blobs, a new ID will be assigned. As a result, the set of moving targets is detected and the corresponding layer proposal is generated.

### 2.2 Layer Refinement and Model Update

After the above mentioned motion target indication step, the blob shape of the moving object may not be accurate enough due to occlusion or textureless. For example, background region may be mis-assigned into the blob, or some portion of the moving object may not be fully detected in the blob. Therefore, we need to refine the blob shape to exclude the background pixel from the blob and also include the nearby undetected object pixels into the blob as many as possible.

In our approach, we first apply a KLT tracking process to re-estimate the motion model of the blob[2,9]. In KLT tracker, a motion model is approximately represented by an affine transformation, such that,

$$I_1(A\mathbf{x} + t) = I_0(\mathbf{x}), \qquad (2)$$

where $A$ is a 2D matrix and $t$ is the translation vector. This equation can be iteratively solved by gradient descent method for the pixels within the blob. Similarly, a residual difference map, $d_f$, is generated as Eq . Then, we apply a graph cut approach by using $d_f$ against $d_b$ to identify the nearby supporting pixels and exclude background outliers

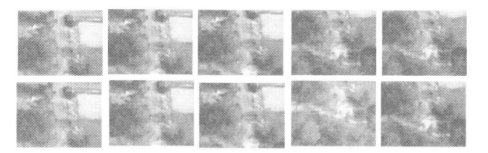

**Fig. 4.** Post linking result. Top: The ID of blue car has been changed several times due to occlusion by trees. Bottom: The car's ID is maintained after linking process.

from the blob[10]. In the graph cut algorithm, a smoothness energy term is introduced to naturally solve the problem. This smoothness energy term fully exploits the similarity information around the neighboring pixels, and constrain the partition more prone to high gradient boundary that is more likely corresponding to object boundary.

### 2.3    Post-linking Process

In order to further reduce false alarm and increase detection rate, we also propose a post-linking process to link the track fragments into a smooth long track with a same identity. In our approach, we mainly employ track kinematic property to evaluate the association probability between different tracks. Our approach includes three main steps. In the first step, we create a mosaic from the input video sequence and re-project the moving object tracks into the mosaic space. Figure 3 shows the mosaic of one video sequence. Next, we smooth the track fragment by using Kalman filter and estimate the speed at each time instance. If the track is missing at certain frames, an interpolation process will be applied to recover the location and speed information for these frames. After that, an extrapolation process is applied for each smoothed track. Finally, a probability association metric is applied for the tracks which are temporal closing or overlapped. In this step, a greedy algorithm is designed to minimize the cost function by the near-neighbor association. Figure 4 shows one result before and after the linking process. With the post-linking process, some missing tracks are recovered and track fragments are dramatically reduced for most cases. Therefore, both the number of ID switching and false alarm rate are reduced to a satisfactory low level.

## 3    SNIFF Object Tracking Algorithm

In this section, we will discuss another tracking algorithm, which was developed at Sarnoff Corporation for real-time application[3,11]. The algorithm is based on robust change detection and optical flow based linkage as shown in Figure 5. At the first stage, a robust change detection is used to find the moving object position every frame or every other fixed number of frames (depending the program configuration). At the second stage, optical flow technique is used to find the association between the detected objects in the frames.

**Fig. 5.** Flow chart of the SNIFF algorithm

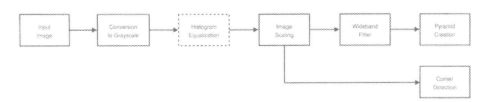

**Fig. 6.** The pre-processing stage for SNIFF tracking. The images are first converted to grayscale format. Then an optional histogram equalization step is applied. A Gaussian pyramid is built for the optical flow computation. Harris corner detection is another option for image alignment in the later stage.

At the change detection stage, the first step is to align the consecutive frames then to subtract the aligned images. In Sniff algorithm, the default image alignment is performed using the direct method or flow-based method. There is another image alignment method, called feature-based method. The benefit of direct method is that it is fast with the help of using pyramids. The drawbacks are that it is sensitive to the large illumination changes, occlusions, low textured surface, or rapid motion. The feature based method such as Harris corner detection can effectively deal with such difficulties. The SNIFF algorithm provides both alignment options for different requirements.

The simple image subtraction is sensitive to the sudden illumination changes, and the vegetable-textured areas. So the SNIFF algorithm chooses normal flow rather than simple image subtraction. The normal flow will generate object masks in the image. Due to noise and/or occlusions and shadows, the masks might be broken. Morphological operation such as dilation is applied to grow the masks back to the original size. In the real implementation, the SNIFF algorithm steps up to one level of the image pyramid then steps down one level to simulate the dilation procedure.

At the association stage, the optical flow is computed between consecutive frames. The correspondences between the pixels in the masks of different frames is associated using the optical flow. To speed up this association processing, every four pixels are glued together to form a super-pixel. The SNIFF also performs an AND operation on the associated multi-frame masks to remove the false alarms.

### 3.1   Post-processing: Use of Global Tracking Trajectory

One of the biggest difficulties in SNIFF algorithm is that it does not handle slowly-moving objects, static objects, and occlusion well, since any broken one frame within the linkage will lose track of the objects. To deal with this problem, the algorithm bookkeeps the lost objects for a fix period of time. Later on, if the lost objects re-appear, then

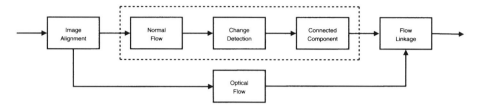

**Fig. 7.** The SNIFF tracking flow chart. Once the images are aligned, the normal flow based change detection is applied to the aligned images. Then morphological operation is used to fill the holes and the broken parts. The connected component algorithm is used to find the blobs in the images. A optical flow method is used to link the blobs in the different frames and assign the ID accordingly.

the lost objects will be re-associated with the current track based on the size of the object and the central moments of the flow vectors.

Even though the SNIFF alleviated the above presented difficulties, it cannot handle the problems due to a long period time of occlusion or slow moving objects. The reason behind is that it is a local method and the global tracking information is ignored. However such global tracking information is vital for object tracking. For instance, human vision system utilizes such global information to find the moving objects, even very small one.

To improve the algorithm, we first build a mosaic of tracking trajectory to exploit global information. However, in the 2D mosaic space, the tracking trajectories may be very ambiguous, since a lot of trajectories are overlapped as shown in Figure 3. We then lift up the trajectories into 3D spatio-temporal space. Such lifting makes the trajectories more distinct even they are overlapped in 2D space. The next stage is to connect the fragmented trajectories in 3D space based on the global proximity, continuation, and collinearity. Usually when the occlusion happens, the position and size of the objects before and after occlusion is not accurate, which makes the association method based on local information such as Kalman filter ineffective. On the other hand, global linkage will overcome such shortcoming using global information, which makes the algorithm more robust, even for very large occlusion.

## 4   Vehicle and Person Classifier

To classify the detected moving objects into vehicle and person, we design a HOG based vehicle v.s. person classifier for this evaluation task. Our approach can effectively handle multi-view, multi-pose object appearance during the classification. [12]. In our approach, we develop separate classifiers for each object class that are each specialized to one specific aspect or pose. For example, we have one classifier specialized to front/rear view of people and one that is specialized to side view of people. We apply these view-pose-based classifiers in parallel and then combine their results. If there are multiple detections at the same or adjacent locations, the system selects the most likely one through non-maximum suppression.

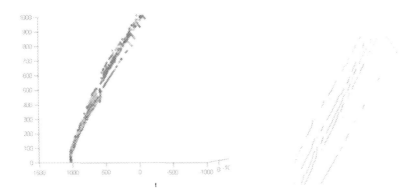

**Fig. 8.** Tracking trajectories in 3D (left). Zoom in view of Tracking trajectories in 3D(right).

We empirically determined the number of views/poses to model for each object. Each of these detectors is not only specialized in orientation, but is trained to find the object only at a specified size within a rectangular image window. Therefore, to be able to detect the object at any position within an image, we re-apply the detectors for all possible positions of this rectangular window. Then to be able to detect the object at any size we iteratively resize the input image and re-apply the detectors in the same fashion to each resized image. To build each view-pose-based classifier, we extend the histogram of oriented gradient (HOG) representation and use support vector machines (SVM) as the classifier. Unlike some commonly used representations, the extended histogram of oriented gradient gives good generalization by grouping only perceptually similar images together. With a support vector machine, this gives rise to a decision function that discriminates object and non-object patterns reliably in images under different kinds of conditions and results good performance on some challenging datasets.

A HOG feature is created by first computing the gradient magnitude and orientation at each image sample point in a region around an anchor point. The region is split into NxN sub-regions. Accumulating samples within the sub-region, weighted by gradient magnitudes, then forms an orientation histogram for each sub-region. Concatenating the histograms from all the sub-regions gives the final HOG feature vector. The standard HOG feature only encodes the gradient orientation of one image patch, no matter where this orientation is from in this patch. Therefore, it is not discriminative enough if the spatial property of the underlying structure of the image patch is crucial. This is especially true for highly structured objects like vehicles. To incorporate the spatial property in HOG feature, we add one distance dimension to the angle dimension in the binning of all the pixels within each sub-region. The distance is relative to the center of each sub-region. We divide the image window into small spatial regions, which consists of a number of sub-regions (or cells). For each cell we accumulate a local 1-D histogram of gradient directions over the pixels of the cell. The combined histogram entries form the representation. For better invariance to illumination, shadowing, etc., it is also useful to contrast-normalize the local responses before using them. This can be done by accumulating a measure of local histogram over somewhat larger spatial regions (or blocks) and using the results to normalize all of the cells in the block.

| Sequence ID | Detection accuracy | Miss detection per frame | False alarm per frame |
|---|---|---|---|
| V4V30002_046 | 0.000 | 0.120 | 0.000 |
| V4V30002_047 | 0.753 | 0.724 | 0.000 |
| V4V30002_048 | 0.876 | 0.331 | 0.005 |
| V4V30002_049 | 0.929 | 0.078 | 0.000 |
| V4V30002_050 | 0.947 | 0.107 | 0.100 |
| V4V30003_011 | 0.966 | 0.006 | 0.067 |
| V4V30003_014 | 0.622 | 2.350 | 0.179 |
| V4V30003_017 | 0.969 | 0.039 | 0.005 |
| V4V30004_005 | 0.789 | 0.202 | 0.157 |
| V4V30003_015 | 0.868 | 0.095 | 0.286 |
| V4V30004_020 | 0.879 | 0.107 | 0.339 |
| V4V30004_021 | 0.889 | 0.084 | 0.241 |
| V4V30004_024 | 0.923 | 0.04 | 0.408 |
| V4V30004_028 | 0.897 | 0.022 | 0.186 |
| V4V30004_029 | 0.894 | 0.404 | 0.061 |
| V4V30004_043 | 0.945 | 0.297 | 0.073 |
| V4V30004_044 | 0.653 | 2.293 | 0.005 |
| V4V30004_046 | 0.826 | 0.655 | 0.293 |
| V4V30004_049 | 0.960 | 0.005 | 0.000 |

**Fig. 9.** Part of vehicle tracking results using our algorithms. The most MOTAs are among the range of $0.65 - 0.95$. For sequence V4V30002_046, the moving vehicles are only available in a very short period and we did not detect the objects, so the score is 0 with very low false alarm and miss detection.

## 5   Experimental Results

In this section, we report our systematical tracking results on VIVID2 aerial video sequences for both our tracking algorithms. In the experiment, we test our algorithms on the large-scale VIVID2 data set which contains more than 10 hours videos and 238 video sequences. Each sequence has more than a thousand frames. With the support of NIST evaluation team, 29 video sequences has been selected for person tracking performance evaluation. For the vehicle tracking, we also use the standard Viper tool to generate ground truth for a small data set selected from VIVID2 videos and evaluate our vehicle tracking performance.

In CLEAR evaluation program, a set of performance metrics has been earlier defined for both vehicle and person tracking evaluation[13,14]. In this paper, we only report three performance metrics from the evaluation program due to the limited space, which include Multiple Object Tracking Accuracy (MOTA), Average Missed Detection per Frame (AMDF), and Average False Alarm per Frame (AFAF). The most important metric MOTA is defined as

$$MOTA = 1 - \frac{\sum_{t=1}^{N}(c_b(B^t) + c_c(C^t) + \log(Id_{switches}))}{\sum_{t=1}^{N}(N_G^t)}, \qquad (3)$$

| Sequence ID | Detection accuracy | Miss detection per frame | False alarm per frame |
|---|---|---|---|
| V4V30003_042 | 0.000 | 0.000 | 0.000 |
| V4V30002_044 | 0.000 | 0.000 | 0.000 |
| V4V30003_012 | 0.000 | 0.000 | 0.000 |
| V4V30003_013 | 0.523 | 0.093 | 0.109 |
| V4V30004_003 | 0.000 | 0.000 | 0.000 |
| V4V30004_023 | 0.000 | 0.000 | 0.000 |
| V4V30005_030 | 0.000 | 0.000 | 0.000 |
| V4V30007_005 | 0.030 | 0.215 | 0.000 |
| V4V30007_006 | 0.000 | 0.000 | 0.000 |
| V4V30007_016 | 0.000 | 0.000 | 0.000 |
| V4V30007_017 | 0.000 | 0.000 | 0.000 |
| V4V30013_053 | 0.000 | 0.000 | 0.000 |

**Fig. 10.** Part of person tracking results using our algorithms

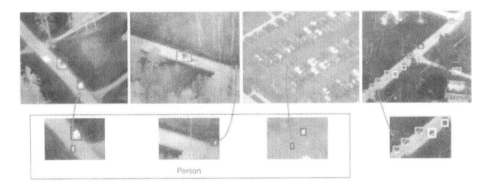

**Fig. 11.** Some tracking results. The moving people are always detected by a red bounding box, while the moving vehicles are detected by other color bounding box.

where $B$ and $C$ are the false acceptance and false rejection counts, $Id_{switches}$ is total number of identity switches made by the system. Hence, if an identity is changed during the tracking process, it will be penalized by a small number. The perfect tracking result will be given a score equal to 1. The tracking performance become worse when the score becomes smaller or negative. Figure 9 shows the partial vehicle tracking results obtained by using our algorithms, where the most MOTAs are among the range of $0.65 - 0.95$ with low false alarm rate. Figure 10 shows the person tracking results. In these result, the MOTAs are quite low due to the small size of moving person and low video quality. Figure 11 shows some frames with detected bounding boxes for both vehicle and person tracking. In the frames, the moving people are always detected by a red bounding box while the moving vehicles are detected by other color bounding box. At the most cases, the moving person has a height of 5-10 pixels and a width of 2-5 pixels. This tiny person is also moving slowly, which creates a serious challenge for the detection stage. In our experiments, we maintain the experimental parameter through all sequences and obtain a stable low false alarm rate, but there are only limited moving person detected in the conducted CLEAR evaluation program.

# 6   Conclusion

Tracking in Aerial video still is a challenging topic in computer vision. In this paper, we present two tracking approaches used in Sarnoff Corporation on a large testing data set. For vehicle tracking, our results demonstrate a reasonable tracking accuracy with low false alarm and missing detection rates. However, for the person tracking, we met a lot of difficulties to achieve good evaluation performance due to the small size of the moving persons, slow motion, and low video contrast. It means a great challenge for person detection and tracking still remained in aerial video. In the future, we will further investigate this challenging case to obtain more stable results for person tracking. We will also integrate the linking process into the online tracking process to improve the tracking performance.

# References

1. Yilmaz, A., Javed, O., Shah, M.: Object tracking: A survey. ACM Journal of Computing Surveys 38 (2006)
2. Shi, J., Tomasi, C.: Good features to track. In: International Conference on Computer Vision, pp. 593–600 (1994)
3. Tao, H., Sawhney, H., Kumar, R.: Object tracking with bayesian estimation of dynamic layer representations. IEEE Trans. on Pattern Analysis and Machine Intelligence 24, 75–89 (2002)
4. Yang, C., Duraiswami, R., Davis, L.: Fast multiple object tracking via a hierarchical particle filter. In: IEEE International Conference on Computer Vision, pp. 212–219 (2005)
5. Perera, A., Srinivas, C., Hoogs, A., Brooksby, G., Hu, W.: Multi-object tracking through simultaneous long occlusions and split-merge conditions. In: Computer Vision and Pattern Recognition (2006)
6. Sawhney, H., Guo, Y., Kumar, R.: Independent motion detection in 3d scenes. IEEE Trans. on Pattern Analysis and Machine Intelligence 22, 1191–1199 (2000)
7. Kang, J., Cohen, I., Medioni, G., Yuan, C.: Detection and tracking of moving objects from a moving platform in presence of strong parallax. In: IEEE International Conference on Computer Vision (2005)
8. Xiao, J., Shah, M.: Motion layer extraction in the presence of occlusion using graph cuts. IEEE Trans. on Pattern Analysis and Machine Intelligence 27, 1644–1659 (2005)
9. Jin, H., Favaro, P., Soatto, S.: Real-time teature tracking and outlier rejection with changes in illumination. In: IEEE International Conference on Computer Vision (2001)
10. Xiao, J., Shah, M.: Accurate motion layer segmentation and matting. In: Computer Vision and Pattern Recognition, pp. 698–703 (2005)
11. Yang, C., Duraiswami, R., Davis, L.: Efficient spatial-feature tracking via the mean-shift and a new similarity measure. In: IEEE Conference on Computer Vision and Pattern Recognition (2005)

12. Han, F., Shan, Y., Cekander, R., Sawhney, H., Kumar, R.: A two-stage approach to people and vehicle detection with hog-based svm. In: Performance Metrics for Intelligent Systems Workshop in conjunction with the IEEE Safety, Security, and Rescue Robotics Conference (2006)
13. Kasturi, R., Goldgof, D., Soundararajan, P., Manohar, V., Manohar, V., Boonstra, M., Korzhova, V.: Performance evaluation protocal for face, person and vehicle detection & tracking in video analysis and content extraction (vace-ii). In: Workshop of Classification of Events, Activties and Relationships (2006)
14. Manohar, V., Soundararajan, P., Raju, H., Goldgof, D., Kasturi, R., Garofolo, J.: Performance evaluation of object detection and tracking. In: Narayanan, P.J., Nayar, S.K., Shum, H.-Y. (eds.) ACCV 2006. LNCS, vol. 3852, pp. 151–161. Springer, Heidelberg (2006)

# Person Tracking in UAV Video

Andrew Miller, Pavel Babenko, Min Hu, and Mubarak Shah

Computer Vision Lab at University of Central Florida

## 1 Introduction

The UAV person tracking task for this evaluation was particularly difficult because of large, complicated, and low-quality videos, with only small images of people. We found that our best results were obtained using a combination of intensity thresholding (for IR imagery), motion compensation, interest-point detection and correspondence, and pattern classification. This can be considered a preliminary exploration into an extremely challenging problem.

## 2 Previous Approaches

Our previous efforts into object detection and tracking in aerial video led to the development of the COCOA system[1], which combines a multi-stage process of detection, tracking, and classification algorithms[2], with a graphical user interface for adjusting parameters.

In the first stage of processing, COCOA performs batch registration of every adjacent pair of frames, using a combination of telemetry information from the aerial vehicle, quick feature correspondence, or dense gradient information. An iterative process is used to maximize the stability of the registration, so that the aligned images can form a seamless mosaic [3].

The second stage of processing involves foreground segmentation, either with Mixture-of-Gaussian (MoG) background modeling (Figure 1), or consecutive frame differencing over a short sliding. In both cases, the information from the registration step is used to align pairs of adjacent frames so the motion of the camera does not affect the segmentation.

Finally objects are tracked from one frame to the next by establishing a correspondence based on similar location and color histogram appearance.

Since the registration stage assumes a planar projective transformation between frames, the algorithm works best when the altitude of the camera is very high, or when the scene is nearly planar. If the scene has lots of three-dimensional artifacts like trees, water towers, or tall buildings, these will show up as false foreground objects because of parallax motion, even if the registration is accurate on the ground plane. Since many of the scenes in CLEAR's dataset had several such artifacts, foreground segmentation produces lots of noisy patches.

An additional problem is the small images of people in most scenes. CO-COA has proven to be fairly robust to this sort of noise in past evaluations involving vehicles because vehicles are very fast moving and large compared to

R. Stiefelhagen et al. (Eds.): CLEAR 2007 and RT 2007, LNCS 4625, pp. 215–220, 2008.

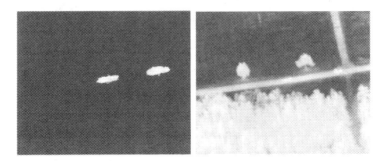

**Fig. 1.** Background modeling is an effective method of detecting vehicles Since the vehicles are large and fast-moving, they appear in the subtraction image as large clearly separated segments.

**Fig. 2.** Background modeling does not work as well for detecting people because the people appear as very small regions that are indistinguishable from clutter noise

the background noise. People are small and slow-moving enough that they are indistinguishable from clutter in the segmentation image.

## 3    Improvements in Static Detection

Rather than rely on foreground segmentation, which proved ineffective, we used a combination feature-point detection and correspondence in each static image with target recognition techniques.

### 3.1    Harris Corner Tracking

Harris corners provide fairly reliable features for tracking. We used greedy correspondence matching, based only on spatial information, similar to the more general approach used in [4]. The X and Y coordinates of each corner in one frame are compared to the coordinates in the next frame. The pair of points with the smallest distance between them are linked to each other by assigning the Object ID of the point in the previous frame to the point in the new frame.

**Fig. 3.** Around 200 Harris corners are typically detected per frame. If a person is present in the frame, then at there will be at least one corresponding Harris corner. In this example, a person is running along the road in the left of the frame.

Then this process is repeated for the remaining unmatched points. When there are no pairs of points with a distance between them less than some threshold, the points in the new frame are given a new ID, and the points in the previous frame are forgotten.

Since the homography of the ground plane is available from the registration step in COCOA, we can project all of the interest points in the previous frame (which are assumed to be on the ground plane) onto the ground plane of the next frame. This allows for correspondence matching to be accurate even when the camera undergoes significant motion between frames.

In general, there are between 100 and 150 detected Harris corners in each frame, as in Figure 3. For each visible person, at least one corner corresponds to a spot on the edge of the person, usually the head or shoulder. Thus the remaining challenge is to suppress the false positives in a later step.

### 3.2 OT-MACH Filter Classification

After obtaining trajectories from Harris corner correspondence, we use an OT-MACH filter (Optimal Trade-Off Maximum Average Correlation Height) to determine whether a track is a person or something else - like a car, or just noise, either of which we should discard. An OT-MACH filter essentially generates a single image template using several training examples of the target, which can be correlated with the image to detect the target.

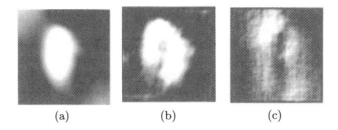

(a)                    (b)                    (c)

**Fig. 4.** OT-MACH Filters generated for: (a) zoomed out IR Intensity, (b) zoomed out IR gradient magnitude, and (c) close up EO gradient magnitude

One filter was generated from a training set of chips of people in all sizes by resizing the images to a common scale. Additional filters were generated by rescaling the original filter to 80% and 120% of the original size. We also used an Edge-Enhanced OT-MACH filter [5] to improve performance in color imagery.

In each frame, the object is compared to the filter to determine whether or not it is a person or not. For each frame when it is classified as a person, a counter associated with the object is incremented. If the counter is greater than a percentage of at least 20% of the total number of frames, then the object is considered a person for its entire duration.

To better localize the tracked person, the filter is correlated with the image in a small spatial window around the feature point, and the location with the highest correlation value is taken as the object's final estimated position.

### 3.3   Intensity and Gradient Histogram

Another way of removing false positives is to compare the the distribution of intensity values and gradient magnitudes of a chip to a generated model. Rather than compare the entire distributions, we can compare only the highest value in the chip as a token for the whole. The histograms for the maximum intensity and gradient magnitude are shown in Figure 5. The intensity histogram is only used for IR imagery, since people in IR will appear very bright, but can be of nearly any color in EO.

These probabilities are thresholded for each frame, and the number of 'passing' frames over an entire trajectory is used to discard more false positives.

## 4   Results

Although there have been difficulties in obtaining a quantitative metric for the performance of our algorithm, our own subjective analysis of our output indicates that there are still very many false positives and some missed detections.

The detection and tracking works fairly consistently, but the classification is still quite poor. The views of people are too small for filters to be meaningful when they are scaled down to an appropriate size.

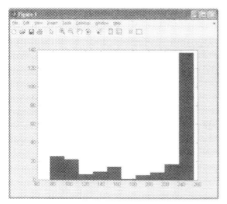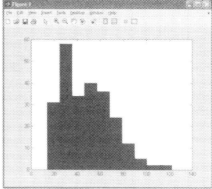

**Fig. 5.** Intensity (left) and gradient magnitude(right) histograms. People appear very bright in IR imagery, thus the intensity histogram is dominated by the upper bin. The gradient magnitude histogram indicates that most chips of people have a maximum gradient magnitude between 20 and 70.

**Fig. 6.** Sample results of combining Harris corner detection and tracking with OT-MACH filter classification. A box is drawn around objects with a track-length of more than 10 frames, and at least 20% classification score. The brightness of the box indicates the classification score beyond 20%.

# 5   Conclusion

Our contribution to this task is the two-part framework of performing correspondence tracking on feature points with lots of positives and then using a combination of classification techniques to suppress the false positives. This approach may prove to be robust in ambiguous scenarios.

Ultimately it seems that the dataset is too difficult to make significant progress in tracking. There were a relatively small number of videos compared to the number of varying conditions. In some cases the camera changed zooms drastically, out of focus, fully occluded, or covered in rain droplets.

As a testament to the difficulty of the dataset, we sat a human volunteer down to watch all of the videos once and asked them to simply point out any people they saw. Later, a larger group watched the videos several times and debated whether or not certain artifacts looked enough like people. The human volunteer only noticed people in 8 of the 30 videos, while the larger group agreed on people in 25 of the videos.

If the dataset is improved and extended in future evaluations, we think it will greatly improve researcher's abilities to make meaningful advances in tracking technology.

# References

1. Ali, S., Shah, M.: Cocoa - tracking in aerial imagery. In: SPIE Airborne Intelligence, Surveillance, Reconnaissance (ISR) Systems and Applications, Orlando (2006)
2. Javed, O., Shah, M.: Tracking and object classification for automated surveillance. In: The Seventh European Conference on Computer Vision, Denmark (2002)
3. Sheikh, Y., Zhai, Y., Shah, M.: An accumulative framework for alignment of an image sequence. In: Proceedings of Asian Conference on Computer Vision (2004)
4. Shafique, K., Shah, M.: A noniterative greedy algorithm for multiframe point correspondence. In: IEEE Trans. Pattern Anal. Mach. Intell. (2005)
5. Ahmed, J., Jafri, M.N., Shah, M., Akbar, M.: Real-time edge-enhanced dynamic correlation and predictive open-loop car-following control for robust tracking. Machine Vision and Applications Journal, Manuscript submission ID MVA-May-06-0110 (accepted, 2007)

# The AIT Multimodal Person Identification System for CLEAR 2007

Andreas Stergiou, Aristodemos Pnevmatikakis, and Lazaros Polymenakos

Athens Information Technology, Autonomic and Grid Computing,
Markopoulou Ave., 19002 Peania, Greece
{aste, apne, lcp}@ait.edu.gr
http://www.ait.edu.gr/research/RG1/overview.asp

**Abstract.** This paper presents the person identification system developed at Athens Information Technology and its performance in the CLEAR 2007 evaluations. The system operates on the audiovisual information (speech and faces) collected over the duration of gallery and probe videos. It comprises of an audio-only (speech), a video-only (face) and an audiovisual fusion subsystem. Audio recognition is based on the Gaussian Mixture modeling of the principal components of composite feature vectors, consisting of Mel-Frequency Cepstral Coefficients and Perceptual Linear Prediction coefficients of speech. Video recognition is based on combining three different classification algorithms: Principal Components Analysis with a modified Mahalanobis distance, sub-class Linear Discriminant Analysis (featuring automatic sub-class generation) with cosine distance and Bayesian classifier based on Gaussian modeling of intrapersonal differences. A nearest neighbor classification rule is applied. A decision fusion scheme across time and classifiers returns the video identity. The audiovisual subsystem fuses the unimodal identities into the multimodal one, using a suitable confidence metric.

## 1 Introduction

Person identification is of paramount importance in security, surveillance, human-computer interfaces and smart spaces. Hence, the evaluation of different recognition algorithms under common evaluation methodologies is very important. Even though the applications of person recognition vary, the evaluations have mostly focused on the security scenario, where training data are few but recorded under close-field conditions. An example of this for faces is the Face Recognition Grand Challenge [1], where facial images are of high resolution (about 250 pixels distance between the centers of the eyes).

The CLEAR 2007 person identification evaluations [2], following the CLEAR 2006 [3] and the Run-1 evaluations [4] of the CHIL project [5], focus on the surveillance and smart spaces applications, where training can be abundant, but on the other hand the recording conditions are far-field: wall-mounted microphone arrays record speech far from the speakers, and cameras mounted on room corners record faces. These two modalities are used, either stand-alone or combined to recognize people in audiovisual streams.

R. Stiefelhagen et al. (Eds.): CLEAR 2007 and RT 2007, LNCS 4625, pp. 221–232, 2008.

The person identification system implemented in Athens Information Technology operates on short sequences of the two modalities of the far-field data, producing unimodal identities and confidences. The system is trained automatically, in the sense that there is no manual operation for the selection of the speech or the faces to be used in the training of the systems. The audio subsystem is analyzed in section 2, while the video one in section 3. The identities produced by the unimodal subsystems are then fused into a bimodal one by the audiovisual subsystem, detailed in section 4. The CLEAR 2007 experiments are presented in section 5. Finally, in section 6 the conclusions are drawn.

## 2 Speaker Identification Subsystem

In the training phase of our system the goal is to create a model for each one of the supported speakers and ensure that these models accentuate the specific speech characteristics of each person. To this end, we first break up the training segments into frames of appropriate size (i.e. duration), with successive frames having a predefined overlap percentage. The samples belonging to each frame are used to calculate a composite feature vector that represents the given frame during the model estimation process. Specifically, a set of Mel Frequency Cepstral Coefficients (MFCC) are extracted from each frame (as in [6]) and augmented by a corresponding set of Perceptual Linear Prediction (PLP) coefficients, in order to model the characteristics and structure of each individual's vocal tract. All composite feature vectors for a given person are collected and used to train a Gaussian Mixture Model (GMM), based on the Baum-Welch algorithm. A GMM is in essence a linear combination of multivariant Gaussians that approximates the probability density function (PDF) of the MFCC+PLP features for the given speaker:

$$\lambda_k = \sum_{m=1}^{M} w_m N\left(o, \mu_m, \Sigma_m\right), \quad k = 1, ..., K \tag{1}$$

where $K$ is the number of speakers (i.e. 28) and $\lambda_k$ is the GMM for the $k$-th speaker. This model is characterized by the number of Gaussians ($M$) that constitutes the mixture, each having its own weight ($w_m$), mean vector ($\mu_m$) and covariance matrix ($\Sigma_m$).

For the identification part, testing samples are again segmented into frames with the same characteristics as the ones created during the training process, and we subsequently extract MFCC and PLP coefficients from each frame and concatenate them into feature supervectors. To perform identification, each of the $K$ GMM's is fed with an array of the coefficients (one row per sample), based on which we calculate two different metrics.

The first one, which is commonly used in MFCC+GMM speaker identification systems [6], measures the sum of log-likelihoods (across all test frames) that this set of observations was produced by the given model. The GMM that produces the highest log-likelihood denotes the most probable speaker according to the system:

$$k_1 = \arg\max_k \left\{ L\left(\mathbf{O} | \lambda_k\right) \right\}, \quad k = 1, ..., K \tag{2}$$

where **O** is the matrix of MFCC+PLP coefficients for the specific test segment and $L(\mathbf{O}|\lambda_k)$ is the total log-likelihood that each model $\lambda_k$ produces this set of observations. We have denoted this standard metric as Maximum Total Likelihood (MTL).

Although the MTL score proves adequate for tests of low duration (i.e., 1 second long), our experiments with this year's development data have shown that for longer durations a different approach is preferable. Specifically, we adopt the video modality identification metric from [6]: for each frame, we find the speaker with the highest log-likelihood, as well as compute a margin that is defined as the ratio of the second-best to best log-likelihood for this frame (since log-likelihoods are strictly negative, this ratio is always greater than one) raised to the sixth power. These margins are then used as weights in a weighted sum score which we denote as Maximum Total Margin – $6^{th}$ power (MTM_6). This second metric is used for tests with durations of 5, 10 and 20 seconds.

All samples are broken up into frames of length 1024 with 75% overlap. Since the data are sampled at 44.1 kHz, each frame has duration of a little over 23 msec. The size of the GMM, as well as the relative numbers of MFCC and PLP coefficients that make up the feature supervectors were determined after experiments conducted on this year's development data. Specifically, all GMM's consist of 32 Gaussians and the number of static coefficients (either MFCC or PLP) per frame has been set to 12, to which we concatenate the log-energy of the frame to create 13D vectors. Depending on the wealth of training data, we have deduced that either MFCC or PLP coefficients must be predominant in the composition of the supervectors. Consequently, for the 15 second training condition (TRAIN_A), each feature vector consists of 39 MFCC (static + delta + delta-delta) and 26 PLP (static + delta) coefficients, whereas for the 30 second training condition (TRAIN_B) we use a complementary setup: 26 MFCC and 39 PLP coefficients. In all cases, both MFCC and PLP coefficients were extracted using the HTK Toolbox [7].

A very crucial step in the creation of a successful GMM is the initialization of its parameters, which will be updated during the iterations of the EM training algorithm. The standard approach is to use the K-Means clustering algorithm to obtain some initial estimates for the Gaussian parameters; this strategy however suffers from the random characteristics of the outcome of K-Means, which in turn lead to a different GMM each time the same data are used for training. Moreover, the identification performance varies considerably across these different models. We have therefore utilized a deterministic initialization strategy for the EM algorithm, based on the statistics of the training data. Specifically, we compute a number of percentiles across all dimensions of the training data set and thus partition the data range in each dimension into as many subsets as the modes of the GMM. The K-Means algorithm is consequently run using the central values of each subset as initial cluster means, and the resulting clustered data are fed into the EM algorithm for parameter fine-tuning.

Our experiments have shown that this strategy gives on average lower error rates than the random K-Means initialization, although there are a few runs using the standard approach that lead to better identification performance.

Automatic identification systems are evaluated based on their response time and error rate. It is obviously important to minimize both these numbers, however in many cases it is not easy or even possible to do that and we must settle for a trade-off between speed and identification accuracy. We have addressed this issue by employing the standard Principal Components Analysis (PCA) as a pre-processing step. Specifically, we compute a transformation (projection matrix) for each speaker based on their training data and use that matrix to perform a mapping to the PCA coordinate system prior to GMM calculation. In the testing phase, we compute the log-likelihood of each speaker by first projecting the MFCC+PLP vectors to the respective PCA space.

The use of PCA introduces one further degree of freedom in the system, namely the dimensionality of the projection space. It is obvious that by keeping an increasingly smaller number of eigenvalues from the PCA scatter matrix we can reduce this dimensionality accordingly, therefore achieving a significant execution speed increase. The choice of the number of discarded eigenvalues will be ultimately dictated by the truncation error introduced due to the reduction of the projection space dimension. Specifically, if the initial space dimension is $d$ and we discard the $q$ smallest eigenvalues, the truncation error will be equal to

$$e = 1 - \frac{\sum\limits_{i=d-q+1}^{d} \lambda_i}{\sum\limits_{i=1}^{d} \lambda_i} \qquad (3)$$

In [6], we had employed an automatic decision process that determines the number of retained eigenvalues in a way that ensures that the average truncation error across all speakers is no more than 0.2%. The maximum value of $q$ that satisfies this condition is chosen, so that we achieve the greatest speed increase possible while retaining (mostly) optimal identification accuracies. Extensive experimentation with this year's development data indicated that the augmentation of the feature vectors with the PLP coefficients forces us to be stricter with this limit, which was ultimately set to 0.1%.

Our experiments indicate that this selection strategy gives a value for $q$ that is at most one above or below the number of eigenvalues that minimizes the error rates. Even if our choice of $q$ leads to slightly sub-optimal solutions, the achieved error rates are still superior to using the standard GMM algorithm approach without PCA pre-processing. We have therefore achieved faster response times as well as enhanced identification performance.

## 3  Face Identification Subsystem

Face recognition on still images has been extensively studied. Given sufficient training data (many gallery stills of each person) and/or high resolution images, the 90% recognition barrier can be exceeded, even for hundreds of different people to be recognized [1]. Face recognition on video streams has only recently begun to receive attention [6, 8-13]. Video-to-video face recognition refers to the problem of training and testing face recognition systems using video streams. Usually these video streams are near-field, where the person to be recognized occupies most of the frame. They are also constrained in the sense that the person looks mainly at the camera. Typical such video streams originate from video-calls and news narration, where a person's head and upper torso is visible.

The CLEAR series of person identification evaluations address a much more interesting application domain: that of the far-field unconstrained video streams. In such streams the people are far from the camera, which is typically mounted on a room corner near the ceiling. VGA-resolution cameras in such a setup can easily lead to quite small faces – down to less than ten pixels between the eyes [3,4], contrasted to over two hundred pixels in many of the latest face recognition evaluations [1]. Also, the people go about their business, almost never facing the camera directly. As a result, faces undergo large pose, expression and lighting variations. Part of the problem is alleviated by the use of multiple cameras; getting approximately frontal faces is more probable with four cameras at the corners of a room than with a single one. The problem is further alleviated by the fact that the goal is not to derive a person's identity from a single frame, but rather from some video duration. Faces to be recognized are collected from a number of frames; the person identity is then established based on that collection of faces. Hence, far-field unconstrained video-to-video face recognition needs to address the following challenges:

- Detection, tracking, segmentation and normalization of the faces from the video streams, both for system training and recognition.
- The face recognition algorithm needs to cope with very small faces, with unconstrained pose, expression and illumination, and also with inaccurate face framing.
- Fusion of the individual decisions on faces, to provide the identity of the person given some time interval.

The video subsystem for person identification utilizes all four camera streams to extract frontal and profile faces for training and testing of the system. The faces are extracted employing the provided face bounding box label files. These are sampled at 200 ms intervals. Cubic interpolation is used between those labels, to get approximate face locations in all frames. Contrary to the CLEAR 2006 AIT system, no geometric face normalization, neither selection of the most frontal faces is applied. The face patches are scaled to a standard size of 48 tall by 32 wide pixels. Intensity normalization to a mean value of 127 and a standard deviation of 40 is applied on every face patch thus obtained. Right profile faces are flipped to become left profile. All these pre-processing steps are based on the analysis of the CLEAR 2006 results, presented in [14].

To cope with different impairments present in the task (pose, expression and illumination changes), three face recognition algorithms are applied and then suitably combined to yield the identity of the person. These algorithms are based on Principal Components Analysis (PCA), subclass Linear Discriminant Analysis (LDA) and intrapersonal differences. They are presented in the next subsections.

### 3.1 PCA Face Recognition

The first algorithm uses Principal Components Analysis (PCA) to find from the gallery faces a recognition subspace of dimension $N_{PCA}$. Classification is done by projecting each probe face in this subspace and then use a nearest neighbor classifier. The distance employed in the classifier is a modification of the weighted Euclidean, with the weights of each dimension depending on the neighborhood of the particular gallery point. The $N_{neib}$ closest neighbors (using Euclidean distance) to the given gallery point are used to estimate the scatter matrix of gallery points in the vicinity of that gallery point. The gallery point-dependant weights are the eigenvalues of that scatter matrix. Although this estimation of point-dependant weights is computationally expensive, it is performed once at system training and the $N_{PCA}$ weights for each of the projected gallery images are stored to be used in the recognition phase.

## 3.2 Subclass LDA Face Recognition

LDA can prove close to useless for class discrimination problems that are non-separable in a linear way [15]. The face manifolds obtained under unconstraint conditions can easily fall in this problem category. For such problems [15, p. 453] suggests sub-class LDA, where training samples belonging to some class are allocated to different subclasses. Even though the resulting classification space is of larger dimension and the training images per subclass are fewer than those per original class, the problem is turned to a linearly separable one that the resulting classifier can cope with. For automatic training of subclass LDA systems, the choice of the split from a class to the subclasses has to be automatic.

Hence an automatic subclass selection process is needed that subdivides each class into subclasses, making no assumption for the number of subclasses or the number of samples in any subclass. These requirements are met using hierarchical clustering trees. During the training phase, PCA is employed to project the faces into a subspace of dimension $N$. The Euclidean distance between all projected faces of each person is calculated, to build a hierarchical clustering tree. The tree is built bottom-up, using a measure of the distance between two clusters of projected faces: At each step up the tree, the two clusters with minimum distance between them are merged into a higher-level cluster. The chosen distance measure is the increase in the total within-cluster sum of squares as a result of joining the two clusters $c_1$ and $c_2$, comprising $n_1$ and $n_2$ projected faces respectively. The within-cluster sum of squares is defined as the sum of the squares of the Euclidean distances between all projected faces in the cluster and the centroid of the cluster. The centroids of the two clusters are:

$$\bar{x}_i = \frac{1}{n_i} \sum_{k=1}^{n_i} x_k^{(i)} , \ i = 1, 2 \tag{4}$$

where $x_k^{(i)}$ is the $k$-th projected faces of the $i$-th cluster. Then, the cluster distance measure is given by:

$$d(c_1, c_2) = \sqrt{\frac{n_1 n_2}{n_1 + n_2}} \|\bar{x}_1 - \bar{x}_2\|_2 \tag{5}$$

where $\|\bar{x}_1 - \bar{x}_2\|_2$ is the Euclidean distance of the two centroids. The hierarchical tree thus obtained is used to cluster the samples of the class in subclasses, by cutting the tree at any distance value $D$. Small cutoff distances result to many subclasses, whereas large cutoff distances result to few subclasses. The PCA subspace dimension $N_{PCA}$ and the tree cutoff distance $D$ are the two parameters of the algorithm.

### 3.3 Bayesian Face Recognition

The images of the face of a person can vary substantially due to pose, expression and illumination variations. Such variations are intrapersonal and should not lead to a decision that a particular face depicted in a probe image is different than those of the same person depicted in the gallery images. A Bayesian face recognition framework can be build by modeling the intrapersonal variations in the gallery images by a Gaussian distribution, and evaluating the probability that the difference of a gallery face from a probe face is indeed intrapersonal [16]. As for the modeling interpersonal differences also proposed in [16], our experiments with the validation set have shown no benefit, at the cost of a significant increase in computation. Hence no such modeling is attempted.

A second deviation from the approach in [16] addresses the computational complexity of modeling the intrapersonal differences. When galleries have many images, as is the case with the training conditions of the CLEAR evaluations, the possible number of differences is overwhelming. To overcome this difficulty, only some of the gallery faces are utilized. The automatic selection of the faces to use is performed by grouping the gallery images of any person using hierarchical clustering trees. The trees are constructed using the projected gallery images onto a PCA subspace of dimension $N_{PCA}$. For every person, $N$ projected images are selected as the median of every of the $N$ clusters obtained by the trees. The intrapersonal differences are formed and modeled at the reduced dimension $N_{PCA}$ of the PCA subspace.

Classification is again based on the nearest neighbor classifier, with the inverse of the intrapersonal probability serving as a distance.

### 3.4 Fusion Across Time and Face Recognition Algorithms

The decisions of the different algorithms for the different images obtained across time and camera views have to be fused into a single identity. The fusion is done in two stages. First, the decisions of each algorithm across time and camera views are fused together. Then, the three decisions of the three different algorithms are fused. Our experiments with the validation dataset indicate that this is a better approach than fussing first across the three algorithms and then across time and views.

The individual decisions of any of the face recognition algorithms are fused across time and camera views using the sum rule [17]. According to it, each decision $ID_i$ in a testing segment casts a vote that carries a weight $w_i$. The weights $w_i$ of every decision such as $ID_i = k$ are summed to yield the weights $W_k$ of each class:

$$W_k = \sum_{i:ID_i=k} w_i \qquad (6)$$

where $k = 1, \ldots, K$ and $K$ is the number of classes. Then the fused decision based on the $N$ individual identities is:

$$ID^{(N)} = \arg\max_{k} \left( W_k \right) \tag{7}$$

The weight $w_i$ in the sum rule for the $i$-th decision is the sixth power of the ratio of the second-minimum distance $d_i^{(1)}$ over the minimum distance $d_i^{(1)}$:

$$w_i = \left[ \frac{d_i^{(2)}}{d_i^{(1)}} \right]^6 \tag{8}$$

This choice for weight reflects the classification confidence: If the two smallest distances from the class centers are approximately equal, then the selection of the identity leading to the smallest distance is unreliable. In this case the weight is close to unity, weighting down the particular decision. If on the other hand the minimum distance is much smaller than the second-minimum, the decision is heavily weighted as the selection of the identity is reliable. The sixth power allows for a few very confident decisions to be weighted more then many less confident ones.

The decisions temporally fused across the whole video duration and four camera views of the PCA, the subclass LDA and the Bayesian face recognition algorithms are $ID^{(\text{PCA})}$, $ID^{(\text{sLDA})}$ and $ID^{(\text{Bayes})}$ respectively. The three are fused, again using the sum rule, to yield the reported identity. For this fusion, the class weights $W_k$ of equation (6) are used instead of the distances in equation (8). Setting:

$$\begin{aligned} k_1^{(i)} &\equiv [\text{best matching class for classifier } i] \\ k_2^{(i)} &\equiv [\text{second-best matching class for classifier } i] \end{aligned}, \ i \in \{\text{PCA, sLDA, Bayes}\} \tag{9}$$

the weights of the PCA, the subclass LDA and the Bayesian decisions become:

$$w_i = \frac{W_{k_1}^{(i)}}{W_{k_2}^{(i)}}, \ i \in \{\text{PCA, sLDA, Bayes}\} \tag{10}$$

As a result, there are $w_i$ votes in favor of identity $k_1^{(i)}$, with a maximum of 3 different identities, as $i \in \{\text{PCA, sLDA, Bayes}\}$. Then the combined decision of the three algorithms to be reported by the visual subsystem $ID^{(\text{visual})}$ is:

$$ID^{(\text{visual})} = k_1^{(i)}, \text{ such as } i = \arg\max_i \{w_i, i \in \{\text{PCA, sLDA, Bayes}\}\} \tag{11}$$

## 4 Audiovisual Person Identification

The audiovisual system is again based on post-decision fusion using the sum rule. The audio and visual weight to be used in the sum rule are computed as follows: The audio weight $w_{\text{audio}}$ is the ratio of the log-likelihood $L(\mathbf{O}|\lambda_{k_1})$ that the best matching model $\lambda_{k_1}$ produces the set of observations $\mathbf{O}$, over the log-likelihood $L(\mathbf{O}|\lambda_{k_2})$ that the second-best matching model $\lambda_{k_2}$ produces $\mathbf{O}$:

$$w_{\text{audio}} = \frac{L(\mathbf{O} \mid \lambda_{k_1})}{L(\mathbf{O} \mid \lambda_{k_2})} \tag{12}$$

The visual weight $w_{\text{visual}}$ is the maximum of the weights corresponding to the three different algorithms employed, as they are given by (10):

$$w_{\text{visual}} = \max\{w_i, i \in \{\text{PCA, sLDA, Bayes}\}\} \tag{13}$$

## 5 Experiments

In CLEAR 2007, training, validation and testing segments have been defined. The two training conditions are 15 and 30 seconds long. Four durations have been defined

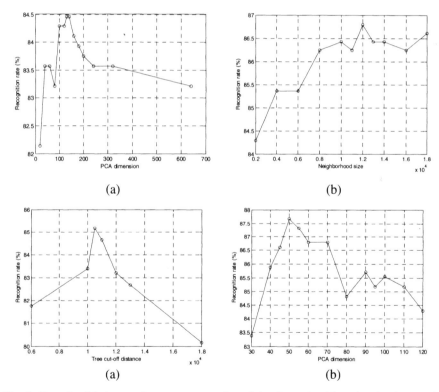

**Fig. 1.** Use of validation set for parameter tuning of the three algorithms involved in the face recognition system. The effect of the various parameters on the fused recognition rate of the whole 1 sec sequence is shown. (a) PCA subspace dimension and (b) neighborhood size for the PCA-based algorithm. (c) Tree cut-off distance for the automatic selection of subclasses in the subclass LDA algorithm. (d) PCA subspace dimension for the projection of the images to the space where representative images for the intrapersonal difference modeling are selected for the Bayesian algorithm.

**Table 1.** Audio, video a006Ed audiovisual recognition performance in CLEAR 2007

| Training duration | Testing duration | Recognition rate (%) | | |
|---|---|---|---|---|
| | | Audio | Video | Audiovisual |
| 15 | 1 | 79.69 | 79.38 | 89.20 |
| | 5 | 90.40 | 86.16 | 94.42 |
| | 10 | 94.64 | 89.29 | 96.88 |
| | 20 | 95.54 | 91.07 | 96.43 |
| 30 | 1 | 84.51 | 86.12 | 92.90 |
| | 5 | 94.87 | 91.29 | 95.98 |
| | 10 | 96.88 | 94.20 | 96.88 |
| | 20 | 99.11 | 94.64 | 97.32 |

both for validation and testing: 1, 5, 10 and 20 seconds long. All these segments contain mostly speech, so a speech activity detection algorithm [18] has not been used.

The development set is used to establish the values of the various parameters of the algorithms. An example of this parameter tuning is shown in Figure 1, for the three algorithms of the face recognition system, 15 sec training and duration of the validation tests of 1 sec. Note that for the longer testing durations, there are not enough validation tests to be performed for trusted analysis. Hence, only the 1 and 5 sec durations of the validation sets are used.

The results of the audio, visual and multimodal person recognition are shown in Table 1 per training and testing duration.

## 6   Conclusions

The results of the person identification system of Athens Information Technology at the development and test sets of the CLEAR 2007 evaluations are quite different. Overfitting to the development set is not a likely cause for the reduced performance on the test set. This is because most parameters have a value region leading to similar recognition performance. The most plausible explanation is the temporal separation of the training, validation and testing sets. Training and testing are chosen as far apart in time as possible, with the validation set being in-between. Also, the small number of segments of the longer durations, render any parameter tuning for these durations very risky from a statistical point of view.

It is not straightforward to judge the relative difficulty of the CLEAR 2007 and CLEAR 2006 person identification evaluations. Although the number of people is slightly increased (28 compared to 26), the sequences are selected keeping a balance between the two modalities (in CLEAR 2006, attention had been paid to the existence of speech) and the video labels are more accurate and are all provided every 200 ms (compared to every 1 sec for the face bounding boxes of CLEAR 2006).

Regarding the performance of the AIT system in the test set, the CLEAR 2007 results are superior to those of CLEAR 2006. The main reason for this is the enhanced algorithms employed, as indicated by the results of the system on the CLEAR 2006 test set.

# Acknowledgements

This work is sponsored by the European Union under the integrated project CHIL, contract number 506909. The authors wish to thank the people involved in data collection, annotation and overall organization of the CLEAR 2007 evaluations for providing such a rich test-bed for the presented algorithms.

# References

[1] Phillips, J., Flynn, P., Scruggs, T., Boyer, K., Worek, W.: Preliminary Face Recognition Grand Challenge Results. In: Proceedings of IEEE Conference on Automatic Face and Gesture Recognition, Southampton, UK, pp. 15–21 (2006)

[2] http://www.clear-evaluation.org

[3] Stiefelhagen, R., Bernardin, K., Bowers, R., Garofolo, J., Mostefa, D., Soundararajan, P.: The CLEAR 2006 Evaluation. In: Stiefelhagen, R., Garofolo, J.S. (eds.) CLEAR 2006. LNCS, vol. 4122, pp. 1–44. Springer, Heidelberg (2007)

[4] Ekenel, H., Pnevmatikakis, A.: Video-Based Face Recognition Evaluation in the CHIL Project – Run 1, Face and Gesture Recognition 2006, Southampton, UK, April 2006, pp. 85–90 (2006)

[5] Waibel, A., Steusloff, H., Stiefelhagen, R., et al.: CHIL: Computers in the Human Interaction Loop. In: 5th International Workshop on Image Analysis for Multimedia Interactive Services (WIAMIS), Lisbon, Portugal (April 2004)

[6] Stergiou, A., Pnevmatikakis, A., Polymenakos, L.: A Decision Fusion System Across Time and Classifiers for Audio-Visual Person Identification. In: Stiefelhagen, R., Garofolo, J.S. (eds.) CLEAR 2006. LNCS, vol. 4122, pp. 223–232. Springer, Heidelberg (2007)

[7] HTK (Hidden Markov Toolkit), http://htk.eng.cam.ac.uk/

[8] Weng, J., Evans, C.H., Hwang, W.-S.: An Incremental Learning Method for Face Recognition under Continuous Video Stream. In: Proceedings of IEEE Conference on Automatic Face and Gesture Recognition, Grenoble, France, pp. 251–256 (2000)

[9] Lee, K.-C., Ho, J., Yang, M.-H., Kriegman, D.: Video-based face recognition using probabilistic appearance manifolds. In: Proceedings of IEEE Conference on Computer Vision and Pattern Recognition, Madison, Wisconsin, USA, pp. 313–320 (2003)

[10] Liu, X., Chen, T.: Video-based face recognition using adaptive hidden markov models. In: Proceedings of IEEE Conference on Computer Vision and Pattern Recognition, Madison, Wisconsin, USA, pp. 340–345 (2003)

[11] Raytchev, B., Murase, H.: Unsupervised recognition of multi-view face sequences based on pairwise clustering with attraction and repulsion. Computer Vision and Image Understanding 91, 22–52 (2003)

[12] Aggarwal, G., Roy-Chowdhury, A.K., Chellappa, R.: A System Identification Approach for Video-based Face Recognition. In: Proceedings of International Conference on Pattern Recognition, Cambridge, UK (2004)

[13] Xie, C., Vijaya Kumar, B.V.K., Palanivel, S., Yegnanarayana, B.: A Still-to-Video Face Verification System Using Advanced Correlation Filters. In: Zhang, D., Jain, A.K. (eds.) ICBA 2004. LNCS, vol. 3072, pp. 102–108. Springer, Heidelberg (2004)

[14] Pnevmatikakis, A., Polymenakos, L.: Far-Field Multi-Camera Video-to-Video Face Recognition. In: Delac, K., Grgic, M. (eds.) Face Recognition", Advanced Robotics Systems, ISBN 978-3-902613-03-5

[15] Fukunaga, K.: Statistical Pattern Recognition. Academic Press, London (1990)
[16] Moghaddam, B.: Principal Manifolds and Probabilistic Subspaces for Visual Recognition. IEEE Trans. Pattern Anal. Mach. Intell. 24(6) (2002)
[17] Kittler, J., Hatef, M., Duin, R.P.W., Matas, J.: On combining classifiers. IEEE Trans. Pattern Anal. Mach. Intell. 20(3), 226–239 (1998)
[18] Sohn, J., Kim, N.S., Sung, W.: A Statistical Model Based Voice Activity Detection. IEEE Sig. Proc. Letters 6(1) (1999)

# Acoustic Speaker Identification: The LIMSI CLEAR'07 System

Claude Barras[1,2], Xuan Zhu[1,2], Cheung-Chi Leung[1], Jean-Luc Gauvain[1], and Lori Lamel[1,*]

[1] Spoken Language Processing Group
LIMSI-CNRS, BP 133, 91403 Orsay cedex, France
[2] Univ Paris-Sud, F-91405, Orsay, France
{barras,xuan,ccleung,gauvain,lamel}@limsi.fr

**Abstract.** The CLEAR 2007 acoustic speaker identification task aims to identify speakers in CHIL seminars via the acoustic channel. The LIMSI system for this task consists of a standard Gaussian mixture model based system working on cepstral coefficients, with MAP adaptation of a Universal Background Model (UBM). It builds upon the LIMSI CLEAR'06 system with several modifications: removal of feature normalization and frames filtering, and pooling of all speaker enrollment data for UBM training. The primary system uses a beamforming of all audio channels, while a single channel is selected for the contrastive system. This latter system performs the best and improves the baseline system by 50% relative for the 1 second and 5 seconds test conditions.

## 1 Introduction

Automatic person identification is a key feature of smart rooms, and in this context the European Integrated Project CHIL[1] has supported the CLEAR'06 and '07 evaluations, where audio, video and multi-modal person identification tasks were evaluated on CHIL seminars. Our work at LIMSI focuses on the acoustic modality. Similar to last year, the CLEAR'07 acoustic speaker identification task is a text-independent, closed-set identification task with far-field microphone array training and test conditions. Enrollment data of 15 and 30 seconds are provided for the 28 target speakers and test segment durations of 1, 5 10 and 20 seconds are considered[2].

This paper describes the LIMSI acoustic speaker identification system, evaluated in the CLEAR'07 benchmark. The system is a standard GMM-UBM system building on the LIMSI CLEAR'06 developments [2]. In the next section, the LIMSI speaker recognition system is presented. Section 3 gives experimental results on the CLEAR development data and evaluation data.

---

[*] This work was partially financed by the European Commission under the FP6 Integrated Project IP 506909 CHIL

[1] CHIL – Computers in the Human Interaction Loop, http://chil.server.de/

[2] http://www.clear-evaluation.org/

R. Stiefelhagen et al. (Eds.): CLEAR 2007 and RT 2007, LNCS 4625, pp. 233–239, 2008.

## 2    Speaker Recognition System

In this section, the LIMSI baseline speaker recognition system used in the CLEAR'06 evaluation and the new system developed for CLEAR'07 are described.

### 2.1    Baseline System

The speaker recognition system developed for the CLEAR'06 evaluation served as the baseline system for this year's evaluation. It is organized as follows:

Acoustic features are extracted from the speech signal every 10ms using a 30ms window. The feature vector consists of 15 PLP-like cepstrum coefficients computed on a Mel frequency scale, their $\Delta$ and $\Delta$-$\Delta$ coefficients plus the $\Delta$ and $\Delta$-$\Delta$ log-energy. Ten percent of the frames with the lowest energy are filtered out, and short-term feature warping [4] is performed in order to map the cepstral feature distribution to a normal distribution.

A Gaussian mixture-model (GMM) with diagonal covariance matrices is used as a gender-independent Universal Background Model (UBM). This model with 256 Gaussians was trained on 90 min. of speech extracted from jun'04 and dev'06 CHIL data. For each target speaker, a speaker-specific GMM is trained by Maximum A Posteriori (MAP) adaptation [3] of the Gaussian means of the UBM. Target models are MAP-adapted using 3 iterations of the EM algorithm and a prior factor $\tau = 10$. The GMM-UBM approach has proved to be very successful for text-independent speaker recognition, since it allows the robust estimation of the target models even with a limited amount of enrollment data [5]. During the identification phase, each test segment $X$ is scored against all targets $\lambda_k$ in parallel and the target model with the highest log-likelihood is chosen: $k^* = \mathrm{argmax}_k \log f(X|\lambda_k)$.

Several optimizations to reduce the training and scoring computational requirements were implemented in the LIMSI CLEAR'06 system in order to carry out identification efficiently, in faster than real-time for realistic configurations. A stochastic frame subsampling was proposed for speeding up the UBM training using a large amount of training data. For the identification stage, top-Gaussian scoring was used, restricting the log-likelihood estimation to the 10 top scoring out of 256 components of the UBM for each frame and resulting in a 13 times speed up, and an auto-adaptive pruning was introduced, resulting in a further factor of 2 speed up for long duration segments [2].

### 2.2    System Development for CLEAR'07

For CLEAR'06 evaluation data, only the 4th channel out of the 64 channels of the MarkIII microphone array was used. Rather than picking a single channel, the ICSI beamforming software [1] was applied to the 64 channels for CLEAR'07 primary submission, with the 4th channel alone being used in a contrastive system. For beamforming, the 1st channel was used as a reference for delay estimation, and other settings were kept identical to the default software configuration, with a delay estimation each 250ms on a 500ms window. In both cases the signal was downsampled from 44kHz to 16kHz. Neither feature normalization nor frame selection were used. Finally, the UBM was trained by pooling all speaker enrollment data instead of using external data, which amounts to 7 minutes for the 15 second training condition and 14 minutes for the 30 second training condition. All other settings were kept unchanged.

# 3   Experimental Results

In this section the impact of the system changes on the CLEAR'06 evaluation and CLEAR'07 validation data are given. Both data sets were used for system development. Results on the CLEAR'07 evaluation data are also provided for the primary and contrastive system.

## 3.1   Experiments with CLEAR'06 Evaluation Data

The results of LIMSI system in CLEAR'06 Acoustic Speaker Identification evaluation are reported in Table 1. The impact of two major changes in the system are given. Discarding feature normalization and UBM training by enrollment data pooling provide a dramatic improvement, an over 50% relative error reduction on the 1 and 5 seconds test conditions.

**Table 1.** Identification error rates on the CLEAR'06 Speaker Identification task for the LIMSI'06 submitted system and for the modified system

| Test duration | 1 second | 5 seconds | 10 seconds | 20 seconds |
|---|---|---|---|---|
| A: LIMSI CLEAR'06 System | | | | |
| Train A (15 s) | 51.7 | 10.9 | 6.6 | 3.4 |
| Train B (30 s) | 38.8 | 5.8 | 2.1 | 0.0 |
| B: A + no feature normalization | | | | |
| Train A (15 s) | 32.8 | 8.0 | 6.2 | 3.9 |
| Train B (30 s) | 20.1 | 3.4 | 2.4 | 1.1 |
| C: B + enrollment data pooling for UBM | | | | |
| Train A (15 s) | 25.0 | 4.9 | 4.8 | 2.2 |
| Train B (30 s) | 16.2 | 1.9 | 0.7 | 0.0 |

## 3.2   Experiments with CLEAR'07 Validation Set

Experiments were conducted using CLEAR'07 validation set in order to assess several settings of the system. Given the size of the validation set, only test durations of 1 and 5 seconds were considered as they provide respectively 560 and 112 samples; fewer than 100 samples were available for other test durations.

As was shown previously, the system is very sensitive to the feature normalization. Table 2 compares the identification error rate on the validation set for cepstral mean substraction (CMS), mean and variance normalization (mean+var),

**Table 2.** Impact of various feature normalizations (CMS, mean+variance, feature warping and raw features) on identification errors for beamformed and single channel audio, for the CLEAR'07 validation data

| Normalization | Train/Test duration | Beamforming | | 4th channel | |
|---|---|---|---|---|---|
| | | *1 sec.* | *5 sec.* | *1 sec.* | *5 sec.* |
| CMS | Train A (15 s) | 38.8 | 6.2 | 46.4 | 11.6 |
| | Train B (30 s) | 28.7 | 3.6 | 38.0 | 4.5 |
| mean+var | Train A (15 s) | 39.6 | 2.7 | 49.8 | 13.4 |
| | Train B (30 s) | 30.2 | 2.7 | 37.7 | 3.6 |
| warping | Train A (15 s) | 39.6 | 2.7 | 48.6 | 9.8 |
| | Train B (30 s) | 28.6 | 0.9 | 39.6 | 4.5 |
| raw | Train A (15 s) | **17.9** | **2.7** | 21.1 | 3.6 |
| | Train B (30 s) | **14.1** | **1.8** | 15.5 | 1.8 |

**Table 3.** Impact of UBM size and MAP prior weight on identification errors on CLEAR'07 validation data

| | MAP prior | $\tau=8$ | | $\tau=10$ | | $\tau=12$ | |
|---|---|---|---|---|---|---|---|
| *UBM size* | *Train/Test duration* | *1 sec.* | *5 sec.* | *1 sec.* | *5 sec.* | *1 sec.* | *5 sec.* |
| 128G | Train A (15 s) | 17.7 | 6.2 | 18.2 | 6.2 | 19.1 | 6.2 |
| | Train B (30 s) | 14.8 | 0.9 | 14.6 | 0.9 | 14.6 | 0.9 |
| 256G | Train A (15 s) | 17.9 | 2.7 | **17.9** | **2.7** | 17.7 | 2.7 |
| | Train B (30 s) | 14.3 | 1.8 | **14.1** | **1.8** | 14.5 | 0.9 |
| 512G | Train A (15 s) | 20.7 | 4.5 | 20.7 | 3.6 | 20.7 | 3.6 |
| | Train B (30 s) | 14.3 | 1.8 | 14.1 | 1.8 | 14.3 | 1.8 |

feature warping and raw features. Avoiding any feature normalization is by far the best. This can be explained by a very limited channel variability per speaker in CHIL seminars. It can also be noted that better results are obtained using beamformed audio data for all configurations.

Keeping raw features, tests were carried out varying the number of Gaussians in the UBM (128, 256 and 512) and the MAP adaptation weights (prior factor $\tau = 8$, 10 and 12) on the validation set with the beamformed audio. As shown in Table 3, the baseline configuration with 256 Gaussians and $\tau=10$ remains a good compromise.

In speaker identification, the GMM-UBM approach generally outperforms a direct training of the target models via maximum likelihood estimation (MLE). For contrastive purposes, identification performance on the validation set for MLE-trained models with a varying number of Gaussians are given in Table 4. The best results are obtained with 32 Gaussians for Train A (15 s) and with 64 Gaussians for Train B (30 s). These results are inferior to those obtained with the GMM-UBM configuration.

**Table 4.** Identification errors on the CLEAR'07 validation data using direct MLE trained models with a varying number of Gaussians

| GMM size | Train/Test duration | Beamforming | | 4th channel | |
|---|---|---|---|---|---|
| | | 1 sec. | 5 sec. | 1 sec. | 5 sec. |
| 16G | Train A (15 s) | 25.4 | 6.2 | 32.1 | 10.7 |
| | Train B (30 s) | 19.8 | 3.6 | 24.3 | 3.6 |
| 32G | Train A (15 s) | 24.6 | 6.2 | 28.2 | 9.8 |
| | Train B (30 s) | 17.3 | 1.8 | 20.5 | 0.9 |
| 64G | Train A (15 s) | 25.2 | 9.8 | 29.8 | 15.2 |
| | Train B (30 s) | 16.1 | 0.9 | 19.1 | 0.9 |
| 128G | Train A (15 s) | 35.4 | 25.0 | 36.1 | 21.4 |
| | Train B (30 s) | 17.9 | 0.9 | 20.7 | 1.8 |

**Table 5.** Identification errors on the CLEAR'07 validation data with and without 10% low-energy frame filtering

| Filtering | Train/Test duration | Beamforming | | 4th channel | |
|---|---|---|---|---|---|
| | | 1 sec. | 5 sec. | 1 sec. | 5 sec. |
| 0% | Train A (15 s) | **19.5** | **0.9** | 21.8 | 2.7 |
| | Train B (30 s) | **13.0** | **1.8** | 14.3 | 1.8 |
| 10% | Train A (15 s) | 17.9 | 2.7 | 21.1 | 3.6 |
| | Train B (30 s) | 14.1 | 1.8 | 15.5 | 1.8 |

The improvement provided by the frame selection was also assessed. Table 5 gives the identification error rate with and without 10% low energy filtering on the validation set. Frame filtering does not seem to significantly help, except for the 15 sec. training / 1 sec. test condition and was thus discarded from the final 2007 system.

### 3.3  CLEAR 2007 Evaluation Results

Table 6 reports the LIMSI results for the CLEAR'07 evaluation for the primary and contrastive systems, along with CLEAR'06 results, on the corresponding evaluation sets, expressed in terms of accuracy. It can be observed that data beamforming, which was effective on validation set, did not work as expected in the test condition. There may be some differences between validation and test data, and the settings of the beamforming were not optimized on the specific task configuration: given that a single speaker can be expected to be found in a segment, a single delay estimation on the whole segment between the reference and the other channels, as was done in [6], may have been a better choice.

There is less degradation for the contrastive system between the validation and test phases, between 25 and 30% relative. In CLEAR'06 evaluation, LIMSI system had rather low identification rates on 1 sec. test segments, below 50% for 15 seconds training and near 60% for 30 seconds training. In CLEAR'07 con-

**Table 6.** Accuracy rates for the LIMSI CLEAR'06 and '07 Acoustic Speaker Identification task on their respective evaluation data sets

| Test duration | 1 second | 5 seconds | 10 seconds | 20 seconds |
|---|---|---|---|---|
| '06 Primary | | | | |
| Train A (15 seconds) | 48.3 | 89.1 | 93.4 | 96.6 |
| Train B (30 seconds) | 61.2 | 94.2 | 97.9 | 100.0 |
| '07 Primary (beamforming) | | | | |
| Train A (15 seconds) | 62.4 | 90.8 | 93.8 | 97.3 |
| Train B (30 seconds) | 69.4 | 92.2 | 95.1 | 95.5 |
| '07 Contrastive (4th channel) | | | | |
| Train A (15 seconds) | 75.0 | 94.9 | 96.9 | 98.2 |
| Train B (30 seconds) | 80.0 | 96.2 | 97.3 | 98.2 |

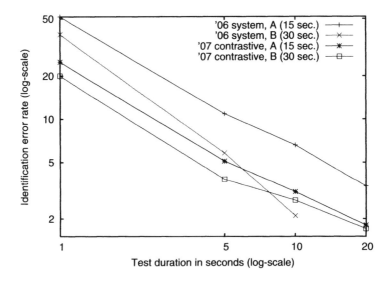

**Fig. 1.** Identification error rates by training and test duration for LIMSI '06 and '07 contrastive systems for CLEAR Acoustic Speaker Identification task

trastive system, these figures have been increased to 75% and 80% respectively. Both evaluations having a similar number of speakers (28 in CLEAR'07 vs. 26 in CLEAR'06), this allows a direct comparison of the results. Figure 1 shows the improvement between the LIMSI '06 and '07 systems, as a function of the training and test durations in a log-log scale.

## 4    Conclusions

LIMSI submitted two systems to the CLEAR'07 Acoustic Speaker Identification task. The contrastive system provides a 50% relative reduction of the error rate compared to previous year results for the 1 and 5 seconds test conditions, resulting in 75% and 80% identification rate for 15 and 30 second training data, respectively.

This improvement is mainly due to modifications in the cepstral feature normalization step and in the UBM training. Feature warping usually improves speaker identification in telephone speech domain, and is also of interest for speaker diarization in broadcast news and meetings. However, discarding any feature normalization proved to be the most successful choice. This may be because a given speaker was generally recorded in a stable acoustic configuration for this evaluation. Training the UBM by pooling all enrollment data was chosen instead of using other available training data. This can only be considered in a closed-set speaker identification context, where the set of possible impostors is fully known in advance. This configuration also outperformed a direct MLE training of the target models.

The primary system, taking advantage of a beamforming of all available 64 channels, performs substancially less well than the contrastive system where only a single channel is selected. This observation is different from the behavior of both systems observed on the validation data, where beamforming always outperformed a single channel. But the beamforming settings we used were not optimized for an array of distant microphones and for the specific evaluation conditions, so there is probably still room for system improvement in this area.

In conclusion, the CLEAR'07 has provided better insight into the speaker identification goals and constraints in the seminar meeting domain. This resulted in a dramatic improvement of the performances of our system for the short test conditions.

# References

1. Anguera, X., Wooters, C., Hernando, J.: Speaker Diarization for Multi-Party Meetings Using Acoustic Fusion. In: Automatic Speech Recognition and Understanding (IEEE, ASRU 2005), San Juan, Puerto Rico (2005)
2. Barras, C., Zhu, X., Gauvain, J.-L., Lamel, L.: The CLEAR 2006 LIMSI Acoustic Speaker Identification System for CHIL Seminars. In: Stiefelhagen, R., Garofolo, J.S. (eds.) CLEAR 2006. LNCS, vol. 4122, pp. 233–240. Springer, Heidelberg (2007)
3. Gauvain, J.-L., Lee, C.H.: Maximum a posteriori estimation for multivariate Gaussian mixture observations of Markov chains. IEEE Transactions on Speech and Audio Processing 2(2), 291–298 (1994)
4. Pelecanos, J., Sridharan, S.: Feature warping for robust speaker verification. In: Proc. ISCA Workshop on Speaker Recognition - Odyssey (June 2001)
5. Reynolds, D., Quatieri, T., Dunn, R.: Speaker verification using adapted Gaussian mixture models. Digital Signal Processing 10, 19–41 (2000)
6. Luque, J., Hernando, J.: Robust Speaker Identification for Meetings: UPC CLEAR 2007 Meeting Room Evaluation System. LNCS, vol. 4625. Springer, Heidelberg (2008)

# MIT Lincoln Laboratory Multimodal Person Identification System in the CLEAR 2007 Evaluation[*]

Kevin Brady

MIT Lincoln Laboratory, 244 Wood Street, Lexington Massachusetts, 02420, USA
kbrady@ll.mit.edu

**Abstract.** A description of the MIT Lincoln Laboratory system used in the person identification task of the recent CLEAR 2007 Evaluation is documented in this paper. This task is broken into audio, visual, and multimodal subtasks. The audio identification system utilizes both a GMM and a SVM subsystem, while the visual (face) identification system utilizes an appearance-based [Kernel] approach for identification. The audio channels, originating from a microphone array, were preprocessed with beamforming and noise preprocessing.

**Keywords:** Gaussian Mixture Model (GMM), Support Vector Machine (SVM), Person Identification, Kernel methods.

## 1 Introduction

Multimodal person recognition is an effective approach to improving overall recognition performance over unimodal approaches, and can address channel-specific performance shortfalls. Speech and visual approaches are popular approaches due to their ubiquity and non-invasive natures. The integration of these two modalities is still an immature research area, though a few reviews are available [11, 12].

The recent person identification task of the CLEAR 2007 Evaluation investigated the closed-set identification task in a small meeting setting. It utilized the CHIL audiovisual corpus for lecture and meeting analysis inside smart rooms [14]. The identification task provided a number of realistic challenges, including the largely uncontrolled nature of the corpus, the paucity of train and test material, low-resolution images, and the pose of facial images.

Our audio recognition approach applied beamforming to reduce the microphone array input to a single-channel audio-channel, which was then noise preprocessed and silence removed. GMM and SVM audio recognition approaches were both evaluated. The visual recognition approach utilized several appearance-based approaches, including Eigenfaces, Fisherfaces, and two Kernel-based methods. Our multimodal recognition approach utilized late-integration (score-level) fusion.

Section 2 of this paper contains a description of the audio identification system utilized in the CLEAR Evaluation. Section 3 contains a description of the video

---

[*] This work was sponsored by the Department of Defense under Air Force Contract FA8721-05-C-0002. Opinions, interpretations, conclusions, and recommendations are those of the authors, and are not necessarily endorsed by the United States Government.

R. Stiefelhagen et al. (Eds.): CLEAR 2007 and RT 2007, LNCS 4625, pp. 240–247, 2008.
© Springer-Verlag Berlin Heidelberg 2008

identification system utilized in the evaluation. Section 4 contains our results from the evaluation, including a brief description of our fusion methodology. Section 5 contains a post mortem evaluation of our system since the conclusion of the evaluation. Section 6 contains our concluding remarks.

## 2 Audio Identification System

As discussed in the previous section, the audio input of the smart room corpus [14] consists of multiple channels of data from a microphone array. A time of arrival based beamformer (BeamformIt) [5] was used to reduce the microphone array output to a single channel of audio data. The beamformed audio was then noise preprocessed using a modified version of the AT&T noise preprocessing algorithm [6] that utilizes a minimum statistics-based approach to noise reduction. Finally, a speech activity detector is applied to the noise preprocessed speech for silence removal.

Two different audio identification systems were investigated. Both systems utilize the Mel Frequency Cepstral Coefficients (MFCC) and delta-MFCCs. The first system utilized was a Gaussian Mixture Model (GMM)-based [8] system. These systems are well established for the speaker recognition task, and a number of excellent tutorials are available [13].

Support Vector Machine (SVM)-based systems have been shown to be highly effective for the speaker and language recognition tasks [9]. Furthermore, this discriminative recognition approach has also been shown to complement generative techniques such as the GMM-based systems. The SVM used in the evaluation uses the same MFCC-based input features as the GMM system. A Generalized Linear Discriminant Sequence (GLDS) Kernel [9] is used for discrimination.

## 3 Visual Identification System

Most modern visual face identification systems utilize appearance-based models that are ultimately based on the work by Turk and Pentland [1] in the mid-1990s resulting in the Eigenfaces approach. More recently, Kernel-based methods [3] have provided significant gains in recognition performance. Much of the research has been on the utilization of high resolution images from one camera such as in the Face Recognition Grand Challenge. The smart room corpus does pose a number of challenges, including recognition from multiple images, using multiple perspectives using different cameras, with low-resolution images.

Face registration information is available for the face images at 5 Hz. This face registration information includes the locations of the eyes, and the coordinates of a bounding box for the face. We only utilized face images that were registered (5 Hz), and did not attempt to utilize the faces at the full sampling rate (15 or 30 Hz). Furthermore, we only utilized frontal face images which we determined using the registration information ---- both eyes are visible (registered).

The face bounding box registration information is refined in scale and location through the utilization of a Distance from Face Space (DFFS) metric [4]. Each face is projected into the Eigenface-based face space. This Face Space was developed on

1180 face images (295 people) from the XM2VTS Corpus [10]. DFFS uses a RMS measure between the face and its projection into the face space to determine how well it matches a 'typical' face. The scale and location of the face is adjusted, and the new face(s) is projected into the Face Space to determine if it is a better match (lower RMS) with the new face(s). This process of adjusting the scale and location is repeated until obtaining the face that best matches its own projection in the Face Space. All faces are mapped to a consistent size and normalized to a zero mean and unitary variance.

Four different appearance-based face recognition approaches were evaluated: Eigenfaces, Fisherfaces, Kernel Eigenfaces, and LDA+Kernel Eigenfaces. The fundamental challenge for these appearance-based face recognition approaches is to find a method to project the typically high-dimensional face images into a low-dimensional feature space where the faces can be effectively discriminated. Eigenfaces, based on the work by Turk and Pentland [1], utilizes Principal Component Analysis (PCA) to determine an optimal linear space (Eigenface space) for the representation of faces. They also applied a simple linear algebra 'trick' to make the problem computationally tractable for typical high-resolution face images. Fisherfaces [2] extends Eigenfaces by applying Linear Discriminant Analysis to the Eigenface space to determine an optimal linear space for discriminating faces. Eigenface and Fisherface test vectors can easily be calculated by a simple projection into the respective space.

Kernel methods [3] have been derived for extending the power of the Eigenface methodology into nonlinear spaces, and have been shown to provide significant performance improvements on several standard visual corpora. Ironically and conceptually this involves first mapping the input features (face image) into a higher dimensional space, by the application of some nonlinear Kernel (ie Gaussian, polynomial) on the input features resulting in a higher dimensional feature set. Fortunately, the Kernel trick obviates the need of projecting the input features into a higher dimensional feature set. Instead, the Kernel can be applied on the dot products of the input features to form a Kernel matrix that can be used in formulating the discrimination problem. The LDA+Kernel Eigenfaces method is the application of LDA to the Kernel Eigenface vectors, much as Fisherfaces is derived from the application of LDA to the Eigenface space.

Visual scoring is applied similarly in each of the four difference face recognition approaches evaluated in the exercise. Each training vector (ie Eigenface vector) is compared to each test vector using a normalized cross correlation metric to determine their similarity. The identity corresponding to the maximum score resulting from the comparison of all test vectors from a test video clip to all of the training vectors is assigned to the test video clip.

# 4  Clear Workshop Results

As noted in the introduction, the Person Identification task of the CLEAR Evaluation 2007 is a closed set identification task broken down into three subtasks: audio identification, video identification, and multimodal identification. There are eight possible testing conditions for the subtasks: using either 15 seconds or 30 seconds of training material, and using 1 second, 5 seconds, 10 seconds, or 20 seconds of testing material.

There are 2240 1 second tests, 448 5 second tests, 224 10 second tests, and 112 20 second tests.

The evaluation utilized a Smart Room Corpus collected at five different sites (AIT, IBM, ITC-IRST, UKA, and UPC), and consists of twenty eight potential clients. No person was collected at more than one site. Audio is collected using a single 64-element microphone array (Mark IV). Video is collected (15 or 30 Hz) by four different wide angle fixed cameras mounted in each corner of the room. As previously mentioned, registration information is available for the video streams at 5 Hz.

The correct identification results for the audio system described in section two are contained in Table 1. Both systems used narrowband (4 kHz bandwidth) speech material preprocessed as described in section 2. The GMM system used 2048 mixture models and a Universal Background Model (UBM) trained primarily on English language telephone speech. The SVM used a third order GLDS Kernel trained on English language telephone speech.

**Table 1.** MIT/LL Audio System Identification Results for 2007 CLEAR Evaluation

|  | Training Duration | 15 Seconds | | | | 30 Seconds | | | |
|---|---|---|---|---|---|---|---|---|---|
|  | Testing Duration | 1s | 5s | 10 s | 20s | 1s | 5s | 10s | 20s |
| ID | GMM | 26.7 | 68.8 | 75.9 | 82.1 | 34.2 | 74.6 | 85.3 | 85.7 |
| Approach | SVM | 26.1 | 69.9 | 76.8 | 84.8 | 30.2 | 73.2 | 83.5 | 86.6 |

The results for the visual identification subtask using the systems described in Section 3 are contained in Table 2. A Gaussian Kernel was used for the Kernel-based visual identification methods shown below. The Kernel-based approaches, unsurprisingly, provided significant performance gains over the Eigenface and Fisherface baseline methods.

**Table 2.** MIT/LL Visual System Identification Results for 2007 CLEAR Evaluation

|  | Training Duration | 15 Seconds | | | | 30 Seconds | | | |
|---|---|---|---|---|---|---|---|---|---|
|  | Testing Duration | 1s | 5s | 10s | 20s | 1s | 5s | 10s | 20s |
| | Eigenfaces | 38.8 | 54.0 | 58.9 | 67.0 | 44.6 | 57.6 | 63.4 | 67.0 |
| | Fisherfaces | 39.9 | 48.4 | 54.0 | 59.8 | 51.7 | 65.8 | 71.4 | 73.2 |
| ID | Kernel Eigenfaces | 57.8 | 70.1 | 75.0 | 82.1 | 64.8 | 75.9 | 80.4 | 86.6 |
| Approach | LDA+Kernel Eigenfaces | 59.0 | 72.1 | 77.2 | 81.3 | 66.4 | 77.7 | 82.6 | 87.5 |

The results for all of the primary systems are contained in Table 3. Note that the audio scores were independently postprocessed using a Normalized Cross Entropy (NCE) criteria [7] to obtain a posterior probability of matched identification. The fused audio score is obtained using score-level fusion where each modality is equally weighted. Note that the visual score (NCC) is a value between 0 and 1 where 1 is a perfect match. The multimodal score is also obtained using score-level fusion, though the weighting for the audio subsystem is 0.6 and the weighting for the visual subsystem is 0.4. These values were arrived at experimentally, based on an evaluation of the results on the VALID development set.

**Table 3.** MIT/LL Primary System Identification Results for 2007 CLEAR Evaluation

|  | Training Duration | 15 Seconds | | | | 30 Seconds | | | |
|---|---|---|---|---|---|---|---|---|---|
|  | Testing Duration | 1s | 5s | 10s | 20s | 1s | 5s | 10s | 20s |
| ID Approach | Audio: GMM+SVM | 38.9 | 73.9 | 82.1 | 93.9 | 36.0 | 77.9 | 87.1 | 89.3 |
|  | Visual: LDA+Kernel Eigenfaces | 59.0 | 72.1 | 77.2 | 81.3 | 66.4 | 77.7 | 82.6 | 87.5 |
|  | Multimodal | 65.8 | 84.4 | 85.3 | 89.3 | 72.5 | 89.7 | 91.1 | 95.5 |

## 5 Post Mortem Results

Since the end of the 2007 CLEAR Evaluation we have completed further analysis on the audio-channel recognition approach. Our intention was to investigate the impact of a number of system parameters on identification performance. One of the basic system parameters of the GMM audio identification system is the number of mixture models. Our evaluation system used 2048 mixture models using a background model trained on telephone speech. This system was designed for an open set detection task, and is not well suited for a closed set identification task. In fact, a much smaller number of GMM mixture models (see Table 4) are appropriate to the CLEAR Evaluation identification task. While we did find that a mismatched background model did degrade performance, we did not find that using a background model trained on the CLEAR Evaluation training material impacted performance.

**Table 4.** Identification Results as a function of number of GMM mixtures on evaluation set (20 s train / 20 s test)

| GMM Mixtures (#) | 16 | 32 | 64 | 128 |
|---|---|---|---|---|
| Percent (Correct Identification) | 92.9 | 96.4 | 92.9 | 89.3 |

We have not compared identification performance on beamformed and non-beamformed signals. When we first received the CLEAR Evaluation material we did complete a comparison of this material using Equal Error Rate (EER) on the 20 seconds VALID [evaluation] set of material (see Table 5). Beamforming provided a large performance gain using this metric. This metric, though, is a detection metric, so no conclusions can be made on its efficacy for the CLEAR Evaluation identification task.

**Table 5.** EER Results on evaluation set (20 s train / 20 s test) for single-channel (channel 1) and beamformed signals

|  | Single Audio Channel | Beamformed Signal |
|---|---|---|
| GMM | 14.3 | 7.1 |
| SVM | 10.7 | 2.8 |

While we can draw no conclusions about whether beamforming affects identification performance, we have completed several experiments on how the processing of the beamformed signal affects performance:

1) Identification performance on the wideband (16 kHz sampling) signal is significantly better than on the narrowband (8 kHz sampling) signal.
2) Noise preprocessing and silence removal provide modest identification performance improvements

We have also drawn several conclusions about the discrimination architectures:

1) A second order GLDS SVM Kernel provides better identification performance than a third order GLDS SVM Kernel
2) Training the GLDS Kernel on the CLEAR Evaluation validation material provides significant performance gains.
3) A GMM background model trained on the CLEAR Evaluation validation material does not strongly impact identification performance.

We have rerun our baseline audio discrimination architectures using the lessons learned in our post mortem experiments:

1) Wideband Signal
2) GMM: Lower Number of GMM Mixture Models (32 instead of 2048)
3) SVM: $2^{nd}$ order instead of $3^{rd}$ order GLDS Kernel
4) SVM: Trained GLDS Kernel on CLEAR Evaluation training material

The resulting identification performance results in Table 6 show strong improvement over the performance shown in Table 1.

**Table 6.** Postmortem results for MIT/LL Audio Identification Systems on 2007 CLEAR Evaluation material •

|  | Training Duration | 15 Seconds | | | | 30 Seconds | | | |
|---|---|---|---|---|---|---|---|---|---|
|  | Testing Duration | 1s | 5s | 10 s | 20s | 1s | 5s | 10s | 20s |
| ID Approach | GMM | 53.5 | 81.9 | 83.5 | 86.6 | 57.3 | 90.4 | 93.8 | 97.3 |
|  | SVM | 20.1 | 71.2 | 87.9 | 93.8 | 20.8 | 77.5 | 92.9 | 96.4 |

## 6 Concluding Remarks

The 2007 CLEAR Evaluation provided an opportunity to evaluate audio, visual, and multimodal evaluation systems on material that is more realistic than typical laboratory collected material. Of particular challenge was the largely uncontrolled nature of the lectures, the paucity of train and test material, low-resolution images, and the pose of facial images.

We have completed an analysis of our audio identification systems from the CLEAR Evaluation identification task. Several system parameters have largely driven system performance, namely the number of GMM mixture models and the size and training material for the SVM Kernel. It is not clear whether beamforming impacts performance, though noise preprocessing and silence removal did provide performance gains.

While we have done no further analysis on our visual identification system, it is apparent that the system did well where it had available face images (train and/ or test) and had no performance where it had little to no available face images. Performance was therefore largely driven by the availability of images. Our system only utilized frontal faces (both eyes present), and therefore sacrificed potential recognition gains from side and back of the head recognition. In practice, though, these gains may not be realistic. Future evaluations should consider the benefits of using less reliable poses (ie side and back images). These poses can improve closed set identification, though are probably less able to determine if an unmodeled person is part of the set (i.e. a secretary who momentarily steps into a meeting). An open set evaluation may be able to consider this question. Finally, the Kernel-based identification approaches provided significant performance relative to the basline Eigenfaces and Fisherfaces approaches.

**Acknowledgments.** I would like to thank Doug Sturim and Bill Campbell of MIT Lincoln Laboratory for their patient assistance in familiarizing me with the inner workings of the MIT/LL audio recognition technologies. I would also like to thank the workshop participants for their helpful interactions, particularly Aristodemos Pnevmatikakis (AIT), Hazim Ekenel (Universitat Karlsruhe), and Claude Barras (LIMSI-CNRS).

## References

1. Turk, M., Pentland, A.: Eigenfaces for Recognition. Journal of Cognitive Neurosciences 3(1), 71–86 (1991)
2. Belhumeur, V., Hespanha, J., Kriegman, D.: Eigenfaces vs. Fisherfaces: Recognition using Class Specific Linear Projection. IEEE Trans. PAMI 19(7), 711–720 (1997)
3. Yang, M.H.: Kernel Eigenfaces vs. Kernel Fisherfaces: Face Recognition using Kernel Mehods. In: Proc. of IEEE Int. Conf. on Face and Gesture Recognition, Washington DC, USA (May 2002)
4. Moghaddam, B., Pentland, A.: Probabilistic Visual Learning for Object Representation. IEEE PAMI 19(7), 696–710 (1997)

5. Anguera, X., Wooters, C., Hernando, J.: Speaker diarization for multi-party meetings using acoustic fusion. In: IEEE Automatic Speech Recognition and Understanding Workshop, Puerto Rico, USA (2005)
6. Martin, R., Cox, R.: New Speech Enhancement Techniques for Low Bit Rate Speech Coding. In: Proc IEEE Workshop on Speech Coding (1999)
7. Campbell, W., Brady, K., Campbell, J., Reynolds, D., Granville, R.: Understanding Scores in Forensic Speaker Recognition. In: IEEE Speaker Odyssey, Puerto Rico, USA (June 2006)
8. Reynolds, D., Quatieri, T.F., Dunn, R.B.: Speaker Verification Using Adapted Gaussian Mixture Models. Digital Signal Processing 10(1-3), 19–41 (2000)
9. Campbell, W., Campbell, J., eynolds, D., Singer, E., Torres, P.: Support Vector Machines for Speaker and Language Recognition. Computer Speech and Language 20(2-3), 210–229 (2006)
10. Messer, K., et al.: XM2VTSDB: The Extended M2VTS Database. In: AVBPA, Washington DC, USA (1999)
11. Chibelushi, C.C., Deravi, F., Mason, J.S.D.: A Review of Speech-based Bimodal Recognition. IEEE Trans. On Multimedia 4(1), 23–37 (2002)
12. Sanderson, C., Paliwal, K.K.: Identity Verification Using Speech and Face Information. Digital Signal Processing Journal 14, 449–480 (2004)
13. Campbell, J.P.: Seaker Recognition: A Tutorial. Proc. of the IEEE 85(9), 1437–1462 (An Invited Paper, 1997)
14. Mostefa, D., Potamianos, G., Casas, J., Cristoforetti, L., Pnevmatikakis, A., Burger, S., Stiefelhagen, R., Bernardin, K., Rochet, C.: The CHIL Audiovisual Corpus for Lecture and Meeting Analysis inside Smart Rooms. Journal for Language Resources and Evaluation (2007)

# Multichannel and Multimodality Person Identification

Ming Liu, Yanxiang Chen, Xi Zhou, Xiaodan Zhuang,
Mark Hasegawa-Johnson, and Thomas Huang

Department of Electrical and Computer Engineering
University of Illinois at Urbana-Champaign
Urbana, IL 61801
mingliu1@ifp.uiuc.edu

**Abstract.** Person's identity is a very important high level information for video analysis and retrieval. Along the growth of multimedia data, the recording is not only multimodality and also multichannel(microphone array, camera array). In this paper, we describe a multimodal person identification system of UIUC team for CLEAR 2007 evaluation. The audio only system is based on a new proposed model – Chain of Gaussian Mixtures. The visual only system is a face recognition module based on nearest neighbor classifier at appearance space. Final system fuses 7 channel microphone recordings and 4 camera recordings at decision level. The experimental results indicate the effectiviness of speaker modeling methods and the fusion scheme.

## 1 Introduction

Person identification is a task of identifying a particular person out of a group of people based on physiology cues such as speech, facial images, finger print and iris, etc. Because of great commercial potential, this topic has brought many research and engineering efforts in both academia and industry. Based on speech signal, the identification of person is also called speaker identification[1][2][3]. Based on facial image, the identification of person is also called face identification [4]. Either category has been extensively addressed, and is traditionally formulated as a pattern recognition problem in some feature vector space, tackled by statistical classification and machine learning algorithms.

Fusing audio and visual cues can substantially boost the performance of the person identification system. The concept of multimodal person identification has been brought to the attention of the speech and computer vision communities. In CLEAR evaluation, the multichannel recordings are also avaiable. To fuse the microphone array recordings and multiple camera recordings is a chanllenge and interesting research problem. This paper describes a system fuse multimodal cues as well as multichannel recording so that person identification achieve significant better performance. The experiemnts are conducted on the CLEAR 2007 Evaluation corpus[5]. The results show that the fusion of multichannel and multimodality do improve the performance significantly. The accuracy of 1sec

R. Stiefelhagen et al. (Eds.): CLEAR 2007 and RT 2007, LNCS 4625, pp. 248–255, 2008.

testing utterance is boosted from 70% to 89%. For longer testing utterance, the fused system can achieve 100% accuracy. These results clearly demonstrate the effectiveness of multichannel and multimodal fusion. The detailed algorithms and implementation of the system are described in the following sections.

## 2  Audio Only Person Identification Subsystem

The Gaussian Mixture Model (GMM) has been considered one of the best modeling method for text-independent speaker identification. In the domain of speaker identification, the Mel Frequency Cepstral Coefficient (MFCC) is widely used as the acoustic feature. Although MFCC is not exclusively designed as a sort of speaker-distinguishing features, it capture the vocal tract structure which is essentially one speaker distinguish feature.

### 2.1  GMM

An $M$-mixture GMM is defined as a weighted sum of $M$ component Gaussian densities

$$p(\bar{x}|\lambda) = \sum_{m=1}^{M} w_m N(\bar{x}|\bar{\mu}_m, \Sigma_m) \tag{1}$$

where $\bar{x}$ is a $D$-dimensional feature vector, $w_m$ is the $m^{th}$ mixture weight, and $N(\bar{x}|\bar{\mu}_m, \Sigma_m)$ is a multivariate Gaussian density, with mean vector $\bar{\mu}_m$ and covariance matrix $\Sigma_m$. Note that $\sum_{m=1}^{M} w_m = 1$.

A speaker model $\lambda = \{w_m, \bar{\mu}_m, \Sigma_m\}_{m=1}^{M}$ is obtained by fitting a GMM to a training utterance $X = \{\bar{x}_1, \bar{x}_2, ..., \bar{x}_T\}$ using the expectation-maximization (EM) algorithm. The log likelihood of a testing utterance $Y = \{\bar{y}_1, \bar{y}_2, ..., \bar{y}_T\}$ on a given speaker model $\lambda$ is computed as follows.

$$LL(Y|\lambda) = \frac{1}{T} \sum_{t=1}^{T} \log p(\bar{y}_t|\lambda) \tag{2}$$

where $p(\bar{y}_t|\lambda)$ is the likelihood of the $t^{th}$ frame of the utterance. To identify an utterance as having been spoken by a person out of a group of N people, we compute its utterance scores against all $N$ speaker models and pick the maximum

$$\hat{\lambda} = \arg \max_{\lambda_n} LL(Y|\lambda_n) \tag{3}$$

where $\lambda_n$ is the model of the $n^{th}$ speaker.

### 2.2  UBM-GMM

The GMM algorithm described in the previous subsection requires that every speaker model be trained independently with the speaker's training data. In the case when the available training data is limited for a speaker, the model is prone to singularity. In the UBM-GMM algorithm, a different scheme is adopted to train the speaker models. A single speaker-independent Universal Background Model (UBM) $\lambda_0$ is trained with a combination of the training data from all speakers, and a speaker model $\lambda$ is derived by updating the well-trained UBM with that speaker's training data via Maximum A Posteriori (MAP) adaptation[6]. The final score of the testing utterance is computed by the log likelihood ratio between target model and background model.

$$LLR(Y) = LLR(\bar{y}_1^T) = \frac{1}{T} \sum_{t=1}^{T} \log \frac{P(\bar{y}_t|\lambda_1)}{P(\bar{y}_t|\lambda_0)} \tag{4}$$

where $(\bar{y}_1^T)$ are the feature vectors of the observed utterance – test utterance $Y$, $\lambda_0$ is the parameter of UBM and $\lambda_1$ is the parameter of the target model. Essentially, the verification task is to construct a generalized likelihood ratio test between hypothesis $H_1$ (observation drawn from the target) and hypothesis $H_0$ (observation not drawn the target).

The UBM is trained with a large amount of data of many speakers. It is considered as a speaker-independent model. Ideally, it describes the all possible acoustic features of human speech. A speaker model, obtained by adapting the parameters of the UBM with a small amount of new data, is expected to be focusing on the difference between this specific speaker and the speaker independent model. Hence, the GMM-UBM can localize the most unique feature for each target speaker.

### 2.3   Chain of Gaussian Mixture

Beside the simplicity and effectiveness of GMM-UBM, the most referred limitation is that the independence between frames is implied. The temporal information of speech signal is found useful in text dependent speaker recognition. In this paper, a new modeling technique named a chain of Gaussian Mixture Model is proposed. The motivation for the new model is to encode the temporal correlation in the chain structure. With this chain structure, a special decoding network is established to ensure that the optimal matches will be found for every segments of test utterance. Instead of conventional frame based system, we are trying to match the trial utterance and the training utterance in segment level. Basically, the goal is to find the longest possible matching segments between training and testing utterances. For example, the training utterance is a phone number sequence "two-one-seven-two-three-four-nine" and the testing utterance is "two-one-seven-three-four-seven-six". The chain model is able to find the first three digits are matched between training and testing, and the 4th and 5th digits in testing utterance match the 5th and 6th digits in training, and 6th digit of testing utterance matches the 3rd digit of training utterance. In this sense, the proposed method is kind of speech decoding with variable length units. Compared with speech recognizer based speaker recognition, our method has the potential advantage of incorporating much long term correlation for speaker recognition. If there are matched long segments between training and testing, the method is going to use the match score of the whole segment. If there are no matched long segments, the method becomes conventional frame based method.

The training of this new model have two steps. First of all, the global Gaussian Mixture is generated by MAP adaptation from the UBM with the whole utterance. Then, the local Gaussian Mixtures are generated by MAP adaptation from the UBM with only the current segment. In our experiment, we set the segment length to be 40 frames(400ms) and overlap between segments are 20frames. After building up the model, to match a test utterance is simply decoding on the chain model with one additional background state which has the global Gaussian Mixture as the observation density.

In order to combine different microphone channel of the microphone array, a linear fusion is adopted to fuse these channels. The MarkIII microphone array in our task has 64 channels which is linear configured with 2cm distance between conjacent channels. In order to have more variety between two channels, we select one channel out of every 10 channels. The channels used in fusion module are 01, 10, 20, 30, 40, 50, 60. The fusion is conducted directly on the log-likelihood score of each individual channel with equal weight.

## 3    Face Recognition

The face recognition subsystem is based on the $K$-Nearest Neighbor (KNN) method in the appearance feature space. The main modules include: cropping, alignment, metric measurement, and KNN modeling. Instead of determining the person ID based on a single face image, we fuse the decision by processing all face samples in a clip of a video.

### 3.1    Face Cropping

For both training and testing videos, the faces are cropped according to the bounding boxes and positions of eye corners manually labeled. In spite of the big variation of the view angles, the face images are then scaled to a fixed size ($20 \times 20$ in our experiment). The face images without the positions of two eye corners are omitted in the experiment because most of those face images have bad quality and may induce extra errors to the system. These cropped images have significant variation on face angles, illumination and background which make the face recognition a big challenge.

### 3.2    Face Alignment

In a typical face recognition system, an alignment procedure should be applied to the cropped faces such that the main facial feature points (such as eye corners, nose point, mouth corners) are aligned cross all images. However, face alignment is extremely difficult for this CHIL data, because face angles vary a lot and face resolution is too low. Therefore we use shifting procedure to partly substitute for the alignment procedure. In detail, the training samples are repeatedly shifted by one or two pixels in all directions to generate new training samples. We assume, after shifting, any test sample has a counterpart in the training data set (including the shifted samples) that both of them come from the same person while having same alignment.

All face recognition algorithms depends heavily on the choice of the metric measurement. we found out that $l^1$ metric works best for our task.

$$d_p(f_1, f_2) = \sum_{i=1}^{D} |(f_1(i) - f_2(i))| \qquad (5)$$

where $f_1$ and $f_2$ are the face samples and the $D$ is the total dimension. $f_1(i)$ is the $i^{th}$ dimension of the face sample.

As mentioned above, unlike the typical face recognition systems, our system makes the decision by processing all face samples in a clip of a video. We call the face samples in the same clip as "test subset". To determine the person ID by considering the entire "test subset", we first apply the KNN algorithm to each sample in subset separately, and then fuse the output of KNN algorithm to make the final decision.

## 4   Audio Visual Fusion

In order to fuse the two modalities for better performance, an audio/visual fusion module is applied to combine these two modalities. There are different kinds of fusion strategies proposed in the literature[7][8][9]. There are mainly three level of fusion: feature-level, state-level and decision level. Fusion at feature-level mainly concatenate the features from different modalities as a single big feature vector. Some dimension reduction techniques such as PCA, LDA can be used to reduce the dimensionality of the final feature vector. The modeling is then conducted on the final feature vectors. Usually the feature level fusion is most simple fusion strategies and often result in moderate improvement after fusion. State-level fusion is considered the best strategies from the reports by audio/visual speech recognition literatures. The basic idea is to fuse the observation likelihood of different modalities on the same state. By searching the right confidence measure of two streams, the fusion can achieve best improvement.

However, the text-independent ID task make it difficult to find the same state for audio and visual streams. To circumvent this difficulties, we explore the decision level fusion for this task. The decision output of audio and visual stream are the similarity scores of the testing utterance on 28 target speaker models. By tuning the weighting factor between two streams, we obtain very good improvement after fusion. Intuitively, the weighting factor should not be static between audio/visual streams. In principle, the optimal weighting factor should be estimated based on the SNRs of different modalities. However, the estimation of SNRs usually is also difficult to obtain. However, the duration of the speech utterance is correlate to the performance of audio-only system in consistent way and so is the number of face frames. In this task, we searched the optimal weighting factor for different testing conditions(1sec, 5sec, 10sec, 20sec) indivisually based on the experiments on CHIL development dataset.

**Table 1.** GMM-UBM vs Chain of GMM on single channel

| Methods | $test_1$ | $test_5$ | $test_{10}$ | $test_{20}$ |
|---|---|---|---|---|
| GMM-UBM | 62.4 | 85.1 | 88.9 | 95.5 |
| Chain of GMM | 69.5 | 89.6 | 92.5 | 95.5 |

**Table 2.** GMM-UBM vs Chain of GMM on multi channels

| Methods | $test_1$ | $test_5$ | $test_{10}$ | $test_{20}$ |
|---|---|---|---|---|
| GMM-UBM | 71.4 | 92.1 | 94.6 | 98.3 |
| Chain of GMM | 76.6 | 93.6 | 95.6 | 98.3 |

## 5 Experiment Results

The CHIL 2007 ID task corpus[5] contain 28 speakers video sequences from 5 cites. The audio recording is far-field microphone array recording. In our experiments, only one microphone array – MarkIII recording is considered. There are 64 channels and linear array configuration with 2cm apart. The video recording includes four cameras located at four corner of ceiling. Both of audio and visual recording are far-field, therefore noisy and low resolution. The performance of each individual modality will not be sufficient. It contains seminar recording as well as interactive discussion recording.

There are two training conditions varying with respect to the duration of the enrollment. The train set A has 15sec training enrollment while train set B has 30 sec enrollment. The testing conditions varies in term of testing durations. The four testing conditions are corresponds to 1sec, 5sec, 10sec and 20sec.

**Table 3.** Microphone Array Audio-only System Performance

| TrainSet | $test_1$ | $test_5$ | $test_{10}$ | $test_{20}$ |
|---|---|---|---|---|
| A | 79.2 | 93.3 | 95.5 | 98.2 |
| B | 82.2 | 97.3 | 97.3 | 100 |

**Table 4.** Visual-only System Performance($N = 1$)

| TrainSet | $test_1$ | $test_5$ | $test_{10}$ | $test_{20}$ |
|---|---|---|---|---|
| A | 58.9 | 65.4 | 67.9 | 70.2 |
| B | 66.2 | 70.6 | 72.6 | 73.7 |

**Table 5.** Final Audio Visual Fusion System Performance

| TrainSet | $test_1$ | $test_5$ | $test_{10}$ | $test_{20}$ |
|---|---|---|---|---|
| A | 85.4 | 95.3 | 96.9 | 99.1 |
| B | 88.7 | 97.5 | 98.7 | 100 |

A 128 component UBM is trained from approximate CHIL development data. To improve the audio only system by multichannel recording, we fuse the channels based on decision level fusion and all 7 channels(01,10,20,30,40,50,60) are treated with equal weighting factor. The experiment results(Table ?? and Table 3) shows the improvement is significance by multichannel fusion, especially for short testing utterarnce conditions(acurracy boost from 69.5% to 79.2%). For visual only part, we have try different distance measure ($l_1, l_2$ and normalized cross correlation) and different neighborhood size ($N = 1, 3, 5, 7, 10$). It turns out the $l_1$ norm combined with $N = 1$ is the optimal based on the CHIL development data, Table 4. The performance of Audio/Visual fusion is listed in Table 5. The improvement due to A/V fusion is as large as 6% in absolete percentage compared to the multichannel fused audio only system and 16% in absolete percentage compared to the single channel audio only system.

## 6   Conclusion and Future Work

In this paper, we describe a Multimodal person ID system base on multichannel and multimodal fusion. The audio only system is combining 7 channels microphone recording at decision output individual audio-only system. The modeling technique of audio system is UBM-GMM and the visual only system works directly on the appearance space via $l_1$ norm and nearest neighbor classifier. The linear fusion is then combining the two modalities to improve the ID performance. The experiments indicate the effectiviness of micropohone array fusion and audio/visual fusion. Although the CHIL07 corpus is quite large database(200 giga bytes for all evaluation data), the number of speakers might be few. In the near future, we are going to including more speakers from CHIL07 development corpus to futher verify our framework. Also, linear fusion is simple yet useful solution for multichannel and multimodal fusion. More sophisticate fusion schemes are under investigation.

## Acknowledgments

This work was supported in part by National Science Foundation Grant CCF 04-26627 and ARDA VACE program.

## References

1. Doddington, G.: Speaker recognition - identifying people by their voices, 1651–1664 (1985)
2. Reynolds, D.A.: Speaker identification and verification using Gaussian mixture speaker models. Speech Communication 17, 91–108 (1995)
3. Furui, S.: An overview of speaker recognition technology, 31–56 (1996)
4. Zhao, W., Chellappa, R., Phillips, P.J., Rosenfeld, A.: Face recognition: A literature survey. ACM Comput. Surv. 35, 399–458 (2003)
5. http://clear-evaluation.org/ (2007)

6. Reynolds, D., Quatieri, T., Dunn, R.: Speaker verification using adapted gaussian mixture models. Digital Signal Processing (2000)
7. Dupont, S., Luettin, J.: Audio-visual speech modelling for continuous speech recognition. IEEE Transactions on Multimedia (to appear, 2000)
8. Garg, A., Potamianos, G., Neti, C., Huang, T.S.: Frame-dependent multi-stream reliability indicators for audio-visual speech recognition. In: Proc. of international conference on Acoustics, Speech and Signal Processing (ICASSP) (2003)
9. Potamianos, G.: Audio-Visual Speech Recognition. Encyclopedia of Language and Linguistics (2005)

# ISL Person Identification Systems in the CLEAR 2007 Evaluations

Hazım Kemal Ekenel[1], Qin Jin[2], Mika Fischer[1], and Rainer Stiefelhagen[1]

[1] Interactive Systems Labs (ISL), Universität Karlsruhe (TH),
76131 Karlsruhe, Germany
{ekenel, mika.fischer}@ira.uka.de
[2] Interactive Systems Labs (ISL), Carnegie Mellon University,
15213 Pittsburgh, PA, USA
qjin@cs.cmu.edu

**Abstract.** In this paper, we present ISL person identification systems in the CLEAR 2007 evaluations. The identification systems consist of a face recognition system, a speaker identification system and a multi-modal identification system that combines the individual systems. The experimental results show that the face recognition system outperforms the speaker identification system significantly on the short duration test segments. They perform equally well on the longer duration test segments. Combination of the individual systems improves the performance further.

**Keywords:** Face recognition, Speaker Identification, Multimodal Person Identification, Person Identification in Smart Rooms.

## 1 Introduction

Person identification for smart environments has become an important application area [1,2,3]. Sample applications can be a smart car that can identify the driver; a smart lecture or meeting room, where the participants can be identified automatically. As can be expected, this group of applications requires identification of people naturally under uncontrolled conditions.

Among the biometric person identification methods, face recognition and speaker identification are known to be the most natural ones, since the face and voice modalities are the modalities we use to identify people in our daily lives. However, doing face recognition or speaker identification in a natural way poses many challenges. In terms of face recognition, there is no cooperation of the subjects being identified, there are no constraints on head-pose, illumination conditions, use of accessories, etc. Moreover, depending on the distance between the camera and the subject, the face resolution varies, and generally the face resolution is low. In terms of speaker identification, again, there is no cooperation, and the system should handle a large variety of speech signals, corrupted by adverse environmental conditions such as noise, background, and channel. The only factors that can help to improve the person identification performance in smart rooms are the video data of the individuals from multiple views provided by several cameras and the multi-channel speech signal provided by

R. Stiefelhagen et al. (Eds.): CLEAR 2007 and RT 2007, LNCS 4625, pp. 256–265, 2008.

microphone arrays that are mounted in the smart room. Furthermore, with the fusion of these modalities, the correct identification rates can be improved further. Sample images from different smart rooms are shown in Fig. 1.

**Fig. 1.** Sample images from different smart rooms

The organization of the paper is as follows. In Section 2, the individual face recognition and speaker identification systems are explained briefly, and the utilized fusion approaches are described. Experimental results are presented and discussed in Section 3. Finally, in Section 4, conclusions are given.

## 2  Methodology

In this section, we present the single modality and multi-modal person identification systems that have been developed at the ISL.

### 2.1  Video-Based Face Recognition

The face recognition system is based on the local appearance-based models and it processes multi-view video data provided by four fixed cameras. In the training stage all the images from all the cameras are put together. Although the manual annotations of the images are available in the database, due to the low resolution of face images these manual labels might be imprecise. In order to prevent the registration errors that can be caused by these imprecise labels, 24 additional samples are also generated by modifying the manual face bounding box labels by moving the center of the bounding box by 1 pixel and changing the width or height by ±2 pixels.

The feature extraction step follows the approach in [7,8], which performs block-based discrete cosine transform (DCT) to non-overlapping blocks of size 8×8 pixels. The obtained DCT coefficients are then ordered according to the zig-zag scan pattern.

The first coefficient is discarded for illumination normalization as suggested in [7] and the remaining first ten coefficients in each block are selected in order to create compact local feature vectors. Furthermore, robustness against illumination  variations is increased by normalizing the local feature vectors to unit norm [8]. The global feature vector is generated by concatenating the local feature vectors. Afterwards, these global feature vectors are clustered using k-means algorithm in order to realize real-time classification with a nearest neighbor classifier.

In the testing stage, at an instant, all four camera views are compared to the representatives in the database. Their distances are converted to confidence scores using min-max normalization [4]. This way, the score is normalized to the value range of [0,1], closest match having the score "1", and the furthest match having the score "0". To have equal contribution of each frame, these scores are re-normalized by dividing them to the sum of their values. We weight each frame using the distance-to-second-closest (DT2ND) metric. In a previous study [9], it has been observed that the difference of the distances, x, between the closest and the second closest training samples is generally smaller in the case of a false classification than in the case of a correct classification. It has been found that the distribution of these distances resembles an exponential distribution:

$$\varepsilon(x; \lambda) = 0.1\lambda e^{-\lambda x} \text{ with } \lambda = 0.05.$$

The weights are then computed as the cumulative distribution function:

$$\omega_{DT2ND}(x; \lambda) = 1 - e^{-\lambda x}.$$

The obtained confidence scores are summed over camera-views and over image sequence. The identity of the face image is assigned as the person who has the highest accumulated score.

## 2.2 Speaker Identification

The speaker identification system is based on Gaussian mixture models (GMM) of Mel Frequency Cepstral Coefficients (MFCC) [10,11]. Feature warping and reverberation compensation are applied on MFCC in order to improve robustness against channel mismatch. Our reverberation compensation approach uses a different noise estimation compared to the standard spectrum subtraction approach [12]. The feature warping method warps the distribution of a cepstral feature stream to a standardized distribution over a specified time interval [12,13,14]. The identification decision is made as follows:

$$s = \arg\max_i \{L(Y|\Theta_i)\} \qquad Y = (y_1, y_2, \cdots, y_N)$$

where $s$ is the identified speaker and $L(Y|\Theta_i)$ is the likelihood that the test feature set $Y$ was generated by the GMM $\Theta_i$ of speaker $i$, which contains $M$ weighted mixtures of Gaussian distributions

$$\Theta_i = \sum_{m=1}^{M} \lambda_m N(X, U_m, \Sigma_m) \qquad i = 1, 2, \cdots, S,$$

where $X$ is the set of training feature vectors to be modeled, $S$ is the total number of speakers, $M$ is the number of Gaussian mixtures, $\lambda_m$ is the weight of the Gaussian component $m$, and $N(X, U_m, \Sigma_m)$ is a Gaussian function with mean vector $U_m$ and covariance matrix $\Sigma_m$. The parameters of a GMM are estimated from speech samples of a speaker using the EM algorithm.

As there are 64 channels for each speech recording, we train GMMs for each speaker on each of the 64 channels. We randomly select channel 7 as the test channel. We apply Frame-based Score Competition approach when computing the likelihood scores of test features given a speaker with 64 GMMs. The idea of the FSC approach is to use the set of multiple GMM models rather than a single GMM model. A multiple microphone setup emits speech samples from multiple channels. As a consequence, we can build multiple GMM models for each speaker $k$, one for each channel $i$ and refer to it as $\Theta_{k, Chi}$. For a total number of 64 channels we get $\Theta_k = \{\Theta_{k, Ch1}, \cdots, \Theta_{k, Ch64}\}$ models for speaker $k$. In each frame we compare the incoming feature vector of channel $Ch7$ to all GMMs $\{\Theta_{k, Ch1}, \cdots, \Theta_{k, Ch64}\}$ of speaker $k$. The highest log likelihood score of all GMM models is chosen to be the frame score. Finally, the log likelihood score of the entire test feature vector set $X$ from channel $h$ is estimated as

$$LL(X \mid \Theta_k) = \sum_{n=1}^{N} LL(x_n \mid \Theta_k) = \sum_{n=1}^{N} \max \left\{ LL(x_n \mid \Theta_{k, Chj}) \right\}_{j=1}^{64}$$

32 Gaussians and 16 Gaussians are trained for each speaker for the training duration of 30-seconds and 15-seconds respectively. 13-dimensional MFCC is used as speaker features.

## 2.3  Fusion

The min-max normalization is used for score normalization. For modality weighting, we used a new adaptive modality weighting scheme based on the separation of the best two matches. It is named as cumulative ratio of correct matches (CRCM) and utilizes a non-parametric model of the distribution of the correct matches with respect to the confidence differences between the best two matches. It relies on the observation that the difference of the confidences between the closest and the second closest training samples is generally smaller in the case of a false classification than in the case of a correct classification. The greater the confidence difference between the best two matches is, the higher the weight the individual modality receives. This weighting model has been computed on a validation set by taking the cumulative sum of the number of correct matches achieved at a confidence difference between the best two matches. Finally, we combined the modalities using the sum rule [6].

## 3  Experiments

The experiments have been conducted on a database that has been collected by the CHIL consortium [15] for the CLEAR 2007 evaluations [16]. The recordings are from lecture-like seminars and interactive small working group seminars that have been held at different CHIL sites: AIT, Athens, Greece, IBM, New York, USA, ITC-IRST, Trento, Italy, UKA, Karlsruhe, Germany and UPC, Barcelona, Spain. Sample images from the recordings can be seen in Figure 1. The used data for the identification task consists of short video sequences of 28 subjects, where the subject is both speaking and visible to the cameras at the same time. The recording conditions are uncontrolled, and depending on the camera view and the position of the presenter/participant, low resolution faces ranging between 10 to 50 pixels resolution are acquired. Two different training and four different validation/testing durations are used in the experiments as presented in Table 1. Identity estimates are provided at the end of each test sequence duration using the available audio-visual data.

**Table 1.** Duration and number of the training, validation and testing sequences

| Sequence ID | Sequence Duration (sec) | No. of Sequences |
|:---:|:---:|:---:|
| Train A | 15 | 28 |
| Train B | 30 | 28 |
| Validation 1 | 1 | 560 |
| Validation 2 | 5 | 112 |
| Validation 3 | 10 | 56 |
| Validation 4 | 20 | 28 |
| Test 1 | 1 | 2240 |
| Test 2 | 5 | 448 |
| Test 3 | 10 | 224 |
| Test 4 | 20 | 112 |

In the database, face bounding box labels are available every 200 ms. We only used these labeled frames for the experiments. The face images are cropped and scaled to 40x32 pixels resolution. They are then divided into 8x8 pixels resolution non-overlapping blocks making 20 local image blocks. From each image block ten-dimensional DCT-based feature vectors are extracted as described in Section 2.1 and they are concatenated to construct the final 200-dimensional feature vector. The classification is performed using a nearest neighbor classifier. The L1 norm is selected as the distance metric, since it has been observed that it consistently gives the best correct recognition rates when DCT-based feature vectors are used.

13-dimensional MFCC, with feature warping and reverberation compensation applied, is extracted from the speech signal as the speaker feature. We trained a GMM with 32 mixtures for each speaker using the expectation-maximization (EM) algorithm under the 30 seconds training condition and 16 mixtures for each speaker under the 15 seconds training condition. The classification is performed as described in Section 2.2.

## 3.1 Experiments on the Validation Set

The correct identification rates of the face recognition and speaker identification systems obtained on the validation set are presented in Table 2. In the table, each row shows the results for a different training-testing duration combination. The letter indicates whether the training is from set A or B which corresponds to 15 and 30 second training durations, respectively. The number indicates the duration of the testing segment in seconds. As expected, as the duration of training or testing increases the correct identification rate increases. Both systems achieve 100% correct identification when the systems are trained with 30 seconds of data and tested with the sequences of 20 seconds duration. Face recognition is found to be significantly superior to speaker identification at the other training-testing duration combinations.

**Table 2.** Correct identification rates of the individual modalities on the validation set

|     | Face Reco. (%) | Speaker Id. (%) |
|-----|----------------|-----------------|
| A1  | 91.4           | 56.4            |
| A5  | 99.1           | 67.9            |
| A10 | 100            | 89.3            |
| A20 | 100            | 92.9            |
| B1  | 94.3           | 61.1            |
| B5  | 100            | 84.8            |
| B10 | 100            | 98.2            |
| B20 | 100            | 100             |

To assess the effect of amount of testing data used for face recognition, we linearly interpolate the manual face bounding box labels and use these interpolated labels for cropping the faces from unlabelled frames during testing. That is, we use not only the labelled frames, but also the frames in between the labelled frames for testing. The obtained results can be seen in Table 3. Compared to the face recognition results in Table 2, a minor increase in correct identification rate in training-testing duration combinations, A1 and A5, and a minor decrease in B1 and B5 are observed. This indicates that using frames every 200ms suffices for face recognition, which provides also a significant drop in processing requirements.

**Table 3.** Correct identification rates of face recognition using every frame in test segments

|                  | A1   | A5  | A10 | A20 | B1   | B5   | B10 | B20 |
|------------------|------|-----|-----|-----|------|------|-----|-----|
| Performance (%)  | 92.1 | 100 | 100 | 100 | 93.9 | 98.2 | 100 | 100 |

Table 4 compares system performances when both training and testing are on channel 7 (CH7-CH7) vs. training using all 64 channels and testing on channel 7 (All

**Table 4.** Comparison of speaker identification performance on validation set

| Test Duration (sec) | Train A (15 sec) | | Train B (30 sec) | |
|---|---|---|---|---|
| | CH7-CH7 (%) | All CHs-CH7 (%) | CH7-CH7 (%) | All CHs-CH7 (%) |
| 1 | 53.6 | 56.4 | 50.9 | 61.1 |
| 5 | 66.1 | 67.9 | 82.1 | 84.8 |
| 10 | 83.9 | 89.3 | 92.9 | 98.2 |
| 20 | 92.9 | 92.9 | 100 | 100 |

**Table 5.** Comparison of modality weighting schemes on validation set

| | DPC (%) | IPF (%) | CRCM (%) | DPC+CRCM (%) | IPF+CRCM (%) |
|---|---|---|---|---|---|
| A1 | 91.8 | 91.6 | 92.0 | 91.8 | 92.7 |
| A5 | 100 | 100 | 98.2 | 99.1 | 100 |
| A10 | 100 | 100 | 100 | 100 | 100 |
| A20 | 100 | 100 | 100 | 100 | 100 |
| B1 | 94.5 | 94.5 | 94.5 | 94.3 | 94.5 |
| B5 | 100 | 100 | 100 | 100 | 100 |
| B10 | 100 | 100 | 100 | 100 | 100 |
| B20 | 100 | 100 | 100 | 100 | 100 |

CHs-CH7) using Frame-based Score Competition (FSC). We can see from the table that combining information from multiple channels provides significant system improvement especially when test duration is short.

Table 5 compares different modality weighting schemes. The correct identification rates in Table 2 are used to determine the fixed weights that each modality receives at each training-testing duration combination. It is done in two different ways. The first way, which is named as DPC, is by determining the weights directly proportional to the correct identification rates. For example, if the face recognition system has 100% and the speaker identification system has 85% correct identification rates, then they are weighted by 1 and 0.85 respectively for that training-testing duration combination. The second way, which is named as IPF, is by determining the weights inversely proportional to the false identification rates. For instance, if the face recognition system has 5% and the speaker identification system has 10% false identification rates, then the face recognition system receives twice as much weight than the speaker identification system. In addition to fixed modality weighting schemes, we also utilized CRCM which is the adaptive weighting scheme explained in Section 2.3. DPC+CRCM and IPF+CRCM are the combinations of fixed and adaptive weighting schemes. According to the obtained results on the validation set, IPF+CRCM has been selected as the modality weighting scheme to be used on the testing set.

## 3.2 Experiments on the Test Set

The correct identification rates of the face recognition and speaker identification systems obtained on the test set are given in Table 6. Similar to the obtained results on the validation set, as the duration of training or testing increases the correct identification rate increases. As can be noticed, on the test set the speaker identification performs as well as or even better than the face recognition at longer duration test segments. In the case of fixed modality weighting, this implies that the validation set is misleading, since on the validation set face recognition has been found to be more successful at these segments. The other observation that can be derived by comparing Tables 2 and 6 is the higher false identification rates obtained on the testing set. The main reason is that the time gap between the training set and test set is greater than the time gap between the training and validation set.

**Table 6.** Correct identification rates of the individual modalities on the test set

|     | Face Reco. (%) | Speaker Id. (%) |
| --- | --- | --- |
| **A1** | 84.6 | 41.9 |
| **A5** | 90.8 | 69.6 |
| **A10** | 93.3 | 92.0 |
| **A20** | 94.6 | 96.4 |
| **B1** | 89.3 | 41.2 |
| **B5** | 94.4 | 78.3 |
| **B10** | 94.6 | 96.4 |
| **B20** | 96.4 | 99.1 |

## 3.3 Fusion Experiments

In the fusion experiments, we analyzed the modality weighting schemes. The results are presented in Table 7. Even with the primitive fixed weights, in most of the training-testing duration combinations the correct identification rates are higher than the ones obtained by the individual modalities. The results with the more sophisticated adaptive modality weighting scheme, CRCM, show a significant increase in correct identification rates. Note that, in terms of performance of each modality, the validation set was not quite representative. As we have seen, under some training-testing duration combinations, face recognition was found superior than speaker identification on the validation set, but on the test set, it was the opposite. Therefore, performance based fixed weighting can be misleading. On the other hand, the results obtained by CRCM indicates that confidence differences are more robust cues for modality weighting. There is no significant performance difference between the CRCM and DPC+CRCM results. The performance degrades with IPF+CRCM, which was chosen as the primary modality weighting scheme for official results submission due to its best performance on the validation set. The

**Table 7.** Correct identification rates of fixed weighting schemes

|     | DPC (%) | IPF (%) | CRCM (%) | DPC+CRCM (%) | IPF+CRCM (%) |
|-----|---------|---------|----------|--------------|--------------|
| A1  | 84.8    | 84.6    | 86.3     | 86.7         | 86.7         |
| A5  | 91.1    | 90.8    | 93.5     | 93.5         | 91.7         |
| A10 | 94.2    | 93.3    | 98.2     | 98.2         | 93.3         |
| A20 | 94.6    | 94.6    | 99.1     | 99.1         | 94.6         |
| B1  | 89.8    | 89.4    | 89.6     | 89.9         | 89.9         |
| B5  | 94.9    | 94.4    | 97.3     | 97.3         | 94.4         |
| B10 | 95.5    | 94.6    | 98.7     | 98.7         | 94.6         |
| B20 | 97.3    | 97.3    | 99.1     | 99.1         | 99.1         |

reason is the hard modality weighting in IPF. Since, on the validation set at some training-testing duration combinations, face recognition reached 0% false identification rate, at these combinations only the face recognition system's decision is trusted.

## 4  Conclusion

In this paper, we presented ISL person identification systems in the CLEAR 2007 evaluations. In Table 8, the false identification rates of the individual modalities and the multi-modal system are listed. The multi-modal system included in the table uses CRCM modality weighting scheme. From the table, it is clear that multi-modal fusion significantly improves the performance compared to each of the single modalities. This also indicates that the face and voice modalities are complementary biometric traits.

**Table 8.** Correct identification rates of individual modalities and the multi-modal system

|     | Face Reco. (%) | Speaker Id. (%) | Fusion (%) |
|-----|----------------|-----------------|------------|
| A1  | 84.6           | 41.9            | 86.3       |
| A5  | 90.8           | 69.6            | 93.5       |
| A10 | 93.3           | 92.0            | 98.2       |
| A20 | 94.6           | 96.4            | 99.1       |
| B1  | 89.3           | 41.2            | 89.6       |
| B5  | 94.4           | 78.3            | 97.3       |
| B10 | 94.6           | 96.4            | 98.7       |
| B20 | 96.4           | 99.1            | 99.1       |

**Acknowledgements.** This work is sponsored by the European Union under the integrated project Computers in the Human Interaction Loop, CHIL, contract number 506909.

# References

1. Vendrig, J., Worring, M.: Multimodal Person Identification in Movies. In: Proceedings of the Intl. Conf. on Image and Video Retrieval, pp. 175–185 (2002)
2. Erzin, E., et al.: Multimodal Person Recognition for Human-Vehicle Interaction. IEEE Multimedia 13(2), 18–31 (2006)
3. Hazen, T.J., et al.: Multi-Modal Face and Speaker Identication for Mobile Devices. In: Hammoud, R.I., Abidi, B., Abidi, M. (eds.) Face Biometrics for Personal Identification: Multi-Sensory Multi-Modal Systems, Springer, Heidelberg (2007)
4. Snelick, R., et al.: Large-scale evaluation of multimodal biometric authentication using state-of-the-art systems. IEEE Trans. on Pattern Analysis and Machine Intelligence 27(3), 450–455 (2005)
5. Brunelli, R., Falavigna, D.: Person Identification Using Multiple Cues. IEEE Trans. on Pattern Analysis and Machine Intelligence 17(10), 955–966 (1995)
6. Kittler, J., et al.: On combining classifiers. IEEE Trans. on Pattern Analysis and Machine Intelligence 20(3), 226–239 (1998)
7. Ekenel, H.K., Stiefelhagen, R.: Local Appearance based Face Recognition Using Discrete Cosine Transform. In: 13th European Signal Processing Conference (EUSIPCO 2005), Antalya, Turkey (September 2005)
8. Ekenel, H.K., Stiefelhagen, R.: Analysis of Local Appearance-based Face Recognition: Effects of Feature Selection and Feature Normalization. In: IEEE CVPR Biometrics Workshop, New York, USA ( June 2006)
9. Stallkamp, J.: Video-based Face Recognition Using Local Appearance-based Models., Thesis report, Universität Karlsruhe (TH) (November 2006)
10. Furui, S.: Recent Advances in Speaker Recognition. Pattern Recognition Letters 18, 859–872 (1997)
11. Reynolds, D.: Speaker Identification and Verification Using Gaussian Mixture Speaker Models. Speech Communication 17(1-2), 91–108 (1995)
12. Jin, Q., Pan, Y., Schultz, T.: Far-field Speaker Recognition. In: International Conference on Acoustic, Speech, and Signal Processing (ICASSP) (2006)
13. Pelecanos, J., Sridharan, S.: Feature warping for robust speaker verification. In: Proc. Speaker Odyssey 2001 Conference (June 2001)
14. Xiang, B., Chaudhari, U., Navratil, J., Ramaswamy, G., Gopinath, R.: Short-time Gaussianization for Robust Speaker Verification. In: Proc. ICASSP (2002)
15. Computers in the Human Interaction Loop –CHIL, http://chil.server.de/
16. CLEAR 2007, Evaluation, http://www.clear-evaluation.org/

# Robust Speaker Identification for Meetings: UPC CLEAR'07 Meeting Room Evaluation System

Jordi Luque and Javier Hernando

Technical University of Catalonia (UPC)
Jordi Girona, 1-3 D5, 08034 Barcelona, Spain
luque@tsc.upc.edu

**Abstract.** In this paper, the authors describe the UPC speaker identification system submitted to the CLEAR'07 (Classification of Events, Activities and Relationships) evaluation. Firstly, the UPC single distant microphone identification system is described. Then the use of combined microphone inputs in two different approaches is also considered. The first approach combines signals from several microphones to obtain a single enhanced signal by means a delay and sum algorithm. The second one fuses the decision of several single distant microphone systems. In our experiments, the latter approach has provided the best results for this task.

## 1   Introduction

The CHIL (Computers in the Human Interaction Loop) project [1] has collected a speaker database in several smart room environments and has organized last two years the Evaluation Campaign to benchmark the identification performance of the different approaches presented. The Person IDentification (PID) task is becoming important due to the necessity of identify persons in a smart environment for surveillance or the customizing of services. In this paper the UPC acoustic person identification system and the obtained results in the CLEAR'07 evaluation campaign [2] are presented.

The CLEAR PID evaluation campaign has been designed to study the issues that cause important degradations in the real systems. One of them is the degradation of performance in terms of the amount of speaker data available for training and testing. In most of the real situations we do not have enough data to obtain an accurate estimation of the person model. Usually, the systems show a big drop in the correct identification rates from the 5 seconds to the 1 second testing conditions.

The second evaluation goal focus on the combination of redundant information from multiple input sources. By means of robust and multi-microphone techniques the different approaches deal with the channel and noise distortion because the far-field conditions. No a priori knowledge about the room environment is known and the multi-microphone recordings from the MarkIII array were provided to perform the acoustic identification, whereas, the previous

R. Stiefelhagen et al. (Eds.): CLEAR 2007 and RT 2007, LNCS 4625, pp. 266–275, 2008.

evaluation only used one microphone in the testing stage. For further information about the Evaluation Plan and conditions see [3].

Two different approaches based on a mono-microphone technique will be described in this paper. The single channel algorithm is based on a short-term estimation of the speech spectrum using Frequency Filtering (FF), as described in [4], and Gaussian Mixture Models (GMM) [5]. We will refer it to as: Single Distant Microphone (SDM) approach. The two multi-microphone approaches try to take advantage of the space diversity of the speech signal in this task. The first approach makes use of a Delay and Sum (D&S) [6] algorithm with the purpose to obtain a enhanced version of the speech. The second approach profits the multi-channel diversity fusing three SDM classifiers at the decision level. The evaluation experiments show that the SDM implementation seems to be suitable to the task obtaining a good identification rate only outperformed by the decision-fusion (D&F) approach.

This paper is organized as follows. In section 2 the SDM baseline is described and the two multi-microphone approaches are presented. Section 3 describes the evaluation scenario and the experimental results. Finally, section 4 is devoted to provide conclusions.

## 2 Speaker Recognition System

Below we describe the main features of the UPC acoustic speaker identification system. The SDM baseline system and the two multi-channel approaches shared the same characteristics about the parameterization and statistical modelling, but they differ in the use of the multi-channel information.

### 2.1 Single Distant Microphone System

The SDM approach is based on a short-term estimation of the spectrum energy in several sub-bands. The scheme we present follow the classical procedure used to obtain the Mel-Frequency Cepstral Coefficients (MFCC), however in this approach instead of the using of the Discrete Cosine Transform, such as in the MFCC procedure [7], the log filter-bank energies are filtered by a linear and second order filter. This technique was called Frequency Filtering (FF) [4]. The filter we have used in this work have the transform frequency response:

$$H(z) = z - z^{-1} \tag{1}$$

and it's applied over the log of the filter-bank energies. By performing a combination of decorrelation and liftering, FF yields good recognition performance for both clean and noisy speech. Furthermore, this new linear transformation, unlike DCT, maintains the speech parameters in the frequency domain. This Filter is computationally simple, since for each band it only requires to subtract the log FBEs of the two adjacent bands. The first goal of frequency filtering is to decorrelate the output parameter vector of the filter bank energies like cepstral coefficients do. Decorrelation is a desired property of spectral features since diagonal covariance matrices are currently assumed in this work [8].

A total of 30 FF coefficients have been used. In order to capture the temporal evolution of the parameters the first and second time derivatives of the features are appended to the basic static feature vector. The so called $\Delta$ and $\Delta$-$\Delta$ coefficients [9] are also used in this work. Note that, for that filter, the magnitudes of the two endpoints of the filtered sequence actually are absolute energies [10], not differences. That are also employed to compute the model estimation as well as its velocity and acceleration parameters.

Next, for each speaker that the system has to recognize a model of the probability density function of the FF parameter vectors is estimated. These models are known as Gaussian Mixture Models (GMM) [5]. A weighed sum of size 64 was used in this work. Maximum likelihood model parameters were estimated by means of the iterative Expectation-Maximization (EM) algorithm. It is well known, the sensitive dependence of the number of EM-iterations in the conditions of few amount of training data. Hence, to avoid over-training of the models, 10 iterations were enough for parameter convergence in both training and testing conditions.

In the testing phase of the speaker identification system, firstly a set of parameters $\mathbf{O} = \{\mathbf{o}_i\}$ is computed from the testing speech signal. Next, the likelihood that each client model is calculated and the speaker showing the largest likelihood is chosen:

$$s = \arg\max_j \left\{ L(\mathbf{O}|\lambda_j) \right\} \tag{2}$$

where $s$ is the score of the recognized speaker. Therefore, $L(\mathbf{O}|\lambda_j)$ is the likelihood that the vector $\mathbf{O}$ has generated by the speaker of the model $\lambda_j$.

## 2.2   Delay-and-Sum Acoustic Beamforming

The Delay-and-Sum beamforming technique [6] is a simple and efficient way to enhance an input signal when it has been recorded on more than one microphone. It does not assume any information about the position of the microphones or their placement.

If we assume the distance between the speech source and the microphones is enough far we can hypothesize that the speech wave arriving to each microphone is flat. Therefore, the difference between the input signals, only taking into account the wave path and without take care about channel distortion, is a delay of arrival due the different positions of the microphones with regard to the source. So if we estimate the delay between two microphones we could synchronize two different input signal in order to enhance the speaker information and reduce the additive white noise.

Hence given the signals captured by $N$ microphones, $x_i[n]$ with $i = 0 \ldots N-1$ (where $n$ indicates time steps) if we know their individual relative delays $d(0, i)$ (called Time Delay of Arrival, TDOA) with respect to a common reference microphone $x_0$ , we can obtain the enhanced signal by adding together the aligned signals as follows:

$$y(n) = x_0[n] + \sum_{i=1}^{N-1} W_i x_i[n - d(0, i)] \tag{3}$$

The weighting factor $W_i$, which is applied to each microphone to compute the beamformed signal, was fixed to the inverse of the number of channels.

In order to estimate the TDOA between two segments from two microphones we have used the Generalized Cross Correlation with PHAse Transform (GCC-PHAT) method [11]. Given two signals $x_i(n)$ and $x_j(n)$ the GCC-PHAT is defined as:

$$\hat{G}_{PHAT_{ij}}(f) = \frac{X_i(f)\left[X_j(f)\right]^*}{\left|X_i(f)\left[X_j(f)\right]^*\right|} \tag{4}$$

where $X_i(f)$ and $X_j(f)$ are the Fourier transforms of the two signals and $[]^*$ denotes the complex conjugate. The TDOA for two microphones is estimated as:

$$\hat{d}_{PHAT_{ij}}(d) = \arg\max_d \hat{R}_{PHAT_{ij}}(d) \tag{5}$$

where $\hat{R}_{PHAT_{ij}}(d)$ is the inverse Fourier transform of $\hat{G}_{PHAT_{ij}}(f)$, the Fourier transform of the estimated cross correlation phase. The maximum value of $\hat{R}_{PHAT_{ij}}(d)$ corresponds to the estimated TDOA. This estimation is obtained from different window size depending of the duration of the testing sentence (1s/5s/10s/20s). In the training stage, the same scheme is applied and we obtain the TDOA value from the training sets of 15 and 30 seconds. Note the difference in the window size in every TDOA estimation because the whole speech segment is employed. A total of 20 channels were used, selecting equispaced microphones from the MarkIII 64 array.

## 2.3    Multi-microphone Decision Fusion

In this approach we have implemented a multi-microphone system fusing three SDM classifiers, each of them as described in Section 2.1, working on three different microphone outputs. The microphones 4, 34 and 60 from MarkIII array have been used. The SDM algorithms are applied independently to obtain an ID decision in matching conditions.

Although they shared the same identification algorithm, the three classifiers sometimes do not agree about the identification of the segment data because of the various incoming reverberation or other noises in the different microphones. In order to decide a sole ID from the classifier outputs, a fusion of decisions is applied based on the following easy voting rule:

$$\begin{array}{lll} \text{if } ID_i \neq ID_j \quad \vee\, i, j \neq i & \text{select the central microphone ID} & (6) \\ \text{if } ID_i = ID_j \quad \text{for some } i \neq j & \text{select } D_i & \end{array}$$

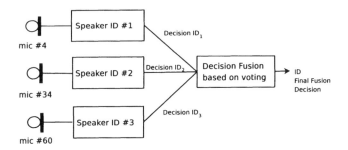

**Fig. 1.** Multi-microphone fusion, at the decision level, architecture

where $ID_i$ is the decision of the classifier number $i$. In other words, an ID is decided if two of them agree, and the central microphone decision is chosen in the case all three classifier disagree. The selection of the central microphone decision is motivated by its better single SDM performance in our development experiments.

## 3    Experiments and Discussion

### 3.1    Database

A set of audiovisual far-field recordings of seminars and of highly-interactive small working-group seminars have been used. These recordings were collected by the CHIL consortium for the CLEAR 07 evaluation according to the "CHIL Room Setup" specification [1]. A complete description of the different recordings can be found in [3].

In order to evaluate how the duration of the training signals affects the performance of the system, two training conditions have been considered: 15 and 30 seconds, called train A and train B respectively. Test segments of different durations $(1, 5, 10$ and $20$ seconds) have been used during the algorithm development and testing phases. There are 28 different personal identities in the database and a total of 108 experiments per speaker (of assorted durations) were evaluated.

For each seminar a 64 microphone channels, at 44.1 kHz and 16 bits/sample, were provided. Each audio signal was divided into segments which contain information of a sole speaker. These segments were merged to form the final testing segments (see the number of segments in Table 1) and the training sets A and B. The silences longer than one second were removed from the data. That is the reason why a speech activity detection (SAD) has been not used in the front-end of our implementations. The metric used to benchmark the quality of the algorithms is the percentage of correctly recognized people from the test segments.

**Table 1.** Number of segments for each test condition

| Segment Duration | Number of segments | |
| --- | --- | --- |
| | Development | Evaluation |
| 1 sec | 560 | 2240 |
| 5 sec | 112 | 448 |
| 10 sec | 56 | 224 |
| 20 sec | 28 | 112 |
| Total | 756 | 3024 |

## 3.2  Experimental Set-Up

The database provided was decimated from 44.1KHz to 16KHz sampling rate. The audio was analyzed in frames of 30 milliseconds at intervals of 10 milliseconds. Each frame window was processed subtracting the mean amplitude and no preemphasis was applied to the signal. Next a Hamming window was applied to each frame and the FFT was computed. The corresponding FFT amplitudes were then averaged in 30 overlapped triangular filters, with central frequencies and bandwidths defined according to the Mel scale. The microphone 4 from the MarkIII array was selected in the SDM algorithm with the purpose of comparing with the CLEAR'06 evaluation.

## 3.3  Results

In this section we summarize the results for the evaluation of the UPC acoustic system and the differences between the previous evaluation are examined. The Table 2 shows the correct identification rate obtained by the UPC acoustic implementations. That Table shows the rates obtained for the single microphone (SDM'07), Decision Fusion (D&F) and Beamforming (D&S) systems in either train A and train B conditions. Furthermore, the results from the single channel system from the previous evaluation (SDM'06) are also provided.

Some improvements have been performed on the system since the CLEAR'06 Evaluation, leading to better results than the ones presented in that. It can be seen that the results are better as the segments length increases. The Table 2 shows

**Table 2.** Percentage of correct identification obtained by the different UPC approaches

| Duration | Train A (15s) | | | | Train B (30s) | | | |
| --- | --- | --- | --- | --- | --- | --- | --- | --- |
| | SDM'06 | SDM'07 | D&F | D&S | SDM'06 | SDM'07 | D&F | D&S |
| 1s | 75.04 % | 78.6 % | **79.6 %** | 65.8 % | 84.01 % | 83.3 % | **85.6 %** | 72.2 % |
| 5s | 89.29 % | **92.9 %** | 92.2 % | 85.7 % | 97.08 % | 95.3 % | **96.2 %** | 89.5 % |
| 10s | 89.27 % | **96.0 %** | 95.1 % | 83.9 % | 96.19 % | **98.7 %** | 97.8 % | 87.5 % |
| 20s | 88.20 % | **98.2 %** | 97.3 % | 91.1 % | 97.19 % | **99.1 %** | **99.1 %** | 92.9 % |

this kind of behavior. In the SDM system, the results reach an improvement of up to 4.5% (absolute) in the recognition, comparing the train A with the train B condition.

On one hand, the decision fusion system seems, even with a very simple voting rule, to exploit the redundant information from each SDM system. This technique achieves the best results in the tests of $1s$ using any training set and in most of the test conditions of the training set B. On the other hand, as we can see in the Table 2, the Delay and Sum system does not provide good results to the task. The low performance of this implementation may be due to a not accurate estimation of the TDOA values. Other possible explanation could be the different background noise and the reverberation effects from the various room setups. The recordings was collected from 5 different sites, which could aid the GMM system to discriminate between the recorded speakers from the different room environments. As we can see in the Figure 2 mostly of the errors occurs between speakers of the same site.

In fact, neither of the systems presented in the evaluation based on any kind of signal beamforming did not show good results. By contrast, the same technique was applied in the Rich Transcription Evaluation'07 [12] obtaining good results in the diarization task.

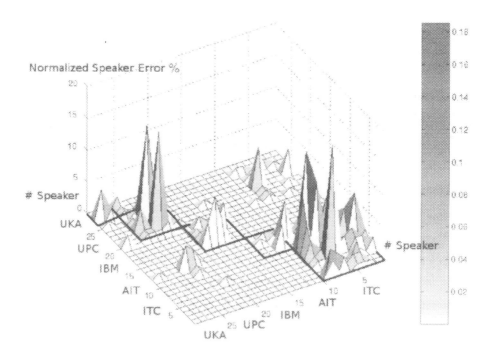

**Fig. 2.** Normalized Speaker Error from SDM in all test conditions. We can see the error mostly appears between the speakers of the same recording conditions.

The Figure 2 depicts the error behavior between speakers from the SDM implementation, a total of 348 over 3024 ID experiments. The boxes around the main diagonal enclose regions corresponding to speakers from the same site, that means, recordings with the same room conditions. As it has been commented above, we can see the number of speaker errors is higher around the main diagonal. The picture shows that the system mostly confuses the speakers from the same site. This kind of behavior could be due to the fact that our system is modelling both the speaker, accent or dialect, and the room characteristics, such as the space geometry or the response of the microphones.

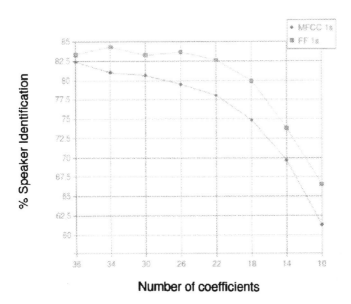

**Fig. 3.** Percentage of correct identification of the SDM approach in terms of the number of front-end parameters. The 30s training set and the 1s test condition from the Evaluation data 07 were employed to draw the figure.

### 3.4   Frequency Filtering Experiments

Some experiments were conducted focusing on the FF front-end. The Figure 3 shows the correct identification rate in terms of the number of parameters. Train A and 1s test condition have been selected to drawn the figure. Note that the number of coefficients are referred to the static parameters, but the total of parameters is three times more, including $\Delta$ and $\Delta - \Delta$. We can see that the optimum value of parameters, 34, is close to the value of 30 tuned during the development and applied in the submitted systems.In addition, the Figure 3 also shows the performance achieved by the MFCC coefficients, which always are lower than the FF results.

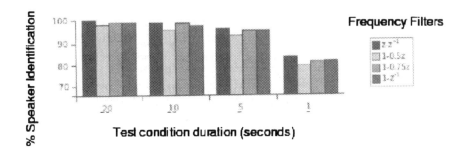

**Fig. 4.** Percentage of correct identification from the SDM approach using four different frequency filters.

Furthermore, a comparison between several frequency filters is provided in the Figure 4. The filter used in the evaluation $z - z^{-1}$ is compared with the first-order filter $1 - \alpha z^{-1}$ for different values of $\alpha$. Summarizing, the best performance is obtained by the second-order filter.

## 4    Conclusions

In this paper we have described three techniques for acoustic person identification in smart room environments. A baseline system based on a single microphone processing, SDM, has been described. Gaussian Mixture Model and a front-end based on Frequency Filtering has been used to perform the speaker recognition. To improve the mono-channel results, two multi-channel strategies are proposed. The first one based on a Delay and Sum algorithm to enhance the signal input and compensate the noise reverberations. The other one, based on a decision voting rule of three identical SDM systems.

The results show that the presented single distant microphone approach is well adapted to the conditions of the experiments. The use of D&S to enhance the signal has not show an improvement on the single channel results. The beamformed signal seems to lose some discriminative information that degrades the performance of the GMM classifier. However, the fusion of several single microphone decisions have really outperforms the SDM results in most of the train/test conditions.

## Acknowledgements

This work has been partially supported by the EC-funded project CHIL (IST-2002 − 506909) and by the Spanish Government-funded project ACESCA (TIN2005 − 08852). Authors wish to thank Dusan Macho for the real time front-end implementation used in this work.

# References

1. Casas, J., Stiefelhagen, R.: Multi-camera/multi-microphone system design for continuous room monitoring. In: CHIL Consortium Deliverable D4.1 (2005)
2. CLEAR-CONSORTIUM: Classification of Events, Activities and Relationships: Evaluation and Workshop (2007), http://www.clear-evaluation.org
3. Mostefa, D., et al.: CLEAR Evaluation Plan 07 v0.1 (2007), http://isl.ira.uka.de/clear07/?download=audio_id_2007_v0.1.pdf
4. Nadeu, C., Paches-Leal, P., Juang, B.H.: Filtering the time sequence of spectral parameters for speech recognition. In: Speech Communication, vol. 22, pp. 315–332 (1997)
5. Reynolds, D.A.: Robust text-independent speaker identification using Gaussian mixture speaker models. In: IEEE Transactions ASSP, vol. 3(1), pp. 72–83 (1995)
6. Flanagan, J., Johnson, J., Kahn, R., Elko, G.: Computer-steered microphone arrays for sound transduction in large rooms. In: ASAJ, vol. 78(5), pp. 1508–1518 (1985)
7. Davis, S.B., Mermelstein, P.: Comparison of parametric representations for monosyllabic word recognition in continuously spoken sentences. In: IEEE Transactions ASSP, vol. 28, pp. 357–366 (1980)
8. Nadeu, C., Macho, D., Hernando, J.: Time and Frequency Filtering of Filter-Bank Energies for Robust Speech Recognition. In: Speech Communication, vol. 34, pp. 93–114 (2001)
9. Furui, S.: Speaker independent isolated word recognition using dynamic features of speech spectrum. In: IEEE Transactions ASSP, vol. 34, pp. 52–59 (1986)
10. Nadeu, C., Hernando, J., Gorricho, M.: On the Decorrelation of filter-Bank Energies in Speech Recognition. In: EuroSpeech, vol. 20, p. 417 (1995)
11. Knapp, C., Carter, G.: The generalized correlation method for estimation of time delay. In: IEEE Transactions on Acoustic, Speech and Signal Processing, vol. 24(4), pp. 320–327 (1976)
12. Luque, J., Anguera, X., Temko, A., Hernando, J.: Speaker Diarization for Conference Room: The UPC RT 2007 Evaluation System. LNCS, vol. 4625, pp. 543–553. Springer, Heidelberg (2008)

# Probabilistic Head Pose Tracking Evaluation in Single and Multiple Camera Setups

Sileye O. Ba and Jean-Marc Odobez

IDIAP Research Institute, Martigny, Switzerland

**Abstract.** This paper presents our participation in the CLEAR 07 evaluation workshop head pose estimation tasks where two head pose estimation tasks were to be addressed. The first task estimates head poses with respect to (w.r.t.) a single camera capturing people seated in a meeting room scenario. The second task consisted of estimating the head pose of people moving in a room from four cameras w.r.t. a global room coordinate. To solve the first task, we used a probabilistic exemplar-based head pose tracking method using a mixed state particle filter based on a representation in a joint state space of head localization and pose variable. This state space representation allows the combined search for both the optimal head location and pose. To solve the second task, we first applied the same head tracking framework to estimate the head pose w.r.t each of the four camera. Then, using the camera calibration parameters, the head poses w.r.t. individual cameras were transformed into head poses w.r.t to the global room coordinates, and the measures obtained from the four cameras were fused using reliability measures based on skin detection. Good head pose tracking performances were obtained for both tasks.

## 1 Introduction

The study of head related-behaviors such as head gestures is of interest in many computer vision related applications. When studying head gestures in a general framework, information about head poses are required. Over at least a decade, many head pose tracking methods have been proposed. However, before being the bases of head gesture studies, the performances of the proposed head pose estimation methods have to be thoroughly investigated. For evaluating head pose estimation methods evaluation databases are required. Efforts have been made to build and make publicly available, a head pose video database with people having their head orientation continuously annotated with a magnetic field location and orientation tracker [1]. Such a database is usefull for comparison of cross-institution head pose evaluation where similar protocols can be used. Therefore, since 2006, the Classification of Events, Activities and Relationships (CLEAR) evaluation workshop has targetted the evaluation of head-pose estimation algorithms. In 2006, the head pose tracking task in the CLEAR evaluation workshop involved estimating the head direction of a person among 8 possible directions

R. Stiefelhagen et al. (Eds.): CLEAR 2007 and RT 2007, LNCS 4625, pp. 276–286, 2008.

(North, North-East, East,..., where the cardinal directions corresponded to the wall of a room). A limitation of this task was that the head directions were annotated by hand and that no precise evaluation was possible. This was remedied in 2007.

In the 2007 CLEAR evaluation workshop, two head pose estimation tasks were proposed. The first task, called the Augmented Multi-party Interaction (AMI) task, was about estimating people's head pose w.r.t. the view from a single camera. The data for this task consisted of 8 one-minute recordings. In each recording, four people are involved in a meeting and two people among the four have their head pose w.r.t. to a camera view annotated using a magnetic field location and orientation tracker [2]. These annotations were used for evaluation as a head pose ground truth (GT). The second task, called the Computers in the Human Interaction Loop (CHIL) task, involved estimating the head pose of a person w.r.t. to a global room coordinate system using four camera views of the person. For this task head pose ground truth was also generated using a magnetic field location and orientation tracker. The two tasks are interesting in the sense that they cover two common scenarii in computer vision applications. The first scenario occurs in a meeting room in which people are mostly seated. The second, occurs in a seminar room or a lecture theatre in which the head is captured at a much lower resolution and the people are mostly standing and moving. Evaluating head pose tracking algorithms in these two situations is important to understand the behaviors of the algorithms for a wide range of potentially interesting experimental setups.

In this work we used a probabilistic method based on a mixed state particle filter to perform head pose tracking w.r.t. a single camera view [3]. Applying this method solves the AMI head pose estimation task. To address the CHIL task, the head pose w.r.t. the camera is transformed to be relative to the global room coordinate system using the camera calibration parameters. Then the head pose estimated w.r.t. to the global room coordinate obtained from the four cameras are fused into a single head pose estimate using the percentage of skin present in the estimated bounding box for the head as reliability measure.

The remainder of this paper describes in more details the methods we used to solve the two tasks. Section 2 describes the estimation method in term of the head pose w.r.t. a single camera view. Section 3 describes the method we used to estimate the head pose w.r.t to a global room coordinate to solve the second task. Section 4 gives the results we obtained for the AMI task and Section 5 the results for the CHIL task. Finally, Section 6 provides some concluding remarks.

## 2   Head Pose Tracking with Respect to a Camera View

In this Section, we summarize the probabilistic method we used to track the head pose of a person w.r.t. a single camera view. This method is more thoroughly described in [3,4].

## 2.1   Probabilistic Method for Head Pose Tracking

The Bayesian formulation of the tracking problem is well known. Denoting the hidden state representing the object configuration at time $t$ by $X_t$ and the observation extracted from the image by $Y_t$, the objective is to estimate the filtering distribution $p(X_t|Y_{1:t})$ of the state $X_t$ given the sequence of all the observations $Y_{1:t} = (Y_1, \ldots, Y_t)$ up to the current time. Given standard assumptions, Bayesian tracking effectively solves the following recursive equation:

$$p(X_t|Y_{1:t}) \propto p(Y_t|X_t) \int_{X_{t-1}} p(X_t|X_{t-1})p(X_{t-1}|Y_{1:t-1})\mathrm{d}X_{t-1} \qquad (1)$$

In non-Gaussian and non linear cases, this can be done recursively using sampling approaches, also known as particle filters (PF). The idea behind PF consists of representing the filtering distribution using a set of $N_s$ weighted samples (particles) $\{X_t^n, w_t^n, n = 1, \ldots, N_s\}$ and updating this representation when new data arrives. Given the particle set of the previous time step, configurations of the current step are drawn from a proposal distribution $X_t \sim q(X|X_{t-1}^n, Y_t)$. The weights are then computed as $w_t \propto w_{t-1}^n \frac{p(Y_t|X_t)p(X_t|X_{t-1}^n)}{q(X_t|X_{t-1}^n, Y_t)}$.

Five elements are important in defining a PF: i) a state model which is an abstract representation of the object we are interested in; ii) a dynamical model $p(X_t|X_{t-1})$ governing the temporal evolution of the state; iii) a likelihood model $p(Y_t|X_t)$ measuring the adequacy of the data given the proposed configuration of the tracked object; and iv) a proposal distribution $q(X|X_{t-1}^n, Y_t)$ the role of which is to propose new configurations in high likelihood regions of the state space v) and a sampling mechanism which defines how the filtering distribution will be approximated using particles. These elements are described in the following paragraphs.

**State Space:** The state space contains both continuous and discrete variables. More precisely, the state is defined as $X = (S, r, l)$ where $S$ represents the head location and size, and $r$ represents the in-plane head rotation. The variable $l$ labels an element of the discretized set of possible out-of-plane head poses. In addition to the set of poses displayed in Fig. 1(a), 3 additional poses at pan values of -135∘, -180∘, and 135∘ (and a 0∘ tilt) were selected to represent the head from the back and allow head tracking when people are turning their head to the camera.

**Dynamical Model:** The dynamics governs the temporal evolution of the state, and is defined as

$$p(X_t|X_{t-1}) = p(r_t|r_{t-1}, l_t)p(l_t|l_{t-1}, S_t)p(S_t|S_{t-1}, S_{t-2}). \qquad (2)$$

The dynamics of the in-plane head rotation $r_t$ and discrete head pose $l_t$ variables are learned using head pose GT training data. Notice that the roll dynamics depend on the out-of-plane appearance (in plane rotation dynamics is different for frontal and profile poses). Head location and size dynamics are modelled as second order auto-regressive processes.

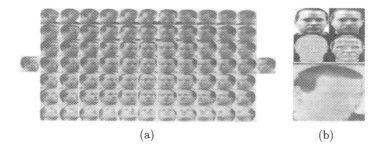

(a)              (b)

**Fig. 1.** a) Training head pose appearance range (Prima-Pointing Database[5] ) and b) texture features from Gaussian and Gabor filters and skin color binary mask

(a)           (b)

**Fig. 2.** a) Silhouette binary features (foreground mask), b) heads detected from the silhouette features

**Observation Model:** The observation model $p(Y|X)$ measures the likelihood of the observation for a given state . The observations $Y = (Y^{tex}, Y^{skin}, Y^{sil})$ are composed of texture features, skin color features (see Fig. 1(b)) and silhouette features (see Fig. 2(a)). Texture features are represented by the output of three filters (a Gaussian and two Gabor filters at different scales) applied at locations sampled from image patches extracted from each frame and preprocessed by histogram equalization to reduce light variations effects. Skin color features are represented by a binary skin mask extracted using a temporally adapted skin color model. The silhouette features are represented by a binary mask which is obtained from foreground segmentation using a temporally adapted background model as presented in [6]. Assuming that, given the state vector, the texture, skin color, and silhouette features are independent, the observation likelihood is modeled as:

$$p(Y|X = (S, r, l)) = p_{tex}(Y^{tex}(S, r)|l)p_{skin}(Y^{skin}(S, r)|l)p_{sil}(Y^{sil}) \quad (3)$$

where $p_{tex}(\cdot|l)$ and $p_{skin}(\cdot|l)$ are pose dependent models learned from the Prima-Pointing Database[5] and $p_{sil}(\cdot)$ is the silhouette likelihood model learned from training data (provided with the two tasks). For a given hypothesized configuration $X$, the parameters $(S, r)$ define an image patch on which the features are computed, while for the pose dependent models, the exemplar index $l$ selects the appropriate appearance likelihood model.

**Proposal Distribution:** The role of the proposal distribution is to suggest candidate states in interesting regions of the state space. As a proposal distribution, we used a mixture between the state dynamics $p(X_t|X_{t-1})$ and a head detector $p(X_t|\hat{\mathcal{X}}_t^d((Y_t)))$ based on the silhouette features according to the formula:

$$q(X_t|X_{t-1}^n, Y_t) = (1 - \alpha)p(X_t|X_{t-1}^n) + \alpha p(X_t|\hat{\mathcal{X}}_t^d((Y_t))) \qquad (4)$$

where $\alpha < 1$ is a mixture weight and $\hat{\mathcal{X}}_t^d((Y_t)) = \{\hat{X}_i^d(Y_t), \ i = 1, ..., N_t^d\}$ is the set candidate head states obtained from the detection procedure illustrated by the green boxes in Fig. 2(b). Qualitatively, the particles drawn from the second mixture components are randomly sampled around the detected head locations. More information about the proposal function can be found in [4]. The state dynamics are used to enforce temporal continuity in the estimated filtering distribution while the head detector's role is to allow automatic re-initialization after short-term failure and to avoid the tracker being trapped in local maxima of the filtering distribution.

**Sampling Method:** In this work, we use Rao-Blackwellization (RB) which is, a process in which we apply the standard PF algorithm to the tracking variables $S$ and $r$ while applying an exact filtering step to the exemplar variable $l$. In the current case, this means that the samples are given by: $X^i = (S^i, r^i, \pi^i(l), w^i)$ instead of $X^i = (S^i, r^i, l^i, w^i)$, where $\pi^i(l)$ represents the posterior distribution of the pose variable given all the other variables and the observations. The method theoretically results in a reduced estimation variance, as well as a reduction of the number of samples. For more details about the RB procedure, the reader is referred to [3].

# 3     Head Pose w.r.t to a Global Room Reference

In section 2 we presented a method to track and estimate head poses w.r.t. to a camera viewing direction. Using the head pose w.r.t. to a camera view, we can estimate it w.r.t. to a global room reference using matrix transformations.

## 3.1     Head Pose Estimation w.r.t to a Global Room Reference Using a Single Camera View

Head poses can be equivalently represented using Euler angles or a rotation matrixes. Denoting by $R_{vdir}^{head}$ the current pose expressed in the local viewing direction coordinate reference system. Then, given the correction matrix $R_{cam}^{vdir}$ that expresses the local reference vectors into the camera reference vector basis (this matrix depends on the image position of the head), and the calibration matrix $R_{3D}^{cam}$ that provides the rotation of the camera reference w.r.t. the global 3D reference, the current pose w.r.t the global reference can simply be computed as: $R_{3D}^{head} = R_{3D}^{cam} R_{cam}^{vdir} R_{vdir}^{head}$.

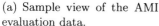
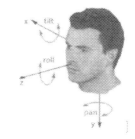

(a) Sample view of the AMI evaluation data.

(b) Head attached basis w.r.t which head rotations are defined.

**Fig. 3.** Example views of two persons in the evaluation data

The pose w.r.t. to the global room reference is then obtained using the Euler angle representation of the matrix $R_{3D}^{head}$.

### 3.2 Head Pose Estimation w.r.t to a Global Room Coordinate Using Multiple Camera Views

The method described in Section 3.1 allows us to estimate the head pose of a person w.r.t. the global room reference using only a single camera. When multiple camera views are available, head poses can be estimated from these sources by defining a procedure to fuse the estimates obtained from the single camera views. Such a fusion procedure is usually based on a measure that assesses how reliable the estimates are for each camera. Assuming the head is correctly tracked, the amount of skin pixels in the head bounding box can be used as a reliability measure. In general, a high percentage of skin pixels is characteristic of near frontal head poses for which head pose estimation methods are known to be more reliable [7], while a low percentage of skin pixels in the head location means the head appears either as a near profile head pose or from the back. Thus, we defined a camera fusion procedure as follows. After tracking the person in each of the camera views and having estimated the head pose w.r.t. to the global room reference, the final head pose is estimated by averaging the estimates from the two cameras for which the percentage of skin in the head bounding box is higher.

## 4 The AMI Head Pose Estimation Task

The AMI head pose estimation task consisted of tracking head poses w.r.t a single camera in a meeting room. In this section we describe the evaluation data and protocols for this task, then give the results achieved by our head pose tracking algorithm.

### 4.1 Evaluation Data and Protocols

The AMI data is composed of 8 meetings recorded from a single camera view. Four people are involved in each meeting. Among the four people, two which are

**Table 1.** Head pose estimation performance for the person left (L) and right (R) in the three test meetings of the AMI data. The last column gives the average pose estimation errors.

| error (in degrees) | 1R | 1L | 2R | 2L | 3R | 3L | average |
|---|---|---|---|---|---|---|---|
| pointing vector | 15. 6 | 17. 5 | 16. 0 | 14. 8 | 8. 4 | 11. 6 | 14. 0 |
| pan | 9. 9 | 13. 4 | 4. 9 | 12. 9 | 4. 4 | 7. 4 | 8. 8 |
| tilt | 11. 2 | 9. 5 | 14. 7 | 6. 7 | 6. 8 | 7. 5 | 9. 4 |
| roll | 10. 4 | 8. 1 | 13. 7 | 8. 2 | 7. 2 | 11. 5 | 9. 8 |

always visible are used for head pose estimation evaluation. Figure 3(a) shows an example view of the two people denominated *person right* and *person left*. The evaluation data consists of 1 minute recordings of 16 people. The head pose annotations of the 16 people used for evaluation were obtained using a magnetic field 3D location and orientation tracker [2], called a flock of bird, that was attached to each person's head. After calibration of the flock of birds to the camera, the outputs of the sensors were transformed to generate the head pose annotations. Among the 16 people available, the data (video recordings and head pose annotations) of 10 people were used as development data, and that of the 6 remaining people were used as test data.

As performance measures, we used four metrics: the head pointing vector error, and the absolute head pan, tilt, and roll estimation error. The head pointing vector is the normal unit vector of the $z$ axis of the basis attached to the head ( see Fig 3(b)). It defines the head pointing direction. The head pointing vector error is the absolute angle between the ground truth head pointing vector and the estimate. The head pan is defined as the rotation w.r.t to the y- axis of the basis attached to the head (see Fig 3(b)), the head tilt is the rotation w.r.t. to the x-axis and the head roll is the rotation w.r.t. to the z-axis. The estimation errors for these angles are the absolute differences between the head pose ground truth and estimates.

### 4.2    Results for the AMI Task

To solve the AMI task, we initialized the head localization manually before applying the head pose tracking method described in Section 2. The performances of the algorithm for the 6 persons in the test set are given in Table 1. Over the whole AMI evaluation dataset, our head pose tracking method achieves an average estimation error of 14° for the pointing vector estimation, 8.8° for head pan estimation, 9.4° for the head tilt estimation and for 9.8° for the head roll estimation. An analysis of the errors according to each individual shows significant variability of the performances due to variations in appearance or sitting attitude. For the head pointing vector estimation, the lowest estimation errors is achieved with the person sitting to the right side in the third test meeting (3R in Table 1) while the highest errors are obtained with person 1L (cf Table 1). This shows that some people are much better tracked than others, which is most

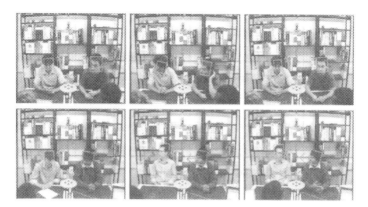

**Fig. 4.** Sample images of head pose tracking results in the AMI data: first row show images of the first test meeting, second row shows images for the third test meeting

probably due to the fact that they are better represented by the appearance models than others.

Fig. 4 gives sample images of head pose tracking results. This figure can be analyzed in parallel with Table 1. The first row of Fig. 4 shows that for person 1L (left person), head localization problems occur in some frames. In the last row of Fig. 4, we can observe that the person sitting to the right side, for whom the best tracking performance are achieved, has his head always correctly localized, even in difficult conditions. This illustrates the correlation between good head pose estimation performance and good head localization performance.

## 5   The CHIL Head Pose Estimation Task

The CHIL task consisted of estimating the head pose of a person w.r.t to a global room coordinate system using single or multiple camera views. In the following subsections, we describe the evaluation data and protocols and show the results using the algorithm described in Section 3.

### 5.1   Evaluation Data and Protocols

The CHIL data involved 15 people recorded in a seminar room. The 15 people were wearing a magnetic field location and orientation tracker, which provided their head pose w.r.t a global room reference. Four cameras located in the upper corners of the room were used to record the whole scene during three minutes in which the people had to move around and orient their head towards all the possible directions. Fig. 5(a) shows a top view of the room with its reference and the four cameras and Fig. 5(b) shows a sample image of all four camera views. In each of the recordings, head location annotations were provided every 5 frames. The recorded data were split into 10 videos with their corresponding annotations for training and 5 videos for testing. Only the frames for which

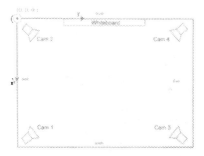

(a) Top view of the room. At the top left corner is the global room reference and at the four corners are the cameras.

(b) Sample images from the 4 camera recordings. First row, camera 4 and 2, second row camera 1 and 3

**Fig. 5.** Top view of the seminar room and sample images from the four camera views

**Table 2.** Head pose estimation average errors over the whole test set of the CHIL data using single camera (CHIL-M1) and the fusion of the four cameras (CHIL-M2)

| method | pointing vector | pan | tilt | roll |
|---|---|---|---|---|
| CHIL-M1 | 30.0° | 24.1° | 14.0° | 7.3° |
| CHIL-M2 | 19.4° | 15.0° | 10.0° | 5.3° |

head location annotations were available were used for head pose estimation evaluation. Similar to the AMI task, the error measures used for evaluation were the head pointing vector, pan, tilt and roll errors in degrees.

### 5.2 Results for the CHIL Task

To solve the CHIL task we used two methods. The first method, denoted CHIL-M1, is based on head pose tracking with respect to a single camera view as described in Section 2. Then the pose w.r.t. the camera are transformed into pose w.r.t. to the global room reference using the methodology described in Section 3.1. For this method, only one camera (cam 3 in Fig. 5(b)) was considered. The second method, denoted CHIL-M2, used the head poses w.r.t. to the global room reference estimated by four cameras and fused the estimates into a single one using the fusion procedure described in Section 3.2. In the following experiments the initial head locations were again provided manually.

Table 2 gives the average head pose estimation errors for the whole CHIL test data using the two methods. From the results, we can conclude that the method based on multiple camera fusion outperforms the method that used a single camera view. The improvements can be explained by the camera selection being implicitly embedded into the fusion process. More precisely, when using only one camera, large errors are produced when the tracked persons are showing the back of their head. On the contrary, in the fusion scheme, only the two cameras

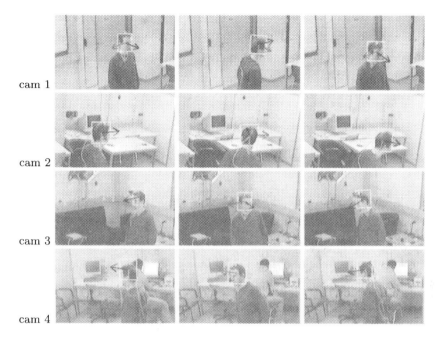

**Fig. 6.** Sample images (cropped from the original images for better visualization) of head pose tracking results for CHIL-M2. Each row displays sample images for the corresponding camera. Images of the same column correspond to a single time frame recorded from the 4 camera views.

with the highest reliability measure -usually the ones that the person is facing- are selected to estimate the head pose, thus providing good results in almost all conditions.

Fig. 6 shows the head pose tracking results for one person and illustrates the usefulness of the fusion procedure. In the second column for instance, camera 3 and 4 were automatically selected to provide the pose results.

# 6   Conclusion

In this paper we described our participation to the two head pose estimation tasks of the CLEAR07 Evaluation and Workshop. We proposed to use an exemplar-based representation of head appearances embedded into a mixed state particle filter framework. This method allowed us to estimate the head orientation of a person w.r.t. to a single camera view, thus solving the first task. The second task was solved by transforming the rotation matrix defining the pose w.r.t. the camera using the camera calibration parameters of a camera to obtain the head pose w.r.t a global room reference. This procedure was improved by fusing the single camera estimates using skin color as a camera fusion reliability measure. Good performances were achieved by the methods we proposed in solving both tasks.

In term of future work, we plan to define the head localization component of the state space of our mixed state particle filter directly in the three-dimensional space rather than in the image plane.

## Acknowledgment

This work was partly supported by the Swiss National Center of Competence in Research and Interactive Multimodal Information Management (IM2), and the European union 6th FWP IST Integrated Project AMI (Augmented Multi-Party Interaction, FP6-506811). This research was also funded by the U.S. Government VACE program.

The authors also thank Hayley Hung and Dr. Daniel Gatica-Perez from IDIAP Research Institute for their fruitfull discussions and usefull comments.

## References

1. Ba, S.O., Odobez, J.M.: A Video Database for Head Pose Tracking Evaluation. Technical Report 04, IDIAP Research Institute (2005)
2. Ascencion Technology (Flock of Birds)
3. Ba, S., Odobez, J.M.: A Rao-Blackwellized Mixed State Particle Filter for Head Pose Tracking. In: ICMI Workshop on Multi-Modal Multi-Party Meeting Processing (MMMP), pp. 9–16 (2005)
4. Ba, S.O.: Joint Head Tracking and Pose Estimation for Visual Focus of Attention Recognition. PhD thesis, Ecole Polytechnique Federale de Lausanne (2007)
5. Gourier, N., Hall, D., Crowley, J.L.: Estimating Face Orientation from Robust Detection of Salient Facial Features. In: Pointing 2004, ICPR international Workshop on Visual Observation of Deictic Gestures, pp. 183–191 (2004)
6. Yao, J., Odobez, J.M.: Multi-Layer Background Subtraction Based on Color and Texture. In: CVPR 2007 Workshop on Visual Surveillance (VS 2007) (2007)
7. Ba, S., Odobez, J.: Evaluation of Multiple Cues Head-Pose Tracking Algorithms in Indoor Environments. In: International Conference on Multimedia and Expo (ICME), Amsterdam (2005)

# Joint Bayesian Tracking of Head Location and Pose from Low-Resolution Video

Oswald Lanz and Roberto Brunelli

Bruno Kessler Foundation - irst
Via Sommarive 18, 38050 Povo di Trento, Italy
{lanz,brunelli}@itc.it

**Abstract.** This paper presents a visual particle filter for jointly tracking the position of a person and her head pose. The resulting information may be used to support automatic analysis of interactive people behavior, by supporting proxemics analysis and providing dynamic information on focus of attention. A pose-sensitive visual likelihood is proposed which models the appearance of the target on a key-view basis, and uses body part color histograms as descriptors. Quantitative evaluations of the method on the 'CLEAR'07 CHIL head pose' corpus are reported and discusssed. The integration of multi-view sensing, the joint estimation of location and orientation, the use of generative imaging models, and of simple visual matching measures, make the system robust to low image resolution and significant color distortion.

## 1 Introduction

Non verbal behavior, which includes gaze and expressions, is one of the most important aspects of human interactions [3]. Its analysis complements the information derived from macro features of verbal behavior, such as speaker turns patterns, supporting group behavioral studies. Automatic analysis of people interaction is then most naturally posed within an audio-visual framework [4]. Mutual distances (proxemics [9]) and orientations (focus of attention) of interacting people provide information valuable in determining group dynamics and roles. Automatic tracking of people location supports proxemics studies while reliable computation of head orientation, that is highly correlated to the real focus of attention of interacting people, provides additional support to behavioral studies.

The CLEAR'06 workshop [10] addressed these tasks and provided a quantitative comparison of several techniques. Many approaches are based on head detection followed by pose estimation, often using neural networks classifiers (e.g. [5,6,7]). A somehow different approach is followed in [8] where pose estimation is computed by Bayesian integration of the response of multiple face detectors tuned to different views. However, the separation into two stages may result into sub optimal performance. A potentially more robust approach proposed in [1,2] is to estimate jointly location and orientation using a mixed-state particle filter.

R. Stiefelhagen et al. (Eds.): CLEAR 2007 and RT 2007, LNCS 4625, pp. 287–296, 2008.

This paper [1] focuses on the joint determination of head position and orientation (horizontal and vertical) of people monitored with multiple cameras. The system relies on a Bayesian framework exploiting probability density distributions in state space. This approach eases the integration of information from multiple cameras (or even heterogeneous sensors) and opens the way to dynamic trade-off between accuracy and computational load. A generative likelihood is proposed that adopts a low-dimensional shape and appearance model of the target with an associated rendering procedure that supports real time processing. Although capable of operating reliably with a single camera, top-level fusion of likelihoods yields improved accuracy.

The next section introduces the model used for visual tracking and the corresponding likelihood measure. The integration of multiple views and of a model of temporal dynamics is then addressed in Sec 3. Experimental results are reported in Sec. 4, and Sec. 5 has the conclusions.

## 2    Appearance Likelihood for Pose Tracking

Following Bayesian approaches to object tracking, we describe the target in terms of a low-dimensional representation of its visual appearance based on color and shape. For a given pose hypothesis, the shape model is used to identify image patches where head and torso are expected to appear. Within these patches we use color histograms to describe the appearance of the body parts. This approach presents the following advantages:

- the use of histograms offers robustness to small misalignments, slight illumination changes and to noise deriving from non-modeled articulated motion;
- part-based definition of the model exploits appearance independence that usually exists between the different body parts due to skin color and clothing;
- the likelihood function built upon such model is sensitive enough to carry out the task, while at the same time remains simple and efficient.

The configuration, or state, of the target is described in terms of its position on a horizontal reference plane (e.g. the floor), horizontal torso orientation, and its head pan and tilt angles (all measured in the 3D space). See Fig. 1 for a graphical presentation of the quantities involved.

### 2.1    Shape

A coarse, part-based 3D model identifying the scene volume occupied by a person in a specific pose is adopted for shape, similar to the generalized-cylinder model proposed in [11]. This model is shown in Fig. 1 and is assembled from a set of rigid cone trunks. To represent a given pose in 3D, these trunks are positioned, scaled and oriented according to floor location, target height and body part orientations. To obtain the image projection corresponding to a pose for a given view,

---

[1] Research partly funded by the European Union under project IP 506909: CHIL - Computers in the Human Interaction Loop.

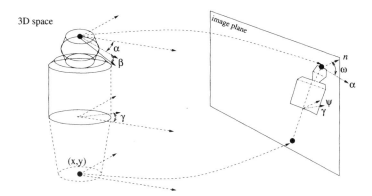

**Fig. 1.** 3D shape model parametrized by floor position $(x, y)$, body orientation $\gamma$ and head pose $(\alpha, \beta)$ (pan and tilt angle), and an approximate, but efficient, rendering implementation which still conveys imaging artifacts such as perspective distortion and scaling. Note the offset of the head patch from the central axis which gives a strong cue for head pose estimation. Angles $\omega, \psi$ involved in the rendering are defined as the angular offsets of body parts to the camera's optical axis $n$.

mesh based rendering techniques taken from the field of Computer Graphics [15] could be applied. More efficiently, we proceed as follow. A triple of 3D points representing the centers of hip, shoulder, and top of head is computed from the pose vector. These points are projected onto the camera frame using a calibrated camera model. The segments joining these image points define the 'backbone' around which the body profile is drawn with a piece-wise linear, horizontal offset. The profile width $W$ of the upper torso changes in accordance with the relative orientation $\omega$ of the body to the observer. More precisely, we modulate the projected physical body width with the factor $W(\omega) = 0.7 + 0.3 \cdot |\cos(\omega)|$. Similarly, the relative head orientation $\psi$ (again relative to the observer) is taken into account to modulate the projected head width. The head patch also has a horizontal offset $O$ from the axis which scales as a function of $\psi$: $O(\psi) = 0.38 \cdot \sin(\psi)$. This rendering procedure is fast and sufficiently accurate on near-horizontal views such as the ones captured by cameras placed in the corners of a room.

## 2.2   Color

To render the color histograms (RGB, $8 \times 8 \times 8$ bins) within the two body parts identified by the shape model we adopt a view-based rendering approach. The basic idea is to record a set of key views of the target prior to rendering, to extract the corresponding descriptions (i.e. color histograms) for each body part and to generate the histograms for a new pose and view by interpolation from these pre-acquired key histograms. How to acquire such key views for a target will be discussed later; for now their availability is assumed. The histogram rendering procedure for a specific pose works for each body part as depicted in Fig. 2. Given the spatial orientation $\gamma$ of the considered body part, the set of neighboring

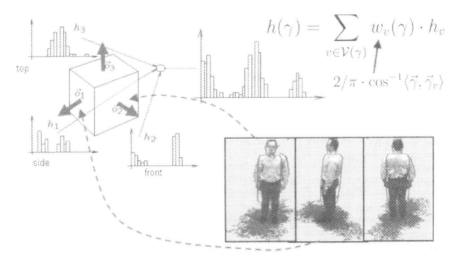

**Fig. 2.** Histogram synthesis. The cube faces represent pre-acquired top, front and side view of the object as seen from a new viewpoint. A weight is assigned to each view according to its amount of visible area (which is proportional to the cosine angular offset to the new views). New object appearance is then generated as a weighted interpolation of these histograms.

model views $v \in V(\gamma)$ that point towards the camera is identified. Corresponding key view histograms $h_v$ are then combined to get the new appearance by linear interpolation

$$h(\gamma) = \sum_{v \in V(\gamma)} w_v(\gamma) \cdot h_v \qquad (1)$$

Interpolation weights $w_v(\gamma)$ sum up to 1 over the set $V(\gamma)$ and account linearly for the angular offset from the current viewing direction

$$w_v(\gamma) \propto 2/\pi \cdot \cos^{-1}\langle \vec{\gamma}, \vec{\gamma}_v \rangle \qquad (2)$$

Here $\langle \vec{\gamma}, \vec{\gamma}_v \rangle$ denotes the scalar product between the 3D versors pointing in the direction of pose orientation $\gamma$ and key view orientation $\gamma_v$. Note that histogram interpolation is required only for body parts on which the appearance changes significantly with the viewing orientation. This is usually only the case for the head (skin color vs. hair color), while for the torso a single histogram should suffice. This method supports histogram rendering from any viewing orientation, including top-down views. In setups where only lateral views are available (typically cameras placed in the corners of a room) it is sufficient to acquire key view histograms for side views only (like those seen in Fig. 2), and interpolation for a new view can only be achieved for the two closest ones. We have used this faster rendering strategy in the implementation of the tracker described briefly later.

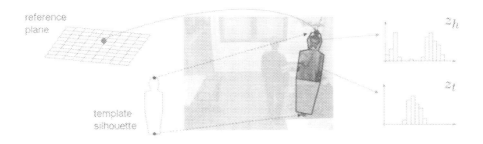

**Fig. 3.** Candidate histogram extraction procedure. The shape model is used to identify candidate body parts from which color histograms are extracted and finally compared to the rendered ones.

### 2.3  Likelihood Extraction

Fig. 3 shows the different steps in the likelihood calculation. To obtain the likelihood $p(z|\mathbf{x})$ of a pose hypothesis $\mathbf{x}$ on a new input frame $z$ we utilize the shape rendering function to identify potential head and upper torso patches within the image. From these regions a pair of color histograms is extracted and compared to the synthetic ones rendered for $\mathbf{x}$ as explained in the previous section. This comparison is made using a sum of Bhattacharrya-coefficient based distances [12] between normalized histograms pairs. If $a^h, a^t$ is the area of body part projections and $h_z^h, h_z^t$ and $h_m^h, h_m^t$ denote normalized extracted and modeled histograms respectively, the likelihood assigned is

$$p(z|\mathbf{x}) \propto \exp\left( -\frac{a^h d^2(h_z^h, h_m^h) + a^t d^2(h_z^t, h_m^t)}{2\sigma^2(a^h + a^t)} \right) \tag{3}$$

with normalized histogram distance given by

$$d^2(h, k) = 1 - \sum_{i=1}^{512} \sqrt{h_i k_i}. \tag{4}$$

Formally, $d$ considers the angle between the two versors $h_i, k_i$. Head and torso distances are weighted according to $a^h, a^t$ because their contribution to the likelihood is assumed to be proportional to their projected image area. Parameter $\sigma$ can be used to control the selectivity of this function and is set empirically to 0.12. This likelihood is background-independent and can therefore be used with active cameras or when the background scene is itself dynamic (containing non-tracked motion, video projector transitions, etc.). Note that the presence of the torso in the model provides a cue that may allow to distinguish between different people in the scene.

It is worth to underline that the use of color histograms as appearance descriptors results in a loss of spatial information. At first sight, this may seem disadvantageous for the task of head pose estimation: symmetric poses map into the same, ambiguous histograms. This ambiguity, however, is resolved by the shape model used to extract the histograms. Since the profile of the upper body of a person is different where head histograms are similar and viceversa, different image regions are taken into account when they are extracted, thus pose can be unambiguously determined from a single view. At the correct configuration the projected shape fits tightly the observed silhouette, thus body part histograms are extracted at the correct regions, providing good matching scores. At the other hand, the histograms extracted for a wrong configuration contain a significant amount of noise due to background contributions and body part misalignment. This explains the method's good performance in spite of using simple features, which is underlined by the experimentations reported in Sec. 4.

## 3    Multi-view Particle Filter

Generative approaches provide a suitable framework for state estimation from multi-sensor streams. Since the likelihoods proposed in this paper refer to the same, spatial, target representation, independently of the camera that is used, their integration becomes particularly simple and remains consistent with the measurement process. Under the assumption that observations are conditionally independent given the signal to be estimated (i.e. pose trajectory in our context), the joint likelihood of a set $\mathbf{z} = \{z^i\}$ of measurements factorizes

$$p(\mathbf{z}|\mathbf{x}) = \prod_i p(z^i|\mathbf{x}). \tag{5}$$

Although not guaranteed in theory, this independence assumption is commonly accepted in sequential Bayesian filtering. The evaluation results reported in Sec. 4 suggest that this is an acceptable approximation for our task.

As common for online estimation, the signal is modeled as a first order Markov process with dynamical model $p(\mathbf{x}_t|\mathbf{x}_{t-1})$ and initial distribution $p(\mathbf{x}_0)$. This enables to compute a new estimate $p(\mathbf{x}_t|\mathbf{z}_{1:t})$ solely from the actual observations $\mathbf{z}_t = \{z^i_t\}$ and its previous estimate $p(\mathbf{x}_{t-1}|\mathbf{z}_{1:t-1})$ using stochastic propagation and Bayes law

$$p(\mathbf{x}_t|\mathbf{z}_{1:t}) \propto p(\mathbf{z}_t|\mathbf{x}_t) \int p(\mathbf{x}_t|\mathbf{x}_{t-1})p(\mathbf{x}_{t-1}|\mathbf{z}_{1:t-1})d\mathbf{x}_{t-1}. \tag{6}$$

This defines the sequential Bayes filter: the integral term represents the prediction $p(\mathbf{x}_t|\mathbf{z}_{1:t-1})$ which is aligned with the evidence contained in the observation by a likelihood. To account for uncertainty and ambiguity, a non-parametric representation of the estimates in form of a set of representative sample states (the *particles*) is adopted. This approximation maps the above recursion into a sampling algorithm known as particle filter [14]. Each particle carries a hypothetic pose defined in terms of ground plane position and head and body orientation, extended with 2D target velocity for the purpose of temporal propagation, resulting in a 7-dimensional state space.

The dynamical model is defined in terms of a first order autoregressive process: each particle is linearly propagated along its velocity component according to the time elapsed, and zero-mean Gaussian noise is added to position, velocity and head orientation (variance is $0.6\text{m/s}$, $0.3\text{m/s}^2$ and $2\pi/\text{s}$, respectively). After sampling a new particle set from $p(\mathbf{x}_t|\mathbf{z}_{1:t-1})$, likelihoods are computed for the different views and particle weights are assigned as their product. Weighted resampling can then be applied in a straightforward manner. The initial particle set is sampled uniformly from the domain. The output of the probabilistic tracker is computed as the expectation over the current, weighted particle set.

## 4    Evaluation Results

The proposed pose tracker has been evaluated on the 'CLEAR'07 CHIL Head Pose' corpus. Projected head bounding boxes provided with the corpus have not been used at all (head position is implicitly estimated by the tracker itself). Since the visual appearance is explicitly modeled in the likelihood, the system does not need any training phase: therefore, we did not utilize the development data set provided with the corpus.

Sequences have been processed on a 2.3Ghz Xeon bi-processor dual core computer, using about 50% of the computing capacity. 1000 particles have been used for jointly tracking target location and head pose, image resolution was sub-sampled to 320x240, processing was done with a real-time factor of 3. Post-evaluation experiments suggest that significantly fewer particles could be used

**Fig. 4.** Model acquisition for target 'person03': frontal, side and back view, and extracted contours used for shape matching

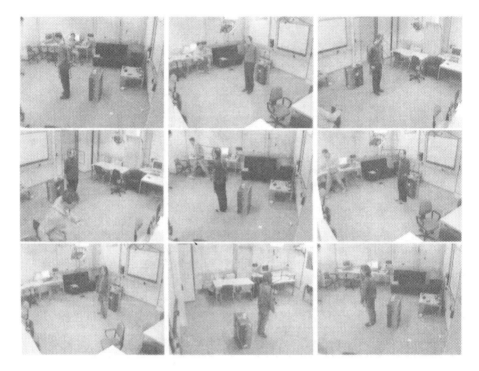

**Fig. 5.** Tracker output for 'person01b', 'person03' and 'person05': the shape model utilized for estimation has been rendered at the configuration computed as the expectation over the current, weighted particle set

achieving comparable performance[2], making real time processing possible on an off-the-shelf PC. Fig. 5 displays some frames of the tracker output on the CLEAR corpus.

Appearance models for the different targets have been acquired prior to tracking, through an automatic procedure, as follows. The entire sequence is first searched independently for each camera for the most frontal face shots by template matching (using a generic face template) and symmetry analysis (within the detected face) [17]. Each single candidate face is then further analyzed jointly in all four corresponding views, by matching extracted contours with the projected shape model outlines (see Fig. 4). Key view histograms for front, side and back views are then extracted from the image quadruple with the best scoring configuration, annotated with shape parameters (target height and width) carried by such configuration. The reader is referred to [16] for details on the model acquisition.

Table 1 presents the performance of the proposed approach on the 'CLEAR'07 CHIL Head Pose' corpus. Reported data include the arithmetic means of pan

---

[2] We have used 500 particles to track in real time at image resolution of $240 \times 180$, obtaining only a slight decrease in accuracy.

**Table 1.** Estimation errors on the CLEAR'07 CHIL Head Pose corpus. The approach does not make use of the hand-labeled head bounding boxes coming with the corpus (head location is jointly estimated from the video rather than provided externally), thus enabling for online elaboration.

|                   | CHIL corpus | person01b | person02  | person03  | person04  | person05  |
|-------------------|-------------|-----------|-----------|-----------|-----------|-----------|
| Mean Error Pan    | 29.52 deg   | 19.93 deg | 30.43 deg | 37.25 deg | 31.95 deg | 26.61 deg |
| Mean Error Tilt   | 16.32 deg   | 8.62 deg  | 23.60 deg | 13.36 deg | 21.53 deg | 12.73 deg |
| Mean Error Joint  | 35.67 deg   | 22.69 deg | 41.27 deg | 40.07 deg | 41.24 deg | 31.45 deg |

and tilt absolute error, and of the joint absolute error $\psi$ computed as

$$\psi(\alpha, \beta) = \cos^{-1}\langle \vec{v}_{\alpha,\beta}, \vec{V} \rangle, \tag{7}$$

where $\langle \vec{v}_{\alpha,\beta}, \vec{V} \rangle$ is the internal product between hypothesis and ground truth normalized orientation vectors, respectively. The dominant information for detecting people's focus of attention is head pan, which is estimated with an average error of less than 30 deg. In spite of using simple, low-dimensional image features and low-resolution input with significant color distortion, the proposed approach achieves sufficiently accurate pose estimation to support automatic behavior analysis in meetings.

## 5   Conclusions and Future Work

Automatic analysis of interactive people behavior is an emerging field where significant research efforts of the audio and image processing communities converge. Data from multiple and heterogeneous sensors may be integrated to obtain detailed reports of people activity enriching the knowledge of people position with additional information such as their relative orientation and their speaking activity.

We described a vision system for tracking at the same time people position and head orientation using multiple cameras. The approach, based on a Bayesian framework, is able to effectively incorporate evidence from multiple sensors, easily trading off accuracy for complexity. Future work will address the integration of audio cues in the estimation process.

## References

1. Ba, S.O., Odobez, J.M.: A probabilistic framework for joint head tracking and pose estimation. In: Proc. of ICPR 2004, vol. 4, pp. 264–267 (2004)
2. Ba, S.O., Odobez, J.M.: A Rao-Blackwellized mixed state particle filter for head pose tracking. In: ACM-ICMI Workshop on Multi-modal Multi-party Meeting Processing (MMMP), Trento, Italy, pp. 9–16 (2005)
3. Parker, K.: Speaking turns in small group interaction: A context-sensitive event sequence model. Journal of Personality and Social Psychology 54(6), 965–971 (1988)

4. Stiefelhagen, R., Yang, J., Waibel, A.: Modeling Focus of Attention for Meeting Indexing based on Multiple Cues. IEEE Transactions on Neural Networks 13(4), 928–938 (2002)
5. Gourier, N., Maisonnasse, J., Hall, D., Crowley, J.L.: Head Pose Estimation on Low Resolution Images. In: Stiefelhagen, R., Garofolo, J.S. (eds.) CLEAR 2006. LNCS, vol. 4122, Springer, Heidelberg (2007)
6. Voit, M., Nickel, K., Stiefelhagen, R.: Multi-View Head Pose Estimation using Neural Networks. In: Proc. of the 2nd Canadian Conference on Computer and Robot Vision CRV 2005, pp. 347–352 (2005)
7. Canton-Ferrer, C., Casas, J.R., Pardas, M.: Fusion of multiple viewpoint information towards 3d face robust orientation detection. In: IEEE International Conference on Image Processing, Genoa, Italy, vol. 2, pp. 366–369 (2005)
8. Zhang, Z., Hu, Y., Liu, M., Huang, T.: Head Pose Estimation in Seminar Room using Multi View Face Detectors. In: Stiefelhagen, R., Garofolo, J.S. (eds.) CLEAR 2006. LNCS, vol. 4122. Springer, Heidelberg (2007)
9. Hall, E.T.: The Hidden Dimension: Man's Use of Space in Public and Private. Doubleday, Garden City
10. Stiefelhagen, R., Garofolo, J.S. (eds.) Proceedings of CLEAR 2006 Workshop: Classification of Events, Activities and Relationships, Southampton, UK. CLEAR 2006. LNCS, vol. 4122. Springer, Heidelberg (2007), http://www.clearevaluation.org
11. Isard, M., MacCormick, J., BraMBLe,: A Bayesian Multiple-Blob Tracker. In: IEEE International Conference on Computer Vision and Pattern Recognition (2000)
12. Comaniciu, D., Ramesh, V., Meer, P.: Real-Time Tracking of Non-Rigid Objects using Mean-Shift. In: IEEE International Conference on Computer Vision (2003)
13. Birchfield, S.T., Rangarajan, S.: Spatiograms versus Histograms for Region-Based Tracking. In: IEEE International Conference on Computer Vision (2005)
14. Doucet, A., de Freitas, N., Gordon, N.: Sequential Monte Carlo Methods in Practice. Springer, Heidelberg (2001)
15. OpenGL: The Industry's Foundation for High Performance Graphics. [Online]: http://www.opengl.org/
16. Lanz, O., Chippendale, P., Brunelli, R.: An Appearance-based Particle Filter for Visual Tracking in Smart Rooms. In: CLEAR 2007 Workshop: Classification of Events, Activities and Relationships. LNCS, vol. 4625. Springer, Heidelberg (2008)
17. Brunelli, R., Poggio, T.: Template Matching: Matched Spatial Filters and Beyond. Pattern Recognition 30(5), 751–768 (1997)

# Learning a Person-Independent Representation for Precise 3D Pose Estimation

Shuicheng Yan, Zhenqiu Zhang, Yun Fu,
Yuxiao Hu, Jilin Tu, and Thomas Huang

ECE Department, University of Illinois at Urbana Champaign, USA
scyan@ifp.uiuc.edu

**Abstract.** Precise 3D pose estimation plays a significant role in developing human-computer interfaces and practical face recognition systems. This task is challenging due to the personality in pose variation for a certain subject. In this work, the pose data space is considered as a union of the submanifolds which characterize different subjects, instead of a single continuous manifold as conventionally regarded. A novel manifold embedding algorithm dually supervised by subjects and poses, called *Synchronized Submanifold Embedding* (SSE), is proposed for *person-independent* precise pose estimation. First, the submanifold of a certain subject is approximated as a set of simplexes constructed using neighboring samples. Then, these simplexized submanifolds from different subjects are embedded by synchronizing the locally propagated poses within the simplexes and at the same time maximizing the intra-submanifold variances. Finally, the pose of a new datum is estimated as the median of the poses for the nearest neighbors in the dimensionality reduced feature space. The experiments on the 3D pose estimation database, CHIL data for CLEAR07 evaluation demonstrate the effectiveness of our proposed algorithm.

**Keywords:** Subspace Learning, Person-Independent Pose Estimation.

## 1 Introduction

A face image encodes a variety of useful information, such as identity [27], emotion [23] and pose [1], which are significant for developing practical and humanoid computer vision systems. The problems of identity verification and emotion recognition have been extensively studied as multi-class classification problems in the computer vision literature. Many commercial systems have been developed for identity verification. However, the research on pose estimation, especially for precise 3D pose estimation, is still far from mature due to the underlying difficulties and challenges. First, the database and ground truth are much more difficult to obtain than the identity and emotion information. Second, the style of pose variation is personalized, and greatly depends on the 3D geometry of the human head. Finally, the pose labels are of real values, and hence the pose

R. Stiefelhagen et al. (Eds.): CLEAR 2007 and RT 2007, LNCS 4625, pp. 297–306, 2008.

estimation problem is essentially a regression problem rather than a multi-class classification problem.

Current research [4] [14] [7] [25] on appearance based pose estimation can be roughly divided into three categories. The first category [13] [14] formulates pose estimation as a conventional multi-class classification problem, and only rough pose information is derived from these algorithms. The second category takes pose estimation as a regression problem, and nonlinear regression algorithms like Neural Network [4] are used for learning the mapping from the original image features to the pose label. The last category assumes that the pose data lie on or nearly on a low-dimensional manifold, and manifold embedding techniques [5] [7] [10] [16] are utilized for learning a more effective representation for pose estimation. In this work, we address the challenging problem of person-independent precise 3D pose estimation, instead of the rough discrete pose estimation in the pan direction as done conventionally, and hence the first category is inapplicable in our scenario. To effectively exploit the underlying the geometry structure information of the pose data space as well as the available subject and pose information, our solution is pursued within the third category.

In this work, we present a dually supervised manifold embedding algorithm for person-independent precise pose estimation motivated from the following observations: 1) the pose sample data are often from multiple subjects, and distributed on distinctive submanifolds of different subjects instead of a single continuous manifold assumed by most conventional manifold learning [3][19][24] algorithms, such as ISOMAP [20], Locally Linear Embedding (LLE) [18], and Laplacian Eigenmaps [2]; 2) these submanifolds commonly often share similar geometric shapes; and 3) a desirable representation for pose estimation should be person-independent, namely the model trained on training data has good generalization capability on data from unknown subject.

Our proposed manifold embedding algorithm is dually supervised by both subject and pose information. More specifically speaking, first, the submanifold of each subject is approximated as a set of simplexes [15] constructed using neighboring samples, and the pose label is further propagated within all the simplexes by using the generalized barycentric coordinates [15]. Then these submanifolds are synchronized by seeking the counterpart point of each sample within the simplexes of a different subject, and consequently the synchronized submanifold embedding is formulated to minimize the distances between these aligned point pairs and at the same time maximize the intra-submanifold variance. Finally, for new data, its pose is estimated as the median of poses for its nearest neighbors measured in the dimensionality reduced feature space.

The rest of the paper is organized as follows. Section 2 introduces the motivations from conventional manifold learning algorithms, followed by the formulation of synchronized submanifold embedding. The pose estimation by local simplex propagation is described in Section 3. Experimental results on precise 3D pose estimation are demonstrated in Section 4. We conclude this paper in Section 5.

## 2   Synchronized Submanifold Embedding for Person-Independent Pose Estimation

Here, we assume that the training sample data are given as $X^c = [x_1^c, x_2^c, \cdots, x_{n_c}^c]$, where $x_i^c \in \mathbb{R}^m, i = 1, 2, \cdots, n_c$, and $c = 1, 2, \cdots, N_c$. $n_c$ is the number of training samples for the $c$-th subject, $N_c$ is the number of subjects, and we have $N = \sum_{c=1}^{N_c} n_c$ samples in total. Correspondingly, the pose labels are presented as $\Theta^c = [\theta_1^c, \theta_2^c, \cdots, \theta_{n_c}^c], c=1, 2, \cdots, N_c$, where $\theta_i^c \in \mathbb{R}^3, i = 1, 2, \cdots, n_c$ and three values of $\theta_i^c$ are the pan, tilt and yaw angles of the sample $x_i^c$. For ease of presentation, we denote the concatenated sample data as $X = [x_1, x_2, \cdots, x_N]$ and the concatenated label matrix as $\Theta = [\theta_1, \theta_2, \cdots, \theta_N]$.

Recent work [5] [7] [16] demonstrated the effectiveness of manifold learning techniques for pose estimation. The high-dimensional pose image data are assumed to lie on or nearly on a low-dimensional smooth manifold, and the manifold learning techniques such as LLE and Laplacian Eignmaps, or their linear extensions [10][7] are used for manifold embedding. Then the Nearest Neighbor criterion [8] or other simple linear regression approach is used for final pose estimation.

Though there were some attempts [17] to develop supervised manifold learning algorithms for multi-class classification problems, most manifold learning algorithms run in an unsupervised manner for regression problems like precise 3D pose estimation. Our work presented in this paper is motivated by the idea that both *subject* and *pose* information are mostly available in the model training stage and they are useful for developing effective person-independent precise pose estimation algorithm.

### 2.1   Synchronized Submanifold Embedding

The pose image data of a certain subject constitute a unique separated submanifold. To obtain a person-independent representation for pose estimation, it is natural to learn a low-dimensional subspace by synchronizing these submanifolds, such that the samples from different subjects yet with similar poses will be projected to similar low-dimensional representations.

Before formally describing our solution to learn such a subspace, we review some terminologies on simplex [15] and generalized barycentric coordinates.

A $k$-*simplex* is a $k$-dimensional analogue of a triangle. Specifically, a $k$-simplex is the convex hull of a set of $(k + 1)$ affinely independent points[1] in some Euclidean space of dimension $k$ or higher. Mathematically speaking, denote the vertices as $Z = [z_0, z_1, \cdots, z_k]$, and then the $k$-simplex is expressed as

$$S_k = \{\sum_{j=0}^{k} t_j z_j : \sum_{j=0}^{k} t_j = 1, t_j \geq 0\}. \tag{1}$$

---

[1]  In this work, the affinely independent property is assumed for the $k$ nearest neighbors of a datum, which is commonly satisfied since $k$ is small in our experiments.

The coordinates $[t_0, t_1, \cdots, t_k]$ in $\mathcal{S}_k(Z)$ are called the generalized barycentric coordinates, which is the generalization of barycentric coordinates, and is used for triangles and without nonnegativity constraints and for simplexes of arbitrary dimension.

**Submanifold Simplexization.** For the precise pose estimation problem, it is often difficult to obtain images of the same poses yet from different subjects. Hence the submanifolds cannot be directly aligned based on these discrete training samples.

In this work, we present a method to transform the labeled discrete samples on a submanifold into a set of continuous simplexes with propagated pose labels. For each sample datum $x_i^c$, the $k$-nearest neighbors of the same subject measured by pose label distance are used to construct a $k$-simplex as

$$\mathcal{S}_k(x_i^c) = \{\sum_{j=0}^{k} t_j x_{i_j}^c : \sum_{j=0}^{k} t_j = 1, t_j \geq 0\}, \tag{2}$$

where $\{x_{i_j}^c, j = 1, 2, \cdots, k\}$ is the $k$ nearest neighbors of sample $x_i^c$ within the same submanifold and $x_{i_0}^c = x_i^c$.

Motivated by the work of LLE [18], we assume in this work that the non-negative linear reconstruction relationship within the $k$-simplex $\mathcal{S}_k(x_i^c)$ can be bidirectionally transformed between features and pose labels. That is, for a point within $\mathcal{S}_k(x_i^c)$, denoted as $y_k^t(x_i^c) = \sum_{j=0}^{k} t_j x_{i_j}^c$, then its pose label can be propagated from the poses of vertices using the corresponding generalized barycentric coordinate vector $t$ as

$$\theta_k^t(x_i^c) = \sum_{j=0}^{k} t_j \; \theta_{i_j}^c. \tag{3}$$

Note that the bidirectional propagation of the generalized barycentric coordinates between features and labels is assumed only within a local neighborhood like the $k$-simplex around a certain sample, which is in accord with the general locally linear assumption of a manifold [18].

In this way, beyond a set of discrete samples, each submanifold is expressed as a set of labeled continuous simplexes, and then for each datum $x_i^c$, it has the potential to find a counterpart point with the same pose within the simplexes of any other subject. Consequently, these submanifolds of different subjects can be synchronized by aligning these data pairs.

**Submanifold Embedding by Pose Synchronization.** As described above, we aim to pursue a low-dimensional representation such that the submanifolds of different subjects are aligned according to the precise pose labels. For each sample $x_i^c$, the point within the reconstructed simplexes of the $c'$-th subject $(c' \neq c)$ and with the most similar pose is calculated in two steps. First, the generalized barycentric coordinates of this point is computed as

$$(\tilde{o}, \tilde{t}) = \arg\min_{o,t} ||\theta_i^c - \theta_k^t(x_o^{c'})||^2, \tag{4}$$

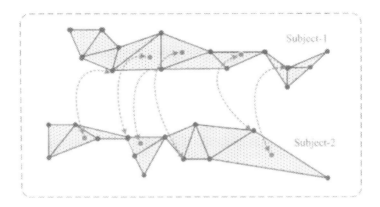

**Fig. 1.** An illustration of submanifold synchronization by simplicization. Note that to facilitate display, we utilize the 2-simplex for demonstration and the Euclidian distance in the 2D plane does not exactly reflect true distance between sample pair. The blue points represent the training samples, and the red points represent the corresponding synthesized points in distinctive submanifolds with the same poses. The dashed bidirectional lines connect the point pairs with the same poses.

and the corresponding datum and label are derived as

$$y(x_i^c, c') = \sum_{j=0}^{k} \tilde{t}_j \, x_{\tilde{o}_j}^{c'}, \tag{5}$$

$$\theta(x_i^c, c') = \sum_{j=0}^{k} \tilde{t}_j \, \theta_{\tilde{o}_j}^{c'}. \tag{6}$$

*Remark:* For a given $o$, the task becomes a standard quadratic optimization problem:

$$\min_{t} \|\theta_i^c - \sum_{j=0}^{k} t_j \, \theta_{o_j}^{c'}\|^2, \quad st. \quad \sum_{j=0}^{k} t_j = 1, \quad t_j \geq 0, \tag{7}$$

which can be solved by general optimization tool, such as the *quadprog* function in Matlab.

There are serval ways to derive a low-dimensional representation for synchronizing these submanifolds, and in this paper, we utilize the linear projection approach, namely, the manifold embedding is achieved by seeking a projection matrix $W \in \mathbb{R}^{d \times m}$ (usually $d \ll m$) and

$$y_i = W^T x_i, \tag{8}$$

where $y_i \in \mathbb{R}^d$ is the low-dimensional representation of sample $x_i$.

On the one hand, the projection matrix $W$ should minimize the distances between each sample to its nearest neighbor (measured by pose label distance) within the simplexes of any other subject. Namely, it should minimize

$$\hat{S}_{syn}(W) = \sum_{c=1}^{N_c} \sum_{i=1}^{n_c} \sum_{c' \neq c} ||W^T x_i^c - W^T y(x_i^c, c')||^2 I(x_i^c, c'), \tag{9}$$

where the indicator function $I(x_i^c, c') = 1$, if $||\theta_i^c - \theta(x_i^c, c')|| \leq \varepsilon$; 0, otherwise. $\varepsilon$ is a threshold to determine whether to synchronize the point pairs, and in this work, $\varepsilon$ is set as 2 for the pose estimation problem.

On the other hand, to promote the separability of different poses, it is desirable to maximize the distances between different sample pairs, namely

$$\hat{S}_{sep}(W) = \sum_{c=1}^{N_c} \sum_{i=1}^{n_c} \sum_{j=1}^{n_c} ||W^T x_i^c - W^T x_j^c||^2. \tag{10}$$

To achieve these dual objectives, the projection matrix $W$ is derived as

$$\arg\max_W \frac{\hat{S}_{sep}(W)}{\hat{S}_{syn}(W)} = \arg\max_W \frac{Tr(W^T S_1 W)}{Tr(W^T S_2 W)}, \tag{11}$$

where

$$S_1 = \sum_{c=1}^{N_c} \sum_{i=1}^{n_c} \sum_{c' \neq c} (x_i^c - y(x_i^c, c'))(x_i^c - y(x_i^c, c'))^T I(x_i^c, c'), \tag{12}$$

$$S_2 = \sum_{c=1}^{N_c} \sum_{i=1}^{n_c} \sum_{j=1}^{n_c} (x_i^c - x_j^c)(x_i^c - x_j^c)^T. \tag{13}$$

The objective function in the optimization problem (11) is nonlinear and commonly there is no closed form solution. Usually, it is transformed into another more attractive form as $\arg\max_W Tr[(W^T S_2 W)^{-1}(W^T S_1 W)$ and solved with the generalized eigenvalue decomposition method as

$$S_1 w_i = \lambda_i S_2 w_i, \tag{14}$$

where the vector $w_i$ is the eigenvector corresponding to the $i$-th largest eigenvalue $\lambda_i$, and it constitutes the $i$-th column vector of the projection matrix $W$.

## 2.2   Pose Estimation by KNN

After we obtain the projection matrix $W$, the sample data are all transformed into the low-dimensional feature space as in Eqn. (8), and then all the training samples are denoted as $Y = [y_1, y_2, \cdots, y_N]$.

For a new datum $x$, first, we also transform it into the low-dimensional feature space as $y = W^T x$. Then, we search for its $k$ nearest neighbors in the low-dimensional feature space, and then its pose is predicted as the median of the poses for its nearest neighbors, namely,

$$\theta_x = \text{median}_{i_j} \theta_{i_j}, \tag{15}$$

where $\theta_{i_j}, j = 1, \cdots, k$, are poses for the $k$ nearest neighbors of $y$.

# 3   Experiments

In this section, we systematically evaluate the effectiveness of our proposed framework, synchronized submanifold embedding (SSE), for person-independent precise pose estimation. We use the latest precise 3D pose estimation database, CHIL data, from the CLEAR07 evaluation [28] for the experiments.

The CLEAR evaluation and workshop [28][21] is an international effort to evaluate systems that are designed to recognize events, activities, and their relationships in interaction scenarios . In this work, we use the latest pose database, CHIL data, in the CLEAR07 evaluation, and this database is intended for precise 3D head pose estimation.

In the CHIL data, observations from four cameras that are placed in a room's upper corners are obtained for each subject. This data set includes 15 different persons standing in the middle of the room, rotating their heads towards all possible directions while wearing a magnetic motion sensor (Flock of Birds) in order to obtain their ground truth head orientations. The task is to estimate the head orientations with respect to the room's coordinate system, thus to obtain a joint estimate from all four views to achieve a hypothesis more robust than estimating from just one single camera. Some sample data are displayed in Figure 2, and the four images in each column are from the same subject and captured by four cameras simultaneously. Precise pose estimation in this scenario is very difficult due to the fact that the images are in a very low resolution and also noisy.

In our experiments, we use the same experimental configuration as designed by the evaluation committees. For training, 10 videos, including annotations of the head bounding boxes and the original ground truth information about the true head pose, are provided. For evaluation, 5 videos along with the head bounding box annotations are provided. The ground truth information is used for scoring. People appearing in the training set do not appear in the evaluation

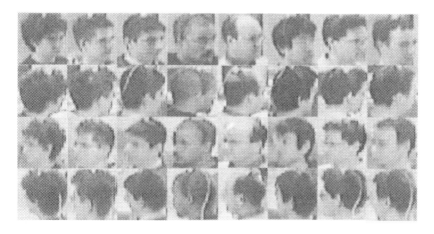

**Fig. 2.** The cropped sample images in the CHIL data for CLEAR07 evaluation. Note that each column contains four images of the same person captured by the four cameras.

**Table 1.** Mean Absolute Errors of the SSE algorithm on the CHIL data of the CLEAR07 evaluation

| Pose Direction | Pan | Tilt | Roll |
|:---:|:---:|:---:|:---:|
| MAE | $6.72^o$ | $8.87^o$ | $4.03^o$ |

set. Since manual annotations of the head bounding box only occur at every 5-th frame of the videos, only hypotheses corresponding to these time stamps are going to be scored [28]. Finally, the training set contains 5348 pose samples (each sample consists of four images captured by four different cameras) from the 10 subjects, and the testing set contains 2402 pose samples. Each image is cropped and scaled to size 40-by-40, and then gray-level values of all the four images are concatenated as the feature vector for each pose sample. For the experiments, we conduct PCA and reduce the feature dimension to 400, and then the algorithm is performed on the dimensionality reduced feature space. The computational cost of the training stage is close to that of the Marginal Fishier Analysis algorithm in [26], and the testing stage is in realtime for our experimental scenario. The Mean Absolute Error (MAE) [12] is used for accuracy evaluation. We conducted pose estimation frame by frame and did no use temporal filtering for smoothing. The detailed MAEs for the pan, tilt and roll directions are listed in Table 1, and the results are very encouraging.

## 4   Discussions

In this paper, we presented a framework for precise pose estimation by seeking effective submanifold embedding with the guidance of both pose and subject identity information. First the submanifolds of different subjects are simplex-ized such that they can be synchronized according to the pose labels propagated within the simplexes. Then submanifold embedding is derived by aligning the pose distribution within different submanifolds, and finally the pose label of a new datum is predicted as the median of the poses for its nearest neighbors in the derived feature space. The effectiveness of the proposed algorithm was validated by the experiments on the latest 3D pose estimation database, CHIL data for CLEAR07 evaluation. Our future work in this direction is to develop dually supervised manifold embedding algorithms which can benefit subject identification and the estimation of pose information simultaneously. Also, how to handle the case with missing views is another our future direction for research.

## References

1. Ba, S., Dobez, J.: A Probabilistic Framework for Joint Head Tracking and Pose Estimation. In: Proceedings of International Conference on Pattern Recognition, vol. 4, pp. 264–267 (2004)
2. Belkin, M., Niyogi, P.: Laplacian Eigenmaps and Spectral Techniques for Embedding and Clustering. Advances in Neural Information Processing System, 585–591 (2001)

3. Bregler, C., Omohundro, S.: Nonlinear image interpolation using manifold learning. Advances in Neural Information Processing Systems, 973–980 (1995)
4. Brown, L., Tian, Y.: Comparative study of coarse head pose estimation. In: Proceedings of IEEE Workshop on Motion and Video Computing, pp. 125–130 (2002)
5. Chen, L., Zhang, L., Hu, Y., Li, M., Zhang, H.: Head pose estimation using fisher manifold learning. In: Proceedings of IEEE International Workshop on Analysis and Modeling of Faces and Gestures, pp. 203–207 (2003)
6. Cootes, T., Edwards, G., Taylor, C.: Active appearance models. IEEE Transactions on Pattern Analysis and Machine Intelligence 23(6), 681–685 (2001)
7. Fu, Y., Huang, T.: Graph embedded analysis for head pose estimation. In: Proceddings of the 7th International Conference on Automatic Face and Gesture Recognition, pp. 3–8 (2006)
8. Fukunnaga, K.: Introduction to Statistical Pattern Recognition, 2nd edn. Academic Press, London (1991)
9. He, X., Yan, S., Hu, Y., Niyogi, P., Zhang, H.: Face Recognition Using Laplacianfaces. IEEE Transactions on Pattern Analysis and Machine Intelligence 27(3), 328–340 (2005)
10. Hu, N., Huang, W., Ranganath, S.: Head pose estimation by non-linear embedding and mapping. In: Proceedings of IEEE International Conference on Image Processing, pp. 342–345 (2005)
11. Jolliffe, I.: Principal Component Analysis. Springer, Heidelberg (1986)
12. Lanitis, A., Draganova, C., Christodoulou, C.: Comparing different classifiers for automatic age estimation. IEEE Transactions on Systems, Man and Cybernetics, Part B 34, 621–628 (2004)
13. Li, S., Fu, Q., Gu, L., Scholkopf, B., Cheng, Y., Zhang, H.: Kernel machine based learning for multi-view face detection and pose estimation. In: Proceedings of the International Conference on Computer Vision, vol. 2, pp. 674–679 (2001)
14. Li, S., Lu, X., Hou, X., Peng, X., Cheng, Q.: Learning multiview face subspaces and facial pose estimation using independent component analysis. IEEE Transactions on Image Processing 14(6), 705–712 (2005)
15. Munkres, J.: Elements of Algebraic Topology. Perseus Press (1993)
16. Raytchev, B., Yoda, I., Sakaue, K.: Head estimation by nonlinear manifold learning. In: Proceedings of the 17th International Conference on Pattern Recognition, vol. 4, pp. 1051–4651 (2004)
17. Ritte, D., Kouropteva, O., Okun, O., Pietikainen, M., Duin, R.: Supervised locally linear embedding. In: Proceedings of Artificial Neural Networks and Neural Information, pp. 333–341 (2003)
18. Roweis, S., Saul, L.: Nonlinear Dimensionality Reduction by Locally Linear Embedding. Science 290(22), 2323–2326 (2000)
19. Saul, L., Roweis, S.: Think Globally, Fit Locally: Unsupervised Learning of Low Dimensional Manifolds. Journal of Machine Learning Research 4, 119–155 (2003)
20. Tenenbaum, J., Silva, V., Langford, J.: A Global Geometric Framework for Nonlinear Dimensionality Reduction. Science 290(22), 2319–2323 (2000)
21. Tu, J., Fu, Y., Hu, Y., Huang, T.: Evaluation of Head Pose Estimation For Studio Data. In: Stiefelhagen, R., Garofolo, J.S. (eds.) CLEAR 2006. LNCS, vol. 4122, pp. 281–290. Springer, Heidelberg (2007)
22. Turk, M., Pentland, A.: Eigenfaces for recognition. Journal of Cognitive Neuroscience 13, 71–86 (1991)
23. Wang, H., Ahuja, N.: Facial expression decomposition. In: IEEE International Conference on Computer Vision, vol. 2, pp. 958–965 (2003)

24. Weinberger, K., Saul, L.: Unsupervised Learning of Image Manifolds by Semidefinite Programming. In: Proceddings of IEEE Conference on Computer Vision and Pattern Recognition, vol. 2, pp. 988–995 (2004)
25. Wenzel, M., Schiffmann, W.: Head pose estimation of partially occluded faces. In: Proceeding of the Second Canadian Conference on Computer and Robot Vision, pp. 353–360 (2005)
26. Yan, S., Xu, D., Zhang, B., Zhang, H., Yang, Q., Lin, S.: Graph Embedding and Extensions: A General Framework for Dimensionality Reduction. Proc. IEEE Trans. Pattern Analysis and Machine Intelligence 29(1), 40–51 (2007)
27. Zhao, W., Chellappa, R., Rosenfeld, A., Phillips, P.: Face Recognition: A Literature Survey. ACM Computing Surveys, 399–458 (2003)
28. http://isl.ira.uka.de/clear07/?The_Evaluation

# Head Pose Estimation in Single- and Multi-view Environments –
# Results on the CLEAR'07 Benchmarks

Michael Voit, Kai Nickel, and Rainer Stiefelhagen

Interactive Systems Lab, Universitt Karlsruhe (TH), Germany
{voit,nickel,stiefel}@ira.uka.de

**Abstract.** In this paper, we present our system used and evaluated on the CLEAR'07 benchmarks, both on single- and multi-view head pose estimation. The benchmarks show a high contrast in the application domain: whereas the single-view task provides meeting recordings involving high-quality captures of the participants, the multi-view benchmark targets at low-quality, unobtrusive observations of people by means of multiple cameras in an unconstrained scenario. We show that our system performs with state-of-the-art results under both conditions.

## 1 Introduction

To obtain information about peoples' visual focus, targets they are referencing to during speeches, actions or interactions, tracking eye gaze is too difficult and obtrusive to capture when allowing natural behaviour patterns in uncontrolled environments. Instead, the estimation of peoples' head orientation easily allows to deduce knowledge about e.g. interaction dynamics without the need of wearing such special gear for detecting explicitly the participant's pupils. One of CLEAR's workshop task is to track head orientation within different domains. Therefore, CLEAR'07 introduced two different datasets, that both aim for separate scenarios: Head pose is to be estimated both for high-quality single-view meeting recordings provided by the AMI project [1], as well as for low-resolution, wideangle multi-view recordings that were captured by four upper-corner cameras during the CHIL project [2]. Whereas multi-view head pose estimation shows to be a rather young research field, head pose recognition on high quality video frames in general, already shows a lot of history both using model- [4,5,6] and appearance-based [3,7] approaches. In this work, we use one same approach for both domains: by training a neural network classifier, we are able to obtain hypotheses on a per-camera basis rather than estimate the overall posterior output immediately. In case of the multi-view scenario, a successive fusion scheme based on bayesian dynamics merges the single estimates into one final, joint system output. For both tasks we show that our technique produces state-of-the-art results.

R. Stiefelhagen et al. (Eds.): CLEAR 2007 and RT 2007, LNCS 4625, pp. 307–316, 2008.

## 2     Task Descriptions

### 2.1     The CHIL Data Corpus - Multi-view Head Pose Estimation

The CHIL subtask in CLEAR'07's head pose estimation benchmark included the use of multiple cameras in order to gather and merge single-view hypotheses into one joint, robust estimate. The CHIL smartroom is equipped with several sensors to gather both audio and visual features about peoples' occupations and activities. Amongst numerous microphones and microphone arrays (both for speaker source localization and far field speech recognition), several cameras are installed to allow unobtrusive visual people tracking, person identification or head pose estimation. Overall, for this task, four fixed and calibrated wideangle

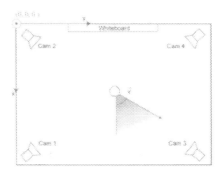

**Fig. 1.** Setup of the CHIL head pose task: four cameras were installed in a room's upper corners to capture the whole area underneath them. This surrounding setup allows people to move and behave without restrictions regarding a specific sensor. Using numerous cameras always guarantees to capture at least one frontal view. However, it is inevitable that some cameras only capture the back of the head, depending on how the head is rotated.

cameras were used, that were installed in the room's upper corners (Figure 1). The cameras do not obtain any zooming abilities and capture with a resolution of $640 \times 480$ pixels at 15 frames per second; hence, concerning where a person is standing in the room, head captures tend to vary strongly in size: overall, head captures as small as $20 \times 30$ pixels can be observed, not allowing any detailed detection of nostrils, eye or mouth corners that might allow for detailed model-based approaches. The use of multiple cameras in a surrounding sensor setup allows people to move without restrictions but guarantees that at least half the sensors capture the back of the respective person's head only. However, always at least one frontal view of the head may be observed. During recording sessions, all people in the dataset were instructed to wear a magnetic motion sensor to in-nitialize their groundtruth head orientation relative to a fixed transmitter, which was aligned with the room's coordinate system (hence, a horizontal head orienta-tion of $0°$ would point straight along the room's positive x-axis). The tracker used

**Fig. 2.** Example captures of one frame from all four views in the CHIL corpus. The person recorded was to wear a magnetic motion sensor to capture his groundtruth head orientation.

allows to capture with 30Hz, thus providing angle annotations as fast as twice the cameras' rates. To avoid dedicated tracking and implicit head alignment, head bounding boxes were manually annotated and provided with the dataset both for training and evaluation. Overall, the final data corpus thus provided 15 recordings with one person each. Every recording was about 3 minutes long. For training, 10 of these 15 people were distributed. The successive evaluation step happened on the remaining 5 videos.

### 2.2   The AMI Data Corpus - Single-view Head Pose Estimation

The AMI task provided single-view camera recordings of simulated meeting scenarios with two people sitting both in front of a table and a camera. Both persons are oriented towards the camera, hence their head orientation only varies within $-90°$ to $+90°$ for both pan and tilt rotations. The dataset included 8 meeting videos, hence 16 persons, to estimate head orientation in total. The overall length of one video is 1 min. As in the CHIL dataset, all persons involved were to wear a magnetic motion sensor for tracking their groundtruth head orientation. The dataset itself was split into one trainingset, containing 5 videos (10 people) and a testing set, including 3 videos (6 people).

## 3   System Overview

We adopted and extended our system already presented in [8,9] to also cope with vertical pose estimation (tilt). The following subsections thus present a brief overview of the previous work.

**Fig. 3.** Example capture of one frame from the AMI data corpus. Two meeting participants are sitting opposite to a camera. Their groundtruth head orientation is captured with a magnetic motion sensor. Due to the meeting scenario, the overall head pose range is limited to profile view reative to the capturing camera.

### 3.1 Single-view Head Pose Estimation Using Neural Networks

Neural Networks have proven, especially because of their generalisation, to be a robust classifier for the estimation of head orientation. We adopted this idea and applied this classifier for each camera view. Both horizontal and vertical head rotation were modeled with one network respectively. Either network follows a three-layered, feed-forward topology, receiving a cropped and preprocessed head image (according to a tightest fitting head bounding box), capturing the current observation at time $t$ and stating a hypothesis of the observed head rotation in either direction (horizontally or vertically).

The cropped head region is preprocessed by grayscaling, equalizing its histogram and resampling to $32 \times 32$ pixels. A Sobel operator computes the normalized head region's edge magnitude image which is concatenated to the normalized appearance, thus retrieving an overall feature vector of 2048 dimensions, derived from a merged head representation of $32 \times 64$ pixels.

The second layer was empirically chosen to contain 80 hidden units, all fully connected to both all input neurons as well as all output neurons.

Depending on the task, the network's output layer was trained to represent either a likelihood distribution or a final, continuous estimation of the observed head orientation. The latter was used for the single-view task involving the AMI data corpus. Since no multiple cameras were used, no fusion scheme to merge numerous hypotheses was required - the networks' output could be used as the posterior system's output. Especially, since no uncertainty resulting from views at the back of peoples' heads is involved. Regarding our multi-view approach, the networks were trained to output a likelihood distribution of the possible head orientation over the whole range of observable rotation angles ($-180°$ to $+180°$ for pan and $-90°$ to $+90°$ for tilt). To achieve sensor-independent classification,

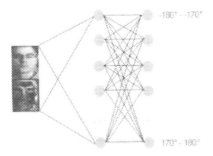

**Fig. 4.** In the multi-view setup, we trained one neural network with 36 output neurons. Each of them represents one discrete head pose class, relative to the camera's line of view (in 10° steps). The network was trained to estimate the likelihood of a possible rotation, given the observation of that camera.

all networks were trained to estimate those likelihoods over the range of relative poses to the respective camera's line of sight. That way, extending the setup by adding further cameras allows for no need of retraining a new classifier. Whereas, in the single-view task, we only used one single output neuron both for a pan as well as a tilt estimating network, the multi-view task thus required numerous output units to approximate the corresponding distribution. We therefore discretised the relative angle space into 36 classes each. Target outputs were modeled as gaussian densities as this uncertainty helps in correlating the single views' hypotheses as described later on.

## 3.2 From Single-view to Multi-view Scenarios

Taking advantage of having multiple views as in the CHIL data corpus, single-view hypotheses are gathered from every available sensor and merged into one joint, final estimation of the current observation. We apply the previously described networks to retrieve single-view distributions and merge and track with a bayesian filter. The bayesian filter resembles a general particle filter setup, omitting the resamling step, since, as described later, we only use a stationary, discrete set of states (thus particles) for pose tracking, which only need for reweighing. In our setup we compute a final estimate within a horizontal head rotation range of 360° (180° for tilt respectively). Hence, we use a fixed set of 360 (180) filter states, each one representing a corresponding head rotation in horizontal (vertical) direction. The task is to compute a posterior likelihood distribution $p(x_i|Z_t)$ over this defined set of states $X = x_i$ for a given time $t$ and single-view hypotheses $Z_t$ . The posterior distribution can thus be described as

$$p(x_i|Z_t) = \frac{p(Z_t|x_i) \cdot P(x_i)}{p(x_i)} \qquad (1)$$

As defined, the joint measurement $p(Z_t|x_i)$ is derived from all single cameras' hy- potheses with observations $Z_t = z_{j,t}$. The prior $P(x_i)$ denotes the probability to be in state $x_i$, modelling diffusion and providing temporal smoothing used for tracking. Each of these factors is going to be described in the following subsections.

### 3.3   Building a Joint Measurement

After mapping each possible head orientation $x_i$ to an orientation $\phi_j(x_i)$, relative to camera $j$'s line of view, we gather a combined measurement over all cameras by averaging the four class-conditional likelihoods, such that

$$p(Z_t|x_i) = \frac{1}{4} \sum_{j=1}^{4} p(Z_t|\phi_j(x_i)) \tag{2}$$

The intuition behind Equation 2 is that the hypothesis $x_i$ is scored higher, the more cameras agree on it, i.e. the respective output neuron exhibits a high value. That means, if two or more hypotheses strongly agree on the very same head orientation, the final sum of these probabilities returns a much higher value than accumulating smaller likelihoods that describe rather uncertain, ambiguous estimates.

### 3.4   Integrating Temporal Filtering

Temporal information is implied by the prior distribution $P(x_i)$ within Equation 1: at each timestep $t$ this factor implies the probability to observe state $x_i$. This factor is derived from the transition probability $p(x_i|x')$ to change from state $x'$ at time $t-1$ into the current state $x_i$ and the a-posteriori distribution $p(x'|Z_{t-1})$ which was computed at time $t-1$:

$$P(x_i) = \sum_{x' \in X} p(x_i|x')p(x'|Z_{t-1}) \tag{3}$$

We applied a gaussian kernel function to provide state change propagation $p(x_i|x')$, hence updating the prior distribution can be defined as a convolution of the gaussian kernel and the previous a-posteriori likelihoods:

$$P(x_i) = \sum_{x' \in X} \mathcal{N}_{0;\sigma}(x_i - x)p(x'|Z_{t-1}) \tag{4}$$

We used the empirically evaluated standard deviation $\sigma = 20°$. By using a gaussian kernel, short-term transitions between neighboring states are more likely than sudden jumps over a bigger range of states, hence the adaptation of the kernel's width directly influences how strong temporal filtering and smoothing of the system's final output takes place.

# 4  Experimental Results

We evaluated our system on both the CHIL [2] data corpus as well as the AMI [1] data corpus. Since we only directly used the neural networks' outputs in the latter task, no temporal filtering was applied here. The CHIL corpus involved our bayesian filter scheme, which showed to improve the overall accuracy by approximately 2°.

## 4.1  Results on the CHIL Corpus

As described in 2.1, the dataset was split into one training set, containing recordings of 10, and one testset, containing videos of 5 individual, different people. Each video was about 3 minutes long, captured with a framerate of 15 frames per second. For every 5th frame, a manually annotated head bounding box was provided. During training stage, all cropped head boxes were mirrored to double the amount of training data. Either network's behaviour was learned in overall 100 training iterations. The training dataset was split into one training and one cross-evaluation subset (90% training, 10% cross-evaluation). Amongst 100 training iterations (in which the network's connectionist weights and activations were learned using standard error backpropagation algorithm), that network minimizing the mean square error over the given cross-evaluation set was saved and extracted for later use, thus avoiding overfitting to the given training samples. As can be seen in Figure 5, the cameras' hypotheses generally seem to follow the unimodal behaviour used during training. The uncertainty displayed in the wide variance of the distribution helps in tracking the head's orientation, since choosing the final head rotation is based on finding that specific system state that maximizes the accumulation of the single-view hypotheses' corresponding likelihoods. Uncertainty in one view tends to be balanced with stronger confidences in the remaining views which leads to an unimodal posterior distribution as shown in Figure 6. The final results are depicted in Table 1: our system showed to perform with an accuracy of 8.5° for horizontal orientation estimation and 12.5° for its vertical counterpart. Omitting temporal smoothing during bayesian filtering resulted in an overall performance loss of 2°.

**Table 1.** Results on the CHIL data corpus. The corpus provided multi-view recordings.

| Mean Error Pan | Mean Error Tilt | Mean Angular Error |
|----------------|-----------------|--------------------|
| 8.5°           | 12.5°           | 16.4°              |

## 4.2  Results on the AMI Corpus

The AMI training corpus included 10 recordings of two persons sitting either to the left or right side of the camera. Because of missing 3D information regarding

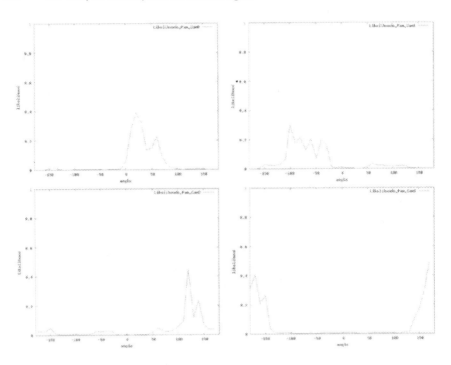

**Fig. 5.** Single-view pan likelihood distributions of the four used cameras for one single frame in the CHIL multi-view head pose task. Each distribution shows a significant cluster of high probability for a specific head orientation, relative to that cameras line of sight.

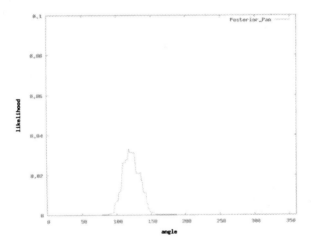

**Fig. 6.** The posterior distribution resulting after applying the bayesian filter on the given single-view likelihoods shown in Figure 5. The distribution is unimodal and un-ambiguous.

**Table 2.** Results on the AMI data corpus. The corpus provided single-view recordings of meeting scenarios.

| Mean Error Pan | Mean Error Tilt | Mean Angular Error |
| --- | --- | --- |
| 14.0° | 9.2° | 17.5° |

the translation of the magnetic sensor to the recording camera, we trained individual classifiers for both the left and the right person in order to avoid including ambiguous head pose appearances from shifted locations. Overall, we evaluated with four neural networks: two for pan (left person, right person) and two networks for tilt estimation (left person, right person). All networks were trained in a similar way to our scheme in the multi-view task: the training set was split into one training and one cross-evaluation subset. Here, too, the cropped head regions during training stage were mirrored to double the amount of samples. Since no bounding boxes were provided, a skin-color classifier helped to detect the corresponding person's head bounding box. Due to the static seating locations of the participants, no tracking became necessary.

The networks were trained with standard error backpropagation algorithm, using 100 iterations to extract that network minimizing the mean square error on the cross-evaluation set. The latter was set to include 10% of the overall training samples.

## 5 Conclusion

In this paper we presented the evaluation of our head pose estimation approach on the CLEAR'07 head pose benchmarks. We adopted our previously presented work for horizontal head pose estimation to hypothesise the vertical rotation, too and evaluated our approach on different multi-view (CHIL data corpus) and single-view (AMI data corpus) recordings. Under both circumstances, our system proved to produce reliable and state-of-the-art results of up to 8.5° mean pan error and 12.5° mean tilt error on the multi-view dataset and 14.0° and 9.2° on the single-view dataset respectively. In the multi-view setup, people were to move their head without any restrictions, views at the head's back were as often observable as profile or frontal views. Since the single-view meeting scenarios only provided fixed locations of the participants, only head rotations within profile range were involved. Whereas the latter benchmark focused on interaction scenarios with multiple people involved, the multi-view recordings were oriented towards unobtrusive head pose estimation in environments where people need to move their head freely without restrictions. Both goals were successively achieved. Our system hereby uses neural networks on each camera view for estimating head orientation in either direction. For the fusion of multiple views', a bayesian filter was applied to both diffuse prior estimates (temporal propagation) as well as search for the most coherent match of overlapping single-view hypotheses over all included sensors.

## Acknowledgement

This work has been funded by the European Commission under contract nr. 506909 within the project CHIL (http://chil.server.de).

## References

1. http://www.amiproject.org
2. http://chil.server.de
3. Ba, S.O., Obodez, J.-M.: A probabilistic framework for joint head tracking and pose estimation. In: Proceedings of the 17th International Conference on Pattern Recognition (2004)
4. Gee, A.H., Cipolla, R.: Non-intrusive gaze tracking for human-computer interaction. In: Proceedings of Mechatronics and Machine Vision in Practise, pp. 112–117 (1994)
5. Horprasert, T., Yacoob, Y., Davis, L.S.: Computing 3d head orientation from a monocular image sequence. In: Proceedings of the 2nd International Conference on Automatic Face and Gesture Recognition (1996)
6. Stiefelhagen, R., Yang, J., Waibel, A.: A model-based gaze tracking system. In: Proceedings of the IEEE International Joint Symposia on Intelligence and Systems, pp. 304–310 (1996)
7. Stiefelhagen, R., Yang, J., Waibel, A.: Simultaneous tracking of head poses in a panoramic view. In: Proceedings of the International Conference on Pattern Recognition (2000)
8. Voit, M., Nickel, K., Stiefelhagen, R.: A bayesian approach for multi-view head pose estimation. In: Proceedings of IEEE International Conference on Multisensor Fusion and Integration for Intelligent Systems (MFI) (2006)
9. Voit, M., Nickel, K., Stiefelhagen, R.: Neural network-based head pose estimation and multi-view fusion. In: Proceedings of the CLEAR Workshop (2006)

# Head Orientation Estimation Using Particle Filtering in Multiview Scenarios

C. Canton-Ferrer, J.R. Casas, and M. Pardàs

Technical University of Catalonia, Barcelona, Spain
{ccanton,josep,montse}@gps.tsc.upc.es

**Abstract.** This paper presents a novel approach to the problem of determining head pose estimation and face 3D orientation of several people in low resolution sequences from multiple calibrated cameras. Spatial redundancy is exploited and the head in the scene is approximated by an ellipsoid. Skin patches from each detected head are located in each camera view. Data fusion is performed by back-projecting skin patches from single images onto the estimated 3D head model, thus providing a synthetic reconstruction of the head appearance. A particle filter is employed to perform the estimation of the head pan angle of the person under study. A likelihood function based on the face appearance is introduced. Experimental results proving the effectiveness of the proposed algorithm are provided for the SmartRoom scenario of the CLEAR Evaluation 2007 Head Orientation dataset.

## 1 Introduction

The estimation of human head orientation has a wide range of applications, including a variety of services in human-computer interfaces, teleconferencing, virtual reality and 3D audio rendering. In recent years, significant research efforts have been devoted to the development of human-computer interfaces in intelligent environments aiming at supporting humans in various tasks and situations. Examples of these intelligent environments include the "digital office" [3], "intelligent house", "intelligent classroom" and "smart conferencing rooms". The head orientation of a person provides important clues in order to construct perceptive capabilities in such scenarios. This knowledge allows a better understanding of what users do or what they refer to. Furthermore, accurate head pose estimation allows the computers to perform Face Identification or improved Automatic Speech Recognition by selecting a subset of sensors (cameras and microphones) adequately located for the task. Being focus of attention directly related to the head orientation, it can also be used to give personalized information to the users, for instance through a monitor or a beamer displaying text or images directly targeting their focus of attention. In synthesis, determining the individuals head orientation is the basis for many forms of more sophisticated interactions between humans and technical devices. In automatic video conferencing, a set of computer-controlled cameras capture the images of one or more individuals adjusting for orientation and range, and compensating for any source motion [22].

R. Stiefelhagen et al. (Eds.): CLEAR 2007 and RT 2007, LNCS 4625, pp. 317–327, 2008.

In this context, head orientation estimation is a crucial source of information to decide which cameras and microphones are more suited to capture the scene. In video surveillance applications, determination of the head orientation of the individuals can also be used for camera selection. Other applications include control of avatars in virtual environments or input to a cross-talk cancellation system for 3D audio rendering.

Methods for head pose estimation from video signals proposed in the literature can be classified as feature based or appearance based [21]. Feature based methods [2, 14, 17] use a general approach that involves estimating the position of specific facial features in the image (typically eyes, nostrils and mouth) and then fitting these data to a head model. In practice, some of these methods might require manual initialization and are particularly sensitive to the selection of feature points. Moreover, near-frontal views are assumed and high-quality images are required. For the applications addressed in our work, such conditions are usually difficult to satisfy. Specific facial features are typically not clearly visible due to lighting conditions and wide angle camera views. They may also be entirely unavailable when faces are not oriented towards the cameras. Methods which rely on a detailed feature analysis followed by head model fitting would fail under these circumstances. Furthermore, most of these approaches are based on monocular analysis of images but few have addressed the multiocular case for face or head analysis [17,6,4]. On the contrary, appearance based methods [24,20] tend to achieve satisfactory results with low resolution images. However, in these techniques head orientation estimation is posed as a classification problem using Neural Networks, thus producing an output angle resolution limited to a discrete set. For example, in [19] angle estimation is restricted to steps of 25° while in [9] steps of 45° are employed. Data analysis methods providing a real valued angle output will be preferred since produce more information for further analysis modules. Recently, a multimodal head orientation estimation algorithm has been presented by the authors [5] based on the output of this video analysis system.

The remainder of this paper is organized as follows. In the next section, we introduce the Particle Filtering theory that will be the basis of the head orientation estimation technique. In Section 3, the monomodal video head estimation algorithm is presented. Finally, in the following section, the performance obtained by our system is discussed.

## 2    Particle Filtering for Head Orientation Estimation

The estimation of the pan angle $\theta_t$ of the head of a person at a given time $t$ given a set of observations $\Omega_{1:t}$ can be written in the context of a state space estimation problem [23] driven by the following state process equation:

$$\theta_t = \mathbf{f}\left(\theta_{t-1}, \mathbf{v}_t\right), \tag{1}$$

and the observation equation:

$$\Omega_t = \mathbf{h}\left(\theta_t, \mathbf{n}_t\right), \tag{2}$$

where $\mathbf{f}(\cdot)$ is a function describing the evolution of the model and $\mathbf{h}(\cdot)$ an observation function modeling the relation between the hidden variable $\theta_t$ and its measurable magnitude $\Omega_t$. Noise components, $\mathbf{v}_t$ and $\mathbf{n}_t$, are assumed to be independent stochastic processes with a given distribution.

From a Bayesian perspective, the pan angle estimation and tracking problem is to recursively estimate a certain degree of belief in the state variable $\theta_t$ at time $t$, given the data $\Omega_{1:t}$ up to time $t$. Thus, it is required to calculate the *pdf* $p(\theta_t|\Omega_{1:t})$, and this can be done recursively in two steps, namely prediction and update. The prediction step uses the process equation Eq.1 to obtain the prior *pdf* by means of the Chapman-Kolmogorov integral:

$$p\left(\theta_t|\Omega_{1:t-1}\right) = \int p\left(\theta_t|\theta_{t-1}\right) p\left(\theta_{t-1}|\Omega_{1:t-1}\right) d\theta_{t-1}, \tag{3}$$

with $p\left(\theta_{t-1}|\Omega_{1:t-1}\right)$ known from the previous iteration and $p\left(\theta_t|\theta_{t-1}\right)$ determined by Eq.1. When a measurement $\Omega_t$ becomes available, it may be used to update the prior *pdf* via Bayes' rule:

$$p\left(\theta_t|\Omega_{1:t}\right) = \frac{p\left(\Omega_t|\theta_t\right) p\left(\theta_t|\Omega_{1:t-1}\right)}{\int p\left(\Omega_t|\theta_t\right) p\left(\theta_t|\Omega_{1:t-1}\right) d\theta_t}, \tag{4}$$

being $p\left(\Omega_t|\theta_t\right)$ the likelihood statistics derived from Eq.2. However, the posterior *pdf* $p\left(\theta_t|\Omega_{1:t}\right)$ in Eq.4 can not be computed analytically unless linear-Gaussian models are adopted, in which case the Kalman filter provides the optimal solution.

Particle Filtering (PF) [1] algorithms are sequential Monte Carlo methods based on point mass (or "particle") representations of probability densities. These techniques are employed to tackle estimation and tracking problems where the variables involved do not hold Gaussianity uncertainty models and linear dynamics. In this case, PF approximates the posterior density $p(\theta_t|\Omega_{1:t})$ with a sum of $N_s$ Dirac functions centered in $\{\theta_t^j\}$, $0 < j \le N_s$, as:

$$p\left(\theta_t|\Omega_{1:t}\right) \approx \sum_{j=1}^{N_s} w_t^j \delta(\theta_t - \theta_t^j), \tag{5}$$

where $w_t^j$ are the weights associated to the particles fulfilling $\sum_{j=1}^{N_s} w_t^j = 1$. For this type of estimation and tracking problems, it is a common approach to employ a Sampling Importance Re-sampling (SIR) strategy to drive particles across time [12]. This assumption leads to a recursive update of the weights as:

$$w_t^j \propto w_{t-1}^j \, p(\Omega_t|\theta_t^j). \tag{6}$$

SIR PF circumvents the particle degeneracy problem by re-sampling with replacement at every time step [1], that is to dismiss the particles with lower weights and proportionally replicate those with higher weights. In this case, weights are set to $w_{t-1}^j = N_s^{-1}$, $\forall j$, therefore

$$w_t^j \propto p(\Omega_t|\theta_t^j). \tag{7}$$

Hence, the weights are proportional to the likelihood function that will be computed over the incoming data $\Omega_t$. The re-sampling step derives the particles depending on the weights of the previous step, then all the new particles receive a starting weight equal to $N_s^{-1}$ that will be updated by the next likelihood evaluation.

The best state at time $t$, $\Theta_t$, is derived based on the discrete approximation of Eq.5. The most common solution is the Monte Carlo approximation of the expectation

$$\Theta_t = \mathbb{E}\left[\theta_t | \Omega_{1:t}\right] \approx \sum_{j=1}^{N_s} w_t^j \theta_t^j. \tag{8}$$

Finally, a propagation model is adopted to add a drift to the angles $\theta_t^j$ of the re-sampled particles in order to progressively sample the state space in the following iterations [1]. For complex PF problems involving a high dimensional state space such as in articulated human body tracking tasks [10], an underlying motion pattern is employed in order to efficiently sample the state space thus reducing the number of particles required. Due to the single dimension of our head pose estimation task, a Gaussian drift is employed and no motion models are assumed.

PF have been successfully applied for a number of tasks in both audio and video such as object tracking tasks with cluttered backgrounds [15]. Information of audio and video sources have been effectively combined employing PF strategies for active speaker tracking [18] or audiovisual multi-person tracking [11].

## 3   Video Head Pose Estimation

This section presents a new approach to multi-camera head pose estimation from low-resolution images based on PF. A spatial and color analysis of these input images is performed and redundancy among cameras is exploited to produce a synthetic reconstruction of the head of the person. This information will be used to construct the likelihood function that will weight the particles of this PF based on visual information. The estimation of the head orientation will be computed as the expectation of the pan angle thus producing a real valued output which will increase the precision of our system as compared with classification approaches.

For a given frame in the video sequence, a set of $N$ images are obtained from the $N$ cameras. Each camera is modeled using a pinhole camera model based on perspective projection. Accurate calibration information is available. Bounding boxes describing the head of a person in multiple views are used to segment the interest area where the colour module will be applied. Center and size of the bounding box allow defining an ellipsoid model $\mathcal{H} = \{\mathbf{c}, \mathbf{R}, \mathbf{s}\}$ where $\mathbf{c}$ is the center, $\mathbf{R}$ the rotation along each axis centered on $\mathbf{c}$ and $\mathbf{s}$ the length of each axis. Colour information is processed as described in the following subsection.

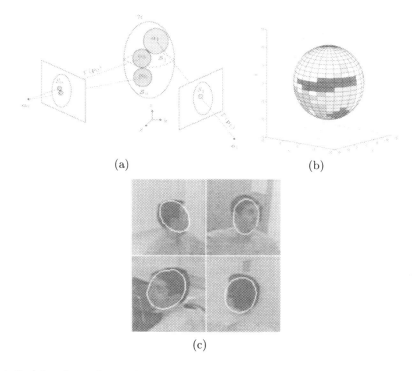

(a)                                                        (b)

(c)

**Fig. 1.** In (a), color and spatial information fusion process scheme. Pixels in the set $\mathcal{S}_n$ are back-projected onto the surface of the ellipsoid defined by $\mathcal{H}$, generating the set $\boldsymbol{\mathcal{S}}_n$ with its weighting term $\alpha_n$. In (b), result of information fusion obtaining a synthetic reconstruction of face appearance from images in (c) where the skin patches are plot in red and the ellipsoid fitting in white.

## 3.1   Color Analysis

Interest regions provided as a bounding box around the head provide 2D masks within the original images where skin color pixels are sought. In order to extract skin color like pixels, a probabilistic classification is computed on the RGB information [16] where the color distribution of skin is estimated from offline hand selected samples of skin pixels.

Let us denote with $\mathcal{S}_n$ all skin pixels in the $n$-th view. It should be recalled that there could be empty sets $\mathcal{S}_n$ due to occlusions or under-performance of the skin detection technique. However, tracking information and redundancy among views would allow to overcome this problem.

## 3.2   3D Head Appearance Generation

Combination of both color and space information is required in order to perform a high semantic level classification and estimation of head orientation. Our information aggregation procedure takes as input the information generated from the low level image analysis for the person under study: an ellipsoid estimation $\mathcal{H}$ of the head and a set of skin patches at each view belonging to this head $\{\mathcal{S}_n\}$, $0 \leq n < N_{\mathrm{CAM}}$. The output of this technique is a fusion of color and space information set denoted as $\Upsilon$.

The procedure of information aggregation we define is based on the assumption that all skin patches $\mathcal{S}_n$ are projections of a region of the surface of the estimated ellipsoid defining the head of a person. Hence, color and space information can be combined to produce a synthetic reconstruction of the head and face appearance in 3D. This fusion process is performed for each head separately starting by back-projecting the skin pixels of $\mathcal{S}_n$ from all $N_{\mathrm{CAM}}$ views onto the 3D ellipsoid model. Formally, for each pixel $\mathrm{p}_n \in \mathcal{S}_n$, we compute

$$\Gamma\left(\mathrm{p}_n\right) \equiv P_n^{-1}\left(\mathrm{p}_n\right) = \mathbf{o}_n + \lambda \mathbf{v}, \qquad \lambda \in \mathbb{R}^+, \tag{9}$$

thus obtaining its back-projected ray in the world coordinate frame passing through $\mathrm{p}_n$ in the image plane with origin in the camera center $\mathbf{o}_n$ and director vector $\mathbf{v}$. In order to obtain the back-projection of $\mathrm{p}_n$ onto the surface of the ellipsoid modelling the head, Eq.9 is substituted into the equation of an ellipsoid defined by the set of parameters $\mathcal{H}$ [13]. It gives a quadratic in $\lambda$,

$$a\lambda^2 + b\lambda + c = 0. \tag{10}$$

The case of interest will be when Eq.10 has two real roots. That means that the ray intersects the ellipsoid twice in which case the solution with the smaller value of $\lambda$ will be chosen for reasons of visibility consistency. See a scheme of this process on Fig.1(a).

This process is applied to all pixels of a given patch $\mathcal{S}_n$ obtaining a set $\boldsymbol{\mathcal{S}}_n$ containing the 3D points being the intersections of the back-projected skin pixels in the view $n$ with the ellipsoid surface. In order to perform a joint analysis of the sets $\{\boldsymbol{\mathcal{S}}_n\}$, each set must have an associated weighting factor that takes into account the real surface of the ellipsoid represented by a single pixel in that view $n$. That is, to quantize the effect of the different distances from the center of the object to each camera. This weighting factor $\alpha_n$ can be estimated by projecting a sphere with radius $r = \max(\mathbf{s})$ on every camera plane, and computing the ratio between the appearance area of the sphere and the number of projected pixels. To be precise, $\alpha_n$ should be estimated for each element in $\boldsymbol{\mathcal{S}}_n$ but, since the *far-field* condition

$$\max(\mathbf{s}) \ll \|\mathbf{c} - \mathbf{o}_n\|_2, \qquad \forall n, \tag{11}$$

is fulfilled, $\alpha_n$ can be considered constant for all intersections in $\boldsymbol{\mathcal{S}}_n$. A schematic representation of the fusion procedure is depicted in Fig.1(a). Finally, after applying this process to all skin patches we obtain a fusion of color and spatial information set $\Upsilon = \{\boldsymbol{\mathcal{S}}_n, \alpha_n, \mathcal{H}\}$, $0 \leq n < N_{\mathrm{CAM}}$, for the head of the person under study. A result of this process is shown in Fig.1(b).

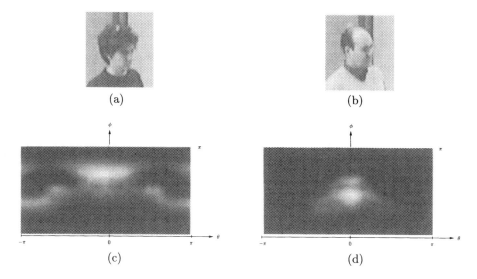

**Fig. 2.** Two examples of the $\Omega_t^V$ sets containing the visual information that will be fed to the video PF. This set may take different configurations depending on the appearance of the head of the person under study. For our experiments a quantization step of $\Delta_\theta \times \Delta_\phi = 0.02 \times 0.02$ rads have been employed.

### 3.3 Head Pose Video Likelihood Evaluation

In order to implement a PF that takes into account visual information solely, the visual likelihood evaluation function must be defined. The observation $\Omega_t^V$ will be constructed upon the information provided by the set $\Upsilon$. The sets $\mathbf{S}_n$ containing the 3D Euclidean coordinates of the ray-ellipsoid intersections are transformed on the plane $\theta\phi$, in elliptical coordinates with origin at $\mathbf{c}$, describing the surface of $\mathcal{H}$. Every intersection has associated its weight factor $\alpha_n$ and the whole set of transformed intersections is quantized with a 2D quantization step of size $\Delta_\theta \times \Delta_\phi$. This process produces the visual observation $\Omega_t^V(n_\theta, n_\phi)$ that might be understood as a *face map* providing a planar representation of the appearance of the head of the person. Some examples of this representation are depicted in Fig.2.

Groundtruth information from a training database is employed to compute an average normalized *template face map* centered at $\theta = 0$, namely $\widetilde{\Omega}^V(n_\theta, n_\phi)$. That is, the appearance that the head of a person would have if there were no distorting factors (bad performance of the skin detector, not enough cameras seeing the face of the person, etc.). This information will be employed to define the likelihood function. The computed template face map is shown in Fig.3.

A cost function is defined as a sum-squared difference function $\Sigma^V$ $\left(\theta, \Omega^V(n_\theta, n_\phi)\right)$ and is computed using

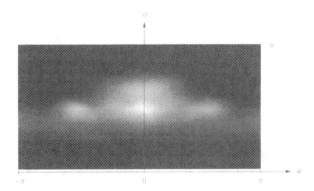

**Fig. 3.** Template face map obtained from an annotated training database for 10 different subjects

$$\Sigma^{V}\left(\theta, \Omega^{V}\left(n_{\theta}, n_{\phi}\right)\right) = \tag{12}$$

$$= \sum_{k_{\theta}=0}^{N_{\theta}} \sum_{k_{\phi}=0}^{N_{\phi}} \left(1 - \left(\Omega^{V}\left(k_{\theta}, k_{\phi}\right) \cdot \tilde{\Omega}^{V}\left(k_{\theta} \ominus \left\lfloor \frac{\theta}{\Delta_{\theta}} \right\rfloor, k_{\phi}\right)\right)^{2}\right),$$

$$N_{\theta} = \left\lfloor \frac{2\pi}{\Delta_{\theta}} \right\rfloor, \qquad N_{\phi} = \left\lfloor \frac{\pi}{\Delta_{\phi}} \right\rfloor, \tag{13}$$

where $\ominus$ is the circular shift operator. This function will produce small values when the value of the pan angle hypothesis $\theta$ matches the angle of the head that produced the visual observation $\Omega^{V}\left(n_{\theta}, n_{\phi}\right)$. Finally, the weights of the particles are defined as

$$w_{t}^{j}\left(\theta_{t}^{j}, \Omega^{V}\left(n_{\theta}, n_{\phi}\right)\right) = \exp\left(-\beta_{V} \Sigma^{V}\left(\theta_{t}^{j}, \Omega^{V}\left(n_{\theta}, n_{\phi}\right)\right)\right). \tag{14}$$

Inverse exponential functions are used in PF applications in order to reflect the assumption that measurement errors are Gaussian [15]. It also has the advantage that even weak hypotheses have finite probability of being preserved, which is desirable in the case of very sparse samples [10]. The value of $\beta_{V}$ is not critical, and it has been empirically fixed at $\beta_{V} = 50$ to allow some useful bias towards lower cost solutions.

## 4   Results and Conclusions

In order to evaluate the performance of the proposed algorithms, we employed the CLEAR 2007 head pose database containing a set of scenes in an indoor scenario were a person is moving his/her head. 10 video segments of approximately 2 minutes each are used for the training phase and 5 segments are used for the testing. The analysis sequences were recorded with 4 fully calibrated and

synchronized cameras with a resolution of 640x480 pixels at 15 fps. Head localization is assumed to be available since the aim of our research is at estimating
its orientation. Groundtruth information of the pan/tilt/roll angles of the head
is available for the evaluation of the algorithm. However, since our algorithm
performs an estimation of the pan angle, only result of this magnitude will be
reported.

For all the experiments conducted in this article, a fixed number of particles
has been set, $N_s = 100$. Experimental results proved that employing more particles does not report in a better performance of the system. Results reported
in Table 1 quantitatively prove the effectiveness of the presented method at
estimating the pan angle orientation of the head of a person.

**Table 1.** Results of the proposed method for the CLEAR Head Pose Testing Database

|  | Pan Mean Error |
| --- | --- |
| person01b | $22.91^o$ |
| person02 | $31.41^o$ |
| person03 | $17.40^o$ |
| person04 | $11.83^o$ |
| person05 | $17.22^o$ |
| **Average** | **$20.48^o$** |

Orientation estimation depends on the detection of skin patches thus being
sensitive to its performance. Typically, skin detection underperforms when the
face is being illuminated by a coloured light, i.e. a beamer. Other effects to be
considered are the hair style, the presence of beard or baldness. Nevertheless,
the proposed particle filter strategy is able to cope with such effects in most of
the cases.

Future work aims at continuing the multimodal head orientation approach already presented by the authors in [5]. Focus of attention in multi-person meetings
based on the information retrieved from head orientation estimation of multiple
people is under study.

# References

1. Arulampalam, M.S., Maskell, S., Gordon, N., Clapp, T.: A tutorial on particle
   filters for online nonlinear/non-Gaussian Bayesian tracking. IEEE Trans. on Signal
   Processing 50(2), 174–188 (2002)
2. Ballard, P., Stockman, G.C.: Controlling a computer via facial aspect. IEEE Trans.
   on Systems, Man and Cybernetics 25(4), 669–677 (1995)

3. Black, M., Brard, F., Jepson, A., Newman, W., Saund, W., Socher, G., Taylor, M.: The Digital Office: Overview. In: Proc. Spring Symposium on Intelligent Environments, vol. 72, pp. 98–102 (1998)

4. Canton-Ferrer, C., Casas, J.R., Pardàs, M.: Fusion of Multiple Viewpoint Information Towards 3D Face Robust Orientation Detection. In: Proc. IEEE Int. Conf. on Image Processing, vol. 2, pp. 366–369 (2005)

5. Canton-Ferrer, C., Segura, C., Casas, J.R., Pardàs, M., Hernando, J.: Audiovisual Head Orientation Estimation with Particle Filters in Multisensor Scenarios. EURASIP Journal on Advances in Signal Processing 1(32) (2008)

6. Chen, M., Hauptmann, A.: Towards Robust Face Recognition from Multiple Views. In: Proc. IEEE Int. Conf. on Multimedia and Expo. (2004)

7. IP CHIL-Computers in the Human Interaction Loop, http://chil.server.de

8. Chiu, P., Kapuskar, A., Reitmeier, S., Wilcox, L.: Room with a rear view: Meeting capture in a multimedia conference room. IEEE Multimedia Magazine 7(4), 48–54 (2000)

9. CLEAR Evaluation Workshop (2006)

10. Deutscher, J., Reid, I.: Articulated Body Motion Capture by Stochastic Search. Int. Journal of Computer Vision, 61(2), 185–205 (2005)

11. Gatica-Perez, D., Lathoud, G., Odobez, J.-M., McCowan, I.: Audiovisual Probabilistic Tracking of Multiple Speakers in Meetings. IEEE Trans. on Audio, Speech and Language Processing 15(2), 601–616 (2007)

12. Gordon, N.J., Salmond, D.J., Smith, A.F.M.: Novel approach to nonlinear/non-Gaussian Bayesian state estimation. IEE Proc. on Radar and Signal Processing 140(2), 107–113 (1993)

13. Hartley, R.I., Zisserman, A.: Multiple View Geometry in Computer Vision, 2nd edn. Cambridge University Press, Cambridge (2004)

14. Horprasert, T., Yacoob, Y., Davis, L.S.: Computing 3-D head orientation from a monocular image sequence. In: Proc. Int. Conf. on Automatic Face and Gesture Recognitio, pp. 242–247 (1996)

15. Isard, M., Blake, A.: CONDENSATION–Conditional Density Propagation for Visual Tracking. Int. Journal of Computer Vision 29(1), 5–28 (1998)

16. Jones, M., Rehg, J.: Statistical Color Models with Application to Skin Detection. Int. Journal of Computer Vision 46(1), 81–96 (2002)

17. Matsumoto, Y., Zelinsky, A.: An algorithm for real-time stereo vision implementation of head pose and gaze direction measurement. In: Proc. IEEE Int. Conf. on Automatic Face and Gesture Recognition, pp. 499–504 (2000)

18. Nickel, K., Gehrig, T., Stiefelhagen, R., McDonough, J.: A joint particle filter for audio-visual speaker tracking. In: Proc. IEEE Int. Conf. on Multimodal Interfaces,, pp. 61–68 (2005)

19. Rae, R., Ritter, H.J.: Recognition of Human Head Orientation Based on Artificial Neural Networks. IEEE Tran. on Neural Networks 9, 257–265 (1998)

20. Voit, M., Nickel, K., Stiefelhagen, R.: Neural Network-based Head Pose Estimation and Multi-view Fusion. In: Stiefelhagen, R., Garofolo, J.S. (eds.) CLEAR 2006. LNCS, vol. 4122, pp. 299–304. Springer, Heidelberg (2007)

21. Wang, C., Brandstein, M.: Robust head pose estimation by machine learning. In: Proc. IEEE Int. Conf. on Image Processing, vol. 3, pp. 210–213 (2000)

22. Wang, C., Griebel, S., Brandstein, M.: Robust automatic video-conferencing with multiple cameras and microphones. In: Proc. IEEE Int. Conf. on Multimedia and Expo., vol. 3, pp. 1585–1588 (2000)
23. West, M., Harrison, J.: Bayesian forecasting and dynamic models, 2nd edn. Springer, New York (1997)
24. Zhang, Z., Hu, Y., Liu, M., Huang, T.: Head Pose Estimation in Seminar Rooms Using Multi View Face Detectors. In: Stiefelhagen, R., Garofolo, J.S. (eds.) CLEAR 2006. LNCS, vol. 4122, pp. 299–304. Springer, Heidelberg (2007)

# The Acoustic Event Detector of AIT

C. Boukis and L.C. Polymenakos

Athens Information Technology, Greece

**Abstract.** In this paper the acoustic event detection and classification system that has been developed at Athens Information Technology is presented. This system relies on the use of several Hidden Markov Models arranged in a hierarchical manner in order to provide more accurate detections. The audio streams are split into overlapping frames from which the necessary for training and testing features are obtained. A post processing scheme has also been developed in order to smooth the raw detections. The results that were obtained from the application of this system on the testing data of the CLEAR evaluation, obtained from five different sites are presented and the performance of this system is discussed.

## 1 Introduction

Acoustic event detection (AED) is a tedious task whose objective is the detection of specific acoustic events within one or more synchronised audio streams. These audio streams can be processed either in an online fashion (while they are captured from the microphones) or offline (after being captured and stored). The list of events that we look for is pre-defined and *a-priori* data for every event are required.

The detection of acoustic events within audio streams and their subsequent classification is a relatively new research area. Existing systems rely on the use of classification techniques. Typical examples is the use of Hidden Markov Models (HMM) [1] or Support Vector Machines (SVM) [2]. These approaches require training data for the optimisation of the parameters of their classification system. These training data are collected from the same environment in which the AED system will be performing, in order to be as coherent as possible with the testing data, covering several noise conditions. Many approaches use a silence detector that prevents the classification of silence intervals as events and thus increases the overall performance of the system [3].

AED can be considered as a generalisation of voice activity detection (VAD) [5, 6], where the objective is the detection of speech intervals within audio signals. VAD can be performed either with unsupervised methods that employ statistical criteria like the Likelihood Ratio Test (LRT) [7], or with supervised methods like Hidden Markov Models (HMM) and Linear Discriminant Analysis (LDA) [4]. Since AED attempts to identify several acoustic events, only supervised methods are used since only these can distinguish adequately various acoustic events. Similarities can be found between AED and face or object recognition within

R. Stiefelhagen et al. (Eds.): CLEAR 2007 and RT 2007, LNCS 4625, pp. 328–337, 2008.

images. In both cases the detection of a specific pattern within a data vector is desired. In object (or face) recognition though, it is assumed that the entire object (or face) is contained entirely in an image; this is not the case in AED where an acoustic event might last from one to several frames.

In this paper the primary and the contrast AED systems that have been developed by Athens Information Technology are presented. These two systems rely on the use of HMMs for the identification of acoustic events. Their difference is that the primary system employs a different set of HMM parameters for every site, which is derived by using only the data derived from this site, while the contrast system uses the same set of HMM parameters for every site, derived by applying a global training scheme using all the available data. The use of hierarchical structures for the improvement of the performance of the system is also proposed and post processing methods that aim at the smoothing of raw decisions are discussed.

This paper is organised as follows: In section 2 the pre-processing of the audio signals for both the development and the testing data is discussed. In section 3 the HMM-based decision-making process is presented. Post-processing of the results is shown in section 4, while the results are presented in section 5. Finally, section 6 concludes the paper.

## 2   Pre-processing

The AED system uses audio signals obtained from one (or more) microphone, which are used either as development data for training, or as hypothesis data for decision making. These audio signals are initially down-sampled (or interpolated) in order for all of them to have the same sampling rate, and subsequently they are split into frames from which the desired features are extracted. More analytically:

Down-sampling: Since the number of samples that are included within a frame has been chosen to be fixed, all the audio signals should have the same sampling rate, so as frames to have the same duration. Therefore, development and hypothesis data should have the same sampling rate. To this cause the hypothesis data are down-sampled by a factor of two, since their sampling rate (44100 Hz) is twice that of the development data.

Framing: Detection using supervised methods, like HMMs or SVMs, requires the processing of data in frames. Every time a frame of available data is passed into the system and either the estimates of the model parameters are improved (training mode), or a decision is made (decision-making mode). in our approach we have chosen the frame length to be 2048 samples and the overlapping between neighbouring frames was 75%, that is 1536 samples. These values correspond to 93 *msecs* duration and 70 *msecs* overlapping and they were chosen so as many short-time acoustics events like door knock, door slam, clapping etc to be included within a single frame.

Feature extraction: In classification applications with unsupervised techniques it is usually more convenient, robust and effective to extract some features from the data frames and process them instead of the raw data (time-domain audio samples in our case). For the sake of acoustic event detection the features that have been chosen to operate with are the first 12 mel frequency cepstral coefficients along with the energy and their $1^{st}$ and $2^{nd}$ order derivatives. These together with the zero-crossing rate consist the 40-elements long feature vectors that have been used in the present AED implementation.

Notice that the down-sampling and the framing process might affect significantly the performance of the AED system.

**Table 1.** Notation of acoustic events

| event | notation |
|---|---|
| door slam | ds |
| steps | st |
| chair moving | cm |
| spoon(cup jingle) | cj |
| applause | ap |
| laugh | la |
| key jingle | kj |
| cough | co |
| keyboard typing | kt |
| phone ringing/music | pr |
| knock (door, table) | kn |
| paper wrapping | pw |
| speech | sp |
| unknown | un |

## 2.1   Development Data

The development data consist of the audio part of five seminars each one recorded at a different site (AIT, IBM, ITC, UKA, UPC) and two isolated events data bases provided by ITC-irst and UPC respectively. The seminar recordings were monophonic, their sampling rate was 22050 Hz and they were captured using the markIII microphone array, while the isolated events databases contained recordings from several microphones (hamerfall and markIII microphone array) at 44100 Hz [Ref]. Accompanying csv files were provided for each recording including time-stamps about the begin and the end of every event.

Using the time-stamps provided in the csv files the occurrences of every event in the seminar files were obtained. These occurrences were subsequently split into frames according to the procedure described earlier. For every frame a set of features was extracted, which were subsequently used for the training of the parameters of the HMMs. Notice that the provided csv files contain information concerning the 12 acoustic events that we are looking for, along with information

concerning speech occurrences and unknown sounds (Table 1). The seminar segments that are not annotated at all were treated as silence and were used for the
training of the HMM that were developed for the modelling and the detection
of silence intervals.

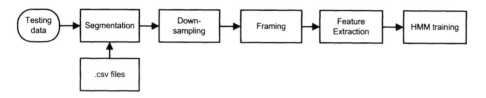

**Fig. 1.** Training of the HMMs for the task of AED

In order for the development and the testing data to be coherent only data
obtained from the markIII microphone array were used. Hence, only the acoustic
events of the UPC database were employed. The procedure that was followed
for the extraction of feature vectors from the isolated events data bases was the
following: the recordings from five different microphones of the array were averaged in order to enhance the waveforms of the acoustic events and to suppress
the ambient noises. The microphones that were used were the $13^{th}$, the $23^{rd}$, the
$33^{rd}$, the $43^{rd}$ and the $53^{rd}$ microphones. The obtained signal was subsequently
down-sampled in order to reduce its sampling rate from 44100 Hz to 22050 Hz.
Using the provided csv files the occurrences of every event were extracted and
they were subsequently split into overlapping frames. Finally, for every frame a
corresponding feature vector was computed. The training process is presented
graphically in the block diagram of Fig. 1. Notice that the silence intervals of
the isolated seminars were not used as training data, since they are not coherent
with the silence intervals of the seminars which would be used for the evaluation
of the system.

### 2.2   Hypothesis Data

The hypothesis data that were used for the evaluation of the developed system
are 20 segments of seminars recorded in 4 different sites: AIT, ITC, UKA and
UPC. The duration of each segment is approximately 5 *mins* (300 *secs*) and the
sampling rate is 44100 Hz. For each seminar segment recordings captured from
the 64 microphones of the markIII array and the hammerfall microphones were
provided.

In order to produce decisions, the signals of the microphones 13, 23, 33, 43 and
53 were averaged. This form of spatial averaging was applied in order to suppress
the ambient noises and enhance the occurrences of the acoustic events. Every
seminar segment was initially down-sampled to 22050 Hz. The down-sampled
signal was subsequently split into frames of length 2048 samples. Neighbouring frames were overlapping by 75% (1536 samples). For every frame a feature

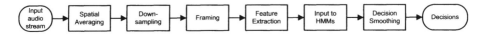

**Fig. 2.** Decision making process

vector was derived that was fed to the acoustic event detector. This process is graphically illustrated in Fig. 2

## 3   Decision Making

The developed AED system relies on the use of HMMs. More specifically left-right (or Bakis) models were employed with continuous observation densities. Each model was characterised by its number of states $N$ and the transition matrix $A$, which is has the form

$$
A = \begin{bmatrix}
a_{11} & a_{12} & 0 & \cdots & 0 \\
0 & a_{22} & a_{23} & \cdots & 0 \\
0 & 0 & a_{33} & \cdots & 0 \\
\vdots & \vdots & \vdots & \ddots & \vdots \\
0 & 0 & 0 & \cdots & a_{N-1N} \\
0 & 0 & 0 & \cdots & 1
\end{bmatrix}
\tag{1}
$$

for left-right model model of order $N$. The initial state probability of the first state is 1, while that of all the other states is zero, that is

$$
\pi_i = \begin{cases}
0 & , \text{ when } i \neq j \\
1 & , \text{ when } i = j
\end{cases}
\tag{2}
$$

The continuous observation density of every state $i$ is modelled with a single Gaussian with mean vector $\mu_i$ and covariance matrix $\Sigma_i$. For the training of the parameters of every HMM the Baum-Welch method was employed. The number of states of every model was deduced heuristically and these are presented in Table 2.

### 3.1   Initial System

Initially an HMM model for every event was developed. Two training policies were applied aiming at the maximisation of the discrimination power of these models

-   Partial training: For every site derive a separate set of HMMs by performing training only with the corresponding development data and the isolated events databases (Primary system). In this case the HMMs that are used for the detection of acoustic events within AIT's seminars were trained using the development data of AIT and the isolated events databases of UPC.

**Table 2.** Number of states of employed HMMs

| Event | Number of states |
|-------|------------------|
| ap    | 3                |
| cl    | 3                |
| cm    | 3                |
| co    | 3                |
| ds    | 3                |
| kj    | 3                |
| kn    | 3                |
| kt    | 3                |
| la    | 4                |
| pr    | 4                |
| pw    | 3                |
| sl    | 3                |
| sp    | 8                |
| st    | 3                |
| un    | 3                |

Similarly the HMM models used for detection of events in the IBM seminars were trained using the IBM development data together with the UPC isolated events databases and so on.

- Global training: In this scenario a unique set of HMMs was used for the detection of events in every site (Contrast system). Their parameters were obtained by performing training using all the available seminar development data along with the isolated events database of UPC.

## 3.2   Hierarchical Detection

The initially developed AED system was under-performing since it was continuously misclassifying silence intervals as event occurrences. To improve its performance the detection process was split into two stages, and thus became a two-step process. In the first step two left-right HMMs were used to detect the presence of an event or silence. The silence model was of order 3 and it was trained using the silence intervals that are inherent in the seminar development data, while for the training of the event HMM, whose order was 8, all the event data were used. In this AED implementation the type of the event is detected in the second stage by using 14 HMM models, provided that the presence of an event has been deduced in the first layer of this structure. The orders of the employed HMMs are presented in Table 2. Partial and global training was applied in this case too and it was found out that performing detection in stages results in improved performance. The system that was derived with partial training is the primary system that was used in the CLEAR evaluation, while the system

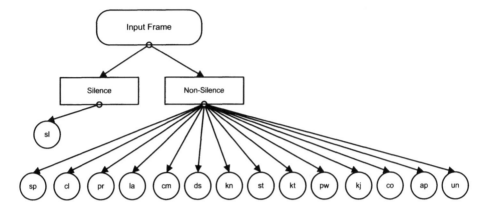

**Fig. 3.** A two-layer hierarchical structure for AED using HMMs

that was derived with global training is the contrast system. This hierarchical structure is depicted in Fig. 3.

Grouping acoustic events together, based on their characteristics can lead to multilayered hierarchical detection approaches that are expected to have improved performance compared to conventional methods. In this approach the existence of an event is examined in the first layer of the hierarchy. If the content of this frame is not silence it is examined whether this is speech or not. The HMM model that is used for the detection of speech is trained using all speech data, while all the other data are used for the training of the coefficients of the non-speech HMM. If the decision is non speech, it is examined whether the frame contains a periodic or a non-periodic event and so on. Every internal layer of decision has two HMMs while the lower layer of the hierarchy (the leafs of the tree) can have several HMMs. An example of a multilayer approach is shown in Fig. 4. This model is still under development and actual results are not available.

## 4    Post-processing

The raw decisions that are produced from the AED system might contain isolated detections of events of very small duration or gaps of small duration between detection of events of the same type, which are usually erroneous. For instance, detection of a speech segment of duration less than 100 *msecs* is probably erroneous since there isn't a word, or even a phoneme with so sort duration. Moreover, several detections of an event that lie in the same neighbourhood, located very close to each other, should be grouped together to form a global event detection.

For the smoothing of the raw detections a finite state model was employed, that was inspired from the hang-over schemes that are used for the smoothing of the detections of VAD systems. The basic idea of this post-processing system is to

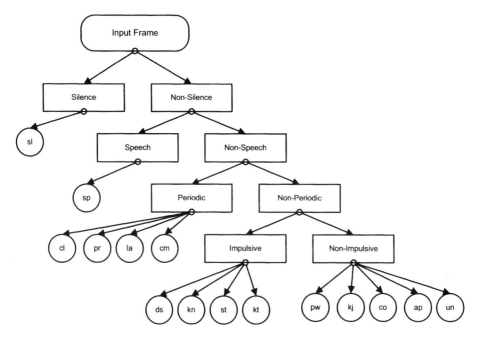

**Fig. 4.** A multiple-layer hierarchical structure for AED using HMMs

- group together detections of the same event that are less than 3 frames far away from each other and
- to remove detections that after the grouping have length less than 5 frames.

It was found out that this smoothing procedure improves significantly the performance of the detector at since many erroneous mis-detections are removed, at the cost of dropping some accurate decisions though.

## 5   Results and Discussion

The performance of the system was evaluated by applying it to the testing data. These were spatially averaged, down-sampled, and separated into frames as described in section 2. From these frames feature vectors were extracted that were fed to the AED system. Finally the decisions were smoothed with the use of a finite state model that imposed time duration constraints, as explained in section 4 and the smoothed decisions were converted into time-stamps. The results that were obtained are presented in Table 3. The metrics that were used for the evaluation of the performance of the system are the AED-ACC and the AED-ER that measure the detection accuracy and the accuracy of the endpoints of the detected acoustic events [8].

The performance of this system is poor, contrary to what has been observed from the developmment data, where for instance the recall metric was lying

**Table 3.** Evaluation results for AIT's AED system

```
AIT_primary

Accuracy=0.044
Precision=0.034 (correct system AEs = 102; number system AEs = 2988)
Recall=0.060    (correct reference AEs = 86; number reference AEs = 1434)
------------------------------------------------------------------------
SCORED ACOUSTIC EVENT TIME = 2167.75 secs ( 36.3 % of scored time)
MISSED ACOUSTIC EVENT TIME = 743.31 secs ( 34.3 % of scored acoustic event time)
FALARM ACOUSTIC EVENT TIME = 2300.64 secs (106.1 % of scored acoustic event time)
EVENT SUBSTITUTION TIME = 1358.96 secs ( 62.7 % of scored acoustic event time)
------------------------------------------------------------------------
OVERALL ACOUSTIC EVENT DETECTION ERROR = 203.11 % of scored time   (ALL)


AIT_contrast

Accuracy=0.055
Precision=0.044 (correct system AEs = 111; number system AEs = 2545)
Recall=0.075    (correct reference AEs = 107; number reference AEs = 1434)
------------------------------------------------------------------------
SCORED ACOUSTIC EVENT TIME =2167.75 secs ( 36.1 % of scored time)
MISSED ACOUSTIC EVENT TIME =921.59 secs ( 42.5 % of scored acoustic event time)
FALARM ACOUSTIC EVENT TIME =1795.63 secs ( 82.8 % of scored acoustic event time)
EVENT SUBSTITUTION TIME =1130.66 secs ( 52.2 % of scored acoustic event time)
------------------------------------------------------------------------
OVERALL ACOUSTIC EVENT DETECTION ERROR = 177.51 % of scored time   (ALL)
```

between 60% and 70%. Moreover, the performance of the constrast system is better than that of the primary, which was not the case when evaluating the performance of the system with the development data. The reasons for this are probably

- The fact that fusion of the data was performed through spatial averaging. Maybe it would have been more appropriate to derive a decision from each employed microphone and then fuse the decisions.
- The use of a small part of the isolated events databases data for training and from the testing data for the extraction of decisions (only the data obtained from microphones 13, 23, 33, 43, 53 of the mark III microphone array were used). This approach was applied in order to increase the coherence between testing and training data, but obviously it did not work.
- The use of a single Gaussian instead of Gaussian mixtures for the modelling of the continuous observation distribution of the states.
- The down-sampling which resulted in dropping information that could have been valuable for more accurate detections
- The choice of the feature vectors.

# 6   Conclusions

In this paper the Acoustic Event Detection (AED) system that was developed in Athens Information Technology (AIT) is presented. The components of this system, which are the pre-processing system, the detection system and the post-processing scheme are discussed into detail. The use of Hidden Markov Models arranged into a hierarchical structure is also presented in order to perform more robust detections. Finally the performance of the system is presented and various aspects that might possibly improve its accuracy are discussed.

## Acknowledgements

This work is sponsored by the European Union under the integrated project CHIL, contract number 506909.

## References

[1]  Rabiner, L.R.: A Tutorial on Hidden Markov Models and Selected Applications in Speech Recognition. Proceedings of the IEEE 77(2), 257–286 (1989)

[2]  Burges, C.J.C.: A Tutorial on Support Vector Machines for Pattern Recognition. Data Mining and Knowledge Discovery 2, 121–167 (1998)

[3]  Temko, A., Malkin, R., Zieger, C., Macho, D., Nadeu, C., Omologo, M.: CLEAR Evaluation of Acoustic Event Detection and Classification Systems. In: Stiefelhagen, R., Garofolo, J.S. (eds.) CLEAR 2006. LNCS, vol. 4122, Springer, Heidelberg (2007)

[4]  Duda, R.O., Hart, P.E., Stork, D.G.: Pattern Classification. John Willey & Sons (2001)

[5]  Mauuary, L., Monné, J.: Speech/non-speech Detection for Voice Response Systems. In: Eurospeech 1993, Berlin, Germany, pp. 1097–1100 (1993)

[6]  Martin, A., Charlet, D., Mauuary, L.: Robust Speech/Non-Speech Detection Using LDA Applied to MFCC. In: ICASSP (2001)

[7]  Ramirez, J., Segura, J.C., Benitez, C., Garcia, L., Rubio, A.: Statistical Voice Activity Detection Using a Multiple Observation Likelihood ratio Test. IEEE Signal Processing Letters 12(10), 689–692 (2005)

[8]  Temko, A.: AED evaluation plan. In: CLEAR (2007), www.clear-evaluation.org

# An HMM Based System for Acoustic Event Detection

Christian Zieger*

FBK-irst,
Via Sommarive 18,
38050 Povo, Trento,
Italy
zieger@itc.it

**Abstract.** This paper deals with the CLEAR 2007 evaluation on the detection of acoustic events which happen during seminars. The proposed system first converts an audio sequence in a stream of MFCC features, then a detecting/classifying block identifies an acoustic event with time stamps and assign to it a label among all possible event labels. Identification and classification are based on Hidden Markov Models (HMM). The results, measured in terms of two metrics (accuracy and error rate) are obtained applying the implemented system on the interactive seminars collected under the CHIL project. Final not very good results highlight the task complexity.

## 1 Introduction

Acoustic scene analysis consists in describing all possible acoustic events in terms of space, time or type by means of a single microphone or a distributed microphone network that constantly monitors the environment [1]. In the CHIL project acoustic scene analysis has been adopted to describe automatically human interactions and interactions between humans and environment. This work focuses on the problem of detecting acoustic events, that is identifying an acoustic event with its timestamps and classifying it selecting among a list of predefined possible events.

In literature acoustic event detection has been studied in different fields: in [2] the authors focus on detecting a single event, in [3,4] speech and music classification is explored, in [5] acoustic events for medical telesurvey are considered, in [6] audio events are detected to automatically extract highlights from baseball, golf and soccer matches and [7] detection of animal sounds is investigated.

This paper addresses the CLEAR 2007 evaluation on acoustic event detection for seminars. In particular, the evaluation considers a list of 12 events (named CHIL events): door or table knock (kn); door slam (ds), steps (st), chair moving (cm), spoon clings or cup jingle (cl), paper wrapping (pw), key jingle (kj),

---

* This work was partially funded by the European Community under the CHIL and DICIT projects.

R. Stiefelhagen et al. (Eds.): CLEAR 2007 and RT 2007, LNCS 4625, pp. 338–344, 2008.

keyboard typing (kt), phone ring/music (pr), applause (ap), cough (co), laugh (la). All recorded interactive seminars are acquired through a distributed microphone network composed by T-shaped arrays, the linear NIST markIII array and tabletop microphones. The proposed acoustic event detector (AED) considers the audio stream of a fixed single microphone, converts it in a feature vector sequence, on which an Hidden Markov Model (HMM) based detection stage is applied. The paper is organized as follows: section 2 will describe the inplemented AED system, section 3 reports on the evaluation results specifying the metrics used to evaluate system performance and finally the last section outlines some conclusions.

## 2    AED Based on HMM

The block diagram of the implemented AED consists in two blocks. The first one, the front-end, converts an audio stream into a sequence of acoustic parameter vectors. The second one, the event detector/classifier, identifies the acoustic events exploiting previously trained acoustic models.

### 2.1    Front-End

The audio signal sampled at 44.1 kHz coming from a fixed microphone is converted by the front-end in a feature vector stream of Mel Frequency Cepstral Coefficients (MFCC), which are widely used in the speech recognition field [8,9]. The Mel frequency equispaced triangular filter used are 24, while the cepstral coefficients extracted after the DCT operation are 12. The analysis window is 20 ms and the step of the sliding window is 10 ms. The hamming window is used. The first and second derivatives of the MFCCs are also computed and appended to the feature vector. The signal energy is not considered since the seminars are characterized by energy conditions that can change considerably from seminar to seminar and even during the seminar. Its first and second derivatives are appended to the acoustic feature vector instead. In conclusion, the acoustic feature vector is composed by 38 elements:

 - 12 MFCCs + first and second derivatives
 - first and second derivatives of the signal energy

In table 1 the system front-end parameters are summarized and in figure 1 the block diagram of the front-end is reported.

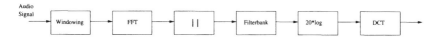

**Fig. 1.** Block diagram of the AED front-end

**Table 1.** Front-end parameters

| front-end parameters | |
|---|---|
| sampling frequency | 44.1 kHz |
| analysis window | 20 ms |
| analysis step | 10 ms |
| window type | Hamming |
| number of MEL filter bank channels | 24 |
| number of cepstral coefficients | 12 |

## 2.2  Acoustic Event Detector

The acoustic event detector implemented is based on HMMs [8,9]. For every event in the list of all possible CHIL events an HMM is trained using the databases available in the development set, which is composed by the isolated acoustic event databases, collected by ITC and UPC (see [10] for a description), and by 4 interactive seminars whose characteristics in terms of length and number of events are reported in tables 2 and 3. The same event type can differ from the acoustic point of view from site to site according to the construction material of the object that produces the acoustic event (steps, chair moving, door slam). For this reason the not uniform distribution of the events among all seminars can give rise to a possible mismatch between acoustic models and test set. Further models for speech and silence are added to the list of all possible events in order to identify and consequently reject speech and silence sequences. The speech model is trained selecting from the interactive seminars those speech sequences that do not temporally overlap with other events.

The HMM topology adopted is left-right, with 3 states. The number of the Gaussian mixtures for each state is 128. Diagonal covariance matrix is adopted. The optimum events sequence is obtained applying the viterbi algorithm to the whole converted audio segment using the models previously trained. Site dependent ($SD$) and site independent ($SI$) systems are implemented. In the former a set of acoustic models is trained for each site using the corresponding training data. Then, in the detection step, the system selects acoustic models according to the prior information about the room type (UPC, ITC, UKA, AIT). Figure 2 reports on the block diagram of the $SD$ AED. In the latter the same acoustic models, trained with all available databases, are used for each room (see figure 3) instead.

## 3  Evaluation Results

In this section the results of the evaluation for the $SD$ and $SI$ systems are reported. Let us notice that $SI$ system results have been submitted after the official evaluation dead line, that is after having the ground truth. According to the evaluation plan, system performance is measured by means of two metrics, called AED-ACC and AED-ER.

**Table 2.** Number of occurrences of each event in single seminar

| event type | ITC | UKA | AIT | UPC |
|:---:|:---:|:---:|:---:|:---:|
| kj | 4 | 4 | 8 | 5 |
| sp | 304 | 435 | 195 | 190 |
| pw | 13 | 61 | 27 | 20 |
| cl | 7 | 0 | 0 | 22 |
| kn | 9 | 18 | 15 | 29 |
| st | 5 | 24 | 16 | 38 |
| cm | 48 | 123 | 16 | 43 |
| kt | 6 | 6 | 15 | 14 |
| la | 4 | 20 | 6 | 12 |
| un | 59 | 154 | 47 | 36 |
| pr | 6 | 0 | 8 | 4 |
| co | 11 | 20 | 4 | 16 |
| ap | 2 | 2 | 0 | 3 |
| ds | 23 | 4 | 18 | 11 |

**Table 3.** Seminar lengths in minutes

| Seminar type | length in minutes |
|:---:|:---:|
| ITC | 30 |
| UKA | 44 |
| AIT | 32 |
| UPC | 23 |

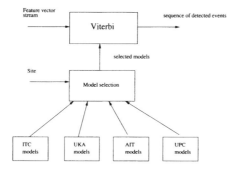

**Fig. 2.** Block diagram of the *SD* AED

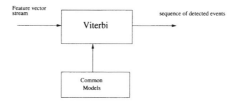

**Fig. 3.** Block diagram of the *SI* AED

## 3.1  Metrics

AED-ACC is defined as

$$AED - ACC = \frac{(1 + \beta^2) \text{ * Precision * Recall}}{\beta^2 \text{ * Precision + Recall}} \tag{1}$$

$$Precision = \frac{\text{number of correct system output AEs}}{\text{number of all system output AEs}} \tag{2}$$

$$Recall = \frac{\text{number of correctly detected reference AEs}}{\text{number of all reference AEs}} \tag{3}$$

A system output acoustic event (AE) is considered correct if there exist at least one reference AE whose temporal center is situated between the timestamps of the system output AE and the label of the system output and the reference AE is the same, or if the temporal center of the system output AE lies between the timestamps of at least one reference AE and the label of the system output AE and the reference AE is the same. A reference is considered correctly detected if there exist at least one system output AE whose temporal center is situated between the timestamps of the reference AE and the label of the system output AE and the reference AE is the same, or if the temporal center of the reference AE lies between the timestamps of at least one system output AE and the label of the system output AE and the reference AE is the same. In this evaluation $\beta$ is set to one.

AED-ER is a metric for measuring the temporal resolution of the detected event and is defined as follows:

$$AED-ER = \frac{\sum\limits_{\text{all seg}} \{dur(seg) * (\max(N_{REF}(seg), N_{SYS}(seg)) - N_{correct}(seg))\}}{\sum\limits_{\text{all seg}} \{dur(seg) * N_{REF}(seg)\}} \tag{4}$$

where $dur(seg)$ is the duration of the segment $seg$, $N_{REF}(seg)$ is the number of reference events in $seg$, $N_{SYS}(seg)$ is the number of system output events in $seg$, $N_{correct}(seg)$ is the number of reference events in $seg$ which have a corresponding mapped system output AEs in $seg$.

## 3.2  Results

The evaluation test set is composed by 20 audio segments of 5 minute length. In table 4 the number of occurences, the total duration in seconds and the percentage of event shorter then 1 second are reported for each transcribed event in order to give an idea about the task complexity. First let us notice that the database is not balanced, in fact there are more frequent events like steps, chair moving, laugh, knock and events that happen rather seldom like applause, phone ring, cup jingle. This unbalancing is not considered in the metric for the system performance. Morover events not to be detected, like speech and unknown, are the most frequent events during the seminar, in fact they doubled the number

**Table 4.** Statistics in terms of number, duration, percentage of short events for each event in the evaluation test set

| event | event number | total duration in s. | % of events shorter than 1 s. |
|---|---|---|---|
| kj | 32 | 32.40 | 46.875 % |
| sp | 1239 | 1241.60 | 19.53 % |
| pw | 88 | 88.71 | 31.81 % |
| cl | 28 | 29.35 | 39.28 % |
| kn | 153 | 153.55 | 88.88 % |
| st | 498 | 503.95 | 53.21 % |
| cm | 226 | 232.64 | 57.07 % |
| kt | 105 | 107.91 | 52.38 % |
| la | 154 | 154.3 | 36.36 % |
| un | 559 | 559.27 | 75.49 % |
| pr | 25 | 26.08 | 40 % |
| co | 36 | 36.77 | 75 % |
| ap | 13 | 17.45 | 23.07 % |
| ds | 76 | 76.51 | 46.05 % |
| total chil events | 1434 | 1459.6 | 53.69 % |
| total non chil events | 3232 | 1798.3 | 36.92 % |

**Table 5.** Evaluation results in terms of AED-ACC, Precision, Recall and AED-ER for the site dependent system (results submitted before the evaluation dead line)

| System type | AED-ACC | Precision | Recall | AED-ER |
|---|---|---|---|---|
| SD | 23.4 % | 35.4 % | 17.5 % | 109.07 % |

of CHIL events and they temporally overlap with CHIL events. Observing the total duration of each event it can be noted that the average duration of every single event is about 1 second. Short events which are the most difficult to detect, represent about the 53 % of the total number of CHIL events. Short events that happen very often are knock, cough, chair moving, keyboard typing.

In tables 5 and 6 the results in terms of AED-ACC, Precision, Recall and AED-ER for both *SD* and *SI* systems are shown. The results confirm the difficulty of the task as previously mentioned. *SD* system guarantees better results in terms of AED-ACC, but the worst ones in terms of AED-ER. It can be useful to compare the results for each single site as reported in table 7. *SD* system reduces the mismatch between training and test data yielding in general better results for UKA and AIT, but worst results for UPC and ITC.

**Table 6.** Evaluation results in terms of AED-ACC, Precision, Recall and AED-ER for the site independent system (results submitted after the evaluation dead line)

| System type | AED-ACC | Precision | Recall | AED-ER |
|---|---|---|---|---|
| SI | 26.3 % | 39.1 % | 19.9 % | 111.33 % |

**Table 7.** Results for diffrent rooms and systems

| Site | AED-ACC (SD) | AED-ACC (SI) | AED-ER (SD) | AED-ER (SI) |
|------|--------------|--------------|-------------|-------------|
| AIT  | 16.8 %       | 9.2 %        | 103.44 %    | 98.80 %     |
| UKA  | 11.8 %       | 6.6 %        | 157.07 %    | 141.32 %    |
| UPC  | 29.0 %       | 39.4 %       | 103.33%     | 116.25 %    |
| ITC  | 30.0 %       | 32.0 %       | 86.93 %     | 93.97 %     |

# 4   Conclusions

In this paper an HMM based acoustic event detector with site dependent and site independent models has been introduced for the CLEAR 2007 evaluation on the acoustic event detection task. System performance have been measured in terms of two metrics using as test set 20 seminars, each 5 minutes long, collected in four rooms under the CHIL project. A description of the test database, characterized by very short events temporally overlapping with other disturbing events, like speech and unknown, let suppose the high difficulty of the considered task. The evaluation results have confirmed this hypothesis. Moreover the low results do not allow to make a good comparison between the *SD* and *SI*.

# References

1. Wang, D., Brown, G.: Computational Auditory Scene Analysis: Principles, Algorithms and Applications. Wiley-IEEE Press (2006)
2. Kennedy, L., Ellis, D.: Laughter detection in meetings. In: NIST ICASSP Meeting Recognition Workshop, Montreal, Canada, pp. 118–121 (2004)
3. Lu, L., Hong-Jiang, Z.J.H.: Content analysis for audio classification and segmentation. IEEE Transaction on Speech and Audio processing 10(7), 504–516 (2002)
4. Pinquier, J., Rouas, J.L., Andrè-Obrecht, R.: Robust speech / music classification in audio documents. In: Proc. ICSLP, Denver, USA, vol. 3 (2002) 2005–2008
5. Vacher, M., Istrate, D., Serigna, J.F.: Sound detection and classification trough transient models using wavelet coefficient trees. In: EUSIPCO, Vienna, Austria, pp. 1171–1174 (2004)
6. Xiong, Z., Radhakrishnan, R., Divakaran, A., Huang, T.: Audio events detection based highlights extraction from baseball, golf and soccer games in a unified framework. In: ICME 2003, Baltimora, USA, vol. 3, pp. 401–404 (2003)
7. Slaney, M.: Mixtures of probability experts for audio retrieval and indexing. In: ICME 2002, Ischia, Italy, vol. 1, pp. 345–348 (2002)
8. Rabiner, L.R., Juang, B.H.: Fundamentals of Speech Recognition. Prentice Hall, Englewood Cliffs (1993)
9. Rabiner, R.L.: A tutorial on hidden markov models and selected applications in speech recognition. Proceedings of the IEEE 77(2), 257–286 (1989)
10. Temko, A., Malkin, R., Zieger, C., Macho, D., Nadeu, C., Omologo, M.: Clear evaluation of acoustic event detection and classification systems. In: Stiefelhagen, R., Garofolo, J.S. (eds.) CLEAR 2006. LNCS, vol. 4122, Springer, Heidelberg (2007)

# HMM-Based Acoustic Event Detection with AdaBoost Feature Selection

Xi Zhou, Xiaodan Zhuang, Ming Liu, Hao Tang,
Mark Hasegawa-Johnson, and Thomas Huang

Beckman Institute
Department of Electrical & Computer Engineering
University of Illinois at Urbana-Champaign (UIUC), Urbana, IL 61801, USA

**Abstract.** Because of the spectral difference between speech and acoustic events, we propose using Kullback-Leibler distance to quantify the discriminant capability of all speech feature components in acoustic event detection. Based on these distances, we use AdaBoost to select a discriminant feature set and demonstrate that this feature set outperforms classical speech feature set such as MFCC in one-pass HMM-based acoustic event detection. We implement an HMM-based acoustic events detection system with lattice rescoring using a feature set selected by the above AdaBoost based approach.

## 1 Introduction

There is a growing research interest in Acoustic Events Detection (AED). Although speech is the most informative auditory information source, other kinds of sounds may also carry useful information, such as in surveillance systems [3]. In a meeting room environment, a rich variety of acoustic events, either produced by the human body or by objects handled by humans, reflect various human activities. Detection or classification of acoustic events may help to detect and describe the human and social activity in the meeting room. Examples include clapping or laughter inside a speech discourse, a strong yawn in the middle of a lecture, a chair moving or door noise when the meeting has just started [12]. Detection of the nonspeech sounds also help improve speech recognition performance [8,1].

Several papers have reported work on acoustic events detection for different environments and databases [13,4]. AED as a task of CLEAR Evaluation 2006 [12] was carried out by the three participant partners from the CHIL project [2]: The UPC system is based on the Support Vector Machine (SVM) [10] discriminative approach and uses log Frequency Filter bank parameters and four kinds of perceptual features. Both the CMU and ITC systems are based on the Hidden Markov Model (HMM) generative approach using Mel-Frequency Cepstral Coefficients (MFCC) features [6]. In these works, we can see that Hidden Marcov Model (HMM) based Automatic Speech Recognition (ASR) framework worked better for detection task while the discriminative SVM approach was more successful for classification task. The main features for acoustic event detection are

R. Stiefelhagen et al. (Eds.): CLEAR 2007 and RT 2007, LNCS 4625, pp. 345–353, 2008.

still complete sets of speech perception features (critical band integration simulated by Mel/Bark filter bank or simple log frequency filter bank parameters) which have been proven to represent the speech spectral structure well. However, these features are not necessarily suitable for AED for the following reasons: 1) Limited work has been done in studying the spectral structure of acoustic events which is obviously different from that of speech. The speech features (such as filter bank parameters and MFCC) are designed according to the spectral structure of speech. Those features neglect the frequency parts that contain less speech discriminant information which may contain much discriminant information for acoustic events. 2) The Signal Noise Ratio (SNR) is low for AED. In the meeting room environment, the speech that co-occurs with the acoustic events most of the time should be seen as noise. Therefore, analysis of the spectral structure of acoustic events and design of suitable features are very important for AED task.

In this study we proposed a new front-end feature analysis and selection framework for AED. We characterize the features by quantifying their relative discriminant capabilities using Kullback-Leibler Distance (KLD) [7]. Adaboost [9,5] based algorithm is used to select the most discriminant feature set from a large feature pool. The acoustic event detection experiments show that the discriminant feature set extracted by the data-driven methods significantly outperform the MFCC features without increasing the parameter number.

This paper is organized as follows: Section 2 analyzes the spectral correlates of acoustic events, and particularly quantifies the discriminant capabilities of all speech feature components in AED task by a KLD based criterion. In Section 3, the new AdaBoost based feature selection algorithm is proposed. Section 4 introduces the HMM-based system architecture for AED task. The experiment results are shown in Section 5, followed by the conclusion and the discussion of future work.

## 2   Spectral Correlates of Acoustic Events

Currently, the speech features are designed mainly based on the properties of speech production and perception. The envelope of spectrogram (formant structure) instead of the fine structure of spectrogram (harmonic structure) is believed to hold most information for speech. Both log frequency filter bank parameters and Mel Frequency Cepstra Coefficients (MFCC) [6] use triangle bandpass filter to bypass the fine structure of spectrogram. Moreover, to simulate the non-uniform frequency resolution observed in human auditory perception, these speech feature sets adopt -uniform critical bands, providing high resolution in the low frequency part. However, the spectral structure of acoustic events is different from that of speech as shown in Figure 1, questioning the validity of using exactly a speech feature set for AED.

To analyze the spectral structure of acoustic events and design suitable features for AED, we carry out KLD based feature discriminant capability analysis. This helps us to understand the salient feature components of speech feature sets in the AED task. Intuitively, a discriminative feature component should separate

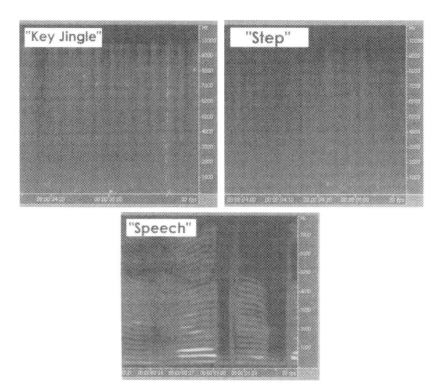

**Fig. 1.** Spectrograms of the acoustic events "Key Jingle", "Step" and human speech

an acoustic event from the other audio events (other events and speech). From a statistical point of view, more difference between the distributions of an acoustic event and the other audio parts results in smaller Bayesian error rates. The distance between the distributions of an acoustic event and the other audio parts reveals the discriminant capability of the feature for that acoustic event. Therefore, we introduce a KLD based analysis method to quantify the discriminant capability of feature components.

KLD $(D(p\|q))$ is a measure between two distributions, $p$ and $q$, and is defined as the cross entropy between $p$ and $q$ minus the self entropy of $p$.

$$D(p\|q) = \int p(x) \log \frac{p(x)}{q(x)} \tag{1}$$

We adopt KL distance to measure the discriminant capability of each feature component for each acoustic event, $d_{ij} = D(p_{ij}\|q_i)$, where $p_{ij}$ denotes the distribution of $i^{th}$ feature component given the $j^{th}$ acoustic event and $q_i$ denotes the distribution of $i^{th}$ feature component given all the audio parts. Then the global discrimant capability of $i^{th}$ feature component is defined by

$$d_i = \sum_j P_j d_{ij} \tag{2}$$

where $P_j$ is the prior probability for the $j^{th}$ acoustic event.

Obviously, a larger global KL distance $d_i$ means that the distributions in $i^{th}$ component have larger difference between different acoustic events, thus having greater discriminant capability. In Figure 2, we show the global KL distances for different log frequency filter bank parameters for AED are different from those for speech digit recognition. The KL distances for speech digit recognition are calculated in the same way as described above, having speech digits in the place of acoustic events. All global KL distances in Figure 2 are mean normalized.

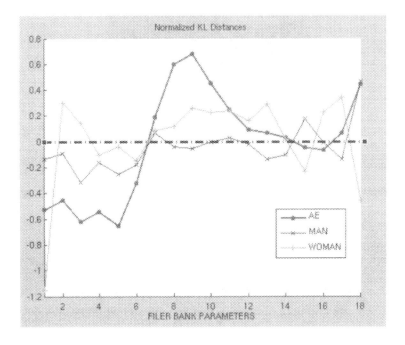

**Fig. 2.** Global KL distances for acoustic event detection, speech digit recognition (Men / Women)

# 3    Adaboost Based Feature Selection

## 3.1    Adaboost Algorithm

The basic Adaboost algorithm [5] deals with a 2 class classification problem. It iteratively selects and combines several effective classifiers among lots of weak classifiers. For each iteration one weak classifier is chosen from the weak classifier pool and the error rate is required to be less than 0.5.

The basic steps of Adaboost are:

1. Given a set of sample $x_1, x_2, ..., x_m$, and the corresponding labels $y_1, y_2, ..., y_m$, where $y_i \in Y = \{-1, +1\}$ for negative and positive examples respectively.
2. Initialize weights $D_1(i) = \frac{1}{m}$ where $m$ is the total number of positive and negative examples.
3. For $t = 1, ..., T$ :
   (a) Find the classifier $h_t$ that minimizes the error with respect to the weight $D_t$. The error of $h_t$ is given by $\epsilon_t = \sum_{i=1}^{m} D_t(i) \left( h_t(x_i) \neq y_i \right)$
   (b) Choose $\alpha_t \in \mathbf{R}$, typically $\alpha_t = \frac{1}{2} \ln \frac{1-\epsilon_t}{\epsilon_t}$
   (c) Update weights $D_t$:

$$D_{t+1}(i) = D_t(i) \frac{\exp\{-\alpha_t y_i h_t(x_i)\}}{Z_t}$$

   where $Z_t$ is a normalization constant, such that $\sum_{i=1}^{m} D_{t+1}(i) = 1$
4. Output the final classifier

$$H(x) = sign \left( \sum_{t=1}^{T} \alpha_t h_t(x) \right)$$

Details about AdaBoost algorithm can be found in [9,5].

### 3.2 Adaboost Based Feature Selection

As described in the earlier section, we need to choose a set of features that can best separate each acoustic event from the other audio part. In this paper, AdaBoost is used to select the feature set but not to linearly combine several classifers. In our framework, each audio utterance in the development set is segmented to several acoustic event instances (as well as silence and speech) according to the labels. These event instances together with their labels serve as the labeled examples in AdaBoost. The weak classifiers in AdaBoost are of just one type: if the log likelihood of a particular example on the one-feature-component correct-label GMM is larger than that on the one-feature-component global GMM, this example is correctly classified.

## 4    HMM-Based AED System Architecture

For the detection and classification of acoustic events, we implement a hidden Markov model (HMM)-based system with lattice rescoring using features selected by AdaBoost (Figure 3).

We formulate the goal of acoustic event detection in a way similar to speech recognition: to find the event sequence that maximizes the posterior probability of the event sequence $W = (w_1, w_2, ..., w_M)$, given the observations $O = (o_1, o_2, ..., o_T)$:

$$\hat{W} = \arg \max_{W} P(W|O) = \arg \max_{W} P(O|W)P(W) \qquad (3)$$

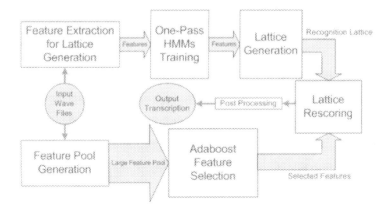

**Fig. 3.** AED System Architecture

The acoustic model $P(O|W)$ is one HMM for each acoustic event, with three emitting states and left-to-right state transitions. To account for silence and speech, we use a similar HMM, but with additional transitions between the first and third emitting states. The structure of HMMs can model some of the nonstationarity of acoustic events. The observation distributions of the states are incrementally-trained Gaussian mixtures. Each HMM is trained on all the segments labeled as this event in the development seminar data. The language model, which is a bigram model, acounts for the probability of a particular event in the event sequence conditioned on the previous event: $P(w_1 w_2 \cdots w_m) = P(w_1) \prod_{i=2}^{m} P(w_i|w_{i-1})$.

Such a language model in acoustic event detection favors those recognized acoustic event sequences that are more similar to the sequences in the development data. Although the language model here does not have those linguistic implications as in speech recognition, it does improve performance, one of the possible reasons being to suppress a long sequence of identical event labels so that the internal structure of HMM can try to fit the temporal structure of the event segment.

In our HMM-based AED System Architecture, the upper part of Figure 3 generates a recognition lattice, which is a compact representation of N-best recognition outputs. Each edge in the lattice is annotated with acoustic model score and language model score. The acoustic features used to train HMMs for lattice generation consists of 26 frequency-filtered log filter-bank parameters or 26 MFCC, their overall energy, delta and acceleration, calculated on 25 ms Hamming windows with 10ms shifts.

The lower part of the architecture in Figure 3 selects the most discriminative feature set according to the AdaBoost approach described in the previous section. This selected feature set is a subset of a feature pool having much more feature components. New HMMs trained using this feature set assign new acoustic scores to each arc in the recognition lattice. The best path in this updated lattice is output as the recognized event sequence.

## 5   Experiments

Our acoustic event detection experiments use about 3 hours development data with event boundaries and labels to train our systems, and test these systems on about 2 hour testing data, which is the official testing data for CLEAR 2007 AED Evaluation [11]. Both the development data and testing data are seminar style, having both speech and acoustic events with possible overlap. The performances are measured using AED-ACC (the first metric in CLEAR 2007 AED Evaluation). This metric aims to score detection of all acoustic event instances, oriented to applications such as real-time services for smart rooms and audio-based surveillance.

The first experiment is designed to compare the performance of one-pass HMM-based AED systems, using either a set of MFCC or the AdaBoost-selected feature set. The baseline set of MFCC (called MFCC13DA) is the widely-used feature set for speech recognition: 13 parameters calculated on 0Hz - 11000Hz band of the audio files. The delta and acceleration of these parameters are also included, forming a whole MFCC feature set of 39 components. The AdaBoost-selected feature set in this experiment (called SELECTED13DA) includes 13 feature components selected using the AdaBoost-based approach in Section 3 from a feature pool of 26 log frequency filter bank parameters and 26 MFCC parameters on the 0Hz-11000Hz band. The delta and acceleration of these selected feature components are also included, forming a feature set of 39 components.

**Table 1.** AED-ACC score of one-pass recognition using MFCC or selected feature set

| AED-ACC | Dev | Test |
|---|---|---|
| MFCC13DA | 38.92 | 25.27 |
| SELECTED13DA | 39.8 | 26.9 |

**Table 2.** AED-ACC scores of one-pass system using the feature set MFCC27DA and complete systems (lattices generated using either the feature set MFCC27DA * or a similar 81-dimension log frequency filter bank feature set **)

| AED-ACC | Test | |
|---|---|---|
| MFCC27DA (one-pass) | 29.51 | |
| Selected 26DA | 31.44** | 33.6* |

Table 1 shows that the AdaBoost-selected feature set outperform the MFCC feature set in recognition on both development data and test data. This indicates that for the AED task, using a complete set of features designed for speech recognition is far from optimal, and a feature set extracted using data-driven approach could yield better performance in AED without parameter increase.

The second experiment is designed to compare the performance of a one-pass HMM-based AED systems using MFCC and our complete system as described in Section 4. Reasonably increased parameter size would lead to better system performance. Therefore, the MFCC feature set used in this experiment (called MFCC27DA) consists of 27 MFCC parameters along with their delta and acceleration, forming 81 feature components. The complete system uses either the feature set MFCC27DA or a similar 81-dimension log frequency filter bank feature set to generate a recognition lattice. Then this system uses 26 feature components selected by AdaBoost from the same feature pool as in the first experiment, together with their delta and acceleration, forming a feature set of 78 dimensions (called SELECTED26DA), to rescore the recognition lattice and obtain the final recognition result.

Table 2 indicates that given a recognition lattice, using the selected feature set could benefit the system by updating the acoustic scores of the lattice and finding the optimal path in the updated lattice.

# 6   Conclusion

In this study, we use KLD to quantify the discriminant capability of all speech feature components in acoustic event detection. Global KLD shows that the speech feature components have different discriminant capabilities for speech recognition and acoustic event detection. The most discriminant feature set is extracted from a large feature pool using AdaBoost based approach. The acoustic event detection experiments show that the discriminant feature set extracted by the data-driven methods significantly outperform the MFCC features without increasing the parameter number in one-pass HMM-based acoustic event detection. And additional performance improvement is achieved by using speech feature set to generate recognition lattice and using the AdaBoost-selected feature set to rescore this lattice.

## Acknowledgement

This research was supported in part by the U.S. Government VACE Program; and in part by National Science Foundation Grants 04-14117 and 05-34106. Findings and recommendations expressed in this paper are those of the authors and do not necessarily reflect the views of the U.S. Government or NSF.

## References

1. Beaufays, F., Boies, D., Weintraub, M., Zhu, Q.: Using speech/non-speech detection to bias recognition search on noisy data. In: ICASSP 2003, vol.I, pp. 424–427 (2003)
2. CHIL. Computers in the human interaction loop (2006), http://chil.server.de/
3. Clavel, C., Ehrette, T., Richard, G.: Events detection for an audio-based surveillance system. In: ICME 2005, pp. 1306–1309 (2005)

4. Cui, R., Lu, L., Zhung, H.-J., Cai, L.-H.: Highlight sound effects detection in audio stream. In: ICME 2003, vol.III, pp. 37–40 (2003)
5. Freund, Y., Schapire, R.E.: A short introduction to boosting. Journal of Japanese Society for Artificial Intelligence 14(5), 771–780 (1999)
6. Hermansky, H.: Mel cepstrum, deltas, double deltas... what else is new? In: Proc. Robust Methods for Speech Recognition in Adverse Condition (1999)
7. Krishnamurthy, V., Moore, J.: On-line estimation of hidden markov model parameters based on the kullback-leibler information measure. IEEE Trans. on Signal Processing 41(8), 2557–2573 (1993)
8. Martin, A., Mauuary, L.: Voicing parameter and energy based speech/non-speech detection for speech recognition in adverse conditions. In: Interspeech 2003, pp. I 3069–3072 (2003)
9. Ratsch, G., Onoda, T., Muller, K.-R.: Soft margins for adaboost. IEEE Trans. on Signal Processing 42, 287–320 (2001)
10. Schòlkopf, B., Smola, A.: Learning with Kernels. MIT Press, Cambridge (2002)
11. Temko, A.: Clear 2007 AED evaluation plan (2007), `http://isl.ira.uka.de/clear07`
12. Temko, A., Malkin, R., Zieger, C., Macho, D., Nadeu, C., Omologo, M.: Acoustic event detection and classification in smart-room environments: Evaluation of chil project systems. Cough 65, 5–11 (2006)
13. Temko, A., Nadeu, C.: Classification of meeting-room acoustic events with support vector machines and variable-feature-set clustering. In: ICASSP 2005, vol. V, pp. 505–508 (2005)

# Acoustic Event Detection: SVM-Based System and Evaluation Setup in CLEAR'07

Andrey Temko, Climent Nadeu, and Joan-Isaac Biel

TALP Research Center, Universitat Politècnica de Catalunya (UPC),
Campus Nord, Ed. D5, Jordi Girona 1-3, 08034 Barcelona, Spain
{temko, climent, albiel}@talp.upc.edu

**Abstract.** In this paper, the Acoustic Event Detection (AED) system developed at the UPC is described, and its results in the CLEAR evaluations carried out in March 2007 are reported. The system uses a set of features composed of frequency-filtered band energies and perceptual features, and it is based on SVM classifiers and multi-microphone decision fusion. Also, the current evaluation setup and, in particular, the two new metrics used in this evaluation are presented.

## 1 Introduction

The detection of the acoustic events (AE) that are naturally produced in a meeting room may help to describe the human and social activity that takes place in it. Additionally, the robustness of automatic speech recognition systems may be increased by a previous detection of the non-speech sounds lying in the captured signals.

After the Acoustic Event Detection (AED) evaluation within the CLEAR evaluation campaign 2006 [1] organized by the CHIL project [2], several modifications have been introduced into the task for the CLEAR evaluation campaign 2007. The old metric has been substituted by two new metrics: Accuracy and Error Rate, which are based, respectively, on precision/recall and on a temporal measure of detection error. Additionally, AED is performed only in seminar conditions, where the AEs are often overlapped with speech and/or other AEs. The definition of the classes of AEs is kept.

In this paper, after presenting the current evaluation setup and, in particular, the two new metrics used in this evaluation, we describe the AED system developed at the UPC and submitted to the CLEAR evaluations carried out in March 2007 along with its results.

The paper is organized as follows. In Section 2 the evaluation setup is presented. Specifically, the definition of the task is given in Subsection 2.1. Subsection 2.2 describes the databases assigned to development and testing. Metrics are given in Subsection 2.3, and Subsection 2.4 states the main evaluation conditions. The detailed description of the proposed system is given in Section 3. The results obtained by the detection system in the CLEAR evaluations are shown and discussed in Section 4. Conclusions are presented in Section 5.

R. Stiefelhagen et al. (Eds.): CLEAR 2007 and RT 2007, LNCS 4625, pp. 354–363, 2008.

## 2  Evaluation Setup

### 2.1  Acoustic Event Classes

The AED evaluation will use the same 12 semantic classes, i.e. types of AEs, used in the past evaluations CLEAR 2006 [1]. The semantic classes with the corresponding annotation label are shown in black in the first column of Table 1. Apart from the 12 evaluated classes, there are 3 other possible events shown in grey in Table 1 which are not evaluated.

**Table 1.** Number of occurrences per acoustic event class for the development and test data

| Event Type | | Number of Occurrences | | | |
|---|---|---|---|---|---|
| | | Development | | | Test |
| | | UPC iso | ITC iso | Seminars | Seminars |
| Door knock | [kn] | 50 | 47 | 82 | 153 |
| Door open/slam | [ds] | 120 | 100 | 73 | 76 |
| Steps | [st] | 73 | 50 | 72 | 498 |
| Chair moving | [cm] | 76 | 47 | 238 | 226 |
| Spoon/cup jingle | [cl] | 64 | 48 | 28 | 28 |
| Paper work | [pw] | 84 | 48 | 130 | 88 |
| Key jingle | [kj] | 65 | 48 | 22 | 32 |
| Keyboard typing | [kt] | 66 | 48 | 72 | 105 |
| Phone ring | [pr] | 116 | 89 | 21 | 25 |
| Applause | [ap] | 60 | 12 | 8 | 13 |
| Cough | [co] | 65 | 48 | 54 | 36 |
| Laugh | [la] | 64 | 48 | 37 | 154 |
| Unknown | [un] | 126 | - | 301 | 559 |
| Speech | [sp] | | - | 1224 | 1239 |
| Silence | | Not annotated explicitly | | | |

### 2.2  Databases

The database used in the CLEAR evaluation campaign 2007 consists of 25 interactive seminars of approximately 30 min long each that have been recorded by AIT, ITC, IBM, UKA, and UPC in their smart-rooms.

Five interactive seminars (one from each site) have been assigned for system development. Along with the seminar recordings, the databases of isolated AEs recorded at UPC [3] and ITC [4] have been used for development.

The development database details in terms of the number of occurrences per AE class are shown in Table 1. In total, development data consists of 7495 seconds, where 16% of total time is AEs, 13% is silence, and 81% is "Speech" and "Unknown" classes.

The remaining 20 interactive seminars have been conditionally decomposed into 5 types of acoustic scenes: "beginning", "meeting", "coffee break", "question/answers", and "end". After observing the "richness" of each acoustic scene type in terms of

AEs, 20 5-minute segments have been extracted by ELDA maximizing the AE time and number of occurrences per AE class. The details of the testing database are given in Table 1. In total, the test data consist of 6001 seconds, where 36% are AE time, 11% are silence, and 78% are "Speech" and "Unknown" classes. Noticeably, during about 64% of time, the AEs are overlapped with "Speech" and during 3% they are overlapped with other AEs. In terms of AE occurrences, more than 65% of the existing 1434 AEs are partially or completely overlapped with "Speech" and/or other AEs.

## 2.3 Metrics

Two metrics have been developed at the UPC, with the agreement of the other participating partners which are involved in CHIL: an F-score measure of detection accuracy (which combines recall and precision), and an error rate measure that focuses more on the accuracy of the endpoints of each detected AE. They have been used separately in the evaluations, and will be called, respectively, AED-ACC and AED-ER.

### AED-ACC
The aim of this metric is to score detection of all instances of what is considered as a relevant AE. With this metric it is not important to reach a good temporal coincidence of the reference and system output timestamps of the AEs but to detect their instances. It is oriented to applications like real-time services for smart-rooms, audio-based surveillance, etc. AED-ACC is defined as the F-score (the harmonic mean between Precision and Recall):

$$AED - ACC = \frac{(1+\beta^2) * Precision * Recall}{\beta^2 * Precision + Recall},$$

where

$$Precision = \frac{number\ of\ correct\ system\ output\ AEs}{number\ of\ all\ system\ output\ AEs}$$

$$Recall = \frac{number\ of\ correctly\ detected\ reference\ AEs}{number\ of\ all\ reference\ AEs}$$

and $\beta$ is a weighting factor that balances Precision and Recall. In this evaluation the factor $\beta$ has been set to 1. A *system output AE* is considered *correct* or *correctly produced* either if there exist at least one reference AE whose temporal centre is situated between the timestamps of the system output AE and the labels of the system output AE and the reference AE are the same, or if the temporal centre of the system output AE lies between the timestamps of at least one reference AE and the labels of the system output AE and the reference AE are the same. A *reference AE* is considered *correctly detected* either if there exist at least one system output AE whose temporal centre is situated between the timestamps of the reference AE and the labels of the system output AE and the reference AE are the same, or if the temporal centre of the reference AE lies between the timestamps of at least one system output AE and the labels of the system output AE and the reference AE are the same.

*AED-ER*

For some applications it is necessary to have a good temporal resolution of the detected AEs. The aim of this metric is to score AED as a task of general audio segmentation. Possible applications can be content-based audio indexing/retrieval, meeting stage detection, etc.

In order to define AED-ER, the NIST metric for Speaker Diarization [5] has been adapted to the task of AED. The audio data is divided into adjacent segments, whose borders coincide with the points whether either a reference AE or a system output AE starts or stops, so that, along a given segment, the number of reference AEs and the number of system output AEs do not change.

The AED-ER score is computed as the fraction of time, including regions of overlapping, in which a system output AE is not attributed correctly to a reference AE, in the following way:

$$AED-ER = \frac{\sum_{\substack{all \\ seg}} \left\{ dur(seg) * \left( \max\left(N_{REF}, N_{SYS}\right) - N_{correct}(seg)\right)\right\}}{\sum_{\substack{all \\ seg}} \left\{ dur(seg) * N_{REF}(seg)\right\}}$$

where, for each segment *seg*:

    *dur(seg)*:    duration of *seg*
    $N_{REF}(seg)$:    number of reference AEs in *seg*
    $N_{SYS}(seg)$:    number of system output AEs in *seg*
    $N_{correct}(seg)$:    number of reference AEs in *seg* which correspond to system output AEs in *seg*

Notice that an overlapping region may contribute with several errors. Also, "Silence" is not explicitly transcribed, but is counted in the context of this metric as an AE.

The numerator of the AED-ER expression includes the substitution time, that corresponds to the wrong AE detection, the deletion time (missed AEs), and the insertion time (AE false alarms).

Only the 12 above-mentioned evaluated classes can cause errors. For example, if the reference label is "Speech" and the system output is "Unknown", there is no error; however if the system output is one of the 12 classes, it will be counted as an error (insertion). Similarly, if the reference is one of the 12 classes and the system output is "Speech", it will be also counted as an error (deletion).

## 2.4 Evaluation Scenario

In order to have systems comparable across sites, a set of evaluation conditions were defined [6]:

- The evaluated system must be applied to the **whole** CLEAR 2007 test DB.
- Only **primary** systems are submitted to **compete**.
- The evaluated systems must use **only audio** signals, though they can use **any** number of **microphones**.

# 3  Acoustic Event Detection System

The general scheme of the proposed system for AED is shown in Figure 1. Firstly, on the data preprocessing step, the signals are normalized based on the histograms of the signal energy. Then, a set of frame-level features is extracted from each frame of 30ms and a set of statistical parameters is computed over the frames in a 1-second window. The resulting vectors of statistical parameters are fed to the SVM classifier associated to the specific microphone. A single-microphone post-processing is applied to eliminate uncertain decisions. At the end, the results of 4 microphones are fused to obtain a final decision.

Our system, written in C++ programming language, is part of the smartAudio++ software package developed at UPC which includes other audio technology components (such as speech activity detection and speaker identification) for the purpose of real-time activity detection and observation in the smart-room environment. That AED system implemented in the smart-room has been used in the demos about technology services developed in CHIL. Also, a specific GUI-based demo has been built which shows the detected isolated events and their positions in the room. The positions are obtained from the acoustic source localization system developed also in our lab [11]. A video showing that demo is being currently recorded and will shortly be made publicly available in the CHIL webpage.

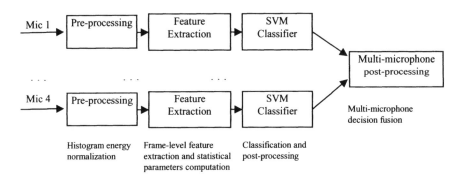

**Fig. 1.** The block-scheme of the developed AED system

## 3.1  Histogram-Based Energy Normalization

As it was mentioned in Section 2.2 the evaluation database has been recorded in 5 different rooms. Due to this fact, the energy level of audio signals varies from one audio file to another. In this work as a preprocessing step we decided to perform energy normalization of all audio files to a predefined level. Because the energy level of a given AE depends both on its type, the manner it is produced, and the position of the person who produces it, the energy normalization is based on the energy level of silence. For this the histogram of the audio signal log-energy calculated each 30ms with 10ms shift has been plotted. The results for one development seminar are shown in Figure 2. The lower-energy hump corresponds to the silence energy level. A 2-

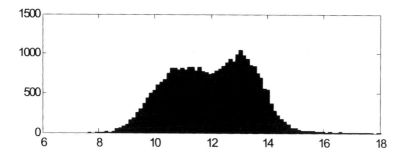

**Fig. 2.** Frame log-energy histograms calculated over the whole seminar signal

Gaussians GMM has been trained on the energy values and the lowest mean has been taken as the estimation of the silence energy. In Figure 2, the estimated silence level corresponds to the point 10.41 whereas the true value of silence energy level, calculated on the annotated silence segments, is 10.43. The normalizing coefficient is then calculated as $coef = \sqrt{\exp(9)/\exp(a)}$, where $a$ is the estimated silence level and 9 is the predefined final silence energy level. The exponential is used to come from the log scale back to the initial signal amplitude scale. Then, the development seminar signal is multiplied by $coef$.

### 3.2 Feature Extraction

The sound signal is down-sampled to 16 kHz, and framed (frame length/shift is 30/10ms, a Hamming window is used). For each frame, a set of spectral parameters has been extracted. It consists of the concatenation of two types of parameters [7]: 1) 16 Frequency-Filtered (FF) log filter-bank energies along with the first and the second time derivatives, and 2) a set of the following parameters: zero-crossing rate, short time energy, 4 sub-band energies, spectral flux, calculated for each of the defined sub-bands, spectral centroid, and spectral bandwidth. In total, a vector of 60 components is built to represent each frame. The mean and the standard deviation parameters have been computed over all frames in a 1-second window with a 200ms shift, thus forming one vector of 120 elements.

### 3.3 One-Microphone SVM System

For AED, SVM classifiers [8] have been implemented. They have been trained using the isolated AEs from the two databases of isolated acoustic events mentioned in Section 2.2, along with segments from the development data seminars that include both isolated AEs and AEs overlapped with speech. The segments that contain the overlapping of two or more AEs with or without speech are not used. In both training and testing processes, a vector of 120 statistical parameters has been computed from each 1-second window. The 1 vs. 1 multiclass strategy has been chosen to classify among 14 classes that include "Speech", "Unknown", and the 12 evaluated classes of AEs. Besides, "Silence" vs. "Non-silence" SVM classifier has been trained where "Non-silence" class includes all 14 classes. In that case, in order to decrease the

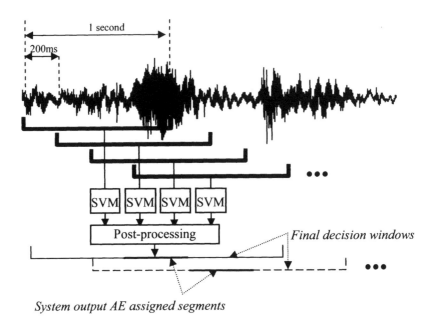

*System output AE assigned segments*

**Fig. 3.** One microphone AED system

number of training vectors and make training feasible, the dataset reduction technique described in [9] has been applied.

The testing stage is shown in Figure 3. An input vector of statistical components computed over the frames from a 1-second window is firstly fed to the "Silence" vs. "Non-silence" classifier and if the decision is "Non-silence", the vector is further fed to a SVM multiclass (14 classes) classifier based on the DAG testing scheme [10]. The most frequent event (the "winner") is taken from the final decision window of 4 decisions that corresponds to the time interval of 1.6 seconds. If the number of votes of the "winner" does not exceed the threshold the event is marked as "Unknown". The threshold has been set in order that the winner has to get at least 3 votes. The final decision window is shifted by 2 decisions, i.e. 400ms. Consequently, the temporal resolution of the produced system output AEs is 400ms, and the corresponding AE label is assigned to the central 400ms of the 1.6-second window.

For instance, for the first window of 4 decisions that corresponds to the time interval from 0 to 1.6s, the starting and ending timestamps of the system output AE will be 0.6 and 1s.

### 3.4 Multi-microphone Processing

The database used in the evaluation has been recorded with a set of microphones. Depending on the site, the following audio equipment has been used: one or two Mark III (array of 64 microphones), 3-7 T-shape clusters (4 mics per cluster), and several tabletop and omni directional microphones. To construct a multi-microphone AED

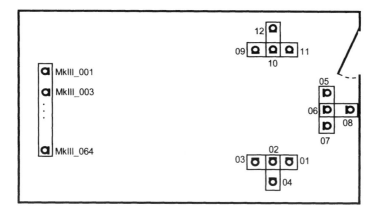

**Fig. 4.** The choice of the microphones for the UPC smart-room

system it has been decided to choose one microphone from each wall of the room and train a SVM classifier for each wall microphone. Due to the different configuration of the rooms where the development and testing data have been recorded and due to different numbering of the microphones, a mapping of the microphones across the sites has been performed. The Mark III microphone array has been chosen as the fixed point. For the remaining walls the T-shape cluster microphones have been chosen. An example of choice of the cluster microphones for the UPC smart-room is shown in Figure 4. The following microphone numbers have been chosen 1-5-9, 6-1-25, 1-5-9, 1-5-9 for the AIT/ITC/UKA/UPC smart-rooms, respectively. For instance, one SVM has been trained on audio signals from microphones 1, 6, 1, 1 taken from AIT/ITC/UKA/UPC, respectively. For the Mark III array the 3$^{rd}$ microphone has been chosen across all sites.

For multi-microphone decision fusion, the voting scheme has been used. The AE label with the largest number of votes is sent to the system output. In case of draw the event is chosen randomly.

## 4 Results and Discussion

The results obtained with the primary system submitted to the evaluation are shown in Table 2. Along with the main metrics, accuracy and error rate, the intermediate values are also given. They are precision and recall for accuracy, and DEL (deletions), INS (insertions), and SUB (substitutions) for error rate. A contrast system has been also submitted, showing little worse results than the primary system: ACC=23, ER=141.57. The difference between the primary and contrast system is that for multi-microphone fusion the former uses voting among the "winners" of the one-microphone systems while the contrast system performs voting adding up the confidences of the "winners" calculated as the number of times the "winner" is found in the 4-decision window.

**Table 2.** Official results obtained by the submitted AED primary system

| Accuracy (%) (Precision / Recall ) | Error Rate (%) (DEL/INS/SUB) |
|---|---|
| 23.0 | 136.69 |
| (19 / 29) | (50.3 / 57.1 / 29.3) |

Table 3 shows the results of each one-microphone SVM system before applying the voting decision. Actually, the final results of the multi-microphone system shown in Table 2 are worse that the results of the one-microphone SVM system obtained on the 3$^{rd}$ microphones of MarkIII array (Mic4). This fact may indicate that simple fusion methods, i.e. voting, do not work properly when the scores of the various systems differ significantly.

**Table 3.** The results obtained with each one-microphone SVM system before applying voting

|  | Mic1 | Mic2 | Mic3 | Mic4 |
|---|---|---|---|---|
| Accuracy (%) (Precision / Recall ) | 20.5 (17/27) | 22.6 (19/28) | 19.9 (15/29) | **26.8** **(34/22)** |
| Error Rate (%) (DEL/INS/SUB) | 145 (51/64/30) | 136 (54/55/27) | 155 (46/74/34) | **98** **(69/13/16)** |

The individual class accuracies are shown in Table 4. Interestingly enough, we have observed that the low accuracy and high error rate are mostly attributable to the bad recognition of the class "steps", which occurs more than 40% of all AE time.

Besides, more than 76% of all error time occurs in the segments where AEs are overlapped with speech and/or other AEs. If the overlapped segments were not scored, the error rate of the primary submitted system would be 32.33%.

**Table 4.** Accuracy scores for each class obtained with the primary system

| ap = 0.81 | cl = 0.29 | cm = 0.22 | co = 0.19 |
|---|---|---|---|
| ds = 0.42 | kj = 0.18 | kn = 0.05 | kt = 0.08 |
| la = 0.38 | pr = 0.28 | pw = 0.12 | st = 0.16 |

## 5   Conclusions

The presented work focuses on the CLEAR evaluation task concerning the detection of acoustic events that may happen in a lecture/meeting room environment. The evaluation has been performed on the database of interactive seminars that have been recorded in different smart-rooms and contain a significant number of acoustic events of interest. Two different metrics have been proposed and implemented. One is based on the precision and recall of the detection of the AEs as semantic instances, and the other is based on a more time-based error. Although the proposed system, which was the only submission not using HMM, ranked among the best, there is still a big room for improvement. Future work will be devoted to search a better way to deal with overlapping sounds, and to improve the algorithms of multi-microphone fusion. Multimodal AED is another approach from which a performance improvement can be expected.

## Acknowledgements

This work has been partially sponsored by the EC-funded project CHIL (IST-2002-506909) and the Spanish Government-funded project ACESCA (TIN2005-08852). Authors wish to thank Djamel Mostefa and Nicolas Moreau from ELDA for their role in the transcription of the seminar data and in the scoring task.

## References

1. Temko, A., Malkin, R., Zieger, C., Macho, D., Nadeu, C., Omologo, M.: CLEAR Evaluation of Acoustic Event Detection and Classification systems. In: Stiefelhagen, R., Garofolo, J.S. (eds.) CLEAR 2006. LNCS, vol. 4122, pp. 311–322. Springer, Heidelberg (2007)
2. CHIL - Computers In The Human Interaction Loop, http://chil.server.de/
3. Temko, A., Macho, D., Nadeu, C., Segura, C.: UPC-TALP Database of Isolated Acoustic Events. Internal UPC report (2005)
4. Zieger, C., Omologo, M.: Acoustic Event Detection - ITC-irst AED database. Internal ITC report (2005)
5. Spring 2007 (RT-07) Rich Transcription Meeting Recognition Evaluation Plan, NIST (December 2007)
6. Temko, A., Nadeu, C.: AED Evaluation plan for CLEAR 2007 (February 2007)
7. Temko, A., Nadeu, C.: Classification of Acoustic Events using SVM-based Clustering Schemes. Pattern Recognition 39(4), 682–694 (2006)
8. Schölkopf, B., Smola, A.: Learning with Kernels. MIT Press, Cambridge (2002)
9. Temko, A., Macho, D., Nadeu, C.: Enhanced SVM Training for Robust Speech Activity Detection. In: IEEE ICASSP 2007, Honolulu, Hawaii, USA (April 2007)
10. Platt, J., Cristianini, N., Shawe-Taylor, J.: Large Margin DAGs for Multiclass Classification. Proc. Advances in Neural Information Processing Systems 12, 547–553 (2000)
11. Segura, C., Abad, A., Hernando, J., Nadeu, C.: Multispeaker Localization and Tracking in Intelligent Environments. In: CLEAR 2007 Evaluation Campaign and Workshop, Baltimore MD, USA (May 2007)

# TUT Acoustic Event Detection System 2007

Toni Heittola and Anssi Klapuri

Tampere University of Technology, P.O. Box 553, 33101, Tampere, Finland
{toni.heittola,klap}@tut.fi

**Abstract.** This paper describes a system used in acoustic event detection task of the CLEAR 2007 evaluation. The objective of the task is to detect acoustic events (door slam, steps, paper wrapping etc.) using acoustic data from a multiple microphone set up in the meeting room environment. A system based on hidden Markov models and multichannel audio data was implemented. Mel-Frequency Cepstral Coefficients are used to represent the power spectrum of the acoustic signal. Fully-connected three-state hidden Markov models are trained for 12 acoustic events and one-state models are trained for speech, silence, and unknown events.

## 1 Introduction

In the meeting room environment, the detection or classification of acoustic events may help to describe human activity that takes place in the room. For example, door slams and chair movements can be used to detect the beginning of the meeting. The event activity information is essential for perceptually aware interfaces in smart meeting rooms.

Computational auditory scene analysis may be used to detect and identify acoustic events. Acoustic Event Detection (AED) and Classification aims to process the acoustic signal and convert it into a symbolic descriptions of the corresponding sound events present in the acoustic signal. Information produced by the AED system can be further used to increase the robustness of automatic speech recognition, for example. Most of the previously presented AED systems rely on the use of traditional classification techniques, using hidden Markov models [1] or support vector machines [2]. Acoustic event detection is closely related to the more general task of noise classification and recognition [3]. Audio-based context-aware systems classify acoustical environments based on the general acoustic information and these systems utilize many of the approaches used in AED systems [4].

In this paper, we present our system for the acoustic event detection task in CLEAR 2007 evaluation [6]. The next section introduces the proposed system. In Section 3, the database and the metrics used in the evaluation will be described along with the results of the evaluation. Section 4 concludes the discussion.

R. Stiefelhagen et al. (Eds.): CLEAR 2007 and RT 2007, LNCS 4625, pp. 364–370, 2008.

## 2   System Description

The proposed system is based on modeling sound events with continuous-density hidden Markov models (HMMs). Mel-Frequency Cepstral Coefficients (MFCCs) are used to represent the power spectrum. Observation probabilities are calculated separately for one channel from each T-shaped microphone array. After that, all the observation probabilities are combined (see Figure 1) and the optimal path through all models (see Figure 2) is decoded.

### 2.1   Features

Mel-Frequency Cepstral Coefficients and their time-derivatives are the most widely-used features in speech recognition [5], and recently these have been successfully used in audio-based context recognition [4] and noise classification tasks [2,3], too. MFCCs are short-term features used to represent the coarse shape of the power spectrum and provide a good discriminative performance with reasonable noise robustness. We used 10 MFCCs calculated from the outputs of a 40-channel filterbank. In addition to the static coefficients, their time-differentials ($\Delta$MFCC) are used to describe the dynamic properties of the cepstrum. Signal's log-energy is also used in the feature vector. Before the feature extraction, the time-domain signals are normalized to have zero mean and unity variance over the training data. Features are extracted in 23 ms frames with 50% overlap. In order to normalize channel effects caused by the frequency responses of the microphones used in the recordings, all the features are mean and variance normalized using global estimates measured over all the training data available from a particular audio channel.

### 2.2   Classification

Hidden Markov models (HMMs) are used to characterize a time-varying series of observations. Fully-connected three-state HMMs having four Gaussians per state are trained for each of the 12 acoustic events. One-state HMMs with 32 Gaussians are trained for speech, silence, and unknown events. Training segments for event models are selected from the development set by preferring event segments which do not overlap with speech. The amount of training segments used per event are shown in Table 1. All the available audio channels are used for the training and HMMs for events are trained with the standard Baum-Welch procedure.

   In the classification stage, observation probabilities are calculated for each microphone channel. These probabilities are then combined by assuming that the microphone channels are independent, i.e. probabilities are multiplied (see Figure 1). At the model decoding stage, all the event HMMs are combined to form a single big transition matrix and one state space. The trained transition matrices for individual events form blocks along the diagonal of the big transition matrix. All transitions between events are set equally probable. An overview of the structure is shown in Figure 2. The optimal path through the combined model is decoded with Viterbi algorithm. The final event sequence is smoothed

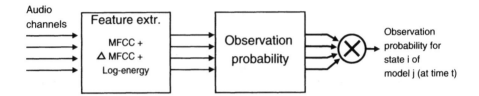

**Fig. 1.** Calculation of observation probability for multichannel audio data

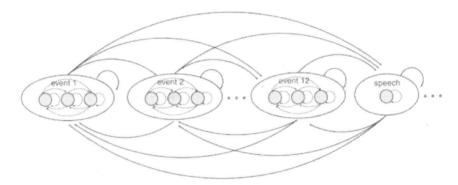

**Fig. 2.** Model overview

by using one-second sliding window where the event in the middle of the window is decided by a majority vote.

## 3   Evaluation

### 3.1   Task

The objective of the task is to detect and recognize acoustic events using only the acoustic data from the multiple microphones placed in the meeting room environment. The evaluation will use the 12 semantic event classes shown in Table 1.

### 3.2   Data

A description about the database used in the system development and performance evaluation is given here. For further details, refer to the CLEAR 2007 evaluation plan [6]. The data is divided into development (Dev) and evaluation (Eval) sets. Segments for these sets are extracted from five interactive seminar databases:

- Politécnica de Catalunya (UPC) Interactive Seminar Database 2006
- Institutino di Cultura (ITC) Interactive Seminar Database 2006
- Athens Information Technology (AIT) Interactive Seminar Database 2006

- University of Karlsruhe (UKA) Interactive Seminar Database 2006
- IBM Interactive Seminar Database 2006

One seminar per database is selected for the development set, and eight five minute long excerpt from each database for the evaluation set. The databases consist of about 30 minutes long multi-channel audio recordings made in the meeting room environment while a presentation is given to a group of 3-5 attendees. There is typical meeting room activity present: discussion among the attendees and the presenter, people entering and leaving the room, people having coffee breaks, chairs moving, paper wrapping, etc. The acoustic events in the recordings may have temporal overlapping with speech and/or other acoustic events. The recordings are annotated by hand with a time resolution of 150 ms. Annotated event classes and the number of segments per event are shown in Table 1. The recordings were made at 44.1kHz sampling rate and 24 bit resolution.

**Table 1.** Number of events in the seminar database

| Event | Total count | Selected for training |
|---|---|---|
| Knock (door,table) | 77 | 36 |
| Door slam (open and close) | 71 | 33 |
| Steps | 89 | 25 |
| Chair moving | 263 | 39 |
| Spoon clings (cup jingle) | 29 | 9 |
| Paper wrapping | 163 | 9 |
| Key jingle | 21 | 4 |
| Keyboard typing | 73 | 8 |
| Phone ringing/music | 27 | 2 |
| Applause | 8 | 2 |
| Cough | 54 | 17 |
| Laugh | 43 | 5 |
| Speech | 1230 | |
| Unknown | 317 | |

## 3.3  Metrics

Two metrics will be used in evaluations. An F-score is used to measure detection accuracy (AED-ACC) and error rate (AED-ER) is used to measure the accuracy of the endpoints of detected acoustic events. Only the 12 evaluated classes can cause errors in the evaluations: speech events are allowed to be confused with unknown events and vice versa.

**Accuracy.** Accuracy (AED-ACC) metric is used to evaluate the detection of all the relevant acoustic events. The metric is oriented to audio-based services in smart meeting rooms and surveillance systems. Therefore a good temporal coincidence of the reference and system output is not important with this metric.

AED-ACC is similar to F-score and it is defined as the harmonic mean between precision and recall:

$$\text{AED-ACC} = \frac{(1+\beta^2) * precision * recall}{\beta^2 * precision * recall}, \tag{1}$$

where

$$precision = \frac{number\, of\, correct\, system\, output\, events}{number\, of\, all\, system\, output\, events},$$

$$recall = \frac{number\, of\, correctly\, detected\, reference\, events}{number\, of\, all\, reference\, events}$$

and $\beta$ is a weighting factor (in the evaluations set to one) that balances precision and recall. An event detected by the system is considered correct if there exist at least one matching reference event having its temporal center within timestamps of detected event. Detection is also considered correct if the temporal center of detected event is within timestamps of at least one matching reference event. A reference event is considered correctly detected if the temporal center of the reference event is within at least one matching system output or if there exist at least one matching system output having its temporal center within timestamps of the reference event.

**Error Rate.** Error rate (AED-ER) metric is used to evaluate temporal resolution. This is done by scoring the accuracy of the endpoints of the detected events. The NIST metric for Speaker Diarization [7] is adapted to the task of acoustic event detection. First an one-to-one mapping of reference events to system output events will be computed. The measure of mapping optimality will be the aggregation, over all reference events, of the time length that is jointly attributed to both the reference events and the corresponding system output events to which that reference events are mapped. This metric is oriented to applications involving content-based audio indexing and segmentation.

The audio signal is divided into contiguous segments whose borders coincide with starts or stops of a reference or a system output event. For a given segment, the number of current reference events and the number of system output events do not change. The AED-ER is defined as the fraction of the time that is not attributed correctly to an acoustic event:

$$\text{AED-ER} = \frac{\sum_{all\, seg} \{dur\,(seg) * (\max\,(N_{REF}, N_{SYS}) - N_{correct}\,(seg))\}}{\sum_{all\, seg} \{dur\,(seg) * N_{REF}\,(seg)\}} \tag{2}$$

where $dur\,(seg)$ is the duration of the $seg$, $N_{REF}\,(seg)$ is the number of reference events in $seg$, $N_{SYS}\,(seg)$ is the number of system output events in $seg$ and $N_{correct}\,(seg)$ is the number of reference events in $seg$ which have corresponding mapped system output events in $seg$. A wrong event detection, the deletion time (missed events), and the insertion time (false alarms) corresponds to the substitution time included in the numerator.

### 3.4   Results

The performance was evaluated based on the AED-ACC and AED-ER metrics. The proposed system obtained accuracy score 14.7 with the AED-ACC metric. The precision was 19.2 (164/853) and recall 11.9 (170/1434). Overall detection error with AED-ER metric was 139.1 percent of scored event time, see detailed results in Table 2.

**Table 2.** Detailed results with the AED-ER metric

| Scored acoustic event time | 2168 s | 37.4 % scored time |
|---|---|---|
| Missed acoustic event time | 1190 s | 54.9 % scored acoustic event time |
| False alarm acoustic event time | 1091 s | 50.3 % scored acoustic event time |
| Event substitution time | 734 s | 33.9 % scored acoustic event time |
| Overall detection error | 139.1 % | |

## 4   Conclusions

A system used for the acoustic event detection task in CLEAR 2007 evaluation was presented. The system utilized widely used classification system scheme: power spectrum based features and a HMM classifier. The evaluations showed that there is still much room for improvement. However, the proposed system performed moderately compared with the other participants in the evaluation.

In general, the acoustic event detection is a difficult task due to overlapping events, noise and acoustic variation. Multi-channel audio information has to be more utilized in the detection in order to achieve a better performance. More robust feature extraction techniques or sound separation are also needed. In addition to this, more specialized detectors e.g. for speech and silence have to be studied.

## References

1. Temko, A., Malkin, R., Zieger, C., Macho, D., Nadeu, C., Omologo, M.: CLEAR Evaluation of Acoustic Event Detection and Classification Systems. In: Stiefelhagen, R., Garofolo, J.S. (eds.) CLEAR 2006. LNCS, vol. 4122, pp. 311–322. Springer, Heidelberg (2007)
2. Temko, A., Nadeu, C.: Classification of acoustic events using SVM-based clustering schemes. Pattern Recognition 39(4), 682–694 (2006)
3. Gaunard, P., Mubikangiey, C., Couvreur, C., Fontaine, V.: Automatic Classification of Environmental Noise Events by Hidden Markov Models. Applied Acoustics 54(3), 187–206 (1998)
4. Eronen, A., Tuomi, J., Klapuri, A., Fagerlund, S., Sorsa, T., Lorho, G., Huopaniemi, J.: Audio-based context recognition. IEEE Transactions on Audio, Speech, and Language Processing 14(1), 321–329 (2006)

5. Rabiner, L., Juang, B.H.: Fundamentals of Speech Recognition. PTR Prentice-Hall Inc, New Jersey (1993)
6. CLEAR:  AED  Evaluation  Plan  (2007),  `http://isl.ira.uka.de/clear07/download=CLEAR_2007_AED_EvaluationPlan.pdf`
7. NIST: Spring (RT-05S) Rich Transcription Meeting Recognition Evaluation Plan (2005),  `http://nist.gov/speech/tests/rt/rt2005/spring/rt05smeetingeval-plan-V1.pdf`

**RT 2007**

# The Rich Transcription 2007 Meeting Recognition Evaluation

Jonathan G. Fiscus[1], Jerome Ajot[1,2], and John S. Garofolo[1]

[1] National Institute Of Standards and Technology, 100 Bureau Drive Stop 8940,
Gaithersburg, MD 20899
[2] Systems Plus, Inc., One Research Court – Suite 360, Rockville, MD 20850
{jfiscus,ajot,jgarofolo}@nist.gov

**Abstract.** We present the design and results of the Spring 2007 (RT-07) Rich Transcription Meeting Recognition Evaluation; the fifth in a series of community-wide evaluations of language technologies in the meeting domain. For 2007, we supported three evaluation tasks: Speech-To-Text (STT) transcription, "Who Spoke When" Diarization (SPKR), and Speaker Attributed Speech-To-Text (SASTT). The SASTT task, which combines STT and SPKR tasks, was a new evaluation task. The test data consisted of three test sets: Conference Meetings, Lecture Meetings, and Coffee Breaks from lecture meetings. The Coffee Break data was included as a new test set this year. Twenty-one research sites materially contributed to the evaluation by providing data or building systems. The lowest STT word error rates with up to four simultaneous speakers in the multiple distant microphone condition were 40.6 %, 49.8 %, and 48.4 % for the conference, lecture, and coffee break test sets respectively. For the SPKR task, the lowest diarization error rates for all speech in the multiple distant microphone condition were 8.5 %, 25.8 %, and 25.5 % for the conference, lecture, and coffee break test sets respectively. For the SASTT task, the lowest speaker attributed word error rates for segments with up to three simultaneous speakers in the multiple distant microphone condition were 40.3 %, 59.3 %, and 68.4 % for the conference, lecture, and coffee break test sets respectively.

## 1 Motivation

The National Institute of Standards and Technology (NIST) has worked with the speech recognition community since the mid 1980s to improve the state-of-the-art in speech processing technologies. [1] To facilitate progress, NIST has worked with the community to make training/development data sets available for several speech domains. NIST collaborated with the research community to define performance metrics and create evaluation tools for technology developers to perform hill-climbing experiments and measure their progress. NIST also coordinates periodic community-wide benchmark tests and technology workshops to facilitate technical exchange and track progress trends over time. The test suites used in these benchmark tests become development resources after the formal evaluations.

R. Stiefelhagen et al. (Eds.): CLEAR 2007 and RT 2007, LNCS 4625, pp. 373–389, 2008.
© Springer-Verlag Berlin Heidelberg 2008

In 2001, NIST began administering the Rich Transcription Evaluation series for the DARPA Effective, Affordable, Reusable, Speech-to-Text (EARS) Program in the Broadcast News (BN) and Conversation Telephone Speech (CTS) domains. The EARS community focused on building technologies to generate transcriptions of speech that are fluent, informative, readable by humans, and usable in downstream processes. To accomplish this, EARS technologies produced transcripts consisting of words and non-orthographic metadata. We refer to these metadata enriched transcripts as "rich transcriptions." While the metadata can take many forms, the EARS program worked on three main forms: which speakers spoke which words, syntactic boundaries, and dysfluent speech detection.

In 2002, the community began investigating the meeting domain as a new evaluation domain because the error rates on BN material approached 6 times that of human performance indicating the community needed a more difficult challenge problem. When error rates come close to human performance, the evaluation costs rise dramatically because transcription ambiguity in the reference becomes a disproportionately large component of the error rates. While large test sets and/or meticulously scrutinized reference transcripts can ameliorate the impact of ambiguity, they both require great expense. Instead, research in the meeting domain became a popular because it provides a unique environment to collect naturally occurring spoken interactions under controlled sensor conditions that presents several challenges to the technologies resulting in higher error rates. These include varied fora, an infinite number of topics, spontaneous highly interactive/overlapping speech, varied recording environments, varied/multiple microphones, multi-modal inputs, participant movement, and far field speech effects such as ambient noise and reverberation.

At roughly the same time in the early 2000's, a number of independent large-scale programs included the meeting domain as a component of their research and evaluation efforts. The programs included the European Union (EU) Computers in the Human Interaction Loop (CHIL), the EU Augmented Multiparty Interaction with Distant Access (AMIDA) program, and the US Video Analysis and Content Extraction (VACE) program. The programs shared many aspects of uni-modal (audio or video) and multi-modal (audio+video) research indicating a strong movement was underway in the research community to focus on building and experimenting with multi-modal technologies. However, little infrastructure was in place to support the research nor was there a public evaluation-based forum for technical interchange.

Beginning in 2005, CHIL, NIST, and VACE orchestrated a multi-year plan to bring together the disjoint speech and video processing communities through common evaluations. In 2006, the CHIL and VACE programs started the Classification of Events, Activities, and Relationships (CLEAR) evaluation [7, 14]. While the 2006 CLEAR Evaluation Workshop was held in conjunction with the 7th IEEE International Conference on Face and Gesture Recognition (FG2006), the shared use of common evaluation corpora for the RT and CLEAR evaluations in 2006 set the stage for the joint CLEAR and RT evaluations and workshops in 2007. [15]

The Rich Transcription 2007 (RT-07) Meeting Recognition evaluation, which was part of the NIST Rich Transcription (RT) series of language technology evaluations [1] [2] [6] [10], included three evaluation tasks:

- Speech-To-Text (STT) transcription – Transcribe the spoken words.
- "Who Spoke When" Diarization (SPKR) – Detect segments of speech and cluster them by speaker.
- Speaker Attributed Speech-To-Text (SASTT) – Transcribe the spoken words and associate them with a speaker.

The first two tasks, STT and SPKR, are component tasks that have always been include in the RT evaluations. The SASTT is a composite task that includes both STT and SPKR tasks. The RT-07 evaluation was the first evaluation to include the SASTT task although ICSI/SRI experiments conducted during the EARS Program [13] were very similar to the presently defined task.

The RT-07 evaluation is the result of a multi-site/multi-national collaboration. In addition to NIST, the organizers and contributors included:

- Athens Information Technology (AIT)
- The Augmented Multiparty Interaction with Distant Access (AMIDA) Program
- The Computers in the Human Interaction Loop (CHIL) Program
- Carnegie Mellon University (CMU)
- Edinburgh University (EDI)
- Evaluations and Language Resources Distribution Agency (ELDA)
- IBM
- International Computer Science Institute (ICSI)
- Infocomm Research Site (I2R)
- Nanyang Technological University (NTU)
- SRI International (SRI)
- The Center for Scientific and Technological Research (ITC-irst)
- Karlsruhe University (UKA)
- The Linguistic Data Consortium (LDC)
- Laboratoire Informatique d'Avignon (LIA)
- Laboratoire d'Informatique pour la Mécanique et les Sciences de l'Ingénieur (LIMSI)
- Sheffield University
- Netherlands Organisation for Applied Scientific Research (TNO)
- Universitat Politècnica de Catalunya (UPC)
- Virginia Tech (VT)

The RT-07 evaluation made use of three test sets: Conference Meetings, Lecture Meetings, and Coffee Breaks from Lecture Meetings. The multiple test sets fostered collaboration by sharing data across programmatic boundaries while accommodating the needs of individual programs and by promoting cross-disciplinary interchange via shared corpora.

## 2 Rich Transcription 2007 Meeting Recognition Evaluation

The RT-07 evaluation was similar to previous RT evaluations except for three changes: the addition of the Speaker Attributed Speech-To-Text task, the deletion of

Speech Activity Detection (SAD) task, and the addition of Coffee Break excerpts as a new test set.

All participating teams were required to submit a single primary system on the required task-specific evaluation condition. Developers selected their primary systems based on their efforts to build their best performing system. NIST's analysis focuses on these primary systems.

The Rich Transcription Spring 2007 Evaluation plan [3] describes in detail the evaluation tasks, data sources, microphone conditions, system input and output formats, and evaluation metrics employed in the evaluation. This section summarizes the evaluation plan by discussing the test sets for the meeting sub-domains, the audio input conditions, the evaluation task definitions, and the evaluation corpora details.

## 2.1 Meeting Sub-domains and Test Sets

The meeting domain is highly variable along several dimensions. Meetings, which are verbal interactions between two or more people, range from brief informal exchanges to extremely formal proceedings with many participants following specific rules of order. However, the variability is so large that it would be impossible to build either training or testing corpora that encompasses all of these factors. Therefore, the RT evaluations have focused efforts on narrowly defined meeting sub-domains to make the problem tractable. The RT-07 evaluation material included data from two meeting sub-domains: small conference room meetings (also occasionally referred to as "board room" meetings) and interactive lectures in a small meeting room setting.

The two sub-domains represent two different participant interaction modes as well as sensor setups. The primary difference between the two sub-domains is in the group dynamics of the meetings. The first sub domain, conference meetings, consists of primarily goal-oriented, decision-making exercises and can vary from moderated meetings to group consensus-building meetings. As such, these meetings are highly interactive and multiple participants contribute to the information flow and decisions. In contrast, the second sub-domain, lecture meetings, consists of educational events where a single lecturer briefs an audience on a particular topic. While the audience occasionally participates in question and answer periods, the lecturer predominately controls the meeting.

The RT-07 evaluation included three test sets: the conference room meeting test set (*confmtg*), the lecture room meeting test set (*lectmtg*), and the coffee break (*cbreak*) test set. The *confmtg* and *lectmtg* data sets are "similar" to previous test sets because the data selection protocol did not change. The *cbreak* data consisted of excerpts selected from Lecture Meetings where the participants took a coffee break during the recording.

The recordings were sent to participants as either down-sampled, 16-bit, 16 KHz, NIST Speech Header Resources (SPHERE) files, the original 24-bit, 44.1 KHz WAV files, or headerless raw files. [12] further documents the *confmtg* data set. [11] further documents the *lectmtg* data set.

**Conference Room Meetings:** The *confmtg* test set consisted of nominally 190 minutes of meeting excerpts from eight different meetings. NIST selected 22.5 minutes

from each meeting to include in the test set. Four sites contributed two meeting recordings for eight total meetings. The four sites were Edinburgh University (EDI),
Carnegie Mellon University (CMU), the National Institute of Standards and Technology (NIST), and Virginia Tech (VT). The Linguistic Data Consortium (LDC)
transcribed the test set according to the "Meeting Data Careful Transcription Specification - V1.2" guidelines [4], [12]. Table 1 gives the salient details concerning the
*confmtg* evaluation corpus.

Each meeting recording met minimum sensor requirements. All meeting participants wore a head-mounted close talking microphone and there were at least three
table-top microphones placed between the meeting participants. The dialects were
predominately American English with the exception of the EDI meetings. In addition
to these sensors, the EDI meetings included an eight-channel circular microphone
array placed on the table between the meeting participants.

**Table 1.** Summary of Conference Room Meeting evaluation corpus

| Meeting ID | Duration (minutes) | Number of Participants | Notes |
|---|---|---|---|
| CMU_20061115-1030 | 22.5 | 4 | Discussion group |
| CMU_20061115-1530 | 22.6 | 4 | Transcription team mtg. |
| EDI_20051113-1500 | 22.6 | 4 | Remote control design |
| EDI_20051114-1500 | 22.7 | 4 | Remote control design |
| NIST_20051104_1515 | 22.4 | 4 | Planning meeting |
| NIST_20060216-1347 | 22.5 | 6 | SWOT analysis mtg. |
| VT_20050408-1500 | 22.4 | 5 | Problem solving scenario |
| VT_20050425-1000 | 22.6 | 4 | Problem solving scenario |
| Total | | 35 | |

**Lecture Room Meetings:** The *lectmtg* test set consisted of 164 minutes of lecture
meeting excerpts recorded at AIT, IBM, ITC-irst, UKA, and UPC. CMU selected and
transcribed 32, 5-minute excerpts for the test set from 20 different meeting recordings
[11]. The lectures were the CHIL "interactive lectures." The lectures involved fewer
people, 3-7 participants, and contained more interactivity than the RT-06 *lectmtg* test
set. The excerpts selected for the *lectmtg* test set were from the core of the meeting
when either the lecturer was speaking or the lecture was answering questions.

The *lectmtg* data included more audio sensors that the confmtg data. They included
four-to-six source localization arrays mounted on each of the four walls of the room,
and one or two Mark III arrays mounted near the lecturer.

**Coffee Break Meetings:** The *cbreak* test set consisted of 41 minutes of lecture
meeting excerpts recorded at AIT, IBM, ITC-irst, UKA, and UPC. CMU selected and
transcribed eight, 5-minute excerpts for the test set from eight different meeting recordings [11]. The data, which came from the same meetings as the *lectmtg* data,
consisted of the coffee break periods when the lecturer took a brief break from the
presentation and participants stood up to walk around the room and get coffee. The

CLEAR evaluation developed the *cbreak* data set as a more challenging video processing meeting data set than the typical lecture meeting videos. While the community at large wanted to build multi-modal data sets, the RT community decided the *cbreak* data did not conform to previously used *lectmtg* test sets. Therefore, the RT community decided to make the coffee break material a separate test set rather than drastically change the makeup of the RT-07 *lectmtg* test set compared to previous years.

## 2.2 Microphone Conditions

The RT-07 evaluation supported seven input conditions. They were:

- Multiple distant microphones (MDM): This evaluation condition includes the audio from at least three omni-directional microphones placed (generally on a table) between the meeting participants.
- Single distant microphone (SDM): This evaluation condition includes the audio of a single, centrally located omni-directional microphone from the set of MDM microphones. Metadata provided with the meetings supplies the information to select the microphone.
- Individual head microphone (IHM): This evaluation condition includes the audio recordings collected from a head mounted microphone positioned very closely to each participant's mouth. The microphones are typically cardioid or super cardioid microphones and therefore of the best quality signal for each speaker. Since the IHM condition is a contrastive condition, systems can also use any of the microphones used for the MDM condition.
- Individual head microphone plus reference segmentation (IHM+REFSEG): This evaluation condition used the IHM audio and reference speech/non-speech segmentations. This evaluation condition is a laboratory control condition. The intent of the IHM condition was to provide clean, near field speech. However, the IHM recordings can at times include a significant amount of cross talk that requires significant effort to ameliorate. This condition provides developers with the opportunity to process clean, near field speech without the need to implement cross talk rejection.
- Multiple Mark III microphone arrays (MM3A): This evaluation condition includes audio from all the collected Mark III microphone arrays. A Mark III microphone arrays is a 64-channel, linear topology, digital microphone array [18]. The lecture domain data contains the data from each channel of one or two Mark-III microphone array per meeting.
- Multiple source localization microphone arrays (MSLA): This evaluation condition includes the audio from all the CHIL source localization arrays (SLA). An SLA is a 4-element digital microphone array arranged in an upside down 'T' topology. The lecture domain data includes four or six SLAs mounted on the walls of the room.
- All distant microphones (ADM): This evaluation conditions permits the use of all distant microphones for each meeting. This condition differs from the MDM condition in that the microphones are not restricted to the centrally located microphones but rather all microphones including the Mark III arrays and Source Localization arrays.

The troika of MDM, SDM, and IHM audio input conditions makes a very powerful set of experimental controls for black box evaluations. The MDM condition provides a venue for the demonstration of multi-microphone input processing techniques. It lends itself to experimenting with beamforming and noise abatement techniques to address room acoustic issues. The SDM input condition provides a control condition for testing the effectiveness of multi-microphone techniques. The IHM condition provides two important contrasts: first, it reduces the effects of room acoustics, background noise, and most simultaneous speech, and second it is most similar to the Conversational Telephone Speech (CTS) domain [1] and may be compared to results in comparable CTS evaluations.

## 2.3 Evaluation Tasks

The RT-07 evaluation supported three evaluation tasks: the Speech-To-Text transcription task, the "Who Spoke When" Diarization Task, and the Speaker Attributed Speech-To-Text task. The following is a brief description of each of the evaluation tasks:

**Speech-To-Text (STT) Transcription:** STT systems output a transcript containing all of the words spoken by the meeting participants. For each word recognized by the system, the system outputs the word's orthography along with the word's start/end times and confidence score. For this task, the system outputs a single stream of words since no speaker designation is required.

The primary metric is Word Error Rate (WER). WER is the sum of transcription errors, (word substitutions, deletions, and insertions) divided by the number of reference words, and expressed as a percentage. It is an error metric, so lower scores indicate better performance. The score for perfect performance is zero. WER scores can exceed one hundred percent since the metric includes insertion errors.

The scoring process consists of three steps: transcript normalization, segment group chunking to reduce alignment computations, and word alignment.

The process for text normalization includes many steps including spelling variant normalization, contraction expansion, optional words, etc. See the evaluation plan for a detailed enumeration of the text normalizations.

The segment group chunking splits a recording into independent units for alignment based on reference speaker segment times. Figure 1 is an example of segment group chunking which shows four segment groups. The number of active speakers in a segment group defines the "Overlap Factor" (OV) of the segment group. The overlap factor is not a measure of absolute speaker overlap (e.g., by time); rather it is a method for counting the dimensions necessary to compute a word alignment. Segment group chunking is consistent across systems; therefore, segment groups provide an effective way to bound computation and score subsets of the recordings consistently across systems. The final step in segment group chunking is to collect the system words whose time midpoints are within the span of a segment group. Each segment group along with the system output words assigned to it form an independent unit for the alignment engine.

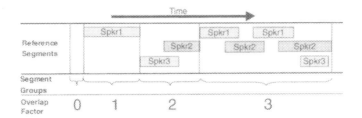

**Fig. 1.** Example segment group chunking analysis

The final scoring step is to align the references and the system output in order to count errors. An alignment is a one-to-one mapping between system and reference words that minimizes the edit distance to convert the system transcript into the reference transcript. NIST used the multi-dimensional, Dynamic Programming solution to sequence alignment found in the ASCLITE tool [8] of the SCTK package [5] to perform the alignment and scoring. The alignments are computationally expensive, $O(N^{\#S+\#R})$ where $N$ is the number of words per speaker, $\#S$ is the number of system speakers, and $\#R$ is the number of reference speakers. The STT systems do not differentiate speakers therefore $\#S$ for the STT task is 1. To reduce the computational burden, several techniques discussed in [8] minimize the computational requirements.

The MDM audio input condition was the primary evaluation condition for the STT task for all test sets. The results reported for all distant microphone conditions include segment groups with up to and including overlap factor 4 ($WER_{(OV\leq4)}$). Standardizing on OV≤4 was empirically determined to be a reasonable cutoff balancing evaluated material vs. the required computational resources for alignment.

**Diarization "Who Spoke When" (SPKR):** SPKR systems annotate a meeting with regions of time indicating when each meeting participant is speaking and clustering the regions by speaker. It is a clustering task as opposed to an identification task since the system is not required to output a speaker name or identify each speaker from a gallery – only a generic id that is unique within the processed meeting excerpt.

The Diarization Error Rate (DER) is the primary metric. DER is the ratio of incorrectly attributed speech time, (falsely detected speech, missed detections of speech, and incorrectly clustered speech) to the total amount of speech time, expressed as a percentage. As with WER, a score of zero indicates perfect performance and higher scores indicate poorer performance.

Incorrectly clustered speech, a speaker error, occurs when a system successfully detects speech but attributes the speech to the wrong speaker. Since the system generates its own clusters and there is no a priori connection between the system and reference speaker clusters, correct speaker attribution is determined by finding a minimal cost, one-to-one mapping between the system speaker clusters and reference speaker clusters using the Hungarian solution to a bipartite graph [16]. This "speaker mapping" is the basis for determining which system speaker is correct – the mapped system/reference speakers are correct.

Preparing reference segment boundaries for the evaluation is an inherently difficult human annotation task because of the ambiguities in pinpointing speech boundaries. Ambiguities include time padding for segment-initial plosives, differentiating independent adjacent segments and single segments, and others. Instead of building arbitrary rules for annotators to follow, the evaluation infrastructure accommodates the variability with three techniques. First, the evaluation tool does not score system performance within 0.25 seconds of each reference segment boundary. This "no score" collar minimizes the amount of DER error due to segment boundary inconsistencies. Second, adjacent reference segments are merged if they are within 0.3 second of each other. Although somewhat arbitrary, 0.3 seconds was empirically determined to be a good approximation of the minimum duration for a pause in speech resulting in an utterance boundary. Finally, the process for constructing the reference segments changed for RT-07. Instead of relying on human segmentations, the reference segment times were derived from automatically computed word occurrence times. NIST used the LIMSI speech recognition tools to align the reference transcript to the speech signals thus generating the word time locations. Using these "forced word alignments," construction of the reference segments consisted of converting each word into a segment and then smoothing the segments with the 0.3 second smoothing parameter.

The MDM audio input condition was the primary evaluation condition for the SPKR task for a test sets.

**Speaker Attributed Speech-To-Text (SASTT):** SASTT systems output a transcript containing all of the words spoken during a meeting and attributing each word to a single speaker. The SASTT task is a joint technology development task that combines both Diarization "Who Spoke When" and Speech-To-Text technologies into a single task.

Speaker Attributed Word Error Rate (SWER) is the primary evaluation metric. SWER is the sum of transcription errors, (word substitutions, word deletions, word insertions, and speaker substitutions) divided by the number of reference words, and expressed as a percentage. WER and SWER are closely related – SWER has an additional error type, "speaker substitutions" (SpSub). Speaker substitutions are correctly recognized words attributed to the incorrect speaker. SWER is an error metric, so lowers scores indicate better performance. The score for perfect performance is zero. SWER scores can exceed one hundred percent since the metric includes insertion errors.

The SASTT scoring process, which is very similar to the STT scoring process, consists of four steps: transcript normalization, speaker mapping, segment group chunking, and word alignment. The transcript normalization and segment group chunking steps are identical to the processes used for STT scoring. The speaker mapping step is an additional step for SASTT scoring and the word alignment process is slightly different for SASTT scoring.

As stated prpeviously, SASTT systems must accurately attribute each word to a speaker. The SASTT scorer uses the SPKR evaluation tool to generate a system-to-reference speaker-mapping list that serves as the definition of a correct speaker: the correct reference speaker for a system speaker is the reference speaker mapped to it. The word alignment process uses the speaker correctness information to determine when speaker substitutions occur. We used ASCLITE's [8] Multiple System Stream-to-Multiple Reference Stream alignment capabilities to compute the word alignments.

Like the STT evaluation, the MDM audio input condition is the required condition. Unlike STT, however, the results reported for all distant microphone conditions include segment groups with up to and including overlap factor 3 (OV≤3). The additional computation burden proved too great to compute overlap factor 4 in reasonable time and with complete coverage. This is because the number of number of system speakers in a segment group can be greater than one. As an example, overlap factor 4 scoring for the AMI SASTT system would require 272 TB of memory search space to complete.

## 3   Results of the RT-07 Evaluation

### 3.1   RT-07 Evaluation Participants

The following table lists the RT-07 participants and the evaluation tasks for which they built systems.

**Table 2.** Summary of evaluation participants and the tasks for which systems were submitted

| Site ID | Site Name | Evaluation Task | | |
|---|---|---|---|---|
| | | SPKR | STT | SASTT |
| AMI | Augmented Multiparty Interaction with Distance Access | X | X | X |
| I2R/NTU | Infocomm Research Site and Nanyang Technological University | X | | |
| IBM | IBM | X | X | X |
| ICSI | International Computer Science Institute | X | | |
| LIA | Laboratoire Informatique d'Avignon | X | | |
| LIMSI | Laboratoire d'Informatique pour la Mécanique et les Sciences de l'Ingénieur | X | | X |
| SRI/ICSI | International Computer Science Institute and SRI International | | X | X |
| UKA | Karlsruhe University (UKA) | | X | |
| UPC | Universitat Politècnica de Catalunya | X | | |

### 3.2   Speech-to-Text (STT) Results

Four sites participated in the STT task: AMI, IBM, SRI/ICSI, and UKA. Figure 2 contains the results of all primary systems.

The WER$_{(OV\leq4)}$s for the MDM audio input condition for the *confmtg* data were 45.6 % and 40.6 % for AMI and SRI/ICSI respectively. The coverage of scoreable meetings for segment groups with OV≤4 was 99.3 %. The differences are significant at the 95 % confidence level using the Matched Pairs Sentence-Segment Word Error (MAPSSWE) test [17].

The WER$_{(OV\leq4)}$s for the MDM audio input condition on the *lectmtg* data were 51.0 %, 49.8 %, and 58.4 % for IBM, SRI/ICSI, and UKA respectively. The coverage of scoreable meetings for segment groups with OV≤4 was 99.6%. All differences are significant according to the MAPSSWE test.

Only SRI/ICSI submitted outputs for the *cbreak* data. Their WER$_{(OV\leq4)}$s for the MDM condition was 48.4, which was 2.8 % (relative) lower than their WER for the *lectmtg* data. While the error rate was lower for the *cbreak* data, it was not a significant different based a 2-Sample T-Test at the 95 % confidence level.

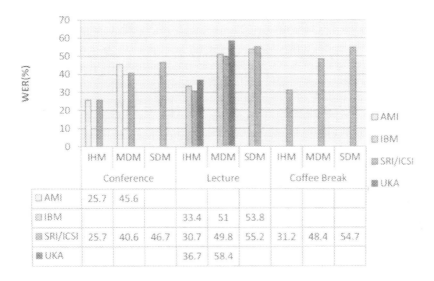

**Fig. 2.** WERs for primary STT systems across test sets and audio input conditions. Overlap Factor 4 and less included in distant microphone conditions.[1]

Figure 3 plots the historical error rates for the MDM and IHM conditions in both domains. For the *confmtg* data, the MDM error rate was 12 % lower than the same condition for '06, but the IHM error rate was 6% higher. For the *lectmtg* data, the MDM error rates dropped 7 % relative while the IHM error rate had no change. Figure 4 sets the *confmtg* '07 results in the context of previous NIST STT evaluations. As evident from the graph, the meeting domain continues to be the most difficult actively researched domain for STT systems.

---

[1] All of SRI/ICSI's submissions were late accept their submissions for the IHM conditions.

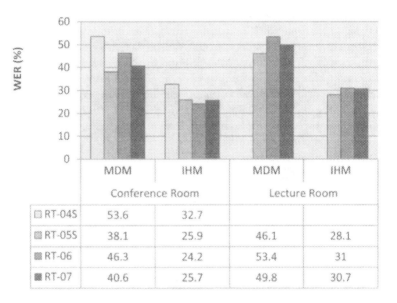

| | MDM | IHM | MDM | IHM |
|---|---|---|---|---|
| | Conference Room | | Lecture Room | |
| ☐ RT-04S | 53.6 | 32.7 | | |
| ▨ RT-05S | 38.1 | 25.9 | 46.1 | 28.1 |
| ▩ RT-06 | 46.3 | 24.2 | 53.4 | 31 |
| ▉ RT-07 | 40.6 | 25.7 | 49.8 | 30.7 |

**Fig. 3.** WERs for the best STT systems from RT-04S through RT-06S. MDM results are for segment groups with OV≤4 while the IHM results include all speech.

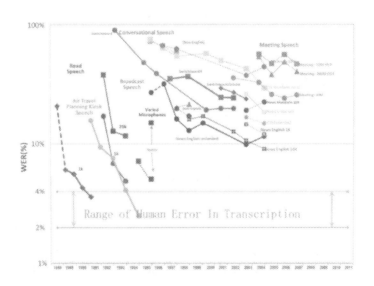

**Fig. 4.** STT Benchmark Test History 1988-2007

## 3.3 Diarization "Who Spoke When" (SPKR) Results

Eight sites participated in the SPKR task: AMDA, I2R, IBM, ICSI, LIA, LIMSI, NTU, and UPC. I2R and NTU collaborated to build a single system. All participants except IBM submitted *confmtg* systems. IBM, LIA, and LIMSI submitted *lectmtg* systems. Figure 5 contains the results of all primary systems. The lowest MDM DERs were 8.5%, and 25.8% for the *confmtg* and *lectmtg* test sets respectively.

The *lectmtg* scores for most systems at the same performance level as the previous year's, however, the 8.5% DER achieved by ICSI is very low. It is half of the closest system and a roughly a third of the rest of the systems. Further, Figure 5 the contains lowest error rate for each of the previous evaluations and shows the result was 76% relative lower than last year's best system.

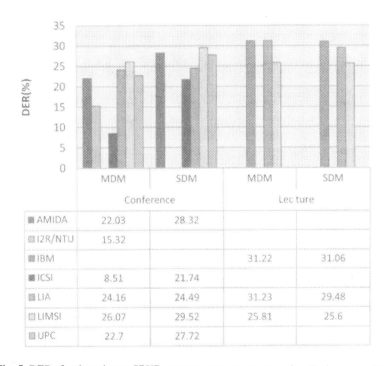

**Fig. 5.** DERs for the primary SPKR systems across test sets and audio input conditions

Extensive discussions of the ICSI *confmtg* results occurred during the workshop. Table 3 compares the performance of the primary *confmtg* systems for differentiating speech vs. non-speech and for the system's ability to cluster speakers.

To evaluate speech/non-speech detection, we scored each SPKR submission as if it were a Speech Activity Detection (SAD) system as defined for the RT-06 SAD evaluation methodology [10]. To evaluate the system's ability cluster speakers, we computed both the average number of system speakers per meeting and the number of meetings with the correct number of speakers. The ICSI system had the second lowest SAD DER score of 3.33% with LIMSI having the lowest at 3.23%. The actual average number of speakers for the *confmtg* test set is 4.4. Six of the eight meetings had 4 speakers, one meeting had 5 speakers, and one meeting had 6 speakers. ICSI had nearly the right average and they correctly predicted the number of speakers in 7 of

**Table 3.** Primary SPKR system performance comparing DET to speech activity detection and speaker count prediction

| Site ID | SPKR DER | SAD DER | Avg. Nbr. Sys. Speakers | Mtgs. With Correct Nbr. Speakers |
|---------|----------|---------|-------------------------|----------------------------------|
| ICSI    | 8.51     | 3.33    | 4.5                     | 87.5%                            |
| I2R/NTU | 15.32    | 8.65    | 4.4                     | 75.0%                            |
| UPC     | 22.70    | 5.39    | 3.9                     | 25.0%                            |
| LIA     | 24.16    | 3.69    | 4.9                     | 12.5%                            |
| LIMSI   | 26.07    | 3.23    | 12.3                    | 12.5%                            |
| AMIDA   | 22.03    | 6.73    | 7.1                     | 0%                               |

the 8 meetings. The combination of good SAD performance and accurate clustering led to ICSI's low overall SPKR DER performance. Other sites did well at one of the aspects, but not both.

The selection protocol for *confmtg* test sets will change in future evaluations. The lack of variability in the number of speakers per test excerpt is not adequately testing the SPKR systems. Next year there will be more excerpts to improve the statistical reliability of the performance estimates. Additionally, next year there will be a wider variety in the number of speakers per excerpt to test the system's ability to predict the correct number of speakers over a broader range of meeting participants.

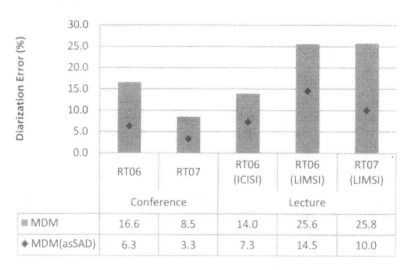

**Fig. 6.** DERs for the best MDM SPKR systems from RT-06 and RT-07 scored against forced alignment mediated references

Figure 5 contains the historical lowest error rates for each year when scored against forced alignment mediated references. As mentioned earlier, the SPKR error rates for the *confmtg* data dropped. The SPKR DER for the *lectmtg* data remained flat when comparing this year's LIMSI system to last year's LIMSI system. However, the LIMSI SAD DER was lower in '07.

Only LIA submitted SPKR results for the Coffee Break data. The DER for their primary, MDM audio condition system on *cbreak* data was 25.5% compared to 31.2% for the same system on the *lectmtg* data. The SAD scores for the LIA system were 7.38 and 9.34 for the *cbreak* and *lectmtg* data respectively. While the error rates for the *cbreak* data are lower, the average SPKR DER by meeting excerpt are not statistically different at the 95% confidence level using a 2-sample T-Test.

### 3.4 Speaker Attributed Speech-to-Text (SASTT) Results

Five sites participated in the Speaker Attributed Speech-To-Text task: AMI, IBM, LIMSI, SRI/ICSI, and UKA. Figure 6 contains the results of all primary systems on the *cbreak*, *confmtg*, and *lectmtg* data for segment groups with OV≤3.

SRI/ICSI had the lowest SWER$_{(OV≤3)}$ of 40.3 % on the *confmtg* data which was statistically different, according to the MAPSSWE test, than AMI's 54.2 %. The coverage of scoreable meetings for segment groups with OV≤3 was 84.5 %.

IBM had the lowest SWER$_{(OV≤3)}$ of 59.3 % on the *lectmtg* data which was not statistically different, according to the MAPSSWE test, than SRI/ICSI's 60.0 %. The rest of the inter-system comparisons on the lecture data were statistically different according to the MAPSSWE test. The coverage of scoreable meetings for segment groups with OV≤3 was 97 %.

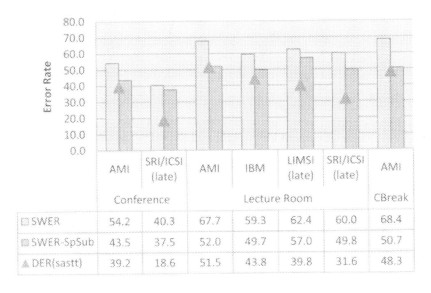

| | AMI | SRI/ICSI (late) | AMI | IBM | LIMSI (late) | SRI/ICSI (late) | AMI |
|---|---|---|---|---|---|---|---|
| | Conference | | Lecture Room | | | | CBreak |
| ☐ SWER | 54.2 | 40.3 | 67.7 | 59.3 | 62.4 | 60.0 | 68.4 |
| ▨ SWER-SpSub | 43.5 | 37.5 | 52.0 | 49.7 | 57.0 | 49.8 | 50.7 |
| ▲ DER(sastt) | 39.2 | 18.6 | 51.5 | 43.8 | 39.8 | 31.6 | 48.3 |

**Fig. 7.** RT-07 Primary SASTT system performance on the MDM condition scored without speaker substitutions and as diarization systems

AMI was the only participant to run their system on the *cbreak* data and achieved a 68.4 % SWER$_{(OV≤3)}$.

The novel aspect of the SASTT task is to combine speaker diarization and STT systems. Figure 6 presents two data points in order to separate the errors due to diarization. The SWER-SpSub bar is the SWER minus the Speaker Substitution rate. The distance between the height of SWER and SWER-SpSub bars indicates the affect of speaker diarization errors on system performance. The second data point is DER(sastt) which is the diarization error using inferred speaker segment boundaries from the SASTT system output[2]. $DER_{(sastt)}$ is not equivalent to the DER for SPKR systems, but it does correlate with Speaker Substitution errors. The notable exception is the LIMSI system where their SpSub errors were relatively low given their high $DER_{(sastt)}$: this is because a large component of the LIMSI's diarization system DER is speech activity detection rather than speaker identification.

This initial evaluation of SASTT systems was a success in that developers built combined systems and the evaluation infrastructure was able to evaluate their performance. Unfortunately, none of the fielded SASTT systems for the 2007 evaluation jointly optimized their STT and SPKR systems, so one would expect future research to include joint optimization to improve error rates.

## 4 Conclusions and Future Evaluations

The 5th RT evaluation occurred during the 1st half of 2007. In order to promote multimodal research, the RT and CLEAR evaluations shared development/evaluation corpora and collocated their evaluation workshops.

The evaluation included three evaluation tasks: Speech-To-Text, Speaker Diarization, and Speaker Attributed Speech-To-Text.

The WERs for the STT task continue to be higher than the WERs for previous Conversational Telephone Speech evaluations by 25 % relative.

The ICSI SPKR team achieved 8.5 % DER on the *confmtg* test set which was 76 % lower than last year's best system. The ICSI system both detected speech accurately and clustered speakers accurately.

This was the first RT evaluation to include the SASTT task. Four out of five STT sites submitted systems for the SASTT tasks. The lowest speaker attributed word error rates for segment groups with OV≤4 for the MDM condition were 40.3 %, 59.3 %, and 68.4 % for the *confmtg*, *lectmtg*, and *cbreak* test sets respectively with relative increases in error of 7.7 %, 17.6 %, and 41.6 % respectively over comparable STT systems.

The Rich Transcription 2008 Evaluation will occur during the Fall of 2008. The SASTT task will likely remain as a task for the next evaluation since the implementation of the evaluation task was successful and there is enthusiasm within the community to continue to work on the task. The selection strategy for the *confmtg* test data will change for the next evaluation to include a wider variety of speaker speech durations and the number of active speakers within each excerpt.

## Acknowledgements

NIST would like to thank AIT, EDI, CMU, IBM, ITC, VT, UKA, TNO, and UPC for donating meeting recordings to the evaluation. Special thanks go to CMU and LDC for preparing reference transcriptions and annotations.

---

[2] The inferred boundaries were generated automatically by converting each recognized word to a speaker segment, then smoothing the segments with the 0.3 second smoothing parameter.

# 5  Disclaimer

These tests are designed for local implementation by each participant. The reported results are not to be construed, or represented, as endorsements of any participant's system, or as official findings on the part of NIST or the U. S. Government. Certain commercial products may be identified in order to adequately specify or describe the subject matter of this work. In no case does such identification imply recommendation or endorsement by NIST, nor does it imply that the products identified are necessarily the best available for the purpose.

# References

1. Fiscus, et al.: Results of the Fall 2004 STT and MDE Evaluation. In: RT-2004F Evaluation Workshop Proceedings, November 7-10 (2004)
2. Garofolo, et al.: The Rich Transcription 2004 Spring Meeting Recognition Evaluation. In: ICASSP 2004 Meeting Recognition Workshop, May 17 (2004)
3. The (RT-07) Rich Transcription Meeting Recognition Evaluation Plan (2007), http://www.nist.gov/speech/tests/rt/rt2007
4. LDC Meeting Recording Transcription, http://www.ldc.upenn.edu/Projects/Transcription/NISTMeet
5. SCTK toolkit, http://www.nist.gov/speech/tools/index.htm
6. Garofolo, J.S., Fiscus, J.G., Radde, N., Le, A., Ajot, J., Laprun, C.: The Rich Transcription 2005 Spring Meeting Recognition Evaluation. In: Renals, S., Bengio, S. (eds.) MLMI 2005. LNCS, vol. 3869, pp. 369–389. Springer, Heidelberg (2006)
7. http://www.clear-evaluation.org/
8. Fiscus, et al.: Multiple Dimension Levenshtein Distance Calculations for Evaluating Automatic Speech Recognition Systems During Simultaneous Speech. In: LREC 2006: Sixth International Conference on Language Resources and Evaluation (2006)
9. http://isl.ira.uka.de/clear06/downloads/ClearEval_Protocol_v5.pdf
10. Fiscus, J., Ajot, J., Michel, M., Garofolo, J.: The Rich Transcription 2006 Spring Meeting Recognition Evaluation. In: Renals, S., Bengio, S., Fiscus, J.G. (eds.) MLMI 2006. LNCS, vol. 4299, Springer, Heidelberg (2006)
11. Burger, S.: The CHIL RT07 Evaluation Data. In: The Joint Proceedings of the 2006 CLEAR and RT Evaluations (May 2007)
12. Lammie Glenn, M., Strassel, S.: Shared Linguistic Resources for the Meeting Domain. In: The Joint Proceedings of the 2006 CLEAR and RT Evaluations (May 2007)
13. Wooters, C., Fung, J., Peskin, B., Anguera, X.: Towards Robust Speaker Segmentation: The ICSI-SRI Fall 2004 Diarization System. In: RT-2004F Workshop (November 2004)
14. Stiefelhagen, R., Bernardin, K., Bowers, R., Garofolo, J., Mostefa, D., Soundararajan, P.: The CLEAR 2006 Evaluation, Proceedings of the first International CLEAR Evaluation Workshop. In: Stiefelhagen, R., Garofolo, J.S. (eds.) CLEAR 2006. LNCS, vol. 4122, pp. 1–45. Springer, Heidelberg (2007)
15. StainStiefelhagen, R., Bowers, R., Rose, R.: Results of the CLEAR 2007 Evaluation. In: The Joint Proceedings of the 2006 CLEAR and RT Evaluations (May 2007)
16. http://www.nist.gov/dads/HTML/HungarianAlgorithm.html
17. http://www.nist.gov/speech/tests/sigtests/mapsswe.htm
18. Stanford, V.: The NIST Mark-III microphone array - infrastructure, reference data, and metrics. In: Proceedings International Workshop on Microphone Array Systems - Theory and Practice, Pommersfelden, Germany (2003)

# The CHIL RT07 Evaluation Data

Susanne Burger

interACT, Carnegie Mellon University
407 South Craig Street, Pittsburgh 15213, USA
sburger@cs.cmu.edu
http://www.is.cs.cmu.edu

**Abstract.** This paper describes the CHIL 2007 evaluation data set provided for the Rich Transcription 2007 Meeting Recognition Evaluation
(RT07) in terms of recording setup, scenario, speaker demagogic and
transcription process. The corpus consists of 25 interactive seminars
recorded at five different recording sites in Europe and the United States
in multi-sensory smart rooms. We compare speakers' talk-time ratios in
the interactive seminars with lecture data and multi-party meeting data.
We show that the length of individual speaker's contributions helps to
position interactive seminars between lectures and meetings in terms of
speaker interactivity. We also study the differences between the manual
transcription of narrow-field and far-field audio recording.

**Keywords:** multi-modal, data collection, transcription, meetings, interactive seminars.

## 1 Introduction

For several years researchers have been interested in different aspects of how
participants in multi-party meetings interact with each other. This has continuously led to the creation of large-scaled research programs, projects and international evaluations of technologies around this topic. One of the recent projects is
CHIL - Computers in the Human Interaction Loop [1], an Integrated Project (IP
506909) under the European Commission's Sixth Framework Programme. CHIL
started in January 2004 and will finish its work in August 2007. 15 partners from
nine countries are jointly coordinated by the Universität Karlsruhe (TH), Germany and the Fraunhofer Institute IITB, Germany. Based on the understanding
of human perception, CHIL computers are enabled to provide helpful assistance
implicitly, requiring minimal human attention or interruptions. To serve development and evaluation of the CHIL technologies, multi-sensory audiovisual lecture
and seminar data was recorded inside smart rooms (CHIL rooms) at five different
CHIL partner sites located in Europe and the United States.

In 2005 CHIL partners started to participate in NIST's rich transcription
(RT) [2] and multi-modal evaluations such as CLEAR [3]. NIST extended their
test and training data sets from multi-party meetings (conference room scenario)
to lecture type data (lecture room scenario) to accommodate new evaluations
such as speaker activity detection and source localization. The basic differences

R. Stiefelhagen et al. (Eds.): CLEAR 2007 and RT 2007, LNCS 4625, pp. 390–400, 2008.
© Springer-Verlag Berlin Heidelberg 2008

between lecture and conference room data are the number and setting of meeting participants, their interactivity and the addition of far-field microphone arrays and extensive usage of video in the lecture data collection.

CHIL contributed a development and test data set to the Rich Transcription 2007 Meeting Recognition Evaluation (RT07) which consists of 25 seminars recorded in 2006 [4], five seminars per recording site. These seminars are supposedly more interactive than the lecture room data CHIL contributed to previous evaluations. This paper describes in a brief summary the technical setup and the situation in which participants were recorded. The following sections report on speaker demagogies, transcription and how test set segments were picked from the recorded episodes. Finally, we compare the ratio of speaker's talk-time in the interactive seminars with the ratios of other lecture- and meeting-type data and show the differences between far-field and narrow-field transcription.

## 2   The CHIL Rooms

The CHIL 2006 seminars [4] were recorded in smart seminar rooms, called CHIL rooms (see also figure 1). These are seminar rooms which provide multiple recording sensors, audio as well as video. There are five different recording sites with completely equipped CHIL rooms:

- AIT: Research and Education Society in Information Technologies at Athens Information Technology, Athens, Greece
- IBM: IBM T.J. Watson Research Center, Yorktown Heights, USA
- ITC-irst: Centro per la ricerca scientifica e technologica at the Instituto Trentino di Cultura, Trento, Italy
- UKA: Interactive Systems Labs of the Universität Karlsruhe, Germany
- UPC: Universitat Politècnica de Catalunya, Barcelona, Spain

Having different sites in multiple countries benefited the variability in the collected data due to the different sizes of the rooms, layouts and light features. In particular, the site variability supplied a range of European English such as British English, American English and and a range of English with foreign accents from all over the world. To ensure a homogeneous technical recording quality, each site equipped its room with a minimum base-set of conformed and identical hardware and software.

### 2.1   Sensor Setup

The minimum video equipment required in a CHIL room includes four fixed corner cameras, a panoramic camera on the table and at least one pan-tilt-zoom (PTZ) camera.

The minimum setup for audio recording comprises far-field and narrow-field sensors. The far-field (FF) data is collected through at least one NIST Mark III microphone array (developed by NIST) [5], which consists of 64 small microphones in a row, and is mounted on the smart room's wall. The Mark III channels

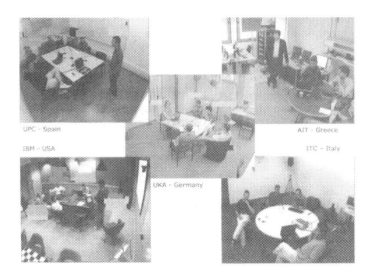

**Fig. 1.** Single-camera views recorded at the five CHIL rooms during interactive seminars

are recorded in SPHERE format via an Ethernet connection to a recording computer in the form of multiplexed IP packages.

A minimum of three T-shaped four-channel microphone arrays are mounted on the room's walls. At least three table top microphones are placed on the meeting table, distributed an appropriate distance from each other.

The narrow-field audio data is collected through close-talking microphones (CTM). The presenter wears a wireless microphone because presenters tend to stay standing and move around more frequently. The basic setup for the other participants consists of one close-talking microphone per participant, wireless if possible. In comparison, the CHIL lectures recorded in previous years had contributions from speakers from the audience which were only picked up by far-field microphones.

The T-shaped arrays, the table top microphones and all CTMs are amplified by RME Octamic 8 channel amplifiers and are recorded via Hammerfall HDSP9652 I/O sound cards. All audio recordings, including the Mark III array channels, were sampled in 44 khz, 28 bits.

As an example for a completely equipped CHIL room, figure 2 shows a sketch of the IBM CHIL room. IBM uses two Mark III arrays, four T-shaped arrays, and three table top microphones.

## 3    Interactive Seminars

The seminars recorded in 2006 are *interactive seminars*: three to five participants sit around a seminar table while one person presents research work. The other

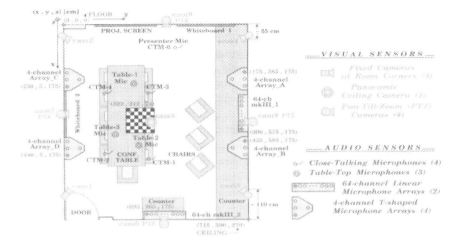

**Fig. 2.** Sketch of the IBM CHIL room

participants may interrupt at any time, ask questions, make comments, give suggestions. This frequently leads to real discussions and meeting-type conversation resulting in frequent interaction between the participants. On the contrary, the CHIL lectures recorded in previous years provided less opportunity for discussion or casual conversation.

The term *scripted* is often used in relation to acted scenarios, where participants' contributions are from following scripts, certain actions are predefined or where participants act in pre-given roles. The CHIL seminars are real seminars which were scheduled without the purpose of data collection. Speaker's contributions occurred naturally and spontaneously. However, to support the evaluation and the development of the multiple CHIL technologies, participants were asked to produce acoustic events from a given list, for example, door slam, chair moving, applause, laugh, cough, keyboard typing. In most of the seminars, a participant would receive a cell phone call. Individuals would come late to the seminar or leave early. There would be a short coffee break in the middle of the seminar. Not all of these extra features were recorded in each seminar. Unexpectedly, these artificially included events elicited spontaneous reactions and contributions of the participant and added humorous scenes. These in turn enriched the naturalness of the data instead of constraining it.

## 4   Speakers

71 individuals spoke in the CHIL seminars. Unfortunately, only five of them are female. The speakers originate from all over the world, mainly from Europe. All of them speak English, most of them with a foreign accent, with the biggest groups being Spaniards (23%), Italians (15%), and Greeks and Germans (each 14%). All sites had visitors, foreign colleagues or students participating in their

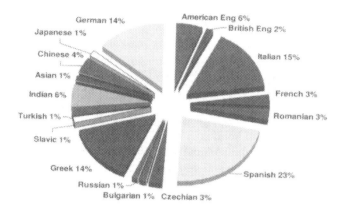

**Fig. 3.** Speaker accents: Distribution of countries of origin in the CHIL RT07 development-set and test-set

recordings so that there is a total of 17 countries represented. Figure 3 shows the distribution of the speakers' countries of origin for the CHIL RT07 test- and development set speakers.

## 5   Transcription

The manual transcription of the speech in the audio recordings was done at Carnegie Mellon University. Transcribers started by transcribing all channels of the close-talking microphones on word level in ISL style (e.g. including labels for vocal noises such as laughter, coughing and filled pauses, tags for word breaks, neologisms, repetitions and corrections). The speaker contributions were manually segmented into talk spurts. In [9], talk spurts have been defined as "speech regions uninterrupted by pauses longer than 500 ms" . The CHIL reference segmentation used a minimum threshold of inter-spurt duration of 300 ms. This value has recently been adapted for the purpose of building speech activity detection references in the NIST RT evaluations.

The transcription of the far-field condition was based on one of the tabletop microphone recordings, usually the most centered microphone or the table microphone channel with the best audio quality. Since a significant portion of the transcription remains the same in both conditions, transcribers adapted the narrow-field transcription to what they perceived from the far-field channel. Changes include removing speaker contributions which were not picked up by the table microphone. Very softly spoken utterances or voiceless laughter which frequently was not audible at all in the far-field recording was also removed. Mumbled utterances or those interfering with noise or speaker overlap were substituted with the label for non-identifiable. In the cases where transcribers could barely recognize a word, they transcribed their best guess and marked the word as hard-to-identify. Contributions or details which were only audible through the table microphone were inserted in the transcription. These were the rare instances where participants had removed their close-talking microphones to leave or to get coffee. Sometimes the CTM recording was too clipped, had technical problems or interfered with another sound source and thus could not be transcribed in the narrow-field condition.

Transcribers used the annotation tool TransEdit[1], a tool developed in-house for multi-channel meeting transcription. It is easy and intuitive to use, independent of the user's education. It focuses on support and convenience for the sole purpose of the transcription and segmentation of speech. It displays all audio channels in parallel which is very helpful when listening to interactive multi-channel conversations. The parallel view also allows the comparison of audio recordings in different qualities.

TransEdit transcriptions result in two annotation files: the actual transcription and the segments' time stamps in sample point values. These files were converted and combined into the NIST STM format. The following section shows a short excerpt of a narrow-field transcription of a CHIL seminar in STM format:

```
...
ait_20060728_ctm ctm_3 ait_20060728_ctm-ait_004 269.69 273.335 <o,male>
so I should sell +/all/+ <uh> all my property in Crete ?
ait_20060728_ctm ctm_1 inter_segment_gap 269.947 273.022 <o,>
ait_20060728_ctm ctm_1 ait_20060728_ctm-ait_005 273.022 277.697 <o,male>
no . <P> build it so that it becomes the basis for knowledge-based
applications .
ait_20060728_ctm ctm_3 inter_segment_gap 273.335 276.206 <o,>
ait_20060728_ctm ctm_3 ait_20060728_ctm-ait_004 276.206 279.724 <o,male>
so% +/I will/+ I will put some *smartness in my olive trees
ait_20060728_ctm ctm_1 inter_segment_gap 277.697 279.825 <o,>
ait_20060728_ctm ctm_4 ait_20060728_ctm-ait_003 279.623 280.631 <o,male>
<Laugh>
...
```

## 6 Evaluation Data Selection

For evaluation purposes, the transcribed data was separated into development-set data and test-set data. The development-set contains a total of 2 hours 45 minutes of recording. It comprises five complete seminars, each recorded by one of the five CHIL room sites. The average duration of a seminar is 33 minutes. Four to five participants spoke at each seminar. The development-set includes 6,656 talk spurt segments, 44,300 word tokens and 2,729 unique word types. 10% of the word types are proper names.

The test-set consists of 40 seminar segments of approximately five minutes each. These segments were selected from the remaining 20 seminars; each of the five recording sites collected four of them. To provide a balanced assortment of the different sections of the seminars, the colleagues of the Universität Karlsruhe developed a system which chooses segments of

---

[1] TransEdit is available for research purposes by sending email to sburger@cs.cmu.edu

- the beginning of a seminar (including the arrival of the participants, welcoming, introduction),
- the actual talk or presentation (including other participants' questions and comments),
- the coffee break or any other section of casual conversation,
- the question and answer part or discussion part at the end of a presentation,
- the end of the seminar (including closing, planning, good-bye, departure of the participants).

Each of the categories was represented at least one time per site and in similar distribution over all sites. The total duration of the test-set is 3 hours 25 minutes. The set consists of 11,794 talk spurts, 56,196 word tokens and 2,870 unique word types. 9.5% of the word types are proper names.

The participants of the RT07 evaluation used development and test-set data of the RT04 and RT05 evaluations as training data for their systems.

## 7   Speaker Talk-Time Ratios

The *talk-time* [6] of a speaker is the total duration of all segmented talk spurts. This includes speech pauses shorter that 300 ms and vocal noises. The ratio of the talk-time of individual speakers during a meeting describes who dominated the meeting in terms of talking for the longest period of time. It also represents how the talk-time was distributed between the participants. The talk-time is calculated as percentage of the total duration of the meeting per individual speaker. A total of all speakers' talk-time will most likely not sum up to 100% because speakers' contributions overlap frequently. The possible pauses between contributions also add to the total duration of a meeting.

To prove that the new interactive CHIL seminars have more interaction between the participants than the previous lecture recordings, we compared speakers' talk-time ratios of the CHIL development- and test-sets with other lecture and multi-party meeting corpora. We looked at six ISL lectures (a total of 6 hours 38 minutes recording), 18 ISL student presentations (8 hours 47 minutes), 27 ISL conference talks (15 hours 45 minutes), 19 meetings of the ISL meeting corpus (10 hours 13 minutes, [7] and [8]) and 28 five-minute segments of 14 of the CHIL 2004 lectures. The latter were part of the CHIL evaluation test-set of the the RT05 evaluation. The ISL lecture, presentation and talk recordings were collected at CMU between 1999 and 2005 for lecture recognition and machine translation projects.

For each corpus, we took the average of the talk-time of the speakers who talked for the longest time (group A), the speakers who talked for the second longest time (group B) and for the third longest time (group C), see figure 4. The CHIL development-set and the CHIL test-set were analyzed separately because the recording setting was slightly changed before and after the collection of the development data. In order to have more data, we looked at the complete 20 test-set seminars, which were the source of the five-minute selections for the CHIL test-set, for a total duration of 11 hours 7 minutes.

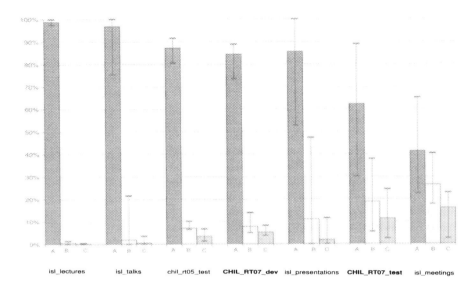

**Fig. 4.** Comparison of speakers' talk time ratio in different data-sets averaged for the speakers with the longest talk-time (A), second longest talk-time (B) and third longest talk-time (C) per data set. Maximum and minimum talk-time duration for each data-set are shown by the little lines on top of each bar.

Figure 4 sorts the seven data sets by duration of talk-time for speakers of the group A.

The ISL lectures and the ISL talks show talk-time durations for group A of 98% and 97%, respectively. The other participants accounted for almost none or only very short talk-time during these recordings. The lectures have a formal teaching session setting; a docent teaches a class to an audience of students. Very rarely do the students ask questions at the end of the lecture. They never interrupt. The talks are research presentations at scientific conferences and workshops. The audience only contributes at the time-for-question period at the end of the talk and also never interrupts during the talk.

The talk-time ratios for the CHIL RT05 lectures and the CHIL RT07 development data seminars look very much a-like with slightly more activity for groups B and C in the RT07 data than in the RT05 data. Participants account for more contributions than in the ISL lectures and talks, because the setting was less formal. The presenter-audience relationship was not always a teacher-student relationship but rather frequently an adviser-student or even peer-to-peer relationship. The RT07 development data were the first recordings done in 2006. At this time, the data collection transitioned to *interactive* seminars. Thus these first recordings were not yet as interactive as the later recorded seminars.

Similar to the RT05 lectures and the RT07 development-set, the ISL presentations were student presentations with an audience of students and advisers who interrupted more frequently. There is also a significantly broader variety between the talk-time durations of groups A, B and C. This is different from all data sets before. It shows that the setting was not as formal or fixed as it was in the lectures and talks.

Each CHIL recording site collected four more seminars during the summer of 2006, the CHIL RT07 test-set. It offered a higher degree of freedom to interact and occasions for casual conversations (as described in section 3). The result for the talk-time ratios in these seminars show much shorter sections of monologue of one single speaker, in average for group A 62%, and longer periods of talk-time for groups B and C. There is also more variety of talk-time ratios of the seminars in this data-set. Some seminars come close to ratios as thus can be seen in the ratios of the ISL multi-party meetings. Here group A's talk-time duration lasts 41% on average, group B speaks for 26% of the meeting on average. Group C still speaks for 16% of the time in the meeting.

As a result, the comparison of talk-time ratios of lecture-type data and meeting-type data positions the CHIL interactive seminars in between. The seminars provide both casual conversation and discussion, as well as monologue-type presentation.

## 8    Far-Field vs Narrow-Field Transcription

The effort to prepare separate transcriptions for the far-field condition as well as for the narrow-field condition is large: the transcription of the narrow-field quality of the CHIL seminars took about 20 times real time including the second passes; the far-field transcription added another 10 times real time on average to the transcription task. To study what was actually changed during the far-

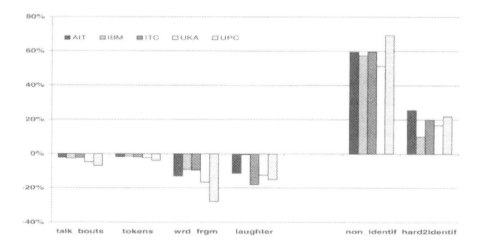

**Fig. 5.** Percentage of loss and gain of transcribed elements of the table microphone transcription compared to the close-talking microphone transcription in average of the CHIL RT07 development and test-set data, for each recording site

field transcription pass, we compared the differences in far-field and narrow-field transcriptions and counted the added and removed elements.

Figure 6 shows the loss and the gain of transcribed elements in terms of what was removed from the narrow-field transcription and what was added. The values are displayed as loss and gain in percentage over both CHIL RT07 data-sets on average, in comparison to the number of elements in the CTM transcription. This is shown for each recording site.

Accordingly, transcribers removed from the close-talking microphone transcription an average of 4% of complete talk spurts, 2% of word tokens, 15% of word fragments (wrdfrgm) and 12% of laughter annotations. The far-field transcriptions show an average of 60% more labels for non-identifiable utterances (non-identif) and 19% more word tokens tagged as hard to identify (hard2identif).

## 9    Conclusion

We described the CHIL evaluation data sets for the RT07 evaluation in terms of recording sensors and setup, scenario, speaker demagogic and transcription process.

We compared speakers' talk-time ratios of the CHIL evaluation data with other lecture-type data and multi-party meeting-type data. The comparison allows us to prove that the CHIL interactive meetings are more interactive than lecture data, but less interactive than multi-party meeting data and, therefore, need to be placed between these categories.

We finally were able to display what is added and what is removed from narrow-field transcriptions when the recording quality is changed to far-field sensors.

The CHIL interactive seminars are publicly available to the community through ELRA's catalog of language resources (`http://catalog.elra.info`).

**Acknowledgments.** We would like to thank Matthew Bell, Brian Anna, Brett Nelson, JP Fridy and Freya Fridy for the transcription of the data and helpful input to this paper. The data collection presented here was funded by the European Union under the integrated project CHIL (Grant number IST-506909).

## References

1. The CHIL Consortium Website: `http://chil.server.de`
2. The NIST RT Website: `http://www.nist.gov/speech/tests/rt/`
3. The CLEAR Evaluation Website: `http://www.clear-evaluation.org`
4. Mostefa, D., Potamianos, G., Chu, S.M., Tyagi, A., Casas, J., Turmo, J., Cristoforetti, L., Tobia, F., Pnevmatikakis, A., Mylonakis, V., Talantzis, F., Burger, S., Stiefelhagen, R., Bernardin, K., Rochet, C.: The CHIL Audiovisual Corpus for Lecture and Meeting Analysis inside Smart Rooms. Journal for Language Resources and Evaluation, Springer, Netherlands (accepted, 2007)
5. The Mark III Website: `http://www.nist.gov/smartspace/cmaiii.html`

6. Nadia Mana, N., Burger, S., Cattoni, R., Besacier, L.: The Nespole! VoIP Corpora In Tourism And Medical Domains. In: Proc. Eurospeech 2003, Geneva, Switzerland (2003)
7. Burger, S., Maclaren, V., Yu, H.: The ISL Meeting Corpus: The Impact of Meeting Type on Speech Style. In: Proc. ICSLP, Denver, CO, USA (2002)
8. Burger, S., Sloane, Z.: The ISL Meeting Corpus: Categorical Features of Communicative Group Interactions. In: NIST Meeting Recognition Workshop 2004, NIST 2004, Montreal, Canada (2004)
9. Shirberg, E., Stolcke, A., Baron, D.: Observations on Overlap: Findings and implications for automatic processing of multi-party conversation. In: Proc. Eurospeech, Aarlborg, Denmark (2001)

# Shared Linguistic Resources for the Meeting Domain

Meghan Lammie Glenn and Stephanie Strassel

Linguistic Data Consortium
3600 Market Street, Suite 810
Philadelphia, PA 19104
{mlglenn, strassel}@ldc.upenn.edu

**Abstract.** This paper describes efforts by the University of Pennsylvania's Linguistic Data Consortium to create and distribute shared linguistic resources – including data, annotations, tools and infrastructure – to support the Spring 2007 (RT-07) Rich Transcription Meeting Recognition Evaluation. In addition to making available large volumes of training data to research participants, LDC produced reference transcripts for the NIST Phase II Corpus and RT-07 conference room evaluation set, which represent a variety of subjects, scenarios and recording conditions. For the 18-hour NIST Phase II Corpus, LDC created quick transcripts which include automatic segmentation and minimal markup. The 3-hour evaluation corpus required the creation of careful verbatim reference transcripts including manual segmentation and rich markup. The 2007 effort marked the second year of using the XTrans annotation tool kit in the meeting domain. We describe the process of creating transcripts for the RT-07 evaluation, and describe the advantages of utilizing XTrans for each phase of transcription and its positive impact on quality control and real-time transcription rates. This paper also describes the structure and results of a pilot consistency study that we conducted on the 3-hour test set. Finally, we present plans for further improvements to infrastructure and transcription methods.

**Keywords:** linguistic resources, transcription, annotation tools, XTrans, Annotation Tool Graph Kit (AGTK).

## 1 Introduction

Linguistic Data Consortium was established in 1992 at the University of Pennsylvania to support language-related education, research and technology development by creating and sharing linguistic resources, including data, tools and standards. Human language technology development in particular requires large volumes of annotated data for building language models, training systems and evaluating system performance against a human-generated gold standard. LDC has directly supported the National Institute of Standards and Technology's (NIST) Rich Transcription evaluation series by providing training and evaluation data and related infrastructure. For the Spring 2007 (RT-07) Rich Transcription Meeting Recognition Evaluation, LDC provided large quantities of training data from a variety of domains to program participants. LDC produced 18 hours of new quick transcripts for the NIST Phase II conference

R. Stiefelhagen et al. (Eds.): CLEAR 2007 and RT 2007, LNCS 4625, pp. 401–413, 2008.
© Springer-Verlag Berlin Heidelberg 2008

room corpus. In addition to that, LDC produced 3 hours of careful reference transcripts of evaluation data to support automatic speech-to-text transcription, diarization, and speaker segmentation and localization in the meeting domain. The RT-07 conference room sets were created by using XTrans, the specialized speech annotation tool that was developed to respond to unique challenges presented by transcription. XTrans supports rapid, high-quality creation of rich transcripts, in the meeting domain and in a wide variety of other genres. It also provides built-in quality control mechanisms that facilitate consistency and improve real-time transcription rates, thereby opening avenues for further experimentation in the reference transcript creation process. This paper also describes a pilot study conducted to begin to understand inter-transcriber consistency. The results show that there are

## 2 Data

### 2.1 Training Data

To enhance availability of high-quality training data for RT-07, LDC coordinated with NIST to distribute eight corpora that are part of the LDC catalog for use as training data by evaluation participants. The data included five corpora in the meeting domain and two large corpora of transcribed conversational telephone speech (CTS) as well as one corpus of transcribed broadcast news (BN). All data was shipped directly to registered evaluation participants upon request, after sites had signed a user agreement specifying research use of the data. The distributed training data is summarized in the table below.

**Table 1.** RT-07S Training Data Distributed through NIST by LDC

| Title | Speech | Transcripts | Volume | Domain |
|---|---|---|---|---|
| Fisher English Part 1 | LDC2004S13 | LDC2004T19 | 750+ hours | CTS |
| Fisher English Part 2 | LDC2005S13 | LDC2005T19 | 750+ hours | CTS |
| ICSI Meeting Corpus | LDC2004S02 | LDC2004T04 | 72 hours | Meeting |
| ISL Meeting Corpus | LDC2004S05 | LDC2004T10 | 10 hours | Meeting |
| NIST Meeting Pilot Corpus | LDC2004S09 | LDC2004T13 | 13 hours | Meeting |
| RT-04S Dev-Eval Meeting Room Data | LDC2005S09 | LDC2005S09 | 14.5 hours | Meeting |
| RT-06 Spring Meeting Speech Evaluation Data | | LDC2006E16 | 3 hours | Meeting |
| TDT4 Multilingual Broadcast News Corpus | LDC2005S11 | LDC2005T16 | 300+ hours | BN |

### 2.2 NIST Phase II Data

LDC transcribed 18 hours of meeting recordings for the NIST Phase II Corpus, using the Quick Transcription (QTR) methodology. The corpus is comprised of 17 files, ranging from 40 minutes to nearly 2 hours in duration. There are between 3 and 6 speakers per session, including native and non-native speakers, and 2 "ambient" speakers who participate via telephone. The topic content varies from business meeting content, product presentations and demonstrations, role playing, and discussions about a prescribed topic.

Before beginning transcription, team leaders scanned each meeting session recording, identified its central topic and various other features of the meeting – for example, the number of speakers, and circulated a table with that information to the group. Transcriber team members chose to work on files with discussion topics that matched their studies or interests. For example, a team member with a finance degree chose to transcribe financial consultant sessions; another transcriber – a freelance journalist with a background in English – selected a literature discussion. This flexible, content-based approach to meetings kept LDC's team members more engaged, consistent and invested in the transcription process.

## 2.3  Evaluation Data

In addition to making the training data available for distribution through NIST, LDC developed a portion of the benchmark test data for this year's evaluation. The RT-07 three-hour conference room evaluation corpus includes nine excerpts from eight meeting sessions contributed by four organizations or consortia: Carnegie Mellon Institute, University of Edinburgh, National Institute of Standards and Technology, and Virginia Tech. The sessions contain an average of six participants and are twenty-two minutes long. In all cases individual head-mounted microphone (IHM) recordings were available and were used for the bulk of transcription. The meetings represent a variety of subjects, scenarios and recording conditions, but contain primarily business content.

As with the NIST Phase II corpus, team leaders scanned the audio recordings before beginning transcription and created a "meeting profile" by noting key features of each discussion: the number of speakers, discussion topic and topic-specific vocabulary, level of interaction, acoustic features, and speaker features. While assignment of

**Table 2.** Profile of a meeting recording in the RT-07 test set

| Filename | CMU_20061115-1530 |
|---|---|
| **# speakers** | Four: 2 males and 2 females. |
| **Topic of conversation** | A group of transcribers discusses things that are difficult to transcribe. Some of these problems include: non-native English speakers, filled pauses, foreign languages, and proper names. They discuss potential solutions to these issues. |
| **Vocabulary** | n/a |
| **Level of interaction** | The level of interaction of this file is 2= Moderately interactive (All speakers participating, some overlap) |
| **Acoustic features** | There are minor background noises. |
| **Speaker features** | One non-native English speaker. All other speakers are native English speakers who are clearly heard and understood. |
| **Other notes** | The speakers in this file know that the file will be transcribed. |

the test set was random, the descriptions of the meetings provided transcribers with important information for each recording. An example of a meeting profile is shown in Table 2.

# 3  Transcription

## 3.1  Quick Transcription (QTR)

The goal of QTR is simply to "get the words right" as quickly as possible; to that end, the QTR methodology automates some aspects of the transcription process and eliminates most feature markup, permitting transcribers to complete a verbatim transcript in a single pass over each channel. [1] Automatic measures include pre-processing the audio signal to segment it into chunks of speech, and post-processing the transcript by running a spell check, data format check and scans for common errors. Manual audio segmentation is an integral part of careful transcription, but is very costly, accounting for 1/4 or more of the time required to produce a highly-accurate verbatim transcript. To reduce costs in QTR, LDC developed AutoSegmenter, a process that uses Entropic's ESPS library to pre-segment a speech file into speaker segments by detecting pauses in the audio stream. AutoSegmenter achieves relatively high accuracy on clean audio signals containing one speaker, and typically produces good results on the head-mounted microphone channels. When the audio is degraded in any way, the quality of automatic segmentation falls dramatically, leading to large portions of missed speech, truncated utterances, and false alarm segments – segments that may have been triggered by other participants in the room, noise, or distortion.

The QTR approach was adopted on a limited scale for English conversational telephone speech data within the DARPA EARS program [2], with real-time transcription rates of seven to ten times real-time. Team leaders monitor progress and speed to ensure that transcripts are produced within the targeted timeframe. The resulting quick transcription quality is naturally lower than that produced by the careful transcription methodology, since accelerating the process inevitably results in missed or mis-transcribed speech; this is particularly true for difficult sections of the transcript, such as disfluent or overlapping speech sections. However, the advantage of this approach is undeniable. Annotators work ten times faster on average using this approach than they are able to work within the careful transcription methodology.

### 3.1.1  Quality Control
Quality assurance efforts are minimized for QTR, since the goal of this approach is to produce a transcript in as little time as possible. However, the meetings in this dataset were reviewed in a quick final pass, which involved a spell check, a data format check and contraction expansion. Transcripts were reviewed again briefly (in a one times real time pass) by a team leader for accuracy and completeness.

## 3.2  Careful Transcription (CTR)

For purposes of evaluating transcription technology, system output must be compared with high-quality manually-created verbatim transcripts. LDC has already defined a careful transcription (CTR) methodology to ensure a consistent approach to the creation of benchmark data. The goal of CTR is to create a reference transcript that is as good as a human can make it, capturing even subtle details of the audio signal and providing close time-alignment with the corresponding transcript. CTR involves multiple passes over the data and rigorous quality control. Some version of LDC's current CTR specification has been used to produce test data for several speech technology evaluations in the broadcast news and conversational telephone speech domains in English, Mandarin, Modern Standard and Levantine Arabic as well as other languages over the past decade. In 2004 the CTR methodology was extended to the meeting domain to support the RT-04 meeting speech evaluation. [3]

Working with a single speaker channel at a time using individual head-mounted microphone (IHM) recordings, annotators first divide the audio signal into virtual segments containing speaker utterances and noise while simultaneously labeling each speaker with a unique speaker ID. At minimum, annotators divide the audio into individual speaker turns. Turns that are longer than 10 seconds are segmented into smaller units. Speaker turns can be difficult to define in general and are particularly challenging in the meeting domain due to the frequency of overlapping speech and the prevalence of side conversations or asides that occur simultaneously with the main thread of speech. Transcribers are therefore generally instructed to place segment boundaries at natural breakpoints like breath groups and pauses, typically resulting in segments of three to eight seconds in duration.

When placing segment boundaries, transcribers listen to the entire audio file and visually inspect the waveform display, capturing every region of speech as well as isolating vocalized speaker noises such as coughs, sneezes, and laughter. Audible breaths are not captured unless they seem to convey some meaning, such as a sigh or a sharp breath. Speaker and ambient noise were annotated on separate virtual channels (VSC) in the XTrans speech annotation tool. The VSC function allows a transcriber to attribute an undetermined number of speakers – or in this case, non-speech events for one speaker – to one audio signal. Segmenting speaker noise in this manner allowed for cleaner speech event segmentation and more accurate non-speech event information. Transcribers leave several milliseconds of silence padding around each segment boundary, and are cautious about clipping off the onset of voiceless consonants or the ends of fricatives.

After accurate segment boundaries are in place, annotators create a verbatim transcript by listening to each segment in turn. Because segments are typically around five seconds, it is usually possible to create a verbatim transcript by listening to each segment once; regions containing speaker disfluencies or other phenomena may warrant several reviews. Though no time limit is imposed for CTR, annotators are instructed to insert the "uncertain transcription" convention if they need to review a segment three or more times. A second pass checks the accuracy of the segment boundaries and transcript itself, revisits sections marked as "uncertain," validates speaker identity, adds information about background noise conditions, and inserts special markup for mispronounced words, proper names, acronyms, partial words, disfluencies and the like. A third pass over the transcript conducted by the team leader ensures accuracy and completeness, leveraging the context of the full meeting to verify specific vocabulary, acronyms and proper nouns as required.

Transcription ends with multiple automatic and manual scans over the data to identify regions of missed speech, correct common errors, and conduct spelling and data format checks, which identify badly formatted regions of each file. These steps are described in more detail in the following section.

### 3.3  Quality Control

To enhance the accuracy of meeting transcription, annotators work with the separate IHM recordings of individual speakers and the merged recording of the all IHM recordings of the meeting participants. Segmentation and first-pass transcription are produced primarily from the individual IHM recordings in the manner described above. Senior annotators listen to all untranscribed regions of individual files, identifying any areas of missed speech or chopped segments using a specialized interface.

Meetings may contain highly specialized terminology and names that may be difficult for transcribers to interpret. To resolve instances of uncertainty and inconsistency, additional quality control passes are conducted using a distant or table-top microphone recording or the merged IHM recording, which conflates all individual speaker transcripts into a single session that is time-aligned with a mixed recording of all IHM channels. This merged view provides a comprehensive inspection of the consistency of terminology and names across the file, and is conducted by a senior annotator who has greater access to and knowledge of technical jargon. Senior annotators also check for common errors and standardize the spelling of proper nouns and the representation of acronyms in the transcript and across transcripts, where applicable.

The final stages of quality control involve multiple quality assurance scans, such as spell checking and syntax checking, which identifies portions of the transcript that are poorly formatted (for example, conflicting markup of linguistic features), and expanding contractions.

## 4  Unique Challenges of Meeting Data

The meeting domain presents a number of unique challenges to the production of highly accurate verbatim transcripts, which motivates the application of quality control procedures as a part of the multi-pass strategy described above. One such challenge is the prevalence of overlapping speech. In meetings, overlap is extremely frequent, accounting for nearly a quarter of the speech on average.[1] Even when transcribing using a speaker's IHM recording, capturing speech in overlapping regions is difficult because other speakers are typically audible on those channels. During all stages of transcription, transcribers and team leaders devote extra attention to overlapping speech regions.

Meeting content may also present a challenge to transcribers. Much of the conference room data is collected during project discussion groups or technical meetings, and frequently involves highly-specific terminology that requires extra care and research to transcribe accurately. Furthermore, meeting attendees show very different levels of participation, and some may not speak at all during a recorded session. While this is not a major roadblock to the production of reference transcription, speakers who do not speak motivate extra care at all phases of transcription, to ensure that no speech event has been missed.

---

[1] This is based on the RT-07 test set, where the amount of overlap ranged from 4.85%-43.04%.

Another challenge fundamental to creating a high-quality meeting data transcript is the added volume of speech, resulting from not one or two but a half a dozen or more speakers. A typical thirty-minute telephone conversation will require twenty hours or more to transcribe carefully (30 minutes, two speakers, 20 times real-time per channel). A meeting of the same duration with six participants may require more than 60 hours producing a transcript of the same quality.

The nature of meeting speech transcription requires frequent jumping back and forth from a single speaker to a multi-speaker view of the data, which presents a challenge not only for the transcribers, but for the transcription tools they use. Many current transcription tools are not optimized for or do not permit this approach. For the most part existing transcription tools cannot incorporate output of automatic processes, and they lack correction and adjudication modes. Moreover, user interfaces are not optimized for the tasks described above.

## 5  Infrastructure

LDC has been using a next-generation speech annotation toolkit, XTrans, to directly support a full range of speech annotation tasks including quick and careful transcription of meetings since late 2005. XTrans, based on QT and implemented in Python and C++, utilizes the Annotation Graph Toolkit [4, 5] whose infrastructure of libraries, applications and GUI components enables rapid development of task-specific annotation tools.

XTrans operates across languages, platforms and domains, containing customized modules for quick and careful transcription and structural spoken metadata annotation. The tool supports bi-directional text input, a critical component for languages such as Arabic. XTrans is being used for full-fledged transcription and a variety of speech annotation tasks in Arabic, Mandarin Chinese, and English at LDC.

XTrans contains user-configurable key bindings for common tasks. All commands can be issued from keyboard or mouse, depending on user preference. This user-friendly tool includes specialized quality control features; for instance speakerID verification to find misapplied speaker labels and silence checking to identify speech within untranscribed regions. The speakerID verification functions include the ability to listen to random segments – or all segments – of one speaker to identify speakerID errors and modify them as necessary. XTrans enables easy handling of overlapping speech in single-channel audio by implementing a Virtual Speaker Channel (VSC) for each speaker, not each audio channel.

To support meeting domain transcription, XTrans permits an arbitrary number of audio channels to be loaded at once. For RT-07, transcribers opened the IHM channels for each meeting recording session. They had access to distant microphone recordings when desired, and could easily toggle between the multi- and single-speaker views, turning individual channels on and off as required to customize their interaction with the data. The waveform markup display makes speaker interaction obvious, showing overlapping segments and assigning a unique color to each speaker. Figure 1 shows a transcription session that is focused on a single speaker (Subj-100).

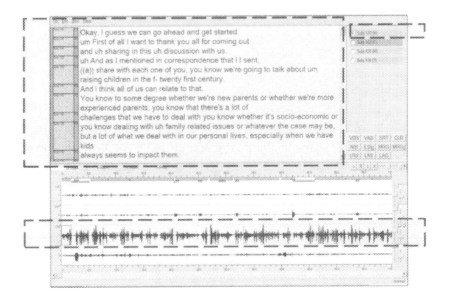

**Fig. 1.** Multiple audio channels, single-speaker transcript view in XTrans. Focus is on one speaker; all non-focal audio channels are turned off.

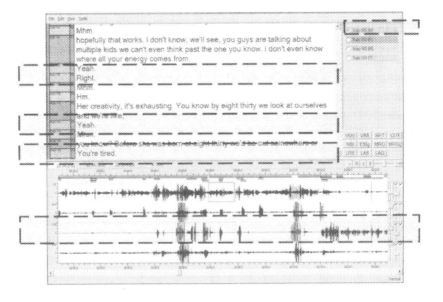

**Fig. 2.** Multiple audio channels, multi-speaker transcript view. Focus is on all speakers; all audio channels are activated.

As shown in Figure 1, the transcriber may choose to show the transcript of only one speaker, and may also mute the audio recordings of the other meeting participants by de-selecting the audio output buttons to the other audio channels. When the transcriber switches to a multi-speaker view of the meeting session, the transcript for all of the meeting participants appears. The transcriber also activates the other audio output for the other speakers' recordings. The multi-speaker view is shown in Figure 2. This image also highlights the speaker featured in Figure 1.

As with LDC's current transcription tools, XTrans is fully integrated into LDC's existing annotation workflow system, AWS. AWS controls work (project, file) assignment; manages directories and permissions; calls up the annotation software and assigned file(s) for the user; and tracks annotation efficiency and progress. AWS allows for double-blind assignment of files for dual annotation, and incorporates adjudication and consistency scoring into the regular annotation pipeline. Supervisors can query information about progress and efficiency by user, language, data set, task, and so on.

## 6 Consistency Pilot Study

### 6.1 Dual Transcription

For the RT-07 test set, LDC implemented the double-blind file assignment function of AWS and performed dual transcription at the first pass level, in order to understand more about inter-transcriber consistency. Seven of the nine file excerpts in the test set were dually transcribed; due to scheduling constraints, the team was not able to finish dual transcription for the entire dataset. The transcription process occurs in two distinct phases: segmentation, then transcription. To facilitate comparison between transcripts, the files were manually segmented by one transcriber. The segmentation file was copied and sent to two independent first pass transcribers. Then one of the first pass files continued through subsequent quality control passes. The file that continued through the pipeline was the one that was completed first. The workflow for the test set is shown in Figure 3.

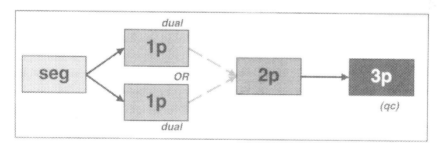

**Fig. 3.** RT-07 test set careful transcription workflow

Careful first pass transcription is typically performed by junior transcribers, since the aim of the first pass is to get a verbatim transcript, ignoring markup. The transcript moves to more senior transcribers for the second pass, where markup is inserted, the transcript is carefully reviewed, proper nouns are checked, and meticulous quality control begins.

## 6.2  Transcript Comparison

We compared the transcripts by asking transcribers to perform a form of "adjudication" by reviewing each segment of the transcripts and coding the differences. Transcribers answered a series of questions about each difference and recorded their analysis inline with the transcript. They determined whether the difference was significant or insignificant, and judged which version was correct. For significant differences, transcribers also described what caused the difference by choosing from the following options: transcriber carelessness, audio quality, the level of speaker interaction, or speaker attributes (voice quality or non-native English speaker). Table 3 shows the key that transcribers used to analyze the differences between files.

We used a modified version of XTrans, shown in Figure 4, to view the files in parallel. The comparison view shows three versions of each line of the transcript: first pass 1, first pass 2, and first pass edit, which allows the adjudicator to correct the transcript or simply take notes about the two versions.

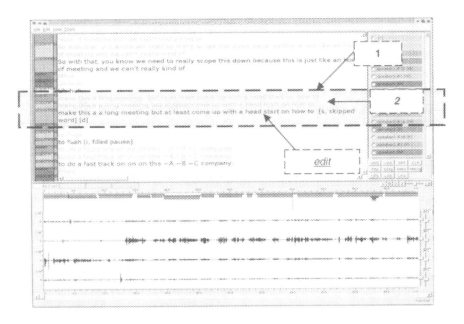

**Fig. 4.** Two transcripts displayed together in a customized version of the XTrans speech annotation too. A script merges the transcripts together and displays the time-aligned segment pairs together, leaving a third transcript line for comments and analysis.

## 6.3  Results

Though the manual comparison of transcripts was more qualitative than quantitative, we made an effort to quantify the findings of this study. To do so, we counted the number of segments, and the number of the significant and insignificant differences in each file.

Across all files, we counted a total of 3495 segments. Among those, 2392 segments differed. Of those differing segments, approximately 36.41% (871) were marked as being insignificant, which means that the differences between segments are spelling errors, punctuation and capitalization differences, lack of markup, or noise annotation. 63.59% (1521) segments that differed were marked as containing significant discrepancies. These were cases where transcriber 1 and transcriber 2 understood an utterance differently. The significant differences between transcribers range from simple – a partial word versus a full word, or "mhm" versus "uh-huh" – to extreme – where the two transcribers wrote completely different utterances. Several examples displaying the range of comprehension deviation are included in Table 3.

**Table 3.** Examples of discrepancies between transcribers during the consistency pilot study with RT-07 test data

| analysis | version id | transcript |
|---|---|---|
| significant, really vs. at least, trans1 | trans1 | at least spell things out and possibly look them up based on that. |
| | trans2 | really spell things out and possibly look them up based on that. |
| significant, three vs. Greek, trans2 | trans1 | We had three %um Spanish, Italian, |
| | trans2 | We had Greek %um Spanish, Italian. |
| significant, missed transcription trans2 | trans1 | (( )) |
| | trans2 | Yeah me too because they s- |
| significant, large portion left out, trans2 | trans1 | you know they're actually saying ^Spain and it's just you know part of sort of their phonetic make up |
| | trans2 | you know they're actually saying ^Spain and it's just you know part of sort of their phonetic makeup to add that *schwa at the beginning and -- |
| significant, comprehension error, trans2 | trans1 | Tha- that's true. ^Alex is kind of ((dead and air looking)). |
| | trans2 | That's true, Alex is kind of debonair looking. |
| significant, trans2 | trans1 | Uh-huh. |
| | trans2 | Mhm. |
| significant, misunderstood word, trans2 | trans1 | Yeah, and it sort of hurts because often you think this is a filled pause. |
| | trans2 | Yeah and it sort of helps because often you think this is a filled pause |
| significant, filled pause, trans2 | trans1 | %ah yes. |
| | trans2 | Ah yes. |
| significant, different segmentation and transcription, trans1 | trans1 | Okay. The memorial is deteriorating. I'd say the %uh problem is the memorial is deteriorating so, |
| | trans2 | Okay. |
| | trans2 | The memorial is deteriorating. I'd say that our problem is the memorial is deteriorating. |

## 6.4 Observations

Upon closer examination of the first pass transcripts, some of the differences seem to stem from a transcriber's lack of understanding of the context of the meeting. First pass transcribers usually focus on only one speaker at a time and do not listen to all participants at once, so these kinds of errors are understandable at this stage. Other differences are simply careless errors or comprehension errors. We did not find that one transcript in a transcript pair was always correct.

The biggest detraction to this pilot study was the segmentation. Transcripts are most easily compared when the segmentation is identical – if the segmentation differs, words are not perfectly aligned across transcripts and it becomes very difficult to see where the primary errors are. Even though the team leader instructed first pass transcribers not to modify segment boundaries, the transcript pairs *did not* end up with identical segmentation. Currently, LDC does not have mechanism for "locking" segmentation in place, which could be useful in future efforts.

We did glean a lot of positive information from this study. It proved to be an instructive management tool. Transcribers were asked to review and adjudicate a large number of careless errors, which reinforced the transcription guidelines for them. For managers, the study highlighted specific areas to underscore during training.

In the future, we would like to compare transcripts that have been transcribed in parallel from first pass through the final stages of quality control so that simple errors are resolved and only serious inconsistencies among annotators remain. We would also like to develop better tools in-house for comparing two transcripts. Analyzing each error in XTrans was constructive, but the results were not easily quantified. Researching ways to improve inter-transcriber consistency is certainly a goal in the future.

## 7  Transcription Rates

LDC careful transcription real-time rates for the RT-05S two-hour dataset approached 65 times real-time, meaning that one hour of data required around 65 hours of labor (excluding additional QC provided by the team leader), which is around 15 times real-time per channel, comparable with rates for BN and slightly less than that for CTS. Using XTrans to develop the RT-06S conference room data, our real-time rates dropped to under 50 times real-time per file (10 times real-time per channel). [6] Careful transcription rates for RT-07 were approximately 50 times real-time, as well.

## 8  Future Plans and Conclusion

LDC's planned activities include additional transcription in the meeting domain and further exploration of segmentation and annotation methods that would enhance the quality or value of reference meeting transcripts. We also plan to explore ways to make Careful Transcription more efficient. XTrans carries many built-in functions that could enrich meeting transcripts, including structural metadata and topic boundary annotation, both of which are currently being annotated under the GALE Quick-Rich Transcription (QRTR) methodology. Porting LDC's expertise in these two areas to the meeting domain may open doors to topic detection research and discourse analysis.

LDC plans to collect new data, as well. Using existing facilities at LDC developed for other research programs, meeting collection is currently opportunistic, with regularly scheduled business meetings being recorded as time allows. As new funding becomes available, we also plan to develop our collections infrastructure with additional head-mounted and lavaliere microphones, an improved microphone array, better video capability and customized software for more flexible remote recording control. While the current collection platform was designed with portability in mind, we hope to make it a fully portable system that can be easily transported to locations around campus to collect not only business meetings but also lectures, training sessions and other kinds of scenarios.

Future plans for XTrans include incorporation of video input to assist with tasks like speaker identification and speaker turn detection. We also plan to add a "correction mode" that will allow users to check manual transcripts or verify output of automatic processes including auto-segmentation, forced alignment, SpeakerID and automatic speech recognition output. Another XTrans feature which we plan to explore is the "adjudication mode", allowing users to compare, adjudicate and analyze discrepancies across multiple human or machine-generated transcripts. This would certainly provide more easily-accessible data on consistency between transcribers.

Shared resources are a critical component of human language technology development. LDC is actively engaged in ongoing efforts to provide crucial resources for improved speech technology to RT-07 program participants as well as to the larger community of language researchers, educators and technology developers. These resources are not limited to data, but also include annotations, specifications, tools and infrastructure.

**Acknowledgments.** We would like to thank Haejoong Lee, primary developer of the XTrans speech annotation tool, for his dedication to improving XTrans. We would also like to thank the LDC transcription team for their hard work in creating the transcripts for RT-07S.

# References

1. Linguistic Data Consortium: RT-07 Meeting Quick Transcription Guidelines (2007), https://projects.ldc.upenn.edu/Transcription/NISTMeet/Meeting DataQTR-V2.0.pdf
2. Strassel, S., Cieri, C., Walker, K., Miller, D.: Shared Resources for Robust Speech-to-Text Technology. In: Proceedings of Eurospeech (2003)
3. Linguistic Data Consortium: RT-07 Meeting Careful Transcription Guidelines (2007), https://projects.ldc.upenn.edu/Transcription/NISTMeet/Meeting DataCTR-V2.1.pdf
4. Bird, S., Liberman, M.: A formal framework for linguistic annotation. Speech Communication 33, 23–60 (2001)
5. Maeda, K., Strassel, S.: Annotation Tools for Large-Scale Corpus Development: Using AGTK at the Linguistic Data Consortium. In: Proceedings of the 4th International Conference on Language Resources and Evaluation (2004)
6. Glenn, M., Strassel, S.: Linguistic Resources for Meeting Speech Recognition. In: Renals, S., Bengio, S. (eds.) MLMI 2005. LNCS, vol. 3869, pp. 390–401. Springer, Heidelberg (2006)

# The 2007 AMI(DA) System for Meeting Transcription

Thomas Hain[1], Lukas Burget[2], John Dines[3], Giulia Garau[4], Martin Karafiat[2],
David van Leeuwen[5], Mike Lincoln[4,3], and Vincent Wan[1]

[1] Department of Computer Science,
University of Sheffield, Sheffield S1 4DP, UK
[2] Faculty of Information Engineering,
Brno University of Technology, Brno, 612 66, Czech Republic
[3] IDIAP Research Institute, CH-1920 Martigny, Switzerland
[4] Centre for Speech Technology Research, University of Edinburgh,
Edinburgh EH8 9LW, UK
[5] TNO,2600 AD Delft, The Netherlands
th@dcs.shef.ac.uk

**Abstract.** Meeting transcription is one of the main tasks for large vocabulary automatic speech recognition (ASR) and is supported by several
large international projects in the area. The conversational nature, the
difficult acoustics, and the necessity of high quality speech transcripts for
higher level processing make ASR of meeting recordings an interesting
challenge. This paper describes the development and system architecture
of the 2007 AMIDA meeting transcription system, the third of such systems developed in a collaboration of six research sites. Different variants
of the system participated in all speech to text transcription tasks of the
2007 NIST RT evaluations and showed very competitive performance.
The best result was obtained on close-talking microphone data where a
final word error rate of 24.9% was obtained.

## 1 Introduction

Transcription of meetings is an interesting task for a wide range of communities.
Apart from face-to-face meetings, telephone conferences are currently replaced
by extended video conferencing which brings new challenges to supportive technologies. Presentations and lectures are more and more available, for streamed
or static consumption or even in the context of global virtual worlds. In most
of these cases it is clear that the lack of personal presence is a deficiency that
hinders both in observation and action. For this purpose meeting analysis, such
as conducted in the AMIDA project[1] is important for all of these tasks. In particular the transcription of the spoken words in meetings is vital to allow higher
level processing, such as for example summarisation or addressee detection.

---

[1] See http://www.amiproject.org

R. Stiefelhagen et al. (Eds.): CLEAR 2007 and RT 2007, LNCS 4625, pp. 414–428, 2008.
© Springer-Verlag Berlin Heidelberg 2008

NIST evaluations on meeting data have been conducted regularly since 2002. During the past two years the meeting domain was split into conference and lecture meeting parts. This year a new component, so-called coffee breaks were added. Whereas the former two are clearly relatively formal events, the idea of the latter was to incorporate more informal settings that would include more lively interactions. There are several other ways by which meeting transcription can be investigated. The most obvious one, a distinction by recording method, i.e. the microphone sources, has been made in NIST evaluations from the start. More recently different ways of measuring performance were added. Whereas until 2005 word error rates (WERs) were measured on speech sections where only a single speaker is talking, more recently speech from multiple voices at the same time is scored. Furthermore, in 2007 the Speaker Attributed Speech To Text (SASTT) task was added where a word also must carry speaker information. A correct word is counted as mis-recognised if it carries an incorrect speaker label and vice versa. Hence naturally SASTT error rates are necessarily at least as high as STT scores.

The development of the AMI(DA) system for meeting transcription is a joint development by several research institutions associated with the AMI/AMIDA projects under the leadership of the University of Sheffield. The first system for participation in NIST evaluations was built in 2005 and the group has contributed data and participated in RT evaluations since, with important help of the ICSI/SRI team on segmentation and data issues. The 2007 system is no exception apart from the fact that the AMI(DA) system now provides all components necessary for transcription of IHM and MDM data, both for conference and lecture room meetings, and STT and SASTT sub-tasks [1]. In this paper we describe the starting point of our work this year, new developments, and the final system architecture, including detailed performance results on the 2006 and 2007 RT evaluation test sets.

## 2 The AMI Systems

The first AMI system for meeting transcription was developed in 2005 [2,3]. The most important technological features were the use of the UNISYN dictionary [4], smoothed heteroscedastic linear discriminant analysis (S-HLDA) [5], adaptation from conversational telephone speech (CTS) data, vocal tract length normalisation (VTLN), discriminative training using the minimum phone error criterion (MPE)[6], and maximum likelihood linear regression (MLLR) adaptation[7]. The system was based on HTK[2] and the SRI language modelling toolkit[3].

In 2006 the system was improved significantly in several areas: automatic segmentation of audio; improved language model data collection; improved acoustic modelling incorporating SAT and adaptation from CTS; and posterior-based feature extraction[8]. Figure 1 shows the associated system diagram. The system

---

[2] The Hidden Markov Model Toolkit. See `://htk.eng.cam.ac.uk`
[3] See `http://www.speech.sri.com/projects/srilm`

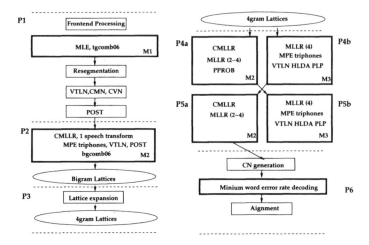

**Fig. 1.** The AMI 2006 RT System architecture. P1-P6 denote system passes, M1-M3 denote different acoustic models which are approximately described in the boxes, all other acronyms can be found in the main text. Re-segmentation is arefinement of the initial output of speech/non-speech detection.

operated in several passes where the initial pass only served for adaptation purposes. Lattices are generated in the second and third passes that are later rescored with different acoustic models. Note that the system also includes confusion network (CN) generation. Originally system combination of the outputs yielded, if any, only minor improvements, and hence the final submitted system included only one branch of the rescoring network. Transcription systems for IHM and MDM were equivalent, the MDM system architecture was a subset of the IHM one. The only difference between IHM and MDM modules, apart from the front-end processing, was the training data for acoustic models. Table 1 shows the system performance of the 2006 system on the 2006 conference evaluation data set (*rt06seval*). On IHM data the final WER was 24.2% , however on MDM (on the same meetings!) the result was 40.9% (For a detailed description of IHM and MDM please refer to [1]). The table also shows first (P1) and third (P3) pass performance. The P1 performance is considerably poorer due to the fact that decoding is performed with unadapted maximum likelihood (ML) trained models. The third pass result is already much closer to the final result and can be obtained with about a third of the processing time (the complete system runs in 60-100 × real-time). Note also that the performance is very similar for all meeting data sources (See Section 3.3 for more detail).

## 3   New Developments in 2007

In the following we give a short overview of the developments that lead to the 2007 AMIDA RT meeting system. Major improvements originate from an increased amount of training data as well as several small, but significant changes

**Table 1.** AMI RT 2006 system performance in %WER on the *rt06seval* test set for the most important passes. Results for both IHM and MDM are shown. CMU/EDI/NIST/TNO/VT denote the different meeting corpora that are part of the test set.

| IHM | TOT | CMU | EDI | NIST | TNO | VT | MDM | TOT |
|---|---|---|---|---|---|---|---|---|
| P1 | **42.0** | 41.9 | 41.0 | 39.0 | 42.1 | 44.8 | P1 | **58.2** |
| P3 | **26.0** | 25.7 | 24.6 | 25.2 | 26.3 | 29.5 | P3 | **42.0** |
| P5a-CN | **24.2** | 24.0 | 22.2 | 23.2 | 23.6 | 28.2 | P4a-CN | **40.9** |

such as a word list cleaning, improved language modelling procedures and data acquisition, enhanced adaptation from CTS, stream-lined discriminative training procedures, new and modified front-ends and system combination.

### 3.1 Word Lists

The selection of word lists and dictionaries for recognition has a considerable impact on performance. Whereas the choice of a pronunciation has an obvious direct effect, the choice of what constitutes a word, i.e. a sensible unit for language models, is often neglected. The wide-spread use of hyphenation of words causes entries in dictionaries which essentially are duplicates. These can only be differentiated by a (then) fixed language model score. Other unusual orthographic forms and mispronunciations also can be found frequently in conversational speech databases and data collected from the Internet. In order to improve the word lists generated for the AMI systems the following procedure was developed: Words for which pronunciations exist (including partial words) are sorted into groups according to their quality, ranging from high quality Q5 to low quality Q1. Words are assigned scores subjectively on the following basis:

Q5. Can be found in a dictionary or encyclopedia
Q4. A spell check will accept these words given less strict settings.
Q3. Variations of words that are unusual, perhaps not in a dictionary or incorrectly conjugated, but may still exist in speech. E.g. verbing in the sentence "The verbing of nouns".
Q2. Highly unusual words that occasionally occur in conversational speech.
Q1. Words to avoid: non words, contain illegal characters or simply wrong, unpronounceable or alternative spellings of existing words.

Q1 exists because training data contains significant numbers of these words. The recognition word list is derived from words of the development text for which pronunciations are available and have a quality of Q2 or greater. The list is then augmented to yield 50,000 words by taking the most frequent words in all our LM corpora for which firstly pronunciations are available and secondly the associated quality is Q2 or higher. To facilitate this process user interface tools were developed and it is planned to make them publicly available. In 2007

**Table 2.** Parameter settings for the IHM segmenter for the RT'06 and RT'07 systems

| Hyper-parameter | P(speech) | Minimum duration (ms) | Insertion penalty | Silence collar (ms) |
|---|---|---|---|---|
| RT'06 | 0.25 | 500 | -15 | 100 |
| RT'07 | 0.25 | 200 | -40 | 200 |

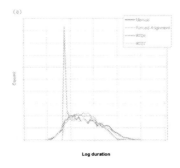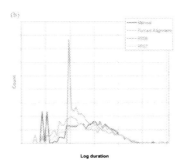

**Fig. 2.** Histograms of (a) speech (b) silence segment durations for manual segmentation, forced alignment and the RT'06 and RT'07 configurations

a total of 1500 new pronunciations were added to account for the inclusion of the Fisher corpus [9](See Section 3.4) in training, plus an additional 1750 words to give full coverage of the AMI corpus [10] including partial words.

### 3.2    Front-End Processing

*IHM speech segmentation* was based on the 2006 system [8]. There a multi-layer perceptron (MLP) consisting of 15 input frames (of feature dimension 51), 50 hidden units and 2 output classes (speech/non-speech) was used that was trained on forced alignment derived segmentation of 150 meetings. Segmentation is performed using Viterbi decoding of scaled likelihoods from the MLP. This system uses several hyper-parameters: the speech/non-speech prior probabilities, segment minimum duration, segment insertion penalty and silence collar. Each of these can be tuned on development data. In previous years the class priors were chosen to minimise the frame error rate (FER). The remaining parameters showed no great influence on performance of the segmenter at the frame level but they still appear to have impact on recognition performance. Hence the remaining parameters were selected to provide a good match of duration histograms from manual segmentation and those obtained for automatically determined segmentation. Table 2 shows the hyper-parameters used in the RT'06 and RT'07 systems that were, obtained using the described approach. Figure 2 illustrates the difference between duration histograms. Note that the minimum duration constraint in RT'06 configuration caused a significant increase in segments of that length. The length of silence segments was also increased.

**Table 3.** %WER and %DER results on the *rt06seval* set using the ICSI RT'06 STT segmentation and several configurations of the TNO diarisation system. Fixed numbers speaker clusters disregard the actual number of people present.

|      |                   | #clusters | WER  | DER  |
|------|-------------------|-----------|------|------|
| ICSI | RT'06 eval        | 4         | 56.8 | -    |
| TNO  | Optimised for DER | -         | 60.1 | 18.1 |
| TNO  | Fixed # clusters  | 6         | 56.2 | 30.9 |
| TNO  | Fixed # clusters  | 5         | 56.1 | 30.1 |
| TNO  | Fixed # clusters  | 4         | 55.6 | 33.6 |
| TNO  | Fixed # clusters  | 3         | 56.3 | 38.9 |
| TNO  | Fixed # clusters  | 1         | 56.9 | 64.0 |

*MDM front-end processing* remained mostly identical to previous years. In contrast to before, if only two omni-directional microphones are present beam-forming is replaced by simple energy based switching. Secondly, in the case of speaker-directed directional no beam-forming is used either. Consistent gains with these simplifications were shown in [8]. In previous years the AMI systems made use of segmentation and speaker clustering information for MDM from ICSI/SRI. This year experiments with using the TNO diarisation system[11]. Table 3 shows WER and diarisation error rate (DER, see [1] for a definition) results using different configurations of the TNO diarisation system. The first line is the baseline performance of a two-pass adapted system with the ICSI segmentation as used in the AMI RT'06 system. Using a system that yields low DER however obtains considerably poorer WER results than a system that uses a fixed number of speaker clusters, which in turn almost doubles the DER.

### 3.3   New Training Data

Due to the recent interest in meetings several corpora are now available: Apart from the ICSI Meeting corpus [12] two phases of the NIST corpus [13], the ISL [14] recordings and the complete AMI corpus [10] contain manually transcribed meeting data. In addition, recordings from Virginia Tech University (VIT) and the Linguistic Data Consortium (LDC) are used in small quantities as test data in NIST evaluations. The main additions in 2007 were the completion of the AMI corpus and the second phase of the NIST corpus, thus adding a total of almost 70 hours of carefully transcribed meetings for training. The AMI corpus consists of 100 hours of meetings where 70 hours follow so-called scenarios where certain roles are acted by the meeting participants. The meetings are recorded at three different sites and due to the proximity to research a large percentage of non-native English speakers was present. Table 4 shows perplexity values of different language models, splitting the corpus along scenario, gender, and language of origin. It is clear that scenario meetings are far less complex than "normal" ones. A rather surprising effect is the difference between languages

**Table 4.** Perplexities of several LMs on the AMI corpus with distinctions on the basis of gender, meeting type and language of origin. LMs are constructed by interpolating the AMI corpus and the listed background material in 5-fold cross-validation.

| Language models | Overall | male | female | Scenario | Non-Scen |
|---|---|---|---|---|---|
| Broadcast News | 99.8 | 99.3 | 100.9 | 87.9 | 137.8 |
| CTS | 100.5 | 100.1 | 101.6 | 88.2 | 140.2 |
| Meetings | 102.7 | 101.6 | 105.4 | 91.2 | 138.8 |
| Combined (inc Web-Data) | 92.9 | 92.8 | 93.2 | 84.1 | 119.7 |

| Language model | English | French | German | OtherEU | S. Asia | Rest of World |
|---|---|---|---|---|---|---|
| Broadcast News | 105.2 | **97.7** | **128.5** | 113.3 | 112.0 | 102.8 |
| CTS | 105.9 | **100.2** | **128.9** | 114.4 | 115.0 | 104.0 |
| Meetings | 110.3 | **98.0** | **126.8** | 115.9 | 113.3 | 103.7 |
| Combined (inc Web-Data) | 96.9 | **90.8** | **111.0** | 103.0 | 104.7 | 94.9 |

**Table 5.** %WER results on rescoring of 4-gram *rt05seval* (NIST 2005 RT evaluation set) lattices. Models are trained on meeting data using the ML or MPE criteria.

| Training | | IHM | | MDM | |
|---|---|---|---|---|---|
| | Iter | 100h | 170h | 68h | 130h |
| ML | - | 24.0 | 23.6 | 39.7 | 38.1 |
| MPE | 1st | 23.2 | - | 39.3 | - |
| MPE | final | 21.7 | 21.5 | 37.3 | 36.0 |

of origin. An investigation of out of vocabulary (OOV) words (not shown here) cannot explain the consider differences, with the speakers of French origin having lowest perplexity (even lower than native English speakers) and German speakers the highest.

In RT'06 the aforementioned corpora amounted to approximately 100 hours of meeting data. The new additions bring the total to approximately 170 hours. The Tables 5 and 7 show the WER gains using the new and old data sets in direct comparison, with ML and MPE training, and for IHM and MDM data. Models are trained on meeting data only and a combination of PLP and LCRC features[15,8]. The MDM data set size is reduced from 170 hours to 130 hours due to the exclusion of overlapped speech (see [8]). Results in Table 5 seem to indicate that the overall gain from the additional data is moderate, at least in the case for IHM. Here both after ML and MPE training the difference in performance between models trained on almost twice as much data is modest. The gain for MDM is higher because the original set of data was very small.

A closer look at performance on AMI data in Table 7 however indicates a different picture. Here the difference for IHM seems to be around 2% WER and for MDM almost 3% WER absolute. In Table 7 the MPE results are compared for all meeting sources. It is clear that the benefit from the new corpora was on

**Table 6.** %WER results on rescoring of 4-gram *rt05seval* lattices using AMI corpus data only

| Training | | IHM | | MDM | |
|---|---|---|---|---|---|
| | Iter | 100h | 170h | 68h | 130h |
| ML | - | 21.7 | 19.9 | 34.6 | 31.8 |
| MPE | final | 19.6 | 18.1 | 32.0 | 29.1 |

**Table 7.** Gain of additional training data in 2007. %WER results on rescoring of 4-gram *rt05seval* lattices.

| | | AMI | CMU | ICSI | NIST | VT |
|---|---|---|---|---|---|---|
| IHM | 100h | 19.6 | 20.1 | 18.3 | 26.9 | 24.3 |
| | 170h | 18.1 | 19.9 | 19.2 | 26.2 | 24.7 |
| $\Delta$ | | -1.5 | -0.2 | +0.9 | -0.7 | +0.4 |
| MDM | 68h | 32.0 | 27.2 | 35.7 | 37.9 | 45.3 |
| | 130h | 29.1 | 27.8 | 34.0 | 35.5 | 45.3 |
| $\Delta$ | | -2.9 | +0.6 | -1.7 | -2.4 | +0.0 |

data from the same source, whereas performance even degraded on others. This is most likely caused by increased under-representation in the overall training data set.

### 3.4   Training on 2000 Hours of CTS Data

In addition to incorporating new meeting data also the adapted model sets were improved. Previously CTS models were trained on the Switchboard and Call-home corpora and adapted to the meeting domain. This year we have included 2000 hours of Fisher corpus recordings [9]. The corpus data was prepared in the usual fashion, including the deletion of non-uniform amounts of silence at segment boundaries. A total of 170 hours of silence based on the manual segmentation was deleted. Table 8 shows results on the NIST CTS 2001 evaluation test sets using 270, 1000, and 2000 hours of training data respectively, where the 270 hour set is identical to the Cambridge University *h5train03* training set and does not include Fisher data. 2000 hour models ware initialised from 1000 hour ML trained models. Overall a 2.1% improvement in WER was observed.

In [8] and [16] we have presented a method to retain the benefit from wide-band data modelling while retaining the gain from CTS data adaptation. Unfortunately a detailed description cannot be given here and the interested reader is referred to those papers. Table 9 shows the performance on the *rt05seval* set using models trained in the mapped NB space on PLP features using VTLN, HLDA and MPE MAP. Note that the baseline performance for CTS models does not change for the 2000 hour models. However, after adaptation a 0.5% difference is observed. This is 1.3% lower than not adapting at all. Note the considerable performance differences across meeting rooms.

**Table 8.** %WER on the 20001 NIST CTS evaluation set with different amounts of training data

|      | #Iter | 270h | 1000h | 2000h |
|------|-------|------|-------|-------|
| ML   | -     | 31.3 | 29.6  | -     |
| MPE  | 1     | 30.3 | 28.6  | 28.5  |
| MPE  | 9     | 28.0 | 26.4  | 25.9  |

**Table 9.** %WER results on *rt06seval* adapting CTS models to meeting data including NB/WB transforms, joined HLDA, and MPE-MAP. 270/100 and 2000/100 refer to the amount of CTS and meeting data respectively

| 270h / 100h | #Iter | TOT | AMI | CMU | ICSI | NIST | VT |
|-------------|-------|------|------|------|------|------|------|
| CTS         |       | 30.4 | 31.4 | 33.0 | 26.4 | 32.5 | 28.3 |
| MAPr-5iter  | 5     | 26.0 | 26.0 | 25.7 | 22.1 | 29.6 | 26.6 |
| MPE-MAP     | 1     | 25.1 | 25.0 | 24.8 | 20.9 | 29.0 | 26.0 |
| MPE-MAP     | 9     | 23.9 | 24.0 | 23.6 | 20.1 | 28.2 | 24.1 |

| 2000h / 170h | #Iter | TOT | AMI | CMU | ICSI | NIST | VT |
|--------------|-------|------|------|------|------|------|------|
| CTS          |       | 30.4 | 30.7 | 31.3 | 27.9 | 32.2 | 30.1 |
| MAP          | 6     | 23.8 | 22.8 | 23.0 | 20.8 | 27.1 | 25.5 |
| MPE-MAP      | 1     | 23.2 | 22.1 | 22.4 | 20.5 | 26.3 | 25.2 |
| MPE-MAP      | 7     | 22.1 | 20.4 | 20.2 | 19.7 | 25.7 | 24.8 |
| No adaptation| -     | 23.4 | 20.5 | 21.2 | 20.2 | 29.0 | 26.6 |

# 4  The 2007 AMIDA System

## 4.1  Acoustic Modelling

As in 2006 models were trained using either meeting data only or adapting from meeting data. The features used were either PLP features ore PLP features together with LCRC posterior features[15]. In addition to these new models were also trained on Mel Frequency Cepstral Coefficients (MFCC) and an alternative posterior based feature vector, the Bottleneck (BN) features. BN features originate from a very similar process than LCRC features, however, instead of using the output of the MLPs the outputs of a hidden layer in a 5 layer network are used directly as features[17]. In detailed experiments these features were shown to yield approximately equivalent performance. Table 10 shows the performance of models trained on the *ihntrain07* training set using both feature representations and identical training style including speaker adaptive training. It can be observed that despite initially poorer performance the MFCC/BN based models yield almost identical error rates after discriminative training. For MDM only PLP/LCRC features were trained, with similar gains in each of the training stages as observed for the IHM models. The final equivalent result is 37.9% which is still substantially higher than the IHM performance.

**Table 10.** Comparison of various front-end configurations. %WER Results on *rt06seval* using models trained on the 170 hour *ihmtrain07* training set.

| Features | Tr | Adapt/Normalise | TOT | CMU | EDI | NIST | TNO | VT |
|----------|-----|-----------------|------|------|------|------|------|------|
| PLP | ML | | 39.0 | 39.0 | 35.4 | 33.7 | 40.3 | 45.6 |
| PLP | ML | VTLN HLDA | 31.8 | 31.9 | 29.0 | 29.1 | 30.0 | 37.9 |
| PLP + LCRC | ML | VTLN HLDA | - | - | - | - | - | - |
| PLP + LCRC | ML | VTLN HLDA SAT | 27.2 | 27.2 | 25.0 | 25.0 | 27.1 | 32.1 |
| PLP + LCRC | MPE | VTLN HLDA SAT | 25.4 | 25.4 | 23.3 | 23.3 | 25.2 | 29.4 |

| Features | Tr | Adapt/Normalise | TOT | CMU | EDI | NIST | TNO | VT |
|----------|-----|-----------------|------|------|------|------|------|------|
| MFCC | ML | | 39.7 | 39.9 | 37.0 | 34.2 | 38.9 | 45.8 |
| MFCC | ML | VTLN HLDA | 34.2 | 34.2 | 32.6 | 29.9 | 32.0 | 41.0 |
| MFCC + BN | ML | VTLN HLDA | 29.4 | 29.3 | 27.5 | 26.6 | 28.1 | 35.6 |
| MFCC + BN | ML | VTLN HLDA SAT | 27.3 | 27.2 | 25.2 | 25.6 | 26.5 | 32.3 |
| MFCC + BN | MPE | VTLN HLDA SAT | 25.6 | 25.6 | 23.0 | 23.6 | 24.9 | 30.1 |

### 4.2  Language Modelling

Language models (LMs) were constructed in a two-stage process. In the first instance out of more than 15 language models the nine most highly weighted LMs are selected and used as background language model for a web data search [18]. 20MW of web data are collected and used to train an additional LM component. In the second stage a new LM is constructed from the ten most highly weighted LMs but components with a weight of less than 1% are removed. Table 11 shows the associated language model weights. Since web-data was already collected multiple times the newly collected data dropped out of the final list. The final LM had a perplexity of 73.1 on the *rt07seval* data.

As in previous years the AMIDA system was tested on lecture room data without training on any acoustic material from that domain. The only change

**Table 11.** LM interpolation weights for the two stages of LM construction. The left table shows the models used in the first stage, on the right are the models for the second stage.

| corpus | weight |
|--------|--------|
| Fisher webdata from UW | 0.220 |
| AMI corpus eval | 0.210 |
| Fisher | 0.186 |
| Meetings webdata from UW | 0.103 |
| ISL meeting corpus | 0.081 |
| Switchboard Callhome | 0.048 |
| Swbd webdata from UW | 0.045 |
| AMI corpus webdata | 0.038 |
| Hub4 1996 LM | 0.035 |
| NIST meetings phase 2 | 0.029 |

| corpus | weight |
|--------|--------|
| Stage 1 *conf LM* | 0.912 |
| rt06s conf webdata | 0.054 |
| ICSI meeting corpus | 0.019 |
| NIST meeting corpora | 0.014 |

**Table 12.** Perplexities using LMs across lecture and conference room domains. *confmtg* and *lectmtg* denote the two domains as defined in NIST RT evaluations.

| 4-gram Models | *confmtg (rt06seval)* | *lectmtg (rt07slmdev)* |
|---|---|---|
| RT06 LM | 75.2 | 125.8 |
| *confmtg* STAGE1 | 73.2 | 144.5 |
| *confmtg* STAGE2 | 73.1 | 140.8 |
| *lectmtg* STAGE1 | 82.9 | 120.4 |
| *lectmtg* STAGE2 | 81.9 | 119.3 |

**Table 13.** %WER results on the NIST RT 2007 conference room meeting test data *(rt07seval)* using trigram LMs of AMI systems in past and the current years. Dictionaries, word lists and language models change, acoustic models are from RT'07.

| LM Year | TOT | CMU | EDI | NIST | VT |
|---|---|---|---|---|---|
| 2005 | 28.7 | 33.6 | 20.7 | 14.7 | 31.7 |
| 2006 | 28.6 | 34.1 | 20.2 | 14.4 | 31.5 |
| 2007 | 28.5 | 34.0 | 20.3 | 14.4 | 31.1 |

was the training of a separate language model. In Table 12 perplexities of models trained and optimised for one domain are tested on the other one. It is clear that perplexities on conference style meetings are substantially lower in general. The models trained on lecture data appear to generalise better to conference room meetings than the reverse. This could be explained by the very generic nature of most conference recordings whereas the lecture room recordings have highly specialist content. Finally we have tested progress in language modelling for the past years. Table 13 shows WER results using the dictionaries and language models developed in each year (trigram). Single pass decoding was performed on the rt07seval data set. The results indicate small improvements each year even though the meeting sources changed considerably in those years.

### 4.3  System Architecture

Figure 3 shows an outline of the complete system. The system operates in a total of ten passes. However, not each pass does generate word level output. The output of a pass can either be word sequences, word lattices or confusion networks. The initial two passes are identical to the 2006 system and ensure adaptation using VTLN and CMLLR. Passes P3, P5 and P8 use PLP/LCRC features, passes P4 P6 use MFCC/BN features and passes P7 and P9 use PLP features only. The models for the PLP/LCRC and MFCC/BN processing stages where described in Section 4.1 whereas the models for P7 and P9 are those outlined in Section 3.4. P3, P4 and P7 generate lattices and the confusion network outputs of P5, P8 and P9 are combined using ROVER to yield the final system result.

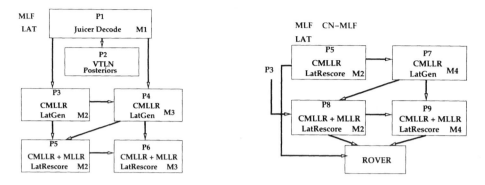

**Fig. 3.** Outline of the system passes of the AMIDA 2007 RT system

### 4.4 STT Results

Tables 14 and 15 show the performance of the 2007 system on IHM and MDM data respectively. These results should be compared with results in Table 1. Overall a reduction of 1.9% in WER is observed on *rt06seval* IHM. On MDM the difference between the 2006 and 2007 system is 3.8% WER absolute. Note that while the overall performance numbers on the *rt06seval* and *rt07seval* IHM sets are very similar. The underlying results for each meeting corpus differ much more on *rt07seval*. The difficulty in the CMU data originates from lower recording quality. Similar to systems before, the result of the third pass is already very close to the results of the final passes. The gap between first and third pass has narrowed due to more training data and MPE trained models. P5 and P6 output yield similar WERs but a combination of the two does not decrease WERs, most likely due to cross-adaptation.

In Table 15 a comparison is made between ICSI/SRI and TNO segmentation and speaker information. Similar performance is observed. However, a comparison with manual segments still shows a substantial difference. The difference between MDM and IHM results is still large with almost 10% WER absolute.

### 4.5 SASTT Results

As mentioned before speaker attributed STT was a new evaluation task in 2007. Systems results were obtained by using the standard MDM systems and attaching speaker labels using a diarisation system. In Table 16 we compare the results with the system as described in 3.2and the TNO and ICSI diarisation systems. It can be observed that with a very low diarisation error rate of 5.1% approximately 1% of loss in WER is obtained.

The MDM system was also used to transcribe the RT'07 lecture evaluation set (*rt07slecteval*). As in previous the acoustic models and all front-end processing was take from the conference domain. Only specific language models were trained (See Section 4.2). ICSI/SRI MDM segmentation optimised for speech recognition (not diarisation!) was used for both recognition and speaker

**Table 14.** %WER results of the AMIDA RT 2007 system on the IHM *rt06seval* and *rt07seval* data sets

|  | rt06seval | | | | | | rt07seval | | | | |
|---|---|---|---|---|---|---|---|---|---|---|---|
|  | Tot | CMU | EDI | NIST | TNO | VT | Tot | CMU | EDI | NIST | VT |
| P1 | 35.4 | 35.4 | 32.5 | 31.5 | 35.2 | 39.8 | 37.4 | 47.7 | 29.3 | 33.8 | 38.4 |
| P3 | 24.9 | 24.9 | 23.0 | 22.4 | 25.0 | 29.3 | 28.2 | 37.9 | 21.9 | 24.6 | 27.9 |
| P4 | 24.4 | 24.4 | 22.7 | 21.7 | 23.9 | 28.8 | 27.9 | 38.0 | 21.7 | 24.1 | 27.4 |
| P5 CN | **23.4** | **23.4** | **21.6** | **20.8** | **24.0** | **27.8** | **25.9** | **35.1** | **20.4** | **21.8** | **25.7** |
| P6 CN | 23.5 | 23.5 | 21.7 | 21.0 | 23.9 | 27.7 | 25.7 | 34.9 | 20.4 | 21.5 | 25.7 |
| P7 | 24.1 | 24.0 | 22.8 | 22.2 | 22.4 | 28.7 | 27.9 | 36.7 | 23.1 | 24.2 | 27.2 |
| P8 CN | 22.9 | 22.9 | 21.1 | 20.7 | 22.5 | 27.3 | 25.4 | 34.5 | 20.4 | 21.1 | 25.3 |
| P9 CN | 23.7 | 23.6 | 22.4 | 21.9 | 22.2 | 27.9 | 26.3 | 35.3 | 22.3 | 21.8 | 25.4 |
| P5 + P8 + P9 | **22.3** | **22.2** | **20.7** | **20.2** | **22.1** | **26.7** | **24.9** | **33.9** | **19.8** | **20.9** | **24.7** |

**Table 15.** %WER on *rt07seval* using MDM data

|  | ICSI S&C | | | | AMI/DA S&C | | | |
|---|---|---|---|---|---|---|---|---|
|  | TOT | Sub | Del | Ins | TOT | Sub | Del | Ins |
| P1 | 44.2 | 25.6 | 14.9 | 3.8 | 44.7 | 25.7 | 16.3 | 2.7 |
| P3 | 38.9 | 18.5 | 16.8 | 3.5 | 34.5 | 19.3 | 12.5 | 2.7 |
| FINAL | 33.7 | 20.1 | 10.7 | 2.9 | 33.8 | 19.2 | 12.2 | 2.4 |
| FINAL manual seg | 30.2 | 18.7 | 9.4 | 2.0 | - | - | - | - |

**Table 16.** %WER, and % speech activity detection (SAD) and % diarisation error rate (DER) results on MDM *rt07seval* using SASTT scoring. SpSub denotes the percentage of cases where the wrong speaker label was assigned to the correct word.

|  | %SAD | %DER | Sub | SpSub | Del | Ins | TOT |
|---|---|---|---|---|---|---|---|
| ASR optimised | - | - | 19.3 | 9.5 | 12.1 | 2.3 | 43.2 |
| TNO 2007 diarisation system | 6.7 | 18.9 | 19.2 | 3.9 | 12.1 | 2.4 | 37.6 |
| ICSI 2007 diarisation system | 3.3 | 5.1 | 19.1 | 0.9 | 12.3 | 2.3 | 34.7 |

assignment. From results shown on conference data it is clear that this is suboptimal. On *rt07slecteval* the STT overall performance was 48.2% WER absolute while the SASTT score was 65.2%.

## 5   Conclusions

We have presented the 2007 AMIDA system for the transcription of meetings and have shown results on the latest evaluation test sets. Major improvements in performance come from new data, fine-tuning of system parameters and a consolidation of system building processes.

# Acknowledgements

This work was largely supported by the European Union 6th FWP IST Integrated Projects AMI and AMIDA (Augmented Multi-party Interaction / with Distant Access). We also would like to thank Andreas Stolcke and Chuck Wooters from the ICSI/SRI team for providing the segments and speaker labels and their diarisation output for MDM data.

# References

1. Fiscus, J.: Spring 2007 (RT-07) Rich Transcription Meeting Recognition Evaluation Plan. U.S. NIST (2007)
2. Hain, T., Burget, L., Dines, J., Garau, G., Karafiat, M., Lincoln, M., McCowan, I., Moore, D., Wan, V., Ordelman, R., Renals, S.: The development of the AMI system for the transcription of speech in meetings. In: Renals, S., Bengio, S. (eds.) MLMI 2005. LNCS, vol. 3869. Springer, Heidelberg (2006)
3. Hain, T., Burget, L., Dines, J., Garau, G., Karafiat, M., Lincoln, M., McCowan, I., Moore, D., Wan, V., Ordelman, R., Renals, S.: The 2005 AMI system for the transcription of speech in meetings. In: Proc. NIST RT 2005, Edinburgh (2005)
4. Fitt, S.: Documentation and user guide to UNISYN lexicon and post-lexical rules. Technical report, Centre for Speech Technology Research, Edinburgh (2000)
5. Burget, L.: Combination of speech features using smoothed heteroscedastic linear discriminant analysis. In: Proc. ICSLP, Jeju Island, Korea, pp. 4–7 (2004)
6. Povey, D.: Discriminative Training for Large Vocabulary Speech, Recognition. PhD thesis, Cambridge University (2004)
7. Gales, M.J., Woodland, P.: Mean and variance adaptation within the mllr framework. Computer Speech & Language 10, 249–264 (1996)
8. Hain, T., Burget, L., Dines, J., Garau, G., Karafiat, M., Lincoln, M., Vepa, J., Wan, V.: The ami meeting transcription system: Progress and performance. In: Renals, S., Bengio, S., Fiscus, J.G. (eds.) MLMI 2006. LNCS, vol. 4299, pp. 419–431. Springer, Heidelberg (2006)
9. Cieri, C., Miller, D., Walker, K.: The fisher corpus: a resource for the next generations of speech-to-text. In: LREC 2004: Fourth International Conference on Language Resources and Evaluatio, Lisbon (2004)
10. Carletta, J., Ashby, S., Bourban, S., Guillemot, M., Kronenthal, M., Lathoud, G., Lincoln, M., McCowan, I., Hain, T., Kraaij, W., Post, W., Kadlec, J., Wellner, P., Flynn, M., Reidsma, D.: The AMI meeting corpus. In: Renals, S., Bengio, S. (eds.) MLMI 2005. LNCS, vol. 3869. Springer, Heidelberg (2006)
11. van Leeuwen, D.A., Huijbregts, M.: The ami speaker diarization system for nist rt06s meeting data. In: Renals, S., Bengio, S., Fiscus, J.G. (eds.) MLMI 2006. LNCS, vol. 4299, pp. 371–384. Springer, Heidelberg (2006)
12. Janin, A., Baron, D., Edwards, J., Ellis, D., Gelbart, D., Morgan, N., Peskin, B., Pfau, T., Shriberg, E., Stolcke, A., Wooters, C.: The ICSI meeting corpus. In: Proceedings IEEE ICASSP (2003)
13. Garofolo, J., Laprun, C., Miche, M., Stanford, V., Tabassi, E.: The nist meeting room pilot corpus. In: Proc. LREC 2004 (2004)
14. Burger, S., MacLaren, V., Yu, H.: The ISL meeting corpus: The impact of meeting type on speech style. In: Proc. ICSLP (2002)

15. Schwarz, P., Matějka, P., Černocký, J.: Hierarchical structures of neural networks for phoneme recognition. In: IEEE ICASSP (accepted, 2006)
16. Karafiat, M., Burget, L., Hain, T., Cernocky, J.: Application of cmllr in narrow band wide band adapted systems. In: Proc 8th international conference INTER-SPEECH 2007, Antwerp, p. 4 (2007)
17. Grezl, F., Karafiat, M., Kontar, S., Cernocky, J.: Probabilistic and bottle-neck features for lvcsr of meetings. In: Proc. ICASSP, vol. 4, pp. IV–757–IV–760 (2007)
18. Wan, V., Hain, T.: Strategies for language model web-data collection. In: Proc. ICASSP 2006. Number SLP-P17.11 (2006)

# The IBM Rich Transcription 2007 Speech-to-Text Systems for Lecture Meetings

Jing Huang, Etienne Marcheret, Karthik Visweswariah,
Vit Libal, and Gerasimos Potamianos

IBM Thomas J. Watson Research Center
Yorktown Heights, NY 10598, U.S.A.
{jghg,etiennem,kv1,libalvit,gpotam}@us.ibm.com

**Abstract.** The paper describes the IBM systems submitted to the NIST Rich Transcription 2007 (RT07) evaluation campaign for the speech-to-text (STT) and speaker-attributed speech-to-text (SASTT) tasks on the lecture meeting domain. Three testing conditions are considered, namely the multiple distant microphone (MDM), single distant microphone (SDM), and individual headset microphone (IHM) ones – the latter for the STT task only. The IBM system building process is similar to that employed last year for the STT Rich Transcription Spring 2006 evaluation (RT06s). However, a few technical advances have been introduced for RT07: (a) better speaker segmentation; (b) system combination via the ROVER approach applied over an ensemble of systems, some of which are built by randomized decision tree state-tying; and (c) development of a very large language model consisting of 152M n-grams, incorporating, among other sources, 525M words of web data, and used in conjunction with a dynamic decoder. These advances reduce STT word error rate (WER) in the MDM condition by 16% relative (8% absolute) over the IBM RT06s system, as measured on 17 lecture meeting segments of the RT06s evaluation test set, selected in this work as development data. In the RT07 evaluation campaign, both MDM and SDM systems perform competitively for the STT and SASTT tasks. For example, at the MDM condition, a 44.3% STT WER is achieved on the RT07 evaluation test set, excluding scoring of overlapped speech. When the STT transcripts are combined with speaker labels from speaker diarization, SASTT WER becomes 52.0%. For the STT IHM condition, the newly developed large language model is employed, but in conjunction with the RT06s IHM acoustic models. The latter are reused, due to lack of time to train new models to utilize additional close-talking microphone data available in RT07. Therefore, the resulting system achieves modest WERs of 31.7% and 33.4%, when using manual or automatic segmentation, respectively.

## 1 Introduction

Meetings and lectures play a central role in human collaborative activities in the workplace, with speech constituting the primary mode of interaction. Not surprisingly, speech processing in such scenarios has attracted much interest, being

R. Stiefelhagen et al. (Eds.): CLEAR 2007 and RT 2007, LNCS 4625, pp. 429–441, 2008.

the focus of a number of research efforts and international projects, for example CHIL [1], AMI [2], and the U.S. National Institute of Standards and Technology (NIST) SmartSpace effort [3]. In these projects, the interaction happens inside smart rooms equipped with multiple audio and visual sensors. The ultimate goal is to extract higher-level information to facilitate meeting indexing, browsing, summarization, and understanding.

Central to this goal is automatic speech recognition (ASR) or *speech-to-text* (STT) technology, and its complementary technologies of *speech activity detection* (SAD) and *speaker diarization* (SPKR). The three partially address the "what", "when", and "who" of human interaction, and are important drivers of additional technologies, for example speaker localization and recognition, summarization, and question answering. Not surprisingly, significant research effort is being devoted to developing and improving these technologies in the meeting scenario. Resulting systems have been rigorously evaluated in the past few years within the Rich Transcription (RT) Meeting Recognition Evaluation campaign series, sponsored by NIST [4].

In this paper, we present a summary of the IBM efforts in developing STT technology and its evaluation in the RT07 campaign. The emphasis of this work is on the "lecture meeting" scenario, central to European-funded project CHIL, "Computers in the Human Interaction Loop" [1]. In this scenario, a subject presents a seminar (lecture) of technical nature in English, with varying interactive participation by a relatively small audience. This represents significant challenges to state-of-the-art STT technology, due to the presence of multiple speakers with often overlapping speech, a variety of interfering acoustic events, strong accents by most speakers, a high level of spontaneity, hesitations and disfluencies, the technical seminar contents, and the relative small amount of in-domain data. Furthermore, the main emphasis is placed on developing STT systems based on far-field microphones, the goal being to achieve interaction with unobtrusive sensors that "fade into the background". This poses additional challenges to the problem, for example low signal-to-noise ratios and reverberation. In particular, the primary evaluation condition in RT07 employs table-top microphones only. These do not have exact positions, therefore their relative geometry is unknown.

In addition to STT, NIST introduced a new variant of it in the RT07 evaluation. This is the so-called speaker-attributed speech-to-text (SASTT) task, which combines both speaker diarization ("Who Spoke When") and STT into a single jointly evaluated task. The purpose of an SASTT system is to correctly transcribe the words spoken, but in addition to also identify the generically labeled speaker of the words. The IBM SASTT system performance will be briefly discussed here, however a detailed description of its speaker diarization component can be found in an accompanying paper [5].

For the IBM team, this effort constitutes the second year of participation in the RT evaluation campaign. A number of technical improvements have been introduced over the IBM STT systems that competed in RT06s [6], most importantly:

- Improved speech activity detection (SAD), which is the very first step for STT, affecting performance of both speaker segmentation and STT.
- Improved speaker segmentation for diarization (SPKR), based on thresholding schemes instead of a fixed number of speaker clusters. Further refinement is achieved through the use of alignment information.
- System combination (via the ROVER technique [7]) of multiple ASR systems, some of which are now built using a randomized decision-tree growing procedure [8].
- Use of two language models (LMs) in the decoding process: Fast decoding employs static graphs with a small LM for the initial decoding phases, whereas on-line dynamic decoding is used for the final recognition step in conjunction with a very large LM. Both LMs are built by introducing an additional source of data mined from the world wide web.

The remainder of the paper is structured as follows: Data resources used for training, development, and evaluation are overviewed in Section 2. Section 3 is devoted to system descriptions, including speaker segmentation, acoustic and language modeling, and the decoding process. Particular emphasis is placed on improvements over the IBM systems evaluated in RT06s. Experimental results on development data, as well as on the RT07 evaluation test set, are presented in Section 4. Finally, Section 5 concludes the paper.

## 2  Data Resources

For the lecture meeting domain of the RT evaluation campaign, development and evaluation data are provided by the CHIL consortium [1], that includes five partner sites with state-of-the-art smart rooms of similar sensory setups. However, for STT system training purposes, the available amount of CHIL data is insufficient. To remedy this problem, additional publicly available corpora [9] are utilized that exhibit similarities to the CHIL scenario, as discussed next.

### 2.1  Training Data

The following data resources are used for system training:

- ICSI meeting data corpus, about 70 hours in duration.
- NIST meeting pilot corpus, about 15 hours.
- RT04 development and evaluation data, about 2.5 hours.
- RT05s development data, about 6 hours.
- AMI meetings, about 16 hours.
- CHIL 2003 and 2004 data, for a total of 4 hours.
- CHIL 2006 and 2007 development data, about 6 hours.
- Part of the CHIL RT06s evaluation test set, consisting of 11 five-minute segments, about 1 hour in total.

All datasets contain close-talking and multiple far-field microphone data. For far-field acoustic model training, we select all table-top microphones present in the corpora, with the exception of AMI data, where two microphones from the eight-element circular microphone arrays are chosen based on their location. This results to approximately 500 hours of far-field data. Notice that additional available resources, such as recently released AMI data and NIST meetings are not used for acoustic modeling; however, their transcripts are employed for language modeling. The TED corpus [10] is also not used, due to its reliance on lapel microphone recordings. Finally, due to time constraints, no new close-talking acoustic model has been developed; instead, the IBM RT06s model is used, trained on a subset of the above-listed resources [6].

### 2.2   Development, Evaluation Data, and Conditions

For system development (tuning), we utilize as development data (dev) the remaining part of the RT06s evaluation test set, not used in system training. This consists of 17 five-minute segments, for a total of 85 mins, recorded in all five CHIL smart room sites. The evaluation data set (eval) is of course the CHIL RT07 test set, which consists of 32 five-minute long segments.

When reporting results, we focus on the following three conditions, two far-field and one close-talking:

(i)  *Single distant microphone* (SDM) condition, with only one table-top microphone used, as specified by NIST.

(ii) *Multiple distant microphone* (MDM) condition, where typically all table-top microphones (ranging from three to five) are used / combined to yield a single transcript. This constitutes the primary evaluation condition.

(iii) *Individual headset microphone* (IHM) condition, where all headsets worn by lecture participants are decoded, with the purpose of recognizing the wearer's speech (i.e. decoding cross-talk is penalized). To facilitate cross-talk removal, both manual and automatic segmentations are provided, the latter kindly contributed by ICSI/SRI [11].

## 3   The IBM Systems

We now proceed to describe the IBM systems developed for the RT07 evaluation on the lecture meeting domain. Since training procedures for both IHM and far-field systems (SDM and MDM conditions) are similar and all share the same language model, the main emphasis of the presentation is placed on far-field STT. Similarly to the RT06s evaluation [6], this is developed around an architecture that combines decoded outputs of multiple systems over multiple table-top microphones (in the MDM case). The section describes front-end processing, speaker segmentation, acoustic and language modeling, and the decoding process, with emphasis on modifications over last year's systems. No description is given for the SASTT system, since this is an obvious union of the far-field STT and SPKR subsystems described in this section.

## 3.1    Acoustic Front-End

The features extracted from the acoustic signal for STT are 40-dimensional vectors obtained from a linear discriminant analysis (LDA) projection. The source space for the projection is 117-dimensional and is obtained by concatenating nine temporally consecutive 13-dimensional acoustic observation vectors based on perceptual linear prediction (PLP). The PLP features are computed at a rate of 100 frames per second from a Hamming windowed speech segment of 25 ms in duration. The vectors contain 13 cepstral parameters obtained from the LPC analysis of the cubic root of the inverse DCT of the log outputs of a 24-band, triangular filter bank. The filters are positioned at equidistant points on the Mel-frequency scale between 0 and 8 kHz. The cepstral parameters are mean-normalized on a per-speaker basis. No noise filtering is applied to the audio.

## 3.2    Speaker Segmentation

The first step of speaker segmentation is speech activity detection (SAD). After SAD, long segments of non-speech (silence or noise) are removed, and the audio is split into shorter segments for fast decoding and speaker segmentation. Last year, IBM developed two schemes for SAD, a complex one used in the RT06s SAD evaluation [12], and a simpler scheme employed for STT [6]. The latter is used again this year, but improved. It basically constitutes an HMM speech/non-speech decoder: Speech and non-speech segments are modeled with five-state, left-to-right HMMs with no skip states. The output HMM distributions are tied across all HMM states, and are modeled with a mixture of diagonal-covariance Gaussians. The non-speech model includes the silence phone and three noise phones, whereas the speech model retains all remaining (speech) phones. Both are obtained by a likelihood-based, bottom-up clustering procedure, applied to the speaker-independent STT acoustic model, MAP-adapted to the available CHIL training data. SAD system details can be found in [5].

The SAD system output is passed as input to the speaker segmenter (SPKR). As compared to our approach last year (part of the IBM RT06s STT system, but not evaluated separately), this year we remove the change-point detection procedure, but keep the simple speaker clustering scheme with few modifications: All homogeneous speech segments are modeled using a single Gaussian and are bottom-up clustered by $K$-means with a Mahalanobis distance measure. Instead of having a pre-set fixed number of clusters, we first over-segment the data into, let's say eight clusters, merge clusters according to the Mahalanobis distance, and stop merging when a threshold value is reached – optimized on development data. We also switch to extracting 19-dimensional MFCC acoustic features (with no energy term), instead of PLP ones, since the former are widely used in the speaker recognition literature. Details of the system are presented in [5].

## 3.3    Acoustic Modeling

The speaker-independent (SI) acoustic model is trained on 40-dimensional features, extracted as discussed in Section 3.1. It employs left-to-right HMMs with

Gaussian mixture emission distributions and uniform transition probabilities. In addition, the model uses a global semi-tied covariance linear transformation [13,14] that is updated at each EM training iteration. The sizes of the mixtures are increased in steps interspersed with EM updates until the final model complexity is reached. Each HMM has three states, except for a single-state silence HMM. The system uses 45 phones, among which 41 are speech phones, one corresponds to silence, and three model noise, namely background noise, vocal noise, and breathing. The final HMMs have 6k context-dependent tied states and 200k Gaussian mixture components. Since a very small portion of the available training data come from CHIL sites, MAP adaptation of the SI model to CHIL data was deemed necessary to improve its performance on lecture meetings.

The SI features are further normalized with a voicing model (VTLN) with no variance normalization. The frequency warping is piece-wise linear with a breakpoint at 6500 Hz. The most likely frequency warping is estimated among 21 candidate warping factors ranging from 0.8 to 1.2 with a step of 0.02. Warping likelihoods are obtained by means of a voicing model, built on 13-dimensional PLP features. A VTLN model is then trained on features in the VTLN warped space. VTLN warping factors are estimated on a per-speaker basis for all training set data using the voicing model. In that feature space, a new LDA transform is estimated and a new VTLN model is obtained by decision tree clustering of quin-phone statistics. The resulting HMMs have 10k tied states and 320k Gaussians.

Following VTLN, speaker adaptive training (SAT) is performed. The SAT model is trained on features in a linearly transformed feature space, resulting from applying feature-space maximum likelihood linear regression (fMLLR) transforms to the VTLN normalized features [14]. The fMLLR transforms are computed on a per-speaker basis, for all training set speakers. The resulting SAT HMMs have 10k tied states and 320k Gaussians.

Following SAT model training, we estimate feature-space minimum phone error (fMPE) transforms [15], and subsequently perform minimum phone error (MPE) training. The fMPE projection uses 1024 Gaussians obtained from clustering the Gaussian components of the SAT model. Posterior probabilities are then computed for these Gaussians for each frame, and time-spliced vectors of the resulting probabilities become the basis for the features subjected to the fMPE transformation. Such transformation maps the high-dimensional posterior-based observation space to a 40-dimensional fMPE feature space. The MPE model is subsequently trained in this space, with MAP-MPE applied to the available amount of CHIL training data [16]. In this implementation, we have changed the MPE objective function to operate on the frame level [17], instead of the utterance level, as this resulted in slight gains.

The above training procedure provides two systems: System (A) with VTLN present, and system (B) without the VTLN step. Based on experience from the RT06s results [6], we do not use variance normalization in the VTLN and SAT models. To yield better gains by ROVER-based system combination [7], we built two additional SAT systems using the randomized decision tree approach [8] (discussed briefly next). For both, the process starts from SAT system (B), followed by fMPE/MPE training. The two additional resulting systems will be denoted by (C) and (D), and – similarly to systems (A) and (B) – they too consist of 10k tied states and 320k Gaussians.

In more detail, randomized decision trees are grown by randomly selecting the split at each node, among the top $N$-best split candidates ($N=5$ in our case). This is in contrast to standard decision trees that are grown by only considering the best split. Systems built on different sets of randomized decision trees will model different clusters of context-dependent units. Multiple systems can then be systematically obtained by simply changing the random number generator seed. It has been experimentally shown that such systems are good candidates to be used in the ROVER voting procedure [8]. Results in Section 4 support this observation.

## 3.4   Language Modeling

To improve language modeling over our RT06s system [6], we complement the four training sources used last year with web data. We thus construct five separate four-gram language models (LMs), all smoothed with the modified Kneser-Ney algorithm [18]: The first LM is based on 0.15M words of CHIL meeting transcript data; the second uses 2.7M words of non-CHIL meeting corpora resources; the third one utilizes 37M scientific conference proceedings (primarily from data processed by CHIL partner LIMSI); the fourth LM uses 3M words of Fisher data [9]; and finally the fifth employs 525M web data available from the EARS program [9]. To construct the LM used for the static decoding graph, we interpolate the five models with weights of 0.31, 0.24, 0.20, 0.06, and 0.19 respectively (optimized on CHIL 2007 development data, as well as 11 segments of the RT06s evaluation test set). We subsequently perform entropy-based pruning [19] to reduce the resulting model to about 5M n-grams. We then employ this LM at the SI and MPE decoding steps (see also Section 3.5). In addition, we consider a much larger LM in conjunction with on-the-fly dynamic graph expansion decoding at the final recognition step (see next subsection). This LM is obtained by pruning only the web data LM, and it consists of 152M n-grams.

A 37k-word vocabulary is obtained by keeping all words occurring in the meeting transcripts and Fisher data and the 20k most frequent words in the other text corpora. Pronunciations use the phone set discussed in Section 3.3, and are based on the Pronlex lexicon, manually augmented whenever necessary.

## 3.5   Recognition Process

After pseudo-speakers are determined following speaker segmentation, for each table-top microphone, a final system output is obtained in the following three decoding passes:

(i)  The SI pass uses MAP-adapted SI models to decode.

(ii) Using the transcript from (i), warp factors are estimated for each cluster using the voicing model, and fMLLR transforms are estimated for each cluster using the SAT model. The VTLN features after applying the fMLLR transforms are subjected to the fMPE transform, and a new transcript is obtained by decoding using the MPE model and the fMPE features. The MPE model is also trained with MAP on the CHIL data. The one-best transcript at this step is referred to as ctm-n, where n stands for model (A), (B), (C), or (D).

(iii) The output transcripts from step (ii) are used to estimate maximum likelihood linear regression (MLLR) transforms on the MPE model. The adapted MPE model together with a large 152M n-gram language model are used for final decoding with a dynamic graph expansion decoder. The final one-best transcript at this step will be referred to as CTM-n, where n stands for model (A), (B), (C), or (D).

For each system at step (iii), instead of using the corresponding decoding output from step (ii), we employ cross-system adaptation as follows: ctm-(A) is used as input to system (C), ctm-(C) to system (B), ctm-(B) to (D), and finally ctm-(D) is used as input to system (A). The above process is shown to be beneficial in Section 4.

For the SDM evaluation condition, all four system outputs are combined using ROVER. For the MDM condition, two rounds of ROVER are applied: First, for each system we combine the outputs from all available table-top microphones; subsequently, we combine the four results across systems to obtain the final transcript.

Concerning runtime performance, the MDM system runs at approximately 90 times slower than real time ($\times$ RT). This can be broken down to 3.6 $\times$ RT for the SI decoding stage, 4.2 $\times$ RT for each of the four MPE system decodings, and 17.5 $\times$ RT for each of the four final MLLR adapted MPE decodings employing the large LM.

### 3.6    The Close-Talking STT System

For the close-talking STT system (IHM condition), we used the acoustic model trained in last year's evaluation (RT06s), in conjunction with the LMs developed for RT07, described in Section 3.4. In particular, our RT06s acoustic model used a subset of the resources listed in Section 2.1 with a total duration of 124 hrs. In contrast to the far-field, only one acoustic model was developed, with both VTLN and variance normalization present, consisting of 5k context dependent states and 240k Gaussians. Details can be found in [6]. For decoding, all three steps described in Section 3.5 are used, with the obvious modification that MLLR adaptation in step (iii) is carried out within the single available system. Furthermore, for cross-talk removal, the ICSI/SRI system output is employed [11].

## 4    Experimental Results and Discussion

We now proceed to present experimental results on our development (dev) set (a subset of the RT06s evaluation test set, as discussed in Section 2.2), as well as the lecture meeting RT07 evaluation test data (eval), for both STT and SASTT.

**Table 1.** STT WERs, %, at various decoding stages, for the RT06s and RT07 systems. For the latter, results with the reference segmentation are also depicted. All WERs are reported on the dev set for the MDM condition, with system (B) considered past the SI decoding level. For the automatic segmentation case, SPKR diarization error is 70.1% for the RT06s system, but only 9.2% for the RT07 one.

| STT system | RT07 | | RT06s |
|---|---|---|---|
| segmentation | reference | automatic | |
| SI | 54.1 | 54.2 | 61.2 |
| MPE - sys. (B) | 45.8 | 46.0 | 50.6 |
| MLLR-MPE - sys. (B) | 43.5 | 43.4 | – |

For the latter task, in addition to the three traditional types of word errors (deletions, insertions, and substitutions), speaker-attributed word errors include speaker label error, i.e. the mapped STT output tokens with matching reference words but non-matching speaker labels. Therefore, SASTT performance really measures both STT word error rate (WER) and diarization error (DER) of the SPKR task. Notice that in this paper, all WER results are reported scored with speech overlap factor set to one [4] – with the exception of Table 6.

We first demonstrate the significant improvement in far-field STT from RT06s to RT07. This is depicted in Table 4 for the MDM condition on our dev set, for one of the four acoustic models (model (B)). For example, SI WER improves from 61.2% (RT06s) to 54.2% (RT07). The improvement is due to a number of factors as discussed in the Introduction, including better acoustic and language modeling, as well as better speaker segmentation. In particular, it is noteworthy that the automatic speaker segmentation scheme used in the RT06s STT system achieves a dismal DER of 70.1%, whereas the RT07 segmentation scheme employed to obtain the tabulated results exhibits a 9.2% DER. The improvement is due to various factors, including the fact that the final number of speaker clusters is no longer fixed to four. Relevant SPKR system experiments can be found in [5]. Notice also, that for the RT07 system, the use of reference (manual) or automatic segmentation results in very similar WERs.

As already mentioned, much of the STT improvement is due to language modeling work. This fact is demonstrated in Table 2, where decoding performance using the RT06s and the two RT07 LMs is depicted, in conjunction with RT07 acoustic model (B). Adding web data to the small LM for SI static-graph

**Table 2.** Dev-set WERs, %, for the MDM STT system developed for RT07, when employing various language models developed for RT06s and RT07. Depicted results are obtained using the reference segmentation.

| Language Model | RT06s LM | RT07 – small LM | RT07 – large LM |
|---|---|---|---|
| SI | 55.2 | 54.2 | – |
| MLLR-MPE - sys. (B) | – | 46.7 | 43.5 |

**Table 3.** Dev-set WERs, %, of the various developed STT systems for the MDM condition using automatic segmentation

| system | (A) | (B) | (C) | (D) |
|---|---|---|---|---|
| MAP-SI | 54.2 | | | |
| MPE | 46.3 | 46.0 | 47.3 | 46.3 |
| cross-MLLR+MPE | 42.9 | 43.4 | 43.3 | 43.0 |
| final ROVER | 41.9 | | | |

decoding achieves a 1% absolute gain in WER (55.2% to 54.2%); employing the very large LM with the dynamic decoder achieves over 3% absolute WER gain, from 46.7% to 43.5%. Clearly, the large LM helps. It is also worth mentioning that decoding with the static graph and the MLLR-adapted MPE model degrades WER from 45.8% (MPE model (B)) to 46.7%, a behavior consistent with the RT06s acoustic model. It therefore seems that our MLLR-adapted MPE model is worth using only with the very large LM.

In Table 3, we depict STT results on the dev set for the various developed systems at the MDM condition. After applying ROVER across all systems, we obtain a WER of 41.9%, which represents a large improvement over the 50.0% WER of our RT06s system – a 16% relative (8% absolute) WER reduction. Clearly, ROVER-based system combination helps, improving performance over the best system by 1% absolute. It is also interesting to remark that cross-system adaptation helps. For example, cross adaptation of system (A) reduces WER from 46.3% at the MPE level to 42.9%. That number would have been 44.1% under a self-adaptation regime.

The observed improvements in the dev set carry over to the eval set. Table 4 presents STT results on the RT07 evaluation test set (eval) for the MDM and SDM conditions. By selecting the highest-SNR microphones to drive the SAD and SPKR subsystems, and by applying ROVER across all available table-top microphones, the final WER at the MDM condition is 3.6% absolute better

**Table 4.** Far-field STT WERs, %, on the eval set at various decoding stages for the MDM and SDM conditions. The final ROVER results are obtained by combining all four systems (A)-(D), and were submitted at the RT07 evaluation with a one week delay. The primary IBM RT07 STT submissions on-time have combined three only systems (due to lack of sufficient time to train the fourth), resulting in WERs of 44.8% and 48.6% for the MDM and SDM conditions, respectively.

| condition | MDM | | | | SDM | | | |
|---|---|---|---|---|---|---|---|---|
| system | (A) | (B) | (C) | (D) | (A) | (B) | (C) | (D) |
| MAP-SI | 55.5 | | | | 58.6 | | | |
| MPE | 48.9 | 48.6 | 48.6 | 48.9 | 53.7 | 53.1 | 53.2 | 53.4 |
| cross-MLLR+MPE | 46.1 | 46.3 | 46.0 | 46.0 | 50.7 | 50.9 | 51.1 | 51.0 |
| final ROVER | 44.3 | | | | 47.9 | | | |

**Table 5.** Eval-set WERs, %, of the IHM system depicted at various decoding stages using both automatic and reference segmentation

| segmentation | automatic | reference |
|:---:|:---:|:---:|
| MAP-SI | 44.1 | 43.2 |
| MPE | 34.6 | 33.4 |
| cross-MLLR+MPE | 33.4 | 31.7 |

**Table 6.** SASTT results on dev and eval data. SPKR and STT system performance is also depicted. STT and SASTT performance is also shown when scoring overlapped speech ("o3" condition).

| data | condition | SPKR DER (%) | STT WER (%) | | SASTT WER (%) | |
|:---:|:---:|:---:|:---:|:---:|:---:|:---:|
| | | o1 | o1 | o3 | o1 | o3 |
| dev | MDM | 9.2 | 41.9 | – | 44.1 | – |
| eval | MDM | 27.6 | 44.3 | 50.0 | 52.0 | 58.4 |
| eval | SDM | 27.4 | 47.9 | – | 55.4 | 60.8 |

than the final WER at the SDM condition. Between SI decoding and the final result, the WER improves by a relative 20% (18%) for the MDM (SDM) condition. These gains are less than the 23% relative observed on the dev set. The reason may be that the DER of the SPKR sybsystem on eval data is much higher (27.6%) than that on dev data (9.2% – see also [5] and Table 6). Further improvements are clearly needed in the SPKR system.

For the IHM condition, we used both the automatic segmentation provided by ICSI/SRI [11], as well as the reference segmentation. Table 5 depicts the eval set results. The final WER using the reference segmentation is about 1.7% better than the WER based on automatic segmentation, with 1.4% more substitution errors but 3.2% less deletion errors. It seems that the automatic segmentation misses some speaker segments.

Finally, Table 6 presents our best WERs for SASTT, as well as DERs for SPKR on both dev and eval sets, with overlapping factor set to one (or three) during scoring [4]. Notice that the WER degradation from the STT to the SASTT task is significantly higher in the eval set than in dev. This is due to the poor performance of the SPKR system on the eval set, as already mentioned.

## 5   Conclusions

We have made significant progress in the automatic transcription of lecture meeting data. Main system advances compared to the RT06s evaluation are improvements in speech activity detection, speaker segmentation, acoustic modeling, system combination, and development of a very large language model that incorporates web data. The effort has led to a 16% relative reduction in word error rate on development data and has resulted in competitive performance in the RT07 evaluation.

## Acknowledgements

We would like to acknowledge support of this work by the European Commission under integrated project CHIL, "Computers in the Human Interaction Loop", contract number 506909.

## References

1. Computers in the Human Interaction Loop, http://chil.server.de
2. Augmented Multi-party Interaction, http://www.amiproject.org
3. The NIST SmartSpace Laboratory, http://www.nist.gov/smartspace
4. Fiscus, J.G., Ajot, J., Michel, M., Garofolo, J.S.: The Rich Transcription 2006 Spring meeting recognition evaluation. In: Renals, S., Bengio, S., Fiscus, J.G. (eds.) MLMI 2006. LNCS, vol. 4299, pp. 309–322. Springer, Heidelberg (2006)
5. Huang, J., Marcheret, E., Visweswariah, K., Potamianos, G.: The IBM RT07 evaluation system for speaker diarization in CHIL seminars (same volume) (2007)
6. Huang, J., Westphal, M., Chen, S., et al.: The IBM Rich Transcription Spring 2006 speech-to-text system for lecture meetings. In: Renals, S., Bengio, S., Fiscus, J.G. (eds.) MLMI 2006. LNCS, vol. 4299, pp. 432–443. Springer, Heidelberg (2006)
7. Fiscus, J.G.: A post-processing system to yield reduced word error rates: Recogniser output voting error reduction (ROVER). In: Proc. Automatic Speech Recognition Underst. Works, Santa Barbara, CA, pp. 347–352 (1997)
8. Siohan, O., Ramabhadran, B., Kingsbury, B.: Constructing ensembles of ASR systems using randomized decision trees. In: Proc. Int. Conf. Acoustics Speech Signal Process, Philadelphia, vol. 1, pp. 197–200 (2005)
9. The LDC Corpus Catalog, Linguistic Data Consortium, University of Pennsylvania, Philadelphia, PA, http://www.ldc.upenn.edu/Catalog
10. Lamel, L.F., Schiel, F., Fourcin, A., Mariani, J., Tillmann, H.: The translanguage English database (TED). In: Proc. Int. Conf. Spoken Language Process, Yokohama, Japan (1994)
11. Boakye, K., Stolcke, A.: Improved speech activity detection using cross-channel features for recognition of multiparty meetings. In: Proc. Int. Conf. Spoken Language Process, Pittsburgh, pp. 1962–1965 (2006)
12. Marcheret, E., Potamianos, G., Visweswariah, K., Huang, J.: The IBM RT06s evaluation system for speech activity detection in CHIL seminars. In: Renals, S., Bengio, S., Fiscus, J.G. (eds.) MLMI 2006. LNCS, vol. 4299, pp. 323–335. Springer, Heidelberg (2006)
13. Gales, M.J.F.: Maximum likelihood linear transformations for HMM-based speech recognition. Computer Speech and Language 12, 75–98 (1998)
14. Saon, G., Zweig, G., Padmanabhan, M.: Linear feature space projections for speaker adaptation. In: Proc. Int. Conf. Acoustics Speech Signal Process, Salt Lake City, UT, pp. 325–328 (2001)
15. Povey, D., Kingsbury, B., Mangu, L., Saon, G., Soltau, H., Zweig, G.: fMPE: Discriminatively trained features for speech recognition. In: Proc. Int. Conf. Acoustics Speech Signal Process, Philadelphia, vol. 1, pp. 961–964 (2005)

16. Povey, D., Woodland, P.C.: Minimum phone error and I-smoothing for improved discriminative training. In: Proc. Int. Conf. Acoustics Speech Signal Process, Orlando, FL, pp. 105–108 (2002)
17. Zheng, J., Stolcke, A.: Improved discriminative training using phone lattices. In: Proc. Eurospeech, Lisbon, Portugal, pp. 2125–2128 (2005)
18. Chen, S.F., Goodman, J.: An empirical study of smoothing techniques for language modeling. Computer Speech and Language 13, 359–393 (1999)
19. Stolcke, A.: Entropy-based pruning of backoff language models. In: Proc. DARPA Broadcast News Transcr. Underst. Works, Lansdowne, VA, pp. 270–274 (1998)

# The LIMSI RT07 Lecture Transcription System

L. Lamel, E. Bilinski, J.L. Gauvain, G. Adda, C. Barras[1], and X. Zhu[1],[*]

LIMSI-CNRS, BP 133, 91403 Orsay Cedex, France
[1] Also with Univ Paris-Sud, F-91405, Orsay, France
{lamel,bilinski,gauvain,gadda,barras,xuan}@limsi.fr

**Abstract.** A system to automatically transcribe lectures and presentations has been developed in the context of the FP6 Integrated Project CHIL. In addition to the seminar data recorded by the CHIL partners, widely available corpora were used to train both the acoustic and language models. Acoustic model training made use of the transcribed portion of the TED corpus of Eurospeech recordings, as well as the ICSI, ISL, and NIST meeting corpora. For language model training, text materials were extracted from a variety of on-line conference proceedings. Experimental results are reported for close-talking and far-field microphones on development and evaluation data.

## 1   Introduction

In the Computers in the Human Interaction Loop (CHIL) project (http://chil.server.de) services are being developed which use computers to improve human-human communication. One of the CHIL services is to provide support for lecture situations, such as providing transcriptions and summaries in close-to-real time for interactive applications or providing off-line support for archiving, search and retrieval, all of which can benefit from automatic processing. One can imagine a future where all public presentations (classes, lectures, seminars, workshops and conferences) are archived for future viewing and selected access. Automatic techniques can provide a wealth of annotations, enabling users to search the audio data to find talks on specific topics or by certain speakers. At LIMSI a transcription system for off-line processing of lecture and seminar has been developed within the context of the CHIL project.

The speech recognizer for CHIL has been derived from the LIMSI Broadcast News transcription system for American English [7]. In addition to the CHIL data available, acoustic and language model training made use of widely available corpora including the TED corpus of Eurospeech recordings, the ICSI, ISL, and NIST meeting corpora. For language model training, in addition to the transcriptions of the audio data, text materials were extracted from a variety of on-line conference proceedings. The LIMSI CHIL speech recognizers used in previous evaluations are described in [9,11,12]. In the remainder of this paper the 2007 speech recognizer is described, and development results are provided.

---

[*] This work was partially financed by the European Commission under the FP6 Integrated Project IP 506909 CHIL.

R. Stiefelhagen et al. (Eds.): CLEAR 2007 and RT 2007, LNCS 4625, pp. 442–449, 2008.

**Table 1.** Summary of audio data sources. The top part of the table lists the audio data available in 2005 (97h of IHM data from 4 sources). The middle lists the additional 76h of data used in training the 2006 system and the bottom lists the additional data used in the 2007 system.

| Source | Microphone | Type | Amount |
|---|---|---|---|
| TED | lapel | 39 speeches | 9.3h |
| ISL | lapel | 18 meetings | 10.3h |
| ICSI | head mounted | 75 meetings | 60h |
| NIST | head mounted | 19 meetings | 17.2h |
| ICSI | tabletop | 75 meetings | 70h |
| CHIL | head mounted | 17 seminars | 6.2h |
| TED | lapel mics, lightly supervised | 190 speeches | 46h |
| Beamformed lecture data tabletop | | rt05s, rt06s, dev07 | <7h |

## 2   Recognizer Overview

The speech recognizer uses the same core technology and is built using the same training utilities as the LIMSI Broadcast News transcription system described in [7]. The transcription system has two main components, an audio partitioner and a word recognizer. Data partitioning is based on an audio stream mixture model [7], and serves to divide the continuous stream of acoustic data into homogeneous segments, associating cluster, gender and labels with each non-overlapping segment. This year the data partitioner was adapted to the MDM beamformed data [18]. For each speech segment, the word recognizer determines the sequence of words, associating start and end times and an optional confidence measure with each word. The word recognizer makes use of continuous density HMMs with Gaussian mixture for acoustic modeling and n-gram statistics estimated on large text corpora for language modeling. Each context-dependent phone model is a tied-state left-to-right CD-HMM with Gaussian mixture observation densities where the tied states are obtained via a decision tree.

The language models (LMs) are interpolated backoff n-gram models estimated on subsets of the available training texts. The recognition word list was selected from the audio transcripts and the proceedings texts so as to minimize the out-of-vocabulary (OOV) rate on a set of development data. The vocabulary contains 58k (case-sensitive) words, including several thousand compound words and acronyms.

Word recognition is performed in multiple decoding passes, where each decoding pass generates a word lattice with cross-word, position-dependent, gender-dependent acoustic models, followed by consensus decoding [14] with 4-gram and pronunciation probabilities. Unsupervised acoustic model adaptation is performed for each segment cluster using the CMLLR and MLLR [13] techniques prior to each decoding pass.

## 3   Training Corpora

One of the challenges of the lecture transcription task is locating appropriate audio and textual resources with which to develop the recognizer models. Although multi-site

**Table 2.** Summary of audio transcripts from various sources (top) and proceedings texts (bottom) along with the number of words by source

| | |
|---|---|
| TED oral presentations | 71k words |
| NIST meetings | 156k words |
| ISL meetings | 116k words |
| ICSI | 785k words |
| CTS | 3M words |
| AMI/IDIAP meeting | 143k words |
| NIST RT04, RT05 data | 57k words |
| CHIL Jun04/Jan05 seminars | 55k words |
| CHIL summer04 seminars | 38k words |

| | | |
|---|---|---|
| TED texts: | 426 papers | 929k words |
| ASRU'99-05: | 427 papers | 1140k words |
| DARPA'97-99,04: | 119 papers | 317k words |
| Eurospeech'97-05: | 3485 papers | 7650k words |
| ICASSP'95-05: | 7831 papers | 14318k words |
| ICME'00,03: | 996 papers | 2101k words |
| ICSLP'96-04: | 3202 papers | 7198k words |
| LREC'02,04: | 891 papers | 2553k words |
| ISCA+other workshops: | 2333 papers | 6077k words |

data collection was carried out in the CHIL project, most of this data was reserved for development and testing purposes with only a limited amount of transcribed data available for speech recognizer training. Therefore a variety of publicly available corpora were used for training. The most closely related audio data are the TED recordings of presentations at the *Eurospeech* conference in Berlin 1993 [10]. The majority of presentations are made by non-native speakers of English. Although there are 188 oral presentations (about 50 hours of audio recordings), transcriptions are only available for 39 lectures [1]. This year a biased-LM version of the LIMSI RT06 close-talking microphone speech system was used to transcribe the remaining 190 speeches (46h) so these could be also used for acoustic model training. Other related data sources are the ISL, ICSI and NIST meeting corpora which contain audio recordings made with multiple microphones of a variety of meetings (3-10 participants) on different topics [5,6,8]. The amount of data per corpus is summarized in Table 1. The first four corpora were used in training the 2005 system and contain data recorded with individual head-mounted microphones (IHM); the middle two entries were added in the 2006 system; and the last two were added in the 2007 system. From the available farfield data in the ICSI corpus for which there are a varying number of channels, the farfield microphone channel with highest likelihood during forced alignment was selected as being the most appropriate for each speaker. The 2007 acoustic models were trained on pooled data from all sources, including close-talking microphone data, tabletop distant microphone data and a small amount of beamformed data. The ICSI delay&sum signal enhancement software [2] was used to process all the available lecture training and test data (rt05s, rt06s, and dev07).

The language model training data are the same as were used in the 2006 system and consist of manual transcriptions of related audio data as well as the proceedings texts from a variety of speech and language related conferences and workshops. The audio transcripts come from the same sources as are used for acoustic training. In addition transcriptions of conversational telephone speech (CTS) from the CallHome, Switch-Board and Fisher collections (distributed by the LDC) were used. The amount of words in the each audio transcript source are given in Table 2. In addition to the audio transcripts, almost 20k papers in the proceedings of workshops and conferences in the audio, speech and language processing domain were used for language modeling. These texts shown in the lower part for Table 2 were processed by tools derived from ones shared by ITC-IRST.

## 4   Audio Partitioner

The LIMSI RT-07S speaker diarization system for the conference and lecture meetings is fully described in [18]. This system builds upon the RT-06S diarization system designed for lecture data. The diarization system combines agglomerative clustering based on Bayesian information criterion (BIC) with a second clustering using state-of-the-art speaker identification (SID) techniques [4,17]. The system has 5 steps which use a 38-dimensional feature vector consisting of 12 cepstral coefficients, $\Delta$ and $\Delta$-$\Delta$ coefficients plus the $\Delta$ and $\Delta$-$\Delta$ log-energy. 1) Speech activity detection (SAD), which locates speech portions in the signal using a Log-Likelihood Ratio (LLR) based speech activity detector [17]. The SAD acoustic models, each with 256 Gaussians, were trained on about 5 hours of conference meeting data from the NIST RT'04 and RT'05 evaluations. 2) Initial segmentation, which is performed by taking the maxima of a local Gaussian divergence measure between two adjacent sliding windows of 5 seconds. 3) Viterbi resegmentation is used to refine the segment boundaries using 8-component GMMs trained from the initial speech segments. 4) BIC clustering which is used to successively merge speech segments, and 5) Speaker clustering is carried out using speaker recognition methods [3,15].

Since the speech activity detection error of the baseline system was relatively high (about 10%) on lecture data, some of the normalization techniques and acoustic representations that were explored to improve performance are described in [18]. The RT07 diarization system integrating these improvements obtains comparable results on both the RT-07S conference and lecture evaluation data for the multiple distant microphone (MDM) condition.

## 5   Acoustic Modeling

The acoustic feature vector has 39-components comprised of 12 cepstrum coefficients and the log energy, along with the first and second order derivatives. The cepstral parameters are derived from a Mel frequency spectrum estimated on the 0-8kHz band every 10ms. For each 30ms frame the Mel scale power spectrum is computed, and the cubic root taken followed by an inverse Fourier transform. Then LPC-based cepstrum coefficients are computed. The cepstral coefficients are normalized on a segment-cluster basis using cepstral mean removal and variance normalization. Thus each cepstral coefficient for each cluster has a zero mean and unity variance.

The acoustic models are context-dependent, 3-state left-to-right hidden Markov models with Gaussian mixture. The triphone-based phone models are word-independent and gender-independent, but word position-dependent. The acoustic models are MLLT-SAT trained, with different sets of tied-state models used in successive decoding passes. State-tying is carried out via divisive decision tree clustering, constructing one tree for each state position of each phone so as to maximize the likelihood of the training data using single Gaussian state models, penalized by the number of tied-states [7]. A set of 152 questions concern the phone position, the distinctive features (and identities) of the phone and the neighboring phones.

Two sets of models were estimated on all the available training data, and MAP adapted with the beamformed data. Since only a very small amount of beamformed data was available, for the final system, the RT06s data used for development was also included in the adaptation data. The small set covers 5k phone contexts and has 5.2k tied states with 32 Gaussians per state. The large set covers 25k phone contexts, with 11.5k tied states and 32 Gaussians per state.

## 6   Language Modeling

The LIMSI RT07 system used two language models, a case-insensitive 35k LM from the 2005 system and the 58k case-sensitive LM from the RT06 system. The recognizer word lists were determined by interpolating unigram language models trained on different subsets of the available training texts listed in Table 2. The proceeding texts are comprised of the proceedings from 54 conferences and workshops in speech and language, which represent about 20,000 PDF documents. While not used for vocabulary selection, the CTS data were used for language model training.

For language model estimation the available corpora were grouped into 3 sources: 1) Seminar and meeting transcriptions (1.42M words); 2) Proceedings texts (46M words); 3) Transcriptions of Conversational Telephone Speech databases available from LDC (29M words). Three backoff n-gram language models were estimated, one on each of the data subsets. The component language models were interpolated [16], and the weights were chosen to minimize the perplexity of the development data. The largest weight is for the transcriptions (0.6), with weights of 0.3 and 0.1 for the proceedings texts and CTS transcripts respectively. The perplexities and OOV rates of the 4-gram LMs are shown in Table 3. The 58k LM contains 8.8M fourgrams, 19M trigrams, 5M bigrams, and the 35k LM contains 6.6M fourgrams, 15M trigrams, 4M bigrams. More information concerning the language models can be found in [12].

## 7   Decoding

Word recognition is performed in two passes, where each decoding pass generates a word lattice which is expanded with a 4-gram LM. The posterior probabilities of the lattice edges are estimated using the forward-backward algorithm. The 4-gram lattices are converted to a confusion network with posterior probabilities by iteratively merging

**Table 3.** Perplexities and OOV rates of the 35k and 58k language models on the development and test data

| Data set | rt06 | | dev07 | | rt07 | |
|---|---|---|---|---|---|---|
| Language Model | OOV | Px | OOV | Px | OOV | Px |
| 35k 4-gram | 0.4 | 157 | 0.9 | 165 | 0.7 | 136 |
| 58k 4-gram | 0.4 | 162 | 0.8 | 163 | 0.7 | 138 |

lattice vertices and splitting lattices edges until a linear graph is obtained. This procedure gives comparable results to the edge clustering algorithm proposed in [14]. The words with the highest posterior in each confusion set are hypothesized.

**Pass 1: Initial Hypothesis Generation -** This step generates initial hypotheses which are then used for speaker-based acoustic model adaptation. This is done via one pass (about 1xRT) cross-word trigram decoding with gender-independent sets of position-dependent triphones (5k contexts, 5k tied states) and a 35k word trigram language model (15M trigrams and 4M bigrams). The trigram lattices are rescored with a 4-gram language model (6.6M fourgrams, 15M trigrams and 4M bigrams).

**Pass 2: Adapted decode -** Unsupervised acoustic model adaptation of speaker-independent models is performed for each speaker using the CMLLR and MLLR techniques [13] with only two regression class. The lattice is generated for each segment using a 58k word bigram LM and position-dependent triphones with 25k contexts and 11.5k tied states (32 Gaussians per state). As in the first pass, the lattices are rescored with a 58k word 4-gram language model (8.8M fourgrams, 19M trigrams and 5M bigrams) and pronunciation probabilities.

# 8   Experiments and Results

Some initial experiments were carried out using the designated RT07 development set comprised of 5 seminars, one from each CHIL data collection site. The seminars have different durations, ranging from 23 to 44 minutes. The baseline results with the LIMSI RT06 farfield system had a word error rate of 64.4% on the beamformed signal. Although results are reported here only for the second decoding pass, the improvement relative to the first pass is in the range of 4-8% depending upon the test set and system configuration. Updating the segmentation gave a slight error reduction (64.0%). Since the development seminars are significantly longer than the test data which consists of 5-min excerpts, these were divided into 5-min chunks. The WER on the chunked data is 63.0% with the RT06 system.

Since this development data is not representative of the test, and in light of the very limited amount of beamformed data that could be used for model adaptation, the RT06s evaluation data was used for all further system development. These data are comprised of 38 5-minute lecture excerpts contributed by 5 of the CHIL partners: AIT, IBM, ITC, UKA and UPC. Table 4 provides some of the development results. The baseline WER with the RT06s MDM acoustic models on the beamformed data was 65.2%. By adding

**Table 4.** Recognition error rates on the RT06s evaluation data for the baseline acoustic models (MDM AM); pooling the beamformed training data (+ pool bmf); MAP adaptation with the beamformed training data (+ MAP with bmf); and decoding tuning (+ tuning)

| RT06s bmf | Corr (%) | Subs (%) | Del (%) | Ins (%) | WER (%) |
|---|---|---|---|---|---|
| RT06s MDM AM | 41.3 | 37.8 | 20.9 | 6.6 | 65.2 |
| + pool bmf data | 41.2 | 35.4 | 23.3 | 5.6 | 64.4 |
| + MAP with bmf data | 43.4 | 34.6 | 22.0 | 5.6 | 62.2 |
| + tuning | 44.4 | 33.2 | 22.4 | 5.4 | 61.0 |

**Table 5.** Official NIST SASTT and STT results on the RT07s evaluation data

| scoring | Cor (%) | Sub (%) | SpSub (%) | Del (%) | Ins (%) | WER (%) | SER (%) |
|---|---|---|---|---|---|---|---|
| SASTT | 47.6 | 29.8 | 4.2 | 18.4 | 5.5 | 57.9 | 40.0 |
| STT | 51.8 | 29.7 | | 18.4 | 5.6 | 53.7 | 38.3 |

the beamformed data to acoustic training data, the WER is reduced by 0.8%. MAP adapting this models with the beamformed data, gives a further error reduction of over 2% and after tuning a word error of 61% is obtained. This represents an error reduction of about 6% relative to the baseline models.

Table 5 reports the official NIST SASTT results, along with the STT scoring. For the evaluation system, MAP adaptation was performed with all the available beamformed data, including RT06s. The SASTT word error rate is 57.9%, including the 4.2% of erroneous speaker associations. The equivalent STT WER is 53.7%. No system development was done this year for the sdm or ihm conditions, but a few contrastive post-evaluation runs were done. Using the segmentations provided by SRI resulted in a 42.2% WER with the LIMSI RT06s ihm acoustic models and a 40.6% WER with the RT07s multistyle acoustic models. Using a single distant microphone with the an STT WER of 60.7% and an SASTT WER of 63.9% were obtained with the RT07s multistyle acoustic models.

# 9  Conclusions

This paper has described the LIMSI RT07 system aiming to automatically transcribe lectures and seminars for off-line applications. Publicly available corpora were used to train both the acoustic and language models, since only a small amount of CHIL data were available for system development. This was LIMSI's second participation to the multiple farfield microphone task. This year the ICSI beamforming software was used to process the lecture training and test data. In addition to including the available beamformed data during acoustic model training, the remaining TED speeches were transcribed and used in a lightly supervised manner. Compared to the LIMSI 2006 system, this year's system also used a revised audio partitioner which significantly reduced the speaker diarization error on the primary MDM test condition.

# References

1. The Translanguage English Database (TED) Transcripts, LDC catalog number LDC2002T03, ISBN 1-58563-202-3
2. Anguera, X., Wooters, C., Hernando, J.: Speaker Diarization for Multi-Party Meetings Using Acoustic Fusion. In: Automatic Speech Recognition and Understanding (IEEE, ASRU 2005), San Juan, Puerto Rico (2005)
3. Barras, C., Gauvain, J.-L.: Feature and score normalization for speaker verification of cellular data. In: IEEE ICASSP 2003, Hong Kong (2003)
4. Barras, C., Zhu, X., Meignier, S., Gauvain, J.-L.: Multi-Stage Speaker Diarization of Broadcast News. The IEEE Transactions on Audio, Speech and Language Processing (September 2006)
5. Burger, S., MacLaran, V., Yu, H.: The ISL Meeting Corpus: The Impact of Meeting Type on Speech Style. In: ICSLP 2002 (LDC2004S05, LDC2004E04, LDC2004E05), Denver (September 2002)
6. Garofolo, J.S., Laprun, C.D., Michel, M., Stanford, V.M., Tabassi, E.: The NIST Meeting Room Pilot Corpus. In: LREC 2004 (LDC2004S09, LDC2004T13), May 2004, Lisbon (2004)
7. Gauvain, J.L., Lamel, L., Adda, G.: The Limsi Broadcast News Transcription System. Speech Communication 37(1-2), 89–108 (2002)
8. Janin, A., Baron, D., Edwards, J., Ellis, D., Gelbart, D., Morgan, N., Peskin, B., Pfau, T., Shriberg, E., Stolcke, A., Wooters, C.: The ICSI Meeting Corpus. In: ICASSP 2003 (LDC2004S02, LDC2004T04), April 2003, Hong Kong (2003)
9. Lamel, L., Adda, G., Bilinski, E., Gauvain, J.L.: Transcribing Lectures and Seminars. In: Proc. ISCA Eurospeech 2005, September 2005, Lisbon (2005)
10. Lamel, L.F., Schiel, F., Fourcin, A., Mariani, J., Tillmann, H.: The Translanguage English Database TED. In: ICSLP 1994 (LDC2002S04), September 1994, Yokohama (1994)
11. Lamel, L., Schwenk, H., Gauvain, J.L., Adda, G., Bilinski, E.: Improvements in Transcribing Lectures and Seminars. In: Renals, S., Bengio, S. (eds.) MLMI 2005. LNCS, vol. 3869, Springer, Heidelberg (2006)
12. Lamel, L., Bilinski, E., Adda, G., Gauvain, J.L., Schwenk, H.: The LIMSI RT06s Lecture Transcription System. In: Proc. RT 2006s Workshop, May 2006, Washington DC, USA (2006)
13. Leggetter, C.J., Woodland, P.C.: Maximum likelihood linear regression for speaker adaptation of continuous density hidden Markov models. Computer Speech and Language 9(2), 171–185 (1995)
14. Mangu, L., Brill, E., Stolcke, A.: Finding Consensus Among Words: Lattice-Based Word Error Minimization. In: Eurospeech 1999, September 1999, pp. 495–498 (1999)
15. Schroeder, J., Campbell, J. (eds.): Digital Signal Processing (DSP), a review journal - Special issue on NIST 1999 speaker recognition workshop. Academic Press, London (2000)
16. Woodland, P.C., Niesler, T., Whittaker, E.: Language Modeling in the HTK Hub5 LVCSR. In: The 1998 Hub5E Workshop (September 1998)
17. Zhu, X., Barras, C., Lamel, L., Gyauvain, J.L.: Speaker Diarization: From Broadcast News to Lectures. In: Renals, S., Bengio, S., Fiscus, J.G. (eds.) MLMI 2006. LNCS, vol. 4299, pp. 396–406. Springer, Heidelberg (2006)
18. Zhu, X., Barras, C., Lamel, L., Gauvain, J.-L.: Multi-Stage Speaker Diarization for Conference and Lecture Meetings. In: Proc. NIST RT 2007, May 2007, Baltimore (2007)
19. Zhu, X., Barras, C., Meignier, S., Gauvain, J.L.: Combining speaker identification and BIC for speaker diarization. In: Proc. Interspeech 2005, Lisbon, September 2005, pp. 2441–2444 (2005)

# The SRI-ICSI Spring 2007 Meeting and Lecture Recognition System

Andreas Stolcke[1,2], Xavier Anguera[2], Kofi Boakye[2], Özgür Çetin[3], Adam Janin[2], Mathew Magimai-Doss[2], Chuck Wooters[2], and Jing Zheng[1]

[1] SRI International, Menlo Park, CA, U.S.A.
[2] International Computer Science Institute, Berkeley, CA, U.S.A.
[3] Yahoo, Inc.
stolcke@speech.sri.com

**Abstract.** We describe the latest version of the SRI-ICSI meeting and lecture recognition system, as was used in the NIST RT-07 evaluations, highlighting improvements made over the last year. Changes in the acoustic preprocessing include updated beamforming software for processing of multiple distant microphones, and various adjustments to the speech segmenter for close-talking microphones. Acoustic models were improved by the combined use of neural-net-estimated phone posterior features, discriminative feature transforms trained with fMPE-MAP, and discriminative Gaussian estimation using MPE-MAP, as well as model adaptation specifically to nonnative and non-American speakers. The net effect of these enhancements was a 14-16% relative error reduction on distant microphones, and a 16-17% error reduction on close-talking microphones. Also, for the first time, we report results on a new "coffee break" meeting genre, and on a new NIST metric designed to evaluate combined speech diarization and recognition.

## 1 Introduction

This paper documents the latest in a series of speech recognition systems [1,2,3] jointly developed by SRI International and the International Computer Science Institute (ICSI) for participation in the annual NIST Rich Transcription evaluations focused on meeting processing (starting with RT-02S in Spring 2002, through RT-07 this year). We give a self-contained overview of the recognition system, while focusing on new aspects of the current version, including several improvements made since the evaluation proper.

Since the beginning of our research on meeting recognition, we have based our systems on existing systems developed for conversational telephone speech (CTS) recognition, by borrowing the decoding architecture and by adapting acoustic models trained originally on telephone corpora. This year, given increasing amounts of in-domain meeting training data, we evaluated if such an adaptation strategy is still worthwhile. We then focused on improvements to the acoustic preprocessing, which aims to minimize the mismatch between meeting speech and our existing acoustic models. New beamforming software for distant microphones and updates to the speech segmenter used for close-talking microphones resulted in improvements in their respective conditions.

R. Stiefelhagen et al. (Eds.): CLEAR 2007 and RT 2007, LNCS 4625, pp. 450–463, 2008.

Next, we applied several techniques to improve the way acoustic models originally trained on CTS and broadcast news (BN) speech are adapted to the meeting and lecture domain. One successful approach was the combination of three discriminative modeling techniques, at the level of features, feature transforms, and Gaussians [4], modified to work in an adaptive fashion. We also achieved gains by paying special attention to nonnative and non-American speakers in model adaptation, since those dialects are underrepresented in our background training corpora while being more pervasive in the meeting test data.

No significant changes were made to the language models, beyond incorporating additional training data from the Augmented Multi-party Interaction (AMI) project. As we will show, this additional data had limited effect, and improved results solely on AMI meeting test data.

## 2   Task and Data

### 2.1   Test Data

**Evaluation data.** The RT-07 evaluation data (eval07) was divided into three portions according to meeting genre: conference meetings (confmtg), lecture meetings (lectmtg), and coffee breaks (cbreak), the latter being a more interactive variant of the lecture room setup. The conference data consisted of excerpts from 8 meetings recorded at 4 sites in the U.S. and Europe (Carnegie Mellon University, Edinburgh, NIST, and Virginia Tech), totaling 3 hours in duration. The lecture data was collected at 5 different "Computers in the Human Interaction Loop" (CHIL) consortium sites and comprised 32 lecture excerpts totaling 2.7 hours. Coffee break data originated from the same 5 sites and added up to 0.7 hour.

Separate evaluations were conducted in three acoustic conditions:

**MDM**   multiple distant microphones (primary)
**IHM**   individual headset microphones (required contrast)
**SDM**   single distant microphone (optional)

Lecture and coffee break rooms had more extensive instrumentation and provided the following additional conditions:

**MSLA**   multiple source localization array microphones (optional)
**MM3A**   multiple Mark-III microphone arrays (optional)
**ADM**   all distant microphones (optional)

Although NIST evaluates recognition error on all speech, including portions where speakers overlap, our recognition system presently ignores this fact, and was optimized for non-overlapping speech. Consequently, all results presented here exclude overlapping speech in the distant-microphone conditions, unless noted otherwise.

**Development data.** The NIST RT-06 (eval06), and to a lesser extent, RT-05 (eval05) evaluation data sets were used as development data. Lecture system development used eval06 only, and confmtg results on eval05 were somewhat discounted since eval05 contains one data source (ICSI) that yields very low error rates and does not occur in more recent test sets. Several system parameters (such as rescoring weights) had been optimized on even older NIST evaluation sets, and have not been re-tuned this year. Also, due to the paucity of lecture development data, those parameters were never tuned specifically for the genre, and simply copied from the confmtg system.

## 2.2   Training Data

In-domain training data for the conference room consisted of the same meeting recordings from AMI, CMU, ICSI and NIST as used in previous years, plus additional data released by AMI and NIST since RT-06. The total amount of IHM data was about 213 hours after speech/nonspeech segmentation (AMI: 100 meetings, 100h; CMU: 17 meetings, 11h; ICSI: 73 meetings, 74h; NIST: 27 meetings, 28h).

The training data aimed at the lecture domain was unchanged from last year—due to time constrains we did not make use of some new lecture and coffee break data released prior to RT-07. As a result, the only lecture-type data used was about 7 hours of CHIL training data (close-talking microphones only), the CHIL dev06 distant-microphone development data, and about 9 hours of transcribed lectures available as part of the Translingual English Database (TED) [5].

As in previous years, we used background models trained on old CTS and BN corpora for adaptation to the meeting and lecture domains. These out-of-domain corpora included about 2300 hours of telephone speech from the Switchboard, CallHome English, and Fisher collections, and about 900 hours of BN data from the Hub-4 and Topic Detection and Tracking (TDT) corpora.

## 3   System Description and Development

### 3.1   Signal Processing and Segmentation

**Distant microphone processing.** All distant microphone channels (in both training and test) were Wiener-filtered for noise reduction using a filter developed for the Qualcomm-ICSI-OGI Aurora system [6], identical to previous years [2].

Subsequently, for the MDM, MDM, MSLA, and MM3A conditions, a delay-and-sum beamforming technique was applied to combine all available distant microphone channels into a single "enhanced" channel. The algorithm used was essentially the same as last year [7], but used a new implementation that is freely available under the name BeamformIt (version 2.0) [8].

Once the enhanced signal was generated, speech regions were identified using a speech/nonspeech two-class hidden Markov model (HMM) decoder. Resulting segments were combined and padded with silence to satisfy certain duration constraints that had been empirically optimized for recognition accuracy. The algorithm and models were unchanged from last year [2]. Finally, the segments were clustered into acoustically homogeneous partitions, which served as pseudo-speaker units for normalization and adaptation. This aspect was also identical to last year's system.

To assess the effect of the new beamforming implementation on recognition performance, we reprocessed the eval06 data with BeamformIt, and then ran RT-06 confmtg

**Table 1.** Comparison of old and new beamforming implementation in terms of word error rates (WER) using RT-06 recognition models

| | eval06 confmtg | eval06 lectmtg | |
| | MDM | MDM | ADM |
|---|---|---|---|
| RT-06 beamformer | 34.2 | 55.5 | 51.0 |
| BeamformIt v2.0 | 33.9 | 55.8 | 46.6 |

**Table 2.** Comparison of IHM speech/nonspeech segmentation without and with per-channel energy normalization for cross-channel feature computation, and for recognition from reference segments. eval06 results were obtained with the RT-06 recognition system, eval07 results with the current system.

| | eval06 | | eval07 | |
| | confmtg | lectmtg | confmtg | lectmtg |
|---|---|---|---|---|
| W/o energy norm. | 24.0 | 30.8 | 25.6 | 29.5 |
| with energy norm. | 22.8 | 31.7 | 25.7 | 30.5 |
| Reference seg. | 20.2 | 29.3 | 22.8 | 28.1 |

and lectmtg systems that were otherwise unchanged. Table 1 shows that MDM performance is virtually unchanged, but that ADM is much improved. This seems to indicate that the new implementation is more robust to heterogeneous and/or very large sets of microphones.

**Close-talking microphone processing.** The IHM input channels are segmented (without Wiener filtering) into speech and nonspeech regions using an HMM-based speech/nonspeech segmenter [9]. The segmenter is a two-class HMM decoder with each class represented by a three-state phone model. The states are modeled by 256-component multivariate Gaussian mixtures with diagonal covariance matrices. The segmentation proceeds via decoding of the full IHM channel waveform, potentially in a multi-pass fashion with decreased transition penalty between the speech and nonspeech classes. This is done so as to generate segments that do not exceed 60 seconds in length.

Last year we had introduced a combination of single- and cross-channel features designed to allow discrimination of foreground speech from cross-talk (which should not be recognized). The single-channel features consist of 12th-order Mel-frequency cepstral coefficients (MFCCs), log-energy, and first and second differences. The cross-channel features are maximum and minimum log-energy differences. The log-energy difference represents the log of the ratio of the short-time energy between a given target channel and a nontarget channel. The maximum and minimum values are selected to obtain a fixed number of feature components, given that the number of channels varies between meetings. All features are computed over a window of 25 ms advanced by 20 ms.

Following RT-06, we modified these features by normalizing the log-energies per channel prior to computing cross-channel features, with the goal of accounting for differences in noise floors and gains. This technique gave excellent results on conference meetings, eliminating cross-talk even from speakers for whom only distant-microphone recordings were available [9]. However, when we evaluated this new

**Table 3.** Effect of adjusting speech/nonspeech prior probabilities. All results obtained with RT-07 recognition systems (hence eval06 results differ from Table 2).

| | eval06 | eval07 | | |
| | confmtg | confmtg | lectmtg | cbreak |
|---|---|---|---|---|
| Old priors | 21.9 | 25.7 | 30.5 | 31.2 |
| New priors | 20.2 | 24.0 | 29.5 | 30.6 |
| Reference seg. | 19.1 | 22.8 | 28.1 | 29.5 |

feature (per-channel energy normalization) on lecture data and current test sets, a mixed picture emerged, as shown in Table 2. It seems that the energy normalization does not improve the result on eval07 confmtg data, and in fact degrades accuracy on lecture data by about 1% absolute. Further investigation is needed to understand the reasons for this inconsistent behavior.

We also observed that there is still a considerable word error rate (WER) gap (1.5-3% absolute) between automatic and reference segmentation, largely because of a high deletion error rate. Running our confmtg recognizer on the AMI system's segmenter output gave a marked improvement, from 25.7% to 24.0% WER. In a post-evaluation experiment we tuned the speech/nonspeech prior probability used by the segmenter on eval06 confmtg data, and were able to obtain the same improvement. Furthermore, as shown in Table 3, the prior adjustment resulted in recognition improvements across all meeting genres.

No speaker clustering was performed on the IHM channels, since it was assumed that each IHM channel corresponds to exactly one speaker.

### 3.2   Acoustic Modeling and Adaptation

**Decoding architecture.** To motivate the choice of acoustic models, we first describe the decoding architecture, which is unchanged from last year, depicted in Figure 1. An "upper" (in the figure) tier of decoding steps is based on MFCC features; a parallel "lower" tier of decoding steps uses perceptual linear prediction (PLP) features. The outputs from these two tiers are combined twice using word confusion networks (denoted by crossed ovals in the figure). Except for the initial decodings, the acoustic models are cross-adapted to the output of a previous step from the respective other tier using maximum likelihood linear regression (MLLR). Lattices are generated initially to speed up subsequent decoding steps. The lattices are regenerated once later to improve their accuracy, after adapting to the outputs of the first combination step. The lattice generation steps use noncrossword (nonCW) triphone models, and decoding from lattices uses crossword (CW) models. Each decoding step generates either lattices or N-best lists, both of which are rescored with a 4-gram language model (LM); N-best output is also rescored with duration models for phones and pauses [10].

The final output is the result of a three-way system combination of MFCC-nonCW, MFCC-CW, and PLP-CW decoding branches. The entire system runs in under 20 times real time (20xRT).[1]

---

[1] Runtimes given assume operation with Gaussian shortlists. Since RT-07 did not impose a runtime limit we ran the system without shortlists, in about 25xRT.

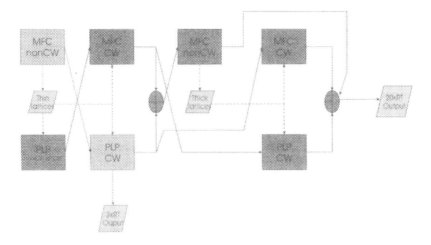

**Fig. 1.** SRI CTS recognition system. Rectangles represent decoding steps. Parallelograms represent decoding output (lattices or 1-best hypotheses). Solid arrows denote passing of hypotheses for adaptation or output. Dashed lines denote generation or use of word lattices for decoding. Crossed ovals denote confusion network system combination steps.

**Baseline models and test-time adaptation.** The MFCC recognition models were derived from gender-dependent CTS models in the RT-04F system, which had been trained with the minimum phone error (MPE) criterion [11] on about 1400 hours of data. (All available native Fisher speakers were used, but to save training time, statistics were collected from every other utterance only.) The MFCC models used 12 cepstral coefficients, energy, first-, second-, and third-order differences features, and $2 \times 5$ voicing features over a 5-frame window [12]. Cepstral features were computed with vocal tract length normalization (VTLN) and zero-mean and unit variance per speaker/cluster. The 62-component raw feature vector was reduced to 39 dimensions using heteroscedastic linear discriminant analysis (HLDA) [13]. After HLDA, a 25-dimensional Tandem/HATs feature vector estimated by multilayer perceptrons (MLPs) [14,15] was appended. Both within-word and crossword triphone models were trained, for lattice generation and decoding from lattices, respectively. PLP models were based on full-bandwidth analysis, producing 12 coefficients, energy, first-, second- and third-order differences, and then reduced to 39 dimensions using HLDA. (No voicing or MLP features were used in this case.) These models were originally trained on about 900 hours of broadcast news data from the Hub4, TDT2, and TDT4 collections. PLP models are gender independent. All models were trained using decision-tree-based state tying.

In testing, all models undergo unsupervised adaptation to the test speaker or cluster, using MLLR with multiple, data-induced regression class trees. The first MFCC and PLP adaptation passes used a phone-loop reference model; later passes adapted to prior recognition output. In addition, all but the first decoding used constrained MLLR in feature space, which was also employed in training (speaker adaptive training) [16].

**Table 4.** Meeting recognition results using CTS training data, using MFCC maximum likelihood models and a simplified, 1-pass recognition system

| Training data | eval05 IHM confmtg |
|---|---|
| Fisher 400h | 34.0 |
| Confmtg 100h, 8kHz | 33.4 |
| Confmtg 100h, 16kHz | 31.7 |
| Fisher + confmtg, 8kHz (pooled) | 31.9 |
| Fisher + confmtg, 8kHz (MAP) | 31.5 |

**MLP feature adaptation.** As in past years, we adapted the MLPs for Tandem and HATs feature computation to the meeting domain by running additional MLP training iterations on meeting data, starting with the CTS-trained MLPs. We showed previously that this type of adaptation yields about the same improvements as MAP adaptation of Gaussians alone [17]. In fact, as an expedient we used the adapted MLPs from last year, that is, without taking advantage of the new acoustic training data and using conference meeting data only. For distant-microphone recognition, the MLPs were adapted to both distant and close microphone recordings, whereas MLPs for IHM recognition were trained on close-talking microphones only.

**Acoustic model adaptation.** In preparation for this year's evaluation, we conducted several experiments to determine the best training strategy. First and foremost, we wanted to confirm that adapting CTS models to the meeting domain was still a profitable approach. It entails downsampling meeting data to 8 kHz, raising the question of whether or not the attendant loss of information was more than compensated for by the added data. Table 4 summarizes some relevant results.

Models were trained on 400 hours of Fisher CTS data, as well as on the 100 hours of meeting speech available for RT-06, and tested on eval05 confmtg. We found that the downsampling of meeting data indeed incurs a significant, 6% relative error rate increase. However, this was almost made up for by simply pooling the CTS and (down-sampled) meeting data. By using MAP adaptation, which gives control over the weighting of the in-domain versus background data, we were able to do slightly better than the meeting-only broadband models (31.5% versus 31.7% WER). Considering that the actual amount of CTS background data available is 5 times the 400 hours used in this experiment, we concluded that it was a safe bet to continue the MAP-adaptation strategy.

The next issue we addressed was the high percentage of nonnative and non-American speakers in the meeting and lecture data. Spot-checking the eval06 lecture data, for example, we found that almost all of it involved speakers with various European accents, most of them nonnative. The mismatch to our CTS background data was exacerbated by the fact that nonnative and non-American speakers had been excluded from our CTS training set (in accordance with past CTS evaluation sets). We therefore collected this previously excluded CTS data in a separate adaptation training set, comprising 220 hours in 1324 conversation sides, and performed tests on eval06 lectmtg data, summarized in Table 5.

The results are quite dramatic, in that adapting the background models to nonnative/non-American CTS data yields better performance than adapting to confmtg

**Table 5.** Meeting recognition results using adaptation to nonnative and non-American CTS speakers, using MFCC ML-MAP models based on native-English Fisher data and a simplified, 1-pass recognition system

| MAP adaptation data | eval06 IHM lectmtg |
|---|---|
| confmtg 100h | 41.9 |
| Fisher nonnative/non-American 220h | 40.5 |
| confmtg + Fisher nonnat./non-Am. | 40.0 |

**Table 6.** Results with different MAP adaptation criteria using complete recognition systems

(a)

| Adaptation method | eval06 IHM | |
|---|---|---|
| | confmtg | lectmtg |
| ML-MAP | 22.8 | 34.1 |
| MMI-MAP | n/a | 29.8 |
| fMPE-MAP | 22.3 | 28.7 |
| fMPE-MAP+MPE-MAP | 22.2 | 26.3 |

(b)

| Adaptation method | eval06 MDM | |
|---|---|---|
| | confmtg | lectmtg |
| ML-MAP | 33.7 | 58.3 |
| fMPE-MAP+MPE-MAP | 30.9 | 48.6 |
| +ML-MAP(lect-dev06) | n/a | 47.8 |

data. This clearly indicates that nativeness is one of the major factors of mismatch between the CTS and meeting data. As is to be expected, combining confmtg and nonnative/non-American CTS data in adaptation yields the best results. As a result of these experiments, we added the previously excluded Fisher speakers to our meeting adaptation data for MFCC model training. Note that this data was not added to the BN-based PLP model training data, both because of the bandwidth mismatch and because BN data is already more heterogeneous in its dialectal makeup.

**fMPE-MAP.** In addition to MLP feature adaptation and MAP adaptation of the Gaussian models, we employed a discriminative feature transform known as fMPE (feature MPE) [18]. A sparse high-dimensional feature vector generated by Gaussian posteriors is mapped to the standard low-dimensional feature space via a transform trained using the minimum phone frame error (MPFE) [11,19] criterion, and combined additively with the standard features. However, we used a novel variant of fMPE called fMPE-MAP, in which the transform is estimated only on adaptation data, based on a pretrained non-fMPE reference model (our CTS and BN background models). We found that fMPE-MAP gave better results than fMPE on the combined background and in-domain data, while taking much less training time [20]. The Gaussian posteriors input to the fMPE transform were based on PLP features from a 5-frame window, for both the MFCC and PLP fMPE-MAP models.

Table 6(a) compares results with ML-MAP, MMI-MAP (the method used last year), fMPE-MAP, and fMPE-MAP followed by MPE-MAP for IHM recognition, using complete recognition systems in which both MFCC and PLP models had been trained using the respective estimation criteria. The discriminative methods yield small gains on confmtg data, but substantial gains on lectmtg data. Recall that almost all the adaptation data is from the confmtg domain, highlighting the fact that discriminative training

**Table 7.** Effect of language model update on recognition performance, differentiated by test data source

| LM | eval06 confmtg | | | |
|---|---|---|---|---|
| | IHM | | MDM | |
| | AMI | non-AMI | AMI | non-AMI |
| 2006 | 20.1 | 23.2 | 28.9 | 32.9 |
| 2007 | 19.6 | 23.1 | 26.9 | 33.4 |

greatly enhances the generalization of acoustic models. Also note that MPE-MAP still gives substantial gains on top of fMPE-MAP in the case of lectmtg test data. The combined WER reduction is by 2.6% relative on confmtg and by 23% relative on lectmtg.

**Adaptation for distant microphone recognition.** Models for recognition from distant microphones were obtained by pooling all close-talking and distant-microphone data for adaptation purposes (similar to MLP adaptation). Table 6(b) shows ML-MAP and fMPE-MAP+MPE-MAP results for MDM recognition. The gains from discriminative adaptation are again substantial: 8.3% for confmtg and 17% for lectmtg. However, since the adaptation set contained only a very small amount of in-domain MDM lecture data (the dev06 set), we felt that the models for that domain might be improved further by giving extra weight to the matched data. This was accomplished by a final ML-MAP step using lectmtg-dev06 data only. As shown in the last row of Table 6(b), this indeed yielded a further 1.6% relative error reduction. The resulting models were used in both lecture and coffee break recognition (since both were recorded under the same acoustic conditions).

### 3.3 Language Models

Language models (LMs) for the RT-07 system had the same structure as in previous years, consisting of an interpolation of various genre-specific LMs, including conference transcripts, lectures, CTS, BN, web data, and conference proceedings [21]. LMs specific to confmtg and lectmtg genres were obtained by finding perplexity-minimizing interpolation weights on held-out data of the respective type.

The only change for this year's system was the addition of new AMI and NIST conference meeting transcripts. While this almost doubled the amount of in-domain LM data, we found only small gains in overall recognition accuracy, as shown in Table 7. Since most of the new data came from the AMI data collection, we broke eval06 recognition results down according to whether or not the test meeting came from an AMI site (Edinburgh or TNO). It becomes evident that the additional training data helps significantly on AMI test data, but not on other data. We attribute this to the special scenario-driven character of the AMI meetings. Still, since the RT-07 test set was expected to contain AMI sources as well, we incorporated the updated LM into our confmtg system. On lectmtg tests, however, the new LM data made no impact whatsoever, so we simply kept last year's lectmtg LM. The lecture LM was also used in coffee break recognition. We again note that, because of time constraints, none of the CHIL lecture data released since RT-06 was used in LM training.

**Table 8.** Effect of acoustic clustering parameters on MDM recognition accuracy. Values chosen in the RT-07 evaluation system appear in boldface.

| | eval06 MDM | | eval07 MDM | | |
|---|---|---|---|---|---|
| Clustering | confmtg | lectmtg | confmtg | lectmtg | cbreak |
| 1 cluster | | 47.8 | | **44.6** | 44.0 |
| 4 clusters | 30.3 | | **26.2** | | **44.7** |
| Unlimited | 30.2 | 48.1 | 26.5 | 44.7 | |
| Combined | 29.4 | 46.9 | 25.8 | 43.7 | 43.5 |

### 3.4 Speaker Clustering Revisited

As mentioned, our distant-microphone recognition system groups waveform segments into pseudo-speaker clusters for feature normalization and model adaptation purposes. However, we had found in previous years that this clustering slightly degrades performance on lecture data, presumably because the lecture is dominated by a single speaker and the clustering algorithm is not accurate enough to identify small sets of non-lecturer speech. Therefore, the RT-07 system again used only a single cluster for lecture recognition.

Post-evaluation we revisited this decision and checked the effect of different clustering parameters for all genres. Three configurations were tried: 1 cluster (the default for lectmtg), 4 clusters (the default for confmtg, close to the average number of meeting participants, and optimized on old evaluation data), and an unlimited number of clusters (constrained only by a minimum amount of data per cluster). The results are summarized in Table 8.

First, we can note that the (blind) choices made for eval07 confmtg and lectmtg turned out to be optimal. The alternative clusterings resulted in minimal degradation only. For coffee break recognition, we had made a poor choice (4 clusters) based on the assumption that they would be more like conference meetings; a single cluster worked best here, too. Most interesting, the error patterns (substitution/insertion/deletion rates) resulting from alternate clusterings were quite different. This suggested combining the different systems by merging the confusion networks produced in their final stages. As shown in the last row of Table 8, this indeed yielded considerable reductions in error over the single best system, of between 0.4% and 1.0% absolute. (Of course, this gain comes at the price of doubled runtime.)

## 4 Overall Results

### 4.1 Conference Meetings

Table 9(a) compares results on last year's and this year's evaluation sets for the conference room condition. For last year's test data we also include results from last year's (RT-06) system, thereby allowing us to assess overall progress made. Furthermore, we list results with both the submitted RT-07 system and the improvements made post-evaluation (the retuned priors for IHM recognition and the cluster combination

**Table 9.** Results on RT-06 and RT-07 test data summarized

(a)

| System | MDM | SDM | IHM |
|---|---|---|---|
| | eval06 confmtg | | |
| RT-06 | 34.2 | 41.2 | 24.0 |
| RT-07 | 30.3 | 40.6 | 21.9 |
| Post-eval | 29.4 | | 20.2 |
| | eval07 confmtg | | |
| RT-07 | 26.2 | 33.1 | 25.7 |
| Post-eval | 25.8 | | 24.0 |

(b)

| System | MDM | ADM | MM3A | SDM | IHM |
|---|---|---|---|---|---|
| | eval06 lectmtg | | | | |
| RT-06 | 55.5 | 51.0 | 56.5 | 57.3 | 31.0 |
| RT-07 | 47.8 | 39.3 | | 49.6 | 26.3 |
| Post-eval | 46.9 | | | | 25.7 |
| | eval07 lectmtg | | | | |
| RT-07 | 44.6 | 42.1 | 54.0 | 50.6 | 30.5 |
| Post-eval | 43.6 | | | | 29.5 |
| | eval07 cbreak | | | | |
| RT-07 | 44.7 | 41.1 | 51.0 | 50.0 | 31.2 |
| Post-eval | 43.5 | | | | 30.6 |

for MDM). On eval06, the progress on MDM data was about 11.4% relative (14.0% post-evaluation), and 8.8% on IHM data (15.8% post-evaluation). We also note that the MDM word error rate on non-overlapped speech is within 8% of IHM performance on eval07, although this looks like an artifact of this particular test set as (eval07 is easier than eval06 on MDM, but harder for IHM recognition).

### 4.2   Lectures and Coffee Breaks

Table 9(b) similarly summarizes all the results for the lecture room task, as well as for the new coffee break genre. For eval06 lectures, MDM word error was reduced 13.9% relative (15.5% post-evaluation), and IHM error 15.2% relative (17.1% post-evaluation). The ADM condition saw an even greater improvement of 22.9% relative, largely because of improved beamforming. Comparing across test sets, we find that IHM became harder this year, whereas MDM became easier, similar to what we saw with conference data.

Finally, we observe that the RT-07 coffee break data shows errors across conditions that are remarkably similar to the corresponding lectmtg results. This, together with the earlier observations about speaker clustering and the fact than these results were obtained with lecture-tuned language model, led us to conclude that, for recognition purposes, the coffee break data is presently not significantly different from lecture data.

### 4.3   Speaker-Attributed Speech-to-Text

This year NIST introduced a new "speaker-attributed speech-to-text" (SASTT) task, combining diarization and speech recognition (speech-to-text, STT). Systems label each recognized word with speaker tags, and the scoring program counts a word as correct only if both the spelling and the speaker label agree with the reference (speaker labels are treated as arbitrary and only significant to the extent that they indicate identity or nonidentity of speakers). The SASTT task is defined only for distant-microphone conditions.

We had not originally planned to develop a system for this task, but after the submission deadline we decided to generate SASTT output by a simple merging of our speech

**Table 10.** Actual and predicted SASTT error rates obtained by a combination of the SRI-ICSI recognizer with the ICSI diarization system. The error rates of the component diarization and recognition systems are also given. Unlike elsewhere in this paper, the scoring here was performed with as many as three overlapping speakers.

| Task | eval07 confmtg MDM | eval07 confmtg SDM | eval07 lectmtg MDM |
|------|------|------|------|
| SASTT (actual) | 40.3 | 51.7 | 56.9 |
| SASTT (predicted) | 41.9 | 55.2 | 58.6 |
| STT | 37.4 | 43.6 | 49.3 |
| diarization | 8.5 | 21.7 | 23.3 |

recognition output with ICSI's diarization output [22]. Each recognized word was labeled with the speaker label that has the longest time overlap with the word. Table 10 summarizes the results, which turned out to be highly competitive even without having performed any joint optimization on the diarization and STT systems.

We also tested a simple model that predicts SASTT error from the error rates and types of the underlying STT and diarization systems. If we assume that diarization errors occur independently of STT errors, we would predict that incorrect speaker labels cause about $ME_{SPKR} + SE_{SPKR}$ correct STT words to be SASTT-incorrect, where $ME_{SPKR}$ and $SE_{SPKR}$ are the diarization miss and speaker error rates, respectively. Therefore, we predict the SASTT WER error to be

$$WER_{SATT} = WER_{STT} + CorR_{STT} \times (ME_{SPKR} + SE_{SPKR})$$

with $CorR_{STT}$ being the STT word-correct rate. As the second row of Table 10 shows, this prediction is only a slight overestimate for the MDM condition. However, for the SDM condition, the formula overestimates SASTT error substantially, probably because under poor acoustic conditions, STT and diarization errors will be more highly correlated.

# 5   Conclusions and Future Work

We have made further progress in the recognition of conference and lecture meetings, with first results on "coffee break" data that are comparable to those on lectures. The most significant contributions this year came from a combination of discriminative techniques in acoustic modeling, including a new method, fMPE-MAP, that showed the most substantial error reductions on the "hard" tasks, namely, distant microphone recognition in general and lecture recognition in particular. Additional acoustic modeling gains came from adaptation to nonnative and non-American English telephone data. Acoustic preprocessing was improved by using a new beamforming implementation (for distant microphones) and retuning the speech/nonspeech priors (for close-talking microphones). We found a simple way to improve distant microphone recognition in combining multiple recognition systems differing only in their speaker clustering constraints. Finally, we constructed a first, yet competitive SASTT system by a straightforward merging of our STT system with ICSI's diarization output.

## Acknowledgments

This work was partly supported by the European Union 6th FWP IST Integrated Project AMI (Augmented Multi-party Interaction, FP6-506811), and by the Swiss National Science Foundation through NCCR's IM2 project. Additional support came from the the Defense Advanced Research Projects Agency (DARPA) to SRI under Contract No. NBCHD030010. Any opinions, findings and conclusions or recommendations expressed in this material are those of the author(s) and do not necessarily reflect the views of the DARPA or the Department of Interior-National Business Center (DOI-NBC). We thank Thomas Hain from Sheffield for making the AMI system's IHM segmenter output available for testing with our system.

## References

1. Stolcke, A., Wooters, C., Mirghafori, N., Pirinen, T., Bulyko, I., Gelbart, D., Graciarena, M., Otterson, S., Peskin, B., Ostendorf, M.: Progress in meeting recognition: The ICSI-SRI-UW Spring 2004 evaluation system. In: Proceedings NIST ICASSP 2004 Meeting Recognition Workshop, Montreal, National Institute of Standards and Technology (2004)
2. Stolcke, A., Anguera, X., Boakye, K., Çetin, Ö., Grézl, F., Janin, A., Mandal, A., Peskin, B., Wooters, C., Zheng, J.: Further progress in meeting recognition: The ICSI-SRI Spring 2005 speech-to-text evaluation system. In: Proceedings of the Rich Transcription 2005 Spring Meeting Recognition Evaluation, Edinburgh, National Institute of Standards and Technology, pp. 39–50 (2005)
3. Janin, A., Stolcke, A., Anguera, X., Boakye, K., Çetin, Ö., Frankel, J., Zheng, J.: The ICSI-SRI Spring 2006 meeting recognition system. In: Renals, S., Bengio, S., Fiscus, J.G. (eds.) MLMI 2006. LNCS, vol. 4299, pp. 444–456. Springer, Heidelberg (2006)
4. Zheng, J., Cetin, O., Hwang, M.Y., Lei, X., Stolcke, A., Morgan, N.: Combining discriminative feature, transform, and model training for large vocabulary speech recognition. In: Proc. ICASSP, Honolulu, vol. 4, pp. 633–636 (2007)
5. Lamel, L., Schiel, F., Fourcin, A., Mariani, J., Tillman, H.: The translingual English database (TED). In: Proc. ICSLP, Yokohama, pp. 1795–1798 (1994)
6. Adami, A., Burget, L., Dupont, S., Garudadri, H., Grezl, F., Hermansky, H., Jain, P., Kajarekar, S., Morgan, N., Sivadas, S.: Qualcomm-ICSI-OGI features for ASR. In: Hansen, J.H.L., Pellom, B. (eds.) Proc. ICSLP, Denver, vol. 1, pp. 4–7 (2002)
7. Anguera, X., Wooters, C., Pardo, J.M.: Robust speaker diarization for meetings: ICSI-SRI RT-06S meetings evaluation system. In: Renals, S., Bengio, S., Fiscus, J.G. (eds.) MLMI 2006. LNCS, vol. 4299. Springer, Heidelberg (2006)
8. Anguera, X.: Beamformit (the fast and robust acoustic beamformer) (2006), http://www.icsi.berkeley.edu/~xanguera/beamformit/
9. Boakye, K., Stolcke, A.: Improved speech activity detection using cross-channel features for recognition of multiparty meetings. In: Proc. ICSLP, Pittsburgh, PA, pp. 1962–1965 (2006)
10. Vergyri, D., Stolcke, A., Gadde, V.R.R., Ferrer, L., Shriberg, E.: Prosodic knowledge sources for automatic speech recognition. In: Proc. ICASSP, Hong Kong, vol. 1, pp. 208–211 (2003)
11. Povey, D., Woodland, P.C.: Minimum phone error and I-smoothing for improved discriminative training. In: Proc. ICASSP, Orlando, FL, vol. 1, pp. 105–108 (2002)
12. Graciarena, M., Franco, H., Zheng, J., Vergyri, D., Stolcke, A.: Voicing feature integration in SRI's Decipher LVCSR system. In: Proc. ICASSP, Montreal, vol. 1, pp. 921–924 (2004)

13. Kumar, N.: Investigation of Silicon-Auditory Models and Generalization of Linear Discriminant Analysis for Improved Speech Recognition. PhD thesis, Johns Hopkins University, Baltimore (1997)
14. Morgan, N., Chen, B.Y., Zhu, Q., Stolcke, A.: TRAPping conversational speech: Extending TRAP/Tandem approaches to conversational telephone speech recognition. In: Proc. ICASSP, Montreal, vol. 1, pp. 536–539 (2004)
15. Zhu, Q., Stolcke, A., Chen, B.Y., Morgan, N.: Using MLP features in SRI's conversational speech recognition system. In: Proc. Interspeech, Lisbon, pp. 2141–2144 (2005)
16. Jin, H., Matsoukas, S., Schwartz, R., Kubala, F.: Fast robust inverse transform SAT and multistage adaptation. In: Proceedings DARPA Broadcast News Transcription and Understanding Workshop, Lansdowne, VA, pp. 105–109. Morgan Kaufmann, San Francisco (1998)
17. Stolcke, A., Anguera, X., Boakye, K., Çetin, Ö., Grézl, F., Janin, A., Mandal, A., Peskin, B., Wooters, C., Zheng, J.: Further progress in meeting recognition: The ICSI-SRI Spring 2005 speech-to-text evaluation system. In: Renals, S., Bengio, S. (eds.) MLMI 2005. LNCS, vol. 3869, pp. 463–475. Springer, Heidelberg (2006)
18. Povey, D., Kingsbury, B., Mangu, L., Saon, G., Soltau, H., Zweig, G.: fMPE: Discriminatively trained features for speech recognition. In: Proc. ICASSP, Philadelphia, vol. 1, pp. 961–964 (2005)
19. Zheng, J., Stolcke, A.: Improved discriminative training using phone lattices. In: Proc. Interspeech, Lisbon, pp. 2125–2128 (2005)
20. Zheng, J., Stolcke, A.: fMPE-MAP: Improved discriminative adaptation for modeling new domains. In: Proc. Interspeech, Antwerp, pp. 1573–1576 (2007)
21. Çetin, Ö., Stolcke, A.: Language modeling in the ICSI-SRI Spring 2005 meeting speech recognition evaluation system. Technical Report TR-05-06, International Computer Science Institute, Berkeley, CA (2005)
22. Wooters, C., Huijbregts, M.: The ICSI RT 2007 speaker diarization system. LNCS, vol. 4625, pp. 509–519. Springer, Heidelberg (2008)

# The ISL RT-07 Speech-to-Text System

Matthias Wölfel, Sebastian Stüker, and Florian Kraft

Interactive Systems Laboratories
Institut für Theoretische Informatik
Universität Karlsruhe (TH)
Am Fasanengarten 5
76131 Karlsruhe, Germany
{wolfel, stueker, fkraft}@ira.uka.de

**Abstract.** This paper describes the 2007 meeting speech-to-text system for *lecture rooms* developed at the Interactive Systems Laboratories (ISL), for the multiple distant microphone condition, which has been evaluated in the RT-07 Rich Transcription Meeting Evaluation sponsored by the US National Institute of Standards and Technologies (NIST). We describe the principal differences between our current system and those submitted in previous years, namely the use of a signal adaptive front-end (realized by warped-twice warped minimum variance distortionless response spectral estimation), improved acoustic (including maximum mutual information estimation) and language models, cross adaptation between systems which differ in the front-end as well as the phoneme set, the use of a discriminative criteria instead of the signal-to-noise ratio for the selection of the channel to be used and the use of decoder based speech segmentation.

## 1 Introduction

In this paper, we present the ISL's most recent lecture meeting speech-to-text system for *lecture rooms*, which has evolved significantly over previous versions [1,2,3,4] and which was evaluated in the NIST RT-07 Rich Transcription Meeting Evaluation. The system described in this paper shares many common elements with last year's evaluation system as described in [1], e.g. the two phoneme sets and the cluster tree. However, it differs from it in several important ways which are the focus of this paper.

This year's system uses decoder based speech segmentation [5] as described in Section 2. Besides our standard *warped minimum variance distortionless response* (WMVDR) [6] front-end we used a signal adaptive front-end provided by *warped-twice warped minimum variance distortionless response* (W2MVDR) [7] spectral estimation. Different front-ends are described and compared in Section 2. To exploit benefits from cross system adaptation and system combination we varied both the front-end and phoneme set [8], described in Section 3.4, which gives an additional accuracy improvement of 0.5% over the usage of a single phoneme-set. To evaluate on different microphones we replaced the *signal-to-noise ratio* (SNR) by a class separability measure for channel selection [9].

R. Stiefelhagen et al. (Eds.): CLEAR 2007 and RT 2007, LNCS 4625, pp. 464–474, 2008.

In addition we improved acoustic models due to *maximum mutual information estimation* (MMIE) training [10] where the speaker dependent adaptation matrices are unchanged during the MMIE training. We also improved our language models by incorporating additional data collected from the world wide web, see Section 3.3. We used only acoustic models which were trained with *vocal tract length normalization* (VTLN) [11], however incremental speaker adaptation in the first pass, as in last year's system, was not used. Last but not least, we used different additional acoustic training material.

Most of the decoding experiments described in this paper were conducted on either the lecture meeting portion of the RT-05S development and evaluation set or the current RT-07 development set.

## 2    Automatic Segmentation

Automatic segmentation follows different strategies for close and distant recordings either by single or by multiple microphone:

For the *individual head-mounted microphone* (IHM) condition, which is particularly difficult due to cross talk from background speakers, we relied on the segmentation and speaker clusters provided by ICSI [12].

For the *single distant microphone* (SDM) and *multi distant microphone* (MDM) condition we used a different approach than in previous years: We used a multi-microphone extended version of the single-microphone system which we used in this year's English European Parliament Plenary Sessions transcription system developed and evaluated under the TC-STAR project [5]. First, from every session, the channel of the unsegmented recording with the highest SNR is selected. In order to determine speech and non-speech regions a decoding pass is performed on the unsegmented audio. Segmentation is then done by consecutively splitting segments at the longest non-speech region that is at least 0.3 seconds long. The resulting segments had to contain at least three speech words and to have a minimum duration of three seconds. The maximum duration was set to sixty seconds.

In order to group the resulting segments into several clusters, with each cluster, in the ideal case, corresponding to one individual speaker we used the same hierarchical, agglomerative clustering technique as last year which is based on TGMM-GLR distance measurement and the *Bayesian information criterion* (BIC) stopping criteria [13]. The resulting speaker labels were used to perform feature and acoustic model adaptation in the multi-pass decoding strategy as described in Section 4.1.

## 3    System Training and Development

All speech recognition experiments described in this paper were performed using the *Janus Recognition Toolkit* (JRTk) and the *Ibis* single pass decoder [14].

### 3.1   Front-End

To increase accuracy via cross system adaptation we used two front-ends and two phoneme sets. One front-end, identical to last year's system, replaces the power spectrum by a WMVDR spectral envelope of model order 30 and drops the filterbank due to the properties of the WMVDR with low model order. The second front-end replaces the power spectrum by a signal adaptive front-end provided by W2MVDR spectral estimation. This is in contrast to our RT-06S system where we used the traditional *mel frequency cepstral coefficient* (MFCC) as the second front-end. Due to the properties of the W2MVDR with high model order, the mel filterbank has to be replaced by a linear filterbank.

The advantages of the WMVDR approach are an increase in resolution in low frequency regions relative to the traditionally used mel filterbanks, and the dissimilar modeling of spectral peaks and valleys to improve noise robustness, as noise is present mainly in low energy regions. The advantage of a signal adaptive front-end is that classification relevant characteristics are emphasized, while classification irrelevant characteristics are alleviated according to the characteristics of the input signal, e.g. vowels and fricatives have different characteristics and therefore should be treated differently.

Both front-ends use a 42-dimensional feature space based on 20 cepstral coefficients with linear discriminant analysis and a global *semi-tied covariance* (STC) transform [15] with utterance-based cepstral mean and variance normalization.

Table 1 and Table 2 compare different front-ends for close and distant data on RT-05S development and evaluation data (lecture meeting). A detailed description about the W2MVDR spectral estimation, the signal adaptive front-end and the training setup can be found in [7]. For close talking microphone data the proposed signal adaptive front-end is superior to all investigated front-ends. On distant speech the proposed signal adaptive front-end is superior to most of the investigated front-ends.

### 3.2   Acoustic Model Training

The training setup was based on last year's evaluation system. However, this year we selected the training data that performs best on distant talking audio. Therefore, we used the following training material: CMU (11 hours), ICSI (72 hours), NIST (13 hours) plus Phase 2 Part 1 — which are recordings of meetings, TED (13 hours), and CHIL (10 hours) plus last year's *lecture meeting* development and evaluation data (6 hours) — which are recordings of lectures. All the acoustic data is in 16 kHz, 16 bit quality and recorded with head-mounted microphones. Far-field data is available for ICSI, NIST and CHIL. Due to channel mismatch between ICSI and NIST data to the lecture meeting data we used only the far-field data provided by CHIL for supervised adaptation of the close talking acoustic models to derive distant speech acoustic models.

The model set used is identical to the model set of our RT-06S evaluation system. In comparison to previous systems, e.g. the RT-04S evaluation system [4], it was augmented by additional noise models for laughter and other human noises

**Table 1.** Word error rates for different front-end types and settings on close recordings

| Spectrum | Order | Cepstra | Word Error Rate % | | | | | |
|---|---|---|---|---|---|---|---|---|
| Test Set | | | Develop | | | Eval | | |
| Pass | | | 1 | 2 | 3 | 1 | 2 | 3 |
| power spectrum | – | 13 | 36.1 | 30.3 | 28.0 | 35.3 | 29.7 | 27.7 |
| power spectrum | – | 20 | 36.0 | 29.7 | 27.7 | 37.2 | 31.3 | 28.4 |
| warped MVDR | 60 | 13 | 35.0 | 30.0 | 28.2 | 35.5 | 29.9 | 27.6 |
| warped MVDR | 60 | 20 | 34.5 | 29.1 | 27.3 | 35.3 | 29.6 | 27.3 |
| warped MVDR | 30 | 13 | 34.6 | 29.8 | 27.8 | 34.7 | 29.6 | 27.2 |
| warped MVDR | 30 | 20 | 33.9 | 29.1 | 27.4 | 34.9 | 29.2 | 26.9 |
| warped-twice MVDR | 60 | 13 | 34.5 | 29.5 | 27.5 | 34.1 | 29.2 | 27.0 |
| warped-twice MVDR | 60 | 20 | 34.1 | 28.8 | 26.8 | 35.4 | 29.0 | 26.3 |

(note that in the WMVDR front-end with model order 30 applies no smoothing and dimension reduction by a filterbank)

**Table 2.** Word error rates for different front-end types on distant recordings

| Spectrum | Order | Cepstra | Word Error Rate % | | | | | |
|---|---|---|---|---|---|---|---|---|
| Test Set | | | Develop | | | Eval | | |
| Pass | | | 1 | 2 | 3 | 1 | 2 | 3 |
| power spectrum | – | 13 | 61.9 | 52.0 | 51.1 | 60.8 | 54.2 | 51.1 |
| power spectrum | – | 20 | 59.8 | 50.4 | 48.9 | 61.0 | 55.0 | 51.7 |
| warped MVDR | 60 | 20 | 60.9 | 51.2 | 49.7 | 59.6 | 51.7 | 49.5 |
| warped MVDR | 30 | 20 | 59.0 | 50.5 | 48.9 | 59.3 | 52.1 | 49.9 |
| warped-twice MVDR | 60 | 20 | 60.3 | 51.1 | 49.8 | 59.9 | 50.4 | 47.9 |

to the existing breath and general noise models, and by a split of the filler model into a monosyllabic and a disyllabic filler model.

Acoustic model training was performed with fixed state alignments, which were written by a small system (2000 codebooks) using a mel frequency cepstral coefficient front-end trained on ICSI, NIST (without Phase 2 Part 1) and TED only. We trained four different acoustic models (varying the two front-ends and the two phoneme sets) for the final evaluation system. All of them are left-right *hidden Markov models* (HMM)s without state skipping with three HMM states per phoneme.

All acoustic models were trained in the same way, resulting in semi-continuous quint phone systems that use 16000 distributions over 4000 codebooks, with a maximum of 64 Gaussians per model.

The adapted gender independent acoustic model training (given the vocal tract normalization values for each speaker by a previous system) can be outlined as follows:

1. Training of the linear discriminant analysis matrix
2. Extraction of samples
3. Incremental growing of Gaussians

4. Training of one global STC matrix
5. Second extraction of samples
6. Second incremental growing of Gaussians
7. Two iterations of Viterbi training to train the distributions for the semi-continuous system and to compensate for the occasionally erroneous fixed-state alignments
8. Four iterations of FSA-SAT speaker adaptive training [16]
9. Decoding of the training data with the previous model and a unigram language model
10. Five iterations of MMIE training [10], leaving the speaker dependent adaptation matrices from the last iteration of the maximum-likelihood speaker adaptive training unchanged during the MMIE training [17]

To adapt to the distant data we adapted the models (after step 7) by

1. Four Viterbi training iterations using the available far-field CHIL data
2. To reduce the impact of distant data on the models we combine the distant adapted models with the clean speech models of step 7 with a weight four times higher than the clean speech models of step 7.

### 3.3   Language Model Training

We used a 4-gram language model trained on the following corpora: A subset of CHIL transcriptions (ISL_20031028, ISL_20031216_A, ISL_20031125_B, ISL_20040614, ISL_20040616, ISL_20040621, ISL_20040721, ISL_20040830), rt04s-dev and rt04s-eval transcripts, meeting transcripts (ICSI, CMU, NIST, AMI), TED transcripts, Hub4 broadcast news, recent proceedings data ranging from 2002 - 2005, web data from University of Washington (150M words related to CMU, ICSI, NIST meetings), two subsets of inhouse Web data collections and a subset of the RT-06S evaluation data.

Subsets of the following pool from an inhouse web data collection were used. Therefore general phrase 3- and 4-grams were combined with topic phrases.

The general phrases in the queries for the corpora webI-III are based on the most frequent n-grams in CHIL transcriptions and for the corpora webIV-V on most frequent n-grams in the meeting transcripts.

The topic phrases were generated by computing bi-gram based tf-idfs for each proceeding paper. After merging them together and skipping bi-grams including stop-words the top 1,400 topic phrases were mixed randomly with the general phrases until the necessary number of queries was generated. For collecting the data we used the scripts provided by the University of Washington [18]. Table 3 gives an overview of the web data collections and the queries they were based on.

We trained one language model component for a subset of webI-III (318M words) and one component for webIV-webV (613M words). The subset selection was performed by skipping data from irrelevant queries, based on their perplexity with an in-domain LM build on the CHIL data used for query generation and the proceedings data.

**Table 3.** Size of collected web data components and number of queries by general and topic phrases

| Corpus | General Phrases | Topic Phrases | Queries | Words |
|---|---|---|---|---|
| webI | CHIL transcripts | CHIL transcripts | 1k | 146M |
| webII | CHIL transcripts | recent proceedings | 4k | 102M |
| webIII | CHIL transcripts | recent proceedings | 10k | 311M |
| webIV | meeting transcripts | recent proceedings | 4k | 398M |
| webV | meeting transcripts | recent proceedings | 10k | 674M |

**Table 4.** Tuning set selection and test of new corpora on the RT-07 development set

| LM Components | Tuning Set | PPL |
|---|---|---|
| LM-A | initial set | 132 |
| LM-A | + RT-06S-dev | 130 |
| LM-A | + RT-06S-dev + RT-06S-eval | 128 |
| LM-A | + RT-06S-dev + RT-06S-eval + NIST07 | 132 |
| + NIST07 | initial set | 132 |
| + RT-06S-dev | initial set | 132 |
| + RT-06S-eval | initial set | 130 |
| + subset(RT-06S-eval) | + RT-06S-dev + subset(RT-06S-eval) | 127 |
| + subset(RT-06S-eval) (i) | + RT-06S-dev + subset(RT-06S-eval) | 120 |
| + subset(RT-06S-eval) (ip) | + RT-06S-dev + subset(RT-06S-eval) | 123 |

Initially all mentioned language model components, except the RT-06S evaluation data, were interpolated (LM-A) according to an initial held-out set consisting of the CHIL transcriptions ISL_20031111, ISL_20031118, ISL_20031125_A, ISL_20031216_B, ISL_20041111_A, ISL_20041111_B, ISL_20041111_C and ISL_20041112_A. We used the resulting language model to update the held-out set with respect to the RT07 development data. By incrementally adding the RT-06S development set and the RT-06S evaluation set to the held-out set, the perplexity on the RT07 development data decreased. However, adding the NIST phase 2 part 1 (NIST07) set hurt as shown in Table 4. The motivation for this procedure is to get a tuning set biased to the RT07 development set, which is not selected too narrow.

The extension of the LM-A with the sets NIST07, RT-06S development set and RT-06S evaluation set revealed, that it was best not to use the new NIST set nor the RT-06S development set for component modeling purpose, but to use the RT-06S evaluation set. Since experiments for held-out set selection also showed an improvement by adding the RT-06S evaluation set, we split it to use for both. Consequently we used the initial held-out set plus the RT-06S development set plus part of the RT-06S evaluation set as tuning set. The final language model consists of all already mentioned language model components without the NIST07 set and only the part of the RT-06S evaluation set not used for tuning.

During the system development we also considered to adapt the language model using a web data collection based on an automated query generation by extraction of topic and style from the hypotheses of previous recognition passes. Unfortunately the methods used lead to no further gain in recognition performance on top of the web data already included.

The final LM was build using the SRILM-toolkit [19]. For discounting we applied the Chen and Goodman's modified Kneser-Ney approach [20], and interpolation of discounted n-gram probability estimates with lower-order estimates was used (marked as (i) in Table 4). Pruning was performed after combining the LM-components (marked as (p) in Table 4) while the threshold was set also with respect to a reasonable decoding time. The perplexities are 123 on the RT-07 development set and 101 on the RT-07 evaluation set.

### 3.4   Phoneme Sets, Recognition Dictionaries and Lexicon

The *first phoneme set* (p1) used is an adapted version of the phoneme set used by the *Carnegie Mellon University* (CMU) dictionary that consists of 45 phonemes and allophones. The *second phoneme set* (p2) used is an adapted version of the Pronlex phoneme set which consists of 44 phonemes and allophones. Common to both phoneme inventories are five diphthongs or vowel-glide sequences, nine fricatives, two affricates, six plosives and three nasals. Both systems contain seven vowels. There are four approximants in both systems. However, Pronlex additionally allows for an allophone of the voiced velar approximant. The phoneme sets also differ in the number of reduced or centralized vowels. Pronunciations of unknown words were either generated automatically by Festival [21] for the CMU dictionary or by Fisher's grapheme-to-phoneme conversion tool [22] for the Pronlex system.

The dictionaries contained 62.4k (p1) and 65.5k (p2) pronunciation variants over a vocabulary size of 51.7k. The vocabulary was automatically derived by analysis of BN, Switchboard, meetings (ICSI, CMU, NIST, AMI), TED and CHIL corpora. After applying individual word-frequency thresholds to the corpora, we filtered the resulting list with `ispell` to remove spelling errors and added a few manually checked topic words from the set of topic bigrams used in web data collection. The OOV-rate on *lecture meeting* development and evaluation was 0.7% and 0.6% respectively.

## 4   Experiments and Results

In this section we present experiments and results on the RT-07 development and evaluation set.

### 4.1   Decoding Strategy

In order to find the best decoding and cross system adaptation strategy, we performed several different experiments on the lecture meeting development set. We found that the best setup in terms of *word error rate* (WER) and complexity for all conditions uses already vocal tract normalized acoustic models in the first pass while following passes use vocal tract normalized and speaker-adapted models (FSA-SAT). For distant speech data, similar to last year's system, we used close talking models which were adapted to distant speech data. However, this year, we switched to the close talking model already in the second pass (which gave significant improvements on the development set). Last year, we switched to the close talking models in the third pass.

In another set of experiments, we followed results presented in [23,24] and experience obtained during the development of a system for transcribing *English European Parliament Plenary Sessions* (EPPS)[25]. A significant gain (approximately 1.5% absolute) from cross adaptation between systems with different front-ends (WMVDR, power spectrum) is reached on EPPS. Cross adapting with the Pronlex system gives additional improves of 0.7% WER after *confusion network combination* (CNC) [26].

On development and evaluation data of the lecture meeting RT-07 data we saw improvements by system adaptation of approximately 2% absolut by the combination of the two front-ends with different phoneme sets for all passes.

The processing steps for decoding can be summarized as follows:

1. Decoder based segmentation
2. Clustering of speaker
3. Estimation of VTLN
4. Calculate of SNR for each individual channel, segment, and utterance
5. Decoding of first pass on combined acoustic channels for WMVDR.p1 and W2MVDR.p2
6. Combination of first passes by confusion networks
7. Select of channel by class separability measures (uses VTLN) for each individual front-end over each segment and utterance
8. Adaptation of VTLN, constrained MLLR and MLLR
9. Decoding of second pass on best channel for WMVDR.p2 and W2MVDR.p1
10. Combination of second passes by confusion networks
11. Adaptation of VTLN, constrained MLLR and MLLR
12. Combination of third pass on best channel for WMVDR.p1 and W2MVDR.p2
13. Combination of third passes by confusion networks

Using an 8 ms instead of a 10 ms frame-shift for the second and third passes, improves the final WER by about 1% absolute [1].

## 4.2    Channel Combination and Selection for MDM

In RT-04S, channel combination was performed by decoding all channels and the combination by CNC on the resulting lattices over all channels. No selection was used, leading to a relatively high computational load for each pass. In the RT-06S system we were able to reduce the computational load by 70% without an increase in WER by performing both channel combination and selection [2].

**Table 5.** Influence of different channel selection techniques, signal to noise and class separability measure, on the *word error rates* (WER)s on development 2007

| Channel Selection | WER % | | |
|---|---|---|---|
| Pass | 1 | 2 | 3 |
| Signal to Noise Ratio | 73.0 | 62.3 | 59.5 |
| Class Separability Measure | 67.4 | 57.8 | 55.1 |

**Table 6.** Overall results and real-time factors on RT-05S Eval and RT-06S Eval. In contrast to previous sections, results for the conference meeting part of RT-05S Eval include meeting NIST_20050412-1303. SDM and MDM results were scored with an overlap of one.

| condition | IHM | | SDM | MDM | | |
|---|---|---|---|---|---|---|
| pass | dev | eval | eval | dev | *compare* | eval |
| 1 | 36.5 | 43.1 | 57.9 | 56.7 | 60.2* | 56.5 |
| 2 | 29.5 | 36.3 | 54.9 | 50.5 | 56.8 | 52.4 |
| 3 | 28.6 | 36.7 | 54.4 | 49.4 | 54.4 | 52.1 |
| RT | | 91 | 113 | | | 114 |

(*compare* give the numbers of last year's evaluation system on the current evaluation set, note that the fist pass marked with * has been adapted incrementally)

This year's scenario is different as such as we can't assume one dominant speaker and that the best possible microphone is changing for each individual speaker due to head orientation. Therefore, in this year's task channel selection is even more important than last year as the signal quality of one channel might be significantly better than those of the other channels. In those cases microphone array or blind source separation techniques might not lead to improvements over the best single microphone.

We presented a novel channel selection method [9], based on class separability, to improve multi-source far distance speech-to-text transcriptions. Class separability measures have the advantage, compared to other methods such as the SNR, that they are able to evaluate the channel quality on the actual features of the recognition system. Note that for different front-ends different channels might be selected.

Table 5 presents results on RT-07 development set. A direct comparison between delay-and-sum channel combination and the proposed channel selection technique on the second pass of the RT-07 evaluation system including both front-ends and phone sets combined by CNC shows a relative improvement of 3.6%, from 52.4% to 50.5% WER.

### 4.3   Overall System Performance

Table 6 lists the overall system results for the development and evaluation RT-07S lecure meeting task. The given WERs per pass are after CNC of the lattices of the WMVDR and W2MVDR front-ends with different phoneme sets. The final pass on the IHM and MDM evaluation set give the official numbers as scored by NIST. All other numbers were scored in our laboratory.

On the MDM task, it can be seen that there is a huge gap between the adapted development and evaluation results. On the development set we gain 7.1% by adaptation, while in the evaluation case we gain only 4.4%. The selection of channels is able to improve the system performance by 2.3%.

## 5  Conclusion

This paper has presented the Interactive Systems Laboratories automatic speech recognition systems with which we participated in NIST's RT-07 evaluation campaign in spring of 2007. This year's system showed performance improvements to last years system mainly by the introduction of novel techniques, namely a signal adaptive front-end and class separability channel selection.

## Acknowledgments

This work was partly funded by the European Union (EU) under the integrated project CHIL [27] (IST-506909).

## References

1. Fügen, C., Wölfel, M., McDonough, J.W., Ikbal, S., Kraft, F., Laskowski, K., Ostendorf, M., Stüker, S., Kumatani, K.: Advances in lecture recognition: The ISL RT-06S evaluation System. In: Proc. of Interspeech (2006)
2. Wölfel, M., Fügen, C., Ikbal, S., McDonough, J.W.: Multi-source far-distance microphone selection and combination for automatic transcription of lectures. In: Proc. of Interspeech (2006)
3. Wölfel, M., McDonough, J.: Combining multi-source far distance speech recognition strategies: Beamforming, blind channel and confusion network combination. In: Proc. of Interspeech (2005)
4. Metze, F., Jin, Q., Fügen, C., Laskowski, K., Pan, Y., Schultz, T.: Issues in meeting transcription – The ISL meeting transcription system. In: Proc. of ICSLP (2004)
5. Stüker, S., Fügen, C., Kraft, F., Wölfel, M.: The ISL 2007 english speech transcription system for european parliament speeches. In: Proc. of Interspeech (2007)
6. Wölfel, M., McDonough, J.: Minimum variance distortionless response spectral estimation: Review and refinements. IEEE Signal Processing Magazine (September 2005)
7. Wölfel, M.: Warped-twice minimum variance distortionless response spectral estimation. In: Proc. of EUSIPCO (2006)
8. Stüker, S., Fügen, C., Burger, S., Wölfel, M.: Cross-system adaptation and combination for continuous speech recognition: The influence of phoneme set and acoustic front-end. In: Proc. of Interspeech (2006)
9. Wölfel, M.: Channel selection by class separability measures for automatic transcriptions on distant microphones. In: Proc. of Interspeech (2007)

10. Povey, D., Woodland, P.: Improved discriminative training techniques for large vocabulary continuous speech recognition. In: Proc. of ICASSP, Salt Lake City, UT, USA (May 2001)
11. Zhan, P., Westphal, M.: Speaker normalization based on frequency warping. In: Proc. of ICASSP (1997)
12. Boakye, K., Stolcke, A.: Improved speech activity detection using cross-channel features for recognition of multiparty meetings. In: Proc. of Interspeech (2006)
13. Jin, Q., Schultz, T.: Speaker segmentation and clustering in meetings. In: Proc. of ICSLP (2004)
14. Soltau, H., Metze, F., Fügen, C., Waibel, A.: A one pass-decoder based on polymorphic linguistic context assignment. In: Proc. of ASRU (2001)
15. Gales, M.J.F.: Semi-tied covariance matrices. In: Proc. of ICASSP (1998)
16. Gales, M.J.F.: Adaptive training schemes for robust asr. In: Proc. of ASRU
17. McDonough, J., Schaaf, T., Waibel, A.: On maximum mutual information speaker-adapted training. In: Proc. of ICASSP (2002)
18. Scripts for web data collection provided by University of Washington, http://ssli.ee.washington.edu/projects/ears/WebData/web_data_collection.html
19. Stolcke, A.: SRILM – an extensible language modeling toolkit. In: Proc. of ICSLP (2002)
20. Chen, S.F., Goodman, J.: An empirical study of smoothing techniques for language Modeling, Computer Science Group, Harvard University, Tech. Rep. TR-10-98, (1998)
21. Black, A.W., Taylor, P.A.: The festival speech synthesis system: System documentation, Human Communciation Research Centre, University of Edinburgh, Edinburgh, Scotland, United Kongdom, Tech. Rep. HCRC/TR-83 (1997)
22. Fisher, W.M.: A statistical text-to-phone function using n-grams and rules. In: Proc. of ICASSP (1999)
23. Yu, H., Tam, Y.-C., Schaaf, T., Stüker, S., Jin, Q., Noamany, M., Schultz, T.: The ISL RT04 mandarin broadcast news evaluation system. In: Proc. of EARS Rich Transcription Workshop (2004)
24. Lamel, L., Gauvain, J.-L.: Alternate phone models for conversational speech. In: Proc. of ICASSP (2005)
25. Stüker, S., Fügen, C., Hsiao, R., Ikbal, S., Jin, Q., Kraft, F., Paulik, M., Raab, M.W.M., Tam, Y.-C.: The ISL TC-STAR spring 2006 ASR evaluation systems. In: Proc. of TC-Star Workshop on Speech-to-Speech Translation (2006)
26. Mangu, L., Brill, E., Stolcke, A.: Finding consensus among words: Lattice-based word error minimization. In: Proc. of EUROSPEECH (1999)
27. CHIL – computers in the human interaction loop, http://chil.server.de

# Progress in the AMIDA Speaker Diarization System for Meeting Data

David A. van Leeuwen and Matej Konečný

TNO Human Factors, Postbus 23, 3769 ZG Soesterberg, The Netherlands
david.vanleeuwen@tno.nl, matej.konecny@gmail.com

**Abstract.** In this paper we describe the AMIDA speaker dizarization system as it was submitted to the NIST Rich Transcription evaluation 2007 for conference room data. This is done in the context of the history of this system and other speaker diarization systems. One of the goals of our system is to have as little tunable parameters as possible, while maintaining performance. The system consists of a BIC segmentation/clustering initialization, followed by a combined re-segmentation/cluster merging algorithm. The Diarization Error Rate (DER) result of our best system is 17.0 %, accounting for overlapping speech. However, we find that a slight altering of Speech Activity Detection models has a large impact on the speaker DER.

## 1 Introduction

The AMIDA speaker diarization system is an ongoing research effort to investigate different approaches to the challenging task of speaker segmentation and clustering of meeting recordings. This year's efforts have been concentrated on the use of multiple microphones recordings and exploring different modelling and initialization approaches.

The task of speaker diarization[1] is commonly summarized as determining *who* spoke *when*, where speakers can be given arbitrary labels, i.e, no absolute identification of speakers is required. This article describes the AMIDA system and its performance in the Spring NIST Rich Transcription 2007 (RT07s) speaker diarization task. As the successor of AMI, the EU-funded project AMIDA attempts to develop tools that allow more effective meetings in so-called smart meeting rooms, which are equipped with many microphones and cameras to record the meeting process. Automatic data processing tools extract and structure information, so that meeting participants, who are not available in place or time, can still benefit from and interact with the meeting process. The AMI consortium has donated evaluation data for the NIST RT series since 2005.

This paper is organized as follows. First, a recapitulation of earlier TNO/AMI work is made, and the 2007 system is described. Then, te evaluation results are discussed, and some experiments with speaker overlap detection are described.

---

[1] The meaning of the term *diarization* may not be very familiar outside this community. The word is related to *diary*, indicating an annotation of events with time marks.

R. Stiefelhagen et al. (Eds.): CLEAR 2007 and RT 2007, LNCS 4625, pp. 475–483, 2008.

## 2   System History and Design Goals

In 2005, TNO participated in the speaker diarization task for the first time [16]. The system consisted of a speech activity detector (SAD), followed by a Bayesian Information Criterion (BIC) based segmentation [8] and clustering [7] system. We had correctly identified the importance of a good SAD as a prerequisite for acceptable speaker Diarization Error Rates (DER), and obtained low SAD error rates. However, we had underestimated the sensitivity of the optimal setting of BIC parameters $\lambda$ to the test set. Merely tuning the two $\lambda$'s from the optimal setting for development test data (RT04s) to evaluation data (RT05s) reduced DER from the evaluation results 34.2 % to a post-evaluation result of 25.4 %.

In 2006, where we participated as AMI referring to the increased effort of co-operation, we attempted to remove the dependence of these parameters $\lambda$ by keeping the number of parameters in the speaker models before and after clustering the same [2]. The influence of $\lambda$, that penalizes such a difference in number of model parameters, is then effectively removed from the BIC. By moving from a full-covariance single-Gaussian speaker model to a diagonal covariance Gaussian Mixture speaker model the system became more in-line with other current approaches [5,10,20], allowing Viterbi re-segmentation to fine-tune speaker change boundaries during the clustering process. These GMM-based re-segmentation systems showed less sensitivity to the evaluation collection [18], and the drop in performance seen in going from development (RT05s) to evaluation (RT06s) data of 7–12 % could partially be attributed to the RT06s data being 'harder.'

In 2007 we re-designed the system and partially re-wrote the code base. This year, for the first time, we utilized more information than just the Single Distant Microphone (SDM) in the Multiple Distant Microphone (MDM) condition, an opportunity provided by ICSI by sharing their beamforming software with the research community [3]. This allowed modeling of the beamformer's delay-parameters as well as provided for better quality cepstral features, by improving the SNR.

The goals of the 2007 AMIDA system were to have almost no tunable parameters, no assumptions on the number of speakers in the meeting, reasonable speed and better utilization of the available microphones.

## 3   System Description

The general design of the AMIDA 2007 speaker diarization system is depicted in Fig. 1.

### 3.1   Signal Processing

For all signal processing steps, we used tools made available by third parties. For the MDM condition we processed the data using the BeamformIt tool [3]. We reduced the analysis window to 32 ms and step size to 16 ms, rather than the default 500 and 250 ms, in order have the delay feature stream synchronous to

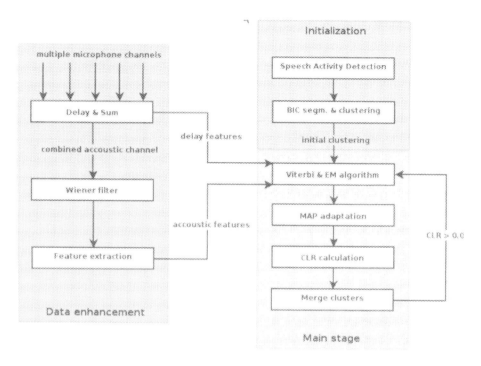

**Fig. 1.** Overview of the AMIDA speaker diarization system

the cepstral features. The single microphone signal output by the beamformer was further enhanced using a Wiener filter, by the Qualcomm-ICSI-OGI Aurora frontend tool [1].

This signal with improved SNR was used to extract 12 PLP coefficients and log energy, every 16 ms, as calculated over 32 ms windows by the ICSI implementation rasta [13,12].

### 3.2   Speech Activity Detection

Only for this step, we augmented the features with 1st order derivatives estimated over 5 consecutive frames. A two-state HMM was used for SAD, with diagonal covariance GMMs (number of Gaussians $N_G = 16$) for a speech and a silence state. Because, since RT06s, the speech activity reference truth is determined from SRI's forced aligned decoding of the Individual Headset Microphones, we experimented with two sets of models for speech and silence. These are indicated in Table 1.

### 3.3   Initial Segmentation and Clustering

In order to speed up the clustering process we used our old BIC system [16] to perform an initial clustering. Respecting silence regions as segment boundaries,

**Table 1.** SAD models and their training data

| Name | $N_G$ | Training data |
|------|-------|---------------|
| AMI-dev | 16 | 10 AMI meetings distributed as development test for RT05s |
| RT-FA | 16 | RT05s and RT06s evaluation data, with force-aligned reference |

we set $\lambda = 1$ for both segmentation and clustering, which typically leads to over-segmentation and under-clustering. If the BIC system was to produce the final clustering, optimal values for segmentation would be $\lambda_s \approx 1.5\text{--}2$ and for clustering $\lambda_c \approx 6\text{--}14$. With the 'ideal' values of $\lambda_{c,s} = 1$ we ended up with typically 40 clusters after this step. The clusters found at this step were used to train initial diagonal covariance GMMs $\Lambda$ for each cluster. We used an occupancy driven approach [4,18] for determining the number of Gaussians $N_G$,

$$N_G = \left\lfloor \frac{N_f}{R_{\mathrm{CC}}} + \frac{1}{2} \right\rfloor, \tag{1}$$

where $N_f$ is the number of frames in the cluster and $R_{\mathrm{CC}}$ is the 'cluster complexity ratio', which we set to 300. This corresponds to about 4.8 seconds/Gaussian.

The clusters are also used to train single Gaussian GMMs for the delay parameters.

### 3.4   Agglomerative Clustering

This is the main step in the speaker diarization system. It consists of several smaller steps.

1. First, all silence frames are removed from the feature stream, making it appear continuous. The silence regions are recovered at the end of the clustering process. Note that the SAD for determining silence frames does not need to be the same as in the BIC segmentation/clustering step.
2. A GMM $\Theta$ with $N_G = 64$ was trained using all acoustic speech frames of the meeting, for later usage in the clustering process. In speaker recognition such a model is known as a 'Universal Background Model' (UBM), which is perhaps too grand a name for a model containing only meeting speakers.
3. Using the $N_C$ initial GMMs $\Lambda$, do a Viterbi decode using GMMs as single states in an $N_C$ parallel state topology. The new segmentation is used to train new GMMs for the clusters, changing $N_G$ according to (1) if necessary. This step is repeated several times, and both the cepstral and delay GMMs are used. We mix the per-frame log likelihoods $\log L$ for the acoustic model $\Lambda_A$ and delay model $\Lambda_D$ using linear interpolation,

$$\log L(a_t, d_t | \Lambda_A, \Lambda_D) = \alpha \log L(a_t | \Lambda_A) + (1 - \alpha) \log L(d_t | \Lambda_D), \tag{2}$$

where $a_t$ and $d_t$ are acoustic and delay parameters at frame $t$. We used a fixed value $\alpha = 0.9$.

4. Using Maximum A Posteriori adaptation [11] of the GMM in step 2 to the data of each cluster, build adapted 64-Gaussian GMMs. For each pair $(i, j)$ of these $N_C$ models $\Theta_i$, calculate the cross likelihood ratio [15]

$$R_{\text{CL}}(i, j) = \frac{1}{N_i} \log \frac{L(x_i|\Theta_j)}{L(x_i|\Theta)} + \frac{1}{N_j} \log \frac{L(x_j|\Theta_i)}{L(x_j|\Theta)}, \tag{3}$$

where $N_{i,j}$ are the number of frames contributing to the clusters $i$ and $j$, respectively. Then, determine the pair $(I, J)$ that maximizes $R_{\text{CL}}$

$$(I, J) = \arg\max_{i,j} R_{\text{CL}}(i, j). \tag{4}$$

If $R_{\text{CL}}(I, J) > 0$, merge the data from $I$ and $J$ to a single cluster, train new GMMs $\Lambda$ and continue with step 3. Otherwise, go to the final step.
5. On finalization, insert the silence frames that were removed in step 1.

### 3.5 Differences from Other Approaches

All steps described here have been used elsewhere [5,20], but with slightly different implementation details. The order of the delay-and-sum beamforming and Wiener filtering is traditionally reversed [19]. We applied the filtering after the beamforming, because we were uneasy about phase difference the Wiener filtering might introduce. We did experiment with the order reversed, but did not see a performance difference. Applying Wiener filtering to only one signal is less computationally expensive.

The current ICSI system [19] uses a linear initial clustering with a fixed number of initial clusters, and many re-segmentation iterations for initial clustering. Our BIC initial clustering does not assume a maximum number of speakers. This approach is similar to the LIMSI system [20].

The use of the UBM/GMM cross likelihood ratio is similar to the LIMSI diarization system for both Meeting [20] and Broadcast News [6] data, but we do not use a tunable threshold as stopping criterion for $R_{\text{CL}}$, but rather 0.

Also note, that we use two sets of GMMs: one set (with lower $N_G$, depending on the amount of data available for the cluster) for Viterbi re-segmentation, and one set (with $N_G = 64$) for determining the cluster to merge and the stopping criterion. This is computationally expensive, but we found this to give us best results for development test data.

### 3.6 Initialization of GMMs

We experienced problems with random $k$-means initialization of the GMMs. It had a strong effect in the segmentation/clustering and led to badly reproducing results. We therefore reverted to a more deterministic estimation of the GMM parameters, starting with a single GMM and doubling Gaussians until the highest power of two below the desired $N_G$, followed by sequentially adding a single Gaussian until reaching $N_G$. In the re-segmentation process, we used existing

GMMs. When $N_G$ had to grow (according to (1)), this was carried out though adding Gaussians by splitting the Gaussian with highest variance of all feature dimensions. In reducing $N_G$, the GMM was retrained from scratch.

## 4   Results

We tabulated the results for development and evaluation data in Table 2, at RT submission time. Results are reported in the primary evaluation measure defined by NIST [9], the Diarization Error Rate (DER), evaluated including overlapping speech.

**Table 2.** Speaker Diarization Error rate (DER) for different data sets (MDM), including overlapped speech. First line is our original BIC-based system from 2005. SAD1 and SAD2 refer to speech activity detection used for initial BIC segmentation and final agglomerative clustering, respectively, see Table 1. The last column shows the SAD error for the evaluation data.

| system | SAD1 | SAD2 | RT05s | RT06s | RT07 | SAD (RT07) |
|---|---|---|---|---|---|---|
| TNO'05 | AMI-dev | AMI-dev | 21.7 % | 32.4 % | 26.2 % | 6.4 % |
| AMIDA'07 | AMI-dev | AMI-dev | 16.3 % | 18.1 % | **22.0 %** | 6.7 % |
| AMIDA'07 | AMI-dev | RT-FA | - | 20.1 % | 17.0 % | 2.9 % |
| AMIDA'07 | RT-FA | RT-FA | - | - | 18.6 % | 2.9 % |

The result of the primary system (in bold), 22 %, is not particularly good. Once again we observe that development test results (16.3 and 18.1 %, respectively) do not generalize very well to the evaluation data. We blame this partly to the unexpectedly bad SAD performance, 6.7 %, which is probably related to the fact that the SAD models used (AMI-dev) are trained on Single Distant Microphone data, without Wiener filtering, and using manually-annotated speech/non-speech labeling. For the RT07s reference, forced-aligned speech/non-speech labeling is used, and models trained on beamformed, Wiener filtered data from RT05 and RT06. This would suggest that the RT-FA SAD models should work better. Indeed, we find lower SAD error for the evaluation data, and a much more improved DER of 17.0 %.

We used RT06s data[2] primarily for development testing, but at a later stage looked at RT05s as well to check for dataset dependence. In retrospect, we should have combined all available proper meetings for development testing, since per-meeting DER tends to vary a lot. Hence, our 'wrong choice' to use AMI-dev SAD models, based on RT06s performance where AMI-dev models scored better with 18,1 % than the RT-FA models, with 20.1 %.

In Table 3 we show the influence of the Delay parameter modeling on DER for RT05s and RT06s. We can clearly observe an improvement including these parameters.

---

[2] Excluding the meeting recorded at TNO, because the wrong MDM microphones had been included in the test set.

**Table 3.** Influence of delay parameters on development test DER

| Delay parameters | RT05s | RT06s |
|---|---|---|
| no | 20.5 % | 24.3 % |
| yes | 16.3 % | 18.1 % |

# 5 Overlapping Speech

Most implementations so far [5,10,20,18] have always interpreted the speaker diarization task as a speaker segmentation and clustering task. Although theoretically possible [18], the segmentation/clustering implementations do not consider the possibility of overlapping speech, i.e., speakers speaking simultaneously. Since the NIST Rich Transcription evaluation in Spring 2006, the primary evaluation measure accounts overlapping speech.

Now, with the new definition of speech/non-speech in the reference, using SRI's forced aligned segmentation, the amount or overlapped speech has reduced from 22 % to 8 % for RT06s, in going from manual to forced alignment. Also the average duration of overlap reduces from 1.57 s to 0.53 s. This appears to make the challenging task of determining the identity of overlapping speakers of less priority. However, in the light of ICSI's very good performance [19], overlapped speech might gain renewed attention. For RT07s, there was a difference in DER with and without accounting overlapping speech of about 3.5 %-point.

Last year we tried to generate, as a post-processing step, 'two-speaker models' by adding the probability density functions of pairs of clusters, and include these $\binom{N_C}{2}$ models in the decoding process, including restrictions for transitions to/from the two-speaker models. Then, we could not obtain better DER values, so this year we tried other approaches.

As a cheating experiment, we used the reference transcription to detect overlapping speech. Then, as a post-processing of normal diarization output, we included the 'most talkative speaker' as a second speaker in the output. This led to a reduction of the DER of 2 %-point. Although not a dramatic improvement, this simple 'guess' helps, if we know the regions of overlapping speech. In order to detect overlapping speech, we tried the following.

- Use the output of the `beamformit` tool [3]. The beamformer can give an indication if there is overlapping speech, presumably because of confusion of the location of the sound source. We determined the detection capability, in terms of False Alarm (FA) and missed time, and obtained 6.65 % and 85.6 % respectively. Having small FA time is good for the DER [16], but the detection capability is really too low to use as input for the 'most talkative speaker guess' algorithm. Assuming equal variance of overlap and non-overlap score distributions, this corresponds to a detector with an EER of 41 %, or $d' = 0.44$ [17].

– Train an overlap/non-overlap speech detector, by training GMMs on RT06s development data, and use a Viterbi decoding to detect overlapping speech. This did not seems to give any reasonable overlapping speech detection capability either.

## 6  Discussion

Our systems that included the newly trained SAD models showed an improvement over our 'baseline' BIC speaker diarization system. Overall, the performance of our system improved a lot since last year by inclusion of the delay parameters and signal to noise ration improvement due to the beamforming and Wiener filtering. However, it is quite unsatisfactory that small changes in the application of SAD give dramatic differences (from 17.0 to 22.0 %) in DER. Another unsatisfactory fact is that our development data set (RT06s) did not indicate correctly what the right SAD models were. Possibly, the development data set was too small (and hence the DER too noisy), and also the 'algorithmic tuning' which had been carried out on the development data with the old AMI-dev SAD models will have had an effect. Even though we have been striving towards as few tunable parameters as possible, there still are the SAD models and $R_{CC}$, as well algorithmic parameter choices and design decisions (number of re-alignment iterations, number of Gaussians in UBM, clustering criterion, etc.) that may overtrain on the development data.

Although the importance of proper SAD is clear from the definition of DER (SAD error is a lower bound to the DER), we have some indication that the SAD used in the clustering process should not necessarily be the same as the SAD used in producing the speaker diarization result. Indeed, this is what has been realized by the ICSI team [14,19]. where very strict speech acceptance thresholds are applied for selecting speech frames that take part in the speaker clustering process. Later, for the final postprocessing of speaker segment timing, the speech/silence boundaries are smoothed.

With the beamforming tools made available by ICSI we now have a chance to work seriously at the problem of overlap detection. We feel that this is an interesting task, and useful by itself: the moments of overlap can be indicative of 'hot spots,' disagreement or social cohesion, in meetings. In the context of diarization, good overlap detection can already be helpful by simply guessing the most talkative speaker as the second speakers. Actually identifying the overlapping speakers from the acoustics and/or delay parameters will remain an even more challenging task.

## References

1. Adami, A., Burget, L., Hermansky, H.: Qualcomm-ICSI-OGI noise-robust front end (September 2002), http://www.icsi.berkeley.edu/Speech/papers/qio/
2. Ajmera, J., McCowan, I., Bourlard, H.: Robust speaker change detection. IEEE Signal Processing Lettres 11(8), 649–651 (2004)

3. Anguera, X.: BeamformIt, the fast and robust acoustic beamformer (2006), http://www.icsi.berkeley.edu/~xanguera/BeamformIt/

4. Anguera, X., Wooters, C., Peskin, B., Aguiló, M.: Robust speaker segmentation for meetings: The ICSI-SRI spring 2005 diarization system. In: Proc. RT 2005 Meeting Recognition Evaluation Workshop, Edinburgh, July 2005, pp. 26–38 (2005)

5. Anguera, X., Wooters, C., Peskin, B., Aguiló, M.: Robust speaker segmentation for meetings: The ICSI-SRI spring 2005 diarization system. In: Renals, S., Bengio, S. (eds.) MLMI 2005. LNCS, vol. 3869, pp. 402–414. Springer, Heidelberg (2006)

6. Barras, C., Zhu, X., Meignier, S.: Multistage speaker diarization of broadcast news. IEEE Transactions on Audio, Speech and Language Processing 14(5), 1505–1512 (2006)

7. Chen, S.S., Gopalakrishnan, P.S.: Clustering via the Baysian Information Criterion with applications in speech recognition. In: Proc. ICASSP (1998)

8. Chen, S.S., Gopalakrishnan, P.S.: Speaker, environment and channel change detection and clustering via the Bayesian Information Criterion. In: Proceedings of the Darpa Broadcast News Transcription and Understanding Workshop (1998)

9. Fiscus, J., Radde, N., Garofolo, J.S., Le, A., Ajot, J., Laprun, C.: The rich transcription 2005 spring meeting recognition evaluation. In: Renals, S., Bengio, S. (eds.) MLMI 2005. LNCS, vol. 3869, pp. 369–389. Springer, Heidelberg (2006)

10. Fredouille, C., Senay, G.: Technical improvements of the e-hmm based speaker diarization system for meeting records. In: Renals, S., Bengio, S., Fiscus, J.G. (eds.) MLMI 2006. LNCS, vol. 4299, pp. 359–370. Springer, Heidelberg (2006)

11. Gauvain, J.-L., Lee, C.-H.: Maximum a posteriori esitimation for multivariate gaussian mixture observations of markov chains. IEEE Trans. Speech Audio Processing 2, 291–298 (1994)

12. Hermansky, H., Morgan, N.: Rasta processing of speech. IEEE Transactions on Speech and Audio Processing, special issue on Robust Speech Recognition 2(4), 578–589 (1994)

13. Hermansky, H.: Perceptual linear predictive (plp) analysis of speech. JASA 87(4), 1738–1752 (1990)

14. Huijbregts, M., Wooters, C., Ordelman, R.: Filtering the unknown: Speech activity detection in heterogeneous video collections. In: Proc. Interspeech, Antwerpen (accepted for publication, 2007)

15. Reynolds, D.A., Singer, E., Carlson, B.A.: Blind clustering of speech utterances based on speaker and language characteristics. In: Proceedings of International Conference Spoken Language Processing (ICSLP 1998), November 1998, pp. 3193–3196 (1998)

16. van Leeuwen, D.A.: The TNO speaker diarization system for NIST rich transcription evaluation 2005 for meeting data. In: Renals, S., Bengio, S. (eds.) MLMI 2005. LNCS, vol. 3869, pp. 400–449. Springer, Heidelberg (2006)

17. van Leeuwen, D.A., Brümmer, N.: An introduction to application-independent evaluation of speaker recognition systems. In: Müller, C. (ed.) Speaker Classification 2007. LNCS (LNAI), vol. 4343. Springer, Heidelberg (2007)

18. van Leeuwen, D.A., Huijbregts, M.: The AMI speaker diarization system for NIST RT06s meeting data. In: Renals, S., Bengio, S., Fiscus, J.G. (eds.) MLMI 2006. LNCS, vol. 4299, pp. 371–384. Springer, Heidelberg (2006)

19. Wooters, C., Huijbregts, M.: The ICSI RT07s speaker diarization system. In: Machine Learning for Multimodal Interaction. LNCS. Springer, Heidelberg (2007)

20. Zhu, X., Barras, C., Lamel, L., Gauvain, J.-L.: Speaker diarization: From broadcast news to lectures. In: Renals, S., Bengio, S., Fiscus, J.G. (eds.) MLMI 2006. LNCS, vol. 4299, pp. 396–406. Springer, Heidelberg (2006)

# Speaker Diarization Using Direction of Arrival Estimate and Acoustic Feature Information: The I²R-NTU Submission for the NIST RT 2007 Evaluation

Eugene Chin Wei Koh[1,2], Hanwu Sun[2], Tin Lay Nwe[2], Trung Hieu Nguyen[1],
Bin Ma[2], Eng-Siong Chng[1], Haizhou Li[2], and Susanto Rahardja[2]

[1] School of Computer Engineering, Nanyang Technological University (NTU),
Singapore 639798
{kohc0026,nguy0059,aseschng}@ntu.edu.sg
[2] Human Language Technology Department, Institute for Infocomm Research (I²R),
Singapore 119613
{hwsun,tlnma,mabin,hli,rsusanto}@i2r.a-star.edu.sg

**Abstract.** This paper describes the I²R/NTU system submitted for the NIST Rich Transcription 2007 (RT-07) Meeting Recognition evaluation Multiple Distant Microphone (MDM) task. In our system, speaker turn detection and clustering is done using Direction of Arrival (DOA) information. Purification of the resultant speaker clusters is then done by performing GMM modeling on acoustic features. As a final step, non-speech & silence removal is done. Our system achieved a competitive overall DER of 15.32% for the NIST Rich Transcription 2007 evaluation task.

## 1   Introduction

Speaker diarization has often been described as the task of identifying "Who Spoke When". When done in the context of the NIST Rich Transcription 2007 (RT-07) Meeting Recognition evaluations [1], this involves indicating the start and end time of every speaker segment present in the continuous audio recording of a meeting. Segments with common speakers have to be identified and annotated with a single speaker identity. This paper describes our system for the RT-07 speaker diarization task for multiple distant microphone (MDM) recordings.

Speaker diarization has traditionally relied on acoustic features such as Mel Frequency Cepstral Coefficient (MFCC) [2] or Perceptual Linear Prediction (PLP) [3] to perform segmentation and clustering. Segmentation is commonly done by employing the Bayesian Information Criteria (BIC) [3,4]. Over-segmentation typically has to be carried out in order to capture most of the speaker turns. This however poses a problem for subsequent clustering as the resulting segments will usually be of short duration and hence do not offer reliable clustering. Our system mitigates this problem by directly using Direction of Arrival (DOA) [5] information to identify speaker transitions and perform clustering.

R. Stiefelhagen et al. (Eds.): CLEAR 2007 and RT 2007, LNCS 4625, pp. 484–496, 2008.
© Springer-Verlag Berlin Heidelberg 2008

Cluster purification using acoustic features is then performed. Our results from the RT-07 evaluation have shown that purification using acoustic features helps to overcome mistakes introduced in DOA estimation. The final Diarization Error Rates (DER) (See Table 1) obtained after subsequent non-speech & silence removal were found to be competitive at 15.32%.

The usage of DOA information in the MDM task is not new. In [3,6], DOA information was used by delay-and-sum beamformers to generate enhanced signals. It has also been used in [7] to augment acoustic features when performing speaker clustering. The key novelty of our system is in how DOA is used early in the diarization process to perform both segmentation and clustering. Acoustic features are then employed to do what DOA alone cannot handle: cluster purification and non-speech removal.

The rest of this paper is organized as follows. Section 2 describes the modules in our system and how speaker diarization was performed using DOA and acoustic feature information. Section 3 then presents our experimental results for the RT-07 evaluation and offers some discussions on the performance of our system. Section 4 then concludes the paper.

## 2   System Description

Fig. 1 illustrates our system, which consists of 4 modules. The NIST Rich Transcription Spring 2006 (RT-06s) corpus was used in the development of the system.

1. DOA estimation
2. Bootstrap clustering
3. Cluster purification
4. Non-speech & silence removal

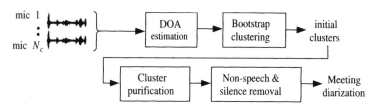

**Fig. 1.** Block diagram of the I²R/NTU RT-07 system

### 2.1   Direction of Arrival (DOA) Estimation

A typical MDM task will have two or more distant microphone recordings. As the microphones are usually placed some distance apart, speech originating from a single source will arrive at the different microphones at different times. The time delay between the arrivals can be exploited to estimate the speech's DOA.

Fig. 2 shows how a pair of microphone inputs are used in our DOA estimation system. $r[n]$ denotes the reference microphone signal at time $n$ and $s[n]$ denotes

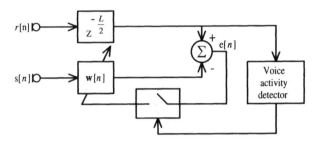

**Fig. 2.** DOA estimation module for a microphone pair

the source microphone. The reference channel is delayed by $L/2$ samples, and the adaptive filter's weights $\mathbf{w}[n]$ is of length $L$. During the presence of speech, the Normalized Least-Mean Square (NLMS) [8] algorithm is used to adapt the filter. DOA estimation is performed by detecting the peak position of the adaptive filter weights when voice activity is present.

Our DOA system operates on a frame-by-frame basis with the number of samples for each frame set to 512. For each frame, voice activity detection (VAD) is first performed by checking if the Teager energy [9] of the current frame is greater than an adaptive threshold. If speech activity is detected, the adaptive filter is allowed to adapt. Otherwise weights decay is applied to $\mathbf{w}[n]$. Our experience suggest that weights decay during silence frames improve the turn detection of short segments.

For the RT-06s task, $L = 250$ was found to be suitable. Given that the sampling rate is 16000 samples/sec, and assuming the speed of sound to be 330m/sec, the length $L = 250$ is able to accommodate a maximum microphone pair separation of 2.7 metres. If microphone pairs are separated by distances larger than 2.7 metres, $L$ should be increased accordingly.

Fig. 3a shows a positive example of how peak detection on $\mathbf{w}[n]$ can be used to find the DOA. In this example, the source and reference signals have good SNR and the recordings are not significantly affected by reverberations. After adaptation, the filter's weights reflects an impulse with peak at index 109. This

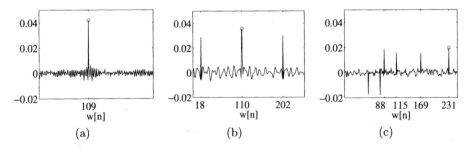

**Fig. 3.** Plot of values for filter coefficients $\mathbf{w}[n]$ at frame instance $n$, (a) showing a clear peak at index 109. (b) where there are 3 simultaneous speakers. (c) showing multiple peaks due to reverberation effects. Index 169 is the true speaker position.

can be interpreted to mean that the reference signal is a delayed version of the source and that the delay is 16 samples (125-109=16).

Given that $K$ pairs of microphones are used to estimate the direction of arrival, the matrix $DOA[n, k]$ stores the DOA values as

$$DOA[n, k] = \arg\max_{j=1..L}\{w_j[n, k]\} \tag{1}$$

where $n = 1..N$ and $k = 1..K$, $N$ being the number of frames and $w_j[n, k]$ the $j^{th}$ filter coefficient for the $k^{th}$ microphone pair at time $n$.

**Microphone Pair Selection.** In cases where many microphone recordings are available, the number of microphone pair permutations may be large. Under such circumstances, we can judiciously choose pairs that exhibit characteristics typical of good DOA estimation. Specifically, we choose microphone pairs that have:

– Large highest-peak to next-highest-peak ratio on $\mathbf{w}[n]$.
– High SNR.
– Large DOA dynamic range.

An example of a SNR estimation algorithm can be found in [10]. To choose the best $K$ pairs, we first rank all the microphone pairs by the above three factors and choose the top $K$ pairs.

## 2.2   Issues Influencing DOA Estimation Accuracy

**Simultaneous Speakers.** In the RT-07 tasks, there are situations when two or more speakers are talking simultaneously. We observed that multiple peaks will be observed for such instances. As can be seen in Fig. 3b, a peak will be registered for each speaker that talks. The filter weights at such an instance appear similar to that when the recordings have reverberations. This thus complicates our selection of the DOA estimate. As our current system is unable to discriminate simultaneous speech instances from reverberant recordings, we only exploit the maximum peak position to identify DOA. To improve system performance, we will develop a simultaneous speech detector to cope with this limitation.

**Presence of Audio Multi-paths.** Fig. 3c shows the adapted filter weights for the case where the recordings have reverberations. The desired peak, although present is less pronounced and multiple secondary peaks are present. The main path is usually represented by the highest peak while the numerous shorter peaks correspond to the other multi-paths. However as is shown in Fig. 3c, the peaks due to multi-paths can sometimes overwhelm the correct primary location, leading to erroneous DOA estimation. We observed that instances like this occured quite frequently for the VT_20050408-1500 task and suggest that this might be the cause of the poor DOA estimation.

**Presence of Frequency Specific Noise.** The impact of frequency specific noise is also an issue that would warrant further examination. Such noise can be observed in the audio spectrogram as "lines" present at certain frequency bands. As was discussed in [11], such noise may be introduced by way of the microphone

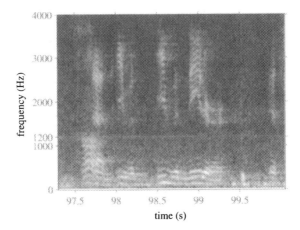

**Fig. 4.** Spectrogram of $1^{st}$ distant microphone for CMU_20061115-1030. Notice a "line" running horizontally at 1.2kHz.

system collecting the recording. In [11], frequency specific device noise was found to be present in a NIST MarkIII [12] microphone array setup. That noise was found to have an effect on the cross-correlation of audio channels. This in turn will also affect DOA estimation.

Our own analysis of the RT-07 audio also suggest the presence of such frequency specific noise. Figure 4 shows a spectrogram of the $1^{st}$ distant microphone of CMU_20061115-1030. In it, a "line" can be observed at the 1.2kHz mark. Similar artifacts can also be found in the recordings for the $2^{nd}$ and $3^{rd}$ distant microphones. We believe that this noise has a detrimental effect on our DOA estimations and further exploration will have to be done to confirm this.

### 2.3   Bootstrap Clustering

This section describes the $2^{nd}$ stage of our diarizaton system. Bootstrap clustering uses the frame-wise DOA information from Eqn. 1 to form initial clusters. Since clustering at this stage forms segments using only spatial location information, impure segments containing different speakers will result if speakers move or change places. The presence of these impurities can be mitigated somewhat during subsequent iterative cluster purification where clustering is performed using speaker dependent acoustic features.

The bootstrap clustering process consists of two sub-steps. The first step quantizes DOA estimates for each microphone pair (the columns of $DOA[n, k]$) to commonly occuring locations. The second step merges DOA information across all $K$ microphone pairs (the rows of $DOA[n, k]$), yielding a set of recurring DOA locations. The number of unique clusters formed after this step is taken by our system to be the final number of speakers. These clusters are used as seeds in the cluster purification step. Speech segments will then be formed by grouping together contiguous frames with a common cluster assignment. The details of the two sub-steps follows.

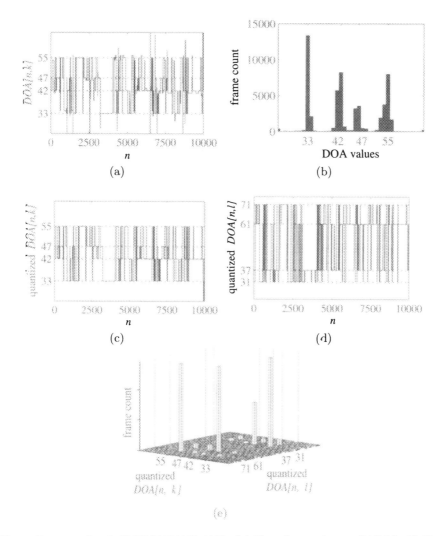

**Fig. 5.** For part of task CMU_20061115-1030 : (a) Plot of one column of DOA$[n, k]$. Horizontal dotted lines correspond to histogram centroids. (b) Histogram of DOA values for selected $k^{th}$ microphone pair. (c) DOA$[n, k]$ values after within-pair quantization. (d) Post-quantization DOA$[n, l]$ values of a different $l^{th}$ microphone pair for the same segment of speech. (e) 2-D histogram of quantized DOA values for 2 microphone pairs ($k^{th}$ and $l^{th}$). 4 peaks are visible.

**Within-Pair Quantization.** For the $k^{th}$ microphone pair, the $DOA[n, k]$ values are quantized to locate frequently occurring DOA positions for this pair. The frequently occurring positions are found by constructing a histogram using the $k^{th}$ column of $DOA[n, k]$. Every peak in the histogram indicates that there is a significant amount of speech originating from that particular location. We make the assumption that speech originating from a single location will very likely belong to a single homogenous speaker. As such, the number of peaks can be used as an estimate of the number of speakers present. The peaks in the histogram are taken as centroids and $DOA[n, k]$ values are quantized to these centroids using a nearest neighbor approach, as illustrated in Fig. 5a-c.

**Inter-Pair Quantization.** The previous subsection discusses quantization along the columns of $DOA[n, k]$. The second step of this module is to perform quantization along the rows of $DOA[n, k]$, i.e., to identify centroids across $K$ microphones pairs. Using the quantized results from within-pair quantization, a $K$-dimension histogram is built across all microphone pairs. Centroids can be readily identified within this high dimension histogram by virtue of their relatively high bin counts. An illustration of this is shown in Fig. 5e where 4 centroids can be observed by quantizing across 2 microphone pairs. The remaining histogram bins with low counts will then be clustered into the nearest centroid.

Our experiments conducted on the RT-07 MDM task showed that segments found after applying the bootstrap clustering were mostly of short durations - almost 90% of the segments are less than 3 seconds long and 71% of all the segments are shorter than 1 second.

It is interesting to note that apart from VT_20050408-1500, the initial clusters resulting after this module were observed to yield reasonably low Speaker Errors (See Table 1). The subsequent step of cluster purification only serves to improve the absolute DER by between 0% to 3.64%. This thus shows the effectiveness of our clustering method when the DOA estimations are accurate.

Clustering using only DOA information however will unlikely be robust towards situations where the speakers move significantly during a meeting. In such situations, speech from a single speaker might span across multiple clusters. The resultant clusters may be impure. Cluster purification will help in such situations to move incorrect speech segments to the cluster that they belong.

## 2.4   Cluster Purification

The $3^{rd}$ module of our system uses acoustic features for iterative re-clustering. This process of re-clustering has the effect of increasing the speaker homogenuity of each cluster. Beamforming is first performed on the available source audio to generate an enhanced recording as described in [6]. MFCC acoustic features are then generated from the enhanced recording. A voice activity detector (VAD) is then applied to retain only the high energy frames.

**Initialization Step.** All the MFCC vectors resulting from acoustic feature extraction are then used to train a root Gaussian Mixture Model (GMM), $\lambda_{Root}$. The $\lambda_{Root}$ has 40 Gaussian components with full covariance matrices and was trained using the Expectation Maximization (EM) algorithm as described in [13].

Segments resulting from bootstrap clustering are then pooled together according to their cluster assignments. Individual GMMs are adapted from $\lambda_{Root}$ for every cluster. Adaptation is performed on the weights, means and variances using the Maximum a Posteriori (MAP) approach [13]. Thus if there are $Q$ speaker clusters resulting from bootstrap clustering, there will be $Q$ GMMs. We denote these $Q$ GMMs as $\lambda_{i,q}$, where $i$ indicates the iteration number and $q = 1..Q$ indicates the $q^{th}$ speaker cluster. For the initialization step, $i = 0$.

**Iterated Steps.** The following is then performed:

1. Let $\mathbf{O}_j$ denote the set of feature vectors extracted from the $j^{th}$ segment. Let $s_{i,j} \in \{1..Q\}$ denote the cluster assignment of $\mathbf{O}_j$ for iteration $i$.
2. Every segment $\mathbf{O}_j$ is scored against models $\lambda_{i,q}$. Each segment is then relabelled by

$$s_{(i+1),j} = \arg\max_{q=1..Q}\{p(\mathbf{O}_j|\lambda_{i,q})\} \tag{2}$$

3. The GMMs $\lambda_{(i+1),q}$ are MAP adapted from $\lambda_{i,q}$ using the segments $\mathbf{O}_j$ corresponding to labels $s_{(i+1),j} = q$.
4. $i = i + 1$; Repeat from Step 2, until the cluster assignments have stabilized and do not vary for successive iterations.

The cluster assignment for segments were found to converge typically within 20 iterations.

## 2.5  Non-speech and Silence Removal

Silence and non-speech events such as coughs, laughter or breathing noises are present intermittently within speech segments. These segments are considered to be non-speech and should not be labeled as speaker segments. Hence, they have to be identified and removed.

**Non-speech Removal.** We performed non-speech identification on a segment-wise basis as it was found that a frame-wise decision was unreliable. The acoustic features used in this stage are the Log Frequency Power Coefficients (LFPC) [14]. A total of 10 coefficients are extracted from each 20 ms frame with a 10 ms overlap between frames. A model based approach was then used to evaluate every segment. Speech and non-speech were modeled by two separate GMMs, $\lambda_S$ and $\lambda_N$. A classification decision can be made for the $j^{th}$ segment, $\mathbf{O}_j$ as follows.

$$p(\lambda_S|\mathbf{O}_j) \geq p(\lambda_N|\mathbf{O}_j) \rightarrow \text{speech} \tag{3}$$
$$p(\lambda_S|\mathbf{O}_j) < p(\lambda_N|\mathbf{O}_j) \rightarrow \text{non} - \text{speech} \tag{4}$$

When expressed as a likelihood ratio, Eqns. 3 and 4 become

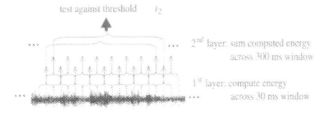

**Fig. 6.** The "Double-Layer Windowing" method of removing silence

$$\frac{p(\mathbf{O}_j|\lambda_S)}{p(\mathbf{O}_j|\lambda_N)} \geq t_1 \rightarrow \text{speech} \tag{5}$$

$$\frac{p(\mathbf{O}_j|\lambda_S)}{p(\mathbf{O}_j|\lambda_N)} < t_1 \rightarrow \text{non} - \text{speech} \tag{6}$$

where $t_1 = \frac{p(\lambda_N)}{p(\lambda_S)}$ is a threshold that was adjusted on the RT-06s corpus.

**Silence Removal.** Silence was removed using a "Double-Layer Windowing" method. In the first layer, audio is divided into frames of 20 ms with 10 ms overlapping. The energy for each frame is computed. In order to remove silences that are longer than the 300 ms tolerance specified for the evaluation [1], a second layer window is applied. This 300 ms long window shifts in 10 ms steps. The energy across all the frames in the window is summed.

When this energy is found to cross a threshold, $t_2$, the region covered by the window will be deemed as silence and dropped. The threshold used to make this decision was determined on the RT-06s evaluation data.

## 3   Experiments

### 3.1   Results on RT-07

The system described in the previous section was entered as our primary entry for the Rich Transcription 2007 (RT-07) Meeting Recognition MDM evaluation. As listed in Table 1, RT-07 consists of 8 meetings from 4 different meeting rooms (i.e. CMU, EDI, NIST & VT). Each meeting evaluation had a duration of about 23 minutes, giving the the entire evaluation a total duration of 3 hours. The number of microphones channels available for each meeting ranged from 3 for the CMU tasks, to 16 for the EDI tasks. All recordings were done using distance microphones, except those for EDI which were made using 2 microphone arrays (8 channels each). The performance of our system was evaluated by computing

**Table 1.** DER and Speaker Error ($SE$) time obtained on the RT-07

| RT-07 Task | Actual number of speakers | DER (%) after | | | $SE$ (s) after | |
|---|---|---|---|---|---|---|
| | | bootstrap clustering † | cluster purification | non-speech & silence removal | bootstrap clustering | cluster purification |
| CMU_20061115-1030 | 4 | 22.8 [4] | 22.7 | 19.4 | 48 | 48 |
| CMU_20061115-1530 | 4 | 17.8 [4] | 17.6 | 12.5 | 8 | 7 |
| EDI_20061113-1500 | 4 | 24.3 [5] | 24.3 | 20.7 | 34 | 34 |
| EDI_20061114-1500 | 4 | 30.6 [4] | 30.2 | 15.0 | 32 | 29 |
| NIST_20051104-1515 | 4 | 23.3 [4] | 22.8 | 12.7 | 18 | 14 |
| NIST_20060216-1347 | 6 | 22.1 [5] | 18.5 | 13.4 | 66 | 39 |
| VT_20050408-1500 | 5 | 46.4 [5] | 19.8 | 11.3 | 234 | 28 |
| VT_20050425-1000 | 4 | 27.4 [4] | 27.1 | 18.5 | 23 | 21 |
| Overall | — | 27.0 | 22.8 | 15.3 | 463 | 218 |

† - Number of resultant clusters for each task is indicated in brackets [ ].

the DER (Diarization Error Rate) against the official RTTM released by NIST. The DER is computed from the following error components.

$$DER = \frac{SE + MS + FA}{SPK}(\%) \tag{7}$$

- Speaker Error time ($SE$): Total time that is attributed to the wrong speaker.
- Missed Speaker time ($MS$): Total time in which less speakers are detected than what is correct.
- False Alarm Speaker time ($FA$): Total time in which more speakers are detected than what is correct.
- Scored Speaker time ($SPK$): Sum of every speaker's utterance time as indicated in the reference.

The DER for every task was found to improve after each subseqent processing step. Non-speech & silence removal yielded the largest overall improvement. It was capable of yielding an absolute improvement in the DER of 7.4%. The final DER of 15.3% was found to be competitive versus the other systems submitted for the RT-07 evaluation.

We observed that after bootstrap clustering, the VT_20050408-1500 task had the worst DER of 46.4%. A clue to its poor performance can be seen in the Speaker Error time ($SE$) component of the DER. It made up almost two-thirds of the diarization errors. As was previously mentioned in Section 2.2, the DOA estimation for this task was highly inaccurate. This resulted in many speech segments being incorrectly attributed to the wrong speaker. The DER for this task however improves considerably to 19.8% after performing cluster purification. The amount of $SE$ fell 88% to 28 seconds. This thus suggests that our cluster purification method is capable of redeeming the speaker assignment errors introduced by inaccurate DOA estimation.

It is noteworthy that after cluster purification, a large DER improvement was observed only for VT_20050408-1500. The improvements for the other tasks were marginal. As can be seen in Table 1, this perhaps is because the Speaker Error time for these tasks were already rather low after bootstrap clustering. Cluster purification thus had little room to improve upon. This thus also suggests that if the meetings recordings are of sufficient quality, DOA estimation alone is capable of producing reasonably pure speaker clusters.

In the course of the review process for this paper[1], it was suggested that further gains may be obtained by moving the cluster purification step to be after Non-Speech & Silence removal. This is a possibility that we are currently studying. The merit of doing so would be that cluster purification will be performed on segments that are free from silence and non-speech. The resultant speaker assignments may be more accurate, and this could be a way of further reducing our $SE$ time.

## 3.2   Performance of Non-Speech and Silence Removal

As was mentioned in Section 3.1, the non-speech & silence removal module produced the greatest improvement to the DER scores for RT-07. This module

---

[1] We would like to thank the anonymous reviewer for this suggestion.

**Table 2.** Before and after non-speech & silence removal

|  | SAD DER Error (%) ‡ | SAD Missed Speaker time (s) | SAD False Alarm Speaker time (s) |
|---|---|---|---|
| Before non-speech & silence removal | 14.5 | 8 | 1005 |
| After non-speech & silence removal | 8.7 | 326 | 280 |

‡ - Speech Activity Detection (SAD) DER error measures the amount of non-speech or silence that is incorrectly attributed to a speaker (SAD Missed Speaker time or $SADMS$ time), and speech that is incorrectly regarded as non-speech or silence (SAD False Alarm Speaker time or $SADFA$ time).

produced an absolute overall DER reduction of 7.4%. Further analysis however suggests that there remains potential for the improvement of this module. The Speech Activity Detection (SAD) error after this module stands at 8.7%. This value is relatively high when compared to the same for the systems submitted by the other RT-07 entrants.

The further removal of non-speech & silence however cannot be done by simply increasing the thresholds $t_1$ and $t_2$. As is reflected in Table 2, the removal of non-speech & silence was done at the expense of increasing the amount of speech misclassified to be non-speech or silence, i.e. the $SADFA$ time. A more aggressive non-speech or silence removal could worsen the system by removing more than it should. Subsequent experiments will thus have to be done to determine the optimum trade-off point where the total error time is lowest.

### 3.3   Number of Detected Speakers

It was observed that the number of unique speakers present in each meeting was determined quite accurately by our system. This number was incorrectly anticipated only in the case of EDI_20061113-1500 and NIST_20060216-1347. For EDI_20061113-1500, our system found 5 speakers when there should be 4. The speech of the longest speaker was found to be divided into two clusters, one containing 441 seconds of speech and other 86 seconds.

The numbers for NIST_20060216-1347 and our previous experience on the RT-06s corpus however suggests a shortcoming of our system. In our RT-06s experiments, it was observed that our system tends to under-estimate the number of speakers for those tasks with a large number of speakers. Speakers who spoke for the shortest durations tends to be found clustered together with a longer speaker. Our results for NIST_20060216-1347 reinforced this observation - only 5 speakers were detected when there should be 6. The speaker who spoke the least (59 seconds of speech) was found merged with a speaker who spoke for 128 seconds.

The reason for these missing short speakers would be due to the histogram quantization used in the bootstrap clustering process. When there is a large number of speakers, the resolution of the histogram becomes inadequate. Adjacent speaker distributions tend to overlap. Those speakers who spoke the least had small bin counts and therefore did not register as a clustering centroid. They were thus absorbed into their neighbours.

Our system currently determines the number of unique speakers present using only the DOA estimation values. This could potentially also result in another shortcoming. The number of unique speakers is approximated using those physical locations where most of the speech originates from. In the event where there is a speaker replacement in the middle of a meeting (e.g. in a lecture), this method will mistake both the speaker and its replacement as a common speaker. A possible solution to this problem would be to use acoustic information to test the homogenuity of each cluster prior to purification. Clusters that are found to be highly impure can be split into smaller parts of higher purity. Purification can then proceed on these smaller clusters.

## 4 Conclusions

The system developed for the $I^2R/NTU$ submission to the RT-07 evaluation was found to yield a competitive overall DER of 15.3%. For 7 of the 8 meetings, the initial clusters obtained after bootstrap clustering had a relatively low Speaker Error time. This indicates that using DOA alone can serve as an effective way of segmenting and clustering speakers.

It was observed however that the usage of DOA information alone is inadequate for the VT_20050408-1500 task. Clustering mistakes introduced by the unreliable DOA estimation could be redeem by performing cluster purification using acoustic features. We thus conclude that the usage of acoustic features to perform purification serves as an effective complement to segmentation and clustering using DOA information.

## References

1. Spring 2007 (RT-07) Rich Transcription Meeting Recognition Evaluation Plan (2007), http://www.nist.gov/speech/tests/rt/rt2007/docs/rt07-meeting-eval-plan-v2.pdf
2. Anguera, X., Wooters, C., Peskin, B., Aguilo, M.: Robust Speaker Segmentation for Meetings: The ICSI-SRI Spring 2005 Diarization System. In: Renals, S., Bengio, S. (eds.) MLMI 2005. LNCS, vol. 3869, pp. 402–414. Springer, Heidelberg (2006)
3. Leeuwen, D.A.v., Huijbregts, M.: The AMI speaker diarization system for NIST RT06s meeting data. In: Proc. NIST Rich Transcription 2006 Spring Meeting Recognition Evaluation Workshop, Washington DC, pp. 371–384 (2006)
4. Istrate, D., Fredouille, C., Meignier, S., Besacier, L., Bonastre, J.F.: NIST RT'05S Evaluation: Pre-processing Techniques and Speaker Diarization on Multiple Microphone Meetings. In: Renals, S., Bengio, S. (eds.) MLMI 2005. LNCS, vol. 3869, pp. 428–439. Springer, Heidelberg (2006)
5. Brandstein, M.S., Silverman, H.F.: A robust method for speech signal time-delay estimation in reverberant rooms. In: Proc. International Conference on Acoustics, Speech, and Signal Processing, Munich, pp. 375–378 (1997)
6. Anguera, X., Wooters, C., Hernando, J.: Speaker Diarization for Multi-Party Meetings Using Acoustic Fusion. In: Proc. IEEE Automatic Speech Recognition and Understanding Workshop, San Juan (2005)

7. Anguera, X., Wooters, C., Pardo, J.: Robust Speaker Diarization for Meetings: ICSI RT06s evaluation system. In: Proc. Interspeech 2006 ICSLP, Pittsburgh (2006)

8. Haykin, S.: Adaptive Filter Theory, 4th edn. Prentice-Hall, Inc., Upper Saddle River, NJ, USA (2002)

9. Kaiser, J.F.: On a simple algorithm to calculate the 'energy' of a signal. In: Proc. International Conference on Acoustics, Speech, and Signal Processing, Albuquerque, pp. 381–384 (1990)

10. Hirsch, H.G.: Estimation of noise spectrum and its application to SNR-estimation and speech enhancement. Technical report tr-93-012, ICSI, Berkeley (1993)

11. Brayda, L., Bertotti, C., Cristoforetti, L., Omologo, M., Svaizer, P.: Modifications on NIST MarkIII array to improve coherence properties among input signals. Journal of Audio Engineering Society (2005)

12. Rochet, C.: Technical Documentation of the Microphone Array Mark III (September 2005), http://www.nist.gov/smartspace/cmaiii.html

13. Reynolds, D.A., Quatieri, T.F., Dunn, R.B.: Speaker Verification using Adapted Gaussian Mixture Models. Digital Signal Processing 10, 19–41 (2000)

14. Nwe, T.L., Foo, S.W., Silva, L.C.D.: Stress classification using subband based features. IEICE Trans. Information and Systems E86-D, 565–573 (2003)

# The IBM RT07 Evaluation Systems for Speaker Diarization on Lecture Meetings

Jing Huang, Etienne Marcheret, Karthik Visweswariah,
and Gerasimos Potamianos

IBM Thomas J. Watson Research Center
Yorktown Heights, NY 10598, U.S.A.
{jghg,etiennem,kv1,gpotam}@us.ibm.com

**Abstract.** We present the IBM systems for the Rich Transcription 2007 (RT07) speaker diarization evaluation task on lecture meeting data. We first overview our baseline system that was developed last year, as part of our speech-to-text system for the RT06s evaluation. We then present a number of simple schemes considered this year in our effort to improve speaker diarization performance, namely: (i) A better speech activity detection (SAD) system, a necessary pre-processing step to speaker diarization; (ii) Use of word information from a speaker-independent speech recognizer; (iii) Modifications to speaker cluster merging criteria and the underlying segment model; and (iv) Use of speaker models based on Gaussian mixture models, and their iterative refinement by frame-level re-labeling and smoothing of decision likelihoods. We report development experiments on the RT06s evaluation test set that demonstrate that these methods are effective, resulting in dramatic performance improvements over our baseline diarization system. For example, changes in the cluster segment models and cluster merging methodology result in a 24.2% relative reduction in speaker error rate, whereas use of the iterative model refinement process and word-level alignment produce a 36.0% and 9.2% speaker error relative reduction, respectively. The importance of the SAD subsystem is also shown, with SAD error reduction from 12.3% to 4.3% translating to a 20.3% relative reduction in speaker error rate. Unfortunately however, the developed diarization system heavily depends on appropriately tuning thresholds in the speaker cluster merging process. Possibly as a result of over-tuning such thresholds, performance on the RT07 evaluation test set degrades significantly compared to the one observed on development data. Nevertheless, our experiments show that the introduced techniques of cluster merging, speaker model refinement and alignment remain valuable in the RT07 evaluation.

## 1 Introduction

There are three tasks evaluated this year in the Rich Transcription 2007 (RT07) evaluation campaign [1], conducted by the National Institute of Standards and Technology (NIST): Speaker diarization (SPKR), speech-to-text (STT), and speaker-attributed STT (SASTT), a task newly introduced this year. The three

R. Stiefelhagen et al. (Eds.): CLEAR 2007 and RT 2007, LNCS 4625, pp. 497–508, 2008.

are very much interconnected, with SPKR being an important pre-processing step to STT, but also a required part of the final SASTT output. The latter is due to SASTT aiming not only to correctly transcribe spoken words, but also to identify the generically labeled speaker of these words. A better SPKR system would therefore produce better SASTT results. An additional pre-processing step in this "cascade" of tasks is speech activity detection (SAD). This has been a separate evaluation task in the RT Spring 2006 (RT06s) evaluation campaign [2], but is now considered a "mature" task and, as such, has been sunset in RT07. Nevertheless, SAD remains an important step prior to speaker diarization.

The goal of speaker diarization is to label each speech segment (as provided by the SAD pre-processing step) with speaker information. The SPKR task is therefore sometimes referred to as the "who spoke when" problem [2]. Typically, the number of speakers present is not known a-priori. Such information needs to be determined automatically in the diarization task. In recent years, significant research effort has been devoted to the problem [3,4,5,6], with progress rigorously benchmarked in NIST speech technology evaluations [7].

There exist two main approaches to speaker diarization: The first is a bottom-up approach, i.e. hierarchical, agglomerative clustering [8,9,10], and the second is top-down, employing evolutive hidden Markov models (E-HMMs) [4], starting with one speaker and detecting and adding speakers in succession. Agglomerative clustering generally involves several steps: Initially, speech segments, as determined from SAD output, are investigated for possible speaker change points [11]. The output of change point detection is then fed into a speaker clustering procedure. Clustering stops when a predetermined criterion is satisfied (for example a drop in overall data likelihood from a merge). The limitation of this approach is that errors in the first two steps carry over to the final clustering step.

An improvement is to jointly optimize segmentation and clustering using an iterative procedure based on Gaussian mixture models (GMMs) of each cluster [12]. Recently, ICSI proposed purification algorithms for the iterative segmentation scheme to improve performance. Impure segments are removed before the cluster merging step, and impure frames are removed from GMM training and cluster merging [8]. LIMSI proposed to use speaker identification combined with the Bayesian information criterion (BIC) to improve performance [9,13]. However, this approach may not work well in lecture data, where many of the speakers (audience members asking questions) do not have enough data to generate reliable speaker models. The same problem occurs with the E-HMM scheme, where speaker models are needed. This approach usually detects the most dominant speakers well, but misses speakers with little data [4].

Although it is allowed to use STT system output to assist speaker diarization in the NIST RT evaluation, most submitted systems do not take advantage of word output from the STT task [2]. To our knowledge, such information has in the past been exploited by LIMSI, for example use of spoken cues ("Back to you, Bob"), as a means to add information to the diarization output for Broadcast News data [14], as well as for removal of short-duration silence segments when training speaker models [9].

In this paper, we present details of our SPKR system evaluated in the RT07 campaign for the lecture meeting domain. This represents the first year that the IBM team participated in the RT SPKR evaluation, although a baseline system has been developed last year as an STT pre-processing step [16] – but not officially evaluated. However, a separate SAD system had been evaluated [15]. A number of modifications have been made to these systems, resulting in the RT07 IBM SPKR system. In summary:

- A simpler SAD algorithm is employed, compared to the one in RT06s [15]. It is based on a speech/non-speech HMM decoder, set to an optimal operating point for missed speech / false alarm speech on development data. Because missed speech cannot be recovered in following speaker segmentation steps, the operating point is selected to miss only a small amount of speech, but at the same time not to introduce too many false alarms.
- Word information generated from STT decoding by means of a speaker-independent acoustic model is used to improve speaker clustering. Such information is useful for two reasons: It filters out non-speech segments, and it provides more accurate speech segments to the speaker clustering step, removing short silence, background noise, and vocal noise that do not discriminate speakers and cause overlaps of cluster models. As a result, only speech frames are used to train and compare cluster models.
- GMM-based speaker models are built from an available segmentation (for example, as provided by SAD), and the labels of each frame are refined using these GMM models, followed by smoothing the labeling decision with its neighbors. A result of re-classification and smoothing is the possibility that the original segments can be further segmented, in effect locating speaker change points within the initial segmentation. This process is significantly better than last year's change point detection approach.

The rest of the paper is organized as follows: Section 2 briefly overviews the baseline SAD and speaker diarization systems developed in RT06s. Section 3 presents RT07 modifications to the components of the baseline systems to improve diarization performance. Section 4 describes two system level variations taking advantage of the improved components. Section 5 is devoted to the experimental study and discussions, and Section 6 concludes the paper.

## 2   Baseline SAD and SPKR Systems

Speech activity detection (SAD) is a prerequisite to both SPKR and STT. After SAD, long segments of non-speech (silence or noise) are removed, and the audio is partitioned into shorter segments for fast decoding and speaker segmentation. For the RT06s evaluation, the IBM team developed two SAD systems: The one was officially evaluated, and it was based on a complex scheme of fusing acoustic likelihood and energy features for modeling three classes by full-covariance GMMs. During testing, the classes were collapsed into speech and silence, and appropriately smoothed to yield the final SAD result. Significant performance gains were observed when combining SAD results across multiple far-field channels by simple "voting" (decision fusion) [15].

The second scheme was employed as a first step in the IBM RT06s STT system, but was not evaluated separately [16]. We use this scheme as the first step for our SPKR/STT development this year. In more detail, it was an HMM-based speech/non-speech decoder; speech and non-speech segments were modeled with five-state, left-to-right HMMs. The HMM output distributions were tied across all states and modeled with a mixture of diagonal-covariance Gaussian densities. The non-speech model included the silence phone and three noise phones. The speech model contained all speech phones. Both were obtained by applying a likelihood-based, bottom-up clustering procedure to the speaker-independent acoustic model developed for STT, but adapted to the CHIL part of the training data by maximum a-posteriori (MAP) adaptation.

Our baseline speaker diarization system was originally developed for the EARS transcription system [17]. The framework is similar to the one described in [10], and it's briefly summarized here: All homogeneous speech segments as determined by the SAD output were modeled using a single Gaussian density function with diagonal covariance, and were bottom-up clustered into a pre-specified number of speaker clusters using $K$-means and a Mahalanobis distance measure. This distance measure between two $D$-dimensional Gaussians of diagonal covariance, denoted by $N(\mu_k, \sigma_k)$, $k = i, j$, is given by

$$dist(i, j) = \sum_{d=1}^{D} \frac{(\mu_i(d) - \mu_j(d))^2}{(\sigma_i^2(d) + \sigma_j^2(d))} \, . \tag{1}$$

For CHIL data, the number of speaker clusters was set to four for each lecture. This particular scheme proved sufficient for STT, but was never evaluated as a separate SPKR system in RT06s. For both SAD and SPKR tasks, 24-dimensional PLP acoustic features were used.

## 3   Improvements over Baseline Systems

We now proceed with details of the improvements introduced in RT07 to our SPKR system.

### 3.1   Improvement on SAD

By varying the number of Gaussians for speech and non-speech models, we are able to obtain different operating points of SAD performance, i.e. the ratio of missed speech vs. false alarm speech. For example, if too many Gaussians are used for speech, then the false alarm rate becomes high; if too many Gaussians are used for non-speech, then the miss rate grows. Because the missed speech cannot be recovered in the following speaker segmentation step, we choose an operating point that would only miss a very small amount of speech, but at the same time would not introduce too many false alarms. In fact, this simple scheme works extremely well. Interestingly, at that operating point, no gain is obtained by combining multiple distant microphone SAD outputs, in contrast to the RT06s system [15]. The output of SAD is purified as discussed next.

## 3.2  Incorporating Word Output Alignments

In general, the speaker diarization task is performed before decoding. Here we propose a slight variation, namely to use the decoded output from a speaker-independent acoustic model in order to further refine SAD output, prior to its use in the speaker diarization step. The information is used in two ways:

- We remove segments with only silence, background noise, and vocal noise. These are segments that SAD failed to identify as non-speech.
- In the subsequent speaker clustering steps, we ignore frames that correspond to silence, background noise, and vocal noise.

The first constitutes a segment-based purification, whereas the second is frame-based purification [8]. By identifying non-speech frames and removing them from the speaker model training step, one expects better speaker clustering.

## 3.3  Clustering and Refinement

An important change from our baseline SPKR system is that instead of using a fixed number of desired speakers, we estimate the initial number of speakers according to a minimum number of expected frames. This process results in an upper bound on the expected number of speakers. Subsequently, speaker clustering and refinement reduce this number, as discussed in this section.

An additional change has to do with the employed acoustic features. Instead of 24-dimensional PLPs, we switch to 19-dimensional MFCCs, with the energy term dropped. Such features constitute the traditional feature space used for speaker recognition.

A crucial step in the whole process is the maximum-likelihood based clustering and GMM refinement. This consists of the following steps:

- *Initialization:* To build the initial speaker models we use the K-means process as follows: We take the segments sequentially partitioned equally to each speaker. A single-mixture full-covariance (FC) Gaussian for each speaker model is then estimated using a maximum likelihood criterion on each of these segments. In parallel, segments generated by the SAD output are modeled by a single mixture FC model. Subsequently, the speaker models are re-estimated by maximum likelihood using the SAD segment sufficient statistics. In more detail, each SAD segment model is assigned to the best speaker model according to a maximum per-frame log-likelihood criterion; i.e., for speaker model $i$ and SAD segment model $j$, the following are used

$$LL_1(i,j) = \Sigma_{SAD(j)} + \left(\mu_{SPK(i)} - \mu_{SAD(j)}\right)\left(\mu_{SPK(i)} - \mu_{SAD(j)}\right)^T$$
$$LL(i,j) = -\frac{1}{2}\,trace\left(\Sigma^{-1}_{SPK(i)}LL_1(i,j)\right) - \frac{1}{2}\log|\Sigma_{SPK(i)}|\,, \qquad (2)$$

where $(\mu, \Sigma)$ denote Gaussian model mean and full covariance. The assignment and re-estimation steps are run for ten iterations.

- *Cluster Merging:* At each step in the bottom-up clustering process, we combine the two nodes that result in the smallest likelihood loss, if merged. We stop, when no two nodes can be combined with a loss smaller than a pre-set threshold. The likelihood loss associated with merging clusters $i$ and $j$ is

$$dist(i, j) = N\left(\log |\Sigma| - p_i \log |\Sigma_i| - p_j \log |\Sigma_j|\right),\qquad(3)$$

where $N = n_i + n_j$ is the total number of frames assigned to clusters $i$ and $j$, and the priors on clusters are determined as $p_i = n_i/N$. Therefore, at each step in the merging process, the smallest $dist(i, j)$ determines which clusters to merge. The result is then compared against a pre-specified threshold $\lambda$, causing the merging process to be terminated if $dist(i, j) > \lambda$.

- *Refinement:* From the merging step we have frame-level assignments to each of the remaining speaker models. Using these indices, we build diagonal-covariance GMMs with ten mixtures (an empirically determined number). This is accomplished by clustering and splitting, running expectation-maximization steps between splits. From the resulting refined models we then compute the per-frame likelihoods. The frame-level likelihoods are subsequently smoothed over a 150 msec window ($\pm$ 75 msec), and the frame is assigned to the appropriate model, according to the maximum score. With these new frame-level assignments the entire refinement process can be re-run. We find that after two iterations frame-level assignments stabilize.

## 4   SPKR System Variations Used

In our experiments, in addition to the baseline, we consider two similar SPKR systems – referred to as "IBM 1" and "IBM 2" – that adopt most of the above improvements. In particular, both take advantage of improved SAD and word-level alignment and employ sequential cluster pre-initialization. The difference lies in the clustering metric and the use of the secondary GMM refinement step:

- *IBM 1:* During cluster merging, the Mahalanobis distance metric (1) is used on the over-segmented input, instead of (3). The merging process is terminated when a pre-specified threshold value is reached – determined on development data. Use of the word-level alignment information results in system "IBM 1 + align". Note that the Mahalanobis distance metric of equation (1) is used in both the SAD segment assignment to a speaker cluster and the distance metric, when deciding which clusters to merge.
- *IBM 2* is generated by the initialization and cluster merging steps, as described in Section 3.3. We denote use of word-level alignments and the GMM refinement step by "IBM 2 + align" and "IBM 2 + refine", respectively.

## 5   Experiments and Results

Our experiments are conducted on the lecture meeting data collected by five partners of the CHIL consortium ("Computers in the Human Interaction Loop")

**Table 1.** Overall diarization error (DER), %, of the baseline and improved (tuned) speech activity detection (SAD) systems on our development set based on input from a single distant microphone (SDM). The two systems use different numbers of Gaussians to model speech and silence. DER break-down into its two components (missed and false alarm errors) is also shown.

| systems | | missed (%) | false alarm (%) | DER (%) |
|---|---|---|---|---|
| sad.16.16 | (baseline) | 0.3 | 16.5 | 16.8 |
| sad.100.32 | (improved) | 1.3 | 3.0 | 4.3 |

[18]. For development data, necessary for SAD and cluster merging threshold tuning, we use part of the RT06s evaluation test set containing 28 lecture meetings recorded in CHIL smart rooms. From this set, 27 lectures are used as the development set, with one lecture excluded due to it being closer to the so-called "coffee-break" scenario [1]. Of course, for final system evaluation the lecture meeting part of the RT07 test set is used. Note that all experiments in this section are reported for the single-distant microphone (SDM) condition, as specified in the NIST evaluation plan [1].

In accordance to NIST scoring, results are reported in terms of diarization error rate (DER). DER is calculated by first finding the optimal one-to-one mapping between reference speakers and the hypothesized ones, and then computing the percentage of time that is wrongly assigned according to the optimal mapping. DER includes speaker error time, missed speaker time, and false alarm speaker time, thus also taking SAD errors into account [2]. SAD performance is measured in DER as well, but with all speakers labeled simply as speech. Segments with overlapping speech are also included in the DER computation.

## 5.1 Development Set SAD and SPKR Results

As already mentioned, there exists a tradeoff in SAD system performance between false accepts and missed speech, with the operating point being a function of the number of Gaussians modeling the speech and silence classes. In our reported experiments, we imply this dependence by denoting the SAD systems as "sad . < number of speech Gaussians > . < number of silence Gaussians >". In particular, the baseline system is "sad.16.16" and the improved (after tuning) is "sad.100.32". Table 1 compares performance of these two systems at the SDM condition. Notice the significant reduction in false alarm rate with a small only impact on missed speech over the baseline. The overall SAD DER is reduced by 74.4% relative.

We now proceed to report experiments on the speaker diarization system. We first investigate the impact on DER of the cluster merging threshold. Fig. 1 illustrates results for three configurations of the "IBM 2" system, namely "IBM 2", "IBM 2 + align", and "IBM 2 + refine". Not depicted is the "IBM 2 + align + refine" system, as no gain was achieved using alignment following refinement. This figure demonstrates that the optimal cutoff threshold lies around 7000.

Table 2 provides a comparison between the baseline SPKR system (the crude RT06s system that uses a pre-set number of speaker clusters) and the "IBM

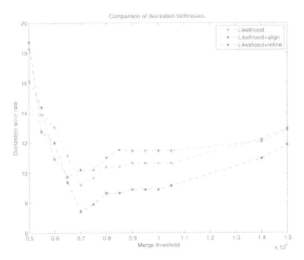

**Fig. 1.** Impact of the cluster merging threshold on DER on our development set, depicted for three variants of the "IBM 2" speaker diarization system

1" and "IBM 2" systems, under various configurations concerning the use of alignment and refinement, but in all cases at their respective optimal cluster merging thresholds. Note that the cluster merging thresholds differ, due to the use of different distance metrics (see (1) and (3)). Unfortunately, due to lack of time, we did not explore the "IBM 1 + refine" system.

Finally, Fig. 2 illustrates the effect of SAD error rate (missed plus false alarm errors) on SPKR DER. In this experiment, we increase SAD error from the 4.3% value of Table 2 to 12.3%, by switching to a "sad.256.16" system. Notice that the average reduction in speaker error rate by employing the selected "sad.100.32" system is 20.3% over the use of "sad.256.16". In particular, at the optimal cluster merging threshold of 7000, we observe a 56.7% relative reduction in speaker error rate (from 7.4% to 3.2%).

## 5.2   Evaluation Results

The IBM team submitted the following systems relevant to speaker diarization for the RT07 evaluation:

**Table 2.** DER and its break-down, %, for various SPKR systems measured on development data, depicted at their optimal cluster merging thresholds (if applicable)

| systems | opt. thresh. | missed (%) | false alarm (%) | speaker error (%) | DER (%) |
|---|---|---|---|---|---|
| IBM baseline | — | 0.3 | 16.5 | 53.3 | 70.1 |
| IBM 1 | 0.6 | 1.3 | 3.0 | 6.6 | 10.9 |
| IBM 1+align | 0.6 | 1.3 | 3.0 | 5.6 | 9.9 |
| IBM 2 | 7000 | 1.3 | 3.0 | 5.0 | 9.3 |
| IBM 2+align | 6500 | 1.3 | 3.0 | 5.5 | 9.8 |
| IBM 2+refine | 7000 | 1.3 | 3.0 | 3.2 | 7.5 |

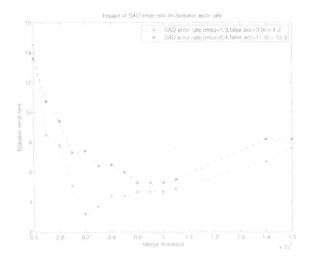

**Fig. 2.** Speaker error rate on development data as a function of the cluster merging threshold for two different SAD systems with error rates of 4.3% and 12.3%

- *Speaker Diarization (SPKR) task:* With the speaker diarization deadline a week before SASTT was due, and owing to the fact that the "IBM 2" system was not ready by the first deadline, for SPKR we submitted the "IBM 1 + align" system. Threshold tuning was applied per recording site, tuned on the development set.
- *Speaker-Attributed Speech-To-Text (SASTT) task:* By the SASTT deadline, the "IBM 2 + refine" system was ready. Results from this system were used in SASTT with a cluster merging threshold of 7000.
- *Speech Activity Detection (SAD) subsystem:* The "sad.100.32" system was used in both cases.

We now proceed to report evaluation set results using the above systems. Table 3 summarizes experiments on the 32-segment RT07 test set. We observe that the overall SAD performance (missed and false alarm errors) remains relatively consistent, degrading from 4.3% on development data to 6.3% on the evaluation set. On the other hand, speaker diarization performance does not show similar stability. It is clear from the table that the chosen thresholds in our submitted systems (SASTT and SPKR), tuned on basis of development data, do not generalize well to the test set. In particular, it seems that our primary system submitted to the SPKR task ("IBM 1 + align") gets penalized by the selection of site-specific thresholds – as compared to the use of a site-independent threshold of 0.6 determined on development data (see also Table 2). In general, it also seems that this system is slightly less sensitive to the tuned threshold than the "IBM 2 + refine" system, submitted to the SASTT task. Nevertheless, the "IBM 2 + refine" system has the potential to generate a lower DER – if only the optimal threshold of 15000 were used!

**Table 3.** DER and its break-down, %, on the RT07 test set for the two IBM systems in various configurations, and for various thresholds tuned on development or evaluation data. The latter are marked with "opt.", and of course constitute a "cheating" experiment. The systems in bold are the ones officially benchmarked in RT07.

| systems | threshold | missed | false alarm | speaker error | DER |
|---|---|---|---|---|---|
| IBM 1 | 0.6 | 2.4 | 3.9 | 21.9 | 28.2 |
| IBM 1 | 0.9 (opt.) | 2.4 | 3.9 | 18.5 | 24.8 |
| **IBM 1+align** | site-spec. (RT07 SPKR) | 2.4 | 3.9 | 23.7 | 30.0 |
| IBM 1+align | 0.6 | 2.4 | 3.9 | 21.0 | 27.3 |
| IBM 1+align | 0.85 (opt.) | 2.4 | 3.9 | 18.7 | 25.0 |
| IBM 2 | 7000 | 2.4 | 3.9 | 24.8 | 31.1 |
| IBM 2 | 15000 (opt.) | 2.4 | 3.9 | 17.6 | 23.9 |
| **IBM 2+refine** | 7000 (RT07 SASTT) | 2.4 | 3.9 | 21.4 | 27.7 |
| IBM 2+refine | 15000 (opt.) | 2.4 | 3.9 | 16.5 | 22.8 |

It is interesting to note that the "IBM 1 + align" system improves performance over its "IBM 1" variant for both development and evaluation data, achieving a relative 9.2% DER reduction (from 10.9% down to 9.9% – see Table 2), and 3.2% (28.2% to 27.3%) respectively. In terms of pure speaker error rate, the relative gains are 15.2% (6.6% to 5.6%) and 4.1% (21.9% to 21.0%), respectively. Similar improvements occur for the "IBM 2 + refine" system over the "IBM 2" one: Namely, for DER, a 19.4% (9.3% becomes 7.5%) and a 10.9% (31.1% to 27.7%) relative reduction are observed on the development and evaluation sets, respectively; in terms of pure speaker error rates, these reductions become even more pronounced, at 36.0% (5.0% to 3.2%) and 13.7% (24.8% to 21.4%) relative. Comparing the baseline IBM 1 and IBM 2 systems, we see a 24.2% (5.6% to 4.0%) relative reduction in speaker error rate on the development test set. On the evaluation test set at optimal thresholds we see a smaller 4.9% (18.5% to 17.6%) relative reduction between the two baseline systems.

This "picture" changes though, if threshold tuning is performed on the evaluation set. Under such scenario, the "IBM 1 + align" shows a 1.1% degradation in speaker error over the "IBM 1" system. Furthermore, the relative DER gain of the "IBM 2 + refine" over the "IBM 2" system is reduced to only 4.6% (23.9% to 22.8%), corresponding to a 6.3% relative gain in speaker error (17.6% to 16.5%).

It is worth making two final remarks. The one is that the DER numbers reported in Table 3 deviate somewhat from the RT07 results reported by NIST for the IBM system. In particular, the official DER number for the RT07 SPKR system is 29.83%, contributed by 2.5% missed, 3.6% false alarm, and 23.7% speaker errors. The reason for the discrepancy in the results is unclear to us, but is most likely due to the scoring software. The second remark has to do with the multiple distant microphone (MDM) condition. In our submitted SPKR MDM system, we have not performed any microphone channel combination (for example, signal-based or decision fusion). Instead, we used a single microphone, selected based on the highest signal-to-noise ratio among the available table-top microphones in each lecture. This turns out to be in almost all cases identical to the channel selected by NIST for the SDM condition. As a result, MDM SPKR performance is very close to the SDM one, exhibiting a DER of 30.00%.

# 6   Conclusions and Future Work

In this paper, we presented the IBM team efforts to improve speaker diarization (SPKR) for lecture meeting data, as part of the RT07 evaluation campaign. We first described the speech activity detection (SAD) subsystem that constitutes a greatly improved version of the one used in conjunction with the IBM speech-to-text (STT) system in the RT06s evaluation. The improvements resulted in a 74.4% relative reduction in SAD error on development data, by appropriately tuning the balance between the number of Gaussians used to model the speech and silence classes. The SAD error rate generalized relatively well from development to evaluation data, achieving a 6.3% "diarization" error on the latter.

For speaker diarization, we developed a new approach that over-segments SAD output, and subsequently initializes, merges, and refines speaker clusters. This results in a varying number of final speakers, as opposed to our simple approach employed as part of the RT06s STT system that derived a pre-set number of speakers. In the newly developed system, we employed different distance metrics (Mahalanobis, likelihood-based) and Gaussian models (with diagonal or full covariance) in the initialization and cluster merging steps, giving rise to two slightly different systems that were submitted to the SPKR and SASTT tasks. The systems dramatically improved performance over our RT06s baseline, achieving diarization errors as low as 7.5% on development data. However, these results do not carry over to the evaluation set, due to system sensitivity to the cluster merging threshold. Indeed, diarization error hovers in the range of 28% and 30% for the two systems.

To reduce such instability, one possibility is to use the modified BIC score [8], which would hopefully remove the need for such threshold altogether. Replacing the refinement step with a speaker identification system, iteratively refining the enrollment against a relevant universal background model may also help. Finally, we would like to investigate the use of multiple microphone input to improve SKPR system performance over the single channel system.

# Acknowledgments

This work was supported by the European Commission under integrated project CHIL, "Computers in the Human Interaction Loop," contract no. 506909.

# References

1. NIST 2007 Spring Rich Transcription Evaluation,
   http://www.nist.gov/speech/tests/rt/rt2007/index.html
2. Fiscus, J.G., Ajot, J., Michel, M., Garofolo, J.S.: The Rich Transcription 2006 Spring meeting recognition evaluation. In: Renals, S., Bengio, S., Fiscus, J.G. (eds.) MLMI 2006. LNCS, vol. 4299, pp. 309–322. Springer, Heidelberg (2006)

3. Anguera, X., Wooters, C., Pardo, J.M.: Robust speaker diarization for meetings: ICSI RT06S meetings evaluation system. In: Renals, S., Bengio, S., Fiscus, J.G. (eds.) MLMI 2006. LNCS, vol. 4299, pp. 346–358. Springer, Heidelberg (2006)
4. Fredouille, C., Senay, G.: Technical improvements of the E-HMM based speaker diarization system for meeting records. In: Renals, S., Bengio, S., Fiscus, J.G. (eds.) MLMI 2006. LNCS, vol. 4299, pp. 359–370. Springer, Heidelberg (2006)
5. Zhu, X., Barras, C., Lamel, L., Gauvain, J.-L.: Speaker diarization: From Broadcast News to lectures. In: Renals, S., Bengio, S., Fiscus, J.G. (eds.) MLMI 2006. LNCS, vol. 4299, pp. 396–406. Springer, Heidelberg (2006)
6. van Leeuwen, D.A., Huijbregts, M.: The AMI speaker diarization system for NIST RT06s meeting data. In: Renals, S., Bengio, S., Fiscus, J.G. (eds.) MLMI 2006. LNCS, vol. 4299, pp. 371–384. Springer, Heidelberg (2006)
7. NIST Rich Transcription Benchmark Tests, http://www.nist.gov/speech/tests/rt
8. Anguera, X., Wooters, C., Hernando, J.: Purity algorithms for speaker diarization of meetings data. In: Proc. Int. Conf. Acoustic Speech Signal Process (ICASSP), Toulouse, France, vol. 1, pp. 1025–1028 (2006)
9. Zhu, X., Barras, C., Meignier, S., Gauvain, J.-L.: Combining speaker identification and BIC for speaker diarization. In: Proc. Interspeech, Lisbon, Portugal, pp. 2441–2444 (2005)
10. Reynolds, D.A., Torres-Carrasquillo, P.: Approaches and applications of audio diarization. In: Proc. Int. Conf. Acoustic Speech Signal Process (ICASSP), Philadelphia, PA, vol. 5, pp. 953–956 (2005)
11. Ajmera, J., Wooters, C.: A robust speaker clustering algorithm. In: Proc. Automatic Speech Recogn. Understanding Works (ASRU), St. Thomas, US Virgin Islands (2003)
12. Gauvain, J.-L., Lamel, L., Adda, G.: Partitioning and transcription of Broadcast News data. In: Proc. Int. Conf. Spoken Language Systems (ICSLP), Sydney, Australia (1998)
13. Sinha, R., Tranter, S.E., Gales, M.J.F., Woodland, P.C.: The Cambridge University speaker diarisation system. In: Proc. Interspeech, Lisbon, Portugal, March 2005, pp. 2437–2440 (2005)
14. Canseco-Rodriguez, L., Lamel, L., Gauvain, J.-L.: Speaker diarization from speech transcripts. In: Proc. Int. Conf. Spoken Language Systems (ICSLP), Jeju Island, S. Korea (2004)
15. Marcheret, E., Potamianos, G., Visweswariah, K., Huang, J.: The IBM RT06s evaluation system for speech activity detection in CHIL seminars. In: Renals, S., Bengio, S., Fiscus, J.G. (eds.) MLMI 2006. LNCS, vol. 4299, pp. 323–335. Springer, Heidelberg (2006)
16. Huang, J., Westphal, M., Chen, S., Siohan, O., et al.: The IBM Rich Transcription Spring 2006 speech-to-text system for lecture meetings. In: Renals, S., Bengio, S., Fiscus, J.G. (eds.) MLMI 2006. LNCS, vol. 4299, pp. 432–443. Springer, Heidelberg (2006)
17. Chen, S.F., Kingsbury, B., Mangu, L., Povey, D., et al.: Advances in speech transcription at IBM under the DARPA EARS program. IEEE Trans. Speech Audio Language Process. 14(5), 1596–1608 (2006)
18. CHIL: Computers in the Human Interaction Loop, http://chil.server.de

# The ICSI RT07s Speaker Diarization System

Chuck Wooters[1] and Marijn Huijbregts[1,2]

[1] International Computer Science Institute, Berkeley CA 94704, USA
[2] University of Twente
Department of Electrical Engineering, Mathematics and Computer Science,
Enschede, The Netherlands
{wooters,marijn}@icsi.berkeley.edu

**Abstract.** In this paper, we present the ICSI speaker diarization system. This system was used in the 2007 National Institute of Standards and Technology (NIST) Rich Transcription evaluation. The ICSI system automatically performs both speaker segmentation and clustering without any prior knowledge of the identities or the number of speakers. Our system uses "standard" speech processing components and techniques such as HMMs, agglomerative clustering, and the Bayesian Information Criterion. However, we have developed the system with an eye towards robustness and ease of portability. Thus we have avoided the use of any sort of model that requires training on "outside" data and we have attempted to develop algorithms that require as little tuning as possible.

The system is simular to last year's system [1] except for three aspects. We used the most recent available version of the beam-forming toolkit, we implemented a new speech/non-speech detector that does not require models trained on meeting data and we performed our development on a much larger set of recordings.

## 1 Introduction

The goal of speaker diarization is to segment an audio recording into speaker-homogeneous regions. This task is sometimes referred to as the "Who Spoke When" task. Knowing when each speaker is speaking is useful as a pre-processing step in speech-to-text (STT) systems to improve the quality of the output. Such pre-processing may include vocal tract length normalization (VTLN) and/or speaker adaptation. Automatic speaker segmentation may also be useful in information retrieval and as part of the indexing information of audio archives.

For the past three years, the US National Institute of Standards and Technology (NIST) has conducted competitive evaluations of speaker diarization systems using recordings from multi-party meetings. For these evaluations, the speaker diarization task must be performed with little knowledge of the characteristics of the audio or of the talkers in the recording. Within the meeting domain, there are several conditions on which diarization systems are evaluated. The primary evaluation condition allows the use of audio recorded from multiple distant microphones. As an optional task, NIST also evaluates the performance of diarization systems when the audio input comes from just a single (distant)

R. Stiefelhagen et al. (Eds.): CLEAR 2007 and RT 2007, LNCS 4625, pp. 509–519, 2008.

microphone. The performance of diarization systems on the multiple distant microphone task is typically better than on the single distant microphone task due to the extra information provided by the additional microphones.

One of the most commonly used techniques for performing speaker diarization is agglomerative clustering, where a large number of initial models are merged pair-wise, until the system arrives at a single model per speaker. Techniques such as agglomerative clustering often call for the use of "tunable" parameters such as: the number of initial models, the number of Gaussian mixtures per model, or the penalty factor used in the Bayesian Information Criterion (BIC) [2]. The choice of the values for these parameters can be vital to the performance of the clustering system. Typically, system designers choose the values for the parameters empirically based on training and development data. It is important that this data be as similar as possible to the data on which the system will ultimately be tested in order to ensure robust behavior.

In this paper, we present the ICSI speaker diarization system used in the NIST RT07s evaluations. The system we present is based on agglomerative clustering and automatically deduces the number of speakers in a recording, along with the information about where each speaker is speaking. The algorithm runs iteratively, alternating model alignment with model merging. The algorithm we use for model merging is a modification of BIC in which we keep the number of parameters between the two BIC hypotheses constant. An important property of this modification of BIC is that it allows us to eliminate the BIC penalty term, thus eliminating one of the parameters that must be tuned.

The system is simular to last year's system [1] except for three aspects. First of all, we used the most recent available version of the beam-forming toolkit. During initial experiments we noticed that the performance of the toolkit has increased significantly. We performed all of our development on a much larger set of recordings compared to earlier years so that the development decisions are less likely based on characteristics of specific meetings. Also, we implemented a new speech/non-speech detector that does not require models trained on in-domain data. The detector does need models, but only to make an initial rough segmentation. The final segmentation is created using models trained on the recording itself.

In section 2, we present an overview of the speaker diarization system that we used for the 2007 evaluation. In section 3 we describe several experiments we ran after the evaluation to examine the behavior of the system in more detail. Finally, we end with some conclusions and future work.

## 2    System Description

### 2.1    Front-End Acoustic Processing

The acoustic processing consists of three steps. First, Wiener filtering [3] is performed on each available audio channel. The goal of the Wiener filtering is to remove any "corrupting" noise from the signal. The noise is assumed to be additive and of a stochastic nature. The implementation of the Wiener filtering we use was taken from the noise reduction algorithm developed for the Aurora 2 front-end proposed by ICSI, OGI, and Qualcomm [4]. The algorithm performs Wiener filtering with typical engineering modifications, such as a noise over-estimation factor, smoothing of the filter response, and a spectral floor. We modified the algorithm to use a single noise spectral estimate for each meeting waveform. This was calculated over all the frames judged to be non-speech by the voice-activity detection component of the Qualcomm-ICSI-OGI front end.

After Wiener filtering, if multiple audio channels (i.e. recordings from multiple microphones) are available, a single "enhanced" channel is created by running delay and sum beamforming on the separate channels. The beamforming was done using the BeamformIt 2.0 toolkit[1] with a 500 msec analysis window stepped at a 250 msec frame rate. Finally, feature extraction is performed on the resulting beamformed channel.

Our system uses two types of acoustic features. The first nineteen Mel Frequency Cepstrum Coefficients (MFCC), created using the HTK toolkit[2], form our standard feature type. These features are created at a 10 msec frame rate with a 30 msec analysis window. The second type of feature we use is only used when multiple audio channels are available (the MDM condition). In this case, we use the BeamformIt tool to calculate the delay values between the different audio channels. When using BeamformIt to produce these delay features, we use a 500 msec analysis but it is stepped at the same frame rate (10 msec) as was used for the MFCC features. The delay factors are then added to the system as a second feature stream.

## 2.2   Speech/Non-speech Detection

One of the improvements we made this year was the creation of a new speech/non-speech detector. The detector we used last year consisted of two stages. It first selected those regions in the audio with high and low energy levels and then in the second stage it trained dedicated speech models on the high energy regions and silence models on the low energy levels. The major advantage of this approach is that it does not use models trained on outside data making it robust to changes in audio conditions. The drawback of using energy however is that it is not possible to use this approach when the audio contains fragments with high energy levels that are non-speech. For another task [5], we developed a new speech/non-speech detector inspired by last year's system. This new system is better able to detect audible non-speech.

The new speech/non-speech detector consists of three steps. First, as in last years system, an initial guess is made about which regions in the audio are speech, silence or non-speech sounds. Only the regions that are classified with a high confidence score are labeled. To create these three regions, an initial segmentation is created with an HMM that contains a speech and a silence GMM that was trained on broadcast news data. The silence region is then split

---

[1] Available at: http://www.icsi.berkeley.edu/x̄anguera/beamformit
[2] Available at http://htk.eng.cam.ac.uk/

into two classes: regions with low energy and regions with high energy and high zero-crossing rates. From the data in each of these two classes a new GMM is trained. The GMM trained on the low energy data contains 7 gaussians, and the GMM trained on the high energy, high zero-crossing rate data contains 18 gaussians (once fully trained.) For the speech regions, a third GMM is trained with 24 gaussians. The gaussians of all three models are built up iteratively, and during this process the audio is re-segmented a number of times [6].

In the second step of the speech/non-speech detector, models are trained from the data in the three regions defined by the first step, and we label these regions: "speech", "silence" and "non-speech sound". We always assume that a recording has all three types of regions. However, if an audio recording does not contain any non-speech sounds, it is possible that the "sound" model will end up containing "speech" data. Therefore, in the third step, the system checks to see if the "sound" and "speech" models are similar. To test for similarity, a new model is trained on the combined speech and sound data, and BIC is used to test whether it is better to model all of the data with one combined model or two separate models (similar to what we do during the diarization process). If the BIC score is positive, the sound model is discarded and a new speech model is trained using all of the speech and sound data.

For all of these steps, we use feature vectors with 12 MFCC components, zero-crossing, deltas and delta-deltas. The underlying system uses a Hidden Markov Model with two (or three) "strings" of states in parallel (in order to enforce a minimum duration for each segment). Each string shares a single Gaussian Mixture Model (GMM) as its probability density function that represents one of the three classes. The segmentation into the two (or three) classes is found by performing a Viterbi search on the data using this HMM.

### 2.3 Cluster Modeling

The Probability Density Function (PDF) used in our diarization system is modeled with a Gaussian Mixture Model (GMM). If multiple audio channels are available, each of the two audio streams (MFCC and delays) are modeled using separate GMMs, and the overall PDF is modeled as a weighted combination of these two GMMs. The weights of the two streams are initially set to fixed values (0.65 and 0.35). Then, during the merging process, the weights are adapted using the algorithm introduced in [7]. This approach makes it possible to automatically find appropriate weights for the two streams during the diarization process and eliminates the need to tune the weights on a development set.

### 2.4 Diarization Algorithm

As explained in [8] and [9], the speaker clustering system is based on an agglomerative clustering technique. It initially splits the data into $K$ clusters (where $K$ should be greater than the number of true speakers), and then iteratively merges the clusters (according to metric based on $\Delta$BIC) until a stopping criterion is met. Our clustering algorithm models the acoustic data using an ergodic hidden

Markov model (HMM), where the initial number of states is equal to the initial number of clusters ($K$). Upon completion of the algorithm's execution, each remaining state is taken to represent a different speaker. Each state in the HMM contains a set of $MD$ sub-states, imposing a minimum duration on the model (we use $MD = 2.5$ seconds). Also, each one of the sub-states shares a single probability density function (PDF).

The following outlines the clustering algorithm step-by-step.

1. Run front-end acoustic processing.
2. Run speech/non-speech detection.
3. Extract acoustic features from the data and remove non-speech frames.
4. Create models for the $K$ initial clusters via linear initialization.
5. Perform several iterations of segmentation and training to refine the initial models.
6. Perform iterative merging and retraining as follows:
   (a) Run a Viterbi decode to re-segment the data.
   (b) Retrain the models using the Expectation-Maximization (EM) algorithm and the segmentation from step (a).
   (c) Select the cluster pair with the largest merge score (based on $\Delta$BIC) that is $> 0.0$.
   (d) If no such pair of clusters is found, stop and output the current clustering.
   (e) Merge the pair of clusters found in step (c). The models for the individual clusters in the pair are replaced by a single, combined model.
   (f) Go to step (a).

For our stopping criteria, we use $\Delta$BIC, a variation of the commonly used Bayesian Information Criterion (BIC) [2]. $\Delta$BIC compares two possible hypotheses: 1) a model in which the two clusters belong to the same speaker or 2) a model in which to two clusters represent different speakers. The variation used was introduced by Ajmera et al. [9], [10], and consists of the elimination of the tunable parameter ($\lambda$) by ensuring that, for any given $\Delta$BIC comparison, the difference between the number of free parameters in the two hypotheses is zero.

## 3 Experiments and Results

### 3.1 Data

All of the experiments reported here were conducted using data distributed by NIST as part of the Rich Transcription 2004, 2005, 2006 and 2007 meeting recognition evaluations [11]. This data consists of excerpts from multi-party meetings collected at eight different sites. From each meeting, an excerpt (chosen by NIST) of 10 to 12 minutes is used.

**RT07s Development Data.** Table 1 lists the names of the 21 meetings we used for our development testing for this year's evaluation. Because of the "flakiness" of the diarization error rate (DER) (see 3.2 for an explanation of DER) that we

**Table 1.** The names of the 21 meetings used for development

| | |
|---|---|
| ICSI_20000807-1000 | ICSI_20010208-1430 |
| LDC_20011116-1400 | LDC_20011116-1500 |
| NIST_20030623-1409 | NIST_20030925-1517 |
| AMI_20041210-1052 | AMI_20050204-1206 |
| CMU_20050228-1615 | CMU_20050301-1415 |
| VT_20050304-1300 | VT_20050318-1430 |
| CMU_20050912-0900 | CMU_20050914-0900 |
| EDI_20050216-1051 | EDI_20050218-0900 |
| NIST_20051024-0930 | NIST_20051102-1323 |
| TNO_20041103-1130 | VT_20050623-1400 |
| VT_20051027-1400 | |

have observed in previous work [12], we believe that it is important to use as many meetings as possible for development. This helps to "smooth" diarization error rates by preventing large variations in the scores of one or two meetings from influencing the overall DER.

We performed all of our development work on the Multiple Distant Microphone (MDM) condition.

**RT07s Evaluation Data.** Table 2 list the eight meetings that were chosen by NIST for this year's evaluation.

**Table 2.** The names of the eight RT07s evaluation meetings

| | |
|---|---|
| CMU_20061115-1030 | CMU_20061115-1530 |
| EDI_20061113-1500 | EDI_20061114-1500 |
| NIST_20051104-1515 | NIST_20060216-1347 |
| VT_20050408-1500 | VT_20050425-1000 |

### 3.2 Error Metric

The metric used to evaluate the performance of the system is the same as is used in the NIST RT evaluations and is called Diarization Error Rate (DER). It is computed by first finding an optimal one-to-one mapping of reference speaker ID to system output ID and then obtaining the error as the percentage of time that the system assigns the wrong speaker label. All results presented here use the official NIST DER metric.

### 3.3 Experiments

**Speech/Non-speech Detection.** This speech/non-speech system described in Section 2.2 outperformed last year's speech/non-speech system on our development set. Although typically in the meeting domain the number of non-speech sounds is negligible, in two of the twenty one meetings of our development set, the system classified part of the audio as non-speech sounds (paper shuffling and doors slamming). In the other meetings, (including all of the meetings in the test set) the BIC score was always positive and each sound model was discarded. The SAD error rate on our development set was 4.40% while the error rate after the first step (using the bootstrap models trained on Dutch broadcast news) was 26.9%. This proves that the first step is really only used as a rough bootstrap for the models trained on the recordings itself [6].

Table 3 contains the results of last year's system and our new system on the test set. The first two rows show the results scored only for speech activity detection. The new system has a slightly lower false alarm rate. The last two rows of table 3 show the results of our current diarization system using either the speech/non-speech segmentation of the RT06 detector or the RT07 detector. On this data, the new detector has a lower false alarm rate. Most of the performance gain though is a result of the reduction in speaker error (diarization). This is partly explainable by the fact that we do not smooth the speech/non-speech data before diarization (see the next experiment). We surmise that the remainder of the gain is due to the reduced number of false alarms. We believe that this helps to make the data used to train the GMMs "cleaner", resulting in better models.

**Table 3.** Performance of the RT06 and RT07 speech/non-speech detectors on the RT07s Eval data. In the first two rows, only the SAD segmentation is scored. The last two rows show the results of the RT07 diarization system using either the RT06 speech/non-speech system or the RT07 speech/non-speech system.

| System | % missed speech | % false alarm | % SAD | % Spkr | % DER |
|---|---|---|---|---|---|
| RT06 (only SAD) | 1.10 | 2.80 | 3.90 | n.a. | n.a. |
| RT07 (only SAD) | 1.20 | 2.10 | 3.30 | n.a. | n.a. |
| RT06 (diarization) | 4.40 | 2.30 | 6.70 | 4.10 | 10.81 |
| RT07 (diarization) | 4.50 | 1.50 | 6.00 | 2.50 | 8.51 |

**Smoothing SAD.** In previous years, we have tuned our speech/non-speech detectors by minimizing the SAD error on a development set. One of the steps that helps in minimizing the SAD error is 'smoothing' the output (NIST provides scripts to do this). During this process, short non-speech segments (shorter than 0.3s) are removed from the segmentation. Smoothing helps to reduce the SAD error because the reference segmentation is smoothed as well, and so these little fragments of non-speech will be regarded as missed speech if no smoothing is performed. On the other hand, adding these short non-speech segments to the speech data that is processed by the speaker diarization system will most likely increase the DER. The non-speech will be assigned to one or more clusters and will "muddy" the data pool, forcing the GMMs to be less specific for a particular speaker. Therefore, this year we decided to use the unsmoothed speech/non-speech segmentation as input to our diarization system and perform smoothing after the diarization process is finished. The improvement over using the smoothed speech/non-speech segmentations on the test set was marginal. On the conference room MDM task, using the smoothed segmentation resulted in a diarization error of 9.03%, and so the improvement by using the unsmoothed speech/non-speech input was only 0.52% absolute.

**Blame assignment.** In order to find out what part of our system is contributing most to the total DER, we conducted a cheating experiment. Instead of using the automatically generated speech/non-speech segmentation, we used the reference segmentation as input for our diarization system. Table 4 contains the error rates of our MDM and SDM submissions and the results of the cheating experiments. All results are scored with and without overlap.

**Table 4.** DER for the MDM and SDM submissions. The rows in bold show the results of the actual submissions. They are scored with overlap and make use of our speech/non-speech segmentation. The systems marked with -ovlp/+ovlp are scored with/without overlap and the systems marked with -ref/+ref make use of the automatic speech/non-speech segmentation or of the reference speech/non-speech segmentation.

|  | %Miss | %FA | %Spkr | %DER |
|---|---|---|---|---|
| **MDM -ref +ovlp** | **4.5** | **1.5** | **2.5** | **8.51** |
| MDM +ref +ovlp | 3.7 | 0.0 | 3.8 | 7.47 |
| MDM -ref -ovlp | 0.9 | 1.6 | 2.6 | 5.11 |
| MDM +ref -ovlp | 0.0 | 0.0 | 3.9 | 3.94 |
| **SDM -ref +ovlp** | **5.0** | **1.8** | **14.9** | **21.74** |
| SDM +ref +ovlp | 3.7 | 0.0 | 12.8 | 16.51 |
| SDM -ref -ovlp | 1.4 | 2.0 | 14.7 | 18.03 |
| SDM +ref -ovlp | 0.0 | 0.0 | 12.7 | 12.75 |

Even if the reference segmentation is used, the percentage of missed speech will not be zero. This is because our diarization system is only able to assign a speech fragment to one single speaker and thus, when scoring with overlap speech, all overlapping speech will be missed. As can be seen in the second row of table 4 the error due to missed overlapping speech is 3.7%. The total error due to missed speech and false alarms is 6.0%. Subtracting the error due to overlap leaves the error contribution of our speech/non-speech system: 2.3%. The remaining 3.8% of the total DER is caused by the diarization step (speaker error). Note that the percentages change slightly if scored without overlap because ignoring segments with overlap will decrease the total amount of speech, which is part of the DER calculation.

The same blame assignment can be done for the SDM task. The error because of missed overlapping speech for the SDM task is 3.7%, and the error due to the speech/non-speech detector is 3.1% (3.4% if scored without overlap). The speaker error caused by the diarization system is 14.9%.

**Noise Filtering.** In a series of experiments, we tested how much the system gains from applying Wiener filtering. Wiener filtering is normally applied to the audio used for the speech/non-speech detector, and on the audio that is used to create MFCC features, and on the audio that is used to calculate the delay features. Table 5 shows the results of several experiments where we omitted filtering for one or more of these components. It shows that filtering helps to reduce the DER considerably. Although it seems that filtering the audio for speech/non-speech helps the most, the SAD error on unfiltered audio only increases marginally (from 3.3% to 3.4%).

**Table 5.** DER for the MDM submission (bottom row) and for the experiments where Wiener filtering is omitted in one or more of the components

| Where do we apply Wiener filtering? | %DER |
|:---:|:---:|
| Nowhere | 15.80 |
| Speech/non-speech | 10.54 |
| Speech/non-speech and MFCC | 12.99 |
| Speech/non-speech and Delays | 13.70 |
| All components | 8.51 |

**Delay Features.** This year we used the algorithm introduced in [7] to automatically determine stream weights for the MFCC and delay feature streams. In last year's submission, the weights were fixed to 0.9 and 0.1. We have conducted an experiment on this year's evaluation data where the weights were fixed (as was done last year) in order to determine if the adaptive weighting was the right choice for the evaluation data. On the MDM conference meeting task the DER was 9.29% using the RT 2006 fixed weights. Thus, the new algorithm improved the DER by 0.78% absolute.

The gap between our results in the SDM task and MDM task is considerably large. This performance difference could be because it is not possible to use the second (delay) feature stream for SDM. To test this hypothesis we have ran the MDM data using only the MFCC stream. The diarization error of this experiment is 14.02%. A difference of 5.51% DER absolute.

## 4    Conclusions

In this paper, we have presented the ICSI RT07s speaker diarization system. This year, we introduced a new speech/non-speech detector that is able to filter out audible non-speech without the need for models trained on "outside" data. This new speech/non-speech system reduced false alarm errors by 0.7% absolute compared to our RT06s speech/non-speech system. Post evaluation experiments showed that by reducing the false alarms, the diarization system also performed better (2.3% DER absolute).

Other post evaluation experiments showed that the use of cross-channel delays as a second feature stream (for the MDM task) improved the system considerably resulting in a gain of 5.51% DER absolute. We also observed that omitting noise filtering in either one of the feature streams decreases the performance of the system by up to 7.29% absolute. We obtained modest improvements (0.52% DER absolute) in system performance by using unsmoothed speech/non-speech segmentations as input to the diarization system. We also achieved another modest improvement (0.78% DER absolute) by dynamically tuning the stream weights as proposed by [7] rather than using fixed stream weights.

The gap in performance of our system between the SDM and MDM tasks is striking. Our post evaluation experiments showed that the errors due to missed overlapping speech and misclassified speech/non-speech are comparable for the two tasks. Thus, the main difference in performance is caused by the diarization system itself (3.8% DER for MDM and 14.9% DER for SDM). We believe that our SDM system can be improved considerably by introducing additional feature streams, similar to what we used in the MDM system. Of course these additional streams would not be based on delays since there is only a single microphone in the SDM condition, but we believe that we could use other acoustic features (e.g. PLP or RASTA features), or even the output of other speaker diarization systems as additional feature streams. For the next evaluation we will concentrate on finding suitable features to add to the primary MFCC feature stream.

Finally, because of the "flakiness" of the diarization error rate, this year we performed all of our development work using a much larger set of recordings (21 in total) than we have used in past evaluations. We believe that using this larger set of data helps to reduce some of the flakiness, thus leading to better decisions about system design and tuning.

## Acknowledgments

This work was partly supported by the European Union 6th FWP IST Integrated Project AMIDA (Augmented Multi-party Interaction with Distant Access, FP6-506811), by the Swiss National Science Foundation through NCCR's IM2 project, and by the MultimediaN project (http://www.multimedian.nl). MultimediaN is sponsored by the Dutch government under contract BSIK 03031.

The work was also partly funded by DARPA under contract No. HR0011-06-C-0023 (approved for public release, distribution is unlimited).

## References

1. Anguera, X., Wooters, C., Pardo, J.: Robust speaker diarization for meetings: Icsi tr06 meetings evaluation system. In: Renals, S., Bengio, S., Fiscus, J.G. (eds.) MLMI 2006. LNCS, vol. 4299, pp. 302–9743. Springer, Heidelberg (2006)
2. Shaobing Chen, S., Gopalakrishnan, P.: Speaker, environment and channel change detection and clustering via the bayesian information criterion. In: Proceedings DARPA Broadcast News Transcription and Understanding Workshop, Virginia, USA (1998)
3. Wiener, N.: Extrapolation, Interpolation, and Smoothing of Stationary Time Series. Wiley, Chichester (1949)

4. Adami, A., Burget, L., Dupont, S., Garudadri, H., Grezl, F., Hermansky, H., Jain, P., Kajarekar, S., Morgan, N., Sivadas, S.: Qualcomm-icsi-ogi features for asr. In: ICSLP (2002)
5. Huijbregts, M., Ordelman, R., de Jong, F.: Speech-based annotation of heterogeneous multimedia content using automatic speech recognition. Technical Report TR-CTIT-07-30, Enschede (2007)
6. Huijbregts, M., Wooters, C., Ordelman, R.: Filtering the unknown: Speech activity detection in heterogeneous video collections. In: Interspeech, Antwerp, Belgium (2007)
7. Anguera, X.: Robust Speaker Diarization for Meetings. PhD thesis, Universitat Politecnica De Catalunya (2006),
   http://www.icsi.berkeley.edu/~xanguera/phd_thesis.pdf
8. Wooters, C., Fung, J., Peskin, B., Anguera, X.: Towards robust speaker segmentation: The ICSI-SRI fall 2004 diarization system. In: Fall 2004 Rich Transcription Workshop (RT 2004), Palisades, NY (2004)
9. Ajmera, J., Wooters, C.: A robust speaker clustering algorithm. In: ASRU, US Virgin Islands, USA (2003)
10. Ajmera, J., McCowan, I., Bourlard, H.: Robust speaker change detection. IEEE Signal Processing Letters 11(8), 649–651 (2004)
11. NIST: Rich Transcription Evaluations (2007),
    http://www.nist.gov/speech/tests/rt
12. Mirghafori, N., Wooters, C.: Nuts and flakes: A study of data characteristics in speaker diarization. In: ICASSP, Toulouse, France (2006)

# The LIA RT'07 Speaker Diarization System

Corinne Fredouille[1] and Nicholas Evans[1,2]

[1] LIA-University of Avignon, BP1228, 84911 Avignon Cedex 9, France
[2] University of Wales Swansea, Singleton Park, Swansea, SA2 8PP, UK
{corinne.fredouille,nicholas.evans}@univ-avignon.fr

**Abstract.** This paper presents the LIA submission to the speaker diarization task of the 2007 NIST Rich Transcription (RT'07) evaluation campaign. We report a system optimised for conference meeting recordings and experiments on all three RT'07 subdomains and microphone conditions. Results show that, despite state-of-the-art performance for the single distant microphone (SDM) condition, in its current form the system is not effective in utilising the additional information that is available with the multiple distant microphone (MDM) condition. With post evaluation tuning we achieve a DER of 19% on the MDM task with conference meeting data. Some early experimental work highlights both the limitations and potential of utilising between-channel delay features for diarization.

## 1 Introduction

The speaker diarization task is an especially important contribution to the overall Rich Transcription (RT) paradigm, as evidenced by the RT evaluation campaigns administered by the National Institute of Standards and Technology (NIST). Also known as "Who spoke When", the speaker diarization task consists in detecting the speaker turns within an audio document (segmentation task) and in grouping together all the segments belonging to the same speaker (clustering task). Algorithms may be restricted to function with a single distant microphone (SDM) or have the potential to use multiple distant microphones (MDM).

Applied initially to conversational telephone speech and subsequently to broadcast news, the current focus is on conference and lecture meetings, tasks which pose a number of new challenges. Meeting room recordings often involve a greater degree of spontaneous speech with overlapped speech segments, speaker noise (laughs, whispers, coughs, etc.) and sometimes short speaker turns. Due to the availability of many different recording devices and room layouts, a large variability in signal quality has brought an additional level of complexity to the speaker diarization task and more generally to the RT domain.

This paper describes LIA's speaker diarization system and our experimental work and results relating to the most recent NIST RT'07 evaluation [1]. The system is developed on the conference meeting room datasets of the two previous RT campaigns and is evaluated on the three subdomains and three microphone conditions of the RT'07 datasets without modification. Results show that our

R. Stiefelhagen et al. (Eds.): CLEAR 2007 and RT 2007, LNCS 4625, pp. 520–532, 2008.

system performs well on the single microphone condition (SDM), giving among the best results reported for the RT'07 evaluation. However, the system is shown not to be effective in utilising the additional information that is available with multiple microphones (the ADM and MDM conditions). Interestingly our system is shown to be relatively robust across the three subdomains including that of the coffee break condition newly introduced this year. Lastly, we present some post evaluation experiments which lead to improved diarization error rates across development and evaluation sets and some additional work that shows the limitations and potential of utilising the between-channel delay information.

The remainder of this paper is organized as follows: Section 2 presents the baseline E-HMM based speaker diarization system that was used for the RT'07 evaluation campaign. Section 3 describes the experimental protocol and presents results on the NIST RT'05 and RT'06 development datasets and the RT'07 evaluation dataset. Our post evaluation improvements are described in Section 4 and some initial experiments to assess potential of delay features in Section 5. Our conclusions are presented in Section 6.

## 2   Speaker Diarization System

In this paper we report experimental work performed on the NIST RT'07 evaluation dataset. This includes three subdomains in addition to three different microphone conditions. These can involve single or multiple microphones. A number of strategies to utilise data from multiple microphones have appeared in the literature over recent years. The simplest involves the selection of a single channel according to some criteria, for example the channel with the highest estimated SNR. The channels may alternatively be combined according to an SNR-dependent weight parameter [2, 3] and finally, with the provision for time delay of arrival (TDOA) estimation, channels may be resolved according to their respective delays before the addition, commonly referred to as the delay and sum beamforming approach [4]. In contrast to the work in [5] in which diarization was performed separately on each channel before fusing the outputs in a final post processing stage, all of these approaches aim to combine the multiple channels into a single channel prior to feature extraction and this seems to be the most dominant in the literature. For the experimental work reported here, where recordings from multiple microphones are available the different channels are processed very simply by summing related signals in order to yield a unique virtual channel which is used in all subsequent stages.

The LIA speaker diarization system was developed using the open source ALIZE speaker recognition toolkit [6]. The system is composed of 4 main steps:

- Speech/non-speech detection
- Pre-segmentation
- Speaker segmentation and clustering
- Post-normalisation and resegmentation

## 2.1   Speech/Non-speech Detection

The speech activity detection (SAD) algorithm employs feature vectors composed of 12 un-normalised Linear Frequency Cepstrum Coefficients (LFCCs) plus energy augmented by their first and second derivatives. It utilises an iterative process based on a Viterbi decoding and model adaptation applied to a two state HMM, where each state represents speech and non-speech events respectively. Each state of the HMM is initialised with a 32-component GMM model trained on separate data using an EM/ML algorithm. State transition probabilities are fixed to 0.5. Finally, some duration rules are applied in order to refine the speech/non-speech segmentation yielded by the iterative process.

## 2.2   Pre-segmentation

The pre-segmentation phase aims to provide an approximate speaker turn labelling to initialise and speed-up the subsequent segmentation and clustering stages. Now the signal is characterised by 20 LFCCs, computed every 10ms using a 20ms window. The cepstral features are augmented by energy but no feature normalisation is applied at this stage. A classical GLR criterion-based speaker turn detection is applied to two consecutive 0.5 second long windows with a 0.05 second step (single diagonal matrix Gaussian components). Relevant maximum peaks of the GLR curve are thus considered as speaker changes. Once speaker turns are detected, a local clustering process is applied in order to group together successive segments that are deemed to be sufficiently similar according to a thresholded GLR criterion.

## 2.3   Speaker Segmentation and Clustering

This step is the core of the LIA system. It relies on a one-step segmentation and clustering algorithm in the form of an evolutive hidden Markov model (E-HMM) [7, 8]: each E-HMM state aims to characterise a single speaker and the transitions represent the speaker turns.

This process, still based on 20 LFCCs plus energy coefficients, can be defined as follows:

**1. Initialisation:** The HMM has only one state, called $L_0$. A world model with 128 Gaussian components is trained on the entire audio show. The segmentation process is initialised with the segmentation outputs issued from the pre-segmentation stage and are utilised for the selection process.

**2. Speaker addition:** a minimum 3 second long candidate segment is selected among all the segments belonging to $L_0$ according to a likelihood maximisation criterion. The selected segment is attributed to $L_x$ and is used to estimate the associated GMM model.

**3. Adaptation/Decoding loop:** The objective is to detect all segments belonging to the new speaker $L_x$. All speaker models are re-estimated through an adaptation process according to the current segmentation. A Viterbi decoding pass, involving the entire HMM, is performed in order to obtain a new segmentation. This adaptation/decoding loop is re-iterated while some significant changes are observed on the speaker segmentation between two successive iterations.

**4. Speaker model validation and stop criterion:** The current segmentation is analysed in order to decide if the new added speaker $L_x$ is relevant, according to some heuristical rules on speaker $L_x$ segment duration. The stop criterion is reached if there are no more minimum 3 second long candidate segments available in $L_0$ which may be used to add a new speaker; otherwise, the process goes back to step 2.

The segmentation stage is followed by a resegmentation process, which aims to refine the boundaries and to delete irrelevant speakers (e.g. speakers with too short speech segments). This stage is based on the third step of the segmentation process only: an HMM is generated from the segmentation and the iterative adaptation/decoding loop is launched. Here, an external world model, trained on microphone-recorded speech, is used for the speaker model adaptation. Compared to the segmentation process, the resegmentation stage does not utilise the pre-segmentation output. Indeed, all the boundaries (except speech/non-speech boundaries) and segment labels are re-examined during this process.

### 2.4 Post-normalisation and Resegmentation

As reported in the literature [9], this last step consists in applying data normalisation drawing upon the speaker recognition domain. The resegmentation phase, described in the previous section, is repeated, but with a different parameterisation and now with data normalisation. Here the feature vector, comprising 16 LFCCs, energy, and their first derivatives, are normalised on a segment-by-segment basis to fit a zero-mean and unity-variance distribution. This segment-based normalisation relies on the output segmentation issued from the first resegmentation phase. The application of such a normalisation technique at the segmental level facilitates the estimation of the mean and variance on speaker-homogeneous data (compared with an estimate on the overall audio file involving many speakers).

## 3   System Evaluation

This section presents the protocols and results for our submission to the NIST RT'07 evaluation campaign. Our development corpus is comprised of the conference meeting shows of the two previous, NIST RT'05 and RT'06 datasets. However, whilst the system is optimised only on conference meetings we have applied our system, without modification, to the three subdomains of the RT'07 evaluation, namely the conference and lecture meetings as in previous RT evaluations and, new to RT'07, data recorded during coffee breaks.

In its current form, our system is not capable of detecting overlapping speaker segments, thus our development work was optimised without scoring overlapping segments. However, since 2006 the primary metric of the RT evaluations includes the scoring of overlapping segments, thus scores are presented here with and without overlapping segments being taken into account. Unless otherwise stated, all scores referred to in the text are the scores *with* overlap taken into account. In addition, our recent research has been focused toward the conference meeting subdomain and the multiple distant microphone (MDM) condition thus we focus on this condition here.

### 3.1   Development Results

Table 1 illustrates diarization results for the NIST RT'05 and RT'06 datasets that were used for development. The second and third columns illustrate the missed and false alarm error as a percentage of scored speaker time and shows relatively stable performance across the two datasets with averages of 4.6% and 6.4% for the two datasets respectively (5.6% overall average) for missed speech errors and averages of 2.3% and 3.6% for false alarm errors (3.0% respectively).

There is, however, much greater variation in the results for speaker errors, as illustrated in the fourth column of Table 1. Across the two databases results range from 1.3% to 33.3%, though reassuringly the averages are relatively stable, at 13.3% and 11.6% for the RT'05 and RT'06 datasets respectively (12.4% overall average).

The final column illustrates the overall DER for each show and illustrates averages of 20.2% for RT'05 and 21.5% for RT'06 with an overall average of 20.9%. Thus across the two development datasets relatively consistent results are obtained.

### 3.2   Evaluation Results

Turning to the RT'07 evaluation we observe similar levels of performance for both missed and false alarm errors with values of 4.5% and 2.0% respectively. However, there is a significant increase in the speaker error which rises from a 12.4% average across the two development sets to 17.7% for the RT'07 evaluation set. Once again there is a high level of variation between the best and worst results which now range from 3.7% to 36.9%. The degradation in speaker error when moving from the development to the evaluation sets accounts for an increase in the overall DER from 20.9% across the two development sets to 24.2% for the RT'07 evaluation set.

Table 3 summarises the results obtained by our system on each of the three subdomains of the RT'07 evaluation for each microphone condition. Only the primary metric which includes overlapped segments is given. The first general observation is that there is very little difference in performance between the different microphone conditions. This indicates that the system is not effective in utilising the additional information that is available in the additional channels. For the conference meeting subdomain a performance of 24.2% with the MDM condition compares to 24.5% with the SDM condition, an insignificant difference. In addition, the missed, false alarm and speaker error rates are close and, with the exception of the false alarms for the lecture meeting condition, this observation is consistent across the three subdomains.

**Table 1.** Missed speaker, false alarm and speaker error rates for the RT'05 and RT'06 datasets as used for development. Also, overall average time weighted across the two datasets. Results with/without scoring overlapping segments.

| Show | Missed | FAlarm | Speaker | Overall |
|---|---|---|---|---|
| **RT'05** | | | | |
| AMI_20041210 | 1.0/0.6 | 0.9/0.9 | 1.3/1.3 | 3.2/2.8 |
| AMI_20050204 | 3.4/1.3 | 0.9/1.0 | 33.3/34.6 | 37.7/36.9 |
| CMU_20050228 | 11.1/5.2 | 0.9/1.0 | 5.7/6.2 | 17.7/12.5 |
| CMU_20050301 | 3.3/0.6 | 1.8/1.9 | 13.0/13.8 | 18.1/16.3 |
| ICSI_20010531 | 6.3/4.3 | 3.0/3.2 | 13.0/13.5 | 22.4/20.9 |
| ICSI_20011113 | 8.0/1.1 | 2.5/2.9 | 29.1/32.3 | 39.6/36.4 |
| NIST_20050412 | 6.8/0.0 | 3.8/4.4 | 1.9/2.1 | 12.4/6.5 |
| NIST_20050427 | 2.9/0.3 | 6.1/6.5 | 6.9/7.3 | 15.9/14.2 |
| VT_20050304 | 0.7/0.4 | 1.1/1.2 | 8.9/8.9 | 10.7/10.5 |
| VT_20050318 | 3.2/2.5 | 2.2/2.3 | 25.8/26.0 | 31.2/30.8 |
| **RT'05 average** | **4.6/1.6** | **2.3/2.5** | **13.3/14.0** | **20.2/18.0** |
| | | | | |
| **RT'06** | | | | |
| CMU_20050912 | 11.1/0.1 | 6.4/8.1 | 10.0/11.3 | 27.5/19.5 |
| CMU_20050914 | 9.8/0.7 | 3.0/3.6 | 4.3/4.2 | 17.1/8.4 |
| EDI_20050216 | 5.0/1.6 | 1.5/1.6 | 21.6/22.6 | 28.1/25.7 |
| EDI_20050218 | 4.4/1.0 | 2.5/2.7 | 10.7/10.7 | 17.6/14.5 |
| NIST_20051024 | 6.6/0.5 | 1.7/2.0 | 8.7/9.3 | 17.0/11.8 |
| NIST_20051102 | 5.1/0.2 | 3.5/3.9 | 21.3/22.9 | 29.9/26.9 |
| VT_20050623 | 4.6/0.4 | 7.4/8.0 | 3.5/3.3 | 15.5/11.7 |
| VT_20051027 | 3.2/1.5 | 2.9/3.0 | 11.0/11.0 | 17.13/15.5 |
| **RT'06 average** | **6.4/0.7** | **3.6/4.0** | **11.6/12.2** | **21.5/17.0** |
| | | | | |
| **Overall Average** | **5.6/1.2** | **3.0/3.3** | **12.4/13.1** | **20.9/17.5** |

**Table 2.** Missed speaker, false alarm and speaker error rates for the RT'07 evaluation as submitted. Results with/without scoring overlapping segments.

| Show | Missed | FAlarm | Speaker | Overall |
|---|---|---|---|---|
| **RT'07** | | | | |
| CMU_20061115-1030 | 7.4/0.2 | 4.6/5.4 | 9.7/9.8 | 21.8/15.4 |
| CMU_20061115-1530 | 3.3/0.0 | 5.1/5.5 | 14.5/15.0 | 23.0/20.6 |
| EDI_20061113-1500 | 8.9/2.0 | 0.8/0.9 | 22.8/25.0 | 32.5/27.9 |
| EDI_20061114-1500 | 3.2/1.1 | 1.8/1.9 | 23.3/23.9 | 28.4/26.9 |
| NIST_20051104-1515 | 3.8/0.6 | 0.9/0.9 | 7.6/8.0 | 12.2/9.5 |
| NIST_20060216-1347 | 2.5/0.7 | 1.4/1.5 | 20.9/21.6 | 24.8/23.8 |
| VT_20050408-1500 | 1.5/1.1 | 0.6/0.6 | 36.9/37.1 | 39.0/38.8 |
| VT_20050425-1000 | 5.5/1.0 | 0.7/0.8 | 3.7/3.9 | 9.9/5.6 |
| **RT'07 average** | **4.5/0.8** | **2.0/2.2** | **17.7/18.6** | **24.2/21.5** |

**Table 3.** Summary of performance for the three conditions as submitted to the NIST RT'07 evaluation

| Subdomain | Mic. Cond. | Missed | FAlarm | Speaker | Overall |
|---|---|---|---|---|---|
| Conference meeting | MDM | 4.5 | 2.0 | 17.7 | 24.2 |
|  | SDM | 4.7 | 2.1 | 17.7 | 24.5 |
| Lecture meeting | ADM | 4.1 | 7.2 | 19.3 | 30.5 |
|  | MDM | 3.4 | 6.9 | 20.9 | 31.2 |
|  | SDM | 3.6 | 6.5 | 19.4 | 29.5 |
| Coffee break | ADM | 3.5 | 3.6 | 19.2 | 26.4 |
|  | MDM | 3.0 | 5.0 | 17.5 | 25.5 |
|  | SDM | 3.3 | 4.6 | 18.4 | 26.3 |

Whilst the best overall performance is obtained with conference meeting data (the same subdomain on which the system was developed), similar levels of performance are observed with coffee break data with only a marginal decrease in performance to 25.5% for the MDM condition. However, for lecture meeting data there is a marked degradation in performance to 31.2% for the same condition. This is attributed predominantly to an increase in the false alarm error rate whilst the missed and speaker error rates remain relatively consistant. An increase in the false alarm error rate could be expected due to increased levels of activity and noise for this condition.

## 4   Post Evaluation Improvements

According to the results of the system on the RT'07 corpus, two aspects of the speaker diarization system have been studied. The first is related to the successive segment clustering of the pre-segmentation step. As reported in Section 2.2, the pre-segmentation phase is applied in order to speed up the segmentation and resegmentation steps, which is the core of the speaker diarization system. It involves both a speaker turn detection and a coarse clustering, applied locally to aggregate successive segments. This clustering is based on a thresholded GLR criterion and provides a segmentation output, which is involved in the subsequent segmentation phase. The quality of this segmentation output is relevant for the later process, and is constrained by the threshold value used for the clustering.

The second aspect on which we focus, is the selection strategy involved in the segmentation process when adding a new speaker to the E-HMM. This selection strategy is still an issue, since it can contribute largely to the overall system performance. Indeed, the selection of an irrelevant segment (for instance, the selection of a non-speech segment, mislabeled by the speech/non-speech detection or of a multi-speaker segment, due to clustering misclassification) may dramatically disturb the segmentation process. Compared with previous versions of the speaker diarization system [3], hypothesized segments for the selection process may be of variable durations (with a minimum fixed to 3 seconds), since they are directly issued from the pre-segmentation step[1].

Both these aspects are strongly correlated since the clustering process will provide the selection strategy with hypothesized segments. According to the clustering threshold, the number of segments may vary as well as their quality (in terms of speaker purity). These two factors are very important for the selection but also for the overall segmentation process. Indeed, the number of segments available for the selection indirectly determines the number of speakers, which may be potentially added to the E-HMM. In the same way, the less pure the segments, the less robust the speaker models.

In this section, we compare performance of the speaker diarization system according to various values for the clustering threshold and two different selection strategies. For the latter, the maximum likelihood criterion, named "Maximum Selection", used for the evaluation campaign as reported in Section 2.3, is compared with an averaged likelihood criterion, named "Median Selection". In the last case, the segment which is close in terms of likelihood to the likelihood mean computed over all the hypothesized segments is selected.

These post-evaluation experiments have been conducted on the RT'07 evaluation data set as well as on the development set proposed by ICSI in [10]. The latter has been chosen in order to be able to compare the performance of the speaker diarization system with that of ICSI's system (named *DevICSI* in the rest of the paper), regarding the performance gap drawn by the evaluation data set.

Figures 1 and 2 provide the speaker diarization performance in terms of DER involving overlapping segments and according to different configurations (threshold values and selection strategies). Different remarks can be pointed out from these figures:

- threshold values may largely influence scores, depending on the files. Regarding *VT-1500/Dev-ICSI*, the DER varies from 2.9% to 38%. On the opposite, some files (e.g. *NIST-1515/RT07*, *CMU-1530/RT07*, or *LDC-1400/Dev-ICSI* are less sensitive to threshold variation, leading to quite stable DER scores whatever configuration used;
- for a given clustering threshold, selection strategies may behave in opposite manner. For instance, given value −600 for the threshold, the median selection gets 50.6% DER on *VT-1430* files against 15.5% DER for the maximum selection;
- optimal (from an empirical point of view) threshold is different according to the selection strategies and data sets observed (−600 for the Maximum selection against −200 or −700 for the Median selection regarding *Dev-ICSI* data set and −300 for the maximum selection and −200 for the median

---

[1] In the previous versions of the speaker diarization system, the hypothesized segments were extracted directly from the speech portions of signal issued from the speech/non-speech detection process. Their length was fixed to 3seconds.

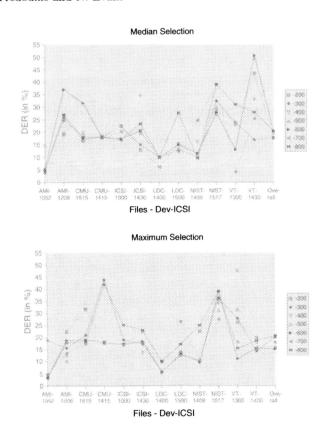

**Fig. 1.** Speaker diarization performance (DER in %) on *Dev-ICSI* according to selection strategies (Maximum or median selection) and clustering thresholds

one for the RT'07 data set). In this way, the official LIA score on the RT'07 is enhanced from 24% to 19.2% DER;

The pre-segmentation responds to its initial goal, which was to speed-up the segmentation step by diminishing hypothesized segments for the selection phase and expanding their length. Compared with previous versions of the speaker diarization system, which will test all the 3second segments available, CPU time was decreased from 3*RT to 0.25*RT (with the clustering threshold fixed to -200). Moreover, speaker diarization tests performed on RT'05 and RT'06 (not reported here) show no loss of performance in this case. Nevertheless, experiments reported in this section outlines an unstable behavior of the speaker diarization system, depending on the clustering threshold value, on the data sets observed or on the selection strategy chosen for the process. Further investigation will focus on novel solutions for pre-segmentation enhancement, which still respond to the speed request while preserving speaker diarization behavior stability.

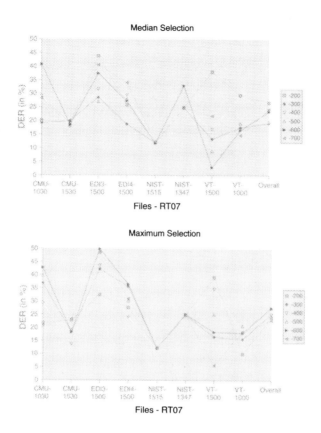

**Fig. 2.** Speaker diarization performance (DER in %) on RT'07 according to selection strategies (Maximum or median selection) and clustering thresholds

## 5   Between-Channel Delay Features

Estimates of the between-channel delay characterise each speaker's position in the room and thus may be utilised as features to assist diarization and in this section we report LIA's early work to assess the potential. The use of delay features has been reported before, for example in [11] and more recently in [12,10] in which a DER of 31% was reported on the NIST RT'05s conference room evaluation dataset. These results do not compare well to a DER of 18% with acoustic-only features following delay and sum beamforming but nonetheless offer additional information which, when used with the acoustic features in a combined log-likelihood, leads to an improved DER of 15%. Thus whilst the delay features produce only a small improvement in DER this work clearly highlights the potential.

Here we report some initial experiments with our diarization system using delay features. This is very much embryonic work and, in moving from acoustic to delay features, we have not modified the underlying diarization system in any

**Table 4.** Diarization performance on the RT'06 database using delay features with SDM channel as reference and segments identified using the key (column 2), the same except with an automatically chosen reference channel (column 3), a real experiment with delay features only (column 4) and for combined acoustic and delay features (column 5)

| Show | SDM ref fake | Auto ref fake | D real | A+D real |
|---|---|---|---|---|
| **RT'06** | | | | |
| CMU_20050912 | 7.8 | 7.8 | 55.6 | 33.8 |
| CMU_20050914 | 3.3 | 3.3 | 28.0 | 22.1 |
| EDI_20050216 | 25.0 | 25.0 | 48.1 | 26.0 |
| EDI_20050218 | 43.7 | 43.7 | 50.4 | 17.6 |
| NIST_20051024 | 10.8 | 2.2 | 24.4 | 46.3 |
| NIST_20051102 | 2.3 | 4.8 | 42.7 | 46.6 |
| VT_20050623 | 6.5 | 13.7 | 43.5 | 15.3 |
| VT_20051027 | 22.7 | 22.7 | 33.7 | 29.6 |
| **Overall average** | **15.3** | **15.2** | **40.8** | **30.5** |

way other than to handle feature vectors of varying order. In all cases delay features are estimated using the conventional generalised cross correlation phase transform (GCC-PHAT) approach [13]. Four different experiments are reported.

We first seek to evaluate the potential of delay features in a 'fake' experiment using the key to identify each speakers' segments, to estimate the delay characteristics of each speaker and then to perform diarization without using the speaker labels but using the segment boundaries identified by the key. Delay features are estimated using whole segments and speaker models are derived from the median between-channel delays. The classifier is based simply on the minimum Euclidean distance between segments and speaker models. The GCC-PHAT algorithm requires a reference channel and results are shown in Table 4 for where the SDM channel is used as a reference (column 2) and where a reference channel is selected automatically (column 3). Here the reference is the channel which exhibits the highest correlation to all other channels. Results show that there is little difference between the two sets of results, each producing a diarization error rate of 15%. The second observation relates to the large variation in the performance, with a best performance of 2% and particularly poor performance being achieved with the two EDI and final VT shows. This leads to the conclusion that in these three shows a number of speakers are difficult to separate in delay space. Given that in these two experiments we have used the key to identify speaker segments these results serve to highlighting the potential limitation and difficulty of using delay features.

The fourth column in Table 4 illustrates the results of a 'real' experiment where now the delay features come from sliding frames of 200 ms in length and with a rate of 100 frames per second. Median filtering is used to smooth the delay profiles. Delay features are calculated with a reference channel that is automatically selected via correlation. As would be predicted the results are much worse and show DERs of between 28% and 56% with an average of 41%. This result does not compare favourably with that of the acoustic-only features (DER of 19%) presented in Section 4 and in the final set of experiments we seek to evaluate the potential of combining the acoutic and delay features.

Using weights of 0.9 for the acoustic and 0.1 for the delay features the two streams are combined in the segmentation and resegmentation stages with a joint log likelihood as in [10]. DER results are presented in the final column of Table 4 which show an overall average DER of 31%. However, without having modified our system in any way other than to fascilitate the combination, this result is hardly surprising. It clearly illustrates the difficulty in accurately estimating and making appropriate use of the delay due to the different nature of acoustic and delay features which are likely to require fundamentally different approaches to handle. This area is a topic of future work.

# 6   Conclusions

This paper presents the results of LIA's speaker diarization system on the NIST RT'07 evaluation dataset. The system is shown to give state-of-the-art performance on the single distant microphone condition but that it is not effective in making use of the additional information provided by multiple channels. An overall average diarization error rate of 24% is reported on the multiple distant microphone condition for conference meeting data. With post evaluation tuning this figure falls to 19% with consistant results obtained across development data. In addition, consistant results are reported across the three subdomain tasks with only a negligible degradation in results observed with lecture meeting data. Finally some of LIA's early experiments with delay features are reported which illustrate the limitations and potential of utilising between-channel delay features for diarization. Our future work is focused toward properly harnessing the additional information in multiple channels in order to improve the stability of the system and hence fully realise the potential of a system proven to give state-of-the-art results for a single microphone channel.

# References

[1] NIST: (RT 2007) Rich Transcription meeting recognition evaluation plan (2007), http://www.nist.gov/speech/tests/rt/rt2007/docs/ rt07-meeting-eval-plan-v2.pdf
[2] Istrate, D., Fredouille, C., Meignier, S., Besacier, L., Bonastre, J.F.: NIST RT'05S evaluation: pre-processing techniques and speaker diarization on multiple microphone meetings. In: Renals, S., Bengio, S. (eds.) MLMI 2005. LNCS, vol. 3869, Springer, Heidelberg (2006)
[3] Fredouille, C., Senay, G.: Technical improvements of the e-hmm based speaker diarization system for meeting records. In: Renals, S., Bengio, S., Fiscus, J.G. (eds.) MLMI 2006. LNCS, vol. 4299, Springer, Heidelberg (2006)
[4] Anguera, X., Wooters, C., Hernando, J.: Speaker diarization for multi-party meetings using acoustic fusion. In: Proc. ASRU 2005 (2005)

[5] Fredouille, C., Moraru, D., Meignier, S., Besacier, L., Bonastre, J.F.: The NIST 2004 spring rich transcription evaluation: two-axis merging strategy in the context of multiple distance microphone based meeting speaker segmentation. In: RT2004 Spring Meeting Recognition Workshop, p. 5 (2004)

[6] Bonastre, J.F., Wils, F., Meignier, S.: ALIZE, a free toolkit for speaker recognition. In: ICASSP 2005, Philadelphia, USA (2005)

[7] Meignier, S., Bonastre, J.F., Fredouille, C., Merlin, T.: Evolutive HMM for speaker tracking system. In: ICASSP 2000, Istanbul, Turkey (2000)

[8] Meignier, S., Moraru, D., Fredouille, C., Bonastre, J.F., Besacier, L.: Step-by-step and integrated approaches in broadcast news speaker diarization. Special issue of Computer and Speech Language Journal 20(2-3) (2006)

[9] Zhu, X., Barras, C., Meignier, S., Gauvain, J.L.: Combining speaker identification and BIC for speaker diarization. In: EuroSpeech 2005, Lisboa, Portugal (2005)

[10] Pardo, J.M., Anguera, X., Wooters, C.: Speaker diarization for multiple distant microphone meetings: mixing acoustic features and inter-channel time differences. In: Proc. ICSLP 2006 (2006)

[11] Ellis, D.P.W., Liu, J.C.: Speaker turn detection based on between-channel differences. In: Proc. ICASSP 2004 (2004)

[12] Pardo, J.M., Anguera, X., Wooters, C.: Speaker diarization for multi-microhpone meetings using only between-channel differences. In: Renals, S., Bengio, S., Fiscus, J.G. (eds.) MLMI 2006. LNCS, vol. 4299, Springer, Heidelberg (2006)

[13] Brandstein, M.S., Silverman, H.F.: A robust method for speech signal time-delay estimation in reverberent rooms. In: Proc. ICASSP 1997 (1997)

# Multi-stage Speaker Diarization for Conference and Lecture Meetings

X. Zhu[1,2], C. Barras[1,2], L. Lamel[1], and J-L. Gauvain[1,*]

[1] Spoken Language Processing Group
LIMSI-CNRS, BP 133, 91403 Orsay cedex, France
[2] Univ Paris-Sud, F-91405, Orsay, France

**Abstract.** The LIMSI RT-07S speaker diarization system for the conference and lecture meetings is presented in this paper. This system builds upon the RT-06S diarization system designed for lecture data. The baseline system combines agglomerative clustering based on Bayesian information criterion (BIC) with a second clustering using state-of-the-art speaker identification (SID) techniques. Since the baseline system provides a high speech activity detection (SAD) error around of 10% on lecture data, some different acoustic representations with various normalization techniques are investigated within the framework of log-likelihood ratio (LLR) based speech activity detector. UBMs trained on the different types of acoustic features are also examined in the SID clustering stage. All SAD acoustic models and UBMs are trained with the forced alignment segmentations of the conference data. The diarization system integrating the new SAD models and UBM gives comparable results on both the RT-07S conference and lecture evaluation data for the multiple distant microphone (MDM) condition.

## 1 Introduction

Speaker diarization, also called speaker segmentation and clustering, is the process of partitioning an input audio stream into homogeneous segments according to speaker identity. It is one aspect of audio diarization, along with categorization of background acoustic and channel conditions. The aim of the speaker diarization is to provide a set of speech segments, where each segment is bounded by speaker change or speech/non-speech change points and labeled with the identity of the speaker engaging in the corresponding speech.

Speaker diarization was evaluated for Broadcast news data in English up to 2004, and the meeting domain became the main focus of NIST evaluations since 2005. Beside the conference room and lecture room sub-domains, a new type of recordings has been introduced into the NIST 2007 Spring meeting recognition evaluation [1], that is, the recordings of coffee breaks. Since the lecture room and coffee break excerpts were extracted from different parts of the same meetings, both sub-domains have the same sensor configurations but these are different from the conference meeting sub-domain. Although these three types of data have different styles of participant interaction, the

---

* This work was partially financed by the European Commission under the FP6 Integrated Project IP 506909 CHIL.

R. Stiefelhagen et al. (Eds.): CLEAR 2007 and RT 2007, LNCS 4625, pp. 533–542, 2008.

RT-07S lecture evaluation data contains more interactions between meeting participants than the previous lecture meeting data.

In the RT-07S evaluation, LIMSI participated to the speaker diarization task on the conference and lecture data and developed a general diarization system for both types of meeting data. As the RT-06S lecture diarization system had a high SAD error that in turn affects strongly final speaker diarization performance, some new acoustic models trained using the forced alignment transcriptions and several different feature normalization techniques are employed to reduce the speech activity detection error. In order to ameliorate the SID clustering performance, several new UBMs were also constructed in a similar manner. For the MDM audio input condition, the RT-07S diarization system uses the beamformed signals generated from the ICSI delay&sum signal enhancement system [2] instead of selecting randomly one channel from all available MDM channels as was done by LIMSI RT-06S lecture diarization system.

The remainder of this paper is organized as follows: Section 2 describes the baseline speaker diarization system for lecture data, and Section 3 presents a proposed acoustic representation for speech activity detection. The experimental results are presented in Section 4.

## 2    Baseline Lecture Diarization System

The baseline lecture speaker diarization system combines an agglomerative clustering based on Bayesian information criterion (BIC) with a second clustering stage which uses state-of-the-art speaker identification methods. This combined clustering technique was first proposed for Broadcast News data [3,4] and was proven to be effective also for lectures data [5]. This baseline system processes 38 dimensional feature vectors consisting of 12 cepstral coefficients, $\Delta$ and $\Delta$-$\Delta$ coefficients plus the $\Delta$ and $\Delta$-$\Delta$ log-energy. The primary system modules are:

- Speech activity detection (SAD): speech is extracted from the signal by using a Log-Likelihood Ratio (LLR) based speech activity detector [5]. The LLR of each frame is calculated between the speech and non-speech models with some predefined prior probabilities. To smooth LLR values, two adjacent windows with a same duration are located at the left and right sides of each frame and the average LLR is computed over each window. Thus, a frame is considered as a possible change point when a sign change is found between the left and right average LLR values. When several contiguous change candidates occur, the transition point is assigned to the maximum of difference between the averaged ratio of both windows. The SAD acoustic models, each with 256 Gaussians, were trained on about 2 hours of lecture data recorded at the University of Karlsruhe (UKA).
- Initial segmentation: the initial segmentation of the signal is performed by taking the maxima of a local Gaussian divergence measure between two adjacent sliding windows of 5 seconds, similar to the KL2 metric based segmentation [6]. Each window is modeled by a single diagonal Gaussian using the static features (i.e., only the 12 cepstral coefficients plus the energy).
- Viterbi resegmentation: an 8-component GMM with a diagonal covariance matrix is trained on each segment resulting from the initial segmentation, the boundaries

of the speech segments detected by the SAD module are then refined using a Viterbi segmentation with this set of GMMs.

- BIC clustering: an initial cluster $c_i$ is modeled by a single Gaussian with a full covariance matrix $\Sigma_i$ estimated on the $n_i$ acoustic frames of each segment output by Viterbi resegmentation. The BIC criterion [7] is used both for the inter-cluster distance measure and the stop criterion. It is defined as:

$$\Delta BIC = (n_i + n_j) \log |\Sigma| - n_i \log |\Sigma_i| - n_j \log |\Sigma_j| - \lambda \frac{1}{2}(d + \frac{1}{2}d(d+1)) \log n \tag{1}$$

where $d$ is the dimension of the feature vector space and $\lambda$ weights the BIC penalty. At each step the two nearest clusters are merged, and the $\Delta BIC$ values between this new cluster and remaining clusters are computed. This clustering procedure stops when all $\Delta BIC$ are greater than zero. This BIC based clustering uses the size of the two clusters to be merged $n = n_i + n_j$ to calculate the penalty term, which is referred to as a local BIC measure. An alternative is to use the all frames in the whole set of clusters to compute the penalty, namely the global BIC penalty. Since the global penalty is constant, the clustering decision is made only by the likelihood increase. It has been experimentally found that the local BIC outperforms the global one on broadcast news data [8,9,10].

- SID clustering: After the BIC clustering stage, speaker recognition methods [11,12] are used to improve the quality of the speaker clustering. Feature warping normalization [13] is performed on each segment using a sliding window of 3 seconds in order to map the cepstral feature distribution to a normal distribution and reduce the non-stationary effects of the acoustic environment. The GMM of each remaining cluster is obtained by maximum a posteriori (MAP) adaptation [14] of the means of an Universal Background Model [15]. This UBM is composed of 128 diagonal Gaussians and is trained on a few hours of the 1996/1997 English Broadcast News data. Then a second stage of agglomerative clustering is carried out on the segments within each gender class (male/female) separately according to the cross log-likelihood ratio as in [16]:

$$S(c_i, c_j) = \frac{1}{n_i} \log \frac{f(x_i|M_j)}{f(x_i|B)} + \frac{1}{n_j} \log \frac{f(x_j|M_i)}{f(x_j|B)} \tag{2}$$

where $f(\cdot|M)$ is the likelihood of the acoustic frames given the model $M$, and $n_i$ is the number of frames in cluster $c_i$. The clustering stops when the cross log-likelihood ratio between all clusters is below a given threshold $\delta$ optimized on the development data (see Section 4.1).

## 3   Applying Voicing Factor to SAD

Normally, the LLR-based speech activity detector is performed on cepstral coefficients with their $\Delta$ and $\Delta\Delta$ plus $\Delta$ and $\Delta\Delta$ log-energy. The reason for not using energy directly is that its level is sensitive to recording conditions, and it needs to be carefully normalized. Experiments on broadcast news data had led us to discard this feature. In order to further improve the SAD performance, a new energy normalization method taking into account a voicing factor $v$ along with the energy $E_0$ is proposed. For each frame, the voicing factor is computed as the maximum peak of the autocorrelation function (excluding lag zero). The harmonic energy is thus defined as the energy associated with the best harmonic configuration, i.e. $E_h = v.E_0$. Finally, the energy of the signal is normalized relative to a reference level determined on the 10% frames carrying the highest harmonic energy. This way, the energy normalization focuses primarily on the voiced frames and may be more robust to varying SNR configurations. This method may be sensitive to music, but this is not expected to be an issue in the context of conferences and lectures.

## 4 · Experimental Results

In the RT-07S meeting recognition evaluation, LIMSI submitted speaker diarization results for both the conference and lecture meeting data on the MDM and SDM audio input conditions. For the MDM test condition, the speaker diarization system is performed on the beamformed signals created by the ICSI delay&sum signal enhancement system (see [2] for details) from all available input signals. Unless otherwise specified, the development experiments were carried out with a BIC penalty weight $\lambda = 3.5$ and a SID threshold $\delta = 0.5$.

Since the RT07S evaluation plans specified the use the word-forced alignment reference segmentations for scoring speaker diarization performance, the SAD acoustic models and UBM employed in the SID clustering stage are retrained using forced alignment segmentations. The forced alignment transcriptions were derived from the manual transcriptions via the ICSI-SRI ASR system [17] that aligns the spoken words to the signal, and therefore segment boundaries are labeled more accurately than the hand-made ones. Based on the aligned segmentations, more precise speech and non-speech models can be estimated and are expected to provide better SAD performances. Instead of training on the UKA lecture data that was used last year and in the baseline system, an union of several previous RT conference datasets consisting of recordings from different sites was used to better approximate this year's test data.

### 4.1 Performance Measures

The speaker diarization task performance is measured via an optimum mapping between the reference speaker IDs and the hypotheses. This is the same metric as was used to evaluate the performance on BN data [18]. The primary metric for the task, referred to as the speaker error, is the fraction of speaker time that is not attributed to the correct speaker, given the optimum speaker mapping. In addition to this speaker error, the overall speaker diarization error rate (DER) also includes the missed and false alarm speaker times.

In addition to the above speaker diarization scoring metrics, the SAD measurement defined in the RT-06S evaluation [19] is used to measure the performance progress of the diarization system. The SAD task performance is evaluated by summing the missed and false alarm speech errors, without taking into account different reference speakers. The SAD error is normally included in the missed and false alarm speaker errors. Although the primary metric used in RT-07S evaluation is calculated over all the speech including the overlapping speech, the DER restricted to non-overlapping speech segments is also given for comparison purposes.

## 4.2 Corpus Description

In order to tune the system parameters, the development experiments were carried out on the RT-06S test data in both the conference and lecture sub-domains. The conference development dataset *conf dev07s* is composed of 9 conference meetings, with a duration of about 15 minutes each. This is the same corpus that was used as the test data in the RT-06s evaluation and were provided by 5 different laboratories: CMU (Carnegie Mellon University), EDI (The University of Edinburgh), NIST, TNO (TNO Human Factor) and VT (Virginia Tech). The lecture development data includes two corpora: the RT-06S lecture evaluation dataset (denoted as *lect dev07s1*) and a new development dataset (denoted as *lect dev07s2*) released in 2007. The *lect dev07s1* consists of 38 5-minutes lecture excerpts contributed respectively by 5 of the CHIL partner sites: AIT, IBM, ITC, UKA and UPC, for which only 28 excerpts reference segmentations are available. The *lect dev07s2* contains 5 lectures with different audio lengths ranging from 23 minutes to 44 minutes, recorded more recently at the same 5 CHIL sites.

## 4.3 LLR-Based SAD with Different Acoustic Features

Although the speech activity detection task is not included in the RT-07S evaluation, a good SAD module is always useful for a speaker diarization system in the sense that it can influence the accuracy of the acoustic models which serve in the subsequent segmentation and clustering stages. Therefore, different kinds of acoustic features were investigated within the LLR-based SAD module. To do this, the SAD stage is separated from the speaker diarization system and assessed as an independent system on the RT-07S development data. However, an optimal SAD is not necessarily the best choice for diarization systems, as false alarm speech will corrupt the speaker models used in clustering stage: the experiments made at ICSI also show that minimizing short non-speech data is helpful to improve diarization performance [20].

Table 1 gives the SAD results with using different acoustic features, where each type of features has its appropriate SAD acoustic models estimated on the training data parameterized by the same features. In all cases, the speech and non-speech models are trained on the same data consisting of 8 RT-04S development conference meetings, 8 RT-04S evaluation conference meetings and 10 RT-05S evaluation conference meetings. It should be noted that the forced alignment segmentations provided by ICSI-SRI were used to estimate the SAD acoustic models. The lack of the forced alignments for the lecture data except the *lect dev07s1* (which serves as development data) is the reason of using only the conference meetings to construct the speech and non-speech models for both the conference and lecture test data.

The SAD results shown in Table 1 are obtained with the same LLR-based SAD configurations: the smoothing window with a size of 50 frames and the prior probabilities for the non-speech and speech models being 0.2 : 0.8 with 256 Gaussians components in each model. The baseline vector consists of 12 cepstral coefficients with their $\Delta$ and $\Delta\Delta$ plus $\Delta$ and $\Delta\Delta$ log-energy and provides a SAD error of 5.6% and 7.8% on the conference and lecture development datasets respectively. When the raw energy is simply appended into the baseline acoustic vectors (c.f. denoted as "baseline+e" in Table 1), the SAD error is reduced to 5.1% for the conference dataset but increases to 11.5% for the lecture data. This degradation of the SAD performance on the lectures is predictable due to the variability of recording conditions in different lecture rooms. The SAD error reduction obtained on the conference meetings implies that the SNR configuration is consistent across the conference audio data. Replacing the energy with the normalized energy relying on the voicing factor $v$ (denoted as "baseline+env") decreases the SAD error to 4.3% on the conference meeting data and 5.7% on the lecture meeting data. Regarding some details, the performance improvement obtained on the conferences comes from the reduction of the false alarm speech error, while the gain observed on the lectures derives merely from the missed speech error. The "baseline+e+mvn" feature set performs a variance normalization of each baseline feature and energy by subtracting their means and scaling by their standard deviations. Using this normalized acoustic representation, a further SAD reduction of absolutely 0.4% is obtained on the conference development data, but no improvement is obtained on the lecture dataset. For the simplicity of the diarization system, the SAD models trained with the "baseline+e+mvn" feature set were used for both the RT-07S conference and lecture evaluation data. Speech and non-speech models with 128 Gaussians were also investigated and although they gave a higher SAD error compared with 256 Gaussians, they perform slightly better on the diarization task.

**Table 1.** SAD results obtained with using different kinds of acoustic features on the RT-07S beamformed MDM development data

| acoustic features | missed speech error (%) | false alarm speech error (%) | overlap SAD error (%) |
|---|---|---|---|
| conf dev07s | | | |
| baseline | 1.3 | 4.3 | 5.6 |
| baseline+e | 1.1 | 4.0 | 5.1 |
| baseline+env | 1.1 | 3.3 | 4.3 |
| baseline+e+mvn | 0.8 | 3.0 | 3.9 |
| lect dev07s1 | | | |
| baseline | 2.4 | 5.3 | 7.8 |
| baseline+e | 0.5 | 11.2 | 11.8 |
| baseline+env | 0.9 | 4.7 | 5.7 |
| baseline+e+mvn | 1.0 | 5.6 | 6.6 |

### 4.4   SID Clustering with UBMs Trained on Different Acoustic Features

The different sorts of acoustic features are also tested for the UBM training. A single gender-independent UBM with 128 Gaussian mixtures is trained for each type of feature, since no gender information is available in the forced alignment segmentations of the training data. Table 2 shows the speaker diarization results on the beamformed MDM development data using different acoustic features to train UBMs. These results are obtained with the same SAD acoustic models that were trained on the normalized features via the variance normalization technique. All UBMs are trained on the same conference dataset that have been used to estimate the speech and non-speech models.

**Table 2.** Diarization results obtained with the UBMs trained on different acoustic representations on the RT-07S beamformed MDM development data (results with '*' were obtained after the evaluation)

| acoustic features | speaker match error (%) | overlap DER (%) |
|---|---|---|
| conf dev07s | | |
| 15plp+w* | 20.5 | 28.3 |
| 15plp+$\Delta$+$\Delta$logE+w | 28.4 | 36.2 |
| 15plp+$\Delta$+$\Delta\Delta$+$\Delta$logE+$\Delta\Delta$logE+w | 23.3 | 31.1 |
| 12plp+w* | 21.3 | 29.0 |
| 12plp+$\Delta$+$\Delta$logE+w | 22.9 | 30.6 |
| 12plp+$\Delta$+$\Delta\Delta$+$\Delta$logE+$\Delta\Delta$logE+w | 27.9 | 35.7 |
| 12plp+mvn* | 28.6 | 36.3 |
| 12plp+$\Delta$+$\Delta$logE+mvn | 33.8 | 41.6 |
| 12plp+$\Delta$+$\Delta\Delta$+$\Delta$logE+$\Delta\Delta$logE+mvn | 32.0 | 39.8 |
| lect dev07s1 | | |
| 15plp+w* | 10.3 | 17.8 |
| 15plp+$\Delta$+$\Delta$logE+w | 10.0 | 17.5 |
| 15plp+$\Delta$+$\Delta\Delta$+$\Delta$logE+$\Delta\Delta$logE+w | 10.2 | 17.7 |
| 12plp+w* | 11.3 | 18.8 |
| 12plp+$\Delta$+$\Delta$logE+w | 10.3 | 17.8 |
| 12plp+$\Delta$+$\Delta\Delta$+$\Delta$logE+$\Delta\Delta$logE+w | 10.2 | 17.7 |
| 12plp+mvn* | 10.1 | 17.6 |
| 12plp+$\Delta$+$\Delta$logE+mvn | 10.5 | 18.0 |
| 12plp+$\Delta$+$\Delta\Delta$+$\Delta$logE+$\Delta\Delta$logE+mvn | 10.2 | 17.7 |

The baseline feature vector is composed of 15 Mel frequency cepstral coefficients plus the $\Delta$ coefficients and the $\Delta$ log-energy with the feature warping normalization (referred to as "15plp+$\Delta$+$\Delta$logE+w" in Table 2). This baseline feature set provides an overlap DER of 36.2% on the conference development data and 17.5% on the lecture development data. Adding the $\Delta\Delta$ coefficients and the $\Delta\Delta$ log-energy, namely "15plp+$\Delta$+$\Delta\Delta$+$\Delta$logE+$\Delta\Delta$logE+w" reduces the DER to 31.1% on the conferences but gives a similar diarization performance as the baseline features for the lectures. When the dimension of cepstral coefficients is diminished to 12, using the "12plp$\Delta$+$\Delta$logE+w" feature set results in a further DER reduction of 0.5% on the conference data but no significant performance change on the lecture meetings. Appending the $\Delta\Delta$ coefficients (denoted as "12plp+$\Delta$+$\Delta\Delta$+$\Delta$logE+$\Delta\Delta$logE+w"), a large increase of DER is observed on the conference data but the DER score rests always very close to the baseline one for the lectures. Finally, we also examined the variance normalization method within the SID clustering stage. As can be seen in Table 2, higher DER rates are provided by this normalization approach than the feature warping technique on both the conference and the lecture development data. For the lecture data, the different acoustic representations are found to give similar diarization results. This may be derived from the mismatch between the conference training data and the lecture test data.

The results of the post-evaluation experiments without the use of derivative parameters are also given in Table 2[1]. Using only static features reduces the diarization error rates on the conference development data and the lowest DER of 28.3% is given by the 15 MFCC with the feature warping normalization. However, no significant difference in diarization performances is observed on the lecture data between using only the static coefficients and by appending the $\Delta$ and $\Delta\Delta$ coefficients.

### 4.5   RT-07S Evaluation Results

The speaker diarization results for the systems submitted to the RT-07S evaluation are given in Table 3. The diarization system uses the same SAD acoustic models and UBM trained on the "baseline+e+mvn" and the "12plp+$\Delta$+$\Delta$logE+w" feature sets respectively for both the conference and the lecture evaluation data. The BIC penalty weight $\lambda$ and the SID clustering threshold $\delta$ were optimized on the development data and set individually for the conference and lecture test data: $\lambda = 3.5, \delta = 0.6$ for the conference dataset and $\lambda = 3.5, \delta = 0.5$ for the lecture dataset. For each type of the data, the same system configurations were used on the MDM and SDM audio input conditions.

For the conference test data, the diarization system has an overall diarization error of 26.1% on the beamformed MDM signals, and the overall DER increases to 29.5% for the SDM condition. The beamformed signals from all available distant microphones are shown to be helpful for improving the diarization performance. For the lecture evaluation data, the diarization system gives similar performances on both the beamformed MDM signals and a single SDM data. This may be because the delay&sum signal enhancement system was not well tuned for lecture data.

**Table 3.** Speaker diarization performances on the RT-07S conference and lecture evaluation data for the MDM and SDM conditions

| data type & condition | missed speaker error (%) | false alarm speaker error (%) | speaker match error (%) | overlap DER (%) | non-overlap DER (%) |
|---|---|---|---|---|---|
| conference MDM | 4.5 | 1.3 | 20.2 | **26.1** | 23.0 |
| conference SDM | 4.9 | 1.3 | 23.3 | **29.5** | 26.6 |
| lecture MDM | 2.6 | 8.4 | 14.7 | **25.8** | 24.5 |
| lecture SDM | 2.9 | 8.1 | 14.7 | **25.6** | 24.3 |

---

[1] We thank the reviewers for suggesting this contrastive experiment.

# 5   Conclusions

The LIMSI speaker diarization system for meetings within the framework of the RT-07S meeting recognition evaluation was described in this paper. The RT-07S diarization system for both conference and lecture meetings keeps the main structure of the RT-06S lecture diarization system except removing the bandwidth detection module, since it is supposed that no telephonic speech would occur during the meetings. The main improvements come from the new SAD acoustic models and UBM that were built on the conference training data with their forced alignment segmentations. Using the speech and non-speech models trained with the variance normalized acoustic features yields the best SAD performance on the development data, i.e. 3.9% for the conference data and 6.6% for the lecture data. The mismatch between the conference training data and the lecture test data results in a relatively higher SAD error on the lecture development data. As for UBMs, the best diarization performance is generated by using the gender-independent UBM trained with 12 Mel frequency cepstral coefficients plus $\Delta$ coefficients and $\Delta$ log-energy with the feature warping technique. The adapted diarization system provides similar diarization results on the beamformed MDM signals for both the RT-07S conference and lecture evaluation data (i.e. an overlap DER of 26.1% for the conference dataset and 25.8% for the lecture dataset). The DER rate increases to 29.5% on the conference SDM data, while for the lecture SDM data, the error rate remains very closely to the one obtained on the beamformed MDM condition.

# References

1. NIST, Spring 2007 Rich Transcription (RT-07S) Meeting Recognition Evaluation Plan (February 2007), http://www.nist.gov/speech/tests/rt/rt2007/spring/docs/rt07s-meeting-eval-plan-v2.pdf
2. Anguera, X., Wooters, C., Hernando, J.: Speaker Diarization for Multi-Party Meetings Using Acoustic Fusion. In: Automatic Speech Recognition and Understanding (ASRU 2005), San Juan, Puerto Rico. IEEE, Los Alamitos (2005)
3. Zhu, X., Barras, C., Meignier, S., Gauvain, J.-L.: Combining Speaker Identification and BIC for Speaker Diarization. In: ISCA Interspeech 2005, Lisbon, September 2005, pp. 2441–2444 (2005)
4. Barras, C., Zhu, X., Meignier, S., Gauvain, J.-L.: Multi-Stage Speaker Diarization of Broadcast News. The IEEE Transactions on Audio, Speech and Language Processing, September 2006 (to appear)
5. Zhu, X., Barras, C., Lamel, L., Gauvain, J.L.: Speaker Diarization: from Broadcast News to Lectures. In: Renals, S., Bengio, S. (eds.) MLMI 2005. LNCS, vol. 3869, Springer, Heidelberg (2006)
6. Siegler, M., Jain, U., Raj, B., Stern, R.: Automatic segmentation and clustering of broadcast news audio. In: The DARPA Speech Recognition Workshop, Chantilly, USA (February 1997)
7. Chen, S., Gopalakrishnan, P.: Speaker, environment and channel change detection and clustering via the Bayesian information criterion. In: DARPA Broadcast News Transcription and Understanding Workshop, Landsdowne, USA (February 1998)
8. Cettolo, M.: Segmentation, classification and clustering of an Italian broadcast news corpus. In: Conf. on Content-Based Multimedia Information Access (RIAO 2000), April 2000, Paris (2000)

9. Barras, C., Zhu, X., Meignier, S., Gauvain, J.L.: Improving speaker diarization. In: The Proceedings of Fall 2004 Rich Transcription Workshop (RT 2004), November 2004, Palisades, NY, USA (2004)

10. Tranter, S.E., Reynolds, D.A.: Speaker diarization for broadcast news. In: Proc. ISCA Speaker Recognition Workshop Odyssey 2004, May 2004, Toledo, Spain (2004)

11. Schroeder, J., Campbell, J. (eds.): Digital Signal Processing (DSP), a review journal - Special issue on NIST 1999 speaker recognition workshop. Academic Press, London (2000)

12. Barras, C., Gauvain, J.-L.: Feature and score normalization for speaker verification of cellular data. In: IEEE ICASSP 2003, Hong Kong (2003)

13. Pelecanos, J., Sridharan, S.: Feature warping for robust speaker verification. In: Proc. ISCA Speaker Recognition Workshop Odyssey 2001, June 2001, pp. 213–218 (2001)

14. Gauvain, J.-L., Lee, C.H.: Maximum a posteriori estimation for multivariate Gaussian mixture observations of Markov chains. IEEE Transactions on Speech and Audio Processing 2(2), 291–298 (1994)

15. Reynolds, D.A., Quatieri, T.F., Dunn, R.B.: Speaker verification using adapted Gaussian mixture models. Digital Signal Processing (DSP), a review journal - Special issue on NIST 1999 speaker recognition workshop 10(1-3), 19–41 (2000)

16. Reynolds, D.A., Singer, E., Carlson, B.A., O'Leary, G.C., McLaughlin, J.J., Zissman, M.A.: Blind clustering of speech utterances based on speaker and language characteristics. In: Proc. of International Conf. on Spoken Language Processing (ICSLP 1998) (1998)

17. Stolcke, A., Anguera, X., Boakye, K., Cetin, O., Grezl, F., Janin, A., Mandal, A., Peskin, B., Wooters, C., Zheng, J.: The ICSI-SRI Spring 2005 Speech-To-Text evaluation System. In: Rich Transcription 2005 Spring Meeting Recognition Evaluation, July 2005, Edinburgh, Great Britain (2005)

18. NIST, Fall 2004 Rich Transcription (RT-04F) evaluation plan (August 2004), http://www.nist.gov/speech/tests/rt/rt2004/fall/docs/rt04f-eval-plan-v14.pdf

19. NIST, Spring 2006 Rich Transcription (RT-06S) Meeting Recognition Evaluation Plan (February 2006), http://www.nist.gov/speech/tests/rt/rt2006/spring/docs/rt06s-meeting-eval-plan-v2.pdf

20. Wooters, C., Huijbregts, M.: The ICSI RT07s Speaker Diarization System. In: Rich Transcription 2007 Meeting Recognition Workshop, Baltimore, USA (May 2007)

# Speaker Diarization for Conference Room: The UPC RT07s Evaluation System

Jordi Luque[1], Xavier Anguera[2], Andrey Temko[1], and Javier Hernando[1]

[1] Technical University of Catalonia (UPC),
Jordi Girona, 1-3 D5, 08034 Barcelona, Spain
luque@tsc.upc.edu
[2] Multilinguism group, Telefnica I+D,
08021 Barcelona, Spain

**Abstract.** In this paper the authors present the UPC speaker diarization system for the NIST Rich Transcription Evaluation (RT07s) [1] conducted on the conference environment. The presented system is based on the ICSI RT06s system, which employs agglomerative clustering with a modified Bayesian Criterion (BIC) measure to decide which pairs of clusters to merge and to determine when to stop merging clusters [2]. This is the first participation of the UPC in the RT Speaker Diarization Evaluation and the purpose of this work has been the consolidation of a baseline system which can be used in the future for further research in the field of diarization. We have introduced, as prior modules before the diarization system, an Speech/Non-Speech detection module based on a Support Vector Machine from UPC and a Wiener Filtering from an implementation of the QIO front-end. In the speech parameterization a Frequency Filtering (FF) of the filter-bank energies is applied instead the classical Discrete Cosine Transform in the Mel-Cepstrum analysis. In addition, it is introduced a small changes in the complexity selection algorithm and a new post-processing technique which process the shortest clusters at the end of each Viterbi segmentation.

## 1 Introduction

Audio segmentation, sometimes referred to as acoustic change detection, consists of exploring an audio file to find acoustically homogeneous segments, detecting any change of speaker, background or channel conditions. It is a pattern recognition problem, since it strives to find the most likely categorization of a sequence of acoustic observations. Audio segmentation becomes useful as a preprocessing step in order to transcribe the speech content in broadcast news and meetings, because regions of different nature can be handled in a different way.

There are two basic approaches to this problem: (1) *model-based* segmentation [3], which estimates different acoustic models for a closed set of acoustic classes (e.g. noise, music, speech, etc.) and classifies the audio stream by finding the most likely sequence of models; and (2) *metric-based* segmentation [4], which defines some metric to compare the spectral statistics at both sides of successive points of

R. Stiefelhagen et al. (Eds.): CLEAR 2007 and RT 2007, LNCS 4625, pp. 543–553, 2008.

the audio signal, and hypothesizes those boundaries whose metric values exceed a given threshold. The first approach requires the availability of enough training data to estimate the models of acoustic classes and does not generalize to unseen conditions. The second approach, sometimes referred as *blind* (unsupervised) segmentation, does not suffer from these limitations, but its performance depends highly on the metric and the threshold. Various metrics have been proposed in the literature. The most cited are the *Generalized Likelihood Ratio* (GLR) [5] and the *Bayesian Information Criterion* (BIC) [4].

The Diarization task assume no prior knowledge about the speakers or how many people participate in the meeting. In order to get acquainted with the problem, the data and the evaluation methodology, we have taken as a baseline a simplified version of the International Computer Science Institute (ICSI) RT06s system as presented in [2]. Our submission still uses the multi-channel and agglomerative clustering capabilities from ICSI's software while using our own Speech Activity Detection (SAD) algorithm, parameterization and avoiding the use of several algorithms in order to make the system more lightweight. Hence we have used an approach which performs the clustering through a modified BIC measure to decide which pairs of clusters to merge and to determine when to stop merging clusters, as in [2].

In addition, some novelties to the diarization system are studied. The use of the Frequency Filtering (FF) parameters instead the classical Mel Frequency Cepstral Coefficients (MFCCs) has been introduced in the speech parameterization. Other of them, a post-processing module is applied after each Viterbi decoding. It looks for orphan speaker segments with small duration and splits them between the adjacent segments. Other new feature is a small modification to the cluster complexity algorithm. It avoids the creation of very small clusters, which do not alter the real system outcome greatly but do pose a burden on execution time.

The following sections give a brief overview of the diarization system focusing in the novelties introduced. Finally, the results section provides the Diarization Error (DER) obtained by the system in the NIST RT07S Evaluation and some comments.

## 2   System Description

The input signal from each one of the multiple distant microphones (mdm) channels, if they are available, is first **Wiener filtered** using the implementation from the QIO front-end [6]. These channels are then fed into the **Beamforming** code implemented by ICSI [7] in order to obtain a single enhanced channel to be further processed. Such output channel is analyzed by the Speech Activity Detector (SAD) from UPC [8] in order to obtain the Speech segments to be fed into the clustering algorithm. The Non-Speech segments are ignored from further processing. The enhanced speech data is parameterized using 30 Frequency Filtering (FF) features as described in [9] and fed into an evolution of ICSI's speaker agglomerative clustering system [2].

**Fig. 1.** Brief scheme of the UPC implementation of the RT'07 diarization system

## 2.1  Wiener Filtering

We used the noise reduction implementation from the QIO front-end [6]. The Wiener filter noise reduction technique was applied on each channel input wave-form. That depends on a noise estimate made over frames judged to be Non-Speech. Despite the SAD used in the next stages of the diarization system, in this phase we used the procedure from the QIO front-end: The noise estimate is initialized from the beginning of each utterance, assuming each sentence starts with a period of Non-Speech, and updated using later frames of the utterance decided to be Non-Speech based on an energy threshold.

## 2.2  Acoustic Beamforming

The Delay-and-Sum (D&S) technique [10] is one of the simplest beamforming techniques but still gives a very good performance. It is based on the fact that applying different phase weights to the input channels the main lobe of the directivity pattern can be steered to a desired location, where the acoustic input comes from. It differs from the simpler D&S beamformer in that an independent weight is applied to each of the channels before summing them. The principle of operation of D&S can be seen in Figure 2.

If we assume the distance between the speech source and the microphones is enough far we can hypothesize that the speech wave arriving to each microphone is flat. Therefore, the difference between the input signals, only taking into account the wave path and without take care about channel distortion, is a time delay of arrival due the different positions of the microphones with regard to the source. So if we estimate the time $\tau$, see Figure 2, we could synchronize two different input signal in order to enhance the speaker information and reduce the additive white noise.

Hence given the signals captured by $N$ microphones, $x_i[n]$ with $i = 0 \ldots N-1$ (where $n$ indicates time steps) if we know their individual relative delays $d(0, i)$ (called Time Delay of Arrival, TDOA) with respect to a common reference microphone $x_0$, we can obtain the enhanced signal using Equation (1).

$$y(n) = x_0[n] + \sum_{i=1}^{N-1} W_i x_i[n - d(0, i)] \qquad (1)$$

The same technique is applied in both training and testing speech leading to matched conditions in the identification. By adding together the aligned signals the usable speech adds together and the ambient noise (assuming it is random and has a similar probability function) will be reduced. Using D&S, according

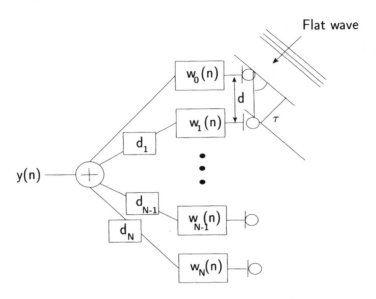

**Fig. 2.** Filter and Sum algorithm block diagram

to [10], we can obtain up to a 3dB SNR improvement each time that we double the number of microphones. In order to estimate the TDOA between two segments from two microphones we used the generalised cross correlation with phase transform (GCC-PHAT) method [11]. Given two signals $x_i(n)$ and $x_j(n)$ the GCC-PHAT is defined as:

$$\hat{G}_{PHAT_{ij}}(f) = \frac{X_i(f)\left[X_j(f)\right]^*}{\left|X_i(f)\left[X_j(f)\right]^*\right|} \tag{2}$$

where $X_i(f)$ and $X_j(f)$ are the Fourier transforms of the two signals and $[]^*$ denotes the complex conjugate. The TDOA for two microphones is estimated as:

$$\hat{d}_{PHAT_{ij}} = \arg\max_d \hat{R}_{PHAT}(d_{ij}) \tag{3}$$

where $\hat{R}_{PHAT_{ij}}(d)$ is the inverse Fourier transform of $\hat{G}_{PHAT_{ij}}(f)$, the Fourier Transform of the estimated cross correlation phase. The maximum value of $\hat{R}_{PHAT_{ij}}(d)$ corresponds to the estimated TDOA.

   In this work we have estimated the TDOA value using a window of 500 ms. at rate of 250 ms. applied on the wiener filtered channels. During the development some experiments were performed with different sizes and shifts of window, but we did not find any improvement in the overall DER error. The weighting factor $W$ applied to each microphone is computed depending the cross correlation between each channel and the reference channel.

### 2.3   SVM-Based Speech Activity Detection

The SAD module used in this work is based on SVM classifier [12]. The developed system showed a good performance in the last RT SAD Evaluations [8], hence we have chosen this SAD implementation due to the fact it is adapted to NIST metric about speech activity detection since it penalizes more the Speech class than the Non-Speech class.

The usual training algorithm of the SVM classifier was enhanced in order to cope with that problem of dataset reduction, proposing a fast algorithm based on Proximal SVM (PSVM). Besides that, the SVM learning process was adjusted in order to take into account the specific characteristics of the metric used in the NIST Rich Transcription (RT) evaluations. The resulting SVM SAD system was tested with the RT06 data and it showed better scores than the GMM-based system which ranked among the best systems in the RT06 evaluation [8].

A set of several hundred of thousand of examples is a usual amount of data for classical audio and speech processing techniques that involve GMM. However, it is an enormous number of feature vectors to be used for a usual SVM training process and hardly makes such training feasible in practice. Alternative methods should be effectively applied to reduce the amount of data.

Proximal Support Vector Machine (PSVM) has been recently introduced in [13] as a result of the substitution of the inequality constraint of a classical SVM $y_i(wx_i + b) \geq 1$ by the equality constraint $y_i(wx_i + b) = 1$, where $y_i$ stands for a label of a vector $x_i$, $w$ is the norm of the separating hyperplane $H_0$, and $b$ is the scalar bias of the hyperplane $H_0$. This simple modification significantly changes the nature of the optimization problem. Unlike conventional SVM, PSVM solves a single square system of linear equations and thus it is very fast to train. As a consequence, it turns out that it is possible to obtain an explicit exact solution to the optimization problem [13].

Figure 3 shows a geometrical interpretation of the change. $H_{-1}$ and $H_1$ planes do not bound the negatively- and the positively-labeled data anymore, but can be viewed as *proximal* planes around which the points of each class are clustered and between which the separating hyperplane $H_0$ lies. In the nonlinear case of PSVM (we use a Gaussian kernel) the concept of Support Vectors (SVs) (Figure 3, in gray) disappears as the separating hyperplane depends on all data. In that way, all training data must be preserved for the testing stage.

The proposed algorithm of dataset reduction consists of the following steps:

– Step 1. Divide all the data into chunks of 1000 samples per chunk
– Step 2. Train a PSVM on each chunk performing 5-fold cross-validation (CV) to obtain the optimal kernel parameter and the C parameter that controls the training error
– Step 3. Apply an appropriate threshold to select a pre-defined number of chunks with the highest CV accuracy
– Step 4. Train a classical SVM on the amount of data selected in Step 3

The proposed approach is in fact similar to Vector Quantization (VQ) used for dataset reduction for SVM in [14]. With Step 2 some kind of clustering is performed, and Step 3 chooses the data that corresponds to the most separable

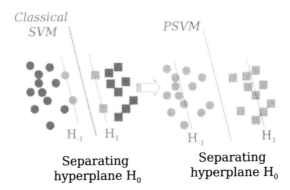

**Fig. 3.** Proximal Support Vector Machine based SVM

clusters. However, unlike VQ, SVs, which are obtained with the proposed algorithm in Step 4, are taken from the initial data. Besides, additional homogeneity is achieved because the PSVM data clustering is performed in the transformed feature spaces with the transformation functions that correspond to the Gaussian kernel and the same kernel type is applied to the chosen data in Step 4.

The second modification makes use of the knowledge of the specific NIST metric during the training phase. The NIST metric depends strongly on the prior distribution of Speech and Non-Speech in the test database. For example, a system that achieves a 5% error rate at Speech portions and a 5% error rate at Non-Speech portions, would result in very different NIST error rates for test databases with different proportion of Speech and Non-Speech segments; in the case of 90-to-10% ratio of Speech-to-Non-Speech the NIST error rate is 5.6%, while in the case of 50-to-50% ratio it is 10%. For this reason, if we want to improve the NIST scores we should penalize the errors from the Speech class more than those from the Non-Speech class. That is possible for a discriminative classifier as SVM in the training stage by introducing different costs for the two classes through the different generalization parameters $C_-$ and $C_+$. In that way, the separating hyperplane $H_0$ will no longer lie exactly in the middle of the $H_{-1}$ and $H_1$ hyperplane (Figure 3). It is worth to mention that favouring a class in the testing stage (after the classifier is trained) could still be done for SVM through the bias $b$ of the separating hyperplane.

## 2.4   Speech Parameterization

The speech parameterization is based on a short-term estimation of the spectrum energy in several sub-bands. The beamformed channel was analyzed in frames of 30 milliseconds at intervals of 10 milliseconds and 16 kHz of sampling frequency. Each frame window is processed subtracting the mean amplitude from each sample. A Hamming window was applied to each frame and a FFT computed. The FFT amplitudes were then averaged in 30 overlapped triangular filters, with central frequencies and bandwidths defined according to the Mel scale.

The squeme we present follow the classical procedure used to obtain the Mel-Frequency Cepstral Coefficients (MFCC), however in this approach, instead of the using Discrete Cosine Transform, such as in the MFCC procedure [15] log filter.bank energies are filtered by a linear and second order filter. This technique was called Frequency Filtering (FF) [9]. The filter $H(z) = z - z^{-1}$ have been used in this work and it's applied over the log of the filter-bank energies. The shape of this filter allow a best classification due it emphasizes regions of the spectrum with high speaker information yielding more discriminative information. This parameters have show a good results in the last CLEAR Evaluation Campaign in the acoustic person identification task [16].

A total of 30 FF coefficients had used in this work and no $\Delta$ or $\Delta - \Delta$ parameters. The choice of this kind of parameters is based on the fact that the using of the FF instead the classic MFCC has shown the best results in both speech and speaker recognition [17]. This features have shown both computational efficiency and robustness against noise than the MFCC. In addition, regarding in the frequency domain imply they have frequency meaning which permits the use of frequency techniques as masking, noise subtraction, etc. We can find other interesting characteristics such as they are uncorrelated, computationally simpler than MFCCs and it does not decrease clean speech recognition results [18]. Summarizing, the FF filter can be seen as a liftering operation performed in the spectral domain equalizing the variance of cepstral coefficients.

## 2.5   Improvements in Agglomerative Clustering

Thequeme we present follow the classical procedure used to obtain the Mel-Frequency Cepstral Coefficients (MFCC), however in this approach, instead approach is based on a iterative segmentation by an ergodic Hidden Markov Model (HMM), which models the acoustic data and their temporal evolution. The system starts with a homogeneous splitting of the data among an initial number of cluster equal to the initial number of states. Next the Viterbi decoding, it merges the pair of cluster more acoustically similar by a modified version of BIC [19]. The BIC measure also handles the stop criterion which occurs if the remaining clusters are below a threshold in the likelihood function. In the end-iteration each remaining state is taken to represent a different speaker.

Changes to the diarization system from ICSI are oriented towards decreasing the runtime of the system while maintaining as much as possible the performance from the original. For instance, in this version it does not use delays as features, does not perform any kind of purification to the clusters and uses linear initialization by splitting evenly all data among the number of determined initial clusters.

In addition, novelties to the diarization system are a post-processing module that looks for orphan speaker segments with small duration and splits them between both adjacent segments and a small modification to the cluster complexity algorithm to avoid the creation of very small clusters, which do not alter the real system outcome greatly but do pose a burden on execution time.

The cluster complexity modification allow drop off small clusters which are modelled by a few Gaussians. The class pruned does not take part in the following segmentations and after the next segmentation step its data is splitted among the remaining classes.

At the end of each segmentation, the final post-processing of the boundaries analyzes whose shortest segments normally associated to false alarms in this kind of tracking implementation. All those segments with duration small than 1.1*MD (Minimum Duration) are processed through a sliding window. From the pre-boundary up to the post-boundary all data inside the window are evaluated using the model of the previous, current and posterior cluster and the new boundary is chosen depending the maximum computed likelihood. Once the last iteration is completed, the system reach the stop criteria and next the last post-processing of the boundaries, the final hypothesis is obtained.

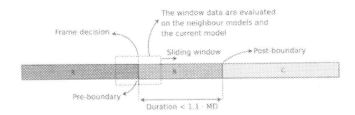

**Fig. 4.** The final stage of the algorithm consists in a post-processing of the short segment boundaries at the final of each segmentation. A sliding windows are applied on the shortest clusters in order to decide with more accuracy the real boundaries.

## 3    Experiments and Results

This section summarizes the results for the evaluation of the UPC diarization system. It examines the differences between the two SAD depending systems as well as the improvement achieved by the mdm systems compared to the sdm approach.

The Table 1 shows the performance of the SAD module in the different Rich Transcription Evaluations conducted in the surrounding of the conference room environment.

The difference between the two mdm systems submitted is the SAD behavior. The bias $b$ of the separating hyperplane, see section 2.3, is chosen according to the speaker time error and false alarms produced in the Non-Speech segments of development data. The weighting which controls the decision boundary between the Speech/Son-Speech classes is chosen according speaker time error and false alarms of Non-Speech using the NIST RT06s Evaluation data. That is the same fashion than the development of the overall diarization system. The conference NIST RT06s evaluation was used to perform all the development experiments for the RT07s.

The Tables 2 and 3 shows the results obtained by the UPC implementation in the RT07s. As we can see, the result from the single distant condition is improved in the multichannel approach. Other interesting feature is the behavior of the diarization system in function of the SAD performance. The system seems

**Table 1.** SAD error results in the previous RT Evaluation Conference data condition

| SAD SVM-based | | | | |
|---|---|---|---|---|
| RT'05 sdm | RT'06 sdm | RT'07 sdm | RT'07 mdm-softsad | RT'07 mdm-hardsad |
| 8.03 % | 4.88 % | 7.03 % | 5.39 % | 4.72 % |

**Table 2.** RT07s Diarization error results of the UPC implementation using the Primary Metric of NIST which considers overlapping of speaker segments

| Overlap SPKR Error, **Primary Metric** | | |
|---|---|---|
| sdm | mdm-softsad | mdm-hardsad |
| 27.72 % | 22.70 % | 22.59 % |

**Table 3.** RT07s Diarization error results of the UPC implementation without considering overlapping of speaker segments

| Non-Overlap SPKR Error | | |
|---|---|---|
| sdm | mdm-softsad | mdm-hardsad |
| 25.06 % | 19.65 % | 19.75 % |

to behave in a similar fashion in spite of the differences of the SAD applied. However, more and accurate experiments must be done in this line trying to find the tradeoff between the speech false alarms and the diarization performance.

Finally, in the Table 4 we can see the RT07s DER per show of the *mdm-softsad* system as well as some experiments performed after the Evaluation. We can observe a high variance between the DER errors from different shows, motivated by the difficulty to tune all the parameters using the RT06s data, around 4 hours of speech. The *mdm-noE* system differs from the *mdm-softsad* only in the number of FF parameters, it uses a vector size of 28. This system does not use the first and last coefficients of the FF. Note that the first and the last coefficients of the FF output of each frame contain absolute energy [20], so they can carry much noise. The last system in the Table, the *mdm-nocomplex* does not implements the modification of the complexity algorithm, it means, no pruning of the small clusters are done.

On the one hand, as we can note in Table 4, the use of the lateral-band coefficients performs badly in the diarization system and, in overall, it is better do not include this features in the speaker modelling. On the other hand, the pruning of small clusters on the complexity algorithm significantly affects the diarization error, over a 5 % of DER fall down by using the complexity algorithm modification, see Table 4 instead the original one from ICSI. Some experiments during the development showed a best behavior of this technique and it could be interesting to find the minimum cluster complexity out to decide the pruning as a tradeoff between the DER degradation and the runtime of the system.

**Table 4.** RT07s Diarization error per show of the (*mdm-softsad*) *system. In addition some experiments posterior to the Evaluation are showed, one of them without using the first and last coefficients of the FF and the other one, without the modification of the complexity algorithm.*

| show | Overlap SPKR Error | | |
|---|---|---|---|
|  | mdm-softsad | mdm-noE | mdm-nocomplex |
| CMU_20061115-1030 | 57.58 % | 39.68 % | 23.51 % |
| CMU_20061115-1530 | 11.46 % | 12.64 % | 15.12 % |
| EDI_20061113-1500 | 24.44 % | 24.53 % | 31 % |
| EDI_20061114-1500 | 17.97 % | 15.39 % | 17.16 % |
| NIST_20051104-1515 | 11.16 % | 11.39 % | 11.23 % |
| NIST_20060216-1347 | 5.62 % | 11.4 % | 10.77 % |
| VT_20050408-1500 | 7.13 % | 6.9 % | 7.44 % |
| VT_20050425-1000 | 49.02 % | 34.3 % | 28.66 % |
| DER global | **22.70** % | **19.36** % | **17.83** % |

# 4 Conclusions

In this work the authors have presented the UPC Diarization system and the results obtained in the NIST RT07s Diarization Evaluation on Conference room data. We have described and implementation of an agglomerative clustering approach based on a software from the ICSI. In addition some novelties are introduced in the diarization system. A Speech/Non-Speech detection module based on a Support Vector Machine is studied. In the speech parameterization the using of Frequency Filtering coefficients is introduced and minor modifications to the complexity selection algorithm and a new post-processing technique are tested looking for a runtime reduction while maintiaining as much as possible the performance of the system. The results obtained in the RT07s show that the fine tuning of the SAD seems not affect significativily the DER of the global system. In addition, in the mdm approach, the DER achieved outperforms the results from the sdm algorithm in all show conditions. Therefore, the using of a simple delay-and-sum algorithm to enhace the signal aids the system to obtain a better clustering. Finally, the main goal of the UPC evaluation is achieved and a diarization system as baseline system for further development and research have been implemented with promising results.

# Acknowledgements

This work has been partially sponsored by the EC-funded project CHIL (IST-2002 – 506909) and by the Spanish Government-funded project ACESCA (TIN2005 – 08852).

# References

1. NIST: Rich transcription meeting recognition evaluation plan. RT-07s (2007)
2. Anguera, X., Wooters, C., Hernando, J.: Robust speaker diarization for meetings: Icsi rt06s evaluation system. In: ICSLP (2006)
3. Gauvain, J., Lamel, L., Adda, G.: Partitioning and transcription of broadcast news data. In: ICSLP, pp. 1335–1338 (1998)
4. Chen, S., Gopalakrishnan, P.: Speaker, environment and channel change detection and clustering via the bayesian information criterion. In: DARPA BNTU Workshop (1998)
5. Gish, H., Siu, M., Rohlicek, R.: Segregation of speakers for speech recognition and speaker identification. In: ICASSP (1991)
6. Adami, A., et al.: Qualcomm-icsi-cgi features for asr. In: ICSLP, pp. 21–24 (2002)
7. Anguera, X.: The acoustic robust beamforming toolkit (2005)
8. Temko, A., Macho, D., Nadeu, C.: Enhanced SVM Training for Robust Speech Activity Detection. In: Proc. ICCASP (2007)
9. Nadeu, C., Paches-Leal, P., Juang, B.H.: Filtering the time sequence of spectral parameters for speech recognition. Speech Communication 22, 315–332 (1997)
10. Flanagan, J., Johnson, J., Kahn, R., Elko, G.: Computer-steered microphone arrays for sound transduction in large rooms. ASAJ 78(5), 1508–1518 (1985)
11. Knapp, C., Carter, G.: The generalized correlation method for estimation of time delay. IEEE Transactions on Acoustic, Speech and Signal Processing 24(4), 320–327 (1976)
12. Schölkopf, B., Smola, A.: Learning with Kernels. MIT Press, Cambridge (2002)
13. Fung, G., Mangasarian, O.: Proximal Support Vector Machine Classifiers. In: Proc. KDDM, pp. 77–86 (2001)
14. Lebrun, G., Charrier, C., Cardot, H.: SVM Training Time Reduction using Vector Quantization. In: Proc. ICPR, pp. 160–163 (2004)
15. Davis, S.B., Mermelstein, P.: Comparison of parametric representations for mono-syllabic word recognition in continuously spoken sentences. IEEE Transactions ASSP (28), 357–366 (1980)
16. Luque, J., Hernando, J.: Robust Speaker Identification for Meetings: UPC CLEAR-07 Meeting Room Evaluation System. In: The same book (2007)
17. Nadeu, C., Macho, D., Hernando, J.: Time and Frequency Filtering of Filter-Bank Energies for Robust Speech Recognition. Speech Communication 34, 93–114 (2001)
18. Macho, D., Nadeu, C.: On the interaction between time and frequency filterinf of speech parameters for robust speech recognition. In: ICSLP, 1137 (1999)
19. Anguera, X., Hernando, J., Anguita, J.: Xbic: nueva medida para segmentación de locutor hacia el indexado automático de la señal de voz. JTH, 237–242 (2004)
20. Nadeu, C., Hernando, J., Gorricho, M.: On the Decorrelation of filter-Bank Energies in Speech Recognition. In: EuroSpeech, vol. 20, p. 417 (1995)

# Author Index

# Lecture Notes in Computer Science

Sublibrary 6: Image Processing, Computer Vision, Pattern Recognition, and Graphics

For information about Vols. 1– 3851
please contact your bookseller or Springer

Vol. 4485: F. Sgallari, A. Murli, N. Paragios (Eds.), Scale Space and Variational Methods in Computer Vision. XV, 931 pages. 2007.

Vol. 4478: J. Martí, J.M. Benedí, A.M. Mendonça, J. Serrat (Eds.), Pattern Recognition and Image Analysis, Part II. XXVII, 657 pages. 2007.

Vol. 4477: J. Martí, J.M. Benedí, A.M. Mendonça, J. Serrat (Eds.), Pattern Recognition and Image Analysis, Part I. XXVII, 625 pages. 2007.

Vol. 4472: M. Haindl, J. Kittler, F. Roli (Eds.), Multiple Classifier Systems. XI, 524 pages. 2007.

Vol. 4466: F.B. Sachse, G. Seemann (Eds.), Functional Imaging and Modeling of the Heart. XV, 486 pages. 2007.

Vol. 4418: A. Gagalowicz, W. Philips (Eds.), Computer Vision/Computer Graphics Collaboration Techniques. XV, 620 pages. 2007.

Vol. 4417: A. Kerren, A. Ebert, J. Meyer (Eds.), Human-Centered Visualization Environments. XIX, 403 pages. 2007.

Vol. 4391: Y. Stylianou, M. Faundez-Zanuy, A. Esposito (Eds.), Progress in Nonlinear Speech Processing. XII, 269 pages. 2007.

Vol. 4370: P.P. Lévy, B. Le Grand, F. Poulet, M. Soto, L. Darago, L. Toubiana, J.-F. Vibert (Eds.), Pixelization Paradigm. XV, 279 pages. 2007.

Vol. 4358: R. Vidal, A. Heyden, Y. Ma (Eds.), Dynamical Vision. IX, 329 pages. 2007.

Vol. 4338: P.K. Kalra, S. Peleg (Eds.), Computer Vision, Graphics and Image Processing. XV, 965 pages. 2006.

Vol. 4319: L.-W. Chang, W.-N. Lie (Eds.), Advances in Image and Video Technology. XXVI, 1347 pages. 2006.

Vol. 4292: G. Bebis, R. Boyle, B. Parvin, D. Koracin, P. Remagnino, A. Nefian, G. Meenakshisundaram, V. Pascucci, J. Zara, J. Molineros, H. Theisel, T. Malzbender (Eds.), Advances in Visual Computing, Part II. XXXII, 906 pages. 2006.

Vol. 4291: G. Bebis, R. Boyle, B. Parvin, D. Koracin, P. Remagnino, A. Nefian, G. Meenakshisundaram, V. Pascucci, J. Zara, J. Molineros, H. Theisel, T. Malzbender (Eds.), Advances in Visual Computing, Part I. XXXI, 916 pages. 2006.

Vol. 4245: A. Kuba, L.G. Nyúl, K. Palágyi (Eds.), Discrete Geometry for Computer Imagery. XIII, 688 pages. 2006.

Vol. 4241: R.R. Beichel, M. Sonka (Eds.), Computer Vision Approaches to Medical Image Analysis. XI, 262 pages. 2006.

Vol. 4225: J.F. Martínez-Trinidad, J.A. Carrasco Ochoa, J. Kittler (Eds.), Progress in Pattern Recognition, Image Analysis and Applications. XIX, 995 pages. 2006.

Vol. 4191: R. Larsen, M. Nielsen, J. Sporring (Eds.), Medical Image Computing and Computer-Assisted Intervention – MICCAI 2006, Part II. XXXVIII, 981 pages. 2006.

Vol. 4190: R. Larsen, M. Nielsen, J. Sporring (Eds.), Medical Image Computing and Computer-Assisted Intervention – MICCAI 2006, Part I. XXXVVIII, 949 pages. 2006.

Vol. 4179: J. Blanc-Talon, W. Philips, D. Popescu, P. Scheunders (Eds.), Advanced Concepts for Intelligent Vision Systems. XXIV, 1224 pages. 2006.

Vol. 4174: K. Franke, K.-R. Müller, B. Nickolay, R. Schäfer (Eds.), Pattern Recognition. XX, 773 pages. 2006.

Vol. 4170: J. Ponce, M. Hebert, C. Schmid, A. Zisserman (Eds.), Toward Category-Level Object Recognition. XI, 618 pages. 2006.

Vol. 4153: N. Zheng, X. Jiang, X. Lan (Eds.), Advances in Machine Vision, Image Processing, and Pattern Analysis. XIII, 506 pages. 2006.

Vol. 4142: A. Campilho, M. Kamel (Eds.), Image Analysis and Recognition, Part II. XXVII, 923 pages. 2006.

Vol. 4141: A. Campilho, M. Kamel (Eds.), Image Analysis and Recognition, Part I. XXVIII, 939 pages. 2006.

Vol. 4122: R. Stiefelhagen, J.S. Garofolo (Eds.), Multimodal Technologies for Perception of Humans. XII, 360 pages. 2007.

Vol. 4109: D.-Y. Yeung, J.T. Kwok, A. Fred, F. Roli, D. de Ridder (Eds.), Structural, Syntactic, and Statistical Pattern Recognition. XXI, 939 pages. 2006.

Vol. 4091: G.-Z. Yang, T. Jiang, D. Shen, L. Gu, J. Yang (Eds.), Medical Imaging and Augmented Reality. XIII, 399 pages. 2006.

Vol. 4073: A. Butz, B. Fisher, A. Krüger, P. Olivier (Eds.), Smart Graphics. XI, 263 pages. 2006.

Vol. 4069: F.J. Perales, R.B. Fisher (Eds.), Articulated Motion and Deformable Objects. XV, 526 pages. 2006.

Vol. 4057: J.P.W. Pluim, B. Likar, F.A. Gerritsen (Eds.), Biomedical Image Registration. XII, 324 pages. 2006.

Vol. 4046: S.M. Astley, M. Brady, C. Rose, R. Zwiggelaar (Eds.), Digital Mammography. XVI, 654 pages. 2006.

Vol. 4040: R. Reulke, U. Eckardt, B. Flach, U. Knauer, K. Polthier (Eds.), Combinatorial Image Analysis. XII, 482 pages. 2006.

Vol. 4035: T. Nishita, Q. Peng, H.-P. Seidel (Eds.), Advances in Computer Graphics. XX, 771 pages. 2006.

Vol. 3979: T.S. Huang, N. Sebe, M. Lew, V. Pavlović, M. Kölsch, A. Galata, B. Kisačanin (Eds.), Computer Vision in Human-Computer Interaction. XII, 121 pages. 2006.

Vol. 3954: A. Leonardis, H. Bischof, A. Pinz (Eds.), Computer Vision – ECCV 2006, Part IV. XVII, 613 pages. 2006.

Vol. 3953: A. Leonardis, H. Bischof, A. Pinz (Eds.), Computer Vision – ECCV 2006, Part III. XVII, 649 pages. 2006.

Vol. 3952: A. Leonardis, H. Bischof, A. Pinz (Eds.), Computer Vision – ECCV 2006, Part II. XVII, 661 pages. 2006.

Vol. 3951: A. Leonardis, H. Bischof, A. Pinz (Eds.), Computer Vision – ECCV 2006, Part I. XXXV, 639 pages. 2006.

Vol. 3948: H.I. Christensen, H.-H. Nagel (Eds.), Cognitive Vision Systems. VIII, 367 pages. 2006.

Vol. 3926: W. Liu, J. Lladós (Eds.), Graphics Recognition. XII, 428 pages. 2006.

Vol. 3872: H. Bunke, A.L. Spitz (Eds.), Document Analysis Systems VII. XIII, 630 pages. 2006.

Vol. 3852: P.J. Narayanan, S.K. Nayar, H.-Y. Shum (Eds.), Computer Vision – ACCV 2006, Part II. XXXI, 977 pages. 2006.